Patterns of Educational Integration

For Jean

PATTERNS OF EDUCATIONAL INTEGRATION: international perspectives on mainstreaming children with special educational needs

Barrie Wade & Maggie Moore

Triangle Books

Triangle Books Ltd
PO Box 65, Wallingford, Oxfordshire OX10 0YG, United Kingdom

Published in the United Kingdom, 1992
© Triangle Books Ltd, 1992

ISBN 1 873927 01 0

Cover and text design by Peter Tucker
Typeset in Palatino by Triangle Books
Printed and bound in the United Kingdom by
Cambridge University Press

Contents

INTRODUCTION

Patterns are essential to processes of careful construction. We have described patterns in this book because we attach maximum importance to the careful construction of school policy for integrating children with special needs into mainstream education. Mainstreaming is, of course, a controversial issue and, in Part 1, we sample international perspectives, (political, economic, legislative and social) on integration and we represent as a continuum those patterns which lie between segregating children and integrating them. Then we outline some of the other forces (curricular, research, comparative, operational and rational) which are accelerating the journey down mainstream currents. Since attitudes (of parents, teachers and students, for example) are crucial to making any system work, we devote Chapter Three to an analysis of what we know about attitudes to children with disabilities, how attitudes may be changed and what their effects on learning and integration might be.

Having discussed these topical issues in Part 1, we move, in Part 2, to a series of case studies in which we analyse how changes towards integration are being effected in Britain, Australia and New Zealand. The pattern for these chapters is a movement from focus on individuals (Chapters Four and Five) to unit or separate provision within a school (Chapters Six and Seven) to liaison between special and mainstream schools (Chapter Eight) to support for special needs within mainstream schools (Chapters Nine and Ten). Chapter Eleven describes a system of continuing mainstream provision for children with disabilities from primary to secondary school and Chapter Twelve examines a parent's viewpoint. The case studies use verbatim accounts to illustrate issues; only the names of participants and their schools have been changed. Special needs vary at an individual level of context, personality, disability, etc., which makes providing for them challenging. The detail of such diagnosis and provision can best be analysed at case study level, so we have given the majority of space to Part 2. Nonetheless this section, from particular cases, raises important general issues: for example, resourcing for special needs; the value of interaction; how best to support children and staff; the need to consult both parents and children. These issues are discussed with their implications for practice in Part 3.

This then is the pattern of our book, but we recognise readers' special needs to begin where they feel most comfortable. In our view, it will be just as valuable to begin at the stories of individual children or at the accounts of school provision and then to return to the legislative, social, political and economic issues. We hope our book will provoke thought and inform practice, but we emphasise that, in construction and in ideas, it offers patterns and not a single blueprint. Rearranging the chapters kaleidoscopically according to need may have more advantage to some readers than following the order we have chosen.

Our own route towards the completion of this book bears striking similarity to the patterns of provision for children with special educational needs that are its subject matter. We too have relied on encouragement, resources, interaction and practical support and without them this book would never have been written.

We received considerable encouragement from individuals, particularly from those who had read *Special Children: Special Needs*, our first book. We were prepared to believe them when they said they had found it entertaining and useful. Our self concepts flourished!

Resources we acknowledge with gratitude in the shape of financial support from the Leverhulme Foundation which enabled us to undertake observational studies in Australia, New Zealand and Singapore as well as in Great Britain. We thank Newman College and the University of Birmingham for resources of time offered by granting a term's secondment to one author and two weeks' leave of absence to the other. These resources provided the launching platform from which we could set out confidently on our journey of enquiry.

We have benefited from interaction with more people than we can mention here who have generously shared ideas with us, stimulated our interest and facilitated our studies in so many ways.

In New Zealand we were helped by John Foster, David and Ketty Philips, Brian Pearl, Rowena Somogyvary, Peter Kohing, Gill Ward, Dr Keith Ballard, Professor Ted Glynn, Dr Keri Wilton, Pat Harrison, Alan Jackson, Dr Geraldine McDonald, Rory Gollop, Graham Murray, Colleen Pilgrim, Yvonne Hope, Geoff Neve, Ross Wilson, Maurice Gianotti, Val Davidson, Pru Ursell, Robin Wright, Tony Stanley, Eric Baker.

In Australia: Ken Watson, John Pimm, Rhonda Brill, Jill Phillips, David Bishop, Professor Diana Davis, Warwick Franks, Rod Leonader, Margaret Swieringa, Jack and Shona Thomson, Ingrid Kaschek, Katherine Stewart.

In Singapore: Angela Khoo, Dr Pamela Sharpe, June Thana.

In Britain: Professor Ron Gulliford, David Cropp, Francesca Healey, Ros Cofield, Stella Bolitho, Pat Burrage, Barbara Johncey.

From interacting with the above we profited immensely. However, since learners must claim ownership of their own learning, we acknowledge that any imperfections or misrepresentations that have crept into the book are our responsibility not theirs.

Finally, we are glad to acknowledge the practical support given by Imogen and Miranda Wade, who transcribed some of our tape-recorded interviews, and by Jean Thompson who expertly prepared our manuscript for publication. It was she who cheerfully shaped the diverse patterns of our handwritten drafts and redrafts into an integrated word-processed form. As a token of our admiration and gratitude this book is dedicated to her.

Acknowledgment

Chapters Four and Five incorporate some material previously published in *Oideas, 33*. The authors are grateful to the journal editor, Patrick Boland, for his early encouragement and interest in our work.

Chapter One

Segregation or Integration

The motives behind integration, just as those behind segregation, are a product of complex social, economic and political considerations which may relate more to the 'needs' of the wider society, the whole education system and professionals working within the system, rather than simply to the 'needs' of individual children.

(Barton & Tomlinson, 1986, p.37)

INTRODUCTION

The shift from total segregation of children with disabilities and learning difficulties towards integration into mainstream education is not a process governed by reason. Barton & Tomlinson (1986) show how a complex mesh of political, economic and social factors influence decision making, attitudes and motives for integrating in much the same untidy way as other developments in education are influenced. Certainly development in special needs education has become influenced by and part of an argument for human rights and for equality of opportunity. In recent years groups of disabled people and parent pressure groups speaking on behalf of their children have added their articulate voices to the argument for better resources, better provision, increased understanding and tolerance from society as a whole. Legislation has been introduced to safeguard newly won rights and educational laws attempt to protect the entitlement of children with disabilities to an education which meets their needs.

We begin by giving examples of how recent legislation affects educational provision and we show how economic and social factors remain involved with political considerations. We then represent the present integration/segregation debate in continuum form, to show how a spectrum of provision is used to meet the needs of children at different stages and in different social and economic contexts. This integration continuum also illustrates the shift that is taking place towards greater integration and it provides a convenient way of placing some of the current types of provision that we evaluate in our later case study chapters.

LEGISLATION FOR SPECIAL NEEDS

It is not our intention here to give full details of special needs legislation which, in any case, is in process of updating and change in several countries. Rather we offer a brief and selective outline in order to illustrate the way social (USA), political (Great Britain), economic (Australia) and procedural (New Zealand) implications are tied in with legislation which aims to facilitate integration.

1. USA

Under US Public Law 94:142 free and equal public education is available for handicapped children. As far as placement is concerned, principles are stated unequivocally:

(a) A handicapped child *as of right* shall, as much as possible, be taught with a non-handicapped peergroup.

(b) If the child's needs can be accommodated in the mainstream classroom (with the support of additional services, materials, aids and special equipment) then the child *must* be placed in the regular classroom with children who are not handicapped.

Only when the child's handicap is too severe for appropriate education as indicated by these principles, may other resources be considered. The guiding principle, therefore, that legislation ensures, is that the child is placed in the least restrictive environment that is possible.

In practice one would expect a certain degree of reluctance – even resistance – on the part of staff unfamiliar with specific handicaps and disabilities. This expectation is supported by Schumaker & Deshler (1988) who note that staff at high school level accept with difficulty the responsibility for teaching handicapped children in their mainstream classes. This is true even when the students' handicaps are not severe. The same authors draw attention to the fact that the personal and social needs of handicapped teenagers may override their academic needs, while Macklem (1988) points out the complex social network that exists in a junior high school. She cites the work of Schneider & Byrne (1984) to illustrate peer group reluctance and resistance:

Students have a large number of teachers to contend with, each having different expectations, content is increasingly abstract, the peer group changes from class to class, and the nontypical student is less accepted by both teachers and peers. (p.10)

This would probably be just as accurate a summary of the position in Britain or Australia or New Zealand and the root causes in all countries are similar. Firstly, secondary schools are necessarily specialist, and many non-handicapped students have problems with a system which brings them into contact with a wider range of adults, expectations and peer group as well as with abstractions. It can be argued that part of normalisation and integration is the chance to confront the same problems that normal adolescents typically face. After all, cocooning, segregating and institutionalising did nothing to integrate handicapped people into society's complexity. In most secondary schools a pastoral care and counselling system exists to support youngsters with adjustment problems: clearly some (but not all) handicapped adolescents will need this existing or additional support.

The second point is that, in each country, there has been a history of stigma related to handicap, so it is hardly surprising that non-typical students are less accepted. In fact, this non-acceptance is a direct result of earlier segregation policies. Ignorance breeds suspicion and, until more people have experience of living, learning and working alongside handicapped people, there will remain a gulf of uncertainty, prejudice and rejecting behaviour. It is therefore important to begin the processes of normalisation and experience through integration despite the social problems involved. We have to begin somewhere and take the problems on board, otherwise nothing will change. Legislation points the way and if, as D.H. Lawrence wrote, "conflict is a part of vital growth", we must accept conflict and social adjustment as part of the process of growing into a healthy society.

2. *Great Britain*
There were two important precursors to the 1981 Education Act. Firstly, the report of the Warnock Committee, *Special Educational Needs* (D.E.S., 1978), signified an important departure from labelling children according to how their handicaps were diagnosed medically. The Committee insisted that about twenty per cent of all children required special help at some time during their schooling and this argument led naturally to the notion of a continuum between handicapped and non-handicapped rather than a strict division into separate categories which the previous legislation of the 1944 Act had assumed. Thus anyone with difficulties in learning was now to be regarded as having special needs. The Warnock Committee recognised the crucial role of parents in the education of their children and argued for an

3

all-round assessment of needs, involving learning, social and psychological factors as well as medical considerations. No longer was the special school and separate provision regarded as the only way to promote learning.

Hard on the heels of this welcome, rational and positive report came more of a disclaimer than a guarantee in a D.E.S. White Paper (1980):

> *Only when the economic situation improves sufficiently will it be possible to bring to fruition all the committed efforts of those engaged in meeting special educational needs. (p.23)*

Since then, political and politico-economic factors have never been far away. The legislation of the 1981 Act broadly followed the Warnock Report's recommendations and placed its emphasis upon integrating children with special needs within the ordinary school system, provided that the school was able to meet those needs and other children's education could still be delivered efficiently. Children with special needs were entitled to Statements of diagnosis and provision, and although parents' views were to be taken into account in the process, so was the efficient use of resources. The criterion of cost effectiveness has offered scope for judgment, rather than a clear cut entitlement, and some children have been disadvantaged because these provisos allow scope for delay in producing Statements or avoidance in meeting some special needs altogether. There is considerable variation in practices in different geographical and political areas. In 1984 Margaret Peter wrote that the Act's provisions would not be met because: (a) no financial resources were made available and (b) complex statementing procedures are time consuming and deflect effort from the 18% of pupils with special needs who remain unstatemented.

Cohen & Cohen (1986) also highlighted another problem precipitated by central government's economic policy and determination to shift power from local education authorities:

> *Since the 1981 Education Act some local authorities are interpreting its findings as a licence to close special schools, sending their former pupils to ordinary schools usually without providing the financial resources, extra equipment, facilities and teachers which are necessary for any integration prospects to have a reasonable chance of success. (p.xix)*

Political concerns hardened during the 1980's into a strategy aimed at offering consumer choice in an educational market economy. Radical changes in curriculum, appraisal, financing schools, examining and reporting results appeared in the 1988 Education Reform Act. The result was a shift of interest, away from making the 1981 Act work, towards a new concern with management of schools, which Coopers & Lybrand (1988) express succinctly:

> *The changes require a new culture and philosophy of the organisation of education at school level. They are more than purely financial; they need a general shift in management. (p.5)*

4

Since 1988 there have developed a good many areas of potential confusion and conflict where the 1988 Act works against the provisions of 1981. Seven of these will illustrate the way political and financial policies can threaten provision for children with special needs.

1. The notion of partnership with all parents in making decisions and assessing children (1981 Act) is shifted to elected parent representation on governing bodies (1988 Act).
2. The emphasis on special needs (1981 Act) has been overtaken by emphasis upon setting standards of attainment (1988 Act).
3. Concentration upon the individual's needs (1981 Act) has given way to concentration upon cost-effectiveness. There is still no proper resourcing for the 20 per cent of children in the Warnock Committee's (D.E.S. 1978) definition of special needs.
4. Notions of integration and collaboration (1981 Act) are threatened by a market-driven competitiveness between schools for pupil numbers and good results, (1988 Act) which might prejudice admission of pupils with learning difficulties.
5. The emphasis on Local Education Authorities meeting special needs by liaison between well-established services (1981 Act) is threatened for pupils with special needs by their schools severing Local Education Authority contact by taking grant maintained status (1988 Act) whereby the school receives its finance direct from central government.
6. The freedom to devise child-centred provision for special needs (1981 Act) has been overtaken by a National Curriculum with a subject-oriented, secondary school dominated framework.
7. The 1981 Act placed emphasis upon diagnosis of children's needs by all-round assessment, but the 1988 Act places emphasis on Standard Assessment Tasks, on which the majority of children with special needs are likely to score badly.

It remains to be seen if pragmatic solutions can be found for such problems of apparent or patent conflict and whether or not progress towards effective integration of children with disabilities is seriously interrupted.

3. *Australia*

Throughout Australia the Australian Commonwealth Schools Commission has supported the integration of students with special needs into the ordinary school since the early 1970's. There is now generally a more pronounced shift towards integration in all states and territories. Policies and practices do, however, differ and the results of a review commissioned by the above body revealed factors of concern expressed as being detrimental to effective integrations (Gow, 1988).

One common view was the lack of funding and the worry that children with special educational needs were being 'maindumped' without the necessary support services. Some states, for example, Victoria, have supplied extra funding, (Safran, 1989) but not all have followed this example.

Australia is different from Great Britain in that it has not introduced national legislation for special needs education. The various states and the two territories have therefore developed somewhat different systems in which state legislation along with good faith and professional judgment (rather than national legislation) regulates the system. Local school authorities are legally entitled to deny children with disabilities an education within their communities, with the State Minister of Education making the final decision. Such denial, according to Safran (1989) is rare, but does occur.

Some states have, however, begun innovative policies to integrate children with special needs into their mainstream schools. Victoria is one of these, having developed a policy based on the principles of the right of education for all and the right, where possible, for that education to take place in mainstream classes. Victoria follows the guide of the Warnock Report (D.E.S., 1978) by abandoning the system of categorising children by types of handicap and, instead, positively identifying their educational needs and the provision necessary to meet them. Different from Britain, integration in Victoria received support of resources, particularly the most crucial resource – that of additional staffing. According to Tarr (1988) 2,950 students in 1,037 schools benefited by the employment of 170 primary integration teachers, 76 postprimary integration teachers and 612 integration aides.

Up to this point the policy appears ideal. Unfortunately, however, because of its non-legislative nature, the authorities could neither close special schools (because jobs had to be protected); nor could they enforce the integration of students with disabilities (as class teachers had the right to refuse to accept them). Additional problems were soon caused by the funding of the integration policy. Since the amount of available finance was finite, competition for funding and support was keen. Many students who were put forward claiming resources had comparatively minor learning or behavioural problems. These children would have been in the 20% of students that the Warnock Committee (D.E.S., 1978) in Britain insisted should receive help, though, as in Victoria, the amount of funding stretched only to a much lower percentage. With the availability of a Statementing procedure to legalise rights to provision to meet needs, we suspect that, to begin with, some British psychologists, determined that their deserving clients should receive the resources necessary for their education, resorted to statementing children whose problems were also relatively minor. Safran (1989) suggests that less deserving cases in Victoria were 'weeded out'. In Britain the complex, time-consuming process of statementing and the administrative burden attached frequently resulted in the same effect through delays and omission. The main point in Victoria is, as Tarr (1988) says, that the additional resources have been accepted by mainstream schools in order to support students with a differing range of disabilities. Possibly, the success of the scheme may have been limited by the financial constraints and the lack of specific legislation. After the first four years of operation the number of students in special schools had not decreased, although some of these students were staying on at school longer and some were actively involved in partial integration schemes. It may be that ultimately provision of resources without legislation is more effective than legislation without the resources to make it work.

4. New Zealand

In New Zealand part of the recent debate has focused on whether more legislation is required to make the shift towards integration more effective or whether the needs of special education students can be met in various forms of 'mainstreaming' through 'consensus decision making'. Don Brown (1989), favouring the latter view, argues for 'enabling' legislation on the British Westminster model rather than the 'legally mandating' US Public Law which defined the categories where federal funding could be used. Gartner & Lipsky (1987), in the USA, had shown how their system in practice meant that students with apparently similar characteristics were allocated different resources and education programmes depending on geographical location and methods of assessment. Brown (1989) articulates his concern that, once special (and specified) assistance is made a legal entitlement, it is difficult to avoid both categorisation and massive amounts of administrative time. He cites survey evidence from the USA (Clement, Zartler & Mulick (1983)) to show that psychologists there are involved in diagnostic activities for 70 percent of their time. A further problem with legislated provision is that it is difficult, if not impossible, to exceed the requirements of that entitlement, even if it appears that the child requires more resources or that flexibility in provision would be beneficial. Brown sums up the tradition in New Zealand since the 1970's which:

> ..has been to lay less emphasis on categorical definitions and more emphasis upon programme development. This is consistent with the wishes and intentions of our North American colleagues but we have the freedom to make these changes since the categories we have are administrative. We do not bear the burden of mandated categories and we should think carefully before adding such a load to the already complex task we have of realigning special education to serve the individual child. (p.167)

Some reform of legislation was necessary, however. The Education Act of 1964 did not include all children in the responsibility that the country had for education: those who were assessed as ineducable (i.e. those with severe disabilities) had no right to receive any education. Even during the period of New Zealand's enabling policy many of these youngsters were confined

7

to hospitals. The Education Act (1989) removed this exclusion. Section 8 states:

> People who have special educational needs (whether because of disability or otherwise) have the same rights to enrol and receive education at state schools as people who do not.

Section 9 emphasises the main attempt to reach consensus in the use of *agree*, but retains final responsibility for the Secretary (Minister of Education) to *direct* in the case of disagreement or non-cooperation:

> The Secretary shall –
>
> (a) Agree with the person's parents that the person should be enrolled, or direct them to enrol the person, at a particular state school, special school, special class, or special clinic;
>
> or
>
> (b) Agree with the person's parents that the person should have, or direct them to ensure that the person has, education or help from a special service.

In keeping with the intention to give more say to parents in education generally, parents may under Section 10's *Right of Reconsideration* appeal against directions by the Minister of Education, when the decision then lies with an independent arbitrator.

Legislation thus provides opportunities for integration to take place by:

- including all children in the state system;
- offering local schooling as a choice for parents, subject to Ministry approval;
- providing an appeals procedure in cases of dispute.

Parents who still want some form of segregated support for their children can opt for it in the system and, in this respect, the solution follows the pragmatism of Britain where few changes have been made to the ways that schools are organised. The legislation is open to criticism on the grounds that it does not do enough to promote 'mainstreaming' of all students. Ballard (1990), for example, criticises the policy documents which preceded the Act because they assigned the word 'mainstreaming' to existing structures that really segregated children. This is an issue that we return to in later chapters. Citing Wang & Birch (1984), Ballard argues that:

> It is well established in the research literature that so-called 'social' and 'locational' arrangements do not work as mainstreaming because when children are segregated for some, or all, of the time, teachers do not make the changes to the curriculum and classroom organisation that would ensure all children are 'full participants in the social and intellectual life of regular classes'. (p.15)

The Act may not go far enough to satisfy all, but it may well result in what, in our next section, we have called the Integration Continuum being telescoped because some of the administrative categories within it simply disappear. Segregation of children in hospitals or at home may soon become a thing of the past. Segregation in a Special School on its own site is also threatened. The 1989 Act in New Zealand became law on 1st January 1990. Three months afterwards we observed the efforts of two new Zealand Special School head-teachers to find new roles through giving itinerant support and advice to main-stream schools which had accepted their students. These head-teachers had themselves recommended closure of their own schools, because the majority of their pupils had been placed in mainstream contexts. So, although legislation did not set out to restrict the spectrum of provision, certain modes of catering for special needs may wither and die. In this way, while parental roles are centralised and applauded, paradoxically parents' actual choices may eventually become more restricted.

We now show this spectrum of provision in diagrammatic form, showing at the same time that the debate about various forms of mainstreaming has little value if it remains at the level of administrative terms. What matters is not what a certain kind of provision is called, but what it looks like behind its label.

THE INTEGRATION CONTINUUM

This book is about integration, but it is also about interaction. It is possible to have individuals (in a marriage), institutions (on the same site) and units (in the same building) that never speak to each other. The interaction of individuals and groups with their environment is necessary for both development and learning as the work of Piaget, Vygotsky, and Bruner

SEPARATION								INTEGRATION
No Contact e.g. Home, Hospital	Special School with own Separate Site	Special School Sharing Site with Mainstream School	Special Unit Sharing Building with Mainstream Classes	Special Unit Sharing Social activities with Mainstream Children	Special Unit with some Mainstream outreach	Mainstream Provision with some withdrawal into Special Classes	Provision for all Special Needs in Regular Classes in Mainstream	

FIG 1. *This conceptualises the continuum in a simplified form and offers a way of showing the spectrum of provision that may be available to cater for a child's individual and changing needs.*

amongst many educationalists have shown. In later chapters we shall discuss various degrees of integration: locational (site sharing), social (sharing of extra curricular activity) and functional (full or partial sharing of ordinary classroom activities with regular classmates). It is helpful at the outset to consider provision as a continuum, as we do in Figure 1, with different methods of provision occupying different positions on an uninterrupted scale between separation and integration.

Figure 1 is helpful also to conceptualise the recent world trend towards integration and away from separation in the direction of the arrow and thus the model may be used as a first categorisation of any provision. For example, two systems that we had first hand experience of in 1990 are in Singapore and New South Wales, Australia. While much excellent work is done at special school level in Singapore, funding is problematic. The mainstream school system is government funded and highly competitive, but special schools must rely on funding from charities and on teachers with little experience or specialist training. Lobbies to government have produced more resources in the way of teachers' salaries, but all education must be paid for and parents have to make some contribution. The stigma of having a child with disability, plus the need to pay for separate provision, possibly deters many parents from sending their children early to school and thus large numbers of children are denied the contacts with adults and peer group which lead to learning. These excluded children have minimal contact with others and would be placed at the extreme of separation on the continuum.

On the other hand, the Australian example, of a purpose-built secondary school to cater for children with a wide range of abilities and the inclusion of children with a range of disabilities in the ordinary classroom, provides complete provision for special needs in the mainstream. This example is at the extreme of integration in the continuum.

While many countries are moving now from separation towards integration, and the continuum, as we have shown, offers a way of categorising such progress, or lack of it, there are two related points which must be remembered. Firstly, every means of provision may have advantages and disadvantages for particular children and these may alter over time. For example, in Chapter 4 we present a case study of Chris who suffered a road accident which at first required an extensive stay in hospital. As his needs changed, he was eventually able to participate in regular class activities and learn alongside able-bodied classmates. Some children may progress or regress through several different kinds of provision. The second point to remember about the integration continuum is that the category labels do not tell us about the quality of interaction that each student enjoys. For example, in a Singapore special school on its own site, we observed constant opportunities for young children with severe disabilities to interact with adults, since every child was accompanied in the classroom by a parent or maidservant who participated in all activities. In

10

this case also, the learning experiences were potentially maximised because of the constant liaison and the likelihood of carry over from school to home. On the other hand, in one integrated North American primary school, two children with disabilities stayed together indoors at recess and lunch break when only adults spoke to them; in the classroom they never contributed to whole class discussion or activity. In one small group discussion, Andy, a child with spina bifida and indistinct speech, was never directly addressed nor included in the talk. He sat patiently until the activity was over while the others talked past him.

Awareness of specific needs is necessary, but the most important ongoing task is to improve the quality of teaching and learning in all schools. Research shows that mainstream teachers frequently hold stereotyped views about what particular pupils can achieve and that these limiting prejudices derive from class, race or gender preconceptions. Patronising and discriminating teacher behaviour towards girls was found by Whyte (1986). Buswell (1984) recorded unfounded beliefs about the limitations of what working class girls could achieve and Kelly's (1986) study showed that girls receive less than their fair share of teacher attention in mixed classrooms. Wright (1986) showed how black children can be unfairly excluded from academic groups because of teacher expectations that they will misbehave and Walkling (1990) identified racism as a cause of Afro-Caribbean children drifting

> ..to the bottom of the education system, and their massive over representation in remedial classes and ESN schools. (pp.83-4)

Schools need to be changed to eliminate these negative features of the system – and this is true also for mainstream schools which cater for children with special needs. All children need positive support, but disadvantaged groups especially need it if they are to develop a clear sense of their own worth and a bright notion of the success and achievement that is within their grasp.

Parents sometimes have reservations about mainstream education for their children because they are fearful of peer group teasing about their disabilities. Evidence about the way mainstream girls can be subjected to peer group labelling and harassment is provided by Lees (1986) and by Jones (1985) respectively. This further evidence of teasing as a general problem rather than one specific to children with disabilities is another indication that schools must work to make mainstream environments welcoming and positive for all children. Creber's (1972) example of mainstream teacher pupil interaction shows how easy it must be for any child to stop making any effort when prevented from making a positive classroom contribution:

Boy: When I was
Teacher: Say Sir when you speak to a member of staff

Boy: Sir.... I was at....

Teacher: And take your hands out of your pockets. I don't speak to the headmaster with my hands in my pockets.

Boy: Sorry –

Teacher: or leaning on a radiator.

Boy: Sorry – sorry Sir. When I was at Blackton

Teacher: .... well boy, get on with it – when you were at Blackton....?

Boy: Yes, Sir, when I was at Blackton primary school.... we used to go birdwatching on the cliffs and ....

Teacher: Jones, I suppose you realise what this lesson is.

    (pp. 21-2)

It is not sufficient to say that the teacher needs a better understanding of the role of anecdote in learning or that his didactic model of teaching needs shifting towards a child-centred, activity one. A significant part of the problem is that of attitudes which we discuss in more detail in Chapter 3. Thus far, however, it has become clearer that providing for children with special needs is part of the whole process of ensuring appropriate resources and learning experiences are made available for all children. There is little point in mainstream schools or classes which really flow in predetermined, separate little streams of opportunity and entitlement. Equally, where teaching is merely perceived as transmission of knowledge and there is no understanding of the kinds of classroom interaction that facilitate collaboration and participation in learning, there will be problems for all children, not just those with special needs. The movement towards integration, therefore, has implications for all schools and for all teachers who must focus on how to help all learners best obtain what they need. As Stainback et al (1985) say, shifts in attitude and practice are necessary to ensure effectiveness even at the integration extreme of our continuum. Other American research that underpins our views here is provided by Ciccelli & Ashby-Davis (1986). They surveyed 600 teachers who were actually in the process of changing to provisions at the integration end of our continuum. Apart from the importance of redefining their own roles, this group of American teachers proposed two major priorities:

1. the necessity of developing appropriate attitudes towards pupils with special needs;
2. the necessity of changing their own traditional ways of teaching. Changing attitudes and changing practice are therefore crucial and must accompany any shift towards integration on our continuum. Salend (1984) proposed certain prerequisites for such changes to integration, for example:

- prior assessment of and preparation for learners with special needs
- peer group preparation to welcome such learners
- further training for mainstream teachers
- efficient monitoring of pupil progress

- better liaison and communication between providers.

We shall return to these issues in the case study section. It is important, though, to take forward the view established here that integration is not an end in itself. The continuum shows that it is an important dimension of practice, a means of recognising that every child is entitled to education in a regular school setting along with his/her peer group. For children with special needs, education in the mainstream is one part of the process that ensures they live their lives with maximum entitlement to normalcy. The aim should be to ensure the fullest development of potential for every learner.

The continuum allows for the fact that the development of some learners may well be best served by hospital care, or residential schools as well as by special support in mainstream classes. However, it is important that no learner is restricted or disadvantaged by the provision and that, where education takes place in the mainstream, everyone, including those without disabilities, gains from the experience. We consider these aspects in detailed case studies later.

Chapter Two

Towards Integration

On a huge hill cragged and steep,
Truth stands, and hee that will
Reach her, about must, and about must goe;
And what the hills suddennes resists, winne so.

John Donne

INTRODUCTION

Having considered the way legislation is bound up with economic, political and social factors, we now proceed in this chapter to outline some of the other forces that are shifting provision for special needs education towards integration with the mainstream. We consider rational arguments as well as those derived from comparative views, curriculum review, management issues and research findings.

RATIONAL PROCESSES

We said in Chapter 1 that educational change is not governed by reason, but rational arguments are used in the process of policy making if only to rationalise decisions that have been influenced by economic, social or political considerations. The examples of legislation we have discussed became necessary to safeguard the essential rights of individuals in contexts where neither attitudes nor resources were conducive to adequate provision. While the argument was often polarised in the 1970s and 1980s into pro-segregation or, increasingly, pro-integration, there were also some careful attempts to study the complex issues rationally and to tease out the strengths and weaknesses of competing claims. One of the more helpful formulations is that by David Thomas (1978) who presents the advantages and disadvantages of segregating handicapped children for their education (pp.137-8).

The advantages of segregation according to Thomas are:
(i) a high ratio of adults to children and the greater attention which individual children can then receive;
(ii) the efficiency of special instructional methods;
(iii) the concentrated availability of medical and therapy services;
(iv) the reduction of pressure on children which gives them the opportunity and time to cope with physical self-care and the psychological opportunity to build up worthwhile levels of self-esteem;
(v) the living in a comprehensive community where needs are acknowledged and catered for.
    A rational approach on its own may leave gaps in the argument. It is possible to add at least three other 'advantages' to Thomas' list:
(vi) economical in terms of concentration of equipment and staff;
(vii) facilitates liaison with medical, psychological and other community services;
(viii) removes difficult children from the mainstream.

On the other hand, what are regarded as advantages from one perspective may, in another context, become regarded in a different way. For example, advantage (ii) above we show to be dubious in the following section on *Curriculum Provision* where special methods restrict learning opportunities. Similarly, advantage (iv) above might be interpreted in some situations as not having expectations high enough for children to reach their true potential.

Thomas gives six disadvantages to segregation of handicapped children:
(i) it places them in a social system largely composed of others similarly handicapped, so that they take the others as their reference group;
(ii) particularly when it is residential, it means a loss of contact with normal peer groups and all that that implies for psychological and social development;
(iii) the children lose friendships in their home neighbourhood;
(iv) there is a sense of stigma;
(v) a too-protective environment is dangerous because of the effect of the loss of protection when the young people have to leave it;
(vi) there are the consequences of a school environment which is uncertain whether it is a branch of the social services, a para-medical aid centre or a teaching institution.

To these six disadvantages we again would add three more:

(vii) a segregation policy does not allow for the needs of those families who want education to be provided in a normal school environment. Therefore some parents may become dissatisfied and unhappy that their children are separated from others;

(viii) the curriculum may be restricted and fail to offer the stimulus and diversity that children with special educational needs require;

(ix) able-bodied children in mainstream schools lose the learning and social benefits derived from interacting with their disabled peers.

A rational approach is helpful in setting out the pros and cons of each system for all concerned, including teachers who can then work to maximise advantages and minimise disadvantages. It may also guide parents in making choices for their children. In this respect it is most helpful where there is a genuine choice to be made between alternatives. We have already said that advantages and disadvantages may be considered differently from different perspectives. We have the benefit of revising Thomas's 1978 outline (with its focus on handicap) from our changed situation of 1991 (with a wider concept of special needs). Rational analyses need to be continually revised as circumstances and opportunities change. Even then they do not necessarily produce educational change which, to restate the view of Barton & Tomlinson (1986), is influenced by a complex of factors, including those which constitute the remaining sections of this chapter.

COMPARATIVE VIEWS

Influences on educational change are no longer confined to those operating within individual states or countries. Educational systems are increasingly open to observation and analysis; innovations developed in one system frequently spread to another. There are, of course, dangers in crude transplantation. Full analysis of any receptive environment (soil or human tissue) is necessary to prevent rejection. Similarly, many adaptations to local factors are required for the successful spread of educational ideas and practices. It is part of our aim for this book that it should contribute to the sensitive and intelligent spread of good practice and encourage the reappraisal, where necessary, of existing policies. The perception of good practice, whenever and wherever it occurs, can have a powerful influence on individuals who then, with new insights, exert pressure for change in their own systems and societies. Considerable pressure towards greater integration into mainstream is provided by observers who see children performing at a higher level than they can envisage in their own more restricted system. A good example of comparative influence is provided by Norway which established non-segregation in its schools as early as 1976 and began to operate a centrally-funded, but locally administered system. Within a few years visitors who came to see how the changes were working were writing appreciatively of the striking, observable new opportunities for children with special needs. Amongst these analysts was Mary Warnock, chair of the committee which produced the influential Warnock Report (1981) in Britain. It is worth quoting her observation in full:

> *We saw Down's Syndrome children working alongside their contemporaries, fully accepted and functioning at a far higher level than they could ever have achieved in a 'special' situation with contemporaries who were themselves all mentally handicapped. Behaviour is largely a matter of imitation, and these children were behaving like the rest of the class. Their contemporaries treated them as real people, not expecting them to be other than they were, different from themselves, but part of the school. Even very severely disabled and mentally retarded children were accepted. No one thought it odd that they should be there; and the system of having more than one teacher in the class, even if one of the teachers was supposed to be working mainly with the disabled child, seemed, on the whole, to operate for the general good. Other children than the 'special' child tended to turn to each of the teachers equally, if they wanted to know something or needed help. We saw some remarkable examples of collaborative or team teaching. (pp.132-3)*

Patent, observable achievement is difficult to ignore and provides an additional spur to re-examine curricula for children with special needs.

CURRICULUM PROVISION

There is extensive, recent criticism of reductive curricula for children with special needs. For example, as early as 1960, Tansley & Gulliford showed how language and number work could form the basis of a curriculum with a series of supplements from other fields including practical, environmental, aesthetic and creative learning experiences. They deplored the paring down process which stripped a mainstream curriculum to an unappetising core for children who were perceived to have difficulties in learning. By the mid-seventies, despite their lead, it appeared that the watering-down process was still flourishing. Brennan (1974) shows there were two powerful reasoning forces which led to typical reduction. Firstly, slow-learners, it was agreed, would only be capable of learning a small amount; that small amount was therefore best if it consisted of the 'basics', divided into small steps and taught with much repetition. Secondly, it was argued, slow learners would only be able to cope with the simplest jobs after leaving school, so school-work should be made both utilitarian and practical. In this way the supplementary curriculum, strongly advised by Tansley & Gulliford (1960), was never experienced by many pupils.

17

The influence of what Brennan identifies as two limiting underpinners of the slow learners' curriculum can still be seen in one of the examples of curricular provision offered by Hegarty et al (1986). A comprehensive school has 60 pupils with moderate learning difficulties whose needs are provided for by a Basic Studies Department. The same department also caters for mainstream children with learning difficulties. For the first three years moderate learning difficulty pupils follow certain subjects (such as games, P.E., drama, music and art) in the main school. However, the programme within the Basic Studies Department is not significantly different from many special schools, comprising literacy, numeracy, social studies, science, woodwork, art, home-management, mural studies and extra sport. Hegarty et al shrewdly note that the department's own programme: "operates in a self-contained way without particular reference to the main school." (p. 324).

They describe the provisions for literacy and numeracy and for practical options in years 10 and 11. As far as literacy is concerned, the provision is as follows:

> Where reading is particularly weak the SRA, Distar and Racing to Read schemes are drawn on, as well as the department's own phonic resource kit, supplemented by a wide range of cassettes, workbooks and reading books. Most pupils are given structured practice in order to acquire word-building skills. Here the department's own reading scheme comes into play. This was developed by the head of department because he considered that existing commercial schemes were insufficiently structured for this type of pupil. The scheme is in two parts: a phonics-based programme, and a section that concentrates on comprehension. It is based on the principles of programmed learning. Pupils work on those aspects of the scheme which relate to their specific area(s) of difficulty. There is a wide array of learning resources (workcards, worksheets and language masters). Pupils whose spelling does not match their reading ability either follow a commercial scheme (Blackwell's Spelling Workshop) or a course specially constructed for them, drawing upon a spelling resource kit developed within the department and designed to facilitate self-help skills in spelling. Once literacy has been attained (defined as reading at the 9-10 year-old level) a range of associated skills are taught, increasingly with a view to the needs of adult life. By the time pupils are in their fourth (i.e. 10th) year the concern is almost exclusively with such aspects of the adult world as writing letters, filling forms and completing job applications. (pp.324-5)

In this account we notice that the teaching of reading is segmented, structured, repetitive and reductive. Reading is taught separately from other language modes and without any context of need or purpose. There is no mention of pleasure or satisfaction in reading, no emphasis upon story structure, no central importance of picture books, rhymes, poems or continuous narrative. Spelling is similarly isolated from purposes of writing and is highlighted; whereas audience and purpose for writing, or drafting, receive no attention. So much for Brennan's first point about restricting a curriculum to what are perceived as basics! His second is illustrated by the reduction of writing entirely to utilitarian, practical exercises such as job applications. What we see in this example is a curriculum and organisation little different from many special schools. It is a salutary warning that, just because unit education takes place in a comprehensive campus, integration does not necessarily occur. Further, the methods used and the assumptions about what children can or cannot learn may actually constrain and inhibit progress. Terminology alone does not indicate the extent of integration. Just as some schools labelled 'comprehensive' could continue to segregate by streaming, banding, and withdrawing pupils, so 'integration' on a unit system may mean continuing division rather than making whole. A different and positive system of whole school support for special needs in a secondary school is analysed in Wade & Moore (1987) and other models are reviewed in Ramasut (1989). It is true that, following the Fish Report on special education in the Inner London Education Authority (ILEA, 1985), "the process of integration should form an essential element in all education wherever it takes place".

However, integration needs to be carefully defined, for segregation can masquerade under many guises.

MANAGEMENT IMPLICATIONS

Curriculum change, to be effective, needs the support of the school management team. Similarly, it is not enough for support teachers and the head of the Special Needs department to have the 'right attitudes' towards the children they teach; positive attitudes must also be in evidence throughout the policies and day-to-day management of the school. We now have a greater understanding of school management (e.g. Everard, 1986; Caldwell & Spinks, 1988) and of the positive force that management can exert in effecting changes in attitudes and practice.

We now recognise that it is not only individuals who can adopt narrow, traditional, defensive or insular postures. Institutions can develop them also and their collective inertia is then difficult and discouraging for individuals to cope with. More needs to be done than mere relabelling of the Remedial Department as the Special Needs Department. In fact, most schools have examples of caring staff, good practice, positive attitudes and significant achievements by pupils with learning difficulties. It is the job of school management to identify and to foreground these growing points, to analyse, foster and develop them, using them as a basis for a whole school policy, but remembering that a policy means more than a reshaping of curriculum and provision of resources. A policy includes, amongst other elements, developing appropriate organisation and liaison, inservice education, community involvement and consultation of the clients – the pupils themselves.

Three essentials lie at the heart of appropriate policies for achieving effective integration:

1. *a welcoming approach* to children with special educational needs. This includes not only such aspects as wheelchair ramps and toilet provision for the disabled, but full inclusion of children with disabilities into the whole life of the school.
2. *tolerance and respect* for individuals and for individual differences. This includes specific curricular provision in personal and social education programmes as well as in pastoral care, plus a rethinking of approaches and teaching methods across the curriculum in all subject areas.
3. *valuing achievements* of children with learning difficulties, recognising the problems they have overcome and, through positive feedback, extending for them the horizons of their potential.

RESEARCH

Research findings may well influence policies, but the relationship is not clear cut. If attitudes and prejudices are deeply ingrained, then results that challenge existing practices may well be ignored. Also research itself is rarely pure and unaffected by assumptions or limitations: sometimes it is even set up to demonstrate that the status quo is effective. Since research findings have to compete with other influences on decision-making, there is often a delay in acting on the conclusions of the most impartial of studies. These issues are illustrated by anthropological, empirical and action research.

Once it was unchallenged that individuals could be assessed as 'imbeciles', 'idiots', 'ineducable' etc. by objective tests given on a single occasion. Since mental ability was also regarded as permanent and unchangeable, testing provided a way of segregating individuals into institutions for permanent stay with little if any stimulus or teaching. What was the point if mental abilities were fixed for all time? In the early part of this century there was great interest in examples of feral children who had been segregated from human beings by living in the wild with animals such as wolves or bears. A useful summary and discussion is provided by the Kellogs (1933). A significant finding which emerged from these individual studies was that the chances of later adapting to civilisation (the ability to learn a human language, for example) seemed to depend upon factors such as the age when children became feral and the length of their period of segregation from human interaction. For the first time isolation was seen as exerting its own pejorative influence. Significantly, progress made in developing human behaviour in feral children was used as evidence for the power of environment to change abilities and capabilities; however, when progress was severely restricted or regressions (howling at the moon, for example) occurred, contrary conclusions could be reached.

At about this time in the 1930's experiments of various kinds were conducted with inmates of institutions. A classical empirical and longitudinal study was conducted in the U.S.A. by Skeels (1966) who compared orphanage children, placed in a caring context with inmates of a mental institution, with a control group who remained in their orphanage. Skeels' early results showed clearly that those given caring attention and human interaction made much better progress than the control group in an institution which only looked after their physical needs. Unfortunately few people wanted to consider the implications of Skeels' results which were criticised as showing mere temporary gains. Persistently Skeels kept contact with his subjects and his 1966 study reports on their progress 25 years later. The results are remarkable. The experimental group had achieved normal, well-adjusted lives, occupations and relationships in society, while the control group recorded only menial occupations and poor relationships, and most control subjects still remained in institutions of one kind or another and some had died. Contradictory evidence seemed to be offered by one control subject: Case 19 had a well paid job and a stable marriage. Skeels, however, discovered that he had been used as a subject in another experiment where he had received individual caring. Thus the evidence pointed overwhelmingly to some harmful effects of institutions and to the crucial importance for children of stable human interactions. Other researchers (e.g. Goffman, 1961; Bowlby, 1953) explored similar avenues. Most significantly people began to trust less in simplistic testing of subjects and were heartened by evidence which showed that, given the right kind of care, children could achieve the potential that institutions and segregation had hitherto repressed.

Such empirical investigations are, perhaps fortunately, no longer possible. Nor are they necessary, for the case against institutional segregation is proven. We now know more than we did about the effects on inmates of the institutions they belong to and various alternatives are being tried out for prisoners, orphans and handicapped persons amongst others. Much still depends on resources available and on the attitudes of society, but since the 1960's research evidence – ethnographic or action research varieties – has confirmed the trend towards integration.

We offer just one relevant example from an observational study. Reporting on their project Special Needs Action Programme (SNAP) and its evaluation in Coventry, Ainscow & Muncey (1988) offer six features which characterise schools successful in meeting special needs:

1. *Effective leadership from a headteacher who is committed to meeting the needs of all pupils.*
2. *Confidence amongst staff that they can deal with children's individual needs.*

3. A sense of optimism that all pupils can succeed.
4. Arrangements for supporting individual members of staff.
5. A commitment to provide a broad and balanced range of curriculum opportunities for all children.
6. Systematic procedures for monitoring and reviewing progress. (pp. 37-8)

Their evaluations, summarised here in the above six features, lead Ainscow & Muncey away from separate provision within the school and towards our own view expressed earlier in this chapter:

> *As we have formulated these ideas we have also realised that special needs are most likely to be met in schools that are responsive to all of their pupils as individuals. The aim, therefore, is not to make separate arrangements for a subgroup of pupils thought to be special, but rather to make all teaching more effective. (p.38)*

The focus of research has recently shifted to a search for those factors which make for effective integration and teaching. Ainscow & Muncey offer a twelve-point analysis of effective teaching whereby teachers are required to:

- emphasise the importance of meaning
- set tasks that are realistic and challenging
- ensure that there is progression in children's work
- provide a variety of learning experiences
- give pupils opportunity to choose
- have high expectations
- create a positive working atmosphere
- provide a consistent approach
- recognise the efforts and achievements of their pupils
- organise resources to facilitate learning
- encourage pupils to work cooperatively
- monitor progress and provide regular feedback

For a fuller discussion of these the reader is referred to their Chapter 5 *Teaching and Learning.* For our purposes the list indicates the shift towards investigating the details of integration policies now that research affirming the value of integration has been accepted and understood. This research will need to take into account social, economic and political issues in relation to legislation as well as the interacting dimensions of the problem that we have considered separately in this chapter. The latter part of this chapter has shown that neither research nor implementation policies are likely to have much effect unless attitudes are favourable. It is to this further complexity that we turn in Chapter 3.

Chapter Three

Attitudes and Integrating

There is one basic and major improvement which can be made which requires no legislation or increase in resources, but would probably bring about the greatest possible change in the lives of those families who have a handicapped member. That is for everyone to accept the fact of handicap in such a way that those who have to suffer the pain of having it in their family do not have to dread the reactions of others, coming to feel that they must either retreat from all contacts or fight to be recognised and accepted and to have their needs appreciated.

(Barbara Furneaux, 1988, p.98)

INTRODUCTION

Attitudes are insidious and all pervasive. Once low status is attached to an individual or group it becomes difficult to escape from the gloomy tunnel of stigma, lack of confidence and despair in which opportunity and possibility are seen only as a distant gleam of light ahead. The tunnel metaphor is appropriate only for the individual who is not valued or treated positively. For others concerned with children with special needs there is also a sideways slippage of attitudes which, amoeba-like, spread to affect them also. Parents are apt to suffer any stigma attaching to their children. Goffman (1968) explains how a stigma tends: "to spread from the stigmatised individual to his close connections". (p.43)

It may be that the strength, resilience and positiveness of particular individuals prevent this sideways slippage in their personal cases, but stigmas have attached to certain groups such as 'remedial teachers' whose work has frequently been hampered by their low status.

Once low status and negative images are assigned they become self perpetuating. Hafftner (1968) suggests that attitudes persist by means of a 'collective unconscious' in society which exerts its influence on our thinking. One might say that it *prevents* us thinking by encouraging us to accept prearranged stereotypes. Since this kind of influence is generally in play, it comes as no surprise when Thomas (1978, p.11) shows how the values and attitudes of society affect both the self-image and the behaviour of disabled people. It is this kind of insight which directs our attention towards uncovering attitudes and beliefs about disability and towards seeking to influence these when they are negative. It is often interesting to determine how attitudes towards the handicapped in society are acquired. It is generally accepted that we all *learn* attitudes – we are not born with them. The initial learning is usually from our homes and families; for example, attitudes towards peoples of different races, of different cultures or of different abilities and disabilities are internalised from the attitudes expressed by family members. As children grow older their social world expands to include school and other groups and their exposure to a different range of attitudes can either strengthen or weaken those that have previously been learned. A child, for example, may have 'learned' that people with a severe hearing impairment are incapable of learning or communicating with other people. Talking to other children or adults who have hearing impaired relatives or friends, or having a hearing impaired child as a class-mate, can alter a previously held attitude to a more positive view towards people with this type of disability. Social interaction can provide a beneficial learning environment and can redress previous misinformation which led to stereotypic views about physical handicap.

Attitude change is not confined to children. Adults too, through social interaction, have opportunities to either update their knowledge and understanding of disability with its consequent acceptance or re-inforce their previously held attitudes. It is the context of the interaction which is crucial. The range of individuals within that context is important in conveying information, acceptance and respect for the disabled either through encounter or conversation. The role of conversation is crucial in determining our attitudes particularly when language is also used as a labelling device for individuals or groups. Words used to describe people can be both a manifestation and a determinant of an attitude. 'Imbecile' and 'idiot' were once officially used (and regrettably sometimes still are) to categorise people of particular IQ measurement, but these categories soon become used as derogatory terms of abuse. The term 'ESN' (Educationally Sub Normal) also segregated huge numbers of children and deprived them, in some cases, of the chance of ordinary schooling. Prevailing attitudes insisted that, since they were not capable of ordinary schooling, such children should be segregated into special schools.

The Warnock Committee (1978) wisely rejected this simplistic notion of categorisation. Nothing is gained by using crude categories and much can be lost when the category names became pejorative and entrenched in negative attitudes.

Negative attitudes do not necessarily constitute dislike or discrimination, but they may set limits on what the child is able to achieve and may add patronisation to the child's learning difficulty. This is particularly true when class teachers are not trained to cope with special needs and when their schools are under-resourced. When they accept children with disabilities they may also accept them with low expectations. Again classroom language can reveal attitudes.

It may be rare to hear:

"You can't do this because you are spina bifida"

but tender solicitations about their abilities also speaks volumes to sensitive children:

"We'll give you something you can do"

"Don't worry about finishing. You've done what I expect from my specials" (teacher overheard referring to a group of children with 'learning difficulties').

Only when teachers have had the necessary training for them to be able to implement their skills will they be confident to tackle the children's education in the most appropriate way. The teacher who values the child as a person and respects what that child can achieve makes a major contribution both to the self-esteem of the child and successful integration.

ATTITUDES IN CLASS

At a school level there are particular difficulties both in clarifying the situation which exists as well as in influencing it. To begin with, it is difficult to obtain clear cut evidence as to how peer groups of normal children relate to classmates with impairments and how teachers relate to children with special needs in mainstream classes. Some studies have been undertaken, but suffer from faulty interpretation and methodology; consequently we need to consider their conclusions carefully. Gottlieb (1975) discussing a range of sociometric studies, notes that evidence indicates that children perceive retarded classmates less favourably than normal peers. Sociometric test results must be treated cautiously, though. We must remember that a child not selected as a 'best friend' may still be held in high regard and treated with consideration and positive respect.

The method tells us nothing about the actual interactions between children. Gottlieb also reports unfavourable teacher attitudes towards retarded children and a reluctance to have them educated in mainstream classes. Similarly, we must realise that measures of attitudes made in isolation from interaction and experience do not say how teachers would, in fact, behave. Experience is likely to change attitudes.

Expressed attitudes in one country may be very different from those conveyed in another and it is unwise to generalise findings from specific studies to wider contexts. For example, attitudes to mentally retarded pupils will be different from those to physically handicapped students. A further problem is that the research, such as it is, travels in one main direction. Few attempts (for an exception see Wade & Moore, forthcoming) have been made to discover how children with special educational needs think and feel about their situation, their teachers and their peer group, yet such information is of great value in maximising the learning potential of all children.

We know, for example, how important the self-concept is to successful learning; we know also how interactions with others – especially how valued persons perceive us and react to our successes and failures - can increase or inhibit our desire to learn and our future achievements. At the macro level, if the community classifies children into groups - handicapped, subnormal, able, maladjusted, spina bifida, etc. – then children can hardly help classifying themselves in the same way, particularly if the school system reinforces the categories by its separatism. A wide range of experiences is required for individuals to recognise the wide-ranging potentials within themselves. Children who have been institutionalised or have been treated stereotypically can hardly help seeing themselves in restricted ways.

Children with handicaps are likely to have adjustment difficulties to schooling even when attitudes and behaviour of teachers and peer group are positive. For a start, many normal children experience problems in adjustment; more important, children with special needs have to come to terms with the nature of their disability and with the contrast between themselves and others in the ordinary classroom. It is a mistake to treat such children 'exactly like the others'. Their disabilities make them different and part of their learning needs is an openness which allows understanding of the nature of their problem and ways of maximising their potentials. Rather the presence of such children should be a constant reminder that all children are different and should help to focus attention on the diversity of potential and need exhibited by normal children.

CHANGING ATTITUDES

The degree to which disabled children are teased or openly rejected in ordinary classrooms has possibly been overstated and some early studies (e.g. Anderson, 1973) have shown handicapped pupils treated fairly by peer group and teachers. A good deal, as has been said already, may depend on previous experience or on the type of disability. How obvious the handicap is appears to affect attitudes to begin with, but Adams & Cohen (1974) discovered that teachers attached less importance to externals as they came to know a child's personality and ways of learning. In this way experience affects attitudes for the better.

This period of adjustment takes time and, although attitudes may ultimately be affected, the period of adjustment for both teacher and pupil may well be difficult. The attitude of the class teacher is crucial for the child's learning. Baker & Gottlieb (1980) maintain that:

> *Teacher attitudes towards integration are expected to influence the extent to which handicapped children become not only physically integrated, but integral members of regular classes benefitting academically, socially and emotionally from the experience. (p.6)*

This contact with pupils with special educational needs certainly provides an educative experience for the teacher. Teachers who do not have contact with such pupils have more negative attitudes to categories of handicap (Brodwin & Gardner, 1978).

It is not only contact that is able to change teachers' attitudes. Knowledge and understanding, not only of the children's disabilities and special needs, but also of the strategies and skills needed to provide appropriate education, have been shown to give teachers not only confidence with, but positive attitudes towards, their pupils with handicaps. Larrivee (1980), for example, compared three degrees of intensity in training on teacher attitudes towards disability. Two groups received training, the third no training at all. Both training groups had training in behaviour management, diagnostic/prescriptive teaching and individual programmes of instruction. The first training group, which received intensive training (summer workshops, weekly training sessions, demonstrations, classroom visits), had significantly more positive attitudes than the second training group (monthly 2-hour sessions throughout the year, 18 hours in all) and the non training group. Leyser & Abrams (1983) also show how attitudes can be changed *before* teachers – particularly those who are prospective teachers of the disabled – enter the profession. A positive attitude can heighten awareness and sensitivity not only to the child's needs but to the needs of the immediate family.

UNDERSTANDING AND PROVIDING FOR DISABILITY

It is not easy to put oneself in the position of a parent who has a handicapped child. Because society has shielded itself for so long by segregating so many groups of people, many of us are unprepared by our experience to empathise. Barbara Furneaux (1988) tells how unprepared, lacking in tact and sensitivity parents found the majority of doctors – and these are the professionals in the front line. It is possible, however, to appreciate the vulnerability of parents torn by despair and grief, confused, blaming themselves and feeling guilty and anxious. We can also appreciate that the reactions of family members, friends and others in the community have a profound effect upon whether parents cope with their own feelings and make the necessary acceptances and adjustments to their own lives. There is a background of stigma and exclusion from normal society to overcome. For example, children with severe mental handicaps were completely excluded from schooling in Britain until recent years. Since the Handicapped Children's Education Act was passed (1971) many families and professionals have been encouraged by what previously rejected children can achieve. However, the stigmas of recent past as well as the painful present still have to be coped with by parents under stress.

Help and understanding should be provided for parents who have children with special needs. However, in many cases, the practicalities of individual initiative and resources mean that help through professional services, family centres or parents' groups is very uneven. Good practice needs to be observed and systematised for the benefits of others. It is fortunate that many parents have not retreated in the face of difficulty, but have followed the second path suggested by Barbara Furneaux by fighting to change prevailing attitudes in society. Frequently that fight has necessitated changes in legislation.

Many of the changes in special educational needs provision in New Zealand have been as a direct result of parents' pressure. Every child, including severely and multiply-handicapped children, now has the right to be educated in a school within their locality. Inevitably there are difficulties in receiving children when staffing and resources are insufficient and schools feel unprepared and inadequate. As parents continue to exercise their choice, schools are preparing their own support programmes in order to meet the needs of the children as fully as they can.

The tensions that these difficulties engender are not restricted to New Zealand schools. Any mainstream school that opens its doors to a special educational needs child without the staff having experience or prior training, inevitably experiences self doubt about its ability to cope. Unfortunately such self doubt can also lead to debates about the child's ability to cope within the mainstream classroom. Research, which we have already referred to on teacher attitudes and expectations, shows how quickly such feelings are transmitted to all pupils within the class. It is essential, therefore, that teachers have sufficient confidence in their own performance in order that they may acquire a positive attitude that is genuine.

As more children with disabling conditions enter the mainstream, more of the prejudice prevailing in society will begin to disappear. Prejudice is, after all, often based on misinformation. As classmates and their parents begin to interact on a day-to-day basis with the children, the differences between fact and myth will become apparent. It is to be hoped that individuals will become part of the social and academic melee of the classroom as a result of their strengths and weaknesses rather than their handicaps. Such positive attitudes towards individuals, developed and demonstrated in many schools, may also permeate through families and society and encourage attitude change towards everyone with disabilities.

ATTITUDES FOR INTEGRATING

Children with special educational needs who start their education in mainstream settings at infant school are perhaps more fortunate than those who make the transition from special schools later in their school career. Any developmental lag as a result of disability is usually less noticeable when children are younger and immediate acceptance by teachers and peers is easier. In many ways they are all in the same coping situation.

For all children the move from home to school can often be a time of confusion and re-orientation. The child is hurled into a situation where the adult in the environment has to be shared with twenty or more other children all vying for attention.

It takes a great amount of learning and adapting in order to adjust to the social melee of the reception infant classroom. In many respects this experience is echoed and relived by children with special educational needs who have made the transition, from the security of a special school or unit, into the hurly burly of the mainstream classroom. Not only do they have to become used to less attention, less help and probably fewer resources, but also to the realisation that, in some way, they are different from the majority of their peers. This is not meant to negate our previously held view (Wade & Moore, 1987) that *all* children are special and, by implication, different in some way. The majority of children, and we as adults, learn to accept these differences, whether physical (Sue is taller and stronger than I am) or academic (David is better at algebra than I am) and relegate them in our consciousness to the position that they deserve. It is very important that children with special educational needs also learn to accept their differences and – as all of us eventually do – to realise that they do not matter all that much when other things are equal. What matters more is their own potential, the realisation of that potential and the self-esteem that is necessary for such realisation. The relationship between self esteem and achievement is symbiotic, one dependant upon the other.

Self concept and self esteem have long been realised as determinants in academic achievement, (Brookover & Patterson, 1964; Coopersmith, 1968). Children with high levels of self esteem, who value themselves as people, often set realistic goals and achieve success through the acquisition of those goals (Coopersmith, 1968) – unfortunately the converse of that is also true. Children with low self esteem frequently set themselves inappropriate goals, either too high and consequently experience failure, or too low and therefore never work to their ability - either way their true potential is never attained.

It is appropriate, therefore, to ask whether the self esteem of children, particularly those with special educational needs, can be enhanced. It has been shown (Chapman, 1988) that children with learning difficulties, for example, generally have lower self-concepts than non-handicapped students. This was particularly true in the area of academic self-concept, as might be expected, but the effects on the self-esteem generally are crucial. The problem is, of course, that school itself can be a determinant of children's self-concept.

The classroom is a very public place, particularly in mainstream where the achievements of a whole range of children are apparent. Areas of knowledge and ignorance are often exhibited in front of peers. Judgements and evaluations are made, skill levels become obvious to groups of friends and systems of self-ranking become apparent – ("the children in Yellow and Blue groups are better than me but I'm better than the children in the Orange group"). This form of ranking might be inescapable, even though teachers do not make it obvious (Nash, 1973), though a lowering of self-esteem need not occur. Self-concept and self-esteem are the result of the internalisation of other people's perceived attitudes towards the individual (Burns, 1982). The people who are of most importance in the formation of the self-concept are the 'Significant Others', described by Kuhn (1964) as: "the others to whom the individual is most fully, broadly and basically committed, emotionally and psychologically.... the others in communication with whom his self-conception is basically sustained and/or changed" (p. 11).

This group contains not only parents but teachers and peers. It is important therefore that, if children are to integrate successfully into the mainstream and fulfil their potential, teachers' and pupils' attitudes towards the special educational needs pupil are positive in order that their self esteem becomes, and remains, at a high level. In the classroom it is initially the teacher's attitude which is crucial. The teacher is a role model for all children and signals which are given to (and about) the special educational needs child are often unconsciously internalised over time by the other class members *as well as* by the individual. Children with special educational needs should be treated the same as other children, but, at the same time, their specific disabilities should be taken into account. This apparent contradiction resolves itself when the 'treatment' is examined - for every child has a right to:

- the acceptance of individual differences
- encouragement of independence and responsibility
- set their own challenges and goals
- realistically high expectations
- encouragement during the learning process
- positive evaluation, praise and constructive criticism

The way in which children are valued and respected as members of the classroom and community not only ensures a positive self-concept, but an acceptance as a participating and functioning contributor to that society. Every child should be seen to have equality of opportunity in the classroom, with individuals receiving education appropriate to their needs. Integration is more than following an entitlement curriculum within the main-stream classroom; it involves the social and emotional components of school life – the components which can determine success in learning, at whatever level is appropriate for the potential of the individual.

CONCLUSION

In order to present such treatments realistically this chapter has shown that teachers need positive attitudes towards all children in their care. Such attitudes are realised through knowledge about children with specific handicaps and a starting point of confidence in their ability to meet the needs of such children. Knowledge encourages high levels of expectation for the children rather than introducing a low ceiling of achievement possibilities. Children with positive self concepts will strive to meet these expectations when teachers and peers alike exert a positive influence. Occasionally the pupils themselves may lift the ceiling of expectation. Peter Spencer (1990), for example, describes how, despite scepticism from staff, conversational French was introduced into his school for children with Moderate Learning Difficulties. It was due to the pupils' (age 15-16) insistence that they learn and their realisation that they were missing out on a curriculum enjoyed by pupils in other schools. The teaching was enjoyable and successful and culminated in a week-end trip to France! One of the most important outcomes noted by the staff was increased motivation and self-esteem among the pupils.

The role of the teacher, therefore, is crucial in determining positive attitudes towards the pupil with special educational needs and a positive self esteem in the pupil. Attitudes are manifested in behaviour; observable treatment of the pupil gives definite messages. Many pupils who are integrated into mainstream classes are, in reality, segregated. Keith Ballard (1990) makes this criticism about some early aspects of New Zealand classrooms and McGrory (1989) shows how one child with moderate learning difficulties, integrated into a primary school, not only received different curriculum work, but sat at a separate table, physically isolated from his peers. Social and academic interaction was minimal. The class teacher had segregated the child with the best of intentions - in order that individual attention could be given. Opportunities for learning through interaction with peers was denied (observation also revealed that teacher help was minimal, as the child worked mainly from worksheets). This type of well-intentioned, but misdirected, treatment reveals neither positive attitudes nor positive expectations. It is easy to understand why teachers who have children with special educational needs group them together for ease of teaching. They can be taught as a group, helped as a group, encouraged as a group, while the rest of the class continues with its set activities. This organisation results from positive intentions, but is not a positive approach to true integration. The prevailing attitude being expressed is that this group is significantly different from the rest of the class in terms of ability and expectation and this difference is underlined daily.

If social interaction and collaborative learning are missing, then the opportunity to gain first hand knowledge about children with, for example, hearing impairment, visual handicap, learning difficulties or physical handicap, is denied to other class members. Also denied is the chance to get to know, accept and value children as people. Those children with special needs also lose since they are denied the frequent satisfaction and encouraging role models that collaboration with mainstream learners provides.

As we discussed earlier, lack of appropriate training and support leads to inappropriate learning opportunities. Teachers work hard, are committed and are usually willing to accept pupils with special educational needs into their classrooms. They cannot, however, realise their own and their pupils' potential unless they have confidence in both.

In the chapters that follow we examine ways in which changes towards integration are being made in individual classrooms, units, schools and local education districts. We use the case study method which is direct and immediate and which provides a convenient way of evaluating whether the needs of pupils are being met and whether the system is supportive and positive.

Chapter Four

Whose Problem is it Anyway?

**Resources for the Disabled Pupil
in the Mainstream Class**

Well it's better than being at a handicapped school/ 'cos here I can mix with children of my own age/ and it doesn't mean that I'm with other people who are handicapped/ so I just think I'm one of them.

(Chris, age 12)

INTRODUCTION

At age 7 Chris sustained a broken neck in a car accident. The injury left him paralysed and without feeling from his neck down. Since he cannot breathe on his own, he has to be ventilated mechanically and relies on his powerdriven wheelchair and on other people for mobility. For three years after his accident he was entirely hospitalised, but for the last five terms he has been attending ordinary school - a middle school, a few miles away from his hospital - and spending Sundays at home. A further stage in the future is to return him to living permanently at home; but there are problems, as his nurse, Rachel, explains:

He lives at the hospital/ his parents are hoping to have him home shortly/ but it is a great responsibility to have a quadriplegic child at home/ fully ventilated/ it means that he's got to have full-time nurses/ somebody behind him all the time/ he's never really on his own.

In many ways the story of Chris and his integration into ordinary school is a success story. The sections which follow describe and analyse the features of his integration as seen from the viewpoints of those who work with him in the classroom and include the perceptions of Chris himself. The viewpoints use verbatim accounts to illustrate issues, but the names of participants have been changed as in all the case studies that follow.

CHRIS AND HIS SITUATION

Without dramatic advances in medical science, Chris's injuries will place permanent handicaps on his mobility and ability to breathe. It is possible that through an operation a battery-operated system could be implanted in his neck to stimulate muscles and make him breathe by electric impulses. Even if that were possible (so far his neck has not grown enough), he would still be placed on a ventilator at night for safety. He regularly practises gulp breathing by blowing out his cheeks and now is capable of breathing in this way for thirty minutes should his ventilator fail. Having a ventilator permanently makes him prone to chest infections which kept him away from school a good deal in his first year. Perhaps because of a developing resistance to infections, he has lost less time in his second year in ordinary school.

Rachel, his nurse, describes Chris variously as:

an intelligent little boy, but he does need pushing; a terrible worrier; he can be awkward; he can be very difficult / and very naughty.

Given Chris's multiple handicaps, it is surprising that Rachel is talking about very infrequent behaviour (though these four statements could apply to almost any adolescent), for, as she adds:

99 per cent of the time he's good.

Rachel is full of admiration for his independence and persistence:

He'll have a good try / I mean like birthday times and Christmas times / he does all his own cards / with our help / we'll steady the card and Chris will write his cards out / he's quite independent in that respect / he's doing really well.

His first teacher, Mrs Buckley, mentions his tremendous sense of humour and his present teacher, Mrs Carson, says

He's treated like any other child in the school / like he gets told off occasionally by me / he doesn't like it / but no other child does.

A rounded picture of Chris emerges from these reactions and clearly he is not patronised or merely 'looked after' in his ordinary school. Mrs Carson makes this point explicitly. Looking after him is:

> not enough / Chris has got a brain / not only that / he wants to succeed / and if we just have this attitude of baby-minding / then that to me is a negative reason for Chris being in the school.

Chris gains much by being treated in a normal, fairminded way. At the same time the special needs of his particular situation have to be taken account of. For example, his start to the day is more demanding than that of most children, as he himself articulately explains:

> Well / the physio has to come / and bang my chest / and then she has to suck me out with a catheter / cos I can't cough myself / to get it up / she has to put a catheter down my throat / and then after that she does my passive movements / just to move my arms and legs about / and then I have to get dressed / and I wear a sheepskin jacket which holds me in place / then they have to lift me into my chair and then get everything done like put my watch on / do my hair / put my tie on / um / then she has to do her jobs / like / we've just started soaking in / um Milton fluid / um / the tubes / she has to put all those in there / and then she has to lock up the door / check my bag to check that everything is in there / and then / we have to go downstairs / get into my van which takes about five minutes / cos they have to drive to school from Churchington / and then get me back out the van / and then I have to drive through the school / to get my lesson / and / it's all such a rush in the mornings.

We suspect that few of us would be good for '99 per cent of the time', if we experienced this routine. Chris's nurse perceptively draws attention to a special need that is more affective than physical. It is normal for adolescents to register protests, to be moody and occasionally to have tantrums. Chris is no exception. He, too, can be moody, even depressed, without being able to talk about it. However, his way of being difficult or naughty is to refuse to eat or to take his medicines. He cannot shout or scream or kick or throw things. This refusal is his only available way of protesting. Similarly he cannot stamp his feet, or run upstairs to his room. As Rachel says:

> he's never really on his own / therefore if he's got / a problem / he has to sort of have his little / paddywack / with you / he can't run away and have it on his own.

From this introduction to Chris - an interesting personality with special needs - it would seem that technology and interaction with others are necessary to expand his horizons and to develop him as a learner. Yet paradoxically continual interaction is shown to be problematic in this one instance:

it's very difficult for us / and it's very difficult for
Chris / cos he's never on his own.

GETTING STARTED ON INTEGRATION

While Chris was still in hospital, the medical authorities regularly met to discuss what could be done to help him. He had some hospital tuition in the mornings and then, for a year or so before he started school, he spent an hour with each of five different tutors in a one-to-one relationship each afternoon of the week. In this way he was prepared for the length of the school day and continuity links were forged. For example, Mrs Fairburn, one of his tutors who taught him Mathematics and Computing in hospital, has continued to give him support teaching all the time he has been in the ordinary school. She supports Chris's regular teachers in a number of ways:

1. She helps him catch up if he misses lessons through illness.
2. She supports teaching and learning:
   I talk to / all his other teachers and ask them if there are any problems / that they feel / could do with a little bit of extra work.
3. She adapts learning experiences to his needs:
   especially in Maths / if he needs something to enable him to carry on with the rest of them / I'm thinking perhaps / when they did graphs in the lesson / he needed a means of representing the graphs on the screen / we make a program / which would help to set out the axes / and plot the points / so we write the programs / and he can help me.
4. She gives him special coaching in his areas of competence, thus expanding his status and confidence.

Perhaps this fourth kind of support is the most important, since it has meant that, from the beginning, Chris has developed computing skills beyond the level of most of his classmates. He does a good deal of programming and Mathematics, he can operate a lead lesson for his classmates from his computer and, with the help of a specially written program, he succeeded in teaching one of the present writers the essentials of binary mathematics! As Mrs Fairburn says:

the better he can use his computer / the better for him.

She helps Chris to write quizzes and to program games that later he can try out on his friends and nurses. The computer is not merely of use intellectually; it is a way by which Chris can interact with others and achieve status and satisfaction.

Chris's first class-teacher, Mrs Buckley, visited him in hospital before he started school partly to prepare Chris, partly to prepare herself:

it was a bit of a daunting prospect / having not taught any handicapped children before / especially with his multiple handicaps really.

She consulted Chris about the new situation and reassured herself:

I had a talk with Chris before he came / and he was such an easy child to talk to / and I said / look I'm going to have problems you're going to have problems and we'll work them out together somehow / and he was quite happy with that.

PROGRESS THROUGH TECHNOLOGY

Ramps had to be built so that Chris could drive his electrically-powered wheelchair (he controls it expertly with his chin) into and around the school building, but other practical problems were not easily anticipated and took longer than necessary to resolve. Mrs Buckley explains:

First we had no computer here for him so we had to use the hospital one which had to be carried in every day / his breathing apparatus on his chair was very noisy / at first / so we had to get that changed / because it made a lot of noise / difficult in the classroom talking to the children / and he didn't have a stand for his computer or anything else / so everything had to be carted about and that made problems at first.

It is inevitable that progress should primarily be seen in terms of technology, for a quadriplegic child is dependent upon equipment for mobility and many learning experiences. Instead of expert educational assessment and anticipation of Chris's needs, there seems to have been a trial and error period, where adaptation and improvisation took place. At last a school computer was obtained and the husband of a staff member fashioned a stand for it. An improved wheelchair with a battery for the ventilator meant Chris could stay in school all day instead of four hours maximum. He was equipped with a specially adapted van for journeys to and from school. Other technological strides forward took time (nine months, in fact) - firstly, because of delays in having Chris's needs assessed outside the school and secondly, because of delays in obtaining equipment. Eventually, however, he obtained a rollerball system which he can rotate to move the cursor on his screen and so draw pictures. Eventually, and perhaps more significantly, he obtained his specially designed mouthpiece - a gumshield attached to a rod - which enables him to tap keys on his computer with speed and efficiency.

Chris is still waiting, however, for a laptop computer which will give him greater flexibility and mobility. At the time of writing this has been 'on order' for eight months. His first class-teacher speaks of the frustration she felt and how lack of technological and educational support added to her difficulty:

> *The only thing I found difficult / as far as getting into school / was the lack of back-up from the education authorities / plenty from the medical side / I didn't see anybody from the education people except the educational psychologist came quite late / he'd been ill / but apart from that there was no real help / we had to fight for everything we've got as far as computers and / that sort of thing / we decided last year / that he needed a lap computer / but we still haven't got that.*

If Chris had not been so cooperative a learner, the practical and technological problems would have had a far greater negative effect. As it was, and without guidance his teacher felt she was 'floundering':

> *I felt I was a bit out on a limb on my own / I was finding out as I went along but / luckily it worked very well.*

There is no necessity to keep reinventing the wheel. Expert advice must be made available to teachers and educational authorities must be sufficiently well organised to supply necessary equipment without undue delay. This was the case as far as Chris was concerned, though his teacher who took responsibility "with no experience and no advice really" is as positive as she can be:

> *because it was a new thing / nobody seemed to know who was actually responsible / for getting the money... I'm not blaming anybody or any authority in particular / but I just feel that / the organisation wasn't there.*

TECHNOLOGY AND INTERACTION

In the case of children with special needs, technology and special equipment are frequently a means to an end rather than an end in themselves. They provide a way of facilitating those kinds of interaction which are essential to the process of learning.

Mrs Fairburn, Chris's support teacher, minimises the role of technology in his learning, preferring to lay the stress upon:

> *the fact that he comes to school / that he gets out / goes on visits / meets more people.*

Interaction with others has changed Chris from an unconfident recluse unwilling to leave his hospital room to a boy eager to learn and enjoying the stimulus and company of others. Mrs Fairburn notes the change she has observed over three and a half years:

> *at first / when he comes to school / he would use / any excuse not to come and play up a little bit / but that's changed / now it's the other way round / he's disappointed if he can't come / last week his car broke down and he had to*

*stay / in the hospital / and he was really / annoyed / because there was
nothing wrong with him*

Here is an example of specialised equipment (his van) being the means to
an end (his interactions within the ordinary school). Herein lies the warning
that we should never try to make new technologies more important than
they are. They may be essential to get children with special education needs
into a context where learning can take place; but they cannot on their own
guarantee that learning. Specialist equipment (whether books, machines,
lenses, recording aids or computers) should not deflect us from our
essential task of ensuring that learners interact appropriately with their
environment and especially with other people. The main purpose of
integrating pupils like Chris into ordinary schools is to provide for them
both educational stimulus and social interaction. In our assessments of
integration we must not be sidetracked from the essential questions: What
learning is taking place? What is the quality of the interactions - specifically
how do they contribute to that learning? It is to some assessment of these
issues that we now turn.

PROGRESS THROUGH INTERACTION AND LEARNING

The fact that Chris's attitude to school has changed dramatically to
wholehearted approval indicates that the educational stimulus and
interactions with others have a positive effect upon his motivation. From
the beginning Mrs Buckley felt that having his nurse in the classroom all the
time would create a barrier between Chris and the rest of the class. She
argued that:

> *it was important that he was integrated as much as possible within the class/
> and didn't feel he was something / extraordinary in the corner.*

Interaction is a two-way process and it was necessary also to discuss
procedures with classmates to allay their concerns:

> *I talked to the rest of the class / about it too because they were rather /
> overawed / with all this / equipment / and Chris being as he was / but they
> were very helpful.*

Consultation and information is necessary to produce understanding and
empathy:

> *They were a little bit reluctant / at first / to be natural with him / so we
> started the system / it was either everybody wanted to stay with him / or they
> all rushed off outside / so we had a system of turns / to be responsible for
> Chris during the day / and they would sit with him / and do his moving
> around / and all that sort of thing / and now / I think he's got really good
> friends / from that time.*

Chris certainly has kept friends from that time though (like other adolescents) has also developed different friends while he has moved away from one or two existing ones. Some friends seem to have moved away from him as Mrs Carson says:

> *as friends do move on / and they've moved on from Chris and Chris has been/ a little bit left high and dry occasionally.*

On the other hand he has more recently been invited to tea at his friends' houses (because he has his little van, his nurse can transport him) and he invites friends to his hospital room. He has a sofa bed so that friends can stay overnight. Frequently they do.

Mrs Carson also recalls how she consulted Chris about entering her class:

> *You will tell me won't you if I'm doing something wrong or whatever / please tell me / or if you find I'm not doing something that's of benefit to you/ if I'm not noticing that you're winking at me / which is how he puts his hand up as it were / just shout my name / don't just sit there.*

It is not workable to tailor every lesson to the needs of one child. If this happened, thirty other children would have no art and craft, model making or cooking, for example. Chris, however, can make important contributions in these areas of the curriculum since much of the point of doing craft work is the planning and decision making about process and order of construction. Chris plays an active part in small groups: exploring, deciding, planning, directing and questioning. Above all, he is constantly socialising and thus engaging in learning through the relevant models of language that Halliday (1969) shows are part of a learner's essential equipment.

From the start he was left with other children who would call his nurse immediately if anything was needed, but who otherwise treated Chris as any other playmate. This was important for Chris, as Mrs Buckley says:

> *He's so much with adults / all the time / that it was a revelation to him to get with children and be part of that.*

At the time of entry to school, she found Chris educationally equal to his classmates because of the good tutoring he had received in hospital, but she adds:

> *Perhaps because of his social isolation from other children / the only area I found he was a little bit immature was in his story writing / he hadn't had the experience of the other children / to draw upon / it was still things / that had happened to him when he was seven.*

Rachel, his nurse, emphasises how difficult it is to provide the firsthand experiences that will encourage learning:

We were going home / and he'd been really depressed all day / it had been absolutely pouring down with rain / and he'd been watching the kids jumping in the puddles / and we were travelling home and he said / will you drive through a puddle / er / and that really touched me / because it was his only way of / being like the rest of the children but we had to do it in the car / because Chris couldn't jump / I had to do it in the car and I felt quite touched by that / and he'll do this quite often / you know ask you to do things which are really for him / and he gets his satisfaction out of watching you do it for him.

Of necessity Chris must obtain a good deal of experience vicariously and his interactions with people are crucial to facilitating this kind of learning. Similarly, interactions with the wider range of people he now meets provide opportunities for first-order experiences. His teacher, Mrs Carson, arranges visitors from the school community and ensures that Chris participates as fully as possible even in sense experiences:

He's touched things with his skin / even though he can't handle things / we had the RSPCA man in / he had a snare and everything / feel how sharp it is / and he (Chris) says well put it against my cheek.

Chris's passion is now story writing - interestingly, since that was regarded as his weakness when he entered school. He contemplates becoming a writer of children's books and his enthusiasm spills over into his leisure time, when he and his friend, Brian, invent adventures and who-dunnits and script them for film or television. He gives an example himself:

Generally we think of an idea / we call it Into The Unknown and we were in the Middle Ages and we're on a ship / and we set off / across the Atlantic and discovered America / we had things like scurvy and shipwreck / mutiny / and the cabin boy was the mate's son / I was the mate / Brian was the captain / and what we do we get all my teddy bears / and make them act it out / Brian does the movements and their voices.

Material from mainstream lessons is activated in this way, Chris takes a role himself in the drama and, through interactions with his friend, has full access to the creative and organising aspects of story making.

CONCLUSION

This brief analysis of progress made by Chris has emphasised the fact that technological features are crucial to provide access to learning opportunities, but that the majority of learning experiences are provided through interactions with friends, teachers and other members of the wider community. Chris himself recognises the broader range of experience available in main stream education and how necessary this is for him:

41

Well it's better than being at a handicapped school / cos here I can mix with children of my own age / and it doesn't mean that I'm with other people who are handicapped / so I just think I'm one of them / I play outside / and things like that.

Mrs Carson, his teacher, views him in the same way, recalling one occasion when she arranged for a blind person and his guide dog to visit the classroom. Discussion following the visit focussed on the blind man's ordinariness:

isn't he normal / just normal / and we all said that / but we all think of Chris/ and I think the class does as well / Chris is normal as well / we just take Chris for granted / and that is a revelation.

One other aspect of learning as an interactional process is that teachers and others frequently learn from students. Chris's classmates have lost their concern and fear for his safety:

now they help / they hold his head / and do all sorts of things, while his nurse changes his tracheostomy tube, for example.

Mrs Carson sums up her own learning and process:

In past years I would have thought twice about speaking to anybody who was different / who / I hate this word different / you know what I mean / he wasn't standing upright like me / and if I did speak to them I'd be awfully nice to them / overly concerned / protective / wary / because I didn't have the knowledge / I was ignorant / I would hope now / if I saw somebody in the street for example / rather than look down I would smile at them.

If discussions of integrating handicapped children into ordinary classrooms have hitherto omitted adequate exploration of the view of some of those most closely concerned with the process, they have also ignored the two-way interaction and the benefits of important learning to others as well as to the learner with special needs. Lest we forget that latter aspect, though, Chris is given the last word:

I really enjoy it here - most of the time.

Chapter Five

Integration and the Specialist Unit: problems of balance

I like it in the classroom because it was great, very interesting.

(Trudy, age 13)

I liked the teachers in the unit because I understand them, but I can't understand the teachers upstairs.

(Sue, age 13)

INTRODUCTION

For hearing-impaired children great strides in technology and the use of resources have made it possible for more to be integrated functionally, rather than merely locationally and socially, (DES, 1978) into the ordinary school.

The use of the radio aid, for example, has allowed the hearing-impaired child to move freely around the classroom while still being able to listen to the class teacher as comprehensively as the hearing impairment will allow. Helpers are often used in the ordinary classroom to ensure that learning is maximised (Wade & Moore, 1987) and help for teachers in the form of specialist support is available, sometimes even on site. This last facility is most effective when the ordinary school has a specialist unit which caters for the hearing-impaired. Even children with profound hearing impairment are able to become part of the ordinary school, ensuring that some of their education, at least, is provided in the mainstream classroom.

Academically, therefore, the needs of these children are being met as fully as possible and, as they are integrating into the ordinary classroom, the assumption is that their social needs are also being met. Yet it is easier to measure academic progress than social development. It is possible to assume that children are interacting socially because of their talking and helping with tasks, but it is the quality and purpose of the social and academic interaction that are more important. As Hodgson (1986) maintains, acceptance within the peer group has a direct and important bearing on the pupil's education. Teachers and researchers can observe peer group interaction and draw conclusions, but because we tend not to ask the children, we are never aware of how they perceive the situation. Perception, of course, is not reality but an amalgamation of responses, emotions and evaluations which then become real to the individual. We can never be sure of a personal response until we question. This chapter, therefore, investigates the perceptions of two hearing-impaired children of their 'integration' at primary school level, in order to evaluate the success of their experience.

The two hearing-impaired children are now in their second year of comprehensive education in Britain. They are both in an 'ordinary' school but are supported by a specialist unit, as they are profoundly deaf. They were each given a questionnaire which they filled in with the help (if necessary) of a teacher whom they knew and trusted. They could either write or dictate their answers and were able to expand their answers if they wished.

The questionnaire focussed on their perceptions of integration in their primary schools. This may have proved initially to be difficult, because of the time gap, but the thoroughness of their answers suggests that this was soon over-come. The time gap could have been beneficial, for remembrance of past events can give an extra dimension to experience. It enables comparisons to be made, it gives time for reflection and it puts the experience into perspective.

This chapter introduces the children and their global perception of the primary school. It then focusses on their views of their teachers and of their friends. Their comments on the classroom environment and the curriculum and finally their experience of school activities are also considered. The chapter discusses their perceptions and concludes with implications for the hearing-impaired child in the ordinary classroom.

THE CHILDREN: TRUDY AND SUE

Trudy and Sue are both thirteen years old and integrate into the mainstream for the majority of their school day, although they also have lessons in the specialist unit. Their teachers state that both appear to be progressing well, academically and socially. They have each experienced integration at primary school level, again with a specialist unit which was an integral part of the main building, not separate. Their perceptions of 'integration', however, varied considerably. We must, of course, remember that hearing-impaired children vary as do any members of a group in terms of their personality; this variation may, of course, account for their differences in perceptions, but nonetheless their reasoning is interesting.

Trudy had entered the primary school when she was seven years old, having previously attended a special school, whereas Sue had attended her primary school from the reception age (5) through to top junior level (11). Recollections of their early days were rather hazy, although Trudy could remember meeting her headmaster for the first time:

The headmaster said "Hello, good morning"

and she felt that he was pleased to see her. She remembers that her parents were 'allowed' (Trudy's term) to go to school with her and even to stay with her at first. This introduction, as well as the fact that her parents were allowed to stay with her, must have been indicative to her that she was welcome and that the headmaster and teachers were interested in her settling into school as quickly as possible.

THEIR VIEWS OF TEACHERS

Teacher/pupil relationships play a vital role in successful integration, not only academically, but socially. Trudy perceived her relationship with staff and pupils in the school in a most positive manner. Although she spent some time in the unit (always at the beginning and end of each day and during specific lessons, for example, reading and language work) she preferred to be in the ordinary classroom:

I like it in the classroom because it was great, very interesting.

She did not necessarily have a good relationship with all her teachers:

One teacher I not like, one teacher shouted and was not nice to me,

but, of course, a child does not have to have a hearing impairment to make that kind of subjective assessment!

One teacher in particular, whom she remembered with affection, had obviously made a conscious effort to communicate with and interest her as fully as possible:

He was very kind and help me a lot. He also learn to do sign language.

On the other hand Sue, who describes herself as 'very profoundly deaf', much preferred to be in the unit than in the ordinary classroom, stating that there she felt more at home:

I liked the teachers in the unit, but I didn't like the teachers upstairs,

and she went on to explain:

I liked the teachers in the unit because I understand them, but I can't understand the teachers upstairs.

She went on to explain that one of the mainstream teachers used to stand over her and mouth (not speak) at her in an exaggerated manner, not only making the communication difficult to understand, but also making her feel 'different' from the other children in her class. In addition, the facility of the radio aid was often not used; therefore she was unable to utilise the little hearing she did have.

This somewhat bizarre approach can only serve to isolate children like Sue even further. Admittedly Trudy's teacher treated her 'differently' by learning and communicating by sign language, but this was, as proposed by Warnock (DES, 1978) *additional* to the verbal communication she was receiving, and not *instead* of it.

It is possible that the children's perceptions of teachers' behaviour could also be interpreted on an emotional plane: Sue, fortunately, did not think that any of her teachers disliked her or her presence in the class, but she attributed that to the fact that she was:

always being good in classes.

She did not like:

being told off because I felt guilty.

Trudy also maintained that her teachers liked her and gave several reasons:

Sometimes they enjoyed having me in their class. I worked hard, I am funny and make jokes. When I was up to mischief they didn't.

Trudy is able to take an objective and humorous view of the teachers' relationship with her. She shows herself able to accept that, at times, she may not have been a favourite member of the class, but she is sufficiently confident of herself to be able to rationalise and put it into perspective.

Relationships with teachers, although social in one sense, are by necessity primarily concerned with 'educational' matters. Relationships with peers, however, are embedded in a social context which then can be a precursor to learning through collaboration. An examination of the friendships of Trudy and Sue gives further indication of the extent of their social and academic integration.

THEIR VIEWS OF FRIENDS

The two girls were asked about their friends at school and how well they got on with them.

Trudy stated that being in the ordinary classroom had become a 'good experience' because she had a lot of friends, both hearing-impaired and hearing, more than if she had remained in the unit and that:

you can have confidence in talking to your hearing friends.

It was clear that she preferred to practise verbal communications and could do this much more easily in the classroom situation. She did not like being confined to the unit:

I don't like sign language.

Her 'best' friends were:

a mixture, because I went round with both hearing-impaired and hearing people.

Sue's experience in the ordinary classroom, however, made her feel 'left out'. She much preferred to be with 'deaf people'. Her best friends were deaf, even those she sat with at lunch-time were hearing-impaired. She would have preferred to have stayed in the unit full time, not only because the teacher there helped her a lot but because she would:

feel not lonely.

Whereas Trudy had the confidence to speak to all of her friends, Sue clearly missed the security of her unit friends when she was in the ordinary classroom situation. Such a sense of isolation and loneliness indicates that the interaction with the hearing children does not necessarily lead to a collaborative learning environment. Sue's loneliness did not stem from a lack of concern by her classmates. The pupils in the ordinary classroom made attempts to help her in her schoolwork; they told her 'things';

they talk very slowly and show what I'm doing.

In the unit, however, she felt that she did not need help:

No-one help me, I knew what I was doing.

Trudy maintained that she did not receive help from her hearing friends in the ordinary classroom. In one class, she remembered, everyone had their own work to do and:

When you finished that you had to say that you finished it and go on to the next subject.

She can, however, remember working with people:

In Maths, Ian and I worked together.

It is possible that Trudy and Sue both received help from their classmates, but that they perceived it differently. Sue obviously resented the fact that she was seen by teachers and pupils to need help, whereas in the unit the work was clearly organised so that help from friends was not necessary. Trudy, on the other hand, insisted that she was able to work either by

47

herself or with other children. The difference in perception of their working relationships with their peers can colour the ways in which they value themselves as learners.

Friendships outside school time were problematic as neither of their schools were local to them. Consequently they were either 'bussed' or 'taxied' to and from school – a factor which placed restrictions on continuation of friendship groupings at the end of the day.

THEIR VIEWS OF CLASSROOM ENVIRONMENTS

The classroom is a place of shared activity between pupils and between teachers and pupils. For many hearing-impaired children, some sharing is missed. One area of classroom interaction where they both expressed dissatisfaction was the missing out of the shared humour between the teacher and the rest of the pupils. Neither understood the jokes or the laughter that resulted from them. On these occasions Sue was lucky, for her classmates often ensured that they repeated the jokes and made sure that she understood them. Trudy was not as fortunate, since her friends did not usually take the time to explain them to her, and she can remember one class in particular:

One year I was made to sit in the back with a hearing-impaired person and everybody else was in groups.

Therefore, the possibility of sharing and comprehending humour was denied to her as a result of the effects of classroom organisation. In many ways Trudy resented any other hearing-impaired children in the class, regarding them in some way as a nuisance:

Some deaf children went a bit silly.

Unlike her classmates, Trudy had little acceptance of the needs of others. In her desire to be seen as 'ordinary' and the same as the rest, she was in danger of being unsympathetic to those children who might have benefited from her example of confident and positive interaction. Fortunately, this attitude was not prevalent at the age of thirteen; perhaps she had to undergo a period of adjustment to the hearing-impaired children in the class. It is likely that by sitting with another hearing-impaired child, Trudy realised the restrictions the situation placed on her interactions with the hearing children.

THEIR VIEWS OF THE CURRICULUM

As with all children, Trudy and Sue had their curriculum preferences. Sue enjoyed painting because it was good fun and craft because it was interesting. She was 'good' at Maths and therefore looked forward to these lessons, unlike English where she felt that everyone was 'better' than she. Trudy, on the other hand, preferred English to Maths and particularly enjoyed project work where she worked with friends. It is, of course, impossible to assess how well they achieved in their particular preferences, but it is clear that their perceptions of their own work was, in the main, creditable. They were positive about most curriculum areas except for games; Sue expressed a severe dislike of games, particularly netball and volleyball:

because no-one threw the ball to me at netball and volleyball was hard for me.

Trudy was not so critical of the games (except outdoors when it was cold) and, in fact, she had joined the badminton club.

It is interesting that Trudy has chosen her favourite subjects in those areas where interaction is most likely (project work and English) whereas Sue has chosen rather more solitary activities where it is more possible to work by oneself. This must have posed a problem for her class teachers (provided that they perceived her difficulty). It is necessary in these cases to encourage interaction with the peer group, although, of course, it is impossible to guarantee success. Her comment about the games lesson is particularly interesting. It may well be, of course, that she was a poor player (everyone tends to pass the ball to those they expect will be able to do something with it), but her perception of the situation is on a more personal level: she does not say that she was poor at games but that she did not like them because her peers did not involve her when they were playing.

THEIR VIEWS ON SCHOOL ACTIVITIES

Trudy and Sue were asked whether they were in a club at school and whether they had ever taken part in an assembly or school play. It had already been mentioned that Trudy belonged to the badminton club at school. Club activities took place at lunch time so that she was able to attend; after-school activities were severely limited because of her need for transport home. Sue, however, not only did not belong to a club at school; she did not have any wish to do so, although she stated that she went to a 'deaf club' after school.

They both took part in school plays, but with different roles. Trudy proudly announced that she had been in lots of plays and had:

a lot of parts, without speaking.

She could remember being the mother of the prodigal son, a poor child in *Oliver*, and

on my last year at school I did the maypole dance.

Sue's experience of plays, however, was more limited.

49

Admittedly she had been in a play, but one produced by 'the unit children' and presented to the rest of the school and parents. She had helped in a full school production:

I only work the lights for the play.

Both, therefore, had taken part in non-academic school activities, but it is perhaps arguable that Trudy's experience had been richer in terms of integration. All of her performances had been with, and for, the ordinary school. The fact that she had not had a speaking part did not appear to concern her and it is highly probable that many other hearing children had non-speaking parts. Therefore, apparently she was offered, and accepted, the same opportunities as the other children in her class.

Sue had had a different opportunity, perhaps one offering less in terms of integration. Although she had performed in a play for the parents and school, she was seen as, and felt, part of the unit, not the school, thus strengthening links with the unit and weakening those with the ordinary school. It is obvious that the school viewed the hearing-impaired children as contributors to the whole school, but continued to create a division between the two. Sue had, of course, also been asked to help with the lights in the 'ordinary' school play, a very important role in any production, needing concentration and a certain amount of mental and manual dexterity. Clearly, however, she had not perceived it as such:

I only work the lights for the play.

Perhaps its importance had not been clearly explained to her, or she was not aware of the responsibility of her task; either way it had lessened the importance and status of her contribution.

Of the two children, only Trudy could remember taking part in a school assembly and that was when the head teacher had read out the names of those who had obtained swimming certificates and she had had to go forward, with other children in her class, in order to receive them from him.

Assemblies, in fact, are an ideal opportunity for all of the children to come together and share in each other's successes and achievements. Assemblies, however, can be problematic for hearing-impaired children, as they often are held in halls with large numbers of children – even when using a radio aid peripheral sounds will be amplified and transmitted and complete understanding may not be possible. Yet it is one other part of the school day where a child with a hearing impairment can be seen to be part of the whole school. This is particularly so when a child has participated in the same activities and shared the same success as his/her peers. Acceptance of achievement in a non-patronising way is another step towards acceptance of the child as an 'ordinary' class-mate who just happens to be hearing-impaired.

TOWARDS EFFECTIVE INTEGRATION

The two girls, Trudy and Sue, are obviously very different in their attitudes, personalities and perceptions. It may well be argued that time has added to, or detracted from, their memories and feelings of the primary school days, as both of them had been away from their primary school for one year and a term. Memory, of course, is selective, and may not present an accurate representation of what actually took place; nevertheless, the very nature of the selective memory would suggest that those events important and crucial to the individual are those which are recollected. In addition, as neither was in the school about which they were being questioned, it could perhaps be said that the answers were more truthful as the girls would not worry about hurting the feelings of staff or fellow pupils. Further, their placement in secondary schools allowed them to make comparisons between institutions and units within them. It is impossible to be critical when only the status quo has been experienced.

In the main, their views on integration appear to be different, Trudy preferring to be in the ordinary classroom whereas Sue obviously found the security of the unit more reassuring. It is, therefore, interesting to speculate: first, why this should be so, and, second, how best we can encourage positive attitudes towards integration, not only by the hearing-impaired children, but by their classmates and teachers.

The Children

First, perhaps we could focus on the children's views of themselves. It appears that Trudy sees herself quite strongly as a member of the ordinary class, preferring to spend most of her time there rather than in the unit where she would receive extra help. She liked her class teachers, particularly one who took the trouble to learn signing so that he could communicate more effectively with her. It is also obvious that, in terms of work, at least, she was treated as any other member of the class, being expected to finish her work and take the responsibility for informing the teacher and starting another project. It is also interesting that she saw herself as equal in status with her peers, working with her friends, unlike Sue who was helped by her classmates. Sue's classmates and teachers apparently had the very best of motives: they were anxious that Sue should be able to cope with the work in her class; they gave her all the help that they thought she needed. However, in so doing, they denied her equal status, relegating her to an inferior rank:

They talk very slowly and show what I'm doing.

51

She states very positively that in the unit she does not need any help; it appears that in this situation at least she is able to view herself as an independent learner.

It is part of a teacher's role to help and encourage children in their learning, but perhaps there are less obvious ways in which this could be done: for example, by getting children to collaborate in the learning, as in project or topic work, where every child's contribution is valued. The teacher may, of course, have to manipulate the size of the group in order that every child may have the opportunity to offer suggestions: initially pair-work might be better, as both members of the pair will have to contribute. Group structure may also have to be predetermined - a dominant hearing child paired with a shy hearing-impaired child would benefit neither! Children usually are sensitive to the needs of others (many children in the ordinary class learn some signing and will naturally and unselfconsciously use it to aid the hearing-impaired child's understanding of their verbal communication). Care should be taken, however, that the hearing-impaired child is not swamped by unlooked-for, and perhaps unnecessary, help.

Ensuring that children have tasks within the boundaries of their capabilities can reduce the need for help and attention from both teacher and peers except when specific instruction is necessary; if there is a unit on site the specialist teachers will offer invaluable advice and support for the class teachers and integrating child.

The Teachers

The fact that adults provide role models is undisputed (Bandura, 1977). Teachers have a powerful effect on children in school. It is important, therefore, that the teacher's interaction with hearing-impaired children should be one of acceptance, respect and value: an acceptance of the children's difficulty, respect for what they are able to achieve and value of them as individuals working alongside other individuals. If the role model is positive, then children in the class will tend to take on the attitudes of the teacher. These three elements also help to formulate teacher expectations, which in themselves can have a significant effect on a child's self-concept (Burns, 1979). Sue's class teacher, who mouthed at her and gesticulated wildly, was undoubtedly treating her as different and, more importantly, conveying this to the rest of her class. Again, he probably had the very best of motives in trying to ensure that he was understood , but the effect would have been directly opposed to that which he had intended. Clearly he never consulted her about how she learned best. Sue became apart from her classmates, preferring the security of the unit where the teachers knew how to speak to her so that she could best utilise her lip-reading skills and also where they used the radio aid to maximise the hearing she did have.

Ignorance is easily overcome if we are aware of it; for example, when Trudy's teacher took active steps to facilitate better communication with her.

Even for Trudy, however, there were faults in the organisational system - placing a hearing-impaired child at the back of the classroom is surely not conducive to clear understanding, particularly when some lip-reading at least is required. Trudy also objected to being placed with another hearing-impaired child. One can understand the reasoning for placing two hearing-impaired children together in the classroom: they are likely to become friends; they will be able to communicate effectively; they will not feel so isolated if they have each other. In fact, they may become *more* isolated because of the physical separation from their peers. Trudy wanted to gain the confidence of and increase the opportunity to talk with her hearing friends; however, this access to opportunity was blocked.

Opportunity

Special education is special in the sense that it can offer children opportunities to be the same as others, in other words to have equal opportunities. It should give opportunities to learn independently, opportunities to volunteer for activities and not be confined to specific roles (for example, only working the lights!), opportunities to be valued and not patronised. Sue's teachers undoubtedly saw her capabilities and gave her the job of working the lights. What they did not do was to offer her choice, or even to explain their reasons for action. The perceptions of the school about the importance of the task clearly did not match those of Sue; consequently her self-concept was undermined.

It is not surprising, therefore, that Sue's perceptions of integration are different from Trudy's and that she relies on the security of the unit rather than seeking the company of her hearing peers. Her unit teachers clearly considered that it was appropriate to integrate her into the mainstream, but if children like Sue are to integrate into school and society successfully, they need active encouragement and we, as class teachers, through our organisation, attitude and commitment, are the ones to provide it.

That is not to say, of course, that on-site units have nothing to offer the integrating child; on the contrary they are available to give their expertise, support and encouragement. Unit staff, too, wish to see their children being as independent as possible. Of course, the children will continue to need extra language help, even when they are integrating into the main classroom, as well as perhaps, additional and supplementary work, but the balance is crucial. Once a child starts to integrate into the ordinary school there needs to be collaboration between members of staff in the unit and those in the mainstream to ensure as successful an interaction as possible, but with the realisation that children like Sue may need, and rely upon, more unit support. We need to think not just of ourselves as teachers in our role as educators, trying to decide on how best to cope with hearing-impaired children, but be able to empathise with them. What do they think of what we are doing? How do they value themselves in our classrooms – as contributing 'full' members, or as 'special' rate members with incomplete access? Although interest, work and commitment among teaching staff may be high, in the eyes of the children it may be viewed quite differently. Good intentions are not enough. Teachers must take into account the social *and* academic needs of the individual child and by doing so maximise not only the quality of the interaction but also the potential of the child as a complete person.

Chapter Six

Opening Doors:
changes of policy

*In our old school they didn't kind of bother with
the children who couldn't do things / they was
too bothered about the kids who could / so you know
by the time I left junior school.... I wasn't that
good / but look at me now*

(Rachel, age 16)

*In the first second and third year you're looked
upon as a bit of a freak really / young kids can
be a bit cruel and they take the mick / but by the
time you're my age they know I'm just as capable as anyone else*

(Barrie, age 16)

INTRODUCTION

In Britain after the Warnock Report (D.E.S., 1978) many units were incorporated into schools to allow access for integration into mainstream for students with disabilities. Some, like the units for the hearing impaired discussed in the previous chapter, offered specific and specialist expertise in one area of disability, while others had a more general policy. These catered for a wider clientele, usually for students with learning difficulties *irrespective of their cause.*

Whatever the type of unit, however, the general aim is the same: greater opportunities for integration. Yet, within the unit system itself, the continuum of integration (Chapter 1) occurs.

There is a variety of ways in which unit provision serves the needs of pupils who are designated as having disabilities and/or difficulties in learning. There are units which educate the child wholly within their confines with perhaps integration occurring at a social level; there are units which integrate their clientele in the less academic subjects in order that they have a participation in mainstream but also receive careful and precise teaching; and there are units which seek to integrate pupils to the greatest possible extent, operating only as a support system where necessary. The extent of integration in any system depends upon the needs of individuals as perceived by the professionals who have contact with them. These perceptions are usually heavily educationally biased and are concerned with how well the pupil will cope with the mainstream curriculum. The degree of success may depend upon many factors, for example, the extent of the liaison between unit and mainstream staff. Evaluating liaison would include such aspects as teaching method and curriculum delivery. Inconsistencies of style and methods of teaching may give an additional burden to those pupils who, for whatever reason, find learning more problematic than others. On the other hand, it could be argued that such variety enables pupils to gain a wider perspective of curriculum content.

Successful integration, however, demands more than being able to cope with subject matter. It involves a degree of interaction within the classroom between teacher and pupil, and between pupils. It involves the valuing not only of the work and responses of children with special needs, but of the children themselves. It involves the recognition of the individual strengths and weaknesses of the integrated pupil and it involves the acceptance of the pupil as a participating member of that class. This acceptance is made increasingly difficult when pupils are viewed as 'visiting' rather than permanent members of the class. If a pupil is not fully integrated, this separation is inevitable. Ideally membership should go beyond that of class or unit so that the pupil is indeed part of the whole school, and is perceived as such.

The assessment of success of an integration policy for a child with special needs is often based on the perceived educational needs rather than these other factors. Although such factors are frequently referred to, it is usually only as side issues. From the pupils' point of view, however, these 'peripherals' may be the most important determinant in assessing their success, pushing the ability to cope with their lessons into second place. If pupils are to learn to their maximum potential, they need to feel confident with their classmates, confident with their teacher and confident with themselves. Self-esteem, as we argued in Chapter 3, is one of the most important factors in achieving success (for example Coopersmith, 1968) and these 'side issues' provide the environment for the developing self-concept.

Most units offer security to their students in terms of smaller classes, more intensive (if restrictive) teaching to their needs and a highly structured environment. There is a growing awareness, however, that this security may be more stifling than enabling and, that for some, a re-assessment of aims and principles is overdue. To this end teaching has been evaluated, procedures discussed and alternative methods proposed - not merely for the sake of change, but because of naturally occurring processes both internal and external to the establishment.

This chapter describes the changes that occurred in a unit attached to a large city comprehensive school shortly after the appointment of a new head of unit. Current practice engendered by the changes is then discussed by some of the students. The chapter concludes with *proposed* changes for the unit which are as a result of continual evaluation of the unit's aims plus the demands of equal access *for all pupils* to a National Curriculum.

PROCESS OF CHANGE

The unit is housed in a large comprehensive school which caters for 1000 pupils in an industrial British city. The unit has taken pains to be as much of the school fabric as possible. There is no separate building or entrance; there are no signposts to, or labels for, the unit; the unit is 'non-specialist' in that it does not cater for one specific area of disability, and this lessens the possibility of the unit pupils being immediately identifiable. The unit staff teach in the mainstream on a regular basis. There are fifty-nine pupils on the roll with a diversity of special needs. These include students with moderate learning difficulties, 'dyslexia', hearing impairment and school phobia. Even prior to the change the policy for such students had always been one of *functional* integration, allowing the students access to mainstream education. It had been based on an inverse relationship of attachment to mainstream school and the unit. During the first three years of the unit students' time at the school, the majority of their time was spent in their 'home base' – the unit. During their fourth year this time was gradually decreased until, for most pupils, the greater percentage was spent in the mainstream. The present head of the unit re-adjusted the focus and took the unit still further in terms of fuller integration for all pupils. He would be the first to admit, however, that many of the changes brought about were not as the result of major pre-planning policies on his part, although his designs for the unit were incorporated into the changes that took place.

The unit, when he arrived, already had a good reputation; the staff was committed and caring, the philosophy positive and structured. Everything was designed to make the students feel secure, yet the students were dissatisfied. It says a great deal for the ethos of the unit that the students felt sufficiently confident to make their dissatisfaction known. Shortly after his arrival, the present head of unit received a 'round robin' from the students – a set of written suggestions for change, passed round and added to by the students and signed by most of them. It was evident that many of them resented the security that the unit had to offer because it made them feel 'different'. There were several written demands, many of them, perhaps surprisingly, asking for more *restrictions* than freedom; for example:

- they wanted to be disciplined in the same way as other members of the school, (even though, at the time, the school had a caning policy);
- they wanted access to dining with their year group rather than going to the dining hall first and missing the rush.

These asked-for restrictions would serve to make the unit students less identifiable as a separate group. In discussion with the staff afterwards, the students talked about the effects of discipline and bad behaviour. If they misbehaved and were excused that behaviour because they were from the unit, the lack of punishment immediately labelled them as *different* from other members of the school. As a result, one of two things usually happened: either their treatment by the rest of the pupils was 'different', thus serving to isolate them even further; or they received their 'punishment' in the playground in order that justice was 'seen to be done'. Therefore punishment on the same lines as other pupils, including detentions and perhaps even caning, was preferable to separate treatment.

The school's policy of allowing the unit students to dine first derived from the caring attitude of the unit (particularly towards the less robust of their members) yet this policy most obviously labelled them as 'Unit' rather than 'Year 7', or 'Year 8' pupils. There was an expressed wish, therefore, to be viewed as part of the *whole* school and not as members of a segregated entity. This wish extended to the academic and social perspective of their schooling, for example:

- they wanted to be allowed *access on merit* to curriculum areas;
- they wanted to have their form titles changed from 'Unit'.

Access to mainstream curriculum was an important consideration. Some pupils, whatever their reason for being in the unit, were academically able and wished to be part of a group of comparable interest and ability. The request had implications however, particularly if a mainstream student was to be dislodged from a top set to make way for a student from the unit. Yet if a student *is* to be viewed as part of the school the equal opportunities and access to the curriculum must be available to all within the school, irrespective of their placement. The change from unit title to a form title, (i.e. identified by a year number) again had the benefit for students that they were no longer immediately identifiable as unit pupils when their name and form were referred to publicly.

During the meeting that took place after the receipt of the round robin, the students discussed these matters at length. The appointment of a new head of unit had led to the realisation that there was now an opportunity for change which they could help precipitate. Interestingly, the students allowed only those who had signed the letter to attend the meeting – an indication of their serious commitment to the requests.

Both the head teacher of the school and the head of unit agreed that these requests were, in the main, reasonable and the head of unit was given permission to implement them, even though some of the other staff, both unit and mainstream, were ambivalent towards some of the ideas. There was certainly the necessity for a re-adjustment of expectation for these students, although the students' professionalism, organisation and articulate requests had already caused some staff to re-assess their capabilities.

The head of unit was not a little worried about the request for punishment, particularly the caning, as there were physically handicapped children attending. The prospect of blaring publicity was daunting.

Eventually the changes worked through and, as a result, the unit changed direction in terms of (1) less identification of unit students, (2) increased pupil access to mainstream, and (3) changed staff roles within the whole school context.

A unit has to be contained within an area of the school building, but this one was not labelled and the students moved in and out quite freely. The students now had an increased commitment to mainstream school policies and curriculum. For example, they were now expected to take both school and public examinations. Previously the students had not been required to take any examinations, not even end of year examinations. This was another aspect of the 'cocooning' of the unit that they found unacceptable as again it had set them apart from the rest of the student body – even when they were mainstreamed in certain lessons. They were now expected to be examined on the work that they completed during the year, including work that was unit based. At examination time, therefore, everyone in the school year group took part.

Public examinations were also made more widely available to the unit pupils. In order to be able to sit for public examinations before the changes in policy, the pupils had to be totally integrated into a mainstream class. It was soon realised, however, that in small group teaching situations in the unit some pupils, irrespective of their disability, could achieve adequate grades but they were being denied the opportunity to do so. Consequently public examinations were introduced into the unit curriculum, initially for English, European Studies and Mathematics. The unit staff were unable to cover all of the areas of specialism, but pupils began to pass examinations. As an incentive to attitude change this was crucial, both for pupils and staff in the mainstream and in the unit. The students realised that if they worked in the unit they were not 'written off' in terms of ability but were capable of achievement there and elsewhere.

The unit staff also had a part to play in the increased integration of the unit as part of the school. It was considered important that not only were the students to be less identifiable, but that the staff should be so too – and should be regarded as staff of the whole school. In schools with units there is often friction between unit staff and mainstream staff members. Even

59

with an understanding of the demands of the post, unit staff are often still viewed by others as teaching smaller groups for larger salaries. The head of unit decided, therefore, that instead of being a 'parasitic' unit, one that was seen as only feeding from the school and its resources, the process should be symbiotic with unit staff integrating with and giving to the mainstream school. There were two main areas in which this was realised. Firstly, the unit staff began to teach some mainstream classes. This proposed change was initially threatening to some unit staff and some found it difficult to achieve in a short space of time. Over several years the staff has taught a whole range of subjects, not in a remedial capacity but in English, Art, French, History, Mathematics, Geography as 'regular' teachers – subjects in which they specialised before graduating to special needs. Therefore their ability and competence were not in doubt and their confidence has increased. The head of unit led by example by teaching in mainstream classes to prove that it could be done *and* that unit teachers were accepted by staff and pupils. Secondly, the expertise of the unit staff as special needs teachers was made available to the whole school. If mainstream staff experienced problems with mainstream pupils with special educational needs, they were able to call on unit staff for advice, support and practical help through classroom collaboration.

The school also began to recognise the benefit of having the unit's resources in that more teachers were available for both teaching and pastoral care. In addition the head of unit tried to ensure that his staff saw themselves as front-runners, as leaders in inservice training and curriculum innovations rather than being peripheral or passive. Staff discussion about special needs teaching has since led to mainstream staff developing a wider perspective about students with difficulties. For example, automatic assumptions about inadequate classroom behaviour are being replaced by consideration of possible causes. Importantly, the unit staff have not been perceived as 'specialists' retaining all responsibility for special needs children. In reality they have moved *away* from this restriction by encouraging collaboration and sharing through discussion. Changes, therefore, have allowed learning in many different ways, not only by the students being given opportunities to work alongside their peers, and to take part in national examinations, but also to learn how to take risks educationally. In this way the students have had chance to grow and develop, to be given, and to respond to, responsibility. This higher profile of individuality within the whole school has led to a greater acceptance of unit students by mainstream pupils, as discussion by the students in this chapter will indicate. Staff, too, have had opportunities to learn from each other as colleagues of a corporate body discussing common issues.

To the staff and the outside observer, therefore, the changes have been successful. Changes were, however, originally pre-empted by the students and it is the students whose judgments are also valid. The following section, therefore, presents students' views about the unit. As the changes began with the appointment of the head of unit eight years prior to their conversation, their views reflect what is now current practice.

THE PUPILS' VIEWS

The students who agreed to take part in discussion were all members of the unit and came from four year groups within the school. The Year Seven pupils (age 12) were Nicholas and Gavin, Year Eight (age 13) Kashif and David, Year Nine (age 14) Michael and Raymond and Year Eleven (age 16) Rachel and Barrie. Year Ten pupils were unavailable at the time of interview. Reasons for being in the unit vary: some students have general learning difficulties; one is terminally ill; another is a school phobic as a result of severe and brutal bullying at a previous school; one has a speech impairment which had contributed to learning difficulties; and another is a 'diagnosed dyslexic'. They all took an active part in discussion and spoke frankly about their experiences, both in mainstream and in the unit. Teachers and teaching proved to be a lively, if inevitable, starting point.

Teachers

Generally, all pupils rated their teachers highly both in and out of the unit. They appreciated those teachers who took their time when explaining and who did not leave learning to chance:

Michael: *I did Biology with one of the teachers and it was / she explained it to you every single detail and it's great*

The unit teachers in particular explained things twice to ensure that everyone understood. Some teachers in mainstream spoke too quickly for the pupils to understand.

Raymond: *they don't give us time / they need to be slower*

They found that most of the mainstream teachers were helpful, if they were asked, but some of the students found asking embarrassing in front of their peer group – an admission that they were unable to cope with their work. Some pupils were too shy to speak out in the mainstream class, but were able to do so in the unit.

Rachel: *if you're a bit shy you can kind of speak up while you're here.*

Rachel and Barrie, the Year Eleven pupils, were more critical of some of the teachers they had had experience of in the mainstream, particularly when compared with the support that the unit teachers had given them. They particularly objected to teachers who treated them 'like babies' or thought that they were 'not capable'. There was the realisation from these students that this may be because mainstream teachers had not had the training to cope with students with special educational needs:

Barrie: *teachers need to be / taught how to handle people with problems ....
you can't blame mainstream teachers because they don't know how to cope I
think what it is / they get a little bit worried*

In spite of these criticisms of some members of staff, however, all of
the students valued the fact that they were in a unit attached to the
mainstream school and that they had the chance to be treated the same as
other students. Barrie found that the experience of being in the unit and in
mainstream had been most beneficial for him, as he had been able to
progress from mainly unit teaching to the majority of his lessons being in
the ordinary school:

Barrie: *they teach you to cope with the rest of the school and that's the good
thing about having a main school and the unit built into the normal school.... they
bring you out / I only come up here for registration now and maths / I progressed a
lot since I first moved into this school / I'm really glad I came because it's given me
a lot of opportunities.*

Lessons

This reflection of the appropriateness of unit placement for himself, and
incidentally, echoed by Rachel, is the result of five years' experience in the
system and the situation that they have experienced and learned from. The
younger pupils are still in the throes of those experiences and, obviously,
have not had the opportunity to view things from a wide perspective.
Nevertheless, their observations are perceptive and reflective. They have
not yet decided whether or not the unit is a good placement educationally.
Some prefer the mainstream lessons although they find the work harder:

Michael: *in mainschool they expect you to know all these different things
and you don't / it's harder in mainschool but it's fun and I'm coping at the
moment.*

Michael refers here to the expectancies of teachers that pupils should
have comparable knowledge of subject areas with the peer group in the
mainstream class. This is a theme further pursued by him and taken up by
the other members of the group. The problem appears to be simple yet
insoluble. The students, on the one hand, greatly appreciate the pace of the
unit teaching:

Rachel: *we get help and we sort of go at our own pace/ and we go through
things so that not just one person understands / but everybody understands;*
but, on the other hand, there is the realisation that the more gentle pace of
the unit makes it difficult to maintain progress with their peers in the
mainstream:

Raymond: *say if you have unit geography you have the same work as
mainstream but they work at a slower pace and in mainschool geography they're
working at a faster pace / and you can't keep up with it.*

An associated difficulty is not being able to attend every lesson in the particular subject area so that the problem of slower pace is compounded by gaps in knowledge:

Michael: *sometimes / in main school / they've been built up to what they're doing more than in the unit and / when you go into mainschool it's harder to understand and catch up ..... sometimes you just don't know what they're on about.*

The split in attendance between main school and unit lessons in many ways adds to the difficulties of the pupils with special needs by inserting more confusion into the learning environment. There must be, for example, a draining of self-confidence in a mainstream lesson if there is a sense of isolation in not understanding an issue or not knowing an answer, when everybody else appears to:

Michael: *the other kids / they (the teachers) ask a question and they (the children) shoot their hands up to say the answer.*

The sense of isolation could well lead to the desire, mentioned earlier, not to admit publicly to a lack of understanding, but to struggle alone even when the students with special educational needs know that teachers are willing to help.

Nicholas: *Maths... sometimes I get them wrong and I have to / figure it again and if I come up with the same answer I just get confused.*

A shift in classroom organisation would be appropriate, not only for the pupils from the unit, but for all the students. Opportunities to discuss work with a small group of peers rather than asking the teacher for help would be less stressful and more conducive to learning. Group work involving collaboration and discussion is a way of ensuring active learning by the pupils involved (see Wade, 1985) and the crucial role of talk in the learning process has been acknowledged by National Curriculum provisions which designate Speaking and Listening as equally weighted with Reading and Writing. The pupils from the unit reinforce the National Curriculum Council's viewpoint when they discuss their own learning and how best they learn. Michael, for example, discusses the changes that he would like to make in the lessons that he attends, but he also makes the point that these are applicable to all schools and to all pupils:

Michael: *I think it's all schools really...if you can talk about it you can get more involved in whatever you're doing / and if you can do more / if you can do something towards it / it's better / if you're writing all the time it's / it does get boring / all kids would say that / if you can do something and talk about it it's different.*

The need to talk about the learning, to sort out problems and arrive at an understanding was echoed by all students. They saw the necessity of writing for recording and other purposes, but suggested that the emphasis on immediate writing, or even always writing, was unbalanced and made the purpose of the task less worthwhile: it was 'just putting it on paper'. It is important to remember also that the physical act of writing is, for some, a tedious business. Again this is not restricted to pupils with special educational needs but for any pupils (and adults!) who have to write at length for the majority of their day. One pupil from the unit perhaps sums it up for all of us:

Gavin: *it makes my hand ache still*

Temporary Classroom Membership

Unless integration is total, the pupil from the unit integrating into the ordinary classroom must initially feel more of a visitor than a permanent class member. The unit provides a securer base for the hesitant learner, but temporary mainstream membership also needs to provide a similar secure environment for the pupil to progress in learning. The other class members pay as great a part in this provision as the class teacher, but the teacher is able to manipulate the organisation of the class environment in order to maximise the pupil-pupil relationship. One way is to encourage pair working in lessons. The pupils from the unit spoke about certain lessons in the mainstream which they enjoyed and it was clear from their comments that it was not just the subject matter that was important, but that the opportunity to work with and alongside their peers contributed greatly to their enjoyment. Practical sessions in Science, for example, provide pair-learning situations.

Nicholas: *I like Science / I like the practical Science / I have them in mainschool / we have a partner from mainschool / he's my friend.*

Working alongside pupils from the unit enables other class members to appreciate the positive aspects of their partners and prompts the realisation that they are not essentially different. Kashnif, for example says that some of his classmates

.....say you're an idiot / you can't read

but they are not the people he works with. Raymond echoes and re-inforces this point:

we reckon we can do as well as they can but they don't know that.

The injustice of being unfairly judged is apparent, but so is the self-confidence in his own ability which he retains in spite of his peers' comments.

Barrie sympathises with the younger pupils. He has had longer in the school and has friends both in the unit and in the mainstream. During lessons he is able to ask for help from his friends if he has problems with his reading – he is self-confident and self-assured about his own ability, but recognises that the younger pupils will have difficulty in being accepted for what they are. He realises also that their mainstream peers have to mature sufficiently in order to appreciate the contributions that pupils from the unit are able to make:

Barrie: *in the first, second and third year you're looked upon as a bit of a freak really / younger kids can be a bit cruel and they take the mick / but by the time you're my age they know I'm just as capable as anyone else.*

The fact that making friends takes time, particularly in a split environment where opportunities are not so numerous, was re-iterated by Rachel: *as soon as you start fitting in with them / after a year or so / they start getting used to you and that's when they start making friends.*

Personal Relationships

The Year Seven pupils, Nicholas and Gavin, both stated that all of their friends were in the unit. Inevitably children will make their initial friendships within their immediate social environment, whether it be a mainstream class or a unit class, and only later widen their scope and initiate new contacts.

Both Nicholas and Gavin appear content with their friends; they had looked forward to making new friends when they arrived at the school. There does, however, seem to be a 'them' and 'us' situation in the early stages of their school career between mainstream and unit pupils:

Nicholas: *the kids in mainschool are okay but sometimes they just run round and torment you.*

Gavin: *I play with some kids in mainschool sometimes / most of them are horrible.*

It is not until, as Barrie states, that the pupils get to know each other that friendships between pupils in different classes can be made. The infrequent integrative opportunities that the early stages of mainstreaming offer do not allow contact to be sustained or friendship to progress at a usual pace. Kashif, for example, mentions the name-calling that unit children experience in the playground. Michael in his third year at the school also refers to playground disturbance:

> *I would prefer to be in mainschool because a lot of the kids cheek you in the playground so we don't hang round with kids in the unit.*

Michael's desire to be part of the mainstream rather than the unit is strongly expressed, leading even to a disassociation from his unit peers at public times. Unlike Raymond, the other Year Nine pupil, his friends are 'mainly in the unit' but he prefers to make new ones in the mainstream because he is conscious of difference. This does not appear to be from choice necessarily, but from circumstance. Initial social groupings of classroom placement inevitably lead to first friendship choices, as mentioned above, but social groupings occur elsewhere within the total environment. Pupils who live near each other, for example, who walk the same route to school or take the same bus journey, have more frequent chance of interaction with members of their peer group other than their classmates. For Michael, however, this is a denied opportunity. Like many children who are pupils in units, he does not live in the local catchment area and therefore has a taxi provided for his journey to and from school.

Inevitably the other pupils in the taxi pick-up service are also unit pupils. The range of friendship choices is severely curtailed. Barrie emphasises this point by putting forward the alternative:

Barrie: *most of my friends are in main school because there are more people out there / I know a lot of people / I get on the same bus and start talking / the last two years I've really begun to know people.*

The ability to establish a wider range of friends encompassing both mainstream and unit pupils therefore seems to depend on two factors: opportunity and time. The school does appear to be providing opportunity when integrating the pupils, but this is restricted to an academic context where inevitably the unit pupils are perceived as visitors to, rather than members of, the class. Although they may be accepted within the confines of the classroom, the amount of time provided does not allow sufficient contact for the division between mainstream and unit children to be bridged. The interactive social occasions for some appear to be restricted to playground activities where the name-calling and teasing take place.

The introduction of greater parental choice in school placement may eventually mean that more mainstream children are unable to take part in joint home-school journeys, if they are driven to schools other than their immediate local school. It is unlikely, however, that their friendship choices will be as limited as all of their classroom interaction will take place within the same boundaries of *one* year group and not two.

Encouragingly, reports from these students point to distinct social improvements as they progress through the school – acceptance, understanding and friendship are extended to Year Eleven students, the result of a maturational process on both sides, perhaps.

We must remember, of course, that a lack of friends in the mainstream does not mean a total lack of friends. The unit's warm, supportive atmosphere ensures that all pupils with disabilities are accepted by each other:

Barrie: *the first year you look around and you see people / all sorts of different people and it seems a bit strange at first and you don't know how to treat them ....*

Rachel: *you get used to them.*

Barrie: *you don't seem to notice them any more / I talk to Mohammed who's quite deaf and as soon as you start talking to him you don't have to think about talking louder and moving your mouth more / you just do it straightaway and you talk different as well / you don't think about it you just do it so he can understand better.*

The maturity and sensitivity of these two pupils is tribute to their years in the unit and the example of the unit staff. Other pupils express similar sentiments. Nicholas, for example, says:

the best thing about the unit is the children.

Kashif realises that part of the unit's function and the pupils within it is to protect the children and

help how they get on.

Michael praises mainstream teachers who, when they have children:

with hearing aids and microphones and things like that / they just pretend it's not there / they're very good.

Their concern, therefore, is not about a *lack* of friends but a wider choice of friends which would ensure total integration and lessen the notion of 'feeling different'. Their educational needs may, for some time, be different from those of mainstream pupils but their emotions, aspirations and even expectations are very similar.

We must not forget mainstream students and their needs too. If they are being deprived of insights such as Rachel and Barrie express above, through lack of sustained integration with students who have special educational needs, then opportunities are being missed.

Expectations

Concern is frequently expressed about the low expectations held by some teachers for their pupils, particularly for pupils with special educational needs, (National Curriculum Council, 1989). Some teachers and some pupils undoubtedly have low expectations, yet the evidence obtained from discussion with students here shows that this is not necessarily so. Their conversation so far suggests that they are expected to work with and keep pace with mainstream students even if they do find it difficult. Their own expectations are similarly high, particularly for their chosen careers. Kashif, for example, with all the confidence of youth, provides a list, in chronological order, of the careers he intends to pursue: a computer operator, a seller of videos, a surgeon and finally, a cricketer. He does, however, suggest that he would need to go to college to get an education! David, in Year Eight, as yet, only sets his sights on his GCSE exams and 'a suitable job'. Michael, in Year Nine, has thought things through more carefully and has decided to utilise his strengths in working out his academic future. He expresses a wish to be a musician, a drummer, as music is his favourite subject:

Michael: *Music's my favourite at the moment because the music teacher says I'm the best drum player in the school / my teacher phoned her (mother) up / I'm one of the best in Birmingham / I'm going to music college in town I've got to get* two 'A' levels to get in there / and art my second one / I'm supposed to be good at art / I don't know 'cos if I can do it it's normal for me / Mrs Mason the art teacher says I should do my 'A' level in it.

Not only are Michael's expectations high, and realistic, for himself; they are bolstered and encouraged by the mainstream teachers. His musical ability has been fostered and extended by the school as there are no facilities for him to play at home:

Michael: *I'd love it but the neighbours wouldn't.*

Barrie's preferred profession is a farrier and again the school has provided encouragement and support for his choice:

Barrie: *I should have a college place soon at the school of farriers and the school has told them the problem and they've said it's fine / I'll have an interview in about three weeks time / as long as they know the problem.*

Obviously the school's liaison with the college has been positive about Barrie as an individual who has strengths as well as weaknesses. The unit has academic expectations equivalent of those in mainstream for these students. This cannot be achieved without a whole school/unit history of acceptance and encouragement for its pupils.

It may be that this is not a typical unit or even typical experiences for pupils with special educational needs. Certainly some of the pupils here give scathing reports of past school experiences. Gavin, for example, was in a primary school unit before his move to secondary school:

Gavin: *at the old school you just stayed there all morning / didn't do any work / stayed there till dinner time then go back to normal classrooms.*

Nicholas referred to the lack of help in his previous school when he was experiencing problems. This was a theme taken up by Rachel and Barrie, but pursued further. Their problem was not just a lack of help, but was compounded by negative attitudes and a lack of recognition and commitment by *some* teachers towards their pupils:

Barrie: *I had a terrible time at my last school*

Rachel: *and I did / it was just awful.... my teacher kept saying she's been a naughty girl and my mum said why / well I was doing my work but the teacher wasn't giving me nothing else so I was playing up so / although they only gave me a minimum of work throughout the day.*

Memory is clouded by time and Rachel's primary school teacher may well have had a different story to tell. However, Rachel's perception of the case is that she was bored and therefore disruptive because she had so little to do. Obviously the work set for any child has to be geared towards the individual's needs and this can often prove to be a difficult task in terms of time for the busy teacher. If expectations are kept realistically high, however, great benefits can accrue for the individual child.

Barrie's early experience is different and more harrowing:

Barrie: *well I was told by a couple of teachers straight off that I was stupid..... I can remember / must have been eight or nine years old / and I couldn't read at all then and the one teacher because he knew it / it was like he got pleasure out of making me embarrassed / he'd call me up and say read this you see / I'd be in front of the class...... I can remember him saying to me I'd never pass the infant stage he don't know why he bothered.*

Painful memories take a long time to eradicate and their effect on self-esteem and future achievement can be catastrophic. Fortunately, as a result of his mother's intervention two other teachers at his primary school took an interest in Barrie's problems:

one of the teachers didn't know what my problem was / he'd never heard of it I don't think but he coped with me pretty well / he helped me a lot.... two of the teachers I owe a lot to / if they weren't there I'd have been in a right mess by now / getting into bother because / out of frustration

THE UNIT AND INTEGRATION

Judging from the pupils' discussion there are both benefits of and disadvantages to being in this type of unit and experiencing this type of integration. Some of the disadvantages are connected with the peer group, although relationships improve as the pupils get older (and are integrated into mainstream for more time). Other disadvantages relate to the different pace of work set by mainstream and unit teachers, the differences in the amount of help given and teacher attitudes to unit pupils. Perhaps, as Barrie suggests, the mainstream teachers should go on a course! Our study suggests that a great deal depends on the teacher in the mainstream, not only in work set and results expected, but in class organisation which enables pupils to work together.

Inevitably the amount of time spent in the mainstream varies with individuals and their needs, but the pupils all agree that their time spent in the unit is beneficial to them. Rachel and Barrie say that everything is more relaxed in the unit which enables them to begin learning under less stress and hold their own in terms of academic progress:

Barrie: *it brings you out slowly / another lesson in the mainschool with support then you do that on your own or you get support then you eventually come away from the unit.*

Success, perhaps, can only be viewed on reflection. Certainly Rachel and Barrie would be considered successes in *any* school. They are mature and supportive, objective in their reflections and are able to sustain calm and reasoned discussion. They are forward looking and positive in their thinking. The last contribution on success, for individuals, the unit and integration is left to Rachel.

Rachel: *in our old school they didn't kind of bother with the children who couldn't do things / they was too bothered about the kids who could / so you know by the time I left junior school.... I wasn't that good..... but look at me now.*

MAKING INTEGRATION WORK

Without a fully integrated organisation the unit and school together are clearly achieving a good deal for children with special educational needs. However, the head of unit sees that progress so far is such that further changes can now be instituted, so that each child can have access to a full curriculum and more students can experience more integration.

It is proposed to change the mainstream teaching organisation for unit staff. Instead of spending part of their time working separately with separate classes in the mainstream, they will use their expertise in team-teaching with mainstream teachers. For example, *all* Year Seven unit students will integrate into mainstream for their science lessons in mixed ability teaching groups and a unit member of staff, with a specialism in science, will be attached to Year Seven for six periods of science per week. The team-teaching may, for example, involve a double period with three different groups, with the unit staff giving help and support to all those who need it. With two teachers, all pupils will have opportunities for more individual attention. In this way, all children with special educational needs will benefit from the expertise of the unit members of staff and not just those from the unit. It is emphasised that in no way will the unit staff be seen as subordinate members of the team or as specialists removing the responsibility for the special educational needs pupils from mainstream staff. They will take an equal part in planning, preparing and teaching the lead lessons. The result, therefore, will be increased pupil integration and increased staff contact. It is envisaged that unit students will still be form-based within the unit, but working with unit staff in the mainstream rather than segregated in the unit. The benefits for all pupils have already been stated, but the benefit for the school additionally is that a five-form entry would have a sixth member of staff throughout the teaching periods. This member of staff will be an integrated specialist in the subject area rather than an 'appendage' who would merely sit and listen and then give separate help when required.

Another major area of change envisaged affects a wider spectrum than that of the main school. In the surrounding area are other schools which have children with special educational needs, but have no recourse to specialist staff within their organisations. Although specialist help is available within the city's resources, it is not necessarily cost effective in that itinerant specialists called in may not know the school or the student who requires help. The head of unit envisages that the unit and its staff can become a major resource, a satellite for support to schools within its locality. It makes more sense for one local primary school, for example, which has a hearing impaired child, to call upon the unit for support in terms of a known teacher of the deaf, as the unit is only 50 yards away, rather than calling on an unknown support teacher from the city centre. Such links between schools offer rich opportunity for collaborative progress towards integration with the unit staff offering support, not only to their main school, but to other schools within a particular segment of the city, giving more specialist help to more pupils with special educational needs and, at the same time, offering natural in-service education to mainstream colleagues.

We consider that these changes are in the right direction, are positive and likely to benefit unit, school and wider community. Additionally, more input from unit staff for non-unit students with special educational needs and more opportunity for all students to work together and to learn from and about each other point towards integration in its truest sense.

Chapter Seven

Mayfield Park: developing an enrichment programme

They need work which they are interested in / which challenges them / which gives them an opportunity to get away from the structure of / the school / and really just lets their minds fly a bit.

Mrs Parr, teacher responsible for enrichment

INTRODUCTION

Provision for so-called 'gifted' children differs in marked respects from other groups with special educational needs. To start with, the labelling of a pupil may have positive effects on the self-concept of the individual and his or her parents, rather than negative influences of terms such as 'disruptive', 'maladjusted', 'slow' or 'remedial'. On the other hand, classmates may resent their own exclusion and teasing behaviour may ensue. This kind of dilemma also colours the decisions of the providers of learning experiences. On the one hand they wish to maximise every child's potential and develop exceptional skills; on the other they may have reservations about creating an educational elite, separate from the mainstream. We examine a school which has faced the need to provide for its ablest students, has given one teacher responsibility for selection and provision and has made resources of time and finance available.

THE SCHOOL

Mayfield Park is a large, Australian, selective, secondary girls' school, where an enrichment programme is being developed. Believing the school was not doing all it could to extend its most able students, the headteacher set up a staff working party which included members of junior (to age 12) school staff. In the process of defining the needs and possible ways of providing for talented children, one teacher, Mrs Parr, obtained a travel grant to study talented children's programmes in the USA and in Israel. Some of the ideas gained from visits - and from conferences such as the World Conference on Gifted and Talented Children are incorporated in the initial exploratory phase of provision. One afternoon per week the normal curriculum includes optional activities (e.g. craft, sports, hospital work, motor mechanics, cooking) for all students. This space was made available for Mrs Parr to organise extension work for the most able. She argues that this is less than satisfactory because of competition from attractive outdoor pursuits such as rowing.

STUDENT SELECTION

Students are selected by Mrs Parr on the results of an aptitude test, but also on term reports and staff recommendation where a girl shows particular imaginative, innovative approaches to work. Mrs Parr is not prepared to rely purely on staff selection:

> *if you ask staff / often the girls that you get are the hard workers / and they're good solid hard workers / and they get good marks / and they're well-balanced in class / but / they're not that highflier and they're a bit frightened of / anything that you can't finish up with a mark out of ten at the end.*

Initial attempts at selection by peer group:

> *led to some very nasty scenes between the girls / and lots of questions which the girls asked and I couldn't really honestly answer / and I decided that / until I knew more about it / until I'd thought more about it / I wouldn't do it again.*

Parents of selected students are informed by letter, after which selectees may opt into the programme or not. Mrs Parr recognises that some girls who might initially have preferred, say, dog-training, have the decision to opt in taken for them by parents. To begin with, 30-40 girls participated from year groups of 140-150.

ORGANISATION

Teaching methods are not markedly different from the rest of the curriculum. However, keystones of the programme are involvement and scope for using initiative. Deliberate attempts are made to make sessions interesting, students are consulted and their suggestions followed wherever practicable. Thus a group of about 15 girls from a particular year group might opt for a term's work in art, drama, philosophy, psychology or problem-solving, for example. Providing an a la carte curriculum option will usually necessitate using expertise from the wider community. In the case of Mayfield Park, funding was made available for teaching fees. Although it was not always possible to predict the effectiveness of particular contributors (and some proved uninspiring), Mrs Parr obtained

> *very positive acknowledgment from the girls that it was interesting and stimulating / in some cases they found it was the best thing / they had done / in the year.*

One variation from normal curriculum times is the weekend workshops into which students may opt and which provide a chance to tackle an activity, not necessarily academic, at depth. A successful writing weekend was led by a professional writer and an ex-student of the school, an expert in fabrics, led a well-received craft workshop. Further plans include photography and cooking.

THE TOURNAMENT OF MINDS

Another way the special provision moved out into a wider community was through team entry in *The Tournament of Minds*, a problem-solving team competition held in the National capital. Two teams of seven volunteers entered in the Mathematics and Engineering section for 13-14 year olds. They were given six weeks to solve a problem of how to propel a golf ball along a metre distance to set off a mousetrap, extinguish a candle and land in a cup in the shortest possible time. One team won the prize for the most innovative and imaginative solution. On the Presentation day their solution only worked at the third attempt, but Mrs Parr thought:

> *that was better than first prize for doing it quickest*

Though competitive, the tournament is made a natural extension of the thinking games, logic problems, charades, etc. that encourage imaginative collaboration in the enrichment programme. Mrs Parr encourages the imaginative achievement of girls working together to spark ideas off each other:

we have games in which I bring in some extraordinary objects / that doesn't look like anything and I say now all right / let's be really wild and work out what this is / and I'm astonished at the really extraordinary ideas that they can come up with.

Other games involve making logical connections, predicting, hypothesising and constructing narrative extensions:

we're going to look at a / mystery movie and stop it half way through and work out the solution before we get to the end.

Equipment is an important ingredient in relaxed learning situations and, for able children, may be crucial to using their full powers without worrying what others may say about outlandish solutions:

they would probably see it as lots of games / but I see it as a chance for some very bright girls to be together / and to / not to be laughed at because they come up with some / really odd ideas / and to think and to enjoy thinking and puzzling.

INDIVIDUAL STUDENTS

Some able students become so wary of peer group scorn that they would rather take no risk and so opt out of even average participation, adopting a careless or sullen attitude, mostly in self defence. Mrs Parr describes one of her students:

Kylie is very very bright / very articulate / very entertaining / but does almost nothing in class / unless she particularly wants to / if she doesn't want to if she's not interested then she doesn't do anything / if she's interested well she'll do a little bit / or she'll do as much as she cares to do.

Along with other girls in the enrichment group, Kylie received help on study skills and an individual counselling session with Mrs Parr. The demonstration that individual needs matter may be more important than any input of information for some able students. Mrs Parr recognises the importance for students like Kylie of an understanding, supportive context for learning, if attitudes are to be altered and confidence developed:

I don't know that I did anything practical for her at all / I don't think I gave her any / extra skills or anything but / at least I made her feel / I think / that she was bright / that if she actually wanted to she could really do whatever she wanted / and it seems to me that her attitude has improved a lot.

Kylie is the kind of student who would never have been selected on teacher recommendation, since her marks were mediocre and her attitude poor. We wonder how many students with similar special educational needs have them overlooked. Kylie was selected through her high aptitude test score and Mrs Parr's subjective assessment from her own class-teaching:

> *you would say something to her that no-one else understood / and her mind made the connection / and she looked at you / she wouldn't say anything because / that would show that she was / actually interested but she would look as if she knew what connection had been made.*

Kylie is typical of the student who is intelligent enough to grasp ideas but either not confident, or not willing enough, to participate. Such students are likely to become disaffected unless something is done to meet their special need. Some students who are unhappy or bored with logical sequential processes are able to make networks of connections in their thinking. Once Kylie was shown how to map networks of ideas, she used this method for her notemaking in most school subjects. A school may have a strong academic tradition but, without flexibility, encouragement and special provision in the system, is unlikely to meet the needs of nonconformist intelligent students. Some students need space creating to make

> *their large jumps in an imaginative way*

as well as having access to the main curriculum and a structured sequence of learning objectives:

> *they need work which they are interested in / which challenges them / which gives them an opportunity to get away from the structure of / the school / and really just lets their minds fly a bit.*

FURTHER DEVELOPMENTS

Presently the school allows no withdrawal from mainstream classes; the special provision outlined here is offered within the option system on an Activities afternoon. However, the headteacher and Mrs Parr would like to experiment with an extension of the enrichment scheme where small groups, say six to eight highly able students from one year, would come together for concentrated attention. Selection would be mainly by aptitude test and the hope is to identify for special attention more underachieving or disaffected students like Kylie. Students would be withdrawn from one period of Mathematics, one period of English and one other period in every two-week cycle over six months. The intention would be to develop students' research skills and for each to become involved in self-selected personal research, thus providing a challenging alternative to the structure of the school.

Problems are envisaged, some additional to the usual difficulties of withdrawal from mainstream classes. Mrs Parr explains:

*I think that will be unpopular amongst many of the staff who see it as / as
elitist and selecting / a few girls and giving them special opportunities.*

Staff attitudes are important to the success of any scheme, but after a trial
period of withdrawing small groups has given a foundation of necessary
experience, the school could move to a system of supporting highly talented
students within the mainstream. This has implications for the role of
co-ordinator. Mrs Parr would need to spend more time working within
other classrooms and with other teachers. There are implications for the
continuing education of teachers too. From the model offered by the way
Mrs Parr works with talented students and from the joint planning,
collaborative teaching and evaluating that her presence in their classrooms
would offer, more teachers could develop their expertise in meeting the
special educational needs of highly talented students.

A STUDENT VIEW

Kylie (age 16) herself reflects on the way she performed below her capacity
in school because she lost interest and gave up. Another reason she gives
was the intense pressure to succeed:

*at times / you just want to break away because / there is so much
competitiveness in the school / cause you know you can't be middle / you've
got to be either the best you know / or else you're just no good at all / and
that makes it a bit hard sometimes to concentrate / if you're doing a Science
or a Maths or something like that / you just have to be the best and if you're
not the teachers think you're not doing your best / you're not working to the
standard that they would like you to / and there is just so much / pressure
from like the school / from friends and home to just do the best.*

The problem for Kylie is the pressure to conform which means increasingly
hard work along traditional lines. However, the enrichment programme
has given her a good deal of confidence in using alternative learning
strategies, as Mrs Parr has already noted. Kylie sees herself as:

*very very unorganised / but I still manage to get like / I get a lot of things
done but not in the way that people would expect it to be done / especially like
you know how you take notes and everything especially like in lines well
mine is like drawings / everywhere / but it makes it more interesting......
it's much better than just like / just writing out notes you sort of get bored
with it so you don't actually take it in / but if you like draw a heading then
draw a picture beside it you sort of remember it more you put the two
together / using both sides of the brain.....
if I write the topic then branch out from it I can usually / write a better essay
than if I just know the information because you don't get the ideas flowing.*

Kylie shows the capacity to work out her own learning strategies and to reflect about them. She has also begun to use experiences from the extension programme and to apply them more generally to her school work.

Kylie clearly profits from the enrichment programme - not least in the way that it has allowed her to be a full (and critical) participant in her own learning. She enjoyed her unit on Psychology, for example, yet was disappointed that after a good start, where students wrote down what they wanted from the course, the tutor took them off in another direction:

> *that sort of let me down a lot because / in the first lesson I was thinking this is going to be so good / and I went back with ideas of what I want to do and what we were going to do together / and all of a sudden it was just like / you know / totally different from what I'd planned and expected.*

Following teachers down tracks which they alone predetermine is difficult enough for many pupils; but, after consultation and agreement to do otherwise, the disappointment is worse. Adolescents, of course, may not realise that some tutors are unconfident about, and unpractised in, teaching in an open, non-directive fashion. However, Kylie and her group, perceptive enough to perceive the mismatch between intentions and actuality, were also committed enough to what they had come to regard as *their* programme to request a full discussion with the external tutor and Mrs Parr. Then followed a discussion with the tutor in which Kylie said they were not getting out of the sessions what they wanted. However Kylie offered a constructive solution:

> *if we think of an idea on the day we'd rather do that than have all these ideas already piled in your head for us to do.*

The tutor responded positively by consulting the group about topics, by providing appropriate resources and by adopting a non-directive approach. Kylie describes the next lesson when, after a short period of relaxation exercises, the group watched a video on sleep:

> *and then we discussed it / and we went off the track totally / going off the track and talking about what we wanted to than we did in the whole time when we were doing what she wanted to do.*

The tutor had learned to meet the girls' needs by presenting interesting, learning experiences in an imaginative way and then allowing the students' minds 'to fly a bit'. Kylie certainly responded to the opportunity. She has left behind her original disaffection and her own evaluation of the whole course is marked with enthusiasm and intelligent appreciation:

> *I really like the enrichment programme because / everyone there sort of / wants to be involved / whereas in other classes people think well I sort of have to do it I have to do English so I'll do it / but they're not really wanting to really get into it.*

The special classes, she says:

> *give you so much more / because they are teaching you what you want to know / which is often / ah / much much more easily received / brilliant / I love it.*

OTHER STUDENTS' VIEWS

Roberta, another 16 year-old, similarly enjoyed the enrichment activities she took, especially etching and drama and appreciated the choice offered:

> *it was really good because it gave us a / wider range of things to choose from / and I did drama which I really enjoyed / ...I really enjoyed it / I thought it was a good programme.*

However, Roberta also reinforces the need to consult properly about the choice of activity:

> *I feel / they ought to / ask you in the beginning what you expect to get out of it / I know a lot of people who did / other courses where they didn't get out what they expected to / and they really ought to find out what people expect before they start off / and then they'd be able to meet their requirements more.*

Three younger girls also talked with similar intelligence, insight and understanding:

> Emily: *I reckon we should do more interesting things*
> Krystal: *I think it would be hard to organise something like that because / all these different people who want a different range of things and / you can only suit so many*
> Anita: *The first four lessons we did practically the same thing every lesson*
> Emily: *and then it got boring*
> Anita: *we got into some of the exciting stuff / and then suddenly she said bang / we can't do any more*
> Emily: *like what*
> Krystal: *I liked constructing things*
> Anita: *the constructing*
> Emily: *oh that was excellent*

Certain aspects of their course provoke enthusiastic response, but the girls agree that there remains a division between the new enrichment programme and the rest of their school-work.

> Anita: *I don't think it helps to make school more interesting /*
> Emily: *It doesn't help /*
>
> Krystal: *It doesn't make school more interesting / it just it's got nothing to do with the school*

It is unfortunate if activities meant to *extend* are perceived as separate, but the organisation of the course in option time contributes towards its being received as just another activity. In order to permeate the school curriculum and to become an integral part of the girls' experience a different approach is needed.

CONCLUSION

It is our contention that children of the highest ability have the same rights as others to have their special needs diagnosed and provided for. We have developed this argument elsewhere (Wade & Moore, 1987) when we pointed out that neither the Warnock Report (D.E.S., 1978) nor the British Education Act, 1981 referred to such children as having special educational needs. These able students frequently fall as far short of fulfilling their potential in schools as do children with disabilities. They are, however, much more difficult to identify. Neither tests nor attainment can be relied upon to reveal exceptional ability and clever children soon learn to keep their motors in low gear if they are apprehensive about peer group teasing or being treated differently. It used to be thought that intellectually gifted children were also likely to be disturbed or to have behaviour problems. In fact, Freeman (1985), reporting on the emotional aspects of giftedness, showed no such direct links and the students we observed at Mayfield Park were well-balanced and mature, as their perceptive comments indicate. If some of them had been disaffected previously, then the enrichment programme must take credit for restoring enthusiasm and confidence and for improving mediocre attainment.

The creative intellects of such students are valuable assets which societies cannot afford to neglect. Progress will only be made through educational provision which offers stimulation, variety, depth, challenge and a questioning approach. Our argument is supported by research (e.g. Rutter, 1983; Whitmore, 1985) which shows that lack of provision can stifle the excitement, curiosity, achievement and development of the gifted.

We should, however, want to extend this argument to all children. Our case-study of Mayfield Park suggests that schools can best provide for the needs of *every* child by making mainstream teaching more interesting and more challenging. All children will benefit from being given more responsibility for their own learning and more choice of activity in programmes which help them to process necessary information for solving problems without taking away the excitement of discovery.

Mayfield Park's provision is experimental, but has strong features which have already achieved significant successes. We mention particularly:
* careful planning
* the expertise of the co-ordinator

- the support of school management
- consultation with students
- choice of activity
- community involvement
- staff who are willing to learn
- opportunity to experiment with teaching methods
- willingness to adapt content and approaches

We have our doubts about the school's contemplated move towards small withdrawal groups and have elsewhere voiced our concern that:

> *often the extension work for the very able is tacked on to the ordinary curriculum instead of being an integral part of it.*

> *(Wade & Moore, 1987, p.146)*

Such a move will probably be unpopular with staff who regard it as elitist, but, more seriously, it will mark off chosen students as being different from others and will intensify individuals' worries about labelling and segregation. It will have no effect on those students who demonstrate creative potential in, say, one subject area, instead of across the board. Not only will the new provision be 'tacked on', but students will have additional problems caused by missing key lessons in major subjects.

A more integrating approach for staff and students would be to adopt the kind of model that we have outlined in our descriptions of whole school policies for support (Wade & Moore, 1987, pp. 170-180). The achievement of Mayfield Park needs an organisation which spreads its effect to all teachers in all subject areas and to more students than small withdrawal groups can cater for. The co-ordinator's role needs to shift emphasis towards co-ordinating staff efforts and towards inservice training. The support for students by community experts, similarly, could shift to support for teachers and students within the ordinary classroom and the regular curriculum. This policy would complement and extend existing provision by offering flexible extension support within the mainstream for all students willing to profit; it would also offer inservice collaborative learning experiences for staff members. In this way the mainstream provision could be made more effective and sensitive to the needs of every student.

Chapter Eight

Working Together: interschool integration

they loved being just anybody else / just being ordinary and people treating them as ordinary people / they just loved it having people around them who didn't / treat them differently

Abigail (age 10)

everyone thought that I was going to / fall off stage when I shouted I say you chaps here comes the mayor / they said Lisa / we thought you was going to fall off stage / I said no / I'm good at running / so I won't fall off stage so don't worry

Lisa (age 10)

INTRODUCTION

It would be unfortunate if, in the shift towards mainstream integration of individuals with special educational needs, existing structures were ignored. There is still, after all, in many countries, separate provision for children in special schools, as our continuum (Chapter One) indicates. Part of the problem is more uncertainty about how to provide for children whose disabilities are intellectual rather than physical or sensory. However, success stories, such as those we have analysed in some of our case studies, have encouraged schools whose experience of mainstreaming physically disabled students or those with, say, hearing impairments, to go further and admit students with intellectual disabilities. Attitudes, in some cases, may change slowly, but they do change, as our studies show.

Where there is still separate provision, we argue that there needs to be liaison and joint enterprise to provide growing points for attitude change, enhancement of self esteem and better provision for students' needs. Some special schools have developed excellent 'outreach' placements for some of their students; but, where mainstream and special schools proceed as if unaware of each other's existence, then both are losers and their students miss valuable opportunities.

Contact is important, even if it begins at an informal level. Our case study in this chapter examines just such an early point of growth between two schools, investigates the gains for all concerned and assesses the potential for further development.

THE SCHOOLS

Both schools are situated in a semi-industrial British town of about 100,000 inhabitants. St. Anne's is a voluntary-aided R.C. middle school catering for some 450 nine to thirteen year-olds in mixed ability, co-educational classes. There is a wide-ranging curriculum and extra-curricular activities. Firtrees, about a mile away, caters for about 200 boys and girls with both moderate and severe learning difficulties. The latter comprise about 25% of the entry, may be admitted from two years old and may remain until the age of nineteen. Most pupils with moderate learning difficulties transfer into the school from mainstream classes from age 7 and onwards. The aims of both schools are similar in that they work to develop each individual to his or her full potential. In the case of Firtrees some pupils will leave to enter full employment; others will require continuing lifetime support for their personal needs.

THE PROJECT

The intention was to develop opportunity for pupils in two schools to work together on a co-operative and creative activity. The Variety Club's theatrical competition provided a focus and it was decided to present the recent musical *Rats* in an adapted version for young children. The rock-pop musical by Nigel Hess and Jeremy Brown was originally intended for secondary schools and professional groups, but the pied piper story interested so many pupils when it was first shared with them that the ambitious project was quickly agreed. The 16 songs and spoken sections portray the feelings of Hamelin people as the story progresses. Instrumentalists from St. Annes and percussionists from Firtrees would accompany some of the musical numbers. There would be ample creative opportunity to develop movement and action to interpret the story and songs. It was hoped that benefits would spread beyond the singing, dancing and acting, with pupils becoming involved in aspects of the *Rats* theme across the curriculum, designing the set, building scenery, collecting costumes and props, making posters and programmes, etc.

THE PARTICIPANTS

Thirty children, (15 from each school) participated, with others from St. Anne's giving choral support. St. Anne's pupils were aged between 11 and 13 and those from Firtrees between 6 and 14. Children of both sexes and a variety of ethnic backgrounds were represented. The intention was that the thirty children would work together from the earliest rehearsals, so that the production could develop as a unified work. Children from Firtrees would develop movement and dance routines to illustrate songs from the musical and children from St. Anne's would be incorporated as ideas and patterns became established. The intention also was that Firtrees pupils would naturally learn words of choruses and become familiar enough with the music so that they could join with the St. Anne's chorus where appropriate. The Firtrees group included both pupils with severe and those with moderate learning difficulties.

ACHIEVEMENTS

The easiest outcome to record is the fact that the joint venture led to successful collaborative productions within the schools and to notable performances at the major theatres both in the town where the schools are situated and in a nearby city where representatives of the Variety Club attended. We cannot underestimate the value for all children of giving pleasure and satisfaction to families, friends and an audience in the wider community. However, there are other important outcomes, some embedded in the process of collaboration, that we will tease out from the participants: first, from staff at Firtrees.

VIEWS OF FIRTREES STAFF

Mrs Page and Mrs Brown, the Firtrees' staff most closely involved with the project, have no doubt of its value to individual students. Mrs Page recalls a conversation she had with a speech therapist who had previously worked with the students:

> she sat in the audience / and watched our children and she said the tears ran
> down my face as I watched children / that I had / struggled with to make
> them even open their mouths seemingly singing every word / I mean folk like
> Samantha and Carrie and Wayne to an extent cos he was such a shy little

boy/ they all have language problems and they loved the singing / and Wayne he opened the show / he was just the little boy who kicked the ball across to the opening bars he just thought it was wonderful it made him feel so important/

Pupils like Wayne *need* to feel important so that their status is raised, through enjoyable achievements. Supported by others and taking a role, his shyness disappears. Similarly some students with severe language problems who have made little progress with decontextualised exercises may only learn how to talk when they have something they want to say - or sing! The joy of participation in song provides a meaningful context where repetition is functional not wearisome. The implications are worth following through to other oral activities in the curriculum.

Mrs Brown speaks admiringly of the dramatic achievement of Firtrees students:

they / had to remember cues / they had to be in the right place at the right time / I think that's what amazed me as much as anything we would tend to panic / where are they / they should be here but nine times out of ten they were a step ahead of us they were there waiting.

Her pupils responded to the opportunity to show responsibility and to learn cues - as many children will when given the chance. Beyond that the same pupils showed the creative ability to adapt and to take different roles, as Mrs Page says:

folks like Lyn and Stuart they just shone as the nasty rats / it's just what they became and that was quite interesting too / yes we did become quite ambitious for them because they started to play two parts / our rats / once they'd drowned in the river those who could cope with it became the children and they made the change from the blackened faces and the snarling round the stage and being thoroughly horrid / they became the most beautiful angelic children /

Both teachers admit to having previously had low expectations for Firtrees' students (Mrs Brown: *we were saying well they won't do it*) and continuing to worry throughout the project. However, Mrs Brown notes with pleasure the children's ability to adapt - especially to problems of staging in different theatres:

they had to improvise each (performance) because things were not standing in the same place / and once upon a time the river was down / and they / jumped into it and the next they had to go underneath / and stay underneath /because obviously / if they jumped over they'd be down in the bandstand / we worried ourselves silly about it / I lay awake at night thinking I could just see one of them forgetting in the excitement and just hurtling down / but not one of them / they all did as they had been directed and we were making changes all the time and they were just accommodating them / it is amazing.

It is not only in special schools that too little is expected of pupils: frequent HMI reports have drawn attention to the same repressive force on pupils' learning in mainstream classes. However, for children whose self concepts may already be fragile, low expectations can have the most seriously depressing and damaging effects. The Firtrees' pupils force both teachers to make this point explicitly in conversation with each other:

> *Mrs Brown: you said you looked at the score originally and thought it was too ambitious and yet everyone coped incredibly well / it wasn't too ambitious / our expectations were perhaps a little low.*

> *Mrs Page: that's right / we tend to feel of our children they will do what we ask and not very much more because they're not terribly imaginative / but / that wasn't so / they were adding touches of their own.*

These perceptions have influenced staff attitudes towards pupils since the project as Mrs Page says:

> *since then we have been a little more ambitious for them.*

The project has been a learning experience for teachers as well as for pupils - particularly important for a special school which, though caring, may have to work to avoid curricular restriction and insularity. Mrs Page says the project was a:

> *good experience for us too / I think that perhaps here / as well as the children being sheltered we are in a way / it's good for us to come back to mainstream.*

The staff at Firtrees now see the links between special and mainstream schools as beneficial, not only for their children, but for themselves too. It is easy to become isolated in a curriculum which, although providing relevance, may not achieve the breadth of mainstream provision. Recent innovations by the National Curriculum Council in Great Britain have legislated for entitlement and access to the National Curriculum for *all* children. The sharing of experience, expertise and even resources between staff on differing sites in joint ventures can make such access easier for pupils with disabilities, particularly when expectations are adjusted upwards.

It is anticipated that many pupils with disabilities will not journey as far through levels of assessment as mainstream pupils and may only ever work towards achieving the lower levels. Yet contact with mainstream pupils is useful for special school staff. Reminders of what is achievable by mainstream pupils can also encourage the setting of higher expectations for pupils with disabilities, thus maximising potential for every pupil within the school. As we have already seen, the teachers from Firtrees are already in the process of re-evaluating the expectations set for their pupils through their experience in *Rats*. Greater interaction with mainstream may encourage further evaluation.

The advantages of inter-school co-operation are not all one way, however. Mainstream teachers, through contact with special schools' staff and pupils, can also profit from a valuable learning experience.

VIEWS OF THE ST. ANNE'S TEACHER

Many teachers, limited by their narrow training and experiences exclusively in mainstream classes, have fears, prejudices and low expectations concerning particular groups of children. Mrs Bedford, the St. Anne's teacher who initiated the collaborative venture, rediscovered how great a teacher is experience and learns from the model of Firtrees teachers:

> *I had no idea what it was like to work with ... Down's Syndrome ... it was quite frightening to be in the middle of a rehearsal / sat at a piano and suddenly to be lifted off / the piano / and the teacher from Firtrees would come along / you know they'd take the child away / just laugh and just sit them down / so calm and patient / that came across with our children as well / we got a lot out of it that way.*

Both Mrs Bedford and the children from St. Anne's learned by example how to relate positively to children with severe learning disabilities.

> *I think I've learned to be a little more patient than I was,*

reflects Mrs Bedford, noting the demands of pupils from Firtrees who accepted her as 'their teacher' and enjoying the informality of being addressed by her first name.

Perhaps, more importantly, she also learned to revise her expectations of what Firtrees' children could do:

> *they picked up the words of the choruses for the songs which many of the children at St. Anne's had found difficult.... they understood the story / behind the songs and from that / they learned.*

Mrs Bedford also draws attention to the value of integration for the parents of both schools:

> *they came along to many rehearsals after school / collecting the children / making their costumes / finding props for them / weekend rehearsals / they'd even wait behind after rehearsals tidying up and of course supporting at every performance.*

Apart from the opportunity for both groups of parents to make contact, to work together and to learn from each other, *Rats* provided an opportunity for parents to take natural pride in their children's achievements. As Mrs Bedford says:

in a normal musical you'd have / the star people / up at the front and the chorus in the background / and I don't think that happened / I think the children from Firtrees were the stars.

This entirely positive response from Mrs Bedford, coupled with the reactions of Mrs Brown and Mrs Page, shows that the success of the venture was not merely in its final performances but, significantly, in the learning that was engendered by the members of staff. The project showed how well pupils of each school could respond and co-operate with each other and they recognised this as a very important spin-off of the production. The children had worked well together and certainly the St. Anne's pupils had been very helpful and considerate towards the Firtrees pupils. We were interested, however, to determine whether *more* than just a caring attitude towards people with disabilities had been developed. Such an attitude, although *positive*, still reflects a 'them and us' dichotomy in society. We therefore asked St. Anne's children to reflect on their experiences of working with the other children.

ST. ANNE'S STUDENTS REFLECT

The *Rats* performances took place in the summer term and there was a time lapse of some six months before the pupils talked to us about their experiences. By that time only seven of the children who had taken part in the production were still at the school; the rest had transferred to secondary education. Of this seven, six had been in the choir. Nevertheless, they had had plenty of opportunity to observe at rehearsals and performances and to draw their own conclusions. Keeley, the seventh student, had been a main performer in the play - she had played the boy who had been left behind. Interestingly, in the story of the Pied Piper the boy who is left behind is lame and cannot keep up with the others, but in the production the character, by agreement, was changed into a day-dreamer so that disability as disadvantage was not a central issue. Keeley herself felt that it would have been insensitive:

if I was disabled / so we had to change that bit

Consideration and appreciation of feelings was much in evidence in the St. Anne's students' group discussion, ranging from pleasure at Firtrees' pupils' enjoyment during their performance to concern about the community's attitude towards them. The process of collaboration was talked about with pleasure and obviously it had been a significant, memorable experience for them. Rebecca, for example, says it 'was a really good experience' and what impressed her most was:

the way they were actually working together.

They recalled their original feelings of surprise that they *could* work together and that it was not really different from working with anybody else. Rebecca went on to say that:

> *the first impression you get is that they'd just be a nuisance around the place and / have to help them out / ... but they're just like ordinary children and they can do anything you want them to.*

Firtrees' students received many favourable comments about their acting; the St. Anne's pupils were genuinely impressed by their ability to perform on stage:

> *Abigail: they did a really good performance / ... they were good actors*

> *Gemma: they knew what was going on / they were there all the time / they were really reliable.*

They seemed to be particularly impressed because all of the pupils in Firtrees had an acting role of some kind, some with speaking parts, whereas they had only had to sing in the choir. They were pleased, however, to be able to say that they had helped some Firtrees' students with their singing and made them more enthusiastic. The area of accomplishment which attracted most admiration was gymnastics. The Firtrees' students had done flic-flacs, backward somersaults and cartwheels with total ease:

> *Gemma: it was amazing the way they just flipped across / they didn't even seem to put any effort into it*

> *Rebecca: I was amazed by the way they could do cartwheels and backward flips / something we couldn't do at all.*

The realisation that their collaborators had talents that they themselves did not possess caused St. Anne's pupils to reflect on the nature of skills and talents:

> *Gemma: they might not be as well as us mentally they are very good at other things so / they've the same amount of skill / just in other areas.*

> *Catherine: it's like...they lose some talents but gain others.*

This constructive ability to perceive positive and superior qualities in others is only one of the outcomes for mainstream students of their joint dramatic venture. Another, closely linked, result is the realisation that these talents need an outlet for appreciation by others:

> *Rebecca: I think doing* Rats *really showed their talents off.*

A venture where special educational needs pupils can be publicly seen as equal, or even superior in some ways, can have positive benefits - for *all* concerned. Certainly at the City Theatre the audience was appreciative. Catherine stated that her parents thought:

> *it was one of the best plays / musicals they'd seen / they thought it was very funny and touching,*

whereas Rebecca's parents noted how well the children from the two schools had worked together. All of the parents and often other members of the family had expressed this kind of praise for the production, thus confirming public interest and awareness of pupils' capabilities as well as disabilities.

The St. Anne's children unanimously affirmed the view expressed by Catherine's parents that it was one of the best productions that their school had done and gave the main credit to the Firtrees' children:

> *Caroline: I think they made the production better.*

> *Catherine: they made the production more interesting / more of a challenge but it was enjoyable all the same.*

We have already recorded how much the St. Anne's children had enjoyed the rehearsal process and the performances, but they were equally gratified that the Firtrees' children appeared also to have enjoyed the experience. They described events which had happened during the three or four months in which shared laughter had been memorable. Gemma summed up for the group when she said:

> *I think they enjoyed mixing with us ... we could see them smiling all the time and having a great laugh with the children from (St. Anne's)*

The perceptions recorded so far come from children who had been in the choir and who had been given no responsibility for the children from Firtrees in terms of partners in the acting roles. Each 'actor', however, had one particular partner from Firtrees to look after and Keeley, the day-dreamer in the play, talked about her experiences of acting and taking responsibility for another person. She described how, at the first rehearsal, members of the two schools sat on opposite sides of the room. Keeley did not say that this separation was because the other students were pupils from a special school; rather that they were students from *another* school whom they did not know. After that first meeting, however:

> *we all got on great.*

Keeley was partnered with Lynn (who remembered her very well) and rationalised her role as carer as follows:

> *we were not older than most of them but because we acted older we had to be responsible for them.*

She admitted that it was difficult in the beginning but, after they got to know each other, relationships were much easier. She spoke also of the learning and the adjustment that she had had to make in order for communication and socialisation to be beneficial:

> *I'm used to having children my age and my capabilities around me so / when I had to / go to them I had to adjust and sort of match their age so they could get used to me.*

Keeley emphasises the shared learning that took place, especially when they had to modify their performance to unfamiliar stage-settings:

> *but at the (City Theatre) we all had to learn to fit together.*

Not only did Keeley have her own responsibility for Lynn, helping her to get changed but she, like the other children from St. Anne's took on a corporate responsibility for the rest of the students by keeping a constant watch and helping them off stage at appropriate times:

> *if we hadn't done that people in the audience would have noticed something had gone wrong.*

Keeley and her co-actors obviously did this with the utmost skill and sensitivity. The teachers from Firtrees have already stated how naturally help was given and, as Keeley said:

> *it just had to blend in.... to look as if it was part of the sequence.*

Keeley enjoyed the extra responsibility of partnering Lynn and helping with the others, as well as learning her own lines and movements. She said it was an experience that she'd like to repeat, particularly with Firtrees because they got on so well. She added that they were genuinely upset when the enterprise came to an end - possibly because of the excitement that rehearsals, production at school and a production at a commercial theatre had generated, but also one suspects because of the genuine friendships that had been made:

> *we were all crying on the last night / we were hoping to keep in touch / but with our music teacher leaving it's a bit hard.*

Rats therefore had been a success in terms of a co-operative venture between two schools, a success in terms of acceptance and friendship and a success in terms of learning about others who are in some ways different, in others very much the same. Such learning has been implicit in what the children have said; their amazement at the things Firtrees' pupils could do that they could not, their appreciation of the children's ability to learn and to act and Keeley's learning of how to 'adjust' and how to care. The group, however, also made explicit reference to what they had learned about the children as people. Most of them commented that the Firtrees' pupils were just like ordinary children:

> *Abigail: they're just / like anybody else.../..they just need more time for people to talk to and learning is just a little bit more difficult for them.*

> *Catherine: they were really like other children / we played games with them.*

Keeley: once you got to know them you realised that they aren't stupid.

Keeley seems to have summed up the most important principle of integration - that 'getting to know' people is crucial for understanding and accepting. True integration cannot be only locational or social; to be effective it must be functional as well. At face value it may seem as if a special school could never integrate functionally; this venture has proved that it can be done and that really it should be done. The St. Anne's pupils have realised that they have learned many positive things about their disabled friends, but have also realised that other people need to learn too:

> *Abigail: they loved being just anybody else / just being ordinary people and treating them as ordinary people / they just loved it having people around them who didn't / treat them differently.*

> *Jonathan: some people in the street actually stop and stare ... I don't think that can make them feel very nice / it might hurt them inside.*

Experience has helped these youngsters to empathise with the students from Firtrees in terms of what is important in social relationships - the need for acceptance and respect of others - particularly those with disabilities.

Keeley re-iterated the group's feelings that people need to learn and in so doing chronicled her own learning. She talked about some others in her school who were not in the production and how they had called the disabled students 'horrible names'. She described how she and her friends found themselves 'sticking up for them' because they did not like the way their visitors were being treated. More importantly perhaps she realised why they were being treated in this way:

> *the other children were spiteful because they didn't know them / they hadn't got used to them*

and later she said:

> *it made me realise / because before I used to be one of the ones that used to call them names and say they're stupid but / when you get to know them / you realise they're not.*

Keeley was the only child who admitted to having a negative attitude towards disabled pupils prior to the co-operative venture. She was brave and honest to do so but it has important implications for the future and society's acceptance of people with disabilities. Keeley's attitude change was brought about by experiencing integration in its truest sense: sharing, collaboration and getting to know each other. If children, both ordinary *and* with special educational needs, are denied the opportunity to integrate and learn about each other there will remain a divide which will be too wide to bridge with understanding. This shared experience was undoubtedly the result of hard work and a great deal of time commitment by pupils, staff and parents. The enthusiasm and dedication of the teachers was, however, the prime driving force of this initiative; without them, their talents and *their* acceptance, it could not have taken place.

This case study so far has analysed people's reactions to a successful collaborative project. Every comment has suggested praise and admiration for those students who achieved much more in terms of memory, social skills, singing and dancing than was originally envisaged.

Finally we consider the experience from the viewpoint of those whom everyone suggested made *Rats* the best production - the students of Firtrees.

THE VIEWS OF FIRTREES' STUDENTS

Eight students from Firtrees sat in a group to share their ideas with us about the performance. Samantha, Lee-ann, Lisa and Neil were Down's Syndrome pupils with severe learning difficulties, Wayne had severe learning difficulties, Andrew's was a language problem compounded by learning difficulties and Claire and Lynn were in what their teachers described as the 'grey' area - not quite severe learning difficulties. All of the children in the performance had been selected on the basis that they would enjoy it and get something out of it. The reactions of the eight pupils here suggests that it was a good basis for selection. Six months had elapsed since the big 'City' production and the Firtrees' staff were concerned how little they would probably remember.

Naturally some students spoke more than others, as in any group interaction, but it was immediately obvious that all of them remembered the performance and remembered it with pleasure. They all talked about what they had enjoyed most, either what they had done as individuals or the pleasure that they had obtained from others. Claire and Lee-ann both liked being the rats with their costumes on. Lee-ann particularly liked:

swinging my tail.

She was obviously well into her part! Neil, Andrew and Wayne referred to the acting that they had had to do. Neil and Andrew had to sweep, but Wayne went into more detail:

I was kicking the ball about / and the rats tried to snatch it off me / I had to go and fetch it.

He not only remembers what he *did* but remembers also his understanding of the complexity of the sequencing and characterisation on stage.

Immediately evident also were expressions of pride in what they had achieved - not just that they had been on the stage and performed well - but that they had done better than other people thought they would do:

Lisa: everyone thought that I was going to / fall off stage when I shouted I say you chaps here comes the mayor / they said Lisa / we thought you was going to fall off stage.

Lisa shows she was well aware of other people's expectations for her in the performance and is probably just as aware of people's expectations for her in school and society. The opportunity that was given to her, however, to perform and to show her potential not only demonstrated to her the trust and support of her teachers and other children but significantly showed her *own* potential to herself. Her pride and her confidence, we feel, are entirely justified.

Lisa: I said no / I'm good at running / so I won't fall off stage so don't worry.

The enhancement of self esteem is as crucial for children with learning difficulties as it is for any child. To realise that they are important and valued for themselves and their abilities, particularly on very special occasions, has obviously had long-lasting effects upon these students:

Samantha: it was nice to be in there / everybody was laughing at me.

Yet it was not just the performance that showed the children that they were accepted in their own right but the friendship and acceptance shown by the St. Anne's children both during rehearsal time leading up to the play and out of school:

Samantha: it was nice being there (St. Anne's) all the children loved us / when we was singing there I didn't know what it would be like / one said do you want to go to tea with me and I said yes.

Both Lynn and Lisa referred to Keeley and the friendship that had grown up between them and which was renewed in chance encounters out of school:

Lisa: I got to know her in Rats */ I've seen Keeley in the library / I was choosing a book / she said Hi Lisa and I jumped a mile / I said Hi Keeley.*

The comments made by the St. Anne's students that they thought the people from Firtrees were ' just like anybody else' and that they were 'really like other children' had also been successfully transmitted to the Firtrees' children through the actions, talk and commitment of the children at St. Anne's. Perhaps Lynn sums it up for *all* of the pupils who took part in the venture:

we all got on with them very well

We made the point earlier (Chapter Three) that it is not easy to be the parent of a handicapped child when society still reacts with stigma and exclusion. This venture, however, heightened pride and awareness of *all* the parents involved: the parents of the Firtrees' pupils and, as we have already seen, the St. Anne's parents. The eight youngsters in our discussion were well aware of the pride that their parents experienced in their performance, even those who could not manage to go to the theatre but saw it televised:

> *Lisa: my mum said quick Matthew press the recorder Lisa's on the telly / so he was shooting from the dining room from having his tea / to a different room / get it here Mum / and put it into the recorder / press the play.*

The heady excitement generated by the family's pleasure is still with Lisa and liable to remain a part of her for a long time to come. The families who saw the performance at the theatre relayed both their pride to their children and their disappointment that not everyone could see them:

> *Lynn : I saw my Dad and my two brothers and my sister and at the end Dad said he was sorry because Mum couldn't come / I said that's all right.*

Lynn's mother, however, went to the school and watched the recording:

> *When it had finished she said I was brilliant.*

Parents of children with disabilities are proud of the progress and achievements that their children make, however small this progress might be when compared with children who have no disability. Achievements can only be measured in terms of the individual - a small step for some may be a great leap for others and parents are aware of this. There is, however, a chance for a wider society than that of the immediate family to appreciate the talents and abilities of children when such a joint venture is made possible. For some, the strain of rehearsals during and after school can become problematic (as in any extracurricular activity):

> *Wayne: Mum said she was pleased with me and happy / I enjoyed it / at the end I said I'd be glad when it was all over / I was tired,*

but the aftermath of perceived attributes in pupils with special educational needs can only be conducive to a more positive attitude and a wider and more genuine acceptance of them as individuals in their own right.

CONCLUSION

The successes of this project in terms of a performance and as a method of integration need no reiteration, but perhaps they need to be underlined and used as pointers for other successful ventures. There were advantages for everyone concerned. The staff and pupils at St. Anne's had had the opportunity of meeting and working with people who have disabilities. The learning that occurred on their own part was apparent to all of them - the realisation that expectations were set artificially low - the acceptance that in some areas the children were more skilled than they could be - the trust that they could put in the pupils to *learn* - to learn songs, words and actions in order to put on a highly creditable performance. Everyone learned that they *could* work together - perhaps not only in this but in other ventures. In addition, the staff at Firtrees continuously upgraded their expectations of the students' potential - and this continued after the stage performance. Parents were able to be publicly and genuinely proud of their children's achievements. The children of Firtrees benefited from having excellent role models in the children from St. Anne's and from having their perceived abilities continually re-assessed and proving that they could reach these new boundaries.

Special schools and mainstream schools can adopt a similar pattern of full, if only temporary, integration. It is good to have a beginning which leaves people wanting more. Yet more is certainly possible. We would argue too that the gains made are too important for such integration to be confined to a small number of students or to depend on the initiative of one teacher. We suggest that such contacts should be part of the development plans of all schools - mainstream or special. Our case study has described only one way in which social and, to some extent, academic integration can take place, but there are certainly others which promise the same degree of success. We shall return to other possibilities of inter-school integration in our final chapter, though without absolute guarantees that all suggestions will enable children from special schools to become - in the words of both staff and children from St. Anne's:

    'the stars'!

Chapter Nine

The Support Team: in-school support

We need to enrich the lives of all of our pupils and you can't do that by having a unit in the middle of a paddock...... I guess the special needs children of years and years ago / we didn't call them special needs / they were just children who came to us with a disability...... we've always done it / I can't understand what all the hoo-hah's about.

(Miss Jacques, Headteacher of Girls' School)

1. Support Teams for Mainstreaming

INTRODUCTION

The New Zealand Education Act (1989) acknowledges the right of all children, regardless of disability or handicap, to be educated at their local school alongside their peers, rather than attending special schools or units.

Mainstreaming in New Zealand receives the support of all areas of the community - parents, professionals and educationalists - but the progression from principle to practice is fraught with difficulty. Many children with disabilities are now entering schools whose staff have neither the experience nor expertise to make provision for their special educational needs. It is, however, the responsibility of the Board of Trustees of the school, and not of a separate education department, to provide for those needs. This presents a challenging, if not daunting, task to fulfil. Within the schools there are now various issues to address, such as, how to achieve *successful* mainstreaming, how best to equip teachers, and how to make a whole school policy out of the needs of a minority of pupils. In order to attain these goals it is envisaged that certain classroom practices and teaching styles will have to be modified; that attitudes of some staff to the inclusion of special educational needs children within their classrooms may have to be skewed to a more positive bias; and that some staff may have to receive some form of in-service in order to enhance appropriate teaching skills, rather than relying on advice from outside experts or by withdrawing pupils from their class. This last point is crucial in the context of movement away from centrally funded services which provide for children on a withdrawal basis.

There have already been attempts to solve the problems caused by withdrawing children. The 1988 Draft Report on Special Education (New Zealand), for example, recommended an extension of the Guidance Unit Model to provide support for the mainstreaming of *all* children with special needs. This Guidance Unit served three schools within the South Auckland area. It operated as a team and provided advice, guidance and support to class teachers with children who were experiencing learning or behavioural difficulties in their classrooms. In addition to providing withdrawal provision for children, the team also devised and implemented learning programmes and behaviour contracts for children. Although it was a valuable asset to the three schools, inevitably members of the team took on the roles of 'expert outsiders'. This often has the effect in schools of taking responsibility of provision for special educational needs children away from the school and its teachers and passing it to the expert who, after all, 'knows best'. Although the approach in many ways was successful the Draft Report recommended its *development* and not its utilisation. One example of a possible development is that of support team provision within individual schools which, although still in its infancy with the associated teething problems, is experiencing a rewarding degree of success and is the subject of a paper by Glynn & Gold (1990) of the University of Otago.

THE SUPPORT TEAM APPROACH

The envisaged role of the Support Team in New Zealand is likely to be crucial in determining how some of the issues that currently beleaguer schools can be resolved. The Support Team is school-based and consists of designated professionals, (both teachers and management) who can, if necessary, liaise with external professionals (educational psychologists etc.). The concept of the Support Team is a *school-based* approach to meet the needs of children with disability. It strives to provide in-school support by utilising a member of the school staff to provide the central and guiding role in the implementation of provision. This provision, although school-based and school-directed, is different from the traditional model of a support teacher who withdraws the child with special needs for extensive and individual tutoring. The latter model works against total integration, as it leads not only to physical segregation (although temporary) but to social segregation. Instead, the Support Team offers a model that supports both children and staff. Central to it is what Glynn & Gold (1990) call a 'Consulting Teacher'. The Consulting or Support Teacher is a member of the school staff who consults and collaborates with all those concerned in the education of children: class teachers, headteachers, other professionals and parents. This consultation ensures a whole school approach for providing for individual children's needs and offers a consistent and secure basis from which to work.

It is inevitable that when children are taught by a variety of teachers, a variety of teaching methods is experienced. Such variety, although usually unproblematic for regular students, may provide a confusing learning environment for children who have to learn to overcome a particular disability. Consistency of method, therefore, should theoretically enable learning to be less confusing. This is not to suggest that a rigidity of style should be enforced but, as Glynn & Gold maintain, that an enhancement of the skills of all of the staff will result. Consultation and collaboration, between all members of staff concerned for the needs of the child, will enable appropriate teaching methods and skills to be formulated, discussed and practised. It is also suggested that an enhancement of teaching skills will benefit *all* children in the school, not only those who are targeted. Enhancement of expertise is beneficial for all.

The Support Teacher has the pivotal role in the team and therefore appropriate selection for this post is crucial. He or she is a permanent teacher on the staff of the local school who is released from a proportion of teaching duties in order to support effectively. The proportion of time might well vary, but, in one example cited by Glynn & Gold, three secondary schools were allocated one Support Teacher post between them, therefore releasing one member of staff from each school from one third of their teaching commitments. It is essential that the Support Teacher should be both highly valued and respected by the other members of staff, both as a teacher and an individual, if successful collaboration between Support Teacher and the team is to take place. A high level of expertise is needed, therefore, not only in teaching but in interpersonal relationships. Further preparation and training for the necessity of working co-operatively with colleagues can be provided through in-service work with the Support Team. Glynn & Gold envisage that such in-service will enable the Support Teacher to achieve the degree of expertise necessary not only in the above areas but in the following:

- consultation and collaboration with other professionals and parents
- advocating and negotiating for changes in school policy and administration

- identifying in-service needs for staff in the school to facilitate mainstreaming
- negotiating for resources through the Ministry of Education on behalf of individual children in their school.

It is also necessary for Support Team teachers to have a period of reflective time in order for them to adjust to the principles of the indirect, collaborative approach rather than the direct, withdrawal approach and to ensure that they are committed to these principles. They may also need time to adjust to new teaching methods, especially individual educational programming for children with special educational needs and disabilities. We observed that the prevalent educational programming in force was behaviouristic in concept, relying on the skills of Task Analysis and evaluation of progress through small step teaching and learning. Some Support Team teachers may have to be strongly convinced by the efficacy of this approach, particularly if they have been accustomed to a holistic approach with its emphasis on the cognitive rather than step by step and reinforcement. Later on, difficulties may arise from those members of staff who prefer a less restrictive view of education, particularly when, even in the world of special education, such methodology is being questioned, (see Ashman & Conway, 1989). Inter-school policy in methodological approaches, therefore, may be more difficult to achieve than the acceptance of the general principles of the Support Team approach and its underlying philosophy of total integration. To begin with, however, it is the consistency of policy within each school that is important.

Perhaps more important than the particular educational orientation are the principles developed for school based team work which are intended to result in positive outcomes for every child with special educational needs: a recognition of individuality, with areas of skill as well as learning difficulties taken into consideration; the recognition of the value of parental contribution to children's learning; the commitment of the school staff to advance children's learning by working systematically as a team, giving appropriate support within classrooms through the implementation of consistent teaching programmes.

Inevitably before such support can be given, collection and collation of necessary information is necessary in order to establish the individuality of the children and their particular educational requirements. Interviews with children and their parents ensure that knowledge of the *whole* child is acquired, with likes and dislikes, attitudes, ambitions and areas of skill, which can then be used constructively to plan for learning.

Records from previous schools and other professional agencies give an indication of the child's reaction to previous educational intervention. In addition, observation by the Support Team of the child in situ provides further information for assessment. Only after such information gathering, can the Support Team check the availability of resources and plan appropriate learning programmes. The Support Team approach envisages that such learning programmes are planned not only in consultation with classroom teachers, but also with parents, who are encouraged to take active responsibility for their children's education and to ensure that a smooth continuation of practice from school to home occurs. Such continuity is invaluable when children are experiencing behavioural difficulties and a consistent approach is necessary to achieve knowledge and rules of acceptable behaviour. It also is beneficial, if the child is given homework or a programme of continuation, that parents and teachers provide a similar approach and support in order to avoid confusion. The recognition of parents as 'other professionals' (Wade & Moore, 1987) is perhaps only slowly being realised, but parents are an invaluable resource if proper consultation takes place.

Once the learning programme is established, continual assessment of the child's progress is crucial. Ideally, assessment gathering comes from a variety of sources, not only from classroom teachers but from the child, the child's parents and perhaps even peers. This assessment would not be restricted to learning programmes, but would include the level of the child's absorption and activity within the whole school programme - a true assessment of successful mainstreaming.

The Support Team approach undoubtedly demands extra commitment from school staff and management, commitment not only of time but of attitude and methodology. Although the model discussed here is directed towards Task Analysis and small step teaching, the choice of methodology appears to be secondary to the general principles. If a school staff is committed to the successful integration and education of every child with special educational needs, is prepared to plan and discuss, is willing to modify and adapt teaching skills and curriculum to meet the needs of the individual, the chosen methodology should stem from expertise of the staff and the needs of the individual.

The sharing of responsibility between staff members ensures support not only for individual children, but for individual members of staff. Too often in schools the teacher with responsibility for special needs has worked in a vacuum with little or no liaison in terms of work set or co-operation between the special educational needs teacher and the school. Support generated by the team model should, if carefully organised, ensure that staff work from a position of knowledge and confidence and, perhaps most importantly, from a positive attitude.

Inevitably, however, even with identical general principles, practices in individual schools vary. The following sections describe and discuss the practice of two schools, which have taken on board the Support Team approach, and evaluate progress as members of the teams attempt to put principles into practice.

2. A Model for Mainstreaming

The Support Team model has formed the basis for a number of schools which are committed to mainstreaming their pupils with special educational needs. Any model that is proposed in education, however, can never be followed exactly, for education deals with people, their perceptions and their circumstances. Any proposed model, therefore, may be *followed* but will be modified to some degree by individual factors.

The rest of this chapter focuses on case studies of two schools in New Zealand, which have adopted the model of the Support Team in their schools. They are both secondary schools catering for a mixed ability intake. The first is a boys' school and the second a girls' school. The information has been collated through interviews and observation.

THE BOYS' SCHOOL

The school is situated on the edge of a town and is bounded by spacious gardens on one side and the beach on the other. It is undergoing extensive renovation and is well resourced. The ability range is wide and includes pupils with specific special educational needs including a cerebral palsy pupil, five intellectually impaired pupils and a number of boys with difficult behaviour problems. The school had only had the Support Team model in situ for about eighteen months and was consequently still experiencing the growing pains that modification and alteration inevitably bring. The changes in the school policy had been brought about by means of a gradual progression of ideas from a system that originally supported and encouraged a rigid demarcation of ability, through to a less rigid streaming policy, followed by a more flexible banding for subject areas. Included in the banding system were special classes for those pupils who were deemed to have special educational needs. The advent of the Support Team, however, encouraged the school to become committed to total mainstreaming for all pupils in each ordinary class, with no special classes or withdrawal classes made available.

The opportunity for change arose when the teacher in charge of special educational needs and slow learners left the school. As the deputy head explained, it was a chance to:

get rid of the tag of slow learners and special needs people

Although there was never any criticism of the teacher or methods used for the pupils, the negative aspects of withdrawal classes and special classes were clearly perceived by the school and its management. The expectations raised (or, more correctly, lowered) by the labelling of 'slow learners' and 'special needs' pupils were reinforced by the different situation and treatment they received. The obvious way to untie and dispose of these labels was by disbanding the special needs class and its associated rooms and resources and by integrating the pupils into the system. The pupils and classes were carefully matched to ensure that each class had a wide ability mix. New boys coming into the school at the beginning of the academic year were also carefully selected for entry to particular classes. The reports written about them by their primary school teachers were taken into consideration and used to place them in their forms. The reports were used, not to segregate one from another, but to ensure again that children of differing abilities were equally distributed between the classes. This was as true for the pupils who needed extra support for their learning as it was for the pupils whose ability was such that they needed extension work in the school curriculum.

This distribution of pupils into the mainstream inevitably produced many problems, particularly for the teaching staff. As a result of the previous systems of streaming and banding, there were teachers who had not only never taught children with special educational needs, but who had not even glimpsed the majority of the spectrum of the ability range, having focussed their expertise on the 'high flyers'. A system of support for teachers was obviously crucial. In some respects the system employed closely follows the model described earlier. It is still in an experimental phase but is working as a teacher support model. Three schools have been given one teacher between them - that is one third of a teacher each for the role of Support Teacher in this school. The designated Support, or Consulting Teacher in this boys' school is the deputy head. One third of his time-tabled teaching hours are committed to this role - the equivalent of eight hours per week. He is the lynch pin of the team and sees his main function as supporting the teachers who are working with mainstreamed children. He feels that he should, in effect, help the teacher to come to terms with what it is like to teach pupils with special educational needs within the class and how best to cope with them. The transition from policy to practice is effected by the help of other team members who are in addition to the permanent members of staff. These team members are not with the school *because of* the change in policy; they were attached to the school before policy changes and it is only their role which has been altered.

The *Resource Teacher*, for example, works at the school for twenty-three hours per week. She now spends her time almost entirely in the classroom working alongside other members of staff. This is contrary to her previous practice which was to withdraw the difficult children from their classes. Working in the ordinary classroom obviously has advantages. Firstly, it reduces the stigma of needing help, particularly as the teacher also helps other boys who are not identified as having special educational needs. This widens the teacher's clientele and can also result in raised expectations for pupils as they work with regular students. Secondly, it provides the special educational needs pupils with appropriate role models rather than the restricted, and often inappropriate role models of withdrawal classes.

A trained *primary school teacher* provides the school with an extra twelve and a half hours per week of teaching reading. She works in whole class groups for at least half of her time, but gives time also to individuals where necessary. The teacher has also introduced the excellent primary practice of inviting and encouraging parents into the school to listen to the pupils read. This stimulates interest from the community and often provides the motivating spur that previously failing readers need.

An extra eight hours of *ancillary help* has been given to the school in the person of another fully-trained primary teacher. The school is very careful about her role and, because of the wide discrepancy in pay between ancillary helpers and teachers, she is not allowed to teach the pupils:

it isn't easy because she's very capable so we have to hold her back.

To the outsider this waste of talent appears to be at odds with the philosophy of the Support Team. A trained primary teacher with a working knowledge of child development, mixed ability teaching and a range of diverse teaching strategies in many areas of the curriculum is an asset to any team that is planning and working to benefit pupils with special educational needs. Relegation to the role of an ancillary helper would suggest that she is unable to utilise all of her skills. One can understand the school's unwillingness to take advantage of her by paying ancillary wages under false pretences, but there must be a great deal of frustration on all sides with a pay system that allows this anomaly.

The aim of all of the support staff mentioned so far is to spend as much time as possible in mainstream classes in order to support and maintain the pupils in the mainstream curriculum. There is, in addition, a guidance counsellor, but the advisory work done tends to be out of classtime.

There are a number of ways in which the Support Team seeks to fulfil its proposed aim and its supporting role. At the time of writing, for example, the team gives three hours a week to each of six Year Nine classes. The three hours consist of one hour each for Maths, English and Social Studies - a total of eighteen hours. In addition, six hours of support a week is divided between two Year Ten classes in the same areas of the curriculum. There is also help given to the pupils in Year 12 and 13 who still need help in reading skills or who are slow developers.

It is interesting to note that the Support Team appears to offer no assistance in the Science curriculum. In Britain, Science is regarded as one of the three major core subjects of the National Curriculum (the other two being English and Mathematics) and as such has a high profile. Pupils with special educational needs, therefore, would be expected to receive assistance in this subject as well as in English and Mathematics. It is not a case, however, of the subject being forgotten in the school but that support is not regarded as necessary. It is reasoned that, as the Science Department has a full time technician (twenty-five hours a week) who can help with the preparation and resources, no extra help is needed.

The deputy head sees many advantages in the present organisation , the major one being that the pupils are no longer so heavily stigmatised by being members of a special class or unit, but are fully integrated into the school. The labelling which *can* occur if pupils receive special help in class is also avoided when, as in the case of the reading teacher, the help is extended to other pupils. A further advantage which he itemised was that of having two teachers in the same class:

> *in case things get a little bit difficult and the staff are able to support each other.*

A good deal has already been achieved, staff are still in the process of learning and the system is undergoing modifications. In any evaluation it is important to remember purposes and overall aims. The Support Team was developed to support the class teacher in the teaching of pupils with special educational needs in the mainstream, to maximise their potential. The type of support offered therefore, is crucial. If 'support' is only seen as help in preparation (which is the reason the Science Department does not need more 'support') then we have to consider *how* this support will eventually help the pupil with special educational needs. The remit of the team is to collaborate with and discuss appropriate methodology for the individual pupil with the mainstream teacher, in order that the teacher is able to provide for the pupil's needs. 'In-class' support is necessary and can provide an excellent role model for the teacher in terms of resources and practice. It can also ensure that the 'specialist' gives help to a wider range of clientele. The problem of the perceived 'specialist', however, is that often the responsibility of the special educational needs pupil remains with that one identified person. This is particularly true when the specialist is not a full time, permanent member of staff. Of all the individual members of the Support Team so far identified, only the deputy head is totally in situ.

It is necessary for the class teacher, for *every* class teacher, to become an expert in appropriate methods and teaching skills so that any support becomes an addition to, rather than separate from, good practice. It is essential that it is perceived as such and not just 'helping the teacher'. The deputy head was concerned with the perceptions of members of staff about the nature of the Support Team. For some traditional thinkers, a teacher receiving 'support' must be a 'weak' teacher:

> *if a support teacher works in class alongside another teacher there's always the temptation for somebody in the system to say hey, how's Mr. Smith getting along / is he coping any better now.*

The assumption seems to be that it is the teacher who needs help rather than the pupil. While this assumption may be true that teachers *do* need help - we all need to continue to learn and develop our teaching skills - it is usually the good teachers who best recognise the fact. The deputy head states very firmly that the team is owned by the teachers who call on them when the necessity arises. It is the teachers' perceptions of whether they need help which is the deciding factor. This can, however, run contrary to the needs of the children in mind:

> *they get help / whether or not they've got any handicapped or emotional / or intellectual or physically handicapped children in their class / so that here it's the teachers on the scheme ..... people opt in ..... sometimes the support team can see that a teacher is clearly under some sort of stress / and they offer to help.*

It appears that here the Support Team may be in danger of moving off target with the needs of the integrated pupils becoming secondary to the needs of the staff. Ideally the two should be satisfied in tandem - though an impossible brief, perhaps, for a Support Team still in process of developing its system. Yet it would be unfortunate indeed if the school did not develop fully into meeting the needs of pupils with disability through the enhancement of the teaching skills of all of the staff. Obviously the teaching staff *is* getting help and support, but it does appear to be aimed more directly at the staff. There is help given in the classroom: the Support Team works with pupils who are problematic, and in this way to some extent the workload is being lessened. However, the question remains: how does this help the classroom teacher to help the pupil with special educational needs? The advantage of the role model is obviously one way but there seems to be the notion that the team acts rather like the cavalry - moving in to sort out the problem and then moving out again. The needs of the teacher have to be met, but the classroom teacher also needs to *learn*. Each individual pupil will have individual problems which need to be discussed by teachers and team members in order that appropriate provision may be made. The class teacher will be aware of how particular problems are manifested in the classroom and shared discussion will enable different strategies to be highlighted, methodologies questioned and, more importantly, modified to suit the needs of the pupil. In this way the class teacher will be perceived as an *active* member of the team rather than a 'weak teacher' and will become an *active* learner able to choose from a variety of strategies based on knowledge and understanding to maximise pupil's learning and become, eventually, an 'in-house' specialist.

The commitment to integration by the school and its staff is genuine; the desire to rid pupils of the 'stigma' of disability is applaudable; and many steps in the right direction are being taken. The school's policy will continue to be evaluated - both by the staff, the team and by representatives of the Ministry which conceived the idea. Nothing can be perfect in development and as long as the steps continue to head for the stated destination, *the needs of the pupil*, then the overall evaluation will be positive.

THE GIRLS' SCHOOL

The girls' school also utilises a Support Team. It is not one of the three designated schools for evaluation but, in many ways, follows the tenets of the Support Team model outlined earlier in the chapter. There are interesting reasons for the differences in the implementation of the model.

The girls' school caters for approximately one thousand girls aged between fourteen and eighteen. It is an urban school and takes its students from the town and its surrounding districts. Its history of meeting the needs of students with disabilities differs greatly from that of the boys' school. It has always had a policy of acceptance and full integration and had previously established a reputation as a caring, as well as an academic, school:

> *the special needs children years and years ago / we didn't call them special needs / they were just children who came to us with a disability.*

This comment by Miss Jacques, the Headteacher, demonstrates the positive attitude to integration which was prevalent throughout the school. Long before government legislation for pupils with special educational needs, the school had accepted visually handicapped students and, without support or resources, had devised its own policy for ensuring their integration. This policy did not include special classes or withdrawal groups, as Miss Jacques had learned from prior experience. Previously the school had employed a withdrawal group policy for remedial groups, but had noted their lack of success:

> *I've watched the remedials regress and that of course / was the determination that we would put resources in the classroom and not withdraw*

To facilitate the students' total integration many of the staff at the school learned Braille and adapted the delivery of their lessons to accommodate the visually impaired pupils' learning.

The determination and willingness of the staff to learn and adapt ensured the success of the original venture. Success led to more students, with a range of disabilities, (for example, hearing impaired, autistic, cerebral palsy) being sent to the school. As their numbers increased, so too did the realisation that more support and resources were necessary if the school was to continue a successful policy of integration into the mainstream. Before legislation, however, this proved to be difficult, but the staff refused to compromise. Miss Jacques, for example, refused to restrict the curriculum for the disabled students even though she was advised to do so:

> *the Education Department told me that I had to curtail some of the subjects*

107

and fought for the right of full access to the curriculum for all of her students in the school:

> *I can remember saying / you are actually denying children their rights in education.*

The recent legislation, however, has led to greater access to resources and support and, for the girls' school, an even wider brief in addressing and meeting the needs of a wide range of students.

Being in advance of the trend towards integration, the school had little need of advice on how to achieve mainstreaming or on how to facilitate a whole school policy on special needs. All staff already had knowledge and experience of, and positive attitudes towards, pupils with disabilities. In these respects, therefore, the school had advantages that the boys' school did not have. The boys' school was still working at the foundation stage of integration, whereas the structure was substantially built at the girls'. Nevertheless, the Support Team at the girls' school is working hard on the final stages towards completion.

THE SUPPORT TEAM

The designated Support Team consists of four teachers and three teaching assistants. The role of the consulting teacher as a team leader is not viewed as a necessity - the team works as equal members with each teacher having responsibility of assessing the needs of the pupils identified as having special educational needs in one of four designated areas of competence for the students with disability. These are not subject areas, but competencies that are interleaved with the school's curriculum. The four areas are:

> *(1) COMMUNICATION: we believe that each child who is suffering from a physical disability needs to be able to communicate as fluently and as confidently as possible*

> *(2) PROBLEM SOLVING: their problem solving skills must be / so highly developed that will allow them independence in living*

> *(3) PHYSICAL FITNESS: it is important for them to be as physically fit as possible*
> and
> *(4) TRANSITION: either to tertiary education or employment:*

> *we want / to take responsibility for these children beyond the walls of school.... we believe that it doesn't stop with schooling*

Each Support Team teacher, with the exception of the physical fitness teacher, has the help of a teaching assistant.

The teachers and assistants work with and alongside the school staff. The focus, however, is not upon a consistency of methodology as proposed by the described model in the first section of this chapter, but on a school philosophy of making the 'mainstreamers' (pupils with disabilities) fit into the school and be:

as normal as possible.

This shared philosophy of acceptance demands that the members of the Support Team are not seen as 'different' from other members of staff. The teachers who teach the 'mainstreamers' must also be seen as mainstream teachers. The Support Team members therefore teach in their specialist subject areas for half of the allotted time-table time and the other half is 'non-contact' time. 'Non-contact' is, in fact, a misnomer as this time is spent in assessing the needs of the pupils in one of the four areas of competence:

if they can build and grow in these areas we are getting them a long way towards functioning independently when they leave school.

The team does not work independently of each other or of other members of staff. The work in the competence areas often takes place in the classes of other colleagues in the team's 'non-contact' time. The team members therefore liaise closely with all colleagues who have concerns about students with special educational needs. Information is collected not only from colleagues, but from all people who are able to provide observations and facts about individuals. These include peer group members and parents. The school recognises the valuable contribution that parents can make - a contribution fully recognised by Glynn & Gold (1990). Parents are asked what their concerns and long term goals are for their daughters and these are responded to:

we take information from all people concerned / asking the parents what are their goals and concerns / observation from the class teacher / putting all the information together.

Once the information has been gathered, the team is then able to itemise and plan appropriate resources. This information is collected and collated by the Director of Student Services (whose responsibilities include pastoral care and discipline within the school) and then distributed to the relevant members of team and staff. This 'networking' system, therefore, ensures that everyone has access to information and knowledge of the goals set. A whole school policy, therefore, works for each individual. In this way, members of the team are able to plan how best they can provide the necessary support - both for teacher and student. The emphasis is less on providing a role model of teaching skill for the class teacher and more on consultation as to the provision of appropriate resource material for the pupil's needs:

building up resources has become a priority / the girls are a priority / we hope to build a bank of resources / where we have to modify a programme for a girl with special needs / that will become available from year to year with adjustments.

The modification of programmes is to ensure that, with support, the pupils with special educational needs achieve the same skills, but perhaps by using different techniques and resources. In an art lesson, for example, one class was involved in screen-printing. One severely handicapped student had neither the strength nor the motor control necessary to make the lino cuts. The Support Team member and the class teacher discussed how best the student could do comparable work and which techniques would be better suited to her needs. The final, successful, solution was for the student to 'dot' polystyrene with a pen to produce a design ready for screen-printing. The resources which had been provided as a result of consultation enabled her to manipulate the tools to achieve the same effect and end product as other members of the class (and, we noted, the same pleasure and sense of achievement). The support given in this example is in making modification and adjustment to a class programme to ensure that the student remains with her group, but with whatever accommodation to her learning that she requires. The support, crucially, is via discussion, co-operation and collaboration by the team member and the class teacher. This is a valuable method of in-service training and a re-affirmation of a whole school policy of team work. The designated Support Team member is not viewed as an outside specialist giving help and advice but as a trusted colleague who is prepared to listen, contribute and extend shared ideas.

This relationship extends to the classroom when the team member works alongside the class teacher. One example of this in-class support was described by Mrs Baines, whose area of competence responsibility was communication. She often spent time with one group during their Drama sessions. One of the members of the group, Donna, has intellectual impairment compounded by a hearing loss. Mrs Baines taught the whole class (and the teacher) some sign language in order that they could communicate with Donna:

> *she signs / so we spent a whole lesson where they individually came up and / they signed their own names / they would sign / hello my name is JULIE / Julie / and she would say Julie / back again / and that broke enormous barriers.*

This shared activity between pupil, peers, teacher and team teacher enhances not only Donna's communication skills but the confidence of pupils and staff in their own skills. The class teacher, a new member of staff, had admitted to feelings of apprehension about her ability to cope with a hearing impaired child in the drama class, but this had changed:

> *it's changed the way I feel about it / I'm just not worried any more.*

ACCEPTANCE

Miss Jacques, the Headteacher, maintains that the support given is wider than that of just the team provision but that the team provides the motivating drive. Part of the aim of the team is to create interdependence so that peer group acceptance is part of the change. This was evident in Drama sessions where the girls worked in groups. We observed Donna in a Drama lesson where enjoyment and learning to take a role were manifested in lively activity. A classroom assistant provided unobtrusive support to Donna, mainly confined to nods of encouragement and smiles. We watched her peer group giving her the same encouragement by giving her props so that she could take an active part. The class teacher was delighted to report that by the end of her lesson she was acting her role:

> she was being Mum and she was cooking the meals / she was waving bye-bye to the children / she just loves it / and she laughs.

The positive acceptance by the peer group indicates that the integration policy of the school is a success, not only at the academic but at the social, interactional level:

> there is a particular group of girls who will always volunteer to work with Donna / bringing her in;

which is reciprocated by Donna:

> she's opened up / her whole body language is much freer / she is becoming very expressive.

The role models provided by the whole staff are obviously very important determinants of attitudes expressed by the peer group to students with disabilities. The Support Team, however, makes active forays in fostering positive, caring attitudes towards the students.

Miss Lewis, whose area of responsibility is physical fitness, is a specialist P.E. teacher. One of her mainstream classes has a girl with autism. The pupils are fourteen to fifteen years old and, in the main, are very keen in their P.E. lessons. Miss Lewis, putting into practice the school philosophy of ensuring that the students 'fit in' and are not seen to be different from the rest, does not give Angela, the student with autism, any overt attention, determined to make her part of the school in every way. In the P.E. lessons, therefore, she receives no adult support at all. Instead Miss Lewis pairs her with Sharon, a very able girl (a proposed member of the under-16 New Zealand basketball team) who encourages her to join in and tells her what to do. We observed Angela participating in ball control games with Sharon alongside, enjoying the activity and communicating naturally with her friend both verbally and non-verbally. Angela has, from this base of confidence, made marked progress in the way she takes part and co-operates in contexts outside the P.E. lessons. The headteacher commented on the changed attitudes of her classmates:

> *When she came / she was sort of a figure of fun / because the school she came*
> *from hadn't the proper atmosphere / so the children who wanted her to sing*
> *and / call out loud at the wrong time / they would coax her to do it / it*
> *allowed taunting / she came to our school with a stigma of special needs / we*
> *all had to work very hard to get to where the girls accepted her / and / as they*
> *accepted her / of course her inappropriate reactions diminished.*

The resolution of the headteacher, the Support Team and school staff that pupils with disabilities should 'fit in' emanates both from a historical context and a shared belief in equality of access and treatment. Individual teaching programmes are drawn up for every pupil with special educational needs in order to ensure that their maximum potential is reached. Specific goals are set for each student after consultation, the steps towards achieving the goals are worked in conjunction with the class teacher, the Support Team constantly assesses and reviews the goals to monitor progress. The information collected by the team is recorded daily and provides feedback for the student, the staff and parents.

Although individual programmes are devised they do not rely on restrictive curriculum practices to ensure that 'basics' are taught and learned. Instead the students receive a rich and varied curriculum: drama, poetry, science, art, exactly the same as their peers. Modifications may have to be made but access is unobstructed.

The realisation of the goals set is a move towards independence for the student. Mrs Carroll, the Support Team member for transition, reflects on its importance:

> *we don't want them over-cossetted / it's timing that's important / knowing*
> *when to withdraw / to be able to cease / to give them independence / when it's*
> *overdone / if it's too great / it's just as bad as neglecting a child.*

Independence of children with special educational needs is encouraged from the beginning when their in-school treatment reflects the same encouragement and discipline as the other pupils. When total integration is a reality with acceptance of all students as individuals, then the lives of all members of the school community are enriched:

> *we need to enrich the lives of all of our pupils / and you can't do that by*
> *having a unit in the middle of a paddock.*

CONCLUSION

Clearly the comment of Miss Jacques above endorses the whole school commitment to integration. The fact that this has always been school policy does not undermine the advantages of having a Support Team on site.

Inevitably the girls' school has evolved its own support provision appropriate to its own needs rather than trying to follow a strictly prescribed model. The boys' school is in the process of adapting the model, but is still coming to terms with the consequences of *total* integration within the school. Miss Jacques and her staff are confident in their abilities to teach and support pupils with disability, but this has consolidated over a number of years:

We've always done it / I can't understand what all the hoo-hah's about.

The deputy head of the boys' school is still in the model of support teacher, having to lead, and hold together, the staff and the team as well as encouraging co-operation and consultation between staff members. The hard work and commitment appear to be working there also. It is possible, however, that the experience of the girls' school could provide some indicators for progression of the integration policy for the boys' school as well as for other schools seeking to adopt some of the ideas and incorporate them into their own practice. From our observations and analysis it is essential that the right kind of support is given and that it is directed correctly; that the support is given only after all the information has been collected and consultation has occurred with the members of staff and parents. It also appears that consistency of methodology in teaching is not necessarily important - as long as the teaching is good, dynamic and creative and attuned to the needs of the individual. It is consistency of attitude which is the overriding factor. Finally, it is crucial that the Support Team does work as a *team* with equal status and responsibility and that this team is only the nucleus of a far larger team which incorporates school staff, parents and pupils.

Schools worldwide are at different stages in forging their systems of collaboration and support. For us the important concern is not how far each school so far has reached in its approach, but that they are heading in the right direction with consistency and a clear aim: that through support given to staff and pupils, students with special educational needs are perceived as equal members of the school and are given equal access to the curriculum and to the varied opportunities of a community of learners and teachers.

Chapter Ten

Educational Programmes: planning for the individual

it's gradually changing their perceptions / it's really nice to see people who are angry and frustrated and irritated with having children in their classroom that they didn't want / and gradually / you go in there and they're saying great..... they're sort of seeing the children in a different light..... and after a while they've forgotten they hadn't used to like them

(Glenys Walsh - Itinerant Resource Teacher)

INTRODUCTION

Within any class of pupils there is a range and diversity of needs which are either covert or overt. The probability that all pupils have needs of one kind or another is an educational tenet constantly referred to by teachers. Teachers attempt to address these needs for all members of the class, but the individual educational needs of pupils with disabilities are paramount - theirs may be over and above the needs of others. The Statementing Procedure in Britain diagnoses, assesses and states the educational provision necessary to foster a pupil's maximum potential. It is a legal document, a contract, as to what should be provided in terms of strategies and resources. The procedure, however, is both complex and time consuming, (between twelve and eighteen months before action is usually taken). As the procedure is so complex, many children with special educational needs are not statemented, since it is determined that the school already has the capability of meeting their needs. Many pupils, therefore, do not have the safeguard of that formal, legal document.

There is no necessity, however, for a document to be legal in order to be effective and provide safeguards. A formal document created in an in-school context and adhered to by staff can work in much the same way. The Individual Educational Programme, described later in this chapter, is such a document. It is a set of strategies and tactics through which a pupil's needs may be met in the mainstream class. The aims and guidelines are practically based for use in the classroom, planned and agreed by a consensus and evaluated by the planning group in which everyone has an important role to play and a contribution to make.

It is important that, when catering for pupils' needs, care is taken that they are not set apart from their peers in terms of activity and interaction - to do so would negate the positive effects of their integration. The case study which follows describes one school's contribution to diagnosing and providing for the needs of their pupils through individual programmes of work but still ensuring entitlement and access to the whole school curriculum.

The School

Te Kanawa is a small suburban school in New Zealand which caters for an age range between five and fourteen years. In addition to the wide ability range common to the majority of schools, it is also a multicultural community and family origins include Samoan, Maori, Indian and South East Asian. For many of these students English is their second language and there is a variance in fluency and understanding.

The school also caters for a range of special educational needs. Attached to the school is a Special Class, an Assessment Unit, a Hearing Impaired Unit and informal facilities for pre-school children with hearing disabilities.

The twelve pupils in the Special Class are assessed as having 'moderate' learning difficulties (having been assessed by an educational psychologist as having an I.Q. score of between 50 and 75) and are on roll at Te Kanawa school. They do not, however, form a class in its own right, but rather a bureaucratic system is in force which, though complex, appears to serve the students well. Four of the twelve pupils are functionally mainstreamed in appropriate age classes at Te Kanawa. The eight remaining children are also functionally mainstreamed, but at one of five other schools.

The hearing impaired pupils are mainstreamed when it is appropriate for them as individuals. They have the support of the specialist teacher and two itinerant resource teachers of the deaf (who also support ten other schools) when they are in the classroom.

115

The Assessment Unit provides support for seven pupils between the ages of five and seven years. These pupils are assessed as having significant and specific teaching needs due to developmental delays. The pupils stay, on average, two years in the unit while assessment is conducted and appropriate provision and placement is decided. Although the pupils are socially mainstreamed (taking part in assemblies, etc.) they are, at times, functionally mainstreamed. We were able to observe two children from the Assessment Unit taking part in a mainstream classroom. All of the children were performing re-enactments of nursery rhymes. Veronica and Georgina from the unit were delighted with the activity and rather excited at being with so many other pupils. They had been encouraged to perform in their group's activity; falling down in 'Ring-a-Ring of Roses', miming the actions in 'Pat-a-Cake'. They were, however, so pleased with their endeavours that it was proving difficult for them to be receptive towards other children's efforts - they preferred to continue their performance! Unobtrusive help in the appropriate behaviour was therefore given. Georgina was being encouraged to sit down when appropriate by the teacher aide from the unit - who was also helping other pupils.

The pre-school children with hearing impairments are brought to school by their parents who remain with them and are helped to engage in language games and activities with their children by a retired teacher of the deaf. In addition the school supports Cerebral Palsy and Spina Bifida children.

Mainstreaming

It is school policy to mainstream pupils whenever possible and this was evident in classroom practice. In Room 10, which housed the eight year old pupils, there were five children who had been assessed as having special educational needs. Ricky, who is hearing impaired, is permanently and fully integrated into the class. He was working alongside his peers, although receiving some language support from a classroom assistant (Teacher's Aide). This help was not exclusive, however, as, in common with other aides at the school, she gave support to other children in the class. Ricky was talked to and signed to simultaneously by his peers and he responded easily and naturally. One child, who described herself as one of Ricky's friends, stated that she had:

learned sign language / from watching other people

She also mentioned that many of the pupils in the class had learned to sign - but she was one of the best!

Two other pupils, Murray and Ian, were from the Special Class and the remaining two, Pepe and Matthew, had English as a second language as a very recent acquisition and were receiving additional support. All these pupils worked and interacted naturally with their peers. They were all involved in the same work as that of their classmates - handwriting, spelling and story writing - although they were also working towards specific goals in their educational programme. Murray read to us a story that he had written. He was very positive about his class:

I like work and my class / I like the new desks

and also very proud of the fact that he had been able to help one of his friends. Our observations and comments from both staff and peer group indicated that all of the children with special educational needs in this class were accepted in terms of learners and friends.

In other classes, a similar wide range of students were working with their peers, but at the same time following an educational programme designed by the staff and catering for their needs. The variety of needs underlined the necessity of adequate resourcing to fulfil stated goals and expectations. The lack of resources was most evident for Chrissy, a twelve year old girl with spina bifida. The restricted human resourcing for her toileting needs (a nurse who came at lunchtime) meant that at times Chrissy had to sit in discomfort for long periods of time. Although this was a physical rather than educational need, the staff were concerned, not only about her discomfort, but about the accompanying effect on her morale and self-esteem - and thus the direct effect on her educational attainment.

The needs of the pupils are so diverse that a variety of strategies is implemented in order to accommodate each individual. Each child is viewed as an individual and therefore their progress is constantly assessed and future action determined particularly to their needs. The school has devised a system of educational programmes for every child who had been assessed as having special educational needs. These programmes are specifically organised and structured for the pupils to enhance their academic progress and to make their integration a positive and successful experience.

INDIVIDUAL EDUCATIONAL PROGRAMMES

All of the mainstreamed children receive support. This is not provided solely by the class teacher or even by a single support teacher, but by a whole team. The model in many ways is similar to that of the support team approach at the secondary girls' school (Chapter Nine). Members of the support team meet together, discuss and plan for each pupil with special educational needs, parents are consulted and goals are reviewed. Unlike the girls' school, however, there is one person who co-ordinates the responsibility for the support in the school and who acts as collator of information and convener of case conferences. She fulfils this role not only in Te Kanawa school, but in seven other schools. Glenys Walsh is this

Itinerant Resource Teacher who visits schools and offers help and support, where necessary, to the mainstreamed children and their teachers.

The balance of her work has shifted, away from previous emphasis on withdrawal and one-to-one tuition with students, to one of discussion and consultation with staff. Glenys does not see her role as merely feeding ideas to teachers, but enabling teachers to provide ideas and strategies of their own:

I see myself as a resource person / so as to give the people the ideas themselves/ to empower them to see that it's not that hard / after all / it's amazing / what kind of a / start off / people get going / and think up much clearer ideas than I can think up myself.

Neither Glenys nor the staff, however, view her role as one of responsibility for the mainstreamed children. This responsibility lies with the school and its staff. Glenys acts as a catalyst for the devising of a classroom programme to meet each child's individual educational needs - the Individual Educational Programme.

The Support Team for each child meets together on a regular basis, at least once a term, and holds a case conference on the pupil's attainment, progress and future goals. The membership of the Support Team varies from one student to another, although Glenys is the nucleus of each team.

The case conference members for Alison, (an eleven year old girl with learning difficulties compounded by a hearing impairment) for example, numbered eight. There were: Glenys Walsh, a psychologist, two team teachers, a speech therapist, the cooking teacher, a maths teacher and Alison's mother.

It is not unusual to have parents at case conferences; indeed their presence is seen as a necessity in order that continuity and corroboration of practice from school to home is ensured, particularly when new skills are being taught, for example in reading or in handwriting. Any decisions about parental involvement, made at the case conference, are written into the document:

We don't just say / no we do it on our own / but it's written down / so that's quite good for them / to feel that they are doing something / and that's okay / it makes the parent feel formally involved.... it's actually contributing to what everybody else is doing.

This involvement of parents alongside professionals is a point we have made earlier (Chapter Nine) and elsewhere (Wade & Moore, 1987) and its importance is recognised by the school. Parental support also allows learning to occur in a more naturalistic setting and also enables concepts to be generalised to non-school activities. One language objective for Alison is written for her mother:

Remember oral language objectives in cooking time. Karen (mother) to
encourage Alison to take part in simple cooking at home (language objectives
provided).

In addition, because of a regular commitment to case conferences, relevant information about the student is continually updated and perhaps more readily given. Certainly parents are pleased to be involved and take their roles as team members conscientiously. In addition, they are aware of and value the support, time and professional expertise given to their children.

One parent, whose child had a hearing impairment commented:

how invaluable it is that everyone's working the same way.

She also said that she found the whole system very supportive and, at her first case conference in particular, she thought:

look at all these people / working together / for my child.

Case conferences for other students involve a variety of staff, perhaps the principal, a teacher aide or physiotherapist, depending on the needs of the child. The case conferences are held out of school time, either before or after school. This enables everyone who is involved to be present without leaving classes (the pupils are able to stay in school if their parents are present). We have said that the conferences are held at least once a term, but, for some pupils, it is more frequent:

there's a child here / he's already had two this term / one in February / he had
one in March / he's got one in May

Each case conference for an Individual Education Programme follows a similar format for areas of discussion. Interestingly, social interaction, a prerequisite for successful integration, is the first area of discussion. Discussion centres upon inter-active response - does the pupil approach and respond to other pupils and is the pupil accepted by the class or by only a small group of children? Any difficulties are noted and strategies are put forward, and commented upon, by the group. Ricky, for example, the hearing impaired student referred to earlier in the chapter, was one pupil whose social interaction with his mainstream peers gave cause for concern. On his arrival at Te Kanawa, he had immediately been put into mainstream as his language development and understanding were very good for his level of hearing. Unfortunately he found the social interaction and level of language use in the classroom too stressful to cope with and his own level of expressive language proved to be inadequate for the situation. As a result of a case conference, which included his mother (who had witnessed the stress caused at home), it was decided to alter his integration pattern. He spent a greater amount of time in the hearing impaired unit consolidating his language work, although he did integrate with his peer group at times. As a result of a year spent partially in the unit, where progress was carefully monitored, his return to the mainstream in his third year has, in his mother's words:

enabled him to blossom.

Not only has he 'blossomed' in his ability to interact with his peers, but his school work has also benefited as a result of his confidence in social situations.

Other areas for discussion at case conferences are the child's language skills, both receptive and expressive. This obviously has close links with the social interaction and, as in Ricky's case, the two cannot be treated as separate issues.

The focus of discussion for reading, written language and maths is upon developing skills, progression, strengths and weaknesses. Final areas for discussion are support and resources, whether or not there is sufficient access and, if not, what needs to be done. If appropriate, further areas of the curriculum, physical skills, for example, are also considered.

As a result of discussion and agreement of strategies, Glenys compiles the Individual Educational Programme (I.E.P.). It is a professional document with attainments, goals and strategies carefully outlined, as the partial example given in Figure 2 indicates.

Individual Education Programme
Date: 15 February 1990

Student	Planning Group	
Name: Ann Green School: Te Kanawa Teacher/s: Mary Brown Class: M/B dob: 25-3-78 Age: 11.11	Glenys Walsh (Itinerant Resource Teacher) John Smith (Psychologist) Mary Brown (Teacher) Pam Green (Parent) Steven Green (Parent) Jo Jones (Teacher Aide)	
Attainments	**Short Term Goals**	**Strategies/Responsibilities**
Written Language: Ann writes 2/3 sentences with help and constant reminding, knows about the use of full-stops and capital letters in a sentence but still needs reminding.	1. Ann will stay on task when writing a story. 2. Ann will consistently write a sentence story.	All language work in class time. Jo to help Mary capitalise on Ann's interest in Nature and Science subjects for stories. Glenys to provide activities if required.

FIG. 2: Partial Example of an Individual Educational Programme (IEP)

This partial example gives the necessary information about the pupil and the members of the planning group. The rest of the I.E.P. is divided vertically into three sections: Attainments, Short Term Goals and Strategies and Responsibilities. It is then sub-divided horizontally into relevant areas; reading, maths, spelling etc. The example given is for Written Language. The attainments that the pupil has achieved are always considered first - Glenys makes the written attainments and goals:

as positive as possible.

This has a double-edged benefit - for the team and for the pupil. For the team it is:

> *gradually changing their perceptions / it's really nice to see people who are angry and frustrated and irritated with having children in their classroom that they didn't want / and gradually / you go in there and they're saying great..... they're sort of seeing the children in a different light..... and after a while they've forgotten they hadn't used to like them.*

and for the pupil it is the raising of self-esteem:

> *When I first saw that kid two and a half years ago he had a real low self-esteem / kicking things / skulking around / beaten dog attitude / he thought he was the boss of the school by the time he left.*

Once the attainments of the pupil have been stated and checked, the forward planning takes place. The checking of attainments is necessary, particularly when the child changes from one teacher to another:

> *we had one child / who went to another teacher / she said a full page story / not my idea / he sat down and wrote a whole lot of words on a page and she thought they meant something / and they didn't.*

Constant checking and evaluation ensures that appropriate goals are set that can be met in the stated time. The expectations for the pupil are realistic as they are set by a number of professionals who have both an objective interest in the pupil and a chance to observe progress. Glenys, for example, endeavours to build upon the pupil's experience:

> *I try and find things that the child will identify with*

We were able to see Ann, the child referred to in the IEP example, in her classroom and talk with her. She was taking part in a reading activity with members of her peer group and receiving help from Jo Jones, the teacher aide, who was also helping others in the group. Ann talked about her reading, which she enjoyed, and her story writing:

> *I like writing stories about animals.*

Glenys' stated strategy in the IEP of capitalising on Ann's interest in nature is paying dividends. When we met Ann at the end of March she was already achieving the first goal in written language - that of staying on task, and the second, of writing a 'sentence story'. Her ability to relate a story to us demonstrated her enthusiasm for the topic which resulted from Glenys' sensitive application of interest to goals. The stated goals are very specific and streamlined as Figure 3 shows.

Attainments	Short Term Goals	Strategies/Responsibilities
Maths Ann needs to continue to consolidate the ground she has covered with money, time and calendars. Is able to count one to one consistently, objects arranged randomly on a page (up to 20 objects). Knows how to order numbers.	1. Ann will find day, date and programme time in TV guide. 2. Ann will continue to choose and pay for one item when shopping with Steven. 3. Ann will consolidate her knowledge of the time of day events take place. 4. Ann will demonstrate addition facts to 10 using concrete materials and then write the equation. 5. Ann will check 2 digit addition to 20 on a calculator. 6. Ann will name o'clock and half past on a digital clock.	1. At home with Pam and Steven, reinforced with Glenys at Maths time. 2. With Steven at weekends. 3. In classroom, at home reinforce what time it is "It's playtime now Ann". "It's time for the taxt". 4. With Glenys at maths time and 5. extension activities for 6. classroom. 7. Clock times at home and at 8. maths time.

FIG. 3: Partial Individual Education Programme Showing Examples of Mathematics Goals

The team members of the planning group are concerned with Ann's academic performance and how this can be observed and evaluated. Inevitably, perhaps, this leads to the goals being stated in behaviouristic terms which might not be entirely appropriate for every teacher or educational programme. However, this was the methodology agreed by this particular team in this particular school. It may be, as we have said earlier in Chapter Nine, that the choice of methodology is less important than the shared philosophy. The philosophy here is that agreed goals are stated for the pupils, goals that everyone knows, understands and can work towards. The important factor is that both teachers and parents are aware of their responsibilities. The parents in this example know how they can help Ann consolidate her learning about Time and Money in a natural context, while Glenys will reinforce these activities in the classroom. Jo Jones, the Teacher Aide, also finds such teamwork very helpful and re-assuring:

> the IEP is very useful as the teacher and part-time teacher and myself / work towards the same goals / not like the usual withdrawal situation / especially if it's tangible and written well / parents also see the IEP so everyone works towards a common aim.

Not only is everyone able to work towards a common aim, but everyone is also aware of their particular responsibility in helping the pupil to achieve that aim: the strategies make it clear *what* is to be done and *who* is to do it. At following case conferences both the pupil's progress is considered and the team's efforts are evaluated in terms of pupil achievement.

Once goals and strategies have been agreed, Glenys writes the IEP and has copies ready for the planning group within a week. Each member of the planning group has a copy of the whole programme, so that they are not only aware of their responsibility in their own area, but also that they can cross-reference and know what other teachers are doing. Consolidation of learning between curriculum areas and reinforcement in all contexts is possible, as Mr King, the headteacher, explains:

> *everyone's aware of what the other care-giver is doing / so we can reinforce and support the other expectations of the other care-givers / so the speech therapist knows what the classroom teacher is doing / the classroom teacher's aware of the parents' obligations and responsibilities and what they're expected to do at home / the parents are aware of what is going on at school / so it's a total support and this way / we feel the child is going to benefit.*

This statement sums up the benefits for the pupil, as they are perceived by the school. Certainly, as Mr King states, it is better than previous practice when everyone was:

> *going their own way / and the poor kid / ....different interpretation at school / different interpretation at home / he goes to speech therapy / different interpretation.....*

The Warnock Report (DES, 1978) considered liaison between professionals to be crucial in the planning for pupils with special educational needs. Certainly at Te Kanawa the liaison plays an important part in providing team support that ensures individual progress. Glenys, the Itinerant Resource Teacher, acts as the link person between the pupils and the professionals and parents. She is also the co-ordinator between the care-givers and her role as facilitator enables the programme to proceed as effectively and efficiently as possible.

In addition she works alongside teachers and teacher aides, supporting both the classroom programme for the child and the class teacher. Through discussion and sharing and enabling of ideas the teachers acquire, develop and extend their skills. Once again we can observe in-service taking place through the school's own staff and resources with all staff developing as teachers and partners and ultimately benefitting, not just those pupils with special educational needs, but all children in the school. As Glenys maintains, the IEP is:

> *based on sound principles of ordinary teaching / ..... that's what mainstreaming is / access to the curriculum and good primary practice.*

and Mr King, the headteacher, states:

> *it's beneficial to the children / in the long run I'm convinced that what we're doing is correct / I'm convinced that ultimately its going to benefit the children.*

CONCLUSION

The Individual Education Programme for pupils with special educational needs in Te Kanawa school certainly has the approval of all members of the planning group. It has enabled greater liaison between staff, external professionals and parents. It has also encouraged a common working purpose for the pupil. Regular evaluation meetings with pre-determined dates also ensure that required support is given to every pupil even when that pupil may be one of thirty-five others. Discussion and shared responsibility also modify teachers' views of, and expectations for, their pupils. At the beginning of the team meeting the emphasis is on positive achievement - what the pupil can do - which is shared and celebrated by all members of the team. Goals and strategies are therefore planned from success towards success. Teachers' perceptions of pupils are changed, as we have seen earlier in this chapter, resulting in a greater acceptance of the pupils in their class and confidence in meeting their educational needs.

The danger of individual programmes, however, is that they can become so individualised that they serve to isolate the learner from the rest of the peer group. In Te Kanawa this danger has been taken on board and dealt with. Even though individually stated goals are very specific, they fit into the planned curriculum for the class. Ann, for example, did her story-writing when the rest of her class was story-writing , and her mathematical Time and Calendar work, when her peers were struggling with similar problems. Interaction with the peer group is viewed as an essential component of the programme by the team: the planned use and integration of IEP's into the curriculum ensures this potential for learning. Individualised does not mean segregated. Neither does it mean inflexible, particularly when evaluations are frequent.

The example of Ricky shows how his distress in communication was noted at school and at home. This wealth of corroborative observation, leading to shared discussion and provision of strategies, allowed Ricky, in a very short time, to be moved into the hearing impaired unit (which catered more specifically for his needs at that time) and moved again, when everyone agreed that it was appropriate for him to do so.

Such flexibility is not apparent in a legal document such as a Statement of Need. The bureaucracy involved cannot allow for speedy change. What a legal document can do, however, is to state the resource provision necessary which Local Education Authorities are under an obligation to provide. Mr King, although pleased with the success of the programme and the support that school staff provided, was concerned about the low level of support and resources that the school received. With extra support and resources the school could enhance the effect of their Individual Educational Programmes:

no allowances are made for our changing role / .... I'm asking for more money .... it's frustrating me in my work / I could be doing other things.

What our case study suggests is that individualised help for special educational needs in integrated contexts requires both legislated and professional support. Adequate resources must be made available as of right, if individuals with diverse special educational needs are to receive appropriate provision. Resources on their own, however, as we have shown elsewhere (Chapter Four, for example), cannot supply the diagnosis, provision, interaction and evaluation necessary for educational progress. Teamwork is crucial for the success of individual students in mainstream classes. Reflection and collaboration are important elements for the professionals who help plan for progress as they are in the process of students' learning.

Chapter Eleven

Continuity of Care: mainstreaming whole persons through their school years

*what I saw as someone coming into this type of system was / students who
had been in special school with a physical disability and a lot of attention and
the focus had been towards / physical disability so there had been time out of
course lots of time for hospitalisation etc / it's like the old system looking at
the disease in the body in the bed / and / somehow or other there seemed to be
lost this whole /looking at the students as a whole / as a whole being / a whole
person /*

(Sheila, occupational therapist)

INTRODUCTION

It is often argued that, despite other disadvantages that they may have,
special schools provide a continuity of care that cannot be matched by
mainstream provision. Many special schools have been designed to take
students throughout the age range, whilst two or three changes of school
are normal for regular pupils. To provide for continuity, therefore, requires
not just positive attitudes, full curriculum, classroom support and adequate
resources - factors already discussed - but sensitive liaison work and
efficient school management. We were fortunate to find two Australian
schools which had recently embarked together to provide for children with
special educational needs throughout their schooling. Excellent liaison work

and caring management characterised the approach of both schools, even though the scheme had been in operation for only two years.

Units for students with severe and profound physical disabilities were established at Birch Grove primary school and at Park Green secondary school in a suburban area with a rising school age population. Birch Grove received some specially designed units to add to its existing buildings. Park Green was in process of being built when the decision was taken and 'where necessary' the building was adapted to its new function. Both schools have therapy rooms and share the services of physiotherapists and occupational therapist who are provided for the schools by the Health Department. The Regional Guidance section retains responsibility for placing students in the two units. The intention is that disabled students will be able to enter Birch Grove at pre-school or any convenient time up to year 6 and then change to Park Green with their peer group in the normal way. A good deal has been achieved in a short time, so that admission is already being extended to students who have sensory and intellectual impairments in addition to their physical disabilities. This early success depends very much on the positive attitude of school staff and enlightened leadership. For example, both schools had clearly worked out policies for integrating students into the mainstream and these were responsible, in our view, for the remarkable early achievements. Birch Grove primary school had published its aims for integration and had set out explicitly the roles and responsibilities of management, unit teachers, mainstream teachers and health professionals, together with practical guides for implementation. Part of the management system for monitoring progress is a review by a regional committee and clear proformas have been constructed to obtain reports from, amongst others, physiotherapist, occupational therapist, other support services, counsellor and teachers. Parents' views are a vital part of the information required for review of a pupil's progress and in Figure 4 (p. 129) we give, as an example, the parents' questionnaire.

Park Green, similarly, has a well-organised approach with a central school policy statement, and various support documents which offer detailed guidelines for teachers aides and therapists, for example. The central policy makes explicit that the school's ultimate aim for integration is full-time mainstreaming of each student and that self-esteem and social acceptance are prerequisites. Five components of success are clarified, thus:

(a) RECOGNITION - the handicapped person must be accorded his/her appropriate status
(b) ACCEPTANCE - the handicapped person must be accepted by others for what he/she is, without fear, anxiety or resentment
(c) RELATIONSHIPS - the handicapped person must have the opportunity for normal, satisfying relationships
(d) EXPERIENCE - the handicapped person must be given the opportunity to have normal experiences, within the limitations of handicap
(e) INDEPENDENCE - the handicapped person must be encouraged to

develop the skills necessary for lifetime independence, within the limitations of handicap.

A reference folder 'Physical Disability: A Reference for Schools' is made available to all staff and individual departments offer guidelines that reinforce and extend the central policy. The following example from the English/History departments indicates how assessment may be modified for individuals, while maintaining for them access to a full curriculum:

Mixed ability classrooms allow for greater flexibility with assessment practices and negotiation of completed tasks. It may be appropriate to designate set tasks in teaching units as compulsory and other tasks as optional - thus allowing all students to complete as best they can tasks appropriate to their ability (intellectual and physical).

Where a test is to be carried out under examination conditions in class, arrangements should be made for a teacher's aide to act as scribe if the student has writing difficulties. Alternatively, the student might be given the option of using a cassette player and completing answers to the test questions orally.

English writing projects (Years 7-10) may be completed by using a word processor, if handwriting is too difficult.

The examples offered so far illustrate the commitment of management to co-ordinate efforts in both schools and to direct these towards the ultimate goals of integration into mainstream classes and continuity of care of students with special educational needs.

Julian Thomas, principal of Park Green, believes that staff skills and resilience of students with disabilities have contributed as much as management policies to integration success so far:

it's recognised as being very successful.... it's good management / but other factors have come into it / the staff are experienced / and prepared to have a try / the other reason is that / the people who are involved / they haven't had the opportunity / to / erm be in a normal situation / and I think they appreciate that chance / if things do go wrong / their personalities are able to say / so what / it's gone wrong / all my life's been wrong / and things are starting to get right now so why worry about little problems

It is to these problems and constraints that we now turn, remembering that the integration project is still in its infancy and that mainstream accommodation was not purpose built. Among the 'little problems' for Julian is the fact that children in wheelchairs cannot manage to drink from

SPECIAL PLACEMENT REVIEW
PARENTS' QUESTIONNAIRE

A MESSAGE TO PARENTS

Twice each year, a REGIONAL REVIEW COMMITTEE examines the placement of all children in Special Education.

For each review, PUPIL PROFILES are updated. These enable the committee to ensure the most appropriate placement for each child.

The Profile consists of reports from:
- the teacher
- the therapists
- the parents
- the counsellor

You are invited to fill out this questionnaire and to add any suggestions or remarks that you feel important to your child's life at school.

PUPIL DETAILS
NAME:

DATE OF THIS REVIEW
......./......./........

PLEASE RETURN THIS REPORT BY
......./......./........

ABOUT YOUR CHILD'S PRESENT PLACEMENT
PLEASE ANSWER THE THREE SETS OF QUESTIONS IN THE FOLLOWING WAY:

A. The first set FROM THE CHILD'S point of view **B.** The second set from YOUR point of view.
and **C.** How you feel about the CHILD'S long term future.

(A) I THINK MY CHILD

enjoys being in the SUPPORT CLASSROOM.... ☐ RARELY ☐ USUALLY ☐ CONSISTENTLY
feels part of the WHOLE SCHOOL...................... ☐ RARELY ☐ USUALLY ☐ CONSISTENTLY
feels safe and happy in the PLAYGROUND...... ☐ RARELY ☐ USUALLY ☐ CONSISTENTLY
works as well as possible for the TEACHER ☐ RARELY ☐ USUALLY ☐ CONSISTENTLY
feels happy with the daily TRAVELLING....... ☐ RARELY ☐ USUALLY ☐ CONSISTENTLY
likes going to THERAPY SERVICES................. ☐ RARELY ☐ USUALLY ☐ CONSISTENTLY
enjoys INTEGRATION with other classes...... ☐ RARELY ☐ USUALLY ☐ CONSISTENTLY

COMMENTS: Please comment about anything you think your CHILD is concerned about.

B. THE WAY YOU FEEL ABOUT

The work in the CLASS................................... ☐ NOT SURE ☐ SATISFACTORY ☐ GOOD
The child's welfare in the CLASSROOM ....☐ NOT SURE ☐ SATISFACTORY ☐ GOOD
The child's welfare in the PLAYGROUND......... ☐ NOT SURE ☐ SATISFACTORY ☐ GOOD
Transport – morning and afternoon................... ☐ NOT SURE ☐ SATISFACTORY ☐ GOOD
Communication with the school......................... ☐ NOT SURE ☐ SATISFACTORY ☐ GOOD
Therapy Services at the school.......................... ☐ NOT SURE ☐ SATISFACTORY ☐ GOOD
Integration into other classes...........................☐ NOT SURE ☐ SATISFACTORY ☐ GOOD
Support from Crippled Childrens' Society...... ☐ NOT SURE ☐ SATISFACTORY ☐ GOOD

COMMENTS: Please comment about anything that YOU are concerned about.

C. THE FUTURE

FOR PRIMARY EDUCATION I feel my child would benefit most by:
☐ attending a SPECIAL SCHOOL for the disabled
☐ continuing in the SUPPORT UNIT attached to this school
☐ integrating FULLY into a mainstream class at his/her neighbourhood school

FOR SECONDARY EDUCATION, I feel my child would benefit most by:
☐ attending a SUPPORT UNIT attached to a High school
☐ integrating FULLY into a mainstream class at his/her neighbourhood high school

AFTER LEAVING SCHOOL COMPLETELY : I feel my child will :
LIVE PERMANENTLY :☐ With a family member ☐ In Group/ Community housing ☐ In a home of his/her own
GET EMPLOYMENT: ☐ In the general workplace ☐ In a sheltered workshop   ☐ None

Signed:..Date:......./......./......

FIG. 4. Birch Grove Parents' Pro-forma for Review of Special Placement.

school water-fountains. Ingenuity and adaptation provides a system of accessible plastic containers, but in subtle irritating ways like this children with disabilities may have their differences reinforced. There are more serious difficulties. Julian again:

> *some of the problems we have had are staffing problems / getting adequate*
> *staffing / and problems with adequate funding / problems within the design /*
> *of the furniture*

It is to these matters that we now turn in a brief analysis of how policies are working in each school.

BIRCH GROVE

Access

Birch Grove is a suburban, Australian primary school in an area with new housing all around. The 'temporary' surge of school population is accommodated in temporary classrooms additional to the main buildings and there are 700 pupils on roll. Birch Grove was chosen to accommodate the special units for disabled children because of its level site and relative ease of accessibility of all permanent buildings. However, wheelchair access to the hall can still involve riding all round the school to avoid steps and a special ramp has had to be built to the library. Temporary classrooms remain inaccessible; this creates problems for the way children can integrate and for which particular children can be admitted to the main school, as the deputy-principal, Rowan Lavery explains:

> *all of these classes / are inaccessible to wheelchair children and some of the*
> *children with walking frames and other disabilities like that / which is a*
> *shame because there is one girl we would love to get into a class / the teacher*
> *is dead keen to have her / we looked at buying a ramp / and with the gradient*
> *that was needed the ramp would have to be twenty-five feet long we couldn't*
> *put it in because it would run into the room on the other side*

Physical problems such as these militate against integrating some children for whom mainstream experience is desirable. Mr Lavery explains the limitation:

> *we try where we can to accommodate the / the children from the unit but we*
> *can't go too far out of our way to do it*

Staffing

The second set of problems concerns staffing. The school had no previous experience of catering for children with disabilities and therefore had to influence attitudes and habits of both existing staff and students who had hitherto been used only to special schools. To begin with, children with severe physical disabilities were admitted; later, children with multi-faceted disabilities began to be placed by the Regional Guidance authority who have responsibility for admissions to the unit.

Progress is being made in shifting the attitudes of mainstream teachers who are now more willing to help with the unit. The main problem is perceived as finding (or educating through in-service training) 'qualified teachers in special education' for the unit itself:

> *I think it will be more successful when we get / um / better levels of training amongst the staff working here / not to take away from what we have because they are working very hard*

Expertise is crucial, though it is perceived by Rowan as necessary within the unit, and confined to it, rather than integrated through the school and affecting mainstream teachers.

Resources
Resources are a third set of problems. We have frequently encountered the suspicion that mainstreaming was a policy set up by an Education Department to save the expensive resources spent on special schools. Clearly lack of communication between administrators and professionals can be inadequate in this respect, and elsewhere in our case studies (Chapter Twelve, for example) we show that equivalent resources were not spent on special school children transferred to local schools. At Birch Grove, early promises of funding had not been kept and some 'maindumping' was suspected. Rowan Lavery again:

> *when they set it up / there were promises about a lot more ongoing support than actually has eventuated / initially a lot of money was given to set up things and to get things working for us / but it hasn't sort of really flowed through right to this stage.*

Apart from the normal requirement of continuous funding that all schools have, special units frequently require ongoing funds, because it is impossible to forecast in advance exactly what resources are required until the specific needs of individuals are assessed. Disabilities and learning difficulties are so various that each new admission to the unit may make different demands on resourcing.

Timetabling
The unit has its own therapy room where occupational and physiotherapy can take place. A physiotherapist is based at Birch Grove, but, of course, any withdrawal of children from timetabled lessons, necessary though it might be, adds another problem for successful integration. Mr Lavery explains how Jean, the physiotherapist works very closely with the teachers trying to co-ordinate her timetable, but experiences difficulty in ensuring:

> *the right amount of time with each child / she talks to them about / their physical handicaps and problems so she can work on that directly and then*

she's got to slot into the teachers' timetable / the general school timetable / as well as the integration timetable / it's very much a shuffling thingy / and that's where we / leads to a lot of inconsistency with their programme.

Thus there are a range of problems, physical, personal, financial and administrative which make it difficult to achieve the ideal for each child. Nonetheless Mr Lavery argues that the flexibility to place each child in either unit or mainstream for certain parts of their curriculum is something no special school can offer. Decisions to integrate can be modified:

it's always a matter of give and take / we'll take a child into a programme / that's not to say they're there for a term or for the year / they're there as long as we feel / that there's a benefit from it / if we find a greater benefit in another area / we'll do that / if we find it's not working we'll change it.

Relationships

Difficulties in providing full integration, as we have seen earlier, can lead to difficulties in relationships. For example, Jenny, almost 11 and in Year 6, has been at Birch Grove unit for almost three years, having transferred from a special school where:

there was no kids like normal kids / they was just / disabled kids and / um / all my friends are there and / in this school I haven't got much / cos some of the normal kids are teasing and all that.

For Jenny, differences between 'disabled' and 'normal' are still reinforced, as they probably are for some mainstream children who, because of infrequent contact, still perceive the unit as segregated and apart. Jenny, after three years, still talks about the school outside the unit as 'the other part'. Confined to her wheelchair and requiring help with feeding at lunchtime, Jenny relies on one of her friends from the unit for help. Asked if there was any way she would change the school, she replied:

strict rules / be nice to the disabled kids / you should hear them / the way they tell my friends names / I just call them back the same.

It is a pity that Jenny will probably leave Birch Grove without much improvement in peer group relationships during the time she has been there. More than occasional contact is necessary for better understanding to develop.

In her case also there seems little continuity between her home and school experience. She is withdrawn from lessons three times a week for physiotherapy (she has her legs moved, hands straightened and back stretched) but she opts out of exercising at home.

I'm supposed to but I don't .... my Dad wants me to do it / but I don't.

Jenny's life seems to be governed by separations: the special provisions given her in the unit and the therapy room do not flow into the rest of her experience. Possibly individual personality factors influence her experience, but some of the difficulties the school faces, notably difficulties of access, reinforce these features rather than influencing them positively.

An Aide's Perspective

Whereas the deputy principal has commented on the difficulties of finding teachers qualified in catering for special needs, Kate, a classroom aide, who has also had the experience of working in a special school, highlights what she calls a certain lack of provision for children in the unit:

> we need a nurse... it's a lot of responsibility to put on aides / the nursing care
> that these children need sometimes / and it's hard to make / teachers and
> headmasters / sometimes senior staff understand that these kids have got that
> extra need.

Spina Bifida children who are particularly susceptible to pressure areas, she says, should have access to nursing care and presently aides do not have these kinds of skills. Skin care is important for children with Spina Bifida. In the Australian climate vigilance is required until these children have learned to cope with their insensitivity to heat, for example. Kate illustrates the problems to avoid and the care required if there are accidents:

> if there was a plastic chair out in the sun and they went and sat on it / they
> could end up with a blister / in five minutes / and then that would take weeks
> and weeks of care / to get rid of and could turn ulcerated.... I've seen a girl
> get a burn / from sitting on a wooden platform / through her uniform and her
> pants / and she ended up having a skin graft / the burning was so bad.

So at more than one level, if Kate is right, there are limitations in staffing provision as well as in the problems previously mentioned. Kate affirms the limitations of a building which makes integration difficult:

> I think if schools could be built / and units could be built into the main part
> of the building it would be / it would be so much better / and normal.

Kate considers there are possibilities for more integration, even given the problems analysed here. The main difficulty, for her, is the ad hoc nature of an organisation where even making a beginning can be vetoed:

> it's really left to the teacher to / be / cajoled / sort of another teacher will you
> take this child into your class / and if that other teacher says no well they
> don't have to / which is rather a shame.

Divisions between mainstream staff and unit teachers reinforce the separateness of unit provision. Even within the unit there may be lack of understanding of the role of aides who may have to spend about a third of their time helping disabled children with toileting:

> it's hard on the teacher / to understand how / you've got to take so much time
> out / and when you're trying to train / a small child to insert a catheter ... I

*mean ... if they can't be taught at home you've got to teach them at school /
for their own benefit.*

Here Kate gets to the heart of what is a complex range of needs for many
children. Frequently their educational progress may depend upon their
social acceptability as far as others are concerned. Certainly independence
and self pride which comes through toileting advances are essential to
make learning smoother - at the very least more time is available to both
children and aides when toileting is mastered. Some of these
misunderstandings will probably be easily resolved through further
discussion of aims and objectives and by specific inservice work and more
contact between mainstream staff and disabled children. Kate points out
that many staff still need to learn:

that those children don't know that they smell

Within the unit Kate had admiration for the teachers who do have day to
day contact:

*I admire the teachers / I don't know how they teach / I don't know how they
finally get through and teach at all because / they just get so many
interruptions / you know because you've got physio / occupational therapy /
toileting / then somebody's got to be fed or somebody's got to take a pill or
something / and all in the middle of this they're trying to teach.*

Discontinuity, in this way, is built into the business of educating children
with special educational needs and particular skills and competences are
required to adapt constantly to individual needs, changing circumstances
and emergencies. For this reason conflicts, misunderstandings and other
problems need to be tackled, otherwise the maximum potential of both
mainstream and unit may never be realised.

Teachers' Views
Elizabeth, a young teacher with previous mainstream experience, newly
appointed to the unit, highlights the problem of learning on the job,
especially the need to work with others:

*I've got a full-time aide / who / I don't know how to use / because I've never /
had an aide in my room before /.... and then also you go on to plan and use
the aide / and you can't rely on the aide because / she goes off / for toileting /
all the time.*

Elizabeth considers her training did not prepare her for a style of teaching
where:

all the children are doing the same work / but at different levels.

Nonetheless her experience at Birch Grove had influenced her positively:

*I just adore this job / and / I've learned to be organised / I'm learning / to be
organised / if I ever went back into a mainstream classroom / it would / I*

*would be super-organised... I've learnt to / not to / judge people / so severely /
I've learnt especially with these kids that / erm / there's so many things that
happen outside school that you've got to consider and it's the same in
mainstream.*

Margaret, the other unit teacher, who has worked at Birch Grove since
children with disabilities were first admitted and is therefore
well-experienced, echoes Elizabeth's commitment, but also her need for
reassurance. Without specific training in special educational needs,
Margaret has developed her expertise from experience, but in isolation,
since no educational adviser has been to visit her in Birch Grove. She
acutely feels the need for:

*just someone to say / am I doing my job right or not / can you help me / or /
you know / nobody's been anywhere near us / and I'm sure that those people
exist.*

We now turn to consider the context of integration at Park Green and
whether similar problems impede full implementation of its integration
policy.

PARK GREEN

Access
Since it is a newly built school and presently has only built up to 50% of its
final roll, Park Green does not have obvious access problems. Although the
special unit was only planned after building work was begun, certain
modifications were made. According to Robin, a Science teacher, they
created ramps and

a door opening wide enough for wheelchairs to have easy access.

However, in a secondary school, students need access to a range of
specialist subject provision such as Science labs and computer rooms, not
merely to the main buildings:

*when it came to the installation of standard fittings in the school / they didn't
take the skills into account / so all the benches are normal height / if we
introduce other benches we don't have enough space for storage / so those
extra details haven't been addressed at all / in the computer area / putting the
computer room upstairs for security is a good thing / but if disabled students
are going to have access to it / we should have had an outside elevator
perhaps// some extra technique to get the students up there / we're fortunate
that we've got the network / that we can run a cable virtually anywhere in
the school / and the students can plug them and have access to the computer
but they / lose a little bit because they don't have that classroom atmosphere
and activity / when a student in a normal classroom situation in a computing
class does something unusual and creative / because there's only two in their*

class / they don't see those things / so they're still missing out a little bit / more than I'd like.

Lack of specific access can therefore create problems of use, as in the case of Science, or problems for interaction in the case of computing. Teacher ingenuity can help resolve the difficulty of unintended segregation, as Robin explains:

actually what I've done is / over the year / I've often sent the able-bodied students down / just to participate in the disabled students' lesson / and be down there with the computer and do the things that we've done upstairs / it's working well / their results are as good as any other student in the school/ the full range / it's terrific.

A different problem of access is that within the classroom itself and Robin has not yet found a satisfactory solution:

I have 30 students / Jenny is in a wheelchair but she lifts out into a normal chair so her wheelchair is in the aisle / that upsets your access to other students in the room / and two others in wheelchairs under tables / and the extra space that they occupy with the wheelchair / wasn't thought about / it's a good designer's problem / it's something that / a professional design team could do / could enjoy doing / because there's a lot of minor problems that need to be solved.

Staffing

Since Park Green is a newly developing school, it has been possible to select able staff committed to making integration work. Further, in a secondary school, staff teaching in their familiar specialist areas usually bring with them confidence and expertise in modifying learning objectives to individuals' needs. Staff expectations of what children could achieve were high at Park Green, since all the teachers were experienced in mainstream mixed ability teaching. When children with severe disabilities produced good work and demonstrated real achievement, this produced pride and considerable satisfaction as in the example given by the teacher of Technical Drawing:

the development of those kids since I saw them at the start of last year / is phenomenal / Mario was the best technical drawer in Year 7 last year / that's using T-square and set- square drawing board / and admittedly it took him forty minutes to do a simple cube / but his work was beautiful / I've still got them hanging up on the wall / and all the new students they all know Mario / know his abilities that / he's a paraplegic / they say did he Mario really draw this / yes he did / because using a T-square and a set-square and a drawing board for anybody the first time is very difficult / he mastered it in very short time and er / his three dimensional knowledge and his comprehension is excellent.

In earlier chapters we have referred frequently to the value of high expectations for students with special educational needs. Such expectations and the achievements which ensue are valuable also for staff and regular students.

Resources

A new school is usually well equipped and Park Green has excellent facilities including computers and well equipped laboratories. A main teaching resource is the availability of space. Some loss of full integration possibilities occurs in craft work, because if a ramp were built to allow disabled students to use specialist machinery, then the space for other students would be restricted; nor would there be space to store the ramp when not in use. Science poses similar problems. Well-equipped laboratories have taps and chemistry-type benches in three corners while in the centre there is a carpeted area with benches for normal seating. Presently all disabled students use the laboratory, but so many wheelchairs make for congestion as the teacher explains:

> *every lesson / I've got to shift this gear in and out of the room and where do I store it when I'm not using it that's our problem here.*

Timetabling

The most serious problems for timetabling stem from the resources issue, for, when the school grows to full complement, it may not be possible to integrate all disabled students in one class. So far there is plenty of space, but, since the special unit was an afterthought, lack of access might well affect timetabling. Bob Taylor, head of the English and History department takes this view, especially with the computer room being on the first floor:

> *in future it's going to cause massive problems when the school gets up to Year 12 / just in terms of timetabling so if we don't get a ramp built / or some form of lift / I think there's going to be less integration than perhaps would otherwise occur.*

One example of timetabling segregation which may easily be overlooked by a school is provided by Mark, aged 15, whose general view, gratifyingly, is:

> *I just feel the same as / you know / everyone else.*

However Mark adds:

> *the only time I feel different is when / like of a Wednesday afternoon ... all the other kids / do sport / they all go to various venues like to other schools and play cricket or / another team'll go to another school and play basketball and stuff like that / where we have to stay back and do lessons ... even if we could just go and watch / I just feel / why should we have to stay back and do work/ if they're out / you know / having fun and stuff.*

He has a point!

Relationships

Mark, whose experience before Park Green was in hospital or special school, reflects about that experience:

> *I didn't like it very much / because they / you know they gave you easy work because they thought cos you were in a wheelchair that / you know / you can only do easy work and stuff like that / but when I've been coming here I've been you know trying harder and / my work's been better.*

A change of relationships and expectations has brought him success. In fact, he explains that it is often ignorance or the absence of a relationship which produces tension and fear. He looks back over his year's attendance at Park Green:

> *when my parents actually come out here and looked at the school / I was going to come out with them but at the time I was in hospital so I didn't really know / you know / what it was going to be like and / when I was first a couple of weeks before I had to come to this school I was you know / sort of scaring / you know will people like me ... but after a couple of weeks I found / you know / it was really good.*

Mark now wants to be included in everything his peer group does and, as Bob Taylor explains:

> *doesn't like being left out / we had a medieval games day / erm / he wanted to charge the target with a broom handle and pretend it was a lance like the other kids / when we had a fight with staves he wanted to have a go at that / tries to the best of his ability to take part in / any activity that we do as normal as the other people in the class.*

A Therapist's Perspective

Sheila is an occupational therapist whose responsibility it is, in both schools, to assess pupils with special educational needs in those areas of the curriculum where they experience difficulty and to devise strategies and programmes by which they achieve as much as possible with due regard to their particular disabilities. Her previous experience had been in special schools where, she says, all the focus was negatively upon deficit and disfunction, so that the wholeness of a student's attributes and personality was not considered:

> *what I saw as someone coming into this type of system was / students who had been / in special school with a physical disability and a lot of attention and the focus had been towards / physical disability / so there had been time out of course lots of time for hospitalisation etc / it's like the old system looking at the disease in the body in the bed / and / somehow or other there seemed to be lost this whole / looking at the students as a whole / as a whole*

being / a whole person / and so there have been deficits / in their education but I think even the focus of/ therapy had been towards the physical disfunction.

Firstly, Sheila argues that most fears of integration had their roots in the old system and were misplaced:

the fears have been the parents' fears and the staff / in the old system / their fears about what would happen to these children / ... the kids loved it / they came to the schools and they love it.

The change of strategy towards integration at Birch Grove and Park Green schools has dispelled those fears. Integration allows more to be done for students in more dimensions, including some that were ignored by their special schools:

there are basic things like decision making skills / conceptual thinking / um all of those areas that are lacking / self confidence self esteem / body image / sexuality / all of those didn't seem to be addressed / and I think it's a fantastic system / it's in its infancy.

Even in the infancy of integration policies, disabled students have a chance to take more responsibility for their learning and for themselves. Sheila generalises about her early therapy sessions:

we went through / a lot of the things that had bugged them / in the past and um / all these things that came up about hospitals and things that they hated/ and other settings and things that they didn't like / and they were very aware / what is so strong / I think is the powerlessness / that they felt.

Her informed view of special schools leads into her concern that forms of segregation should not be allowed to re-establish themselves in regular schools:

one fear that I have is with the development of these types of settings / and the employment of staff who have come from the special schools / that we're not setting up a semblance of the same / just in a different setting.

Attitudes are notoriously difficult to change, as we said in Chapter Three, and Sheila's view is that, unless we are careful, some special school staff may reintroduce outmoded, unhelpful practice:

they bring old attitudes / old ways of doing things / old relationships / long term relationships with youngsters that they've known from very young / and that's not always to the benefit of the child.

Although she is clear about what practice and attitudes should *not* be encouraged, Sheila does not argue only for integration that is at the extreme of our continuum (Chapter One). Instead she takes a pragmatic view that integration depends upon available resources and individual needs. She argues for appropriate flexibility of provision:

there has to be gradations of care / I think one just can't say that everyone moves across / um otherwise some / students that I know that are really

*physically impaired and really will require a one to one / we're wondering
whether we're going to disadvantage them or disadvantage the others in the
group with them / if the staff isn't supplied / if they need a one to one / then /
there's insufficient staff at the moment.*

A Teacher's View

It seemed appropriate, since Park Green special students were all physically
disabled, whether or not they were also intellectually or sensorily impaired,
to seek the views of a teacher who has potentially the most problems - a
teacher of Physical Education. In fact, Jan shows how she includes disabled
students in her regular programme, where she can, and makes appropriate
modifications, where she cannot:

*if I'm doing / major ball skills with the regular students / then the disabled
students follow a / modified programme of major ball skills / they can do
dance / so whenever there's a dance unit on / they can be involved in dance /
and gymnastics is probably / a little more difficult but / we do a lot of
balancing and flexibility exercises when gymnastics is on for the rest of the
school.*

Inclusion with modification is appropriate for severely disabled students as
earlier chapters (for example Four and Nine) have illustrated. Jan
encourages participation in all school activities such as swimming and
athletics; she encourages competition at carnivals which have:

events tailored to suit

and allows students to make their own choices:

*when they do discus they throw a quoit rather than a discus / shotput / they
throw a tennis ball in place of a / shotput and javelin / they have the option to
use a beanbag / some of them prefer to throw the full equipment.*

We have said that successful mainstreaming depends upon a teacher's skill
in choosing strategies and modifying programmes to suit the educational
needs of individual learners. Jan explains how she learned to do this
successfully:

*because I had to restructure everything / I started from their level and worked
up rather than looked at / well this is what I'd be teaching the regular kids
now how can I modify that / so I learnt to work in reverse / here's a lesson
that would suit / the intellectually disabled kids / now what can I do to
extend it for the others / which was a far better way of teaching / than trying
to water something down.*

Jan has found her own way to successful teaching through placing students
with disabilities at the centre of her concern: it is a route that others can
follow.

CONCLUSION

We began this chapter with an exploration of how far effective management was responsible for early success in the attempts to provide continuity of care at Birch Grove and Park Green schools; and we put forward the view that staff abilities and commitment and students' persistence and motivation contributed to this success. Then we assessed progress at each school through a consideration of

- access
- staffing
- resources
- timetabling, and
- relationships

Additionally, for each school, we explored the views of
- teachers
- aides or therapists

Through this analysis we gained a more precise view of achievements and we confirmed that considerable progress had indeed been made by individuals and groups of students who might well have languished in special schools if the expressed views of experienced teachers, professionals and students have validity. We gained insight into particular problems which, in some cases, inhibited or blocked the way towards full integration of students with special educational needs. We suggest that information from the issues we have explored and the views of participants (including students themselves) form an ongoing resource which enables management to inform and develop constructive policies for achieving the ultimate aim of integrating all support class students into mainstream.

In Part 3 we offer some practical, constructive suggestions.

Chapter Twelve

A Parent's Perspective

I feel just his pure happiness / the fact that his friends here go to Boy's Brigade / he is part of the community / he is known around the school and in the community / that has to be / on its own almost enough / to warrant being here.

(Angela, mother of Steven, age 10)

PARENTS' RIGHTS

Parents who have children with special educational needs sometimes still feel excluded from their children's education without just cause. Until comparatively recently, however, there were obstacles which were even embedded in legislation. The 1944 Education Act in Britain, for example, allowed parents very few rights - not even the right of being consulted about their child's progress. Basically the Local Education Authority made decisions and allocations to special schools without the need to consult parents who could only appeal to the Minister of Education. Many parents knew nothing of even this right; others chose not to exercise it. In this way the legal system underpinned the separation already existing in society and sometimes exacerbated the isolation, exclusion and resentment felt by many families. Further, since the special educational needs of only about one in fifty children were considered by the Act, large numbers of pupils with less severe, intermittent or temporary needs were ignored or received scant attention.

Nowadays, by contrast, under U.S. Public Law 94:142, American parents are involved in the process of diagnosis and identification (Comprehensive Individual Assessments) and in decision making. The child's parent attends the meeting where the Individualised Education Plan is developed. Significantly provision is made for the child to attend the meeting when this is thought to be appropriate.

In Britain, too, the 1981 Education Act specified parents' rights. For example, parents who require a formal assessment of their child's educational needs (which may or may not lead to a formal written statement of those needs) can insist on this, even if the Authority has previously declined. Parents can appeal to the Secretary of State, if the Authority does not take action. If the Local Authority takes the initiative in assessment and statementing, then parents must be carefully informed at all stages within a specified time schedule. Parents may now also make representations, appeals and obtain relevant information and advice from 'named persons'. A further important change is the institution of a local appeals committee which can refer back contested decisions for further consideration before parents appeal to the Secretary of State.

The role of the 'named person', who would explain to and help parents in the processes leading to provision for their children, has been clarified in the report on special needs provision published by the Inner London Education Authority (ILEA, 1985). That report suggested:

(a) the appointment of a panel of named persons with expertise from a range of ethnic and social backgrounds;
(b) these advisers should be trained but would then operate on a voluntary basis in the way British magistrates do;
(c) their role would be to advise, befriend and counsel families in their negotiations with Local Education Authorities;
(d) they should have no power of decision-making.

Reviewing the appeals procedure, Philippa Russell (1988) makes the interesting point that bureaucracy is likely to make the role of the 'named person' similar to that of the American 'parent counsellor' (Public Law 94:142), noting that the American system already operates successfully. An appeals procedure is likely to be lengthy and costly. Russell convincingly argues:

LEA's, like parents, would prefer not to enter into proceedings which must at times be contentious and inevitably expensive. (p.14)

If this proves to be the case, parents will be guaranteed the right to express their views plus help and support in the process of decision-making.

Parents have always played a crucial role in the development of children with disabilities, but it has not always been a central one in terms of decision making. Recently the position has changed drastically. In many countries parents are now legally entitled to consultation and to a part in decision making about provision for their children. This shift has placed more responsibility on the parents of children with disabilities, but has also given them the ability to take initiatives and to feel a part of the process of helping their children to educational success. We illustrate these points from the point of view of Angela who has taken the decision to move her son from special school to their local primary school in New Zealand; the chapter touches also on the importance of providing adequate resources to underpin parental choice.

STEVEN (age 10)

Steven, with spina bifida, is severely handicapped in that he is paraplegic from just above the waist. There are neurological problems with his left arm, which, while it looks undamaged, is very weak indeed. His right arm is similarly affected, leaving him only two working fingers with which he can hold a pencil, but in a very clumsy way. He is successfully integrated into a welcoming primary school, but his disability makes it difficult to keep up with the written work required. His slow eye movement makes reading laborious and painstaking.

PROGRESS IN THE MAINSTREAM

Angela, his mother, describes the effect that his disabilities have on his progress and attainment in the kinds of topics required in the primary school curriculum:

> if they are given a topic for example / the pond / to work on and they have to do an appointed number of studies / they have to write on say two creatures and draw pictures of them / Steven's um / final result would be a quarter of what any other child could do mainly because he can't handle the pencil fast enough / he hasn't the physical ability / at home even / to go to a shelf / take a book off / take it back to his desk / organise a book next to it / look from one to the other / he needs help all along the way you have to go with him / to the encyclopaedia find it / carry it because he couldn't possibly lift anything that heavy / even scanning a page with his eye / he has a great amount of trouble for example with the dictionary um / so he needs help in locating information on a page / and if it's very small print you really need to / read through it and then perhaps read it again and ask him now what can you remember write down the points for him / at which stage he'll copy them / um and then even perhaps organise a piece of tracing paper over a picture and clip it because / he can't hold the tracing paper on the picture it'll slip so / it has to be / you know / secured and in that way my involvement in his projects is quite large.

Angela knows more about Steven's disabilities than anyone and, like many parents, is prepared to spend considerable amounts of her time helping him to overcome his handicap and to work to the limit of his potential. She recognises how crucial to learning is the interaction with print in both writing and reading and she knows how best to help with the physical and organisational features of topic work. She gives this essential assistance to Steven at home, but regrets it cannot always be offered at school where it is just as crucial. Steven's work is always assessed highly on the amount of effort he puts into it, but the required assessments, which compare his work normatively with others in his class, always place him in the lowest category of 'experiences great difficulty'. This is discouraging, particularly when a parent sees the school cannot provide the required level of support that she can give at home:

> he will only I suppose make / better headway there if there was someone who was always around / but that's just not possible.

Steven is allocated classroom support for a fixed number of hours per week by an educational award. He is given extra help with Mathematics, but for the rest he shares the three-fifths weekly allocation of a classroom helper with another disabled pupil in another school. Three tenths of his week theoretically is supported, but some of this is lost because the helper has to commute by bus between schools.

CHOICE OF SCHOOL

Steven's parents decided that he should receive his education integrated with his peer group. He went to special school from the age of 6 for about three and a half years and has now been full-time in his mainstream school for one year and a term. He had started on an outreach programme in his local mainstream school first for a morning, gradually working up to two days, with three days in his special school in the town. His mother explains why they wanted him full-time in the mainstream:

> he had a foot in one school and a foot in the other ... he didn't belong to either/ he'd start a unit in one school and never finish it / he'd get a notice for an outing at one school and never go to it / because he was at the other / it was a very unhappy situation.

Previously he had had to spend up to 2 hours 20 minutes per day being transported to and from his special school, whereas his local school is just 5 minutes away. Angela says:

> there is no comparison as far as that's concerned / he has far more leisure time / far more time just to cope.

Continuity and time-saving are strong advantages, important to parents caring for someone like Steven. His parents also felt that he could achieve more in mainstream and wanted to develop more of his potential without making him lose heart. This is a delicate issue, as Angela explains:

> while he had one to one / help in the special school / and he did have physio twice a week there / I think he was lulled into a feeling / because he was /

doing well in relation to the other children / some of them / especially the ones with cerebral palsy weren't able to articulate themselves as well as Steven can/ and perhaps because he had the use of those two fingers he could do things for himself that others couldn't / he felt that he was really rather clever / when he came here it was quite a shock to see that er / he was behind um / in some ways I guess he might feel oh dear I can't do that / in others it / it prompts him to realise he's got to make an extra effort.

The balance between that 'prompting' and loss of confidence is delicate, as Angela realises. They have decided in favour of the necessary prompting in order to give Steven his best chance of achievement. It is necessary to have realistic expectations, but not to be satisfied unless everything possible is being done to overcome the limitations of disability:

scholastically he's not really doing very well / um but then again I'm not sure what we should expect.

For many parents, who may not spend the amount of time in school that Angela does, it may be even more difficult to make decisions on academic grounds. Angela acknowledges that the special school had advantages over the local school, and vice versa. The final decider, though was Steven's social adjustment rather than the physical and educational factors that we have mentioned:

I feel just his pure happiness / the fact that his friends here go to Boys' Brigade / he is part of the community / he is known around the school and in the community / that has to be / on its own almost enough / to warrant being here.

WHAT STEVEN NEEDS

In the process of change from a segregated system to integration of students like Steven into local schools, it is crucial to consult parents about needs. Equally important is necessary funding to make mainstreaming work. There are frequent complaints that children with special educational needs are transferred to mainstream without appropriate resources. Such 'maindumping' creates additional problems. Temporary difficulties and confusion are sometimes caused when the process of funding schools changes towards Local School Management, with each school responsible for its own budget, as has been the recent case in Great Britain and New Zealand, for example. Funding decisions will increasingly be made by School Boards, but whoever makes them, children should not be shortchanged.

In Steven's case, he originally had one-to-one special care in school plus transport provision, but that equivalent in resources has not been passed on to his local school. Angela suggests three improvements which, although relatively modest, would significantly help in caring for Steven:

> *if I was to be asked what / what would you really want for your child well I would say I would like an aide at the school nine to three / um who is there for the handicapped children so you know there is somebody there who could look after him if he needs / special help / I would love / when there was a need for a special resource like toilet arrangements / if that becomes necessary / for that to be easily available / um and I would love to have a visit twice a week from a / a physiotherapist / at home / (laughs) that's what I would love / at home.*

These are relatively modest requests. The full-time aide is no more than the one-to-one care that Steven was previously receiving, but Angela suggests sharing the resource with other disabled children *within* the school. This would be an improvement on the current low provision with the wastage of hours caused by the aide's commuting. Proper toilet facilities are a prerequisite for children with disabilities, but may not receive high priority when there are only one or two such children in a school. Angela made these points at a time when she said that visiting physiotherapists were being phased out. This change seems short-sighted and likely to lead to less flexible provision. It is also likely to discriminate against Steven if he has to miss classes for physiotherapy sessions.

Steven's main need, apart from minimum resources, as Angela sees it, is to grow up in a community that is understanding and caring. Having children like Steven in local schools is a helpful part of the process of changing attitudes. As she says:

> *I think it's got to come from the young kids.*

Steven requires competent, sympathetic teachers too, who have the skills to cater for his specific educational needs:

> *even if the others in his class are doing / advanced division if Steven has to sit with counters / well so be it / forget about / um / having him seen to be doing (what the others are doing) he's got to be doing what he is able or almost able to reach / it can't be so out of his reach that he just gets lost.*

Angela has an informed view of her son's needs and her willingness to help in school has given her an understanding of educational needs and resourcing. As parents come to have a greater say in managing schools, experience and articulateness such as Angela's will be a valuable asset to School Boards which want to make integration really work.

From the family's point of view there is much to gain when parents are in touch with their child's education, as Angela is. She has a sympathetic, informed understanding of specific and more general educational issues and she requires such understanding if she is to help make responsible decisions. The heavy load on parents has not decreased, but at least they have the motivation for commitment to support their children educationally, knowing that they have essential rights and an active role in the process.

CONCLUSION

We have no doubt that the views of parents are essential to decisions about their children, because only parents have access to crucial information and observations about their children's needs. Parents also carry the main responsibility for aiding their children's development and for maximising their potential. Not every parent has Angela's ability to argue intelligently or her experience in presenting ideas and feelings articulately. Legislation is therefore welcome which provides help for the less experienced and the less articulate. All parents have views and attitudes and many will need 'named persons' or 'parent counsellors' to assist them to contribute to the collaborative process of providing for children's educational needs. Such help is valuable not only from the point of view of parents themselves, but also for the likely benefits that commitment and exchange of information bring to their children's education. Parents of children with special educational needs must not be categorised as a single group just because their rights have at last been institutionalised in law. In reality they are as diverse in abilities, income, class, experience and in every other aspect, including the ways they accept and adjust to their children's needs.

Chapter Thirteen

Ways Forward: implications and practical strategies for successful integration

By being conveniently herded together into segregated units we can often become socially crippled as well.

Emma Satyamurti (age 17)

INTRODUCTION

During our research we have been particularly impressed with the positive nature of the responses we have received. The challenge of educating pupils with special educational needs in the mainstream has been taken by teachers and pupils alike with enthusiasm and commitment and we observed many successes in the systems in practice. Although many schools thought that they were moving in the right direction, none was entirely satisfied with what they had achieved. Management and staff constantly evaluated their practice, support and resourcing to ensure that the current educational needs of their students were being met. They did this through a desire to integrate pupils as fully as was practically possible for them. For some students this meant special school placement but having temporary, functional mainstreaming with a local school in joint projects; for others, a unit was still the home base with functional mainstreaming taking place as frequently as possible; while, for a growing number of students a full-time placement in a mainstream school gave the greatest access to total integration.

Evaluation of provision indicates that many schools are in process of developing their provision rather than presenting a final product; in all of the schools in our case studies this process was developing. This final section examines the ways in which schools are moving forward and makes suggestions for integration that arise from that examination. We emphasise that the suggestions we make are not exhaustive. We present them as prompts to further thinking - an opportunity for readers to make their own patterns.

We have sub-divided our concluding analysis into seven broad sections:

- attitudes
- teaching
- curriculum
- resources
- interaction
- whole school policy and management
- pupils' views

Inevitably these categories overlap and cannot be discussed in isolation, but we discuss the broad principles of each. In each section we first address the implications of the category, drawing, where relevant, from earlier chapters for examples, and then we give suggestions - some of which deliberately appear in more than one category to emphasise the interactive nature of the categories themselves. It is our intention that these *Ways Forward* will enable us all to further our knowledge and skills, to stimulate new thinking and to enhance the integration possibilities that we offer our pupils with special educational needs.

Attitudes

Chapter Three underlines the importance of positive attitudes in determining the successful integration and interaction of pupils with special educational needs in the mainstream class. The chapter indicates that the attitudes of everyone in the school, staff and pupils alike, affect all elements of learning and interaction. We stress the importance of teacher attitude in acceptance of pupils with special educational needs and in setting expectations for them that are realistically high rather than artificially low. Teachers, however, are not born with positive attitudes towards people with disabilities. For many, their teacher training is an important factor in setting attitudes, as Leyser's & Abrams' research (1980) shows. The importance of teacher training is further underlined by Barman's (1986) study of fourteen countries in which he demonstrates that teacher attitudes towards integration varied in different countries and are accounted for by preparation during training.

Most colleges of education in English speaking countries do provide courses on special educational needs for their undergraduates but often in an already tight, overcrowded teaching package. These courses are recognised by students as insufficient for their needs, yet they still maintain a positive interest in the subject. Many serving teachers also opt for in-service courses to increase and update their knowledge. We refer to Larrivee (1980) to show the effect of in-service training on teachers' attitudes to mainstreaming. Harvey & Green (1984) also record how training courses in special education led to more positive attitudes, not necessarily towards specific disabilities, or acceptance of such students in the classroom, but to professional competence, confidence and a positive 'philosophical position' on mainstreaming.

There remain teachers in schools, however, whose attitude, although not negative to the individual, is not conducive to successful integration. Glenys Walsh, for example, in Chapter Ten comments on attitudes that some colleagues had prior to their receiving pupils with disabilities in their classroom. Unlike some schools, the staff at Te Kanawa were not given the choice of whether or not to accept them. Their rather negative attitudes must have, initially, caused some concern, but because of the total support of Glenys and members of the planning group, where concerns, strategies and attitudes were discussed, attitudes changed. The teachers eventually accepted, and delighted in, those pupils with disabilities in their classrooms. With in-service courses and in-school support there is no need, as Bender (1987) suggests, to evaluate teacher attitudes prior to integrating pupils in their classrooms, for, as Glenys demonstrates, attitudes can change.

Just as important as teacher attitudes are the attitudes of the peer group towards pupils with special educational needs. The students in Chapter Six, for example, refer to their peer group who make unfair judgements and whose behaviour is unaccepting:

> Raymond: we reckon we can do as well as they can but they
> don't know that.
> Nicholas: the kids in the mainschool are OK / but sometimes
> they just run round and torment you.

The teacher can provide a positive role model for changing the attitudes of the peer group. Strict avoidance of the labelling that can occur in schools ('thick', 'specials', 'remedials') and an overt appreciation of what all pupils contribute can start a change to the positive. The peer group that is not encouraged in this way may, through their lack of understanding, socially isolate a pupil with disability even though that pupil may be a permanent member of their class - thus negating the benefits of integration. Some children may not be able to see beneath the surface of a disability to the depth and quality of the individual and, as we suggest, the teacher may provide the motivating force for fostering positive attitudes. Nicholas, in Chapter Six refers to how his teacher puts the pupils in pair learning situations (one of the pair has special educational needs and the other does not):

I like Science..... we have a partner from mainschool / he's my friend.

This example shows how teacher intervention in the classroom is vital for maintaining interaction. Sensitive organisation of pairs and groups within the mainstream setting can help the interaction that is necessary for acceptance and successful integration. Fox (1989), in her work on peer acceptance, suggests that pairing can work exceptionally well if the children participate in activities which are designed to promote discovery of mutual interests or with an academic task. She found that not only did the acceptance of the partner increase, but the social acceptance of the rest of the class was also increased. A public appreciation of different skills that pupils with special educational needs possess can help the peer group to recognise abilities, which they perhaps do not have. The teachers in Chapter Six encourage Michael with his drumming and the pupils of St. Anne's are genuine in their praise for the gymnastic abilities of the pupils from Firtrees (Chapter Eight).

The attitudes of the community also affect the acceptance of pupils with disability in school. Parents can be concerned that the presence of a pupil with disability may mean that the teacher's time is unequally distributed. Their concern is for the education of their own children and whether or not they are being deprived. The parents of St. Anne's only recognised the Firtrees' pupils talents because they were able to witness them. Similarly, parent volunteers in schools, as in the Girls' school and Te Kanawa (Chapters Nine and Ten) can encourage both recognition of achievements and positive attitudes.

Ways Forward

Teacher attitudes
- show respect for the individual
- show consideration for the dignity of the student
- update knowledge
- discuss attitudes with other staff
- share skills and attitudes with other staff
- give in-school support to colleagues

Pupil attitudes
Teachers need to:

- become a positive role model in valuing and respecting pupils with special educational needs
- intervene sensitively in grouping of pupils
- encourage collaborative pair work
- promote collaborative and co-operative work
- provide opportunities for pupils with special educational needs to demonstrate their skills
- make opportunities for pupils with special educational needs to demonstrate responsibility

Community attitudes
- invite the community into school; have an open day or exhibition to which *all* pupils have contributed
- encourage members of the community to help in shared reading schemes and other projects
- parents of pupils with special educational needs to be included in review procedures
- ensure a positive welcome to all visitors from all members of the school, including pupils with special educational needs

TEACHING

As important as positive attitudes are the teaching skills which enable pupils with special educational needs to embrace the same curriculum as their peers. In order to achieve maximum access teachers need to help and support all pupils in their learning and, in so doing, achieve the necessary balance between 'normal' treatment and recognition of a special educational need.

The pupils from the secondary school unit (Chapter Six) have interesting comments to make about those teachers who had not achieved that balance. One area of comment is the speed of presentation - some teachers go too fast for the pupils to fully understand. Riding (1977) also demonstrates that the comprehension of pupils with learning difficulties increased when the speed of presentation was decreased. As teachers it is important to be aware of pupils' perspectives; it is too easy to make false assumptions about speed of learning and understanding. We also need to be aware of the embarrassment that pupils experience if they have continually to ask questions for clarification in front of their peer group. Clarity of instruction and explanation aids understanding, but there are times inevitably, when pupils need further assistance. Although pupils do appreciate this, it is important to give only the assistance that is needed - and not, as the unit pupils state (Chapter Six) to treat them 'like babies'. Over-helping is as bad as no help, for over-helping denies opportunities for pupils to learn. Many of us are unable to operate some aspect of technology, or investigate our car engines, because there is always someone there to help us!

The context for learning is crucial if success is to be achieved. Any learning becomes easier when it is meaningful for the pupil. Wayne, for example, in Chapter Eight, spoke when he had something to say in a context that he understood and enjoyed, rather than in an unrealistic setting of practising sentences. The provision of new experiences within a meaningful context, as the shared production provided, proved beneficial in terms of knowledge and self-esteem. Working from children's own experience, however, also ensures that learning can be meaningful and purposeful by providing the necessary links between old and new learning. Glenys Walsh, the itinerant teacher in Chapter Ten, realises the importance of relating work to the pupils' experiences and interests, when she determines topics for their individual programmes and incorporates them into her plans.

We have already stressed the importance of collaboration for promoting attitude change, but in learning it is crucial. With positive attitudes the peer group can be sensitive to the needs of pupils with disabilities and are willing to give their classmates responsibility in a shared task. Chris, in Chapter Four, is very limited in what he can physically offer in the classroom, yet he plays a full and active role in discussion with his friends. In Chapter Nine we describe how Donna's classmates encourage her to take part in a drama session and how well she manages to contribute. Through collaboration with sensitive friends, the pupils with special educational needs exhibit and begin to fulfil their potential. Chris, for example, shows promise in writing.

On many occasions so far we have recorded teachers' surprise at how much their pupils have achieved. It is continually necessary to evaluate pupils' progress, as the teachers in Chapters Nine and Ten demonstrate, and to revise expectations upwards. Expectations of pupils' capabilities are often undesirably low, as the staff of Firtrees, (Chapter Eight) discovered when their pupils not only coped with change, responsibility and extra learning, but excelled. Revision of expectations is as important for mainstream teachers as it is for teachers in special schools. It is part of the process of improving the mainstream for all children. Providing challenges to meet raised expectations for the whole ability range, including those who have developed exceptional abilities (Chapter Seven), enables all children to let 'their minds fly a bit'.

The fundamental premise is that all students are capable of learning, irrespective of the degree of disability or the complexity of their difficulties. Once this premise is accepted, then the only way is forward!

Ways Forward

- know and understand individual pupils
- accept that all youngsters can learn
- respect individuals and their achievements
- make appropriate modification of learning objectives to suit the students' needs
- adopt appropriate teaching strategies to suit the learners
- provide challenges in learning
- promote active and experiential learning
- utilise pupils' prior learning, experience and interests
- provide opportunities for new experiences
- continually evaluate students' progress
- revise expectations for students upwards
- record and celebrate students' progress
- ensure clarity of explanation and instruction in teaching to maximise understanding
- make aims clear to the students
- be prepared to repeat, rephrase if necessary
- be aware of optimum speed of delivery
- give help unobtrusively - and only what is needed
- organise resources, classroom and groups efficiently
- be well planned, well organised and well prepared
- when giving feedback of results, concentrate on the positive, what the student *can* do
- offer independence rather than too much security
- organise pair and group work sensitively
- plan opportunities for collaborative learning in which students with special educational needs can make meaningful contributions
- ensure a naturalistic context for learning where pupils can utilise the skills and knowledge they already possess
- liaise with parents to maximise learning opportunities at home
- plan for success
- make learning enjoyable and fun

CURRICULUM

Teachers' and pupils' views, together with observations of practice, demonstrate the necessity, for all students, of following the same broadly based curriculum. Not only does this ensure equality and the right of access (which is stipulated by law in several countries) to all aspects of the curriculum, but it also fosters and underlines similarities rather than differences between pupils.

The curriculum for students with special educational needs has, for too long, been restricted to the 'basics': life skills, or an insistence on the teaching of 'relevant' reading and writing skills, to the exclusion of the expressive and more stimulating areas of the school curriculum. Yet we have seen this changing dramatically. The most severely disabled pupils in the Girls' school (Chapter Nine) take part in the Art, Music, Poetry and Drama lessons. They show how well they are able to take part and contribute to class activities. A restricted curriculum is both socially and educationally unsound, as Rachael demonstrates in Chapter Six. It denies opportunities to take part in the normal classroom activities with the peer group.

Collaborative work in pairs and groups gives access to positive attitudes, interaction and learning. It also enables pupils with special educational needs to share in a full curriculum, supported by their peers. Cross-curricular themes which permeate several subject areas (a philosophy endorsed by the National Curriculum Council of Great Britain) allow all students, whether in primary or secondary schools, to use their particular skills when contributing to a group effort:

> *The world in which pupils live is not compartmentalised into subjects. Their curiosity, questions and ways of thinking transcend subject barriers.*
> *Cross-curricular activities should enable them to understand the relevance of Mathematics to work in Science, English and the other foundation subjects. Such activities also allow pupils to draw on their strengths in other subjects.*
>
> (A Curriculum for All - Special Educational Needs in the
> National Curriculum, p.31, National Curriculum Council, 1989).

Access to a full curriculum and therefore to a wider environment maximises potential for learning, even if that curriculum may have to be adapted to address the needs of the pupils, as in the Art lesson described in Chapter Nine. Pupils engaged in the same kind of task, although perhaps at varying levels of competence and ability, have greater opportunity to interact than if specific and restrictive individual programmes of work are implemented. We see how in Te Kanawa school (Chapter Ten) that, although Individual Educational Programmes are implemented for pupils with individual special educational needs, they are carefully tailored to fit in with the curriculum followed by the peer group. Pupils experience the same activity, but at their own level. We have seen that adaptations may sometimes have to be made to teaching methods and resources within the classroom to ensure that the same skills are being fostered and that an equitable 'end product' (if that is the objective) is achieved. The severely disabled pupil at the Girls' school described in Chapter Nine is able to produce a screen print with the rest of her peers, but only as a result of imaginative adaptation of resources and the support of her teachers.

In addition, Chris the quadriplegic boy discussed in Chapter Four, shows how he is able to adapt to the demands of the curriculum when he has specific aid from adequate resources.

Ways forward

- tailor individual programmes to the mainstream curriculum as well as the needs of the individual
- adapt curriculum to meet the pupils' needs but with the same learning skills and outcomes as other pupils
- provide access to a broad and varied curriculum
- adapt and modify resources to enable pupils access to the same curriculum opportunities as their peers
- make opportunity for cross-curricular themes
- make access to an environment which broadens and expands the student's experience

RESOURCES

The provision of resources, either in material or human terms, is a necessity if integration is to achieve maximum effect. The advantages of mainstreaming can be limited if support services and conditions are inadequate. We have seen how teachers and headteachers are aware of the drawbacks of poor resourcing for the pupils. The lack of back-up from education authorities has motivated schools to fight for adequate provision. Mr King (Chapter Ten) and Miss Jacques (Chapter Nine) are still fighting for the resources that they consider are necessary for their pupils, and Chris (Chapter Four) has suffered from the delays in providing necessary equipment for his full interaction with both his peers and the curriculum. A lap-top computer, although an expensive item, is not extravagant when compared with the resources which cater for his medical needs. Adequate resources affect not only his school and education, but also the quality of his life. Minimum resources are a pre-requisite if mainstreaming is to be successful: for example, ramps for pupils who are confined to wheelchairs, radio-aids for pupils with hearing impairment, computers for those who are severely disabled. Without these resources, access to learning is restricted or obstructed. Even when these resources are available, they need to be kept constantly under review for assurance that they are still meeting students' needs. Resources need updating and need to be on-going as students progress or their needs alter - a once and for all injection of resource does not ensure continuation of provision (Chapter Eleven).

The provision of resources is required not only at the level of immediate contact with the pupil, but also for the teacher. Resources support the teacher and make mainstream provision more effective for all pupils. Such support is often given by specialist teachers who form part of a team, as in Te Kanawa school (Chapter Ten) and in the Boys' and Girls' schools referred to in Chapter Nine. Many teachers in the mainstream do not receive adequate support. Teachers of pupils with special educational needs are regarded as self-reliant and committed professionals, prepared to inform themselves (Panckhurst et al, 1987) through literature, conferences and visits and, we would add, frequently at their own expense; but without availability of equipment and class support their skills are constrained. While both teachers and school may be positive and welcoming, such efforts may be hindered by an authority's lack of recognition of the resources that a pupil needs. Resourcing in special schools is often good, catering for the individual needs of the pupils, but similar availability of resource is restricted when pupils transfer to a mainstream school. Angela, the parent in Chapter Twelve, is discouraged by the lack of required level of support at school and recognises that her son's learning is being hindered because of that lack. Her view of what her son needs is no more than he received at his special school and she suggests that this could be shared between other pupils with disabilities in the school. Such sharing of resources makes practical and economic sense.

It is possible that, even if some resources are unavailable, learning can be achieved if there is sufficient interaction between pupils. Lack of resources can be compensated for to some extent by caring, committed and ingenious staff, as the staff in Park Green school show by adapting the drinking fountains for the needs of their students who are in wheelchairs. Lack of interaction, however, cannot be compensated for. The same staff respond to this area of need by ensuring that students with physical handicap interact with their peers by moving the peer group to work with them in their room, as the school building denies them access to the computer room (Chapter Eleven).

Ways forward

- argue for recognition that minimum resources are a prerequisite for learning
- find out about the hierarchy of the system that makes resources available
- be determined to fight for at least the equivalent of support that is available in special schools
- set up a resource centre (e.g. between schools) that acts as a library for loaning resources as necessary
- share resources and support in school
- constantly review effectiveness of resources for students
- ensure resources are on-going as a result of the review
- seek specialist advice for appropriate resources and technology

- be prepared to be innovative and to adapt
- create space as a resource to enable easy access for pupils who are in wheelchairs

INTERACTION

The importance of interaction in integration pervades all of our chapters. Our view is that, without social and educational interaction, integration cannot be said to be fully functional. The practice of withdrawing students for extra activities serves to reduce opportunities for interaction in the classroom and also emphasises differences between students rather than their similarities. We can see in Chapters Five, Six and Eleven how pupils from the units experience problems of interaction with their mainstream peers. Integration of pupils into mainstream has given increased opportunities for social and informal contact, but these opportunities need to be skilfully handled by the teacher to ensure that the pupils do not feel different and that their peers accept them as classmates. Without opportunities for collaborative learning, shared practices, mutual respect and understanding, pupils with special educational needs are effectively segregated within their mainstream classrooms. Such unofficial, and often unnoticed segregation, for example, denies pupils the chance to test, rehearse and consolidate their learning through discussion with their peers. We see how necessary it is for Chris, in Chapter Four, to verbalise all of his learning and how the acceptance and co-operation of his peer group enable him to do this. His personal relationships within the class are formulated on the basis of equal acceptance. It is important that the relationships are non-patronising as this quickly shifts the balance of equality, to the detriment of the student with disability. Teachers are important role models in promoting peer group equality of acceptance in the classroom by their own acceptance of, and positive attitudes towards, their students.

Although pupils from the units speak of some of their problems, we can see how increased and increasingly successful integration within the mainstream can lead to greater motivation, commitment and educational success. The older students, particularly, show self-confidence, their self esteem is high and their expectations for the future are positive and valid. Opportunities for social interaction with a variety of individuals greatly enhance and extend experience and learning potential for any pupil. Any educational system that denies this opportunity is detrimental to the potential of the whole student. Jenny, in Birch Grove school, (Chapter Eleven) experiences very little interaction and is disaffected towards her school and peer group, while the differing experiences of Trudy and Sue show how crucial acceptance and understanding are in determining the positive perceptions of such integration (Chapter Five).

Ways forward

- encourage everyone to make pupils with special educational needs feel welcome in the school
- use intervention strategies to aid collaborative learning in groups
- emphasise similarities not differences
- make opportunities to verbalise learning
- make non-patronising responses to pupils
- create a flexible learning environment
- make opportunities for shared experiences
- provide opportunities for social and informal contact
- give pupils with special educational needs a low profile in and around school to make them less identifiable and less different from their peer group
- provide maximum numbers of lessons within the mainstream but with adequate support for pupil and teacher from specialist or ancillary staff
- put emphasis on areas of competence rather than on disability
- provide adequate resourcing for pupils to learn in the mainstream
- ensure liaison between class teacher and classroom aide/support teacher
- use two-way interaction, for example, pair work located in a unit situation to use resources, work with the partner in quieter surroundings (emphasis needs to be on the positive benefits for all pupils)
- involve members of the community to allay fears that pupils with special educational needs restrict the progress of others
- encourage independence

Units may have problems in successfully integrating their students, but, for special schools, the problem is more complex. The experiences of Firtrees School and St. Anne's School (Chapter Eight) demonstrate, however, that it is possible for functional mainstreaming to be achieved by a special school if only on a temporary or part-time basis. Not only can it be achieved, but it should be achieved, since locational and social integration cannot offer the same benefits as functional integration which encourages collaborative and co-operative learning experiences. Chapter Eight describes one way in which functional integration of pupils with disabilities and their non-disabled peers was successfully achieved. The benefits were not all for the staff and pupils of Firtrees, but also for those at St. Anne's. The improvements for the mainstream can be seen by the open acceptance of pupils with disabilities, a re-examination of their capabilities and also the desire to maintain social contact. Mrs. Bedford, the St. Anne's teacher, now feels more confident to deal with a wider range of children than before.

Special and regular schools therefore, working together, can offer opportunities for interaction with all the benefits that we have described for pupils and staff. A joint drama production is one opportunity; there are other possibilities.

Ways Forward

- sharing of on-site facilities
- shared in-service days for staff
- cross-site teaching (short term teacher exchange)
- cross-site learning (short term pupil exchange)
- joint projects involving problem-solving at levels designed for individual capabilities
- working co-operatively in physical education
- collaborative art and design projects
- shared educational outings for everyone to extend their experience

WHOLE SCHOOL POLICY AND MANAGEMENT

Another important component for successful integration is a whole school policy where there is a shared philosophy of provision and acceptance. Chapters Nine, Ten and Eleven demonstrate that such a policy is advantageous for all pupils in a school. Consultation, collaboration and co-operation between all staff encourage sharing of attitudes, problems and strategies. A carefully planned programme of intervention and management to which staff are wholeheartedly committed is more likely to achieve success than ad hoc ideas (no matter how brilliant) presented in isolation.

The staff at the Girls' school and at Te Kanawa said how crucial team work was in providing for their pupils' educational needs, how this team work inspired confidence in teachers and fostered their teaching abilities. It is interesting to note too, how 'whole school' in these examples, includes parents; for it is recognised that the home context must be taken into consideration in order to maximise and support teaching.

Support teachers, teachers' aides, psychologists, social workers and everyone involved in the welfare of pupils need to be part of the evaluative and planning process of the whole school. In this way a picture of the whole student emerges, which is clear to everyone, and this policy prevents a narrow focus on the learning disability. Close liaison between professionals therefore is essential.

The full support of school management is implicit in many of our chapters. Management is often the prime mover in requesting resources and building adaptations. This cannot be done without consulting the staff who are part of the support system which caters for the pupils' needs. Staff and management need to work together to overcome design faults in buildings which inhibit the access of pupils with disabilities. Chapter Eleven demonstrates this essential need.

The important consideration is that the whole school moves forward in the same direction to promote and consolidate pupils' learning.

Ways Forward

- there should exist a whole school policy agreed by all
- an agreed and explicit school policy for achieving integration must be published
- individual departments/groups should be encouraged to develop and publish their own specific guidelines
- all staff must be committed to the policy and to the students
- management must be committed to the integration policy
- close liaison between professionals must be part of the policy
- team planning and implementation of agreed programmes is central to development
- collaboration and co-operation are essential between staff
- parents need to be consulted and be part of the planning process
- sharing of teacher expertise should be encouraged
- school staff need the support of advisers and specific training
- collaboration (including team-teaching) between professionals needs to be fostered by school-based in-service training
- specialist teachers need to ensure that they are integral members of the team
- guidelines for teachers, teachers' aids, therapists and others should clarify their various roles and reinforce school policy
- identification of priorities is necessary for appropriate provision
- regular reviews and assessment of student progress by all professionals are a priority
- communication and consultation with all concerned with students (and with students themselves) must be encouraged
- continuity of care for students should be worked for
- school policies should emphasise treating students as whole persons
- consultation about building adaptations or extensions should extend to all staff
- management should identify features of building design, equipment provision and timetabling which restrict access for students with special educational needs, and therefore their successful integration. Steps should be taken to eradicate or minimise these effects.

PUPILS' VIEWS

It is a strange anomaly in education that the people on the receiving end of carefully planned, argued and legislated provision are rarely consulted about their views. We have made it clear so far that our 'clients' have much to tell us that we can learn from; their views are important and we should listen to what they have to say. Those who have listened (for example, the Head of Unit in Chapter Six) and have had the courage to implement change as a result, have achieved a workable integration policy, even when the integration is not a permanent feature for every individual. Chapter Five, on the other hand, shows the disadvantages of not taking the pupils' viewpoint into account. The students, Trudy and Sue, are well able to evaluate their experience of integration; their views of teachers, peer groups, activities, environment and learning experiences are reflective and objective. If we listen it makes us aware, as teachers, that pupils are sensitive to people's expectations of them. Lisa demonstrates this beautifully when she talks meaningfully about her achievement in the production (Chapter Eight) and of other people's fears about her capabilities. Pupils' perceptions of others' views can affect their self concepts; they are sensitive to people's expectations for them. The pupils from the unit (Chapter Six) demonstrate how they are able to judge teachers' expectations, attitudes and ability and are able to assess their own learning experiences as a result of being taught by different teachers.

Self-esteem and confidence are vital components of learning for all pupils, but particularly for pupils who are aware that, in some respects, they are at a disadvantage, yet who are also aware that they are able to achieve. It is up to us to show our students that their viewpoints are valid and that we have sufficient respect for them as individuals to try to act upon those viewpoints. An overt recognition of their worth stimulates the students' self-esteem and encourages confidence and motivation. In Chapter Eleven we see how attention is drawn to Mario and his ability in technical drawing. His peer group colleagues not only wonder how he can do it, but recognise that he is the best.

Integration and interaction are important considerations for all pupils. There are students in special schools whose placement is as a result of economic necessity (availability of resources), rather than as a provision for a learning need. If their views are not made known, and not acted upon, frustration and denial of opportunity can result. Emma Satyamurti (1990), a seventeen-year old disabled student now integrated into a local school, writes of the dangers of segregation and isolation. As she points out, disabled people are not a special breed:

by being conveniently herded together into segregated units we can often become socially crippled as well.

We recommend that we listen when pupils have something to say, for then we might also learn.

Ways Forward

- consult pupils about their needs
- ask questions about their learning
- involve pupils in planning for their needs
- take note of what they say
- be sufficiently far-sighted to implement change
- include pupils' views in evaluation and records of achievement
- show you have taken notice by implementing some of their suggestions
- organise class and school councils which include some students with special educational needs.

CONCLUSION

We have given this chapter the title 'Ways Forward: implications and practical strategies for successful integration'. The 'ways forward' derive from our observations, analyses and reflections in earlier chapters. As we said earlier, however, the ways forward are not presented as an exhaustive document, but as patterns for you to build from, adding your own ideas derived from the students and contexts that you know best. We are of the same opinion as the teachers and pupils in our case studies, that the best way to learn is to share ideas and good practices. We hope that we have made a beginning in this book and that, in some way, you, the reader, have learned from our experiences. We also hope that this process of sharing with us and fashioning your own patterns for action gives you confidence in your own skills and abilities to cater effectively for students with special educational needs. The best way is forward and we wish you success as you continue to reassess, reorganise and reconstruct your own patterns for integration.

References

Acker, S., Mejarry, J., Nisbet, S. & Hoyle, E. (Eds.) (1984) *World Yearbook of Education 1984: Women and Education*. London, Kogan Page.

Adams, G.R. & Cohen, A. (1974) Children's physical and inter-personal characteristics that affect student-teacher interactions, *Journal of Experimental Education*, 43, pp.1-5.

Ainscow, M. & Muncey, J. (1988) *Meeting Individual Needs in the Primary School*. London, Fulton.

Anderson, E.M. (1973) *The Disabled Schoolchild*. London, Methuen.

Ashman, A.F. (Ed.) (1988) *Integration 25 years On*, The Exceptional Child Monograph No. 1, St. Lucia, Queensland, Fred & Eleanor Schonell Special Education Research Centre.

Ashman, A.F. & Conway, R.N.F. (1989) *Cognitive Strategies for Special Education*. London, Routledge.

Baker, J.L. & Gottlieb, J. (1980) Attitudes of teachers towards mainstreaming retarded children, in Gottlieb, (Ed.) *Educating Mentally Retarded Persons in the Mainstream*. Baltimore, University Park Press.

Ballard, K.D. (1990) Special education in New Zealand: disability, politics and empowerment , *International Journal of Disability, Development and Education*, 37, 3

Bandura, A. (1977) *Social Learning Theory*. Englewood Cliffs, N.J., Prentice-Hall.

Barton, L. & Tomlinson, S. (1986) The politics of integration in England, in Cohen & Cohen (Eds.).

Bender, W.N. (1987) Effective educational practices in the mainstream setting: recommended model for evaluation of mainstream teacher classes, *Journal of Special Education*, 20, pp.475-488.

Bowlby, J. & Fry, H. (1953) *Child Care and the Growth of Love*. Harmondsworth, Penguin.

Bowman, I. (1986) Teacher training and the integration of handicapped pupils: some findings from a 14-Nation UNESCO study, *European Journal of Special Needs Education*, 1, pp.29-38.

Brennan, W.K. (1974) *Shaping the Education of Slow Learners*. London, Routledge & Kegan Paul.

Brodwin, M.G. & Gardner, G. (1978) Teacher attitudes towards physically disabled, *Journal of Teaching and Learning*, 3, pp.40-45.

Brookover, W.B., Thomas, S. & Patterson, A. (1964) Self concept of ability and school achievement, *Sociological Education*, 37, pp. 271-8.

Brown, D. (1989) The influence of the American Public Law on New Zealand special education, in Philips et al (Eds.).

Burns, R.B. (1979) *The Self Concept. Theory, Measurement, Development and Behaviour*. Harlow, Longman.

Burns, R. (1982) *Self Concept Development and Education*. London, Holt, Rinehart & Winston.

Buswell, C. (1984) Sponsoring and stereotyping in a working-class English secondary school, in Acker et al, pp.100-109.

Caldwell, B.J. & Spinks, J.M. (1988) *The Self-managing School*. Lewes, Falmer Press.

Chapman, J.W. (1988) Learning disabled children's self-concepts, *Review of Educational Research*, 88, pp.347-371.

Ciccelli, R. & Ashby-Davis, C. (1986) *Teaching Exceptional Children and Youth in the Regular Classroom*. Syracuse, Syracuse University Press.

Clement, D.B., Zartler, A.S. & Mulick, J.A. (1983) Ethical considerations for school psychologists in planning for special needs children, *School Psychology Review*, 12, pp.452-457.

Cohen, A. & Cohen, L. (Eds.) (1986) *Special Educational Needs in the Ordinary School*. London, Harper & Row.

Coopersmith, S. (1968) Studies in self esteem, *Scientific American*.

Creber, J.W.P. (1972) *Lost for Words*. Harmondsworth, Penguin.

D.E.S. (1978) *Special Educational Needs*. The Warnock Report. London, H.M.S.O.

D.E.S. (1980) *Special Needs in Education*. White Paper 7996. London, H.M.S.O.

Eggleston, J., Dunn, D. & Anjali, M. (1986) *Education for Some: the educational and vocational experiences of 15-18 year-old members of minority ethnic groups*. Stoke-on-Trent, Trentham Books.

Entwistle, N. (1990) *Handbook of Educational Ideas and Practices*. London, Routledge.

Everard, K.B. (1986) *Developing Management in Schools*. Oxford, Blackwell.

Freeman, J. (Ed.) (1985) *The Psychology of Gifted Children*. Chichester, Wiley.

Furneaux, B. (1988) *Special Parents*. Milton Keynes, Open University Press.

Gartner, A. & Lipsky, D.K. (1987) Beyond special education: toward a quality system for all students, *Harvard Educational Review*, 57, pp.367-394.

Glynn, T. & Gold, M. (1990) *Support teams for mainstreaming children with special needs* (unpublished paper)

Goffman, E. (1961) *Asylums: essays on the social situation of mental patients and other inmates.* Harmondsworth, Penguin.

Goffman, E. (1968) *Stigma.* Harmondsworth, Penguin.

Gottlieb, J. (1975) Public, peer and professional attitudes towards mentally retarded persons, in Begab, M.J. & Richardson, S.A. (Eds.) *The Mentally Retarded and Society.* Baltimore University

Gow, L. (1988) Integration in Australia, *European Journal of Special Needs Education,* 3, pp.1-12.

Hafftner, C. (1968) The changeling: history and psychodynamics of attitudes to handicapped children in European folklore, *Journal of History of Behavioural Sciences,* 4, pp.55-61.

Halliday, M.A.K. (1969) Relevant Models of Language, in Wade, B. (Ed.) (1982) *Language Perspectives.* London, Heinemann.

Harvey, H. & Green, C. (1984) Attitudes of New Zealand teachers, teachers in training and non-teachers towards mainstreaming, *New Zealand Journal of Educational Studies,* 19, pp.34-44.

Hodgson, A. (1986) How to Integrate the Hearing-Impaired, in Cohen, A. & Cohen, L. (1986).

Inner London Education Authority (ILEA) (1985) *Educational Opportunities for All?* Report of the Committee reviewing provision to meet special educational needs (The Fish Report). London, ILEA.

Jones, C. (1985) Sexual tyranny: male violence in a mixed secondary school, in Weiner, G. (Ed.), pp.26-39.

Kellog, W.N. & Kellog, L.A. (1933) *The Ape and the Child.* McGraw-Hill.

Kelly, A. (1986) Gender differences in teacher-pupil interaction: a meta-analytic review. Paper presented at the Bristol Conference of the British Educational Research Association.

Kuhn, M.H. (1964) The reference group reconsidered, *Sociological Quarterly,* 5, pp.6-21.

Larrivee, B. (1981) Effect of inservice training intensity on teachers' attitudes towards mainstreaming, *Exceptional Children,* 48, pp.34-39.

Lees, S. (1986) *Losing Out.* London, Hutchinson

Leyser, Y. & Abrams, P.D. (1983) A Shift to the Positive: an effective programme for changing pre-service teachers' attitudes towards the disabled, *Educational Review,* 35, pp.35-43

Macklem, G.L. (1988) *Innovative programs that meet complex needs of children in their home communities.* Paper presented at Project Link Symposium, University of East Anglia, Norwich, March 1988.

McGrory, M. (1989) *Integration not isolation : an observation of a child with moderate learning difficulties.* Unpublished B.Ed.Hons. dissertation, University of Birmingham

Nash, R. (1973) *Classrooms Observed.* London, Routledge & Kegan Paul

National Curriculum Council (1989) Curriculum Guidance 2. *A Curriculum For All: special educational needs in the national curriculum.* York, N.C.C.

Peter, M. (1984) A hard act to follow, *Times Educational Supplement,* March 30, p.23.

Philips, D., Lealand, G. & McDonald, G. (1989) *The impact of American ideas on New Zealand's educational policy, practice and thinking.* Wellington, NZ; US Educational Foundation/New Zealand Council for Educational Research.

Ramasut, A. (Ed.) (1989) *Whole School Approaches to Special Needs.* Lewes, Falmer Press.

Riding, R.J. (1977) *School Learning: Mechanisms and Processes.* London, Open Books.

Russell, P. (1988) *The Education Act 1981 - Opportunities for Partnership or Bureaucracy and Confrontation?* Paper presented at Project Link Symposium, University of East Anglia, Norwich, March 1988.

Rutter, M. (1983) School effects on pupil progress: research findings and policy implications, *Child Development,* 54, pp.1-29.

Safran, S.P. (1989) Special Education in Australia and the United States: a cross-cultural analysis, *Journal of Special Education,* 23, pp.330-341.

Satyamurti, E. (February 1990) 'I wanted to be educated in normal schools', *Disability Now,* p.9.

Schneider, B.H. & Byrne, B.B. (1984) Predictors of successful transition from self-contained special education to regular class setting, *Psychology in the Schools,* 21, pp.375-380.

Schumaker, J.B. & Deshler, D.D. (1988) Implementing the regular education initiative in secondary schools: a different ball game, *Journal of Learning Disabilities,* 21, pp.36-42.

Skeels, H.M. (1966) *Adult status of children with contrasting early life experiences,* Monograph of the Society for Research in Child Development, 31, No. 105.

Special Educational Needs in the Ordinary School: a source book for teachers. London, Harper & Row. See A. Cohen & L. Cohen (Eds).

Spencer, P. (1990) 'Vive le francais!' at Priory School, *British Journal of Special Education,* 17, No. 2, pp.51-52.

Stainback, W., Stainback, S., Courtnage, L. & Jaben, T. (1985) Facilitating mainstreaming by modifying the mainstream, *Exceptional Children*, 52, pp.144-152.

Tansley, A.E. & Gulliford, R. (1960) *The Education of Slow Learning Children*. London, Routledge & Kegan Paul.

Tarr, P. (1988) Integration Policy Practice in Victoria: an examination of the Victorian government's educational provision for students with impairments, disabilities and problems in schooling since 1984, in Ashman (Ed.), pp.63-67.

Thomas, D. (1978) *The Social Psychology of Childhood Disability*. London, Methuen.

Wade, B. (1985) *Talking to Some Purpose*. Birmingham, *Educational Review* Occasional Publications.

Wade, B. & Moore, M. (1987) *Special Children...Special Needs: provision in ordinary classrooms*. London, Cassell.

Wade, B. & Moore, M. (forthcoming) *The Experience of Special Education*. Milton Keynes, Open University Press.

Walkling, P. (1990) Multicultural Education, in Entwistle (Ed.), pp.82-90.

Wang, M.C. & Birch, J.W. (1984) Effective special education in regular classes , *Exceptional Children*, 50, pp.391-399.

Warnock, M. (1978) *The Warnock Report (DES) - Special Educational Needs*. London, H.M.S.O.

Weiner, G. (Ed.) (1985) *Just a Bunch of Girls*. Milton Keynes, Open University Press.

Whitmore, J.R. (1985) New Challenges to Common Identification Processes, in Freeman (Ed.).

Whyte, J. (1986) *Girls into Science and Technology*. London, Routledge & Kegan Paul.

Wright, C. (1986), in Eggleston et al.

Index

Educational Psychology

For Teachers
in Training

EDUCATIONAL PSYCHOLOGY

For Teachers in Training

Steven R. Banks
Marshall University

Charles L. Thompson
University of Tennessee–Knoxville

WEST PUBLISHING COMPANY

Minneapolis/St. Paul   New York
Los Angeles   San Francisco

PRODUCTION CREDITS

Copyediting Allen Gooch
Text Design Diane Beasley
Cover Image © David Bishop/Phototake, NYC
Cover Design Roz Stendahl, Dapper Design
Page Layout DeNee Reiton Skipper
Composition Parkwood Composition Services, Inc.
Photo Credits follow the index.

WEST'S COMMITMENT TO THE ENVIRONMENT

In 1906, West Publishing Company began recycling materials left over from the production of books. This began a tradition of efficient and responsible use of resources. Today, up to 95 percent of our legal books and 70 percent of our college and school texts are printed on recycled, acid-free stock. West also recycles nearly 22 million pounds of scrap paper annually—the equivalent of 181,717 trees. Since the 1960s, West has devised ways to capture and recycle waste inks, solvents, oils, and vapors created in the printing process. We also recycle plastics of all kinds, wood, glass, corrugated cardboard, and batteries, and have eliminated the use of Styrofoam book packaging. We at West are proud of the longevity and the scope of our commitment to the environment.

Production, Prepress, Printing and Binding by West Publishing Company.

BRITISH LIBRARY CATALOGUING-IN-PUBLICATION DATA

A catalogue record for this book is available from the British Library.

LIBRARY OF CONGRESS CATALOGING-IN-PUBLICATION DATA

Banks, Steven R.
Educational psychology/ Steven R. Banks, Charles L. Thompson.
p. cm.
Includes bibliographical references and index.
ISBN 0-314-04443-4
1. Educational psychology: for teachers in training.   2. Classroom management
3. Learning, Psychology of.   4. Educational tests and measurements.   5. Special
education.   I. Thompson, Charles L.   II. Title.
LB1051.B2455   1995
370.15—dc20

94-34058
CIP

CONTENTS

Section II
Managing the Classroom 100

4 Classroom Management— Theory and Practice 102

SECTION III
The Basis for Learning 214

8 Behavioral Approaches to Learning 216

9 Cognitive Approaches to Learning 250

12 Effective Classroom Evaluation 363

13 Children at Risk and Children with Disabilities 388

PREFACE

Educational Psychology: For Teachers in Training is designed primarily as an introductory educational psychology textbook for teacher education students. This text focuses on what educational psychology can provide to teacher education. It is for a "first course" in educational psychology, traditionally taught during the sophomore or junior years. However, this book is also well suited to alternative certification programs, such as a Masters of Arts in Teaching program.

This book differs from other educational psychology texts in at least three ways. First, the organization and sequence of the chapters are somewhat different. We believe that an educational psychology book should address the major concerns of beginning teachers. A number of research studies of beginning teachers indicate that their biggest problems are classroom management, motivating students, and diversity issues.

Because of the importance of these issues we have included them immediately after the basic developmental section. To a large extent the three issues of management, motivation, and diversity form a theme of this text. Every chapter attempts to address these central themes.

Secondly, every chapter is organized in certain specific ways to help students understand the information. One organizational method is as follows: each chapter begins with a case study drawn from a real-life classroom situation. Each case study previews the subject of the chapter and shows its relevance to life in the classroom. Each chapter then moves to theoretical/historical issues, then to applied/practical components, and ends with an epilogue that reformulates the case study. This type of organization provides an advanced organizer with the case study, a framework for moving from theory to practice, and an application of the content of the chapter to each case study.

Another organizational technique used in every chapter is SQ3R (Survey, Question, Read, Recite, and Review). SQ3R is a study method that promotes active learning and helps students retain information. The structure of each chapter is designed to follow the format of SQ3R as closely as possible. For example, within each chapter, headings are framed as questions whenever appropriate. SQ3R is also discussed in Chapter One.

A third component of this text is its focus on current issues in education and how these issues are addressed by psychological research. Included among these current issues are the topics of developmentally appropriate curriculum, whole language instruction, Constructivism, Vygotskyan model of thought and language, the decline of college aptitude scores, tracking versus detracking students, educating at-risk children, and full inclusion.

Thus, the vision of this book is a practical, prescriptive approach, linking educational psychology to teacher education. If there is anything that our students want from an educational psychology text, it is a readable, pragmatic manual for dealing with the problems of teaching and learning. It is our hope that this book provides such an approach.

We would like to acknowledge the encouragement and support of our work from the following people: from Marshall University, Dean Carole Vickers, from the University of Tennessee at Knoxville, Dean Richard Wisniewski, and colleagues and students who have contributed to the book and have participated in teaching educational psychology to our teacher evaluation majors. We extend a special note of thanks to: William A. Poppen, professor at the University of Tennessee, for significant contributions to the book; Donna A. Henderson, professor at East Tennessee State University, for her contribution on Piaget; and Beverly Dupré, professor at Southern University, for writing the Instructor's Manual for the text. Three doctoral students at the University of Tennessee made significant contributions to the book: Vivian Haun for the classroom application sections; Sharon Rostosky for her assistance with the chapters on memory, development, and motivation; and Will Batts for developing the index sections.

Appreciation is also extended to our reviewers for their helpful comments and suggestions:

Julius Gregg Adams
SUNY—Fredonia

Debra J. Anderson
St. Olaf College

George M. Bass, Jr.
College of William & Mary

Gary D. Brooks
University of Texas at El Paso

Beverly B. Dupré
Southern University at New Orleans

Lee K. Hildman
University of Southern Mississippi

Eileen S. Kelble
University of Tulsa

Catherine King
Elon College

Charles LaBounty
Hamline University

Fredric Linder
Virginia Commonwealth University

Joseph H. Maguire
College of the Holy Cross

Janet C. Richards
University of Southern Mississippi

Steven M. Ross
Memphis State University

Jay Samuels
University of Minnesota

Sandra L. Stein
Rider College

M. Mark Wasicsko
Texas Wesleyan University

We also want to thank the excellent, efficient, and experienced editorial and production department at West Publishing Company, headed by editor Clark Baxter, editorial assistant Patricia MacDonald, production editor Emily Autumn, and promotion manager Carol Yanisch. All four know the business of publishing textbooks and have given generously of their time and expertise in bringing our book to completion. Appreciation and recognition also go to those who assisted with the typing and general manuscript preparation: Millie T.

Cheatham, Tinah Rhee Utsman, R. Wade Austin, Sandra Hutchison, and Karen Bradley.

Finally, to our spouses, Janice and Harriet, we give our love and appreciation for your continuing patience, support, understanding, and encouragement given to our work.

Steven R. Banks
Charles L. Thompson

CHAPTER 1

EDUCATIONAL PSYCHOLOGY FOR TEACHERS IN TRAINING

Chapter Outline

WHO WILL BECOME A SUCCESSFUL TEACHER?

Henrietta E. Scott is an African American student who returned to the university setting in 1989. She had taken time out from her studies at college to marry and become a mother and somehow never returned to complete her degree in Music Education. She has lived throughout the eastern part of the United States and in Europe—London, England, and Germany. She has traveled extensively throughout the world. After studying for two years at the university she was selected to participate in the International Student Exchange Program, where she studied German at the University of Bonn, Bonn, Germany.

She did some substitute teaching in city schools while visiting her parents during the illness of her father. She was amazed and appalled at the deterioration of the school system. The teaching methods of the teachers and the interactions between teacher and students were sad and anemic. Because of the length of her dad's illness, she found herself still substitute-teaching two years later. As a substitute, she was able to reach the students and establish rapport. The principals at the various schools where she taught observed her abilities and encouraged her to return to school and complete her education.

Henrietta was able to substitute-teach kindergarten through grade twelve. She spent a great deal of time talking to the students inquiring about their hopes, dreams, and aspirations. After talking with the students in depth, she saw a tremendous need and place for herself. She then chose the elementary level because the younger minds are like sponges ready to soak up all that is about them—good, bad, and indifferent. These young minds are not hampered by the rush of hormones as in the middle school years; nor do they have a false sense of knowing it all as with the secondary years. Hopefully, she will be able to open the exciting door of learning to her young charges to show the positive aspects of living.

She sees the positive aspects of teaching as the eagerness of the children and their willingness to learn. She believes her knowledge of how they learn and the pleasure of watching them learn will be a great motivation and will encourage them to explore and learn. She understands the need for preparing each child for her place in this interdependent world after spending so much time in other cultures and carrying out a research project on the German education system. Henrietta's main concern as she moves about this cam-

INTRODUCTION

Three topics in educational psychology are presented in chapter 1. The chapter begins with an overview of what defines educational psychology, where education has been, and where it is today. Next, the reader will examine the process of becoming a teacher and how this differs from previous decades. The various roles teachers perform also are discussed in light of current changes in education. The chapter ends with a summary of how a knowledge of educational psychology can help teaching be more effective and how it can help students make better grades at all educational levels.

pus and the College of Education is the white men who teach and are quite old and come from another era. They are espousing an ideology but are unable to implement it in their teaching. We learn by example, not by what we hear. The students (her peers) are another major concern. Many (unfortunately too many) are unable to interact with her during the normal course of studying, so she shudders at the prospect of them entering a classroom with an African American child and is afraid to think of what they will be like in a classroom with an African American child.

Sharon Lindsey is a twenty-year-old student in her first year of the teacher education program. Sharon became interested in teaching while tutoring in a special education classroom her junior year in high school. She was encouraged by the special education teacher at her high school to pursue her education at the University. After graduating from high school in Tennessee she began attending a community college. She worked as a substitute teacher for two years. She then transferred to the University. She loves her education classes. She really wishes that she already was teaching. She is convinced that she will be a great teacher.

She loves children and wants to be able to make a difference in students' lives. Sharon loves to help disabled children; they have a special place in her heart. She looks forward to watching kids grow and learn. She thinks that is the most rewarding aspect of being a teacher. One thing that Sharon is very worried about is school violence. In fact, while watching the news one evening, she learned that by 1995, many high school students will be carrying weapons to school. She thinks that this is the most frightening subject facing education today.

Christopher Carpenter is a twenty-two-year-old student in his fourth year of the teacher education program at the University. Chris decided to be a teacher from the experience he had as a private tennis coach. From there he worked in extended child care in the local school system. Through these working and field experiences, volunteer work, and knowledge in the mathematics field, Chris believes that he can show that math is fun and very useful for every student he teaches. He also believes it is important to integrate mathematics with other school curricula.

KEY CONCEPTS

- The relationship between education and psychology has a long and rich heritage.
- Some unresolved issues and problems in education provide a fertile field for the personal growth and development of all professional educators willing to undertake the challenge of resolving these questions and problems.
- The rewards of teaching include a wide range of extrinsic as well as intrinsic benefits.
- Our favorite teachers tend to exhibit the same qualities.

- Beginning teachers list classroom discipline and student motivation as their two most serious problems.
- Applied educational psychology can help teachers work more effectively and can help students learn more and make higher grades.

■ ■ ■

WHAT IS EDUCATIONAL PSYCHOLOGY?

Do you believe that psychology is useful today? Describe some alternative ways that psychology can be applied in educational settings.

One way of defining educational psychology is to define education and psychology. Education is defined as the profession that develops, applies, and researches methods of teaching and learning in schools. Psychology is defined as the profession that studies human behavior. Educational psychology, then, becomes the profession that studies a range of human behavior involved in the educational process including human development, learning, memory, motivation, classroom management, and the evaluation of learning.

The focus of this book will be on what educational psychology has to offer practitioners about becoming effective teachers, classroom managers, and motivators of student learning. Each chapter will be devoted to answering these questions about how one becomes an effective teacher. The discussion of the historical development and current issues in the field of educational psychology will be followed by an examination of the teaching profession.

What Is the Historical Relationship Between Education and Psychology?

Education in America can be traced back to the times when families, who could afford such, hired a live-in tutor for their children. Public education was an attempt to bring the tutor to all children. Naturally, as the number of children per tutor increased, so did the difficulty level of the tutor's job. For assistance with the increasing problems, people looked to psychology for assistance. In fact, the education-psychology partnership in the United States can be traced through the contributions of four men: William James, Edward L. Thorndike, John Dewey, and B.F. Skinner.

William James. William James (1842–1910) is recognized as the first American psychologist. He established the first psychological laboratory in the United States, developed the first psychology course, and, in 1890, wrote the book *Principles of Psychology.* William James is known for developing psychological principles particularly for teachers to apply to their teaching. He was famous for his ability to observe the strengths and weaknesses of various educational practices. For example, in his *Talks to Teachers,* James wrote:

> A friend of mine, visiting a school, was asked to examine a young class in geography. Glancing at the book, she said: "Suppose you should dig a hole into the ground, hundreds of feet deep, how should you find it at the bottom—warmer or colder than on top?" None of the class replying, the teacher said: "I'm sure they know, but I think you don't ask the question quite rightly. Let me try." So, taking the book, she asked: "In

Henry James, the novelist, with brother William James, founder of American psychology (right) (1899).

what condition is the interior of the globe?" and received the immediate answer from the class at once: "The interior of the globe is in a condition of igneous fusion" (1899, p. 150).

Clearly, James was developing the idea of lower and higher levels of learning. The students, by committing the words to memory, were operating at the lowest level of learning. The examiner was testing the children for comprehension and understanding, which generally are regarded as the next level of learning in many such hierarchies.

James also was one of the first psychologists to suggest the importance of individualizing instruction and starting with the learner's current readiness level. James, viewing psychology as a primitive science and teaching as an art, believed that good teachers would have to be highly creative in applying their principles to the art of teaching.

Edward L. Thorndike. Edward L. Thorndike's (1874–1949) principal contribution to educational psychology was his emphasis on studying and researching the learning process in a laboratory setting. He believed that observational studies in the classroom failed to control the many variables affecting the behavior of teachers and students.

Thorndike used cats to study behavior and reinforcers. He was interested in how quickly cats could learn to escape from puzzle boxes when food was used as a reinforcer. Thorndike's research led to his development of the Law of Effect. Briefly, the law states that a connection between a stimulus and a response is strengthened when a response is accompanied or closely followed by a satisfying state of affairs (reinforcement). Likewise, a connection is weakened when the response is accompanied or closely followed by an annoying state of affairs (punishment). He modified the latter half of the Law of Effect to redefine punishment as an annoying event that increases the probability that a cat or person will choose a response leading to a satisfying state of affairs. Once the cats learned or made

Is James correct that teaching is an art? Do you believe that great teachers are born, or, are they made?

Thorndike believed that all learning can be traced back to variations on the Law of Effect. Can you think of situations where learning occurs without reinforcement?

the connection that pulling a rope opened the cage door and a pathway to food, they rejected other "escape" behaviors in favor of rope pulling. Thorndike also defined and described the field of educational psychology in a text by the same name in 1903.

John Dewey. John Dewey (1859–1952), siding with William James, believed that learning could best be studied in the actual classroom. Also like James, he believed that the best learning occurred when instruction was geared to a student's interests and abilities. Two of Dewey's principal publications were *Democracy and Education* (1916) and *Logic: The Theory of Inquiry* (1938). Perhaps Dewey's learning-by-doing concept was his most lasting contribution. This concept states that true learning occurs when the learner can actually apply what has been learned. Dewey's pragmatic approach to learning remains a hallmark of American education. Anytime students are able to apply what they have learned, they have moved to a third level of learning—application, which is above memorization and comprehension mentioned earlier.

Hopefully each reader of this book will be able to move to the application level of the ideas and principles presented. Readers may move to even higher levels of learning, which include (a) analysis (the ability to cite the opposing sides of educational issues and to form solid conclusions from the debate); (b) synthesis (the ability to develop creative solutions to educational problems); and (c) evaluation (the ability to develop the criteria for what constitutes effective educational practice and the ability to evaluate methods and programs in the light of these criterion standards). The six levels of learning described here were derived from Bloom's taxonomy of educational objectives (Bloom, Englehart, Furst, Hill, & Krathwohl, 1956).

B. F. Skinner. Burrhus F. Skinner's (1904–1990) principal contribution to the teaching profession was refining the technology of behavioral psychology into methods that were easy to apply in educational settings. Skinner defined learning as any activity that produced new behavior or modified an existing behavior. Behavior was defined as any observable or measurable action displayed by human and animals. He defined operant or instrumental behavior as behavior that operates or changes the environment or is instrumental in the achievement of a goal. Almost any task-directed behavior such as painting a picture, building a fence, or working on a crossword puzzle can be defined as operant behavior or behavior that is not connected with an obvious stimulus. Those behaviors connected with a stimulus, such as blinking your eyes when you hear a loud noise, are defined as respondent or stimulus-response behavior.

Skinner developed his technology based on the idea that reinforcement and punishment were the two ways to modify behavior. Reinforcement, designed to increase the frequency of a certain behavior, consists of presenting something positive or removing something negative after a desired behavior is performed. Punishment, designed to decrease the frequency of a certain behavior, consists of presenting something negative or removing something positive after a behavior is performed.

A young B. F. Skinner (age 29) in a laboratory at Harvard (1933).

Skinner was able to show how various contingencies (or schedules) of reinforcement could be used to shape desired behaviors. He developed shaping (rewarding successive approximations of the desired behavior) as a method for helping pigeons and people learn difficult tasks that were too difficult to learn in one big step. For example, a child can be reinforced for learning each of the several steps required in long division mathematics problems. Skinner also contributed to the refinement of computerized teaching machines, suggesting that computers offer a way to bring individual tutors to all students. Skinner's book, *The Technology of Teaching* (1968), is perhaps his most helpful publication for the teaching profession and an excellent example of his talent for translating behavioral theory into practice.

In summary, the contributions of James, Thorndike, Dewey, and Skinner formed the foundations of the discipline of educational psychology. The contributions of Thorndike and Skinner will be expanded in the learning theories section. Contributions of other psychologists to the current status of educational psychology will appear throughout the book.

Skinner once said that if you use reinforcement appropriately, you would never have to use punishment. Do you agree?

What Are the Current Issues in Educational Psychology?

An issue can be defined as an unresolved debate containing a pro and a con point of view. Issues in educational psychology include the following questions:

What do you consider the most critical issue in American education?

a. Why have the test scores of American students dropped?
b. What should be done about the declining test scores?
c. What are the best ways to teach the basic skill subjects of reading, writing, and mathematics?
d. How should teaching methods differ for each age level or for each stage of development?
e. How should teaching methods differ, if at all, for students from different cultures?
f. What are the best ways to motivate students to learn?
g. How should our educational system be evaluated or how should learning be evaluated?
h. What are the best ways to manage discipline in the classroom?
i. How much attention should be given to educational topics outside the basic skill areas? For example, how much, if any, time should be given to sex education, drug education, career development, entrepreneurial training, and personal growth and development?
j. Should America 2000 and the other twenty-first century educational reform plans include a social curriculum designed to teach caring for others and other social interest topics?

These are some of the issues that will be discussed in this book. Attention will be given to presenting the pro and the con side of the various answers and proposed solutions for each question we have raised.

For example, on the issue regarding declining test scores, the authors believe that the American public has overlooked some interesting facts. From 1900 to

1963, the United States experienced a highly productive period of educational growth and development. However, baby boomers who entered first grade in 1951 graduated in 1963, the first year the United States lost its first-place ranking in academic achievement (Glenn, 1991). Class size doubled when baby boomers started school. Classes of sixteen to eighteen suddenly became thirty-two to thirty-six. Most teachers will agree that even one or two additional students make teaching significantly more difficult. Class sizes continued to double as the baby boomers moved through twelve years of school. One may argue that teachers, faced with these double-size class loads, were not able to provide the individualized instruction and attention required to continue the higher levels of be able to rely on your "stolen" test and answers if you wrote correct answers to your questions. Should your reading assignment have very few topic headings, you can write your questions from the topic sentences in the major paragraphs.

Review

Before moving to the next topic in your reading, be sure to cover your written answer and check yourself to see if you can recite it correctly. When you complete the chapter, test yourself by covering the answers and reciting the correct answer to each of your questions.

Again, once the questions have been written and answered for each topic in your reading assignment, you will not need to reread the assignment. As we mentioned before, the process works even better in small study groups if each member can be trusted to write good questions and answers. Recitation also can be done in your study group. Remember, the more recitation you do, the longer you will remember your answers.

At this point you may be saying, "This all sounds good for studying the textbook, but what about my classes where the professor tests on the lectures and the textbook?" The same procedure can be used on your lecture notes. The main topics in the lecture can be written in question form and answered just as they were in your readings. Most professors will be happy to evaluate your questions (legally stolen test) and tell you if you are covering important parts of the lecture material.

In summary, if you alone or you and your study partners do the work required in the SQ3R method of study, your grades should improve, and you should retain more of your learning for future use. Try SQ3R yourself by writing one question on each topic heading in this chapter and writing brief, correct answers to each question. The authors made it easier to get started by writing topic headings in question form. Study your legally stolen test until you can recite each answer correctly. Then, when you begin your teaching career, teach your students how to steal your tests legally. That will be a lesson that will serve them well throughout their academic career in so far as making good grades is concerned. However, if you, as a student, want more out of a course than a good grade, you will have to develop an interest in the subject you are studying. When such an interest occurs, the need for SQ3R seems to vanish. The same will hold true for the students you teach. If you are successful in stimulating an interest in what you teach, your students will be motivated to learn and apply their learning even without the aid of the SQ3R method. However, SQ3R can be a valuable system for organizing the information to be learned and remembered.

academic achievement that were achieved before 1963. Even though the baby boomers have come and gone, class sizes have remained the same.

Another factor related to class size is the breakdown of family units. Some examples are the increase of nontraditional family systems with their corresponding lack of extended family support often provided by grandparents and other relatives. Smaller class sizes would make it possible for teachers to provide some of this missing care and attention formerly provided by families. Word (1989) and Nye, Achilles, Zaharias, Fulton, and Wallenhorst (1993) found significant differences in achievement favoring smaller classes (thirteen to seventeen) over larger classes (twenty-two to twenty-five). As mentioned earlier,

Describe classes that you liked. Was there a relationship between the class size and whether or not you personally liked the class?

*Too many students in one class-
room can lead to a breakdown in
the educational process.*

teachers do not need to see research data to appreciate the benefits of smaller
class sizes. Regarding the issue of declining test scores, one could take the position
that large class sizes are primary contributors to this situation and, therefore,
support efforts to return to the pre-baby boomer era of class sizes numbering
sixteen to eighteen. Perhaps the one-room school, with its small pupil-teacher
ratio, built-in peer tutoring, and cooperative learning with lots of personal caring,
may become the educational model of the future. In fact, similar models have
been proposed as solutions to educational problems in inner-city schools and to
the problems involved in retaining and educating the "students at risk" populations (Tindall, 1988).

Of course, powerful arguments can be made for many other reasons for the
decline of test scores and performance on other measures of educational achievement. These arguments range from poor teacher training programs and inadequate curriculum design to the loss of traditional values and the breakdown of
family support systems.

Berliner (1994) raised several questions about a possible disinformation campaign being directed toward public schools by people who stand to profit from
the privatization of schools. He pointed out that actual raw scores on college
board tests only have declined by about five points and that scores have actually

risen for many minority groups. During the time span of 1970 to 1990, Berliner pointed out that we have done exceedingly well in meeting our two national goals of increasing the number of high school and college graduates. In addition, he made the point that the average scores on national achievement tests have increased at a steady rate over the past several decades, and that the average score will always have fifty percent above it and below it. So, if a school should have only forty percent below average on some test, the faculty and community should celebrate their achievement.

The preceding discussion about declining test scores illustrates one purpose of this book—presentation of debated educational issues. Readers are encouraged to consider relevant data in discovering viable solutions to the problems surrounding these issues. Readers are also encouraged to consider other components to the teaching profession: the rewards, the problems, the characteristics of successful teachers, and the requirements to become teachers.

ON BECOMING A TEACHER
Why Would a Person Choose to Be a Teacher?

When the above question was posed to those who had been accepted into a university teacher education program, answers covered the full range of extrinsic and intrinsic reasons. From the extrinsic answers we find that salary levels are becoming more competitive with the other professions. Average teacher salaries have risen above $35,000 (Haselkorn & Calkins, 1993). Some school systems have developed a lead teacher position that pays an annual salary in the seventy-thousand dollar range. Opportunities to earn more money in the teaching profession are opened by qualifying for higher salaries by earning advanced degrees, qualifying for higher merit ratings, and making teaching a full-time job. In fact, the public seems to be more sympathetic to raising teacher salaries as teachers are beginning to extend their teaching time into the summer months. Even with opportunities to teach more weeks, teachers still have considerable time off for personal renewal and rest, both an extrinsic and an intrinsic reward. Some teachers supplement their income with royalties by writing their own textbooks and teaching materials.

Other rewards in the teaching profession involve job benefits. Job security also is a benefit for teachers who have proved themselves worthy of higher employment levels and of tenure. Retirement and health benefits seem to be holding up in the teaching profession at a time when such benefits are being cut by many businesses and industries. In fact, a husband and wife teaching team should do quite well in the area of extrinsic rewards of salary and benefits, as well as the intrinsic rewards of making a significant contribution to society through the profession.

Perhaps the key to success in any profession is the degree of enjoyment one finds in the work itself. Enjoyment of one's work is a major part of intrinsic motivation and a principal key to good mental health. Career satisfaction is one of the basic intrinsic rewards available to teachers. Herr and Cramer (1992), sum-

Take a minute and consider why you want to be a teacher. List and rank your reasons.

marizing several studies on job satisfaction, reported that satisfaction with one's work is directly related to longevity, productivity, tenure, physical health, and mental health.

The teaching profession is especially well suited to the individual who likes to respond to the challenge of taking a demanding job that offers opportunities to make significant positive impacts on the lives of many people. People who want to evaluate their lives by how much they were able to help others may find a very comfortable home in the teaching profession. The opportunities for gaining a sense of self-satisfaction and self-worth abound.

The respect accorded excellent teachers continues to grow. No longer can the average college student become a teacher. Teacher education programs are beginning to adopt rigorous admission standards, including intensive admission board interviews. Admission to teacher education is competitive and generally follows successful completion of the first two years of college with grade point averages ranging from 2.7 to 4.0. Teacher education is being extended into five-year programs culminating in the earning of a master's degree. Teaching is moving from certification programs to professional licensing standards and national tests designed to guarantee better-prepared teachers. Graduation and licensing have become accomplishments worthy of note.

In summary, the rewards of being a successful teacher are many. Benefits include many opportunities for professional and personal growth and development. Today's teachers will have many skills transferrable to other careers should the need arise for them to do so. Teaching offers the opportunity to earn a living by learning things well enough to teach them to others. Perhaps the best benefit from teaching is that teaching a subject is the best way to learn it. Education will become more competitive with the best teachers and best schools reaping most of the extrinsic as well as intrinsic rewards. Exceptional teachers will be rewarded with promotions such as career ladder programs that provide opportunities to earn additional salary. Student academic-gain scores will be used to ensure that teacher evaluation will be fair to those teachers who are teaching large numbers of low-achieving students in lower-achieving schools.

Making a significant contribution to someone's life is one of the rewards of teaching.

What Qualities Will the Successful Teacher Have?

Compile a successful teacher profile. First, list the names of your favorite elementary, middle, and high school teachers. Next, under each name list the reasons why you chose that teacher as your favorite.

Every time this list is prepared by various student, teacher, and parent groups, a fairly consistent list of ten to fifteen teacher behaviors emerges. Favorite teachers are generally viewed as follows:

a. They cared about me.

b. They helped me feel successful.

c. Their classroom was a good place to be and a place where important things happened.

d. They made learning interesting, exciting, and even fun.

e. They taught me how to learn and how to solve problems.

f. They treated me fairly.

g. They were interested in my opinions and ideas.

h. They made me feel good about myself and never "put me down."

i. They challenged me to do my best.

j. They listened to me.

The teacher behaviors listed here help define the traits successful teachers have. For teachers to accomplish a large number of the listed behaviors, they would need to be:

a. enthusiastic people with high energy levels and good health;

b. quality communicators and listeners (That is, they would need to be equally well skilled in sending as well as receiving information.);

c. intelligent and knowledgeable scholars who have important things to teach;

d. creative people who can find new solutions to old problems;

e. people with positive self-esteem who hold optimistic views about others and who prefer working with people in helping relationships;

f. people who love challenges and who are skilled problem solvers;

g. effective leaders with skills in group dynamics;

h. patient, tolerant people who will take the time to help slower learners find the mediating steps in learning difficult material.

Having considered the characteristics of favorite teachers, it is only fair to give teachers the opportunity to list the traits of their ideal students. Bellon (1990), in his research on the attributes teachers desire in their students, found that five traits emerge. Teachers want students who:

Do some students like a class because their personalities are congruent with the teacher's?

a. are motivated to learn;

b. make a commitment to lifelong learning;

c. are self-regulated and independent learners who can function on their own, yet know when they can profit from the help teachers offer;

d. have positive self-esteem;

e. feel empowered to take responsible control of their lives.

The challenge Bellon presented to all teachers is that if educators value these traits in students, they must model these same attributes. Lest teachers forget,

EXCERPTS FROM AN 1887 OHIO TEACHERS EXAMINATION

I. Arithmetic

A. Two men working together built a wall in 12 days. The first, working alone, could have built it in 32 days. If $96 is paid for building the wall, how much should each man receive?

B. The circumference of a dome in the shape of a hemisphere is 66 ft. How many square feet of tin roofing are required to cover it?

C. A vessel can be filled in 57 minutes by one pipe which discharges 6 gals. a minute, and empties in 38 minutes by another. Let the vessel be full, and both pipes be opened at the same instant. How long would the vessel be in emptying?

II. Geography

A. Give proof that the earth rotates.

B. Name the states that border on the Great Lakes, and give their capitals.

C. Define the form of government in England, Russia, and the United States.

III. United States History

A. In whose administration, of whom, and when was the Florida Territory purchased?

B. When was the Fourteenth Amendment adopted? What was the purpose of that amendment?

C. Name the two most prominent American Generals of the Mexican War. Who commanded the Mexican forces?

IV. Grammar

A. Illustrate in sentences the possessive, singular, and plural of mercy, authoress, and ox.

B. Define syncope, antithesis, hypothesis, and coordinate.

C. How many absolute tenses are there? What are they? What are other tenses called? Why?

V. Theory and Practice

A. Give a general classification of the powers of the mind.

B. Define perception, memory, and imagination.

C. Explain the word method of teaching reading.

---

students will probably model good and bad traits. In fact, students often treat teachers the way teachers treat them. Therefore, if teachers desire a cooperative learning environment, they would do well by modeling cooperation and enthusiasm for education.

The American Psychological Association (APA) Task Force on Psychology in Education (1992), the National Board for Professional Teaching Standards support many of Bellon's points. They reported that effective instructional practices result from teachers who (a) are interested in what they teach, (b) respect and value their students as individuals, (c) are positive role models and mentors, (d) employ constructive and regular student evaluations, (e) have high expectations for their students, and (f) use questioning skills to actively involve their students in the learning process. Both groups recommend that teacher education should include instruction on how teacher beliefs, attitudes, and motivation affect student motivation, learning, and performance in the classroom.

How Do Today's Requirements for Successful Teaching Differ from the Early Days of Teaching?

Although teaching has always been a demanding profession, today's teachers are facing many more difficult problems than did their predecessors. Earlier, the basic preparation for teachers consisted of high school graduation and passing an examination compiled by a board of school examiners. The excerpt from an examination given in 1887 in Bellefontaine, Ohio, is presented in application 1.2 (Elliot 1991). You may want to take the test to see if you would have been qualified to teach over one hundred years ago. Five subject categories were tested with each category containing ten questions.

The 1887 examination may seem ludicrously easy compared with the National Teachers Examination. Other teaching requirements also have increased in complexity to meet present-day problems.

What Are the Problems Faced by Beginning Teachers?

Any discussion of problems faced by beginning teachers should start with the problems students bring to school. Academic success cannot be isolated from the student's family, peer, and community relationships. A Children's Defense Fund (1990) publication listed the following facts about the problems occurring in our student population:

a. Every day, 2,989 American children see their parents divorced.
b. Every 26 seconds, a child runs away from home.
c. Every 47 seconds, a child is abused or neglected.
d. Every 7 minutes, a child is killed or injured by a gun.
e. Every 53 minutes, a child dies because of poverty.
f. Every day, 100,000 children are homeless.
g. Every school day, 135,000 children bring guns to school.
h. Every 8 seconds of the school day, a child drops out.
i. Every day, 6 teenagers commit suicide.

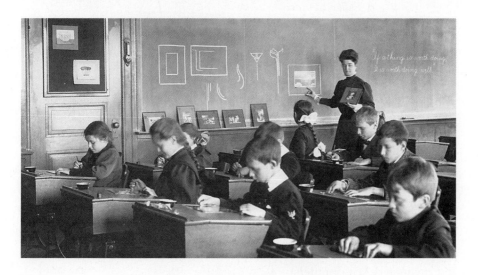

A New England classroom during the 1890s.

Family

a. Divorce and single-parent homes
b. Death, loss, and grief
c. Parent's job loss
d. Substance abuse
e. Physical, sexual, emotional abuse
f. Poverty
g. Homelessness
h. Change of residence and school
i. Incarceration
j. Both parents working

Interpersonal

a. Communication skills
b. Peer pressure
c. Accepting responsibility for behavior
d. Respecting the rights of others
e. Understanding and accepting individual differences
f. Getting along with others

School

a. Attitudes about school
b. Competition
c. Failure
d. School phobia
e. Learning styles
f. Behavior
g. Conflicts with teachers
h. Test anxiety

Personal

a. Stress management
b. Depression
c. Suicide
d. Eating disorders
e. Addictions
f. Health problems

Do you think that teachers and schools are expected to step in and help children when the family system fails?

Bennett (1993) compiled data that support the view that conditions for our youth have been in a downward spiral over the past fifty years. In 1940, teachers identified their top school problems as talking out of turn; chewing gum; making noise; running in halls; cutting in line; dress code infractions; and littering. In 1990, teachers identified drug and alcohol abuse; pregnancy; suicide; rape; robbery; and assault as the most serious problems in America's public schools.

Glenn (1991), quoting the surgeon general, pointed out that one thousand youth between the ages of twelve and twenty-three die each week in the United States. The first "crack" babies (children born to parents addicted to the "crack" form of cocaine) entered school in 1992 with problems involving hyperactivity and attention deficit disorders.

Basically our students' problems fall into four general areas: family, interpersonal issues, school, and personal adjustment. The American School Counselor Association (1990) listed several specific problems under each area (see figure 1.1).

Although all problems can have an impact on the learner, teachers cannot be expected to be experts in all the problem areas listed here. The importance of the counselor's role is clearly evident in our schools. Therefore, the authors take the position that teachers need to understand the impact various problems will have on their students so the teachers will know when to seek help from the counselor for their students. One focus of this book will be directed toward school-related problems.

Veenman (1984) has compiled some data on the twenty-four problems most frequently cited by beginning teachers. Over the past several years, classroom discipline continues to be the problem most frequently cited by teachers at the primary and secondary school levels. In fact, classroom discipline is ranked nearly twice as often as the second-ranked problem, which is motivating students. The remaining twenty-two problems, which range from dealing with individual differences to large class size, are listed in figure 1.2. Another goal of the authors is to provide helpful information on those problems in the remaining pages of the textbook.

What Mistakes Do Beginning Teachers Make?

Many of the mistakes teachers make can be deduced from what was written about the traits of effective teachers. Shortcomings in any one area will cause problems for beginning teachers.

Specifically, beginning teachers may model their teaching style and behavior after former teachers who were not especially effective. For example, beginning

In some of today's high schools students must pass through a security checkpoint to enter school.

teachers may give true/false tests every Friday because when they were in school, they had true/false tests every Friday. Instead of adhering to such traditions, beginning teachers may choose to reconsider their past educational experiences to discover what worked well and what did not. Once again, beginning teachers would do well to remember that students will tend to give to you what you give to them. A caring teacher who plans useful, interesting, and even fun learning experiences will do well, while those who don't, won't.

Many beginning teachers err by not entering their first job with a workable instructional plan and with an effective classroom management program. Without such plans, beginning teachers may try to maintain control of their classes by using the boss-manager style of management rather than the lead-manager style advocated by Shanker (1989) and Glasser (1990). Boss managers try to overpower rather than empower their students. They fail to win their students' cooperation and tend to focus more on failure and wrong answers rather than emphasizing success by building on right answers. In summary, beginning teachers who are thoroughly prepared to teach their subject and who have a person-oriented approach to managing their classrooms should avoid many first-year pitfalls.

What Roles Do Teachers Perform?

Scholar. The teaching profession is becoming so complex that one can argue that effective teachers will have to be both specialists and generalists. The spe-

FIGURE 1.2
A Ranking of Problems
Experienced by Beginning
Teachers

1.	Discipline
2.	Motivation
3.	Individual differences
4.5	Assessment
4.5	Parent relationships
6.5	Organization
6.5	Insufficient materials and supplies
8.	Student problems
9.	Teaching load
10.	Colleague relationships
11.	Planning
12.	Effective use of different teaching methods
13.	Awareness of school policies and rules
14.	Determining student learning levels
15.	Knowledge of subject matter
16.	Clerical work
17.	Administrator relationships
18.	Inadequate equipment
19.	Working with slow learners
20.	Working with cultural differences
21.	Effective use of text and curriculum guide materials
22.	Lack of spare time
23.	Inadequate guidance and support
24.	Large class size

JOB STRESS AND JOB BURNOUT IN TEACHERS

Herbert Freudenberger coined the term job burnout in 1975. According to Freudenberger (1975), job burnout is a syndrome of persistent physical and emotional exhaustion produced by excessive demands on the energy, strength and resources of the individual. Certain helping professions, such as nurses, counselors and teachers, seem particularly susceptible to this type of syndrome.

For instance, when teachers encounter a high level of job stress for a sustained period of time, their ability to cope with that stress may become exhausted. They may begin to display psychosomatic complaints, such as headaches or sleep disorders. They may also exhibit other stress-related physical illnesses, work absenteeism, or a complete lack of concern about their work. When these responses persist over time they may develop into a syndrome labeled job burnout.

One finding in the research (Banks & Necco, 1990; Maslach & Jackson, 1986) is that younger, less experienced teachers report more job stress and burnout. Beginning teachers must develop their own instructional methods, learn to cope with student misbehavior, and deal with motivating recalcitrant students.

Thus, their level of stress is greater than with more experienced teachers.

Another possible contributing factor in producing burnout in beginning teachers is inflated expectations about work. Schwab, Jackson, and Schuler (1986) contended that many individuals begin a teaching career with great expectations of making a contribution to society and their school. After a year or two on the job they realize that they are not living up to these expectations. Such a discrepancy may produce a great deal of stress and frustration about the job.

Weinstein (1988) indicated that unrealistic expectations by new teachers may be due to a lack of realistic exposure to the job during preservice teacher training programs. After entering the work force these teachers experience "reality shock" which forces them to markedly revise their goals and expectations.

It appears that beginning teachers must acquire a variety of skills, both professional and psychosocial, in their early years. If they can effectively "learn the ropes" during the first three years on the job, their reported level of stress should subsequently decline.

cialist role demands both scholarship and instructional expertise. Naturally, teachers need to be subject-matter specialists who stay current with the content and research in their teaching fields. They are scholars who function as models for their students. They know their subject well enough to make it understandable and meaningful to their students. Specifically, they are able to find those mediating learning steps that help students move from what they know to what they need to understand.

Instructional Specialist. Effective teachers are, by definition, instructional specialists. Instructional specialists know how to teach in ways to accommodate a variety of student learning styles. They know how to incorporate a variety of teaching aids in their instructional plan, including computers, films, videotapes and audiotapes, and overhead projectors. They also use a variety of teaching formats, including independent study, cooperative learning (dyads and teams), and peer tutoring. As instructional specialists, they are able to apply remedial as well as developmental methods in helping their students take that next step in learning. Most importantly, instructional specialists know how to strike a productive balance in their teaching in relation to how much time is spent in "tell me," "show me," and "let me do it" activities.

Psychologist. Although teachers do not practice as unlicensed psychologists, they do rely heavily on psychology. Teachers may be the frontline mental health workers in our culture. Students' mental health relates directly to how well they are doing with school work and peer relationships, and teachers can have a powerful influence on both.

The APA (1992) Task Force on Psychology in Education highlighted the teacher's contribution to students' mental health. It reported that self-esteem and learning are mutually reinforcing and that both are heightened when teachers establish respectful and caring relationships with their students. Acceptance of their students as individuals with unique talents and potential is another way teachers can build the self-esteem and learning relationship.

Effective teachers practice good listening and counseling skills and teach problem-solving methods. Effective teachers understand and apply the principles of group dynamics in their classroom. The same is true for applying the principles of motivation and learning theory to the classroom setting. Finally, effective teachers are knowledgeable about testing and assessment procedures for evaluating their students' learning.

Scientist and Practitioner. Teachers are scientist-practitioners when they use research methods and models in their work. For example, teachers may research the effectiveness of their teaching. They also use research models when they analyze a student's learning problem, plan an intervention, and evaluate the intervention procedure. Teachers actually may conduct research in their teaching field. However, it would seem that the teacher's role leans more to the practitioner's side of the continuum. Most of the teacher's day is concerned with the application of the many principles listed in the other roles. Many teachers, though, do use the scientific method of hypothesis testing as well as other problem-solving models in their teaching. Also, it is not uncommon to find considerable student research culminating in science fair projects.

Career Educator. On May 4, 1994, President Clinton signed the School to Work Opportunities bill, which was designed to build partnerships between school and business and to develop educational programs leading to high-skill, high-wage careers. Teachers will be given opportunities to spend their summers working in businesses and professions related to the subject matter they teach. Teachers will be expected to bring their summer learning experiences back to their classrooms and to integrate them with their subject matter. In fact, business and professional people will team teach much of the subject matter with the classroom teacher. Students will be given more opportunities to spend one-half of each school day working in a business or professional setting. Such employer and educator partnerships will provide students with opportunities to complete a career major, to prepare for work after high school, to prepare for postsecondary education, and prepare them for productive lives of continued work and learning. Both students and teachers will be paid for the work they do in a business or professional setting. The passage of the School to Work Opportunities bill will provide an opportunity for teachers to increase their effectiveness in connecting classroom learning to rewarding and high-paying careers; in doing so, teachers may become a primary source of career education for their students.

However, while the "schools to work" focus seems to be a step in the right direction, it may not address the critical issues of creating a new job for newly trained workers. In this regard it would be useful to expand and create programs, such as those offered by Junior Achievement, which teach students how to organize and run their own business. To focus time, energy, and money exclusively on teaching students how to work for someone else may miss the more important point of how to create jobs for others.

In summary, the many and varied roles teachers perform could transfer to a variety of other careers requiring the same skills teachers perform on a daily basis. However, the authors are doubtful that the transfer to teaching from other careers is done as easily. The days of "Those who can, do; and those who can't, teach" are long gone.

What other roles do teachers play? Should teachers play a surrogate parent role?

SUMMARY

Education and psychology have close ties. Students learn various ways to meet their needs. Some of these ways are counterproductive and create more problems. For instance, one major challenge currently faced is the task of serving "at-risk" children. These are the children who are in danger of leaving school before they have the necessary skills to function successfully in today's world. Students need to learn better ways to meet their needs. Education is about learning and psychology is about human behavior, emotions, and thoughts. Teaching brings the best of both disciplines together to accomplish the most important task of our time: the education of our children.

CHAPTER REVIEW

1. Define educational psychology in your own words by describing the relationship between education and psychology.
2. List the three educational issues you believe to be most critical and defend your answers.
3. How would you sell a career in teaching to a colleague who would be an excellent teacher?
4. As a beginning teacher, list the best two ideas you have for overcoming the top two problems beginning teachers face.
5. Considering the various roles teachers perform, select the one you consider to be your greatest strength and describe how you would capitalize on this strength in the classroom.
6. Describe how you could adapt the SQ3R study method to fit your learning style and consequently raise your own academic performance.

OVERCOMING PROBLEMS FOR BEGINNING TEACHERS

EPILOGUE

From our case study at the beginning of this chapter, we learned that Henrietta Scott, Sharon Lindsay, and Christopher Carpenter want to be teachers. They all believe they have what it takes to be successful teachers. Two of the three have some concerns about problems of violence, hate, and crime in our schools. From your study of chapter 1, what degree of success do you believe each of the three prospective teachers will have? Rank them first, second, and third depending on how you view their potential success as teachers. Explain how you arrived at your ranking from the material presented in this chapter.

Finally, you may want to order the Careers in Teaching Handbook by David Haselkorn and Andrew Calkins, which will be sent to you at no cost by Recruiting New Teachers, Inc., of Belmont, Massachusetts. You can get your copy by calling 1-800-45-TEACH.

REFERENCES

American Psychological Association. (1992). *Learner-centered psychological principles: Guidelines for school redesign and reform (Draft #3)*. Washington, DC: American Psychological Association.

American School Counselor Association (1990). *The professional development guidelines for elementary school counselors: Self-audit*. Alexandria, VA: American School Counselor Association.

Banks, S. R., & Necco, E. G. (1990). The effects of special education category and type of training on job burnout in special education teachers. *Teacher Education and Special Education, 13,* 187–191.

Bellon, J. (1990, June). *Some thoughts about teacher renewal*. Paper presented at the meeting of the Southeastern Consortium for Minorities in Engineering, Knoxville, TN. The University of Tennessee, SECME Conference.

Bennett, W. (1993). *The index of leading cultural indicators*. Washington DC: The Heritage Foundation.

Berliner, D. (1994, April). *The misinformation campaign against public education*. Paper presented at Bristol, TN, for an education conference sponsored by the East Tennessee State University College of Education, Johnson City, TN.

Bloom, B., Englehart, M., Furst, E., Hill, W., and Krathwohl, O. (1956). *Taxonomy of educational objectives: The classification of educational goals. Handbook 1: The cognitive domain*. New York: Longman.

Children's Defense Fund. (1990). *Children 1990: A report card, briefing book, and action primer*. Washington, DC.

Dewey, J. (1938). *Logic: The theory of inquiry.* New York: Holt.

Dewey, J. (1916). *Democracy and education.* New York: MacMillan.

Elliott, M. (1991). *History of bokescreek township school.* West Mansfield, OH: Alumni Association of West Mansfield, OH.

Freudenberger, H. J. (1975). The staff-burnout syndrome in alternative institutions. *Psychotherapy: Theory, Research and Practice, 12,* 72–83.

Glasser, W. (1990). *The quality school: Managing students without coercion.* New York: Harper & Row.

Glenn S. (1991, June). *Developing capable people.* Paper presented at the meeting of the American School Counselor Association Conference. Des Moines, IA.

Haselkorn, D., & Calkins, A. (1993). *Careers in teaching handbook.* Belmont, MA: Recruiting New Teachers, Inc.

Herr, E., & Cramer, S. (1992). *Career guidance and counseling through the life span* (4th ed.). New York: Harper Collins College.

James, W. (1899). *Talks to teachers on psychology: And to students on some of life's ideals.* New York: Holt. (Reprinted in *The Works of Williams James,* 1983, Cambridge, MA: Harvard University Press).

James, W. (1890). *Principles of psychology.* Two volumes. New York: Holt.

Maslach, C., & Jackson, S. E. (1986). *Maslach burnout inventory manual* (2nd ed.). Palo Alto, CA: Consulting Psychologists Press.

National Board for Professional Teaching Standards. (1994). What teachers should know and be able to do. Washington, DC: National Board for Professional Teaching Standards.

Nye, B., Achilles, C., Zaharias, J., Fulton B., & Wallenhorst, M. (1993). Tennessee's bold experiment: Using research to inform policy and practice. *Tennessee Education, 22*(03), 10–20.

Robinson, F. (1961). *Effective study.* New York: Harper & Brothers.

Schwab, R. L., Jackson, S. E., & Schuler, R. S. (1986). Educator burnout: Sources and consequences. *Educational Research Quarterly, 10,* (3), 14–30.

Shanker, A. (1989, March). *The class of 2001: Standards and values in a multicultural society.* Paper presented at the meeting of the American Association of Colleges for Teacher Education. Anaheim, CA.

Skinner, B. (1968). *The technology of teaching.* New York: Appleton-Century-Crofts, Educational Division, Meredith Corporation.

Thorndike, E. (1903). *Educational psychology.* New York: Lemcke & Buechner.

Tindall, L. (1988). *Retaining at risk students: The role of career and vocational education.* Information series No. 335. Columbus OH: ERIC Clearinghouse on Adult, Career, and Vocational Education, the Center on Education and Training for Employment, The Ohio State University, (ERIC Document Reproduction Service No. ED 303 683)

Veenman, S. (1984). Perceived problems of beginning teachers. *Review of Educational Research, 54,* 143–78.

Weinstein, C. S. (1988). Preservice teachers' expectations about the first year of teaching. *Teaching and Teacher Education, 4,* 1, 31–40.

Word, E. (1989). *Project star: Final report.* Knoxville, TN: Bureau of Educational Research and Service, The University of Tennessee, Knoxville, TN.

SECTION I

DEVELOPMENTAL ISSUES

CHAPTER 2

Child and Adolescent Development

■ ■ ■

Chapter Outline

A Teenager's Struggle with Adolescence

You are the teacher of a thirteen-year-old girl named Janice B. During the past semester, Janice's behavior has markedly changed. Previously, Janice's school records indicated that her grades were A's or B's with an occasional C in mathematics. Her attendance was excellent. Former teachers characterized her as "easy to instruct," "willing to accept guidance," and "a class favorite."

In the past few months, Janice has become very critical of herself and of those around her. She speaks out of turn in class and puts down other children. She has grown physically to the extent that she is one of the tallest children in the class. The other students occasionally make jokes about her size. This has further isolated Janice from her peers. She also has missed a number of classes without any excused absence. Her grades have suffered accordingly.

When you tried to talk to her privately about her schoolwork, Janice sat and glared at you without comment. After school she hangs out with a gang of older students from the local high school. Her parents are divorced. Janice lives with her mother, who works two jobs to support them. Janice appears to have little supervision or guidance at home.

As her teacher, what should you do about Janice's attitude and behavior?

INTRODUCTION

Reflect on your own life history or the life histories of people with whom you grew up. Did biological and environmental determinants seem more important in childhood? Did historical forces seem more important during adolescence?

The study of human growth and development focuses on the interaction of our biological endowment with our social environment. A traditional view of development stresses the growing and changing student in a static world. The current view is one of the changing student in a changing world.

Three major influence patterns are said to affect the interactive and dynamic relationship between the changing student and the changing world. One of these is called the *normative, age-graded influence,* which consists of biological and environmental determinants that generally are correlated with age. Examples are maturational events (changes in height) and socialization events (dating) that tend to occur at approximately the same time during the life span and last for a similar period for most students.

A second influence is called *normative, history-graded influence* and consists of biological and environmental factors that are correlated with a historical time. For example, the "baby boomers" were products of a particular time in history and were influenced by a variety of factors that did not influence their parents, such as the cold war, a polluted environment, and the sexual revolution.

The third set of influences, *nonnormative, life-event factors,* are not related to age or biological factors. In fact, they may not occur for all students. Having parents who divorce is an example.

Baltes, Reese, and Lipsitt (1980) contend that these sources of influence have various impact over the life span. *Normative, age-graded influences* are said to be significant during childhood and again in old age. *Normative, history-graded factors* are said to be particularly important during the adolescent period. *Nonnormative, life event* influences are said to be most prominent during middle adulthood and again during old age.

Thus, every student has a specific developmental profile produced by each of these patterns of influences. In addition, these separate patterns of influences interact to produce a unique developmental history for each student in a classroom. A major focus on this chapter is to detail these influences and how they impact on individual students in the classroom.

KEY CONCEPTS

- Knowledge about developmental stages is very complex and unlikely to be learned only through observation.
- Knowledge of developmental stages and theories is essential in planning developmentally appropriate educational practices.
- Adolescence is a developmental period when many new abilities and behaviors emerge.
- Early or late development has the potential for significant impact, both psychologically and socially, on the developing adolescent.
- Children progress through a series of stages of moral development.

The study of identical twins provides one of the best methods for distinguishing between the biological and environmental determinants of behavior.

CHAPTER 2
Child and Adolescent Development

31

WHAT IS THE STUDY OF DEVELOPMENT?

Describe the crucial events in early or middle adulthood that seem to occur for all or nearly all people. Do these events form a sequence of stages similar to developmental stages in childhood?

Developmental psychology concerns investigating aspects of human psychological development and change. The study of development includes changes in behavior, thinking, emotions, physical features, and social relationships. Traditionally, the study of developmental psychology was concerned only with childhood and the terms developmental psychology and childhood were practically synonymous. Adolescent development gradually became included as an area of study at colleges and universities. Developmental psychology now includes the entire life span and recently books on adult development or life-span psychology have become popular.

You might be surprised to learn that there is disagreement on a definition of psychological development (Hoppe-Graff, 1989). Developmentalists currently seem to be focusing on two broad questions. The first question is: "What is the sequence of stages during development?" In effect, the task is to determine what stages of development occur first, second, third, etc. The second question is about transitions and concerns how transitions from one stage to another happen: "How and why does change in a person (the developing system) come about?" This chapter will detail some significant developments that happen for children and adolescents at various ages. It also presents some major explanations about transitions from one stage to another or from one level of development to another.

■ ■ ■

WHY LEARN ABOUT DEVELOPMENTAL STAGES?

There are several advantages to knowing developmental stages. Knowledge about developmental stages is not "common sense", nor is it possible to learn these very complex factors through mere observation. One of the valuable products of knowing principles and facts about developmental psychology is that we can get an idea of what is "normal" for a child or adolescent at a given age. These age-related norms (Gesell, 1954; Ilg, 1984) give parents, teachers, and psychologists the standards needed to identify those students who are performing tasks well above or below the average. Early identification of abnormal development combined with thoughtful interventions can help children reach their full potential.

The test by Horrocks, Horrocks and Trayer (1960) in the Applications section illustrates some of these basic developmental questions. For instance, the answer to one question indicates: As children approach adolescence, they increasingly turn to social groups of their own age. Another illustration from the Applications is: Leadership roles among peer groups during the pre-adolescent period often are determined by physical size and strength. While some of the test questions and answers are not quite as valid as in 1960, they still illustrate the reasons for completing research and establishing norms for appropriate development.

Horrocks, Horrocks, and Trayer (1960) developed a test to aid teachers and counselors in understanding developmental principles. Many of these items, taken from the original test, serve to illustrate the point that there are many facts and principles in the field of human growth and development that are important knowledge for teachers and others who work with children and adolescents.

Take the following eight-item test about human growth and development.

How Knowledge Can Help You

1. The majority of adolescents practice masturbation:
   a. infrequently or not at all
   b. only if they have been under the influence of bad company
   c. to some extent
   d. only if they are physically abnormal
2. As children approach adolescence, conduct is increasingly dictated by:
   a. spontaneous social groups
   b. the home
   c. sex differences
   d. the child himself
3. Rapid growth in height through adolescence:
   a. occurs just prior to puberty
   b. occurs during the year following pubescence
   c. is unrelated to pubescence, but occurs in the early teens
   d. occurs earliest in small individuals
4. Normal growth and development in school are:
   a. more important than knowledge of subject matter
   b. not nearly so important as earning good grades
   c. in many ways blocked by conventional procedures
   d. the natural outcome of conventional teaching methods
5. A good teacher realizes that normal physical development is highly desirable but:
   a. that emotional guidance is a greater concern of the school
   b. it must be considered second to academic learning
   c. that attention to it should be left to the home
   d. it is of first importance in relation to other aspects of development
6. Leadership among preadolescents is most often dependent upon:
   a. mental precocity
   b. social status
   c. physical size and strength
   d. willingness to extend fair treatment to followers
7. The relation between physical growth and intelligence is such that on the average:
   a. brighter children tend to develop faster
   b. brighter children develop slower, but for a longer period
   c. dull children develop faster
   d. no conclusions can be drawn
8. Differences in interests between preadolescents and postadolescents are due:
   a. for the most part to cultural influences
   b. for the most part to maturational factors
   c. to a combination of maturational and cultural changes
   d. inheritance through combination of the genes

The answers to the items are: No. 1 (c), No. 2 (a), No. 3, (a), No. 4 (c), No. 5 (d), No. 6 (c), No. 7 (a), and No. 8 (c).

How did you do on the test? These items are among the very few that still apply today. Many other items from the original eighty-item test not included in the sample are still good items but the answers have changed as a result of new findings. In addition, the answers to some of the questions have changed because of changing factors affecting the developmental process. Some of these changing factors are biological, nutritional, and environmental. In short, the answers have changed because we do not live in a static world.

DEVELOPMENTALLY APPROPRIATE EDUCATIONAL PRACTICES

The current view of many educational psychologists is that educational goals should be based on developmental factors rather than on arbitrary decisions. Educational methods, as well as goals, should rely on biological and experiential maturity (readiness rather than age) (Elkind, 1987). The traditional school approach, especially at the early grades, is said to place children under excessive pressure that in turn thwarts learning. The alternative is to adapt developmentally appropriate practices in classrooms through the use of multiple work areas. In these areas, children can move about and interact with learning materials. Of course, this takes place under the guidance and supervision of a skilled teacher. There is considerable disagreement about what constitutes a good definition of developmentally appropriate educational methods during the early childhood years. There is, however, general agreement about certain practices that should be used and others that should be avoided (Bowman, 1993). Retention in kindergarten and the early grades and standardized achievement testing are deplored. Both are opposed because they may have negative effects on the social-emotional development of children. Performance assessment gained via parent interviews, direct observations of children and reviewing portfolios of each child's work is favored. Heterogeneous age and ability grouping is favored instead of teaching children in groups of high and low performance.

Providing Extra Help with Tutoring

A number of studies have demonstrated the value of tutoring, especially peer tutoring approaches. A number of carefully designed programs have proved to be a good approach for students in the upper elementary grades and the middle school years. Significant gains in achievement are obtained by both the students being tutored and the student doing the tutoring (Cohen, Kulic, & Kulic, 1982). Many of the benefits also extend to social and motivational areas.

Presented here is a systematic approach that can be used as a peer tutoring model or with volunteer tutors.

The first step to a good tutoring program is organization. The tutor must have access to learning materials. For example, if the program is for tutoring in reading, the tutor would need a book or other reading materials for the student to read. It is also a good idea to have paper handy for noting new words to be learned or new problems to work on if the tutoring is in mathematics. A supply of three by five cards and a felt-tip pen can be useful for making flash cards in math or new words in reading. A folder, two-pocket style, serves as a place to keep the materials between tutoring sessions. Other supplies to consider are a dictionary, calculator, or other useful tools.

The next step, and the first activity, is to establish a personal and friendly relationship. The student to be tutored might tell some things about herself, especially any positive aspects or experiences. Boser and Poppen (1978) have found that an underestimated skill in establishing new relationships between adults and youth is for the adult to share some important things about himself without dominating the conversation. It is useful to try to identify commonalties.

The next step is when the first actual tutoring begins. If the tutoring is in reading, the student should start by reading. Likewise if math is the subject, the student should attempt some math problems. It is important that the tutor check with the teacher to be sure that the student can demonstrate some success at this level. Missing every problem can be deflating! In other words, the materials used at this level should not be too difficult. The tutor should listen as the student reads or watch while a math problem is attempted. Assistance can be given if a student has trouble attacking a word or a problem. The tutor should give the answer (either say the word or solve the problem) if the student is stumped. The tutor would ask the student to tell him the word, letter by letter, or the problem, digit by digit, while the tutor writes the word or problem on a separate sheet of paper called a word or problem list. The student would watch the tutor write out the word, letter by letter, while the student says each letter. It is a good idea to put the page number next to the word or problem so you can find where you are in the learning materials. Stop this process whenever a predetermined number of words or problems have been missed. Five is a good number. Ten probably is too many for one tutoring session. The idea is that if a student can learn five new words or can solve five problems, she is making a good start. It might be a good idea to end this part of the tutoring by talking about the story being read or the problems being done to be sure that the student comprehends what it is you are trying to teach.

Right after that it is a good idea to make flash cards for the five words or problems missed. Ask the student to tell you the words or problems while you write them on the cards. Make the words or problems large so that they are easy to read.

After the cards have been made, it is good to review them one more time. Keep a record of the student performance. For example, place a small one in the corner of the flash card if the student reads the word correctly. Use a zero for misses. After a student has identified a word correctly five times, consider it learned. It might be good to place them in a "word bank" to show the student how many new words have been learned.

If a student is having particular difficulty with learning to read a new word, she might try tracing the letters of the word one by one while the two of you spell out and then say the word. Any good reward system can be used to enhance the tutoring approach.

Each following tutoring session would be the same as described here except it might begin with a review of the flash cards from the previous sessions. In summary, the process starts by establishing a relationship

01011111 ㉞

understand

Sample Flash Card

(It is a good idea to plan ways to maintain it, too.), doing a study phase while noting problems and writing them down in a special and systematic way, making new flash cards for review, and reviewing words. Thereafter, each session might start by reviewing words or problems to be learned, doing some new reading or math, making flash cards, and reviewing them.

Tutoring Approach

Described here is an approach to helping students learn new words. The method could be modified for use with simple math problems or any assignment.

The method starts by engaging the tutor and the student in reading or whatever is assigned. The assumption is that a student learns to read by reading or learns to do math by doing math problems.

It also is a good idea to take the words learned (the ones in the word bank) and review them from time to time. It also is a real ego boost for the student to see how many words she has actually learned during tutoring. (See the figure illustrating what a flash card might look like in a reading tutoring program).

By having data that show the range of behaviors typical for a certain age, inexperienced teachers and first-time parents may accept actions that might otherwise seem problematic. One example is when children who are beginning to learn to write reverse letters and do mirror-image copying at ages five or six. Such behavior is normal and will be ignored by the informed adult unless it persists until age seven. If so, a learning or perceptual disability may be present.

Adults who know what developmental tasks are awaiting students in the next few months can better plan educational programs that, in effect, pave the way for smooth developmental progress. Such programs are called *developmentally appropriate* educational opportunities. Current studies that gather data for age-related norms show that the normal course of growth changes over time. A good example is presented by Berryman, Hargreaves, Herbert, and Taylor (1991), who try to answer the question, 'When is puberty?" Records from 1860 England indicate that girls began menstruation on the average at age sixteen. The age of menarche has dropped since that time to twelve years-six months. One argument is that improved nutrition, medical care, and standard of living have effected the change. Other changes in age-related norms could be noted. For example, full adult height occurs earlier now than formerly. The point is that age-related norms change, sometimes markedly, depending on several biological and environmental factors (Brooks-Gunn & Warren, 1989).

There are some major cautions about taking a description of children at a certain age and applying it strictly to all individuals. Developmentalists study and see a growing person who is a complex intermixture of behavioral, emotional, moral, and intellectual systems. Yet, other disciplines constantly challenge these developmental principles because of their simplicity. Anthropologists highlight cultural diversity by pointing out that cultural and ethnic factors influence growth patterns. Biologists remind us of the profound effects of genetics and suggest that we underestimate the predictability of these factors. Social historians detail the effect of historical forces on physical and emotional development. Also, feminists refute data gathered to note gender differences, and family theorists contend that we underestimate the results of people trying to satisfy their needs within social systems, especially the family system (Damon, 1989). Mindful of this caveat, we present information about various stages (or ages) of development in children and adolescents.

In this chapter, the definition of developmental theory is the principles of and influences on the person throughout the life span. However, we will focus primarily on the time from preschool through adolescence. Growth and development is onward during this period, as height, weight, and abilities all increase. Reversals do occur, usually as catabolism, which is a form of destructive metabolism or change in living tissue. Growth and development are characterized within this chapter as (1) a series of identifiable stages, (2) a forward progression, (3) an increasing specialization, and (4) a set of causal forces that can be either genetic or environmental.

Presented are various principles, norms, and expectations about development for children who are preschool through the secondary grades. Each description will present certain facts about the average child at a specific chronological age and some major patterns of development occurring during that age.

Do theories involving development stages simply end up labeling children? Is there an unintentional stereotyping of children when they are categorized as being in one stage or another stage?

WHAT ARE SOME OF THE GENERAL PRINCIPLES OF DEVELOPMENT?

The following are statements of general principles of development that apply to the growth of children and adolescents. The American Psychological Association (APA) Task Force on Psychology in Education has developed *Learner-Centered Psychological Principles*. Principle eight, which is a statement on developmental factors, notes that students "proceed through orderly, identifiable progressions of physical, intellectual, emotional, and social development that are a function of unique genetic and environmental factors" (1992). We include below a somewhat more comprehensive list of developmental factors and principles of growth.

Developmental Factors

Childhood is the foundation period of life. Early patterns of behavior continue throughout life. Personality traits, attitudes, habits, even health status established in the first five to six years correlate highly with level of development and adjustment to life as an adult.

Growth and development are continuous but occur in spurts instead of a progressive, upward direction. Physical, emotional, or mental growth may appear to be at a standstill for periods of time. Growth is uneven and occasionally very rapid.

Development is definable, predictable, sequential, and continues through adulthood. Persons progress through the same stages but at individual rates because of the intertwining of inherent capacities with the physical and social environment. The stages of physical, emotional, social, and mental development are overlapping. The transition from one stage to another usually may be either a gradual or a dramatic process.

There are times when heavy demands are placed on the person and change is rapid and critical to continuing development. During these critical times, children are especially vulnerable to adverse environmental conditions. For example, during adolescence, quick physical growth may negatively affect self-concept development or peer relationships.

Mastering developmental tasks for one period serves as a basis for smooth transition through the next developmental stage. There are times when a developmental task can best be accomplished. If the task is not accomplished during a period of equilibrium, the process may become hard to master. Hazards exist both from the environment and within the person.

Physical gender differentiation appears to be greater as children near adolescence. Do you think that certain aspects of psychological development, such as gender role differentiation, follow a similar pattern?

Principles of Growth

There are many ways that development is shown to be orderly, not random. Below are some of the rules that apply to growth.

The principle of differentiation. This principle of growth means that development proceeds from the simple to the complex, from homogeneous to heterogeneous, and from the general to the specific. Simple to complex growth is shown when babies first wave their arms and then later learn to control their fingers. Another example is in the growth of language. Babies progress from cooing to babbling to words—again from the simple to the complex.

The body configuration of boys and girls at birth is much more similar than during adolescence, thereby indicating homogeneous to heterogeneous growth. Babies display general to specific development by moving their whole bodies in response to stimuli and only later will they react with a more specific body part.

Cephalocaudal, proximodistal, and bilateral principles. Major physical and motor growth invariably occur in three bipolar directions. One direction is head-to-toe, which means that the embryo's head and eyes develop more rapidly and before the lower part of the body. Babies learn to control their head before they can master control of their trunk. The proximodistal influence means that development begins at the central axis of the body and progresses toward the extremities. Bilateral (side-to-side) means that physical growth is symmetrical: if growth occurs on one side of the body, it will occur simultaneously on the other.

Asynchronous growth. Young children are not "small adults." Proportions of the various body parts change in relation to one another. Length of limbs in comparison with torso length is smaller in the infant than the schoolchild and greater in the aged than the adolescent because of the biological principle of asynchronous growth.

These principles listed here may not seem important for you to commit to memory, but there is a basic concept that is important for you to remember when working with growing, changing adolescents and children. The point is that these changes are inevitable. With each change is the potential for both positive and negative outcomes. The adult who can influence the environment of the student so that there is a good "fit" between the stage of development and the environment surrounding the student can increase the odds of more positive outcomes (Eccles & Midgley, 1989).

Charlotte Buhler (1968), a developmental theorist during the first half of the 1900s, studied four hundred biographies and autobiographies and identified a basic structure and direction that repeatedly appeared in the lives that were analyzed. Buhler described a biological life cycle and psychological development as different in important ways. For example, psychological development is continuous while biological is not. Although these two major courses of development are not parallel, both are divided into five phases. These five phases are presented in figure 2.1.

Buhler's work sparked several life-span theories, some of which are discussed later in this chapter. First is information related to normative, age-graded characteristics (the ideas about what is typical for children and adolescents at various chronological ages).

In this area one of the major questions about development and growth is: what is a typical rate of growth? The traditional view of physical growth during infancy and childhood is that such changes occur at a relatively continuous, consistent and constant rate. A recent study by Lampl, Veldhuis, and Johnson (1992) challenged this concept of constant, consistent growth.

Until the nineteenth century, children were considered "small adults." Are there still ways in which society considers children as "small adults?"

FIGURE 2.1
Buhler's Biological
and Psychological
Phases of Life

Approximate Age	Biological Phase	Psychological Phase
0–15	Progressive growth	Child at home, prior to self-determination of goals
16–25	Continued growth and ability to reproduce sexually	Preparatory expansion, experimental determination of goals
26–45	Stability of growth	Culmination
46–65	Loss of reproductive ability	Self-assessment after striving for goals
Over 65	Regressive growth and biological decline	Experience of fulfillment or failure

Modified from Buhler, 1968.

Lampl, Veldhuis and Johnson measured 31 infants during their first 21 months of life. Length and weight measurements for the infants were assessed at either weekly, semiweekly, or daily intervals. These researchers found that: "human length growth during the first two years occurs during short (less than 24 hours) intervals that punctuate a background of stasis" (p. 802).

Lampl, Veldhuis and Johnson indicated that infants have short bursts of growth on a given day, followed by long periods of no growth that range from 2 to 63 days in duration. The typical pattern was a one day period of growth in body length of about 1 centimeter with two weeks of no growth.

Such a finding of short periods of rapid growth with long periods of stasis lends support to research conducted by Gesell (1954). The view taken by some researchers in this area is that psychosocial development also may be characterized by a similar pattern. The next section presents a sequence of child and adolescent development based on a pattern of age-specific, rapid growth interspersed with periods of stability.

Imaginary play is a frequent activity for a four year old child.

WHAT ARE THE MAJOR DEVELOPMENTAL CHARACTERISTICS ASSOCIATED WITH A PARTICULAR AGE?

Four-year-old Children. Ilg, Ames, and Baker (1981) believe that it is possible to identify one or two words that are descriptive of the child or adolescent at a specific age range. These "key" words can help us develop a better sense and comprehension of what children are like at a particular time in their development. For age four, at least for the first half of the year, the key words are "out-of-bounds" and "expansive." The four-year-old's movements and emotions are out-of-bounds. Four is a time for hitting, kicking, throwing, running, and breaking

Research indicates that about one-fourth of all children will have an imaginary playmate during the ages of four to six. Do you remember having an imaginary playmate? Such playmates appear to be more common in firstborn or only children.

things. Children at four are constantly on the move. The hustle is undirected and disorganized.

The high drives are both physical and mental. The language of a four-year-old is very expansive! His conversation jumps from one topic to the next with little or no transition. Talk is a steady stream of imagination that has few boundaries. Imaginary playmates or stuffed animals fill the void of absent friends. Simple toys or objects, in the imagination, become elaborate schools, homes, offices, hospitals, cars, doctor's instruments, or food to serve. Language includes the first real attempts at naughty words that shock most adults. Children at this age love to rhyme bad words with other silly words. What is especially maddening to teachers and parents is the persistence and repetition of four-year-olds.

Equally shocking to adults are the tall tales, lies, and other falsehoods that four-year-olds find more interesting than facts and reality. There seems to be no boundary between the imaginary and reality. Fantasy includes inflating their own abilities and, consequently, bragging is common. Four-year-old children think that they can do it all! If they can imagine doing it, they will tell you they did it!

Obviously, dramatic play and artwork are exciting for this age. A drawing that was started as a person may become a house before it is completed as a train or airplane. Also, emotions seem to run hot or cold. Silliness and rage are two very common emotional expressions during this stage of development.

The average four-year-old is 40.9 inches and weighs 36 pounds (Hamill, Drizd, Johnson, Reed, Roche, & Moore, 1979). Milestones of gross motor skill development around age four are skipping, hopping on one foot, and catching a large ball by moving both hands in response to the oncoming object. Fine motor skills that may develop at four are buttoning large buttons and copying simple drawings.

Are preschool children usually able to distinguish between reality and fiction? What impact does this distinction have on young children viewing TV violence?

Four-and-one-half-year-old Children. This is the time best labeled "fitting together." The four-and-one-half-year-old borrows the expansiveness of the four-year-old and the smooth growth stage that is around the corner at age five. There is a pulling in from the out-of-bounds ways of the four-year-old. One task is making a transition to the upcoming quiet times of five.

The four-and-a-half-year-old becomes concerned about what is real and begins to recognize that the fantasy of four was make-believe. Television shows provoke questions about "What is real and what is pretend?" Parents, teachers, and other adults are bombarded with questions from the four-and-a-half-year-old about any possible topic, especially facts about birth and death. Talking becomes a two-way discussion at this age and often includes wanting to see two sides of things. For example, what is good and what is bad about rain or storms.

At this age, children are better able to complete a task, such as building something with blocks or coloring a picture. They will create jobs for themselves and finish many of them. Considerable time is spent on gross motor activities. Hopping on one foot now becomes a short two-footed broad jump (Espenschade & Eckert, 1980). Play is less out-of-bounds than it was and fine motor skills are improving. Drawing and counting, even learning the letters, become interests. Generally, activities are aimed at gathering new information and sharpening old skills.

Emotions remain quite variable. Laughter and tears can still follow each other in quick succession. Fears might become a problem, especially at bedtime. Both nightmares and night lights are common at this age.

Five-year-old Children. The key word used to describe this age is "smooth." Age five is a time of balance and equilibrium. Five-year-old children are almost too good to be true. Major characteristics for five-year-olds are well adjusted, stable, and reliable. Children at five are happy most of the time, or at least they say that they are "fine" or "good." The exuberance and unpredictability of age four is gone. The contented five-year-old stays close to the center of her existence and likes to be in the "here and now."

Play consists of emulating what happens around them in their world. Playing house, or being mom or dad at work, is of more interest than the fantasy world they explored at four and four and a half. Mother is usually the center of the child's world. Obeying orders, asking for permission to do things, requesting instruction, and going places with parents are frequent behaviors. To the observer it seems the child is getting organized in every way. Generally, five-year-old children respond better to small tasks than to a challenge. During this stage of development, children set personal limits rather than taking risks or asserting themselves.

The five-year-old has accomplished something during this stage of development, which is more organizational than expansive. Language vocabulary is about twenty-two hundred words compared with fifteen hundred at age four. Usage of grammar in speech has improved, and children who are five can make five-word sentences, count to ten, name objects upon request, and recall their name, address, and phone number easily.

The "smooth" stage at five lasts for only a short five to six months, which is much too short for most adults, especially when they become aware of what will happen at five and a half. The next stage is a period of disequilibrium and branching out into new areas. The initially enjoyable and calm fifth year will be sorely missed by the child's caregiver.

Five-and-a-half-year-old Children. The only thing constant at this age is the inconsistency of the child's behavior. It is as though they don't know which way to go or what way to do things. Indecisiveness, dawdling, and hesitancy are exhibited one moment, but the next may be a time of high demands and volatility. Children are extremely difficult to deal with at this time because emotions swing from love to hate, even for mother, in a matter of moments. Gone is the cooperative child of five. Arrived are children who want to be the center of their world. Mother, father, and siblings come second. Anyone who thwarts the child's goals is blamed and others are expected to adapt to the child's wants.

Some major physiological disorganization is happening during this stage of development. One area of concern is the visual. Children have difficulty adjusting their focus from near to far objects, consequently eyestrain is common. Imbalance of eye muscles, or strabismus (both eyes do not work together), can occur and lead to amblyopia or "lazy eye." Eye exercises and wearing a patch over the better or stronger eye is the usual treatment regimen, although in serious cases either glasses or surgery is required.

Six-year-old Children. The most descriptive word for this stage of development is "sorting out." Action and real growth changes launch the child into many new areas. The six-year-old will react with the whole body. Emotional expressions are extreme. At six, children do not just cry, they sob. Anger includes hitting, kicking, and seething. Because it is a time of disorganization, six-year-old children benefit from organizational reminders from adults. "In five minutes it will be time to go to recess" helps children finish what they are doing and be ready for the transition to the next activity.

Children, at this time in life, are aware of more than they can do. They have so many new experiences to try to assimilate that they like routines. Praise is a good form of reward for this age group. They want to be first and will often tell tall tales or tattle on others to assure their own value. It is hard to get a six-year-old to admit a misbehavior.

Energy levels seem to be higher in the morning and lower in the evening hours. Ownership of objects is important at age six. Conversely, they exhibit little respect for the property of others and will often claim any money or valuables left lying around. They like to win and will at times cheat to try to avoid losing. They also desire to be right and are more reluctant to accept punishment or blame than they were at five.

This is an expansive age! Readiness for new experiences has replaced the homebody five-year-old. Vocabulary development may reach thousands of words by the end of the period. The basic rules of grammar, such as the use of plurals, possessives, verb tense, and sentence structure, are set. Most girls have mastered all speech sounds by age seven, and the boys will accomplish it soon.

By now you probably have determined that there are better and worse stages and that expansive stages precede and follow a quiet, calmer stage. You are right about these shifts from equilibrium to disequilibrium and back to equilibrium. During the next stage, one of the better ages, the seven-year-old takes in more than he gives out.

Seven-year-old Children. The focal point of the seven-year-old is inward, with the child having long periods of self-absorption. Solitude is prized, while intrusions and interruptions are resented. Thinking moods, when the child is working, lead to slow work habits and methodical completion of tasks. Assignments are worked through over and over until they are nearly perfect. Sometimes the seven-year-old becomes pensive, moody, and negative.

At seven, children like to be around adults, especially their teachers. Any adult who will read to them is admired. The child will request the same story, from either a book or television, over and over. Because they are becoming logical thinkers, they will begin to listen to reason The seven-year-old can be very self-critical, but also is apt to blame others or to give up on a task whenever problems develop.

Some research indicates that children who participate in preschool and day care programs have a slightly higher level of aggressive behavior as they enter the school-age years. List some reasons why these children may demonstrate more aggressive behavior.

By age seven, the development of mental and physical abilities provides new opportunities for learning a variety of skills.

Many self-care habits are finally learned and practiced. Table manners begin to improve, and table conversation becomes amiable. At seven, it is important that others follow "the rules" and even small infractions can become big issues. Seven also is the age when children are relatively illness free but may complain about fatigue and sore muscles (growing pains). The fatigue will leave for most children when they reach the age of eight and the general healthiness will continue. Except for this continuity, there are some big changes in store for adults who spend time with children who are eight years old.

Eight-year-old Children. The key word for year eight is again expansion. Energy, curiosity, and robustness are characteristic of the eight-year-old. The big transition for this age is to more reliance on peers and less on parents. Dependence on parents decreases as eight-year-olds become more of a member of their peer group. At eight, children begin to identify themselves as "children" who have different values and interests than adults.

This age is a prime time for academic growth with reading, writing, and language skills moving ahead at a rapid pace. While the seven-year-old was very here-and-now oriented, at eight, punctuality becomes important. Maps, trips, geography, and compasses are examples of new areas of interest.

Eight is a time of high emotion and sensitivity. This is a dramatic and expressive age. Feelings are easily hurt by jokes or name-calling. Praise is valued because there is a tendency for these children to be self-deprecating.

Some important physical changes are happening in the vision of the eight-year-old. Most eight-year-olds experience changes in the shape of the eye, and the normal farsightedness of the preschool ages is replaced with 20/20 vision. Movement shows more balance and grace than the previous clumsiness.

Nine-year-old Children. At nine, the cycle changes to an integrative phrase that might be labeled "fitting together." Energy rates are high, but they are needed because competitiveness and self-motivation are equally prominent. Responsible use of time is even better than at eight, although children at this age still tend to plan to accomplish more than is possible in a day (some of us never outgrow this, evidently). At nine, children like to make plans and carry them out to show responsibility. Appetite and eating habits are very adultlike at this age.

A major gauge for emotion is fairness. If a nine-year-old child suspects unfairness, expect a strong emotional outburst! Fair treatment results in nine-year-old children reacting realistically and reasonably, but unfair treatment leads to disruptions.

Nine years of age also is a time of worry and fears. Most data show a gradual decrease in fears from early childhood to early adolescence, but there are exceptions. Barnett's (1969) findings indicate that there is, with increasing age, a general decline in the fear of animals, but an increase in school and social fears. Girls are more fearful than boys and all children generally are more fearful than they will be in a year or two (Davidson, White, Smith & Poppen, 1989). Nine is a good time for children to develop pen pals and further their interest in history and foreign cultures.

Ten-year-old Children. Ten is best characterized as smooth, productive, and cooperative. Adults working with this age group find that they tend to be generally well adjusted and content. Adults find this to be the best stage since five and the best to come until sixteen. To the ten-year-old, the adult's word, especially the parent's, is the final authority. Most ten-year-olds are functioning at Kohlberg's third stage of moral development (see later section in this chapter) and, therefore, try hard to be a good boy or a good girl. Furthermore, they understand the logic that says that a person should be good because it is the right thing to do.

Friends are quite important at this age, but there is considerable squabbling. Large group activity is foremost and a major goal is to belong.

Reading, storytelling, and small group discussions are major academic activities. Memorizing generally is considered to be enjoyable and synonymous with learning; however, the attention span is still short. Ten-year-olds like a challenge as long as abstract thought is not required. Abstract reasoning, such as comparing and contrasting ideas, is not usually developmentally attainable. Concrete, literal-minded thinking is still the predominant mode of thinking in most ten-year-old children.

Do you agree with the statement that girls generally are more fearful than boys? If you agree with this statement, what factors might cause girls to be more fearful?

IS THERE A RELATIONSHIP BETWEEN STUDENT LEARNING AND BRAIN DEVELOPMENT?

How brain growth occurs and correlates with age can provide one possible explanation for the stops and starts in student learning. Fischer and Pipp (1984) and Epstein (1978) believe that brain growth is another example that supports the developmental principle that "There are optimal periods of growth and development." Epstein (1978) has devised a description of brain development in normal children from birth to age sixteen (see figure). What is presented is a normative sequence. There is a variation in the rate of growth within each child and between children. We know, for example, that weight and height increase rapidly during infancy, moderately in the preschool years, and slowly during middle childhood. The rate of growth again becomes rapid during adolescence and slows thereafter.

The contention is that brain growth from birth to sixteen follows a cycle of a slow-growth plateau to a growth spurt to a plateau, etc. Significant spurts in brain development happen for most children from three to ten months, from two to four years, from six to eight years, from ten to twelve, at fourteen, and at sixteen. Between these periods, plateaus lasting as little as seven months occur. Plateaus in brain growth are accompanied by children practicing and enhancing recently acquired intellectual skills and knowledge.

The acceleration periods are characterized by considerable axon and dendrite growth. Myelinization, the insulation process of covering nerve fibers that transmit electrical and chemical impulses, is significant. To summarize, millions of new connections form between neurons. This change, plus other brain changes, is indicative of times when children are most apt at accommodating new concepts and ideas. The process is exceedingly complex, however, and Fischer and Bullock (1984) caution that educators should not plan school curricula around these very tentative findings. One erroneous assumption has been that middle school students cannot learn very much because brain growth is in a plateau stage. Current thinking about this issue is much like the "chicken or the egg argument." Which comes first, the brain growth or the behavioral change?" One argument is that behavioral changes are probably ". . . just as likely to precede brain changes as to follow them" (Fischer & Bullock, 1984, p. 112).

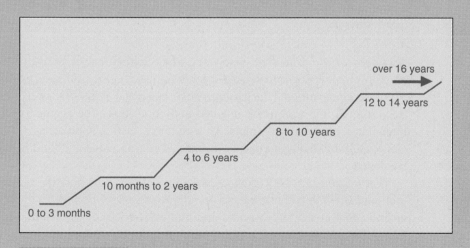

Plateau and Acceleration Periods of Brain Growth (Epstein, 1978).

A number of studies indicate that children now enter puberty earlier than did previous generations. What changes need to be made in elementary schools when children as early as nine are entering puberty?

Junk food may become a special interest at this age and sweets are a real temptation. At ten, the child is less driven by time than the nine-year-old but still is punctual and takes initiative.

Eleven-year-old Children. Key words to describe eleven-year-old children are "rapid change" and "breakup." Eleven is a time of intense physical, emotional, and cognitive growth. Therefore, motion abounds! Social, assertive, moody are all characteristics of the social-emotional pattern of behavior during this stage. These changes affect social relationships greatly. Havoc in peer and family relationships becomes the norm.

At eleven, children will do things just to see how adults and peers will react. Cruel behavior to both friends, teachers, and parents is a result of the child's curiosity and moodiness. Cliques, even more exclusive than those at ten, are common. Problems, which are frequent, come and go before they are solved. The problems are more developmental than situational. Counseling eleven-year-old students can be frustrating to adults because the friend that was berated during the morning will suddenly be a best friend by afternoon.

For girls this is the time of drastic physical changes; breasts develop and menses starts. Boys, on the average, must wait until twelve before testes, scrotum, and penis undergo changes.

For many students, this is a time for transition to a new school, a middle school. Others will wait until twelve to move to a junior high school. This happens at a time when eleven-year-old students like routine and like to know what is going to be expected of them. Advance warnings of changes are especially appreciated at this age.

Academically, the interests of eleven-year-old children are changing. They are entering a developmental period where they will begin to use and understand abstractions. They will begin to comprehend and appreciate the allegorical and figurative uses of language. Remembering facts will become less important to them. Stories about themselves and others in their age group will increasingly spark their interest.

Twelve-year-old Children. Twelve-year-old children are in an age of "sorting out." Twelve is action oriented and peer dominated. Great strides are made in the basic development and integration of the personality. Youth at twelve are less self-centered but more self-contained and competent. The aggressiveness and moodiness of eleven are replaced with more tactful approaches to gaining approval from adults and peers. At times, even reasonable and kind behavior is exhibited.

Peer relationships happen more easily than at eleven because the twelve-year-old is girded with enthusiasm and an improved sense of humor. The peer group is influential in shaping attitudes and interests, especially the "chum" relationships that usually have developed during this stage. This is also a time when many will accept guidance in developing social skills and solving interpersonal problems.

Are there other factors besides the onset of puberty that cause difficulties for eleven- to thirteen-year-olds?

Children, at eleven, twelve, or thirteen, usually are required to make a transition from elementary school to the next educational level. What are criteria for a successful transition? Ward, Mergendoller, Tikunoff, Rounds, Mitman, and Dadey (1982) asked parents what they considered to be criteria for a successful transition. Eight criteria, listed in order of importance to parents, were identified: (1) academic success or grades as good as elementary school, (2) low anxiety, (3) successful peer relationships, (4) good management of time, (5) a positive attitude toward school, (6) involvement in school activities, (7) positive relationships with teachers, and (8) motivation. Students in the seventh grade (age twelve) report that their teachers care less about them and that they have more homework for school than they did previously (Benson, Williams, & Johnson, 1987).

The conceptual thinking abilities of twelve-year-old students are increasing and they seem ready to accept projects and problems that are challenging. Because they are so action oriented, teachers should not make assignments that require prolonged periods of sitting and concentrating.

Thirteen-year-old Adolescents. Thirteen is the beginning of what is often called "early adolescence." The peer group is a primary influence.

Boys and girls conform more at this age than they did earlier and more than they will over the next three or four years (Costanzo & Shaw, 1966). The feelings of such adolescents are easily hurt because thirteen-year-olds are becoming more introspective and are highly critical of themselves. Abstract reasoning is still a newly found intellectual skill that is used to worry about the many transitions occurring, both mentally and physically. Frequent periods of intense introspection among students of this age result in times of moody behavior and irritability. Generally, the reasoning is critical not only of self but of others, too. Reluctance to rely on adult authority is characteristic of both males and females of this age.

Introspection, characteristic of thirteen-year-olds, often takes the form of inspection in front of the mirror. Boys and girls will comb their hair and contemplate their appearance repeatedly each day. There also is an increased interest in the world around them. More than 50 percent watch more than three hours of television a day. Hard rock music and telephone conversations with their current friends also consume large amounts of time (Benson, Williams, & Johnson 1987).

Boys seem to be less able to talk about themselves, while girls seem to thrive on discussing their inner feelings with friends or even amiable adults, such as a school counselor.

Thirteen-year-olds are often challenged by intellectual activities that previously "turned them off." The ability to concentrate for a longer time allows children of this age to enjoy planning and completing "major" projects. One of the authors recently observed a small group of thirteen-year-old boys spend three hours one day and five the next working on a bridge that was to be tested in front of the class by seeing how much weight it could support. Thirteen-year-olds do not seem to suffer from a lack of energy, rather it appears to be boundless when they are truly interested in what they are doing.

Fourteen-year-old Adolescents. Fourteen is a "smoother" year than thirteen. Fourteen, like thirteen, is a year of rapid physical growth, especially for males.

Some research seems to indicate an increasing sense of alienation from school during this age period. This alienation causes lower grades and greater absenteeism. What factors might cause this alienation?

In your own experience, do boys seem less able to talk about their feelings than girls? What factors might cause this?

What can teachers do to reduce negative peer influences?

Many consider it to be a peak year of growth for males. Peer relationships become a greater concern than physical appearance. Belonging to a group or the right clique is a critical need at this age. Boys usually belong to larger groups than do girls, who form a more exclusive and intimate group of friends. Fourteen-year-olds are fairly cooperative, energetic, and content. There generally is less conflict with parents; however, fourteen-year-olds will go to great lengths to dissociate themselves from their parents. Interest in the opposite sex is a consuming interest! Boys begin to take on a manly appearance, with adolescent fat turning to muscle. Nearly all girls have established their regular menstrual cycle and have developed the secondary sex characteristics of a mature female (Ames, Ilg, & Baker, 1988).

Intellectually, fourteen-year-olds become more able to see both sides of an issue and to tolerate the different thinking of others. Disorganized and disjointed thinking still persists but to a lesser degree. Evaluating the self in comparison with others becomes a consuming interest and sparks serious thought about what career to pursue as an adult.

Fifteen-year-old Adolescents. Fifteen is a difficult year! It is a time similar to nine and is characterized as a period of "neurotic fitting together." The focus at this age is inward. Noncommunication is typical of fifteen-year-old adolescents, especially if adults appear to want them to talk.

At fifteen, the desire to be independent and "free" is primary. Because the family is the major source of limitations, fifteen-year-olds typically abhor both parents. Arguing has been perfected to an art. They do seem to get along better with other members of the family than with their parents. Consequently, a few good friends are a source of mutual help. Concerns about self and one's opinions are shared with one or two personal friends (usually age-mates).

Dating and relationships with members of the opposite sex are areas of experimentation at this age. Drinking and dancing are other typical party activities. Educational and career planning are considered but remain unresolved primarily because of conflict with parents and teachers. Although they seldom exhibit them to adults, they report that honesty and fairness are important values.

Certain studies indicate that girls are realistic about their career goals. Boys tend to be more likely to have fantasy careers. How would this research relate to the research on being unsure about a career?

Sixteen-year-old Adolescents. The Gesell system indicates that ages five, ten, and sixteen are "smooth" periods of development. Sixteen is a period of equilibrium. The sixteen-year-old has an improved sense of self and is secure in interpersonal relationships. Family relationships are decidedly better than during fourteen and fifteen. Sixteen-year-old adolescents really prefer peers to family, but they are amiable and appreciative of their parents. Parents describe sixteen as a time when children are cheerful, positive, and outgoing. Brothers and sisters are tolerated and the sixteen-year-old's temper is less out of control.

Both boys and girls rely on a best friend as a confidant but tend to have many friends. Friends of the opposite sex are a definite interest, with over 60 percent of the boys and 75 percent of the girls reporting that they "go steady." Although this is a good time of life for the sixteen-year-old and his teachers and parents, there are important decisions facing the adolescent. A major area of choice is what career to pursue. Girls appear more indecisive than boys. Thirty-five percent of

USING SOCIOMETRIC ASSESSMENT IN THE CLASSROOM

One way to measure friendships in the student's peer group is to use a "sociometric" assessment measure. A sociometric technique is a measure of peer relationships or interpersonal attraction among members of a specified group (Hymel, 1983). There are three common types of sociometric measures One, the most traditional and frequently used, is the nomination method. The nominating method asks each member of the group to identify in some way three to five peers in response to a statement or question. For example, students are asked to complete three blanks indicating fellow students they would like to sit near. Directions are to list or identify the names of only those persons in the group. Procedures are used to be sure that those who are absent are included (students are given a list of all class members). If more than one question is asked, students may use the same nominations for each question. Younger students might be given photographs of the members in the group to help them to remember to consider all members.

Questions may be about students who are liked (accepted) or those who are disliked (rejected). Both acceptance and rejection scores can be obtained from sociometric assessment, although Perry (1979) has developed a method of combining these scores to measure "social impact." Traditional categories of student scores are "stars" (those with the higher scores) and "isolates" (those with few or no nominations). Sometimes the less discriminatory words "overchosen" and "underchosen" are used. Charting the mutual choices of the students produces a graphic display of who is attracted to whom. Cliques, subgroups who interact with each other, can be identified.

Two other methods of sociometry are the use of paired-comparisons methods and use of rating scales. Both allow researchers to use sociometry with children as young as four. The methods are more time-consuming to administer and score than the nomination method, so they are predominantly used by teachers who teach young children.

The results of the nomination method are fairly reliable, at least with groups of children in grade school. The younger the child, especially preschool, the more unstable the scores. One explanation is that the younger children actually change friendships and establish new enemies frequently. The scores are unstable but so are the relationships! Older children, those past middle and junior high school, often establish relationships with persons outside their classroom groups. Furthermore, their school is organized into many class groups, making it hard to obtain accurate results about the student's social support network. Despite these factors, teachers may still be interested in social networking in their class. Teachers experienced with sociometric assessment know how important it is to identify and use the sociometric "stars" to establish a positive peer group environment. In effect, the teacher uses the "power group" to support his goals for the class. Likewise, it is important to identify any cliques that can be a negative influence on the classroom climate.

Social status, or the lack thereof, correlates with a number of factors (Johnson, 1980; Hartup, 1984). For instance, these researchers indicate that there is a relationship between low social status in the classroom and low self-esteem. Another finding is that low social status is related to low school achievement. There also appears to be a relationship between low social status and acting-out behaviors. The importance of student-student interactions in the school setting are often underestimated. Johnson (1980) notes that most educators assume that the important relationship is between the teacher and the student and that this relationship is the locus of learning. Considerable evidence exists supporting the impact of the student-student relationship, which is more frequent and intense than the teacher-student relationship. Who determines what hairstyles and clothes are worn by students? Research supports your obvious answer to the previous question; these are based primarily on imitation of peers. Adult mental health is related to peer acceptance. Poor peer acceptance as early as the third grade is a good predictor of emotional difficulties and delinquency (Cowen, 1973). Acquiring social competencies, managing aggressive behaviors, and tolerating the views of others are all social skills that are learned in the context of peer relationships. Peers also influence the level of educational aspirations and the values obtained during college. Not only are peers often more significant than teachers in social and cognitive development, they also outrank parents in major areas. Hartup (1976) has been bold to say that if parents were given sole responsibility for the socialization of children in the area of sexuality, humans might not survive as a species!

Johnson (1980) has listed a number of contributions that peers make to the cognitive and social development of children and adolescents. First, peers are of primary importance in socialization because interactions with peers are more frequent, intense, and varied than interactions with teachers and other adults in the school. Attitudes, values, and information about sex are critical areas in which peers "teach" each other how to think and behave. The considerable influence of peers is maintained through the college years.

Peers serve as models and sources of reinforcement and thereby teach social behaviors and attitudes that are essential for maintaining interdependent, cooperative relationships. There is evidence that the behavior of someone who is dominant and liked leads to modeling and contagion of the dominant person's behavior (Parke, 1985). As indicated previously, peer adjustment is a good predictor of emotional relationships, during the life span (Cowen, 1973).

Peers have considerable influence on students' achievement motivation and educational aspirations. Actual achievement is more affected by fellow students than by other factors in the school (Damico, 1975). The peer group influence can be desirable or undesirable; however, some studies imply that when students who have poor study habits are associated with peers in moderate-size groups, achievement increases (Stallings & Kashowitz, 1974).

Why give the sociometric test? Sociometric scores provide new information to the teacher, information that is different from the teacher's perceptions. The evaluations are from the peers themselves rather than from the perspective of the teacher. Results have shown consistently that teachers do not accurately rate how their students will nominate each other. The correlation is positive, but a low positive. One study by Vosk et al. (1982) compared "popular" and "unpopular" students on sociometric measures. The unpopular children, third- and fourth-grade students in rural Georgia, spent significantly less time on-task and had more negative interactions than did their popular classmates. Teachers correctly identified the students as unpopular but also saw them as depressed and deviant. Unpopularity is indicative of childhood depression and may be cause for teacher referral for further testing by a school psychologist.

Other interventions are available to teachers beyond referral. At the elementary level, the teacher can be careful about classroom seating arrangements. The "stars" can be placed at strategic locations in the room rather than allowing them to sit together. One teacher in a fourth-grade class arranges the desks in clusters of four and changes the placements every six weeks. She contends that this results in better overall group relationships and fewer cliques, especially those negative groups that tend to cluster together. Isolates or rejectees may need to be referred to the school counselor. Parent consultation may be useful to encourage more appropriate interactive behavior.

Middle and junior high schools can be organized so that many academic and social clubs are open to all students. The first term of middle or junior high school enrollment is a time when many students are able to change unpopular status to popular. A good approach for this age is indirect. Cooperative learning groups or peer tutoring methods are indirect strategies that can help students with their academic concerns while giving them a chance to form new relationships.

girls have no career choice, while only 17 percent of the boys say they are undecided (Ames, Ilg, & Baker, 1988). Other major choices for many sixteen-year-olds are whether to "make out" or whether they should "go all the way."

In summary, specific features of the different ages have been noted. Caution is urged in treating these ideas as absolutes. The point is for you as a prospective teacher to observe students with an eye for the student's level of development and maturity. We have ended these descriptions at age sixteen because the literature seldom contains information about specific ages of adolescents past sixteen. There are some additional points about the period of adolescence.

What Is Important about Adolescence?

Adolescence is a developmental period when many new abilities and behaviors emerge. Technically it is the time between childhood and adulthood. That time seems to be extending as youngsters are maturing earlier each decade and delaying the time they finish schooling and enter an occupation. Some definitions of adolescence extend the period to age twenty-five. Puberty and adolescence have been, but are no longer, equated. Some developmentalists divide adolescence into the following four stages.

Preadolescence or the age of prepuberty usually ends for females sometime between ten and fourteen and for males sometime between twelve and sixteen. Early adolescence begins with puberty and lasts for several years, usually ending at about fourteen for females and sixteen for males. Middle adolescence starts when physical growth is completed (by age sixteen for females and eighteen or twenty for males). Late adolescence may occur from about twenty to twenty-five.

Adolescence is a time of enormous psychological development brought on by two interrelated processes, the growth spurt and sexual maturation (Malina, 1990). The adolescent growth spurt places the teenager in the center of considerable physical and social disequilibrium and puberty results in more than changes in size and shape of the body. Other physiological developments happen, too. New hormones are secreted that affect sexual functions. Boys, for example, until puberty produce nearly as much estrogen (the female hormone) as androgen (the male hormone). Definite increases in the male production of androgen at puberty lead to heightened sexual arousal and greater physical and verbal assertiveness (Paikoff & Brooks-Gunn, 1990).

At various times between twelve and sixteen, the size of a boy's testes, scrotum, and penis will increase. Girls between ten and fourteen develop the breasts, ovaries, and uterus and become physically capable of childbirth. Growth for both sexes includes broader shoulders and hips, longer arms and legs, and increased height and weight (Malina, 1990).

Adolescents report that the most satisfying time of their typical day is the time they spend with their friends (Csikszentimihalyi & Larson, 1984). Yet, many adolescents, especially girls, report that they feel lonely (Brennan, 1982). How vital are peer relationships and friends to the teenager's growth and development? Only recently have developmentalists attempted to answer questions about friendships. Hartup (1978) reports that this area did not gain much prominence until the late 1970s.

Is adolescence always associated with self-esteem problems:? Reflect on your own adolescent years. What were your anxieties and worries?

Is it inevitable that teenagers will turn away from their parents and toward their peers as sources of influence? Is there anything that parents can do about this tendency?

Adolescents who are lonely tend to do very little of the following behaviors: (1) self-disclose, (2) take an interest in others, (3) be assertive, (4) reward others, and (5) send friendly nonverbal signals. They also do not have good ideas about what is involved in being a friend (Argyle, 1985).

What about Those Adolescents Who Mature Early or Late?

Maturity doesn't happen overnight! Nor does it happen at the same age for all adolescents. There is roughly a five-year variation in the age at which puberty is reached (Malina, 1990). Is it better to mature early or late? This is an interesting question about which educational psychologists and developmentalists have gathered considerable data. Of course, there is not a lot that can be done to intervene in the process. Adolescents themselves contend that they would like to be older or more mature and will attempt to dress so as to appear older. Some teenagers appear to be ambivalent about whether they want to mature early or late and admit to close friends, counselors, or parents that they would like to remain their current age forever. One of the authors, the father of two boys, remembers how one son would hide a razor for months so that his parents would not know he was becoming more grown-up and actually shaving. A second son, however, started telling everyone he was shaving even though he needed a magnifying glass to see the peach hairs on his chin. How many boys have asked how to get their beards to grow more quickly or girls have stuffed socks into their bras to appear that their breasts were fully developed?

The research supports early maturity as beneficial for boys but not for girls. Those students, both male and female, who mature early physically tend to score higher on tests of mental ability (Fein, 1978). Yet, as Berryman et al. note (1991), early maturing boys tend to cope better than early maturing girls. Why do early maturing girls seem to have difficulty and what difficulties do they have?

Perhaps the most extensive and current research on this topic has been completed by Stattin and Magnusson (1989), who have developed a theoretical framework to explain how problem behavior arises among teenage girls and how these social behaviors are linked to early physical development. The model describes the interactions of four factors (see figure 2.2). One factor is early *biological maturation,* which corresponds to certain social behaviors being displayed earlier than normal for adolescents. Physical development also is thought to be related to the teenage girl's self-conception of maturity. The earlier the onset of menarche, the earlier the self-conception of being a female and being an adult. Reaching puberty before one's age-mates also has an effect. Social comparison is as important as self-perception. Brooks-Gunn and Peterson (1984) have suggested that the perception of pubertal timing compared with peers might be highly influential on psychosocial functioning. Consequently another factor, the *peer network* comes into play. Stattin and Magnusson (1989) have demonstrated that early maturation results in older friends, many outside the class and school realm. The interaction of these factors results in social transition behavior. According to Stattin and Magnusson's research, early social transition leads to problem behaviors such as drinking alcohol and establishing earlier dating

Is there a relationship between early biological maturation and early social/psychological maturation?

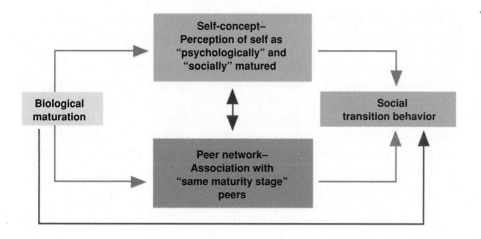

FIGURE 2.2
A Path Model for the
Influence of Biological
Maturation on Social
Transition
Stattin and Magnusson (1989).

behaviors. Although the data verified that early maturing females acted more like older girls, there was no evidence of long-term negative effects, such as greater alcohol abuse or more registered crime as adults.

Although early maturing girls seem to be at some disadvantage, boys appear to benefit by early development. The early maturing male is likely to feel more comfortable around the female who is, on the average, a year or two ahead of the male, at least physically. Livson and Peskin (1980) suggest that adults respond more favorably to the more adultlike appearance of early maturing males. They also have advantages of strength and size, which help them to achieve in sports activities, at least during the stage of midadolescence (Malina, 1983).

A PSYCHOSOCIAL THEORY OF DEVELOPMENT (ERIKSON)

Psychosocial theory covers the life span of human growth and development and includes the assumptions that people are active in directing the course of their own development and that society sets expectations that affect each individual's development. Societies have certain standards for parenting, education, sex, work, etc., as a means to maintain a culture. According to Erikson (1963), individuals incorporate these standards and attitudes to some extent and simultaneously establish a personal identity. A set of continuous challenges are presented to people in eight stages from infancy to later adulthood (see figure 2.3). Each of these eight stages presents the opportunity for new personal skills and abilities to develop within the social context. Tension or conflict is set up for people at every life stage and creates what Erikson called a psychosocial crisis. Each crisis has the potential for the individual to demonstrate successful achievement or an unsuccessful resolution of the challenge.

The order of the stages is set and each new stage will come regardless of how the previous and present psychosocial crises are completed. Of course a more successful resolution of the challenges of each stage will better suit a person to accomplish the tasks of the next stage.

Some psychologists believe that childhood traumas cause a fixation in development. Do you believe that such traumas inevitably cause people to have serious problems as adults?

What Are These Stages and Which Ones Are Particularly Pertinent to School-age Children and Adolescents?

The first stage is *basic trust versus basic mistrust.* If mistrust wins out over trust, the child will become frustrated, withdrawn, and lacking in self-confidence. Problems also will develop with each of the other upcoming psychosocial crises. You might imagine a continuum from trust to mistrust and assume that the individual will develop somewhere between the two extremes. More healthy development will occur if the person learns the ability to trust others but still maintains a realistic attitude toward the dangers that exist in the world.

Parents and other care-giving adults play the dominant role in how infants do in resolving this conflict. Mistrust can come from within the child (from feelings of anger and rage whenever her needs are unfulfilled) or from adults who lack confidence in their own ability to care for the child or who neglect the child's physical and emotional needs.

At the next stage of development, the struggle is between *autonomy versus shame and doubt.* If shame and doubt win out over autonomy, children develop overwhelming feelings of self-doubt and lack confidence in their abilities. At age two, children can walk and communicate. They have developed some incredible skills in a relatively short period of time. The child's psychosocial task involves gaining control over his bodily muscles (Erikson, 1963), including the important ability of bowel control.

A sense of autonomy develops as the child feels in control of these various muscles of the body. If the child is unable to exert what parents expect to be proper control, a feeling of doubt in one's own ability results. A sense of shame can occur when the child sees others doing for her what should be accomplished without help. Near the end of this stage, assuming the child has achieved a sense of autonomy, the child learns that "I am a person."

The third stage, *initiative versus guilt,* is one in which the child must find out what kind of a person he will become. Children want to be like their parents:

FIGURE 2.3
Erikson's Psychosocial
Crises of the Eight Life
Stages

Life Stage/Approximate Age	Psychosocial Crisis
Infancy—0 to 1 1/2	Trust vs. mistrust
Early Childhood—1 1/2 to 3	Autonomy vs. doubt
Preschool age—3 to 6	Initiative vs. guilt
School age—6 to 12	Industry vs. inferiority
Adolescence—12 to 18	Identity vs. identify confusion
Young adulthood—19 to 40	Intimacy vs. isolation
Adulthood—40 to 65	Generativity vs. stagnation
Later adulthood—65 to death	Integrity vs. despair

Modified from Erikson, 1980, 178.

Learning to trust one's parents or caregivers is a major developmental hurdle during infancy.

large, powerful, and somewhat dangerous. Children live literally in a "land of giants." The child's focus is upon investigating what is around her. The attempt is to find some stability and consistency in her environment. Children who have a firm sense of autonomy and confidence will allow new feelings of curiosity and initiative to take over. Experiments with the environment will be conducted to discover if it holds the same regularity and order they found during the second stage in themselves and during the first stage in their parents. If initiative wins out over guilt, the child becomes an active and questioning investigator of the world surrounding him.

Every social order has limits on how intrusive others should be when they are investigating the world. When severe limits are placed on a child's questions and explorations, a sense of guilt over wanting to know about things is formed and the child is left dependent on others. In short, for initiative to overbalance a sense of guilt, children need care from adults who allow them the freedom and opportunity to follow through on self-initiated activities.

The fourth stage is characterized by a struggle between *industry and inferiority*. The child is entering into the larger world of knowledge and work. The child's basic attitude toward work is said to be established during these school-age years.

Erikson claims that autonomy precedes initiative. Would you agree with this idea or do you think that these two stages are really about the same?

Some people believe that children who are retained in school will develop a sense of inferiority. Do you agree?

Successful experiences can bring about a sense of industry and a feeling of competence. Failure, on the other hand, brings about feelings that she is inadequate and inferior. The question is, "How much do I count?" Mastery of new skills leads to increased feelings of independence. Being given new responsibilities can lead to an enhanced sense of worth and can result in the child entering a cycle of success begetting success.

Feelings of inadequacy can be reinforced both internally and externally. Peers, parents, and teachers can promote social comparisons through various systems of obvious and subtle rewards and punishments. Children are grouped, graded, and rewarded for everything from how cute they are, to how fast they run, to how accurately they can spell.

The child also can establish internal "self-talk" that reinforces or negates accomplishments. In this battle, if the struggle between industry and inferiority is not resolved with the balance on the side of industry, the child becomes reluctant, withdrawn, and filled with self-doubt.

Identity versus role confusion is the critical challenge of the adolescent years. Rapid physiological changes produce a "new" body with sexual urges and the capability of a serious response to those urges. The challenge or struggle, much

Adolescence is often characterized as a period of rebellion and alienation.

like those in the past, continues to be promoted by both internal tensions and outside pressures. Adolescents search to find themselves in school, sports, music, religion, political movements, and so on. Many times the skills the adolescent has honed during childhood are not given as much social value as others. Faced with these new insights, and with key educational and occupational choices, adolescents develop at least temporary, if not enduring, confusion and depression. Negative experiences that do not result in a clear self-definition leave adolescents entering the next stage of development with a sense of fear about themselves and their future.

In a comprehensive exploration of Erikson's theory, at least as it applies to adolescence, Marcia (1976) determined that there were four possible "statuses" for dealing with the identity crisis. These statuses can apply to any choice to be made, such as an occupational choice. One status is *identity achievement,* wherein the adolescent wrestles with the decision and makes a firm commitment to an occupation. A second status is called *identity diffusion.* In this case there is a lack of commitment to any choice and a reluctance to face the decision. The third is *identity foreclosure* and indicates an adolescent who makes a commitment to an occupation but has not looked at alternatives. Many times this comes about because of overreliance on the outside pressure of a parent or friend. The fourth status is one of *moratorium.* Under this condition there is an ongoing attempt to decide; however, no commitment has been made to a specific choice. Continuing research still supports Marcia's views about how adolescents resolve the identity crises (Waterman, 1982).

Newman and Newman (1986) disagree with most of traditional psychosocial theory about adolescence being a single stage. They contend that one stage begins at puberty and ends with graduation from high school or about age eighteen. A second stage continues, they say, for another three or four years and is very much like Erikson's description of the entire stage of adolescence. The focus of this second stage of adolescence is on developing a sense of personal identity. The earlier-stage adolescent must resolve issues about his relationship with peers or what the Newmans call the issue of group identity. Thus, the two stages of adolescence involve first developing a sense of group identity before later obtaining a sense of personal identity.

The other three stages of Erikson's theory of psychosocial development occur after adolescence. Stage six, *intimacy versus isolation,* is usually the first task of the young adult as she strikes out to establish a life away from the family. Stage seven deals with the issue of having a family and rearing children. The classic question is, "Can I have it all?" In other words, the choice is between devoting one's life to having a career, focusing on the family, or trying to resolve the issue through some sort of compromise, such as becoming a working mother. The stage is called *generativity versus stagnation.* Stage eight presents the person in later adulthood with thoughts about the meaning of one's life. The struggle is *integrity versus despair.* Integrity, according to Erikson, means accepting the facts about one's life and coming to face death without great fear. Despair, on the contrary, is having deep feelings of regret over one's life and speculating about how things might have been different.

Erikson's model has been criticized for being biased toward Western culture. Is his model oriented only toward Western culture and not applicable to other cultures?

How Do Children Learn Right from Wrong?

Another major area of development that has not yet been discussed is moral development. A number of models and theories attempt to answer the question about how children learn right and wrong.

Piaget (1973) was one of the first to develop a scientific answer to this question. Known for his work in developing a theory of cognitive development in children, he also is prominent because of his study of children's moral judgment, especially how they develop respect for rules and a sense of solidarity with their society. His original studies focused on the rules children used in playing street games. Children from ages three to five, according to his theory, think egocentrically. Consequently, they are self-centered when playing with other children in a group. They imitate the players of games without completely understanding the rules or the purpose of the game. Reimer, Paolitto, and Hersh (1983) describe how a child this age throws a ball without aiming it or closes both eyes when trying to catch a ball thrown at him. At this age, children don't understand teamwork or cooperation as necessary to winning the game. Playing games could best be described as "egocentric imitation."

One of the authors remembers having "marble races" with a group of four-year-old boys. There was no single winner in the game. When the first marble crossed the finish line, that marble was declared the winner. But the boy who rolled another marble would shout, "My marble won, too," even though it crossed the finish line a distant second. The boys at this age had little need for rules or even the concept of a winner.

Seven and eight-year-olds play a game with a purpose, playing together as a team and cooperating to win the game. The children argue about rules usually because they try to follow them exactly. Few adaptations are made to accommodate special circumstances or settings. The rules are followed like "law," which cannot be changed. Piaget called this a stage of moral thinking and named it heteronomous morality, which means a morality of constraint.

Eleven-and twelve-year-olds play "with" the rules instead of strictly by the rules. They follow the rules but are able to modify them to fit the needs of the time, place, or situation. For example, baseball might be played with a rule that "over the fence" is an out instead of a home run if some of the players have an exceedingly higher level of skill at hitting the ball than do most of the players. This stage of thinking is labeled autonomous morality or a morality of cooperation. It is the highest level of moral development in Piaget's model.

Are these really two stages of moral thought that develop in sequence and how do children move from one stage to the next? The argument is that children learn the morality of cooperation through the examples of their parents and through experiences with other children. Children learn the value of using more democratic methods to solve problems in game and play settings. Karniol (1980) has found evidence to support the idea that autonomous morality exists more frequently among older than younger children, thereby lending support to Piaget's concept of moral thinking as developmental stages.

Piaget indicates that children have a fundamentally different sense of right and wrong than adults. Do teachers usually understand that children are fundamentally different?

Helping Children with the Stress of Divorce

Nearly half of the children born after 1970 will experience the crisis of divorce and remarriage (Poppen & White, 1986). Two myths exist about how children view their parents' divorce. One is that they are relieved, as are the parents, to see the end of a bad relationship. The other is that because divorce is becoming so common, there is no longer a stigma for the child to overcome. A fact about divorce is that children need one to two years to adjust to the trauma of being in a divorce situation. Teachers can help them make an easier transition if they follow a few guidelines for helping the child think about the divorce. Also, it is helpful if the teacher or adult is aware of the various reactions of children at different age levels.

A few general rules apply to help children modify some of the erroneous thoughts they have about being from a family of divorce. (1) It helps to talk. Teachers can help children at any age by encouraging them to discuss their feelings with any trusted peer or adult. (2) You are loved and you will be cared for. Children benefit by adult reassurance that adults care for them and will take care of them. (3) You didn't cause the divorce, nor are you responsible for trying to get your parents back together. You can't fix it.

Children's and Adolescents' Reactions to Divorce

Three to Five
Fear of abandonment
Prolonged periods of silence
Worry about causing the divorce
Sadness and confusion; may be more forgetful
Anxiety; sleeping difficulties
Exhibits behaviors similar to a younger child

Six to Eight
Loyalty conflicts
Inhibits anger at departed parent; expresses anger at custodial parent
Fantasy about reconciliation of parents; other unrealistic fantasies
Disorganized behavior
Sadness; crying, especially among boys
Guilt

Nine to Twelve
Shame over what is happening; covers up feelings
Supportive of one parent while blaming the one they think caused the divorce
Headaches, stomachaches, etc.
Outwardly shows courage, poise

Thirteen to Eighteen
Delay of entrance into adolescence coupled with worry about sex and marriage
Sexual acting out
Anger at parents and parents' dates or marriage partners
Mourning; sense of loss for the good parent, family they had before divorce
Withdrawal from family activities; independent behavior

Modified from Kostelnik, Stein, Whiren, and Soderman, 1988, 260–261.

Kohlberg's Theory of Moral Development

Kohlberg's (1981) theory of moral development, a cognitive-developmental theory, is an extension of Piaget's ideas. The six stages of moral reasoning serve to describe a sequence of how children change their thinking about moral issues as they grow (see figure 2.4). In other words, the stages form a progression that may span about twenty-five years.

Kohlberg presented situational moral dilemmas to students and asked them to tell what they would do in these hypothetical situations. The responses determined the level of reasoning. Here is an example:

> Holly is ten years old. A kitten is stranded high in a treetop right above her. Should she climb the tree to rescue the kitten or should she keep a promise made to her father not to climb trees anymore?

Children are asked to respond to these questions and to give the reasons for their answer. The reason is what is evaluated. A stage-one answer would indicate a decision based on what a person in authority (her father) would think. Would he punish or reward her for rescuing the cat? If the child answers: "No, Holly might get into trouble with her father if she rescued the cat" the answer would be an example of a stage-one response.

Describe a recent moral dilemma that you faced. Classify your response based on Kohlberg's model.

FIGURE 2.4
Kohlberg's Stages of
Moral Judgment

Stage	Nature of stage
Preconventional Level (avoiding punishments and getting rewards)	
Stage 1: Heteronomous morality:	What is right or wrong is determined by punishment. If I am punished, I must have done something bad. If not punished, I did something good.
Stage 2: Morality is instrumental:	Right means looking after one's own self and need-satisfying interests; "If I do you a favor, I expect one in return."
Conventional Level (following social rules)	
Stage 3: Interpersonal conformity:	What is right is what brings approval from the immediate peer group. Good girls do what the good girls group says is right.
Stage 4: Conformity to the social order:	What is right is determined by the society. My country right or wrong is the orientation.
Postconventional Level (following moral principles)	
Stage 5: Ethics of social contract:	What is right is determined by an agreed-upon social contract between individuals and the society in which they live.
Stage 6: Ethics of self-chosen:	What is right is self-chosen universal principles that are consistently applied by the individual. "All men are created equal."

Modified from Reimer, Palolitto, and Hersch, 1982.

Stage-two reasoning might follow along the line of thought that, if Holly helped the kitten, it might somehow return the favor. The stage-two child would answer: "Holly should rescue the kitten. Perhaps the kitten would then stay with Holly and warn her of a fire or some other danger."

With stage-three reasoning the child might answer: "it would be a nice thing for a good girl to save the kitten." Stage four reasoning might indicate a consideration of the law. The child might answer: "I think Holly can get arrested for climbing trees in the park. She better not save the kitten."

Although it is unlikely that children before age 12 would reason at stages five or six, a stage-five response would be: "Cats have a right to live, even if Holly does get into trouble." A stage-six response would be: "Animals have as much right to live as we do. Holly should get the kitten down even if she risks her own life."

In their studies, Kohlberg and Blatt (1972) found that people seldom reasoned consistently at only one level, consequently, there were variations in how results were scored. Some researchers used the most frequent stage of thinking given in response to the dilemmas while others used the highest level of thinking demonstrated by any response. Nor have psychologists been able to find a clear correlation between level of moral reasoning and consistent moral behavior. There are still many unanswered questions about Kohlberg's theory. Variations in scoring procedures and complaints that he used only boys in the original research of his work are two of the major criticisms (Gilligan, 1982).

What Factors Contribute to Moral Development?

Several things seem to contribute to growth of moral thinking. There is a relationship between chronological age, intelligence, and higher levels of moral thinking (Froming & McColgan, 1979). An educational experience that allows the student to see a situation from another person's perspective can help promote moral growth. One interesting study supported the idea that counseling someone does more to elevate moral reasoning than does being counseled (Kohlberg & Blatt, 1972). Discussions about moral issues, especially those that present ideas at the next stage ahead of a student's own thinking, enhance moral development. Kohlberg vehemently points out that the best discussions are those that are frequent and an integral part of the school curriculum rather than separate units taught in isolation. Involvement in real decision making is even better!

Not all adults reach the higher stages of moral reasoning; in fact, studies indicate that the number who do is small. The majority of adults operate in stages three and four.

Would you accept Kohlberg's findings that older individuals tend to have higher levels of moral judgment?

■ ■ ■

WHAT IS A "STAGE" THEORY?

You probably have noticed the similarity in the ideas of Piaget and Kohlberg concerning moral development. Erikson's psychosocial theory, like the theories of Piaget and Kohlberg, is a stage theory. Stage theories have at least four common elements. Crain (1985) lists them.

Compare and contrast
Erikson's model with
Kohlberg's model. Do
these models overlap?
Are they mutually
exclusive?

1. Stages refer to qualitatively different cognitive or behavior patterns. At each stage, the major patterns are distinctive from those shown during the previous stage of development. For example, according to Kohlberg (1976), the concept of fairness, a stage-four concept, is not understood by young children who are still reasoning at stage one.

2. Stages describe general issues. A specific characteristic or issue is a dominant theme for each stage. Learning to depend on the predictability of adults is a main issue for the child in the first stage (trust) of Erikson's theory of personal and social development.

3. Stages follow an invariant sequence. Major issues and distinctive behavior patterns happen because of, among other factors, biological maturation. Consequently, stages will follow a definite order. According to Erikson (1980), there are forces that push one along according to a timetable regardless of whether or not one adequately achieves the challenges of the previous stage. In other words, persons must go through all the stages. Kohlberg and Piaget establish stages that are invariant, however they do not contend that persons must go through all the stages. Kohlberg's research verifies that many persons do not reach a level of moral reasoning equal to level five or six.

4. Stages are cultural universals. Do the concepts developed apply to all cultures? If not, a stage would not qualify as legitimate. Kohlberg has demonstrated through research that the level of moral reasoning generally increases as age increases. As a group, teenagers reason at higher levels than do children ages eleven and twelve. Erikson claims that all cultures address the same issues but in different ways. The Sioux of South Dakota, one group that Erikson studied (1975), have a longer and more indulgent nursing period for their children than many other cultures, thereby encouraging dependency upon adults. Other cultures, white American for example, wean children much sooner; consequently, less dependency is encouraged. The issue of dependency at this age is faced by both cultures but with different practices and with different results.

What Are Some Gender Differences in Development?

It appears that females have a slight developmental advantage in terms of the maturation of their physical systems during prenatal and postnatal development. This trend in favor of the female increases from a slight advantage in the preschool period to a quite obvious difference in the average onset for puberty. As previously noted, girls enter puberty almost two years earlier than boys. Girls also achieve their maximum height earlier than boys. This finding of early developmental advantages for girls may explain some of the early verbal and academic advantages that girls appear to enjoy.

Average annual mortality rates for boys are considerably greater than that for girls throughout childhood and adolescence (Smart & Smart, 1975). Accidental death rates account for a large part of the difference between genders. Greater physical activity levels for boys may account for some of the gender differences in accidental deaths.

Considerable research has also been completed on gender differences in self-esteem. As noted by the American Association of University Women (AAUW) (1992), there do not appear to be significant gender differences in self-esteem among elementary students. However, by the sophomore year in high school, girls report a much lower sense of self-esteem than boys. The reasons for these gender differences in self-esteem are not presently clear from the research evidence. However, such findings may indicate that the adolescent years are a more difficult psychosocial time for girls than for boys.

SUMMARY

In this chapter, human growth and development is viewed as an interaction of internal, biological factors with external, social factors. Teachers need to understand both aspects of development to understand the needs of their students. Teachers also need information about developmental factors to design a curriculum that is "developmentally appropriate."

This chapter provides a detailed account of the major characteristics for each age period of the school-aged child. Some of the major developmental models of psychosocial development and moral development also are provided. Both psychosocial and moral development appear to proceed from the externalized control by others, particularly by one's parents, to internalized, self-controlling, self-chosen factors.

Practical information about applying developmental principles to such areas as the curriculum, social problems, and divorce also are provided. This part of the chapter indicates the methods in which research on educational psychology can be effectively used in the classroom.

CHAPTER REVIEW

1. Why should educators learn about developmental stages?
2. What are the general principles of development?
3. What are the principles of growth?
4. What are the characteristics of children and adolescents at various ages?
5. What are some of the major characteristics of the adolescent years?
6. What is critical about either early or late maturing?
7. How can an understanding of the psychosocial theory of development help teachers better understand their students?
8. How do children learn right from wrong?
9. How should an understanding of Kohlberg's theory of moral development influence the practice of teachers at various grade levels?

CONSULTATION COULD MAKE A DIFFERENCE

In reviewing this chapter what types of recommendations would you now make in the case study of Janice at the beginning of the chapter?

The issues raised in the case study can be addressed by some of the following information contained in the chapter.

1. The major characteristics of students at different ages and stages of growth: Was Janice merely "going through the trials of turning thirteen?" Did she need time to work her way through the maturation process and would her disposition and achievement return to normal as she settled into her teenage period?

2. Knowledge about adolescents who mature early or late: Was Janice struggling because she was maturing earlier than her female peers? Was she beginning to feel out of place with her peers and more comfortable with older students?

3. Understanding of the critical challenge of adolescent years: Identity versus role confusion: Was Janice reluctant to make firm commitments to herself and her future? Was she needing help, perhaps counseling, to cope with identity diffusion?

4. Understanding of the importance of the peer group to the developmental process of the individual student: Was Janice experiencing rejection from her peer group? If so, was this rejection somehow related to her early maturing?

It would be important for you as her teacher to seek help in answering these questions. Sociometric data might be useful to see whether Janice has attachments with the other students in her class. An interview with the student, a parent conference, or consultation with specialists in the school (school psychologist or school counselor) might result in a plan to provide experiences for Janice that would help her move through her role confusion and come to accept herself as an achieving and productive adolescent. Using Janice to tutor slightly younger students is perhaps a good choice because it may help her to maintain contact with other age groups. Furthermore, Janice may gain from the experience of tutoring a sense of doing meaningful work and achievement.

REFERENCES

American Association of University Women (1992). *How schools shortchange girls*. Washington, DC: American Association of University Women Educational Foundation.

American Psychological Association (1992). *Learner-centered psychological principles: Guidelines for school redesign and reform* (Draft #3). Washington, DC: American Psychological Association.

Ames, L., Ilg, F., & Baker, S. (1988). *Your ten-to-fourteen-year-old*. New York: Dell.

Argyle, M. (1985) Social behavior problems and social skills training in adolescence. In B. Schneider, K. Rubin, & J. Ledingham, (Eds.) *Children's peer relations: Issues in assessment and intervention* (pp. 207–224). New York: Springer-Verlag.

Baltes, P. B., Reese, H. W., & Lipsitt, L. P. (1980). Life-span developmental psychology. *Annual Review of Psychology, 31,* 65–110.

Barnett, J. (1969). *Development of children's fears: The relationship between three systems of fear measurement.* Unpublished M.A. thesis, University of Wisconsin.

Benson, P., Williams, D., & Johnson, A. (1987). *The quicksilver years: The hopes and fears of early adolescence.* San Francisco: Harper & Row.

Berryman, J., Hargreaves, D., Herbert, M., and Taylor, A. (1991). *Developmental psychology and you.* London: Routledge.

Boser, J., and Poppen, W. (1978). Identification of teacher verbal response roles for improving student-teacher relationships. *Journal of Educational Research, 72* (2), 90–93.

Bowman, B. (1993). Early childhood education. In L. Darling-Hammond (Ed.), *Review of research in education.* Washington, DC: American Educational Research Association.

Brendt, T. (1983). Correlates and causes of sociometric status in childhood: A commentary on six current studies of popular, rejected, and neglected children. *Merrill-Palmer Quarterly, 29* (4), 439–448.

Brennan, T. (1982). Loneliness at adolescence. In A. Peplau & D. Perlman (Eds.), *Loneliness.* New York: Wiley.

Brooks-Gunn, J., & Peterson, A. (1984). Problems in studying and defining pubertal. *Journal of Youth and Adolescence, 13,* 181–196.

Brooks-Gunn, J., & Warren, M. (1989). Biological contributions to effective expression in young adolescent girls. *Child Development, 60,* 372–385.

Buhler, C. (1968). The developmental structure of goal setting in group and individual studies. In C. Buhler & F. Massarik (Eds.), *The course of human life.* New York: Springer.

Cohen, P., Kulic, J., & Kulic, C. (1982). Educational outcomes of tutoring: A meta-analysis of findings. *American Educational Research Journal, 19,* 237–248.

Costanzo, P. R., & Shaw, M. E. (1966). Conformity as a function of age. *Child Development, 37,* 967–975.

Cowen, E., (1973). Long-term follow-up of early detected vulnerable children. *Journal of Consulting and Clinical Psychology, 41,* 3, 438–445.

Crain, W. (1985). *Theories of development: Concepts and applications* (2nd ed.), (pp. 173–175). New York: Prentice Hall.

Csikszentimihalyi, M., & Larson, R. (1984). *Being adolescent: Conflict and growth in the teenage years.* New York: Basic Books.

Damico, S. (1975). The effects of clique membership upon academic achievement. *Adolescence, 10,* 37, 93–100.

Damon, W. (1989). Introduction: Advances in developmental research. In W. Damon (Ed.), *Child development today and tomorrow* (pp. 1–13). San Francisco: Jossey-Bass.

Davidson, P., White, P., Smith, D., & Poppen, W. (1989). Content and intensity of fears in middle childhood among rural and urban boys and girls. *Journal of Genetic Psychology, 150* (1), 51–58.

Eccles, J. S., & Midgley, C. (1989) Developmentally appropriate classrooms for early adolescents. In R. E. Ames & C. Ames (Eds.), *Research on motivation in education: Goals and cognition* (Vol. 3, pp. 139–186). San Diego, CA: Academic Press.

Elkind, D. (1987). *Miseducation: Preschoolers at risk.* New York: Knopf.

Epstein, H. T. (1978). Growth spurts during brain development: Implications for educational policy and practice (pp. 343–370). In J. Chall & A. Mirsky (Ed.) *Education and the Brain.* Chicago: University of Chicago Press.

Erikson, E. H. (1980). *Identity and the life cycle* (2nd ed.). New York: Norton.

Erikson, E. (1975). *Identity: youth and crisis.* New York: Norton.

Erikson, E. (1963). *Childhood and society* (2nd ed.). New York: Norton.

Espenschade, A., & Eckert, H. (1980). *Motor development* (2nd ed.). Columbus, OH: Merrill.

Fein, G. (1978). *Child development.* Englewood Cliffs, NJ: Prentice Hall.

Fischer, K., & Pipp, S. (1984). Processes of cognitive development: Optimal level and skill acquisition. In R. J. Sternberg, (Ed.), *Mechanisms of cognitive development.* San Francisco: W. H. Freeman.

Fischer, K., & Bullock, D. (1984). Cognitive development in school-age children: Conclusions and new developments. In W. Collins (Ed.), *Development during middle childhood: The years from six to twelve.* Washington, DC: National Academic Press.

Froming, W. J. & McColgan, E. B. (1979). *Comparing the defining issues test and the moral dilemma interview.* Developmental Psychology, 15, 6, 658–659.

Gesell, A. (1954). The ontogenesis of infant behavior. In L. Carmichael (Ed.), *Manual of child psychology* (2nd ed.). New York: Wiley.

Gilligan, C. (1982). *In a different voice: Psychological theory and women's development.* Cambridge, MA: Harvard University Press.

Hamill, P., Drizd, T., Johnson, C., Reed, R., Roche, A., & Moore, W. (1979). Physical growth: National Center for Health Statistics prevention. *Clinical Nutrition, 32,* 607–629.

Hartup, W. (1984). The peer context in middle childhood. In W. Collins, (Ed.), *Development during middle childhood: The years from six to twelve.* Washington, DC: National Academic Press.

Hartup, W. (1978). Children and their friends. In H. McGurk (Ed.), *Issues in childhood social development.* London: Methuen.

Hartup, W. (1976). Peer interaction and the behavioral development of the individual child. In E. Schopler & R. Reichler (Eds.), *Psychopathology and child development.* New York: Plenum. Pp 203–218.

Horrocks, J. E., Horrocks, W. B., & Trayer, M. E. (1960). *Tests of human growth and development: Form A.* Columbus: Charles E. Merrill.

Hoppe-Graff, S. (1989). The study of transitions in development: Potentialities of the longitudinal approach. In A. de Ribauprierre (Ed.), *Transition mechanisms in child development: The longitudinal perspective* (pp. 1–30). Cambridge: Cambridge University Press.

Hymel, S. (1983). Preschool children's peer relations: Issues in sociometric assessment. *Merrill-Palmer Quarterly, 29,* 237–260.

Ilg, F., Ames, L., & Baker, S. (1981). *Child behavior: Revised edition.* New York: Harper and Row.

Ilg, F. (1984). *Scoring notes: The developmental examination.* New Haven, CT: Gesell Institute. (rev. ed.).

Johnson, D. (1980). Group processes: Influences of student-student interaction on school outcomes. In J. McMillian (Ed.), *The social psychology of school learning* (pp. 123–168). New York: Academic Press.

Karniol, R. (1980). A conceptual analysis of imminent justice responses in children. *Child Development, 51,* 118–130.

Kohlberg, L. (1981). *The Philosophy of moral development: Moral stages and the idea of justice.* New York: Harper & Row.

Kohlberg, L. (1976). Moral stages and moralization: The cognitive-developmental approach. In T. Lickona (Ed.), *Moral development and behavior* (pp. 31–53). New York: Holt, Rinehart & Winston.

Kohlberg, L., & Blatt, M. (1972). The effects of classroom discussion on level of moral development. In L. Kohlberg & E. Turiel (Eds.), *Recent research in moral development*. New York: Holt, Rinehart & Winston.

Kostelnik, M., Stein, L., Whiren, A., & Soderman, A. (1988). *Guiding children's social development*. Cincinnati, OH: South-Western Publishing.

Lampl, M., Veldhuis, J. D., & Johnson, M. L. (1992). Saltation and stasis: a model of human growth. *Science, 258,* 5083, 801–803.

Livson, N., & Peskin, H. (1980). Perspectives on adolescence from longitudinal research. In J. Adelson (Ed.), *Handbook of adolescent psychology*. New York: Wiley.

Malina, R. (1990). Physical growth and performance during the transitional years (9–16). In R. Montemayor, G. Adams, & T. Gullotta (Eds.), *From childhood to adolescence: A transitional period?* (pp. 41–62). Newberry Park, CA: Sage.

Malina, R. (1983). Menarche in athletes: A synthesis and hypothesis. *Annals of Human Biology, 10,* 1–24.

Marcia, J. E. (1976) Identity six years after: A follow-up study. *Journal of Youth and Adolescence, 5,* 145–160.

Newman, B., & Newman, P. (1986). *Adolescent development* (pp. 95–100). Columbus, OH: Merrill.

Paikoff, R., & Brooks-Gunn, J. (1990). Physiological processes: What role do they play during the transition to adolescence? In R. Montemayor, G. Adams, & T. Gullotta. (Eds.), *From childhood to adolescence: A transitional period?* (pp. 63–81). Newberry Park, CA: Sage.

Parke, B. (1985). A field adaptation of the SYMLOG adjective rating form suitable for populations including children. *International Journal of Small Group Research, 1,* 89–95.

Perry, J. (1979). Popular, amiable, isolated, rejected: A reconceptualization of sociometric status in preschool children. *Child Development, 50,* 1231–1234.

Piaget, J. (1973). *The moral judgment of children*. New York: Free Press.

Poppen, W., & White, P. (1986). Stepfamilies. In L. Golden & D. Capuzzi (Eds.), *Helping families help children: Family interventions with school-related problems*. Springfield, IL: Charles C. Thomas.

Reimer, J., Paolitto, D., & Hersh, R. (1983). *Promoting moral growth: From Piaget to Kohlberg*. New York: Longman.

Smart, M. S., & Smart, R. C. (1975). *Children: Development and relationships* (3rd edition). New York: MacMillan Publishing Company.

Stallings, J., & Kashowitz, D. (1974). *Follow-through classroom observation evaluation*. Menlo Park, CA: Stanford Research Institute.

Stattin, H., & Magnusson, D. (1989). Social transition in adolescence: A biosocial perspective. In A. de Ribauprierre (Ed.), *Transition mechanisms in child development: The longitudinal perspective* (pp. 147–190). Cambridge: Cambridge University Press.

Vosk, B., Forehand, R., Parker, J., & Rickard, K. (1982). A multimethod comparison of popular and unpopular children. *Developmental psychology, 18* (4), 571–575.

Ward, B., Mergendoller, J., Tikunoff, W., Rounds, T., Mitman, A., & Dadey, G. (1982). *Junior high school transition study: Volume VII, executive summary*. San Francisco: Far West Laboratory for Educational Research and Development.

Waterman, A. (1982). Identity development from adolescence to adulthood: An extension of theory and a review of research. *Developmental Psychology, 18,* 341–358.

CHAPTER 3

Cognition, Constructivism and Language

■ ■ ■

Chapter Outline

NEW TEACHING METHODS INTRODUCED

You are a second-grade teacher at a suburban school in a large, Southeastern city. Your principal has just returned from a state department of education workshop. Because of the workshop, your principal has become enthusiastic about some new educational practices. These are "whole language instruction" and "developmentally appropriate curriculum."

Your principal wants to implement these two practices and believes that they will help the children. Your principal also believes that they will help the school with its accreditation review by the department of education during the next school year.

Your principal claims that whole language instruction focuses on integrating the language arts curriculum and on whole class instruction (there will no longer be any in-class groups based on reading level). A developmentally appropriate curriculum focuses on determining the individual's developmental level, such as the level of cognitive development of the student. Then the teacher designs the instruction to match each individual student's ability level.

How will these new policies affect your curriculum and teaching methods? What changes will occur in your classroom in regard to tracking or grouping? How do you determine the child's level of cognitive development? Is there a contradiction between having whole language instruction and a developmentally appropriate curriculum? Can the two policies be integrated together in the classroom?

INTRODUCTION

The purpose of this chapter is to review the psychological aspects of cognition and language with a focus on individual development. A second purpose is to analyze the relationship between cognition and language. In particular, this chapter examines how the interrelationship of thought and language affects learning in children.

In the first part of this chapter, the Piagetian model of cognitive development is presented. This model and its application to the field of teaching are addressed. An emerging model in the field of cognition, Constructivism, is reviewed. The Vygotskian model of thought and language is presented.

In the second part of this chapter, three different models of language development are reviewed. These are the behavioral model, the psycholinguistic model, and the interactionist model. The sequence for individual language acquisition also is examined.

Other areas presented include an examination of second language learning; a survey of the different dialects in the United States; and a review of gender differences in the language area.

COGNITION AND COGNITIVE DEVELOPMENT

Cognition and Language

Higher-order cognition and abstract language comprise two key distinctions between Homo sapiens and other species. Although other species clearly have thought and communication systems, these systems do not appear to have the flexibility or complexity of human cognition and language.

How does thought, language and development come together?

In particular, other species do not show evidence of the ability to form abstract concepts. Abstract concepts are critical to the development of such areas as science, mathematics, religion, and the arts.

Vygotsky (1962) explained the ability to form abstract concepts in the following manner. In developing the capability to create abstract concepts, both thought and language are crucial. In humans, thought and language have different roots, but at some point in development they come together. In effect, thought becomes largely verbal in adults and language becomes largely rational.

By adulthood, Vygotsky indicates that our thought processes are governed by verbal categorizations. Our words are governed by linear, abstract, and logical thought processes. Thus, this coming together of thought and language in development is the key to some of the most distinctive aspects of being human.

The interaction between thought and language in the individual plays a crucial role in maturation and socialization. For instance, the level of vocabulary knowledge is one of the best predictors of school achievement. Conversely, a problem in normal language development is often the first sign that the child may have a disability. As we enter the adult years, our communication skills are often considered a key predictor of vocational success.

What Is the Process of Cognitive Development?

Cognitive development is the process by which mental abilities are constructed during the developing years. The interest in cognitive development and cognition has ebbed and flowed in American psychology during the twentieth century. For many years, the study of cognitive development and cognition existed outside the behaviorist mainstream. However, since the 1960s, there has been a strong and consistent interest in cognitive development.

This interest is largely due to the impact of Jean Piaget's model of cognitive development. As Crain (1992) stated: "Today, there is hardly a study of children's thinking that does not refer to Piaget" (p. 102).

Jean Piaget

Jean Piaget probably is the best-known name in the field of developmental psychology. Piaget's professional career stretched from the 1920s until his death in 1980. In all likelihood, he will be remembered as one of the most influential psychologists of the twentieth century.

Jean Piaget is a major figure in both cognitive development and in cognitive learning theory. In fact, Piaget could be considered one of the founders of the Cognitive Psychology paradigm, as well as of the Constructivist model. (In order to cover the complexity of Piaget's model, his cognitive learning theory is presented in chapter 9.)

What Are the Major Points in Piaget's Model of Cognitive Development?

How does Piaget view the overall process of cognitive development?

Piaget's model of cognitive development can be characterized as an invariant sequence of increasingly complex and sophisticated ways of thinking about the world. In effect, as individuals develop through childhood, their cognitive abilities proceed in a set sequence. The individual's cognitive repertoire becomes more complex and varied during development.

Piaget claimed that the sequence for cognitive development is universal and cross-cultural. However, Piaget did not, as many writers state, indicate that cognitive development was tied to a specific biological timetable (Crain, 1992). Rather, Piaget's stages of cognitive development are viewed as the way that children must progress as they increasingly refine their thinking. Piaget was opposed to specific age-based timetables in his model. Thus, age values presented with Piaget's model are relative rather than absolute.

What Characteristics Are Associated with the Four Stages of Cognitive Development?[1]

Piaget described four basic stages of cognitive development, which represent the basic ways that children construct their understanding of the world. Each peri-

1. Donna A. Henderson Ph.D. wrote the material on Jean Piaget. Henderson is a professor in the Department of Human Development and Learning at East Tennessee State University in Johnson City, Tennessee.

od involves a reorganization in the child's thinking. The ages of children in each stage are approximations of when such changes in cognitive structures occur.

Specifically, the child progresses through the thinking stages of:

1. sensorimotor thinking;
2. preoperational thinking;
3. concrete operational thinking;
4. formal operational thinking.

Transitions during these periods move from action-based thinking processes into symbolic, then logical, and finally abstract thinking.

Sensorimotor Stage. The sensorimotor stage (birth to roughly two years) is characterized by physical actions and sensations, such as touching, hitting, sucking, listening, and seeing. At first, movements are reflexive rather than planned. As children progress, their actions become more goal directed. This accomplishment is a move to means-ends behavior: in effect, the understanding that certain events lead to other events.

At some point during the sensorimotor stage, children begin to distinguish self from the environment, recognizing themselves as separate from mother or bottle or other externals. Children also gain the notion of object permanence, the recognition that something exists even if it is not in sight.

Piaget suggested that object permanence occurs when a child begins to look for something that is hidden. Before object permanence is attained, the child does not look for or pursue hidden objects. The acquisition of the understanding of object permanence is the key development in the sensorimotor period.

As children begin to acquire language in the latter part of the sensorimotor period, symbolic activity (using words and numbers to represent objects) is increased. By the end of this stage, children have an emerging ability in dealing symbolically with the immediate environment.

Preoperational Stage. During the preoperational stage (two to roughly seven years), the development and use of internal images are most clearly demonstrated. The ascendancy of vivid mental imagery in children's mental life is more evident in the first half of this stage than at any other time. Children will often seem preoccupied with their imaginative abilities in the preschool period. They may report seeing things in the dark and may have imaginary playmates.

Children in this stage are described as egocentric. This means they see things from one point of view, their own, and assume everyone else has the identical viewpoint they do. They cannot separate other perspectives from their own view. Egocentrism is often thought of from an emotional viewpoint: the child cannot understand how Mom can be tired when the child is not tired and still wants to play.

However, egocentrism also has a linguistic, a perceptual, and a behavioral basis. For instance, Piaget claimed that the language of preschool children was fundamentally egocentric. Children during this stage frequently engage in what are termed "collective monologues." They verbalize about what is on their own mind without regard to what others are saying or doing.

What is the key development in the sensorimotor stage?

Describe the role of egocentrism during this stage.

Piaget also demonstrated perceptual egocentrism in his own research. He showed that when children view an object or a building from one perspective, they think that all other perspectives look the same. It is not until the latter stages of the preoperational period that the ability to overcome egocentrism is fully possible. The ability to overcome egocentrism is considered the key development during the preoperational period.

Another characteristic of the preoperational stage is children's logic, which is described as transductive. This means that they draw inferences about the relationship of objects based on only a single attribute. For example, all women are mothers. Children in this stage classify objects by some common feature such as shape, texture, or size but will seldom use more than one criterion for classification.

During this stage, children are capable of understanding simple rules. They consider the rules fundamental and inflexible. Cognition in this stage is often described as prelogical thinking.

Concrete Operations Stage. During the period of concrete operations (roughly age seven to eleven/fifteen), a child develops systematic, logical thinking capabilities. These capacities are generally limited, however, to concrete objects and activities. An operation is an activity that is carried out mentally and is reversible. This means that children understand that actions that affect an object (tying a shoelace)—if reversed—(untied) will return the object to its original state.

Children in this period develop an understanding of other people's feelings and thoughts. They can use reasoning skills to solve problems. They can move from specific cases to derive a general principle.

They have conservation skills. According to Piaget, conservation is one of the most important of all mental operations. Understanding the concept of conservation is the key development during this stage. One aspect of conservation means that the child understands that changing some characteristics of an object does not change other characteristics. For instance, understanding conservation means recognizing that the amount of something stays the same even if some other dimension is changed.

Piaget discussed three types of conservation:

1. Conservation of number is illustrated in the following example. A certain number of pennies are lined up with their sides touching. Exactly the same number of pennies are then lined up with space between each penny. The preoperational child will state that the longer row has more pennies. Successfully recognizing that the number has not changed by the new configuration is conservation of number.
2. Conservation of volume occurs when a child can recognize that the amount of liquid in two containers of different shapes is the same even if one level is higher than the other. An example of this is to have two identical containers filled with water. The child will agree that the containers have the same amount. However, if water from one is poured into a tall, thin glass

Discuss the relationship between conservation and learning mathematics.

Until conversation is acquired, children tend to focus on a single feature of an object. In this case the boy indicates that the tall glass contains more liquid even though both glasses have the same amount.

and water from the other is poured into a shorter, wider glass, the child will say the taller glass has more.

3. The final type of conservation Piaget discussed is conservation of area. Pennies once again can be used as an illustration. Conservation of area means that children can recognize that the area within the shapes (pennies) remains the same whether or not the pennies are touching each other or in a different configuration.

During the concrete operations period, children can understand that rules are changeable. Children are fully capable of distinguishing reality from fantasy. Children have increased capacities for memory, attention, and concentration. Children in this stage are able to use logical thought in solving problems that are tied to reality.

Formal Operations Stage. Children in the period of formal operations (roughly eleven, fifteen years of age through adulthood) are in the most advanced stage of cognitive development. They are capable of systematic abstract thought. This means they can think about possibilities—"What if I were president?" "What will happen during an economic depression?"—and other types of abstractions. This ability to understand and generate hypothetical abstractions is the key development during this period.

People in this stage are able to understand similes, metaphors, and analogies in terms of figurative, abstract thinking. For instance, they can understand that the simile,"Her lips were as sweet as red ripe cherries" is purely figurative with no basis in any concrete sense.

What is the key development during formal operations?

The implications of Piaget's work on cognitive development for teachers are significant. Two important aspects are that there are fundamental, qualitative differences in the thinking processes of children when compared with adults and that children are sometimes at different stages of cognitive development even though they are at the same age. Some recommendations for teachers are:

1. Teachers should be aware of the child's current stage of development as classroom activities are planned.
2. Teachers should structure their curriculum to the child's developmental level. A developmentally appropriate curriculum is now being mandated by federal guidelines for preschool and special education programs. A developmentally appropriate curriculum emphasizes formative evaluations, such as readiness tests, that indicate the child's level of ability. Children are then instructed at that level.
3. Piaget emphasized that children must be instructed at their present level of development. Attempts to accelerate or skip stages of cognitive development are doomed to failure. They only increase a child's frustration with the learning tasks.
4. Teachers should recognize that what a child already knows will influence what new information can be absorbed.
5. To maximize learning, education should promote the active participation of the child. Piaget believed that children construct or organize their own cognitive view of the world. Piaget believed that children generally learn at a higher rate by active discovery than by lecture or demonstration.

Individuals in the formal operations stage understand that multiple factors can interact to produce an outcome. They can use deductive reasoning to go from a general proposition to a particular application. In addition, they can generate and test hypotheses. Rules are understood as principles, and they are capable of establishing and revising standards. They have achieved what Piaget considered the highest level of cognitive functioning.

Criticisms of Piaget

One of the major criticisms of Piaget has revolved around the issue of how "invariant" the stages of development are. Do children really stay in these stages in such a definitive manner? What does the research on children indicate on this point?

In their review of the research, Flavell, Miller, and Miller (1993) noted:

> The problem is that children often do not act as though they belong in that stage. "Conservers" do not always conserve; formal operations thinkers often think very concretely. The particular materials, tasks, social contexts, and instructions appear to influence the children's performance (pp. 11–12).

Flavell, Miller, and Miller also indicated that young children appear to be more competent and older children appear to be less competent than Piaget originally postulated. For instance, Flavell, Miller, and Miller stated that children in the preoperational period are able to complete more mental activities than

Piaget asserted. Older children in the concrete operational period and formal operational period are less able to complete the cognitive activities indicated by Piaget.

Another problem with Piaget's model is that many, if not most, adults never fully demonstrate formal operational thinking. Thus, the attainment of the formal operations stage often remains a capability rather than a demonstrated ability.

Therefore, a series of difficult questions are raised about Piaget's model. Some developmental psychologists believe that Piaget's overall model does not stand up to scientific scrutiny. They believe enough problems are found with the model to justify a new approach to cognitive development.

Other researchers believe that though parts of the model should be discarded, the general outlines of Piaget's model of cognitive development have held up quite well (Crain, 1992). They believe that generally children do pass through the stages in a manner that basically follows Piaget's theory. They believe that classroom instruction and curriculum decisions should be based on Piagetian approaches. The child's cognitive developmental level should be ascertained and a developmentally appropriate level of instruction should then be used.

Recently, a number of other models of cognition and cognitive development have been derived from Piaget's work. Some of these developmental psychologists are considered Neo-Piagetian (Flavell, Miller, & Miller, 1993).

Other psychologists take another approach, in part derived from Piaget's model. This group emphasizes the individual's ability to cognitively construct his own view of and understanding of the world. This model is called Constructivism.

What Is the Basis for Constructivism?

Constructivism is an emerging theoretical model that stems from a number of academic areas. These areas are philosophy, philosophy of science, psychology, anthropology, and sociology. In the educational psychology field, Constructivism has its roots in a number of paradigms, including those of Piaget, Dewey, Vygotsky, and Montessori. In the education and psychology fields, some of the current writers in the area of Constructivism are: Kamii (1985); Fosnot (1989); and O'Loughlin (1992).

While there is a divergence of opinion as to what Constructivism means as a theory, there also appear to be some common points. These commonalties are:

1. Constructivism is based on the belief that the cognitive development of a child is due to a continuous process of construction and reconstruction of the child's sense of reality.
2. The cognitions of children reflect this continuous process of trying to organize and make sense out of the world. This process of organizing and constructing cognitive models of the world is inherent in the mental life of humans.
3. Once a cognitive model of the external world is created, it undergoes reality testing by the child. Models are discarded when they fail to correctly match the child's actual observations of the external world. New cognitive constructions are created and the process of reality testing continues.

What are some ways that Constructivism can be applied in the classroom?

4. In applying this process to learning, it is clear that the Constructivist approach encourages an active, creative process in the student.

As stated by Black and Ammon (1992), Constructivism in the educational area is:

> more concerned with understandings achieved through relevant experience than with accumulated facts received from others, more imbued with meaning, more domain or situation specific, more influenced by social and cultural contexts, and, in general, less purely cognitive and less governed by abstract principles than traditional conceptions of learning (p. 324).

Such an approach is clearly influenced by Piaget. However, there are some differences. Constructivism is a model that is not necessarily bound by the fixed cognitive stages seen in Piaget's model. Constructivism also grants a greater influence to the social/cultural aspects of development than Piaget acknowledged. For instance, Constructivism emphasizes an understanding of how the social constructions created by one's society appear to define our own views of what is reality.

Constructivist approaches have been applied to a number of different academic fields. Recently, Constructivism has been applied with increasing frequency to the mathematics and science disciplines.

Mosenthal and Ball (1992) presented a math program that used a Constructivist model. They stated that in this type of program:

> learners develop conceptual understanding and the ability to solve mathematical problems when they are actively involved and their engagement moves from the concrete to the abstract level. Applying mathematics to novel situations, inventing strategies, and assessing the reasonableness of one's solutions are among the hallmarks of understanding. Telling and explaining are less the teacher's trade in this approach. Instead, the teacher serves as a guide, fostering students' learning by posing problems and asking questions aimed at helping students clarify their thinking (p. 348).

Mosenthal and Ball continued:

> The primary criterion for understanding is no longer correctness, but the ability to show the coherence or logic of the problem, a solution path, and a solution. For example, a child who, in computing 32 + 19, makes 32 little slashes and 19 little slashes and then circles groups of 10 likely understands place value better than the one who uses the standard carrying procedure. A child who can use blocks to model 32/7 understands division better than one who can simply compute the answer (p. 350).

Black and Ammon (1992) presented a different type of program that used Constructivism. Their program was designed to train teachers in a Developmental-Constructivist approach to teaching. This approach used a combination of Piagetian and Constructivist views as part of a teacher education curriculum.

As part of this curriculum, Black and Ammon developed a sequence of how teachers change their attitudes in moving from a more traditional, teacher-centered approach to a Constructivist approach. Figure 3.1 presents this sequence.

FIGURE 3.1
Development of Teachers' Conceptions of Teaching and Learning

Goals of Instruction	Requirements for Learning	Nature of Teaching
1. A large store of facts and procedures	1. Be able and receptive	1. Telling and showing
2. Essential skills for attaining and using facts and procedures	2. Practice new skills, having first acquired prerequisite skills	2. Giving students practice, with corrective feedback and positive reinforcement
3. Correct understandings of concepts underlying facts, procedures, and skills in a subject	3. Manipulate and explore relevant aspects of reality, having reached the required developmental stage	3. Giving students opportunities to explore and manipulate developmentally appropriate materials
4. Improved conceptual understandings	4. Use best thinking to construct understandings consistent with present level of development	4. Engaging students in thought-provoking activities and guiding their thinking toward better understandings
5. Ways of thinking that can lead to better understandings	5. Reflect on general characteristics of best current thinking	5. Helping students examine their own thinking

Black, A. & Ammon, P. *Journal of Teacher Education,* November–December 1992, Vol. 43, 323–335.

Criticisms of Constructivism

Like many emerging theoretical models, Constructivism suffers from something akin to an identity crisis. Is Constructivism a rehash of the Socratic method? Is it another version of John Dewey's discovery learning—a model of learning by doing? Or is it simply Piaget warmed-over? Clearly, there are many different views of Constructivism that are rampant today. As to whether these different views will coalesce into a coherent theoretical model remains to be seen.

Perhaps a more telling criticism is made in questioning whether the academic content of a course will suffer in order to use the process involved in a Constructivist classroom. In effect, by emphasizing process, will content suffer in classrooms using this model?

Mosenthal and Ball (1992) make the point that the relationship of academic content knowledge and the use of Constructivism is still an unresolved issue. Thus, it remains unclear as to whether the actual knowledge base and basic skills level of students will suffer from the use of a Constructivist approach.

> Is Constructivism too process oriented? How can it be used to teach basic skills?

Lev Vygotsky

The Vygotskian approach to cognition and language provides an interesting counterpoint to Piaget. Vygotsky was a Russian psychologist whose professional career spanned little more than a decade. Born in 1896, he died of tuberculosis at the age of thirty-eight. Because of Soviet political censorship, Vygotsky's works were suppressed and unavailable in the West until the late 1950s.

The recent interest in the United States with Vygotsky's work apparently stems from a number of sources. The fall of the Soviet Union and the ebbing of Marxist ideology makes Vygotsky more palatable in today's world (Vygotsky,

Vygotsky believed that a complete understanding of the child can only occur through an understanding of the child's social context.

after all, was a Marxist). Publication of his collected works in English in the last decade has been another factor. An increased interest in the interrelationship between cognition and language also has contributed to Vygotsky's resurgence.

What Are the Important Aspects of Vygotsky's Approach to Cognition and Concept Development?

Vygotsky's seminal book was *Thought and Language* (Vygotsky, 1962). Along with his collected writings, this book first presents the paradigm now sometimes referred to as the Contextual model (Flavell, Miller, & Miller, 1993). Other writers refer to Vygotsky's approach as the Social-Historical theory (Crain, 1992).

As both titles imply, Vygotsky's model viewed the child within the framework of a specific cultural context. In fact, Vygotsky was clear that the child-in-society must be the unit of analysis. Neither social environment by itself (as the behaviorists examined development) nor the child by herself (as the Piagetians viewed development) could actually explain the complexity of cognitive development.

Much of Vygotsky's analysis of cognition involved concept development. In terms of concept development, Vygotsky distinguished between spontaneous concepts (everyday concepts) that are learned independently by the child and scientific concepts that are taught through external instruction.

Spontaneous concepts stem naturally from the social development of the child. Vygotsky used the example of the development of the spontaneous concept of brother. This type of concept is based on the experiences and images of one's own brother. It is internally generated.

The abstract or scientific concept of brother (as in brotherly or brotherhood) is developed through outside instruction, usually with adults.

According to Vygotsky, concept development begins with spontaneous concepts. During childhood and particularly during the school-age period, children build on the spontaneous concepts by using scientific concepts to categorize and generalize the spontaneous concepts.

Vygotsky stated that Piaget focused solely on how children develop spontaneous concepts. Vygotsky criticized Piaget for not focusing more on the development of scientific concepts. Vygotsky (1962) believed that the reason for this was:

> he (Piaget) assumes that development and instruction are entirely separate, incommensurate processes, that the function of instruction is merely to introduce adult ways of thinking, which conflict with the child's own and eventually supplant them. Studying child thought apart from the influence of instruction, as Piaget did, excludes a very important source of change and bars the the researcher from posing the question of the interaction of development and instruction peculiar to each age level (pp. 116–117).

Describe the differences between spontaneous and scientific concepts.

Much of Vygotsky's work on cognition examined this interaction of development and instruction. One of the more important ideas derived from this work is the concept of the Zone of Proximal Development.

When children's academic skills are measured, each child is measured separately. Thus, children independently take tests, such as an achievement test. Such tests are used to measure a child's progress and sometimes to predict his academic future.

Vygotsky pointed out that a more useful predictor of a child's potential is the Zone of Proximal Development—the distance between the child's ability when working independently and the child's ability when working with assistance. Thus children who cannot solve fractions on their own but can solve the answers with assistance have the ability to solve fractions within their Zone of Proximal Development. Their potential contains the ability to solve fractions. Infants, who cannot eat on their own but can eat with assistance, have within their zone the potential to eat on their own.

How would the zone of proximal development be used in the classroom?

How Did Vygotsky View the Acquisition of Thought and Language?

It is perhaps the relationship between cognition and language where Vygotsky has had his greatest impact. In exploring the relationship between thought and language, Vygotsky's model begins with a hypothesis about the development of language in Homo sapiens.

The creation and use of tools in our species is believed by Vygotsky to have been crucial to the development of thought and language. As our species created new tools for dealing with its world, it became increasingly aware of the properties of these tools. This brought about new modes of thinking to deal with these tools. New methods of communication also had to be developed to more effectively use the tools in group situations.

At some point our species also learned to create tools to make other tools. (This is a distinctive trait of Homo sapiens. We appear to be the only species to create tools to make other tools.) This step involved another elaboration of both thinking and communication skills. In particular, this step increased the need for foresight, for placing oneself in the future, or for visualizing a created outcome when a tool is used to make another tool.

Vygotsky applied these insights from species development to individual development. The tools that we use today are what Vygotsky called "psychological tools" such as maps or mnemonic memory aids. Using a term from semiotics, Vygotsky called such psychological tools "signs or sign systems." The most important sign system is speech.

What Are the Developments That Bring About Abstract Thinking and Language in Child Development?

Although tool use triggered a series of evolutionary adaptations leading to thought and language, Vygotsky believed that in child development thought and language begin as separate tracks.

Vygotsky (1962) made four conclusions about the early relationship of thought and language:

1. In individual development, thought and speech have different roots.
2. In the speech development of the child, we can with certainty establish a preintellectual stage, and in thought development, a prelinguistic stage.
3. Up to a certain point in time, the two follow different lines, independent of each other.
4. At a certain point, these lines meet, whereupon thought becomes verbal and speech rational (p. 44).

One of the crucial aspects of this coming together of thought and language is the role of inner speech. For Vygotsky, an infant's speech patterns have primarily a social quality to them, though Vygotsky did acknowledge some biological role to language. Thus, the first type of speech pattern to arise is social speech, which is triggered through the infant's interaction with the parents. Social speech is used to identify the basics in life: mama, dada, milk, etc.

Egocentric speech develops out of social speech. However, unlike Piaget, Vygotsky believed that egocentric speech helped children to orient or self-regulate their behavior. Egocentric speech is children talking to themselves in a self-help manner. Egocentric speech continues to develop throughout childhood, but it increasingly becomes silent speech—nonvocal inner speech.

Thus, egocentric speech develops into inner speech. Eventually, inner speech develops into the primary form of cognition in people: "thinking words." This becomes qualitatively different from social speech—the language we use to communicate with other people. Yet there remains some relationship between the two. As Vygotsky (1962) states:

Describe the differences between Piaget and Vygotsky.

The relation between thought and word is a living process; thought is born through words. A word devoid of thought is a dead thing, and a thought unembodied in words remains a shadow (p. 153).

Criticisms of Vygotsky

While Constructivism lacks cohesiveness because it is still emerging as a model, Vygotsky's model suffers from the untimely death of its author. Thus, the incompleteness of Vygotsky's model is perhaps its biggest problem.

Another criticism that may be leveled at this model is the degree to which it supports the acceleration of cognitive functions. Vygotsky appears to have endorsed the view that cognitive development may be accelerated through instruction. This viewpoint has been sharply criticized by those from the Piagetian perspective. The question focuses on the developmentally appropriate level of instruction that should be given to children: Do we take children at the level that they appear to be or do we attempt to take them beyond that level?

Vygotsky's model has a considerable influence on today's educational psychology. As indicated, the relationship between thought and language devised by Vygotsky remains a major contribution. The next section further explores the relationship between thought and language with a particular focus on language development.

Lev Vygotsky (1896–1934) made a number of important insights concerning the relationship between thought and language.

LANGUAGE AND LANGUAGE DEVELOPMENT

What Are the Differences between Language and Communication?

Linguists, psychologists, and anthropologists have traditionally made a distinction between a language system and a communication system (Lieberman, 1984). According to this viewpoint, human languages have the following characteristics that distinguish them from the communication systems of other species:

1. A language is self-generative. From a finite number of phonemes an infinite number of words can be generated. Phonemes are basic sound units, such as the "b" sound. There are approximately forty-five phonemes in the English language, which are combined to generate all the words in the language.
2. Language is made up of arbitrary agreements between words and their referents. There is no direct correspondence between the sounds we make when we say the word "mom" and the actual person. We agree that the word "mom" will be used to designate that person, just as we agree that "chair" will be used to refer to that particular object.
3. A language is flexible and is continuously changing. Languages are constantly being transformed. New words are being created, while other words are being discarded. The English language has undergone such profound changes. For instance, Modern English probably would be unintelligible to an individual speaking Old English at the time of William the Conqueror.

4. A language is capable of forming abstractions and concepts. In this sense a human language is capable of forming a new word to abstract out commonalties from a given group of concrete objects. For instance, a desk, a table, and a sofa have in common the concept or abstraction of furniture. There is no such concrete object as furniture. It is an abstraction formed by deriving the commonalties of chair, table, and sofa.

What Are the Major Theories of Language Acquisition?

One of the perennial questions about human language acquisition centers on whether language is learned or innate. The theories of language acquisition can be distinguished on the basis of how they stand on the nature/nurture issue. The models presented in this chapter range across the spectrum on the issue of whether language is learned, is innate, or is an interaction of learning and innate aspects.

The behavioral theory of language acquisition states that language acquisition is all or nearly all due to learning from environmental stimuli. In this viewpoint, language is fundamentally a cultural trait that is handed down from generation to generation by conditioning and imitation.

On the other hand, the psycholinguistic theory of language states that language acquisition is largely developed through innate neural processes. In this theory, language development is much like physical development. There is an inborn genetic program for language learning that is triggered through interaction with other humans.

The interactionist theory of language is a model that states that language acquisition is the result of a more or less balanced interaction between innate processes and environmental experiences. In this model, the interaction between innate abilities and the environment is the key aspect of language learning.

Behavioral Theory of Language Acquisition. The behavioral theory of language acquisition was generally the result of B. F. Skinner's work on language development (Skinner, 1957). This viewpoint on language acquisition stems from previous positions taken by behaviorists with regard to human development.

The position taken by the behaviorist school on human development, including language acquisition, is perhaps best summarized in a famous quotation by John Watson. Watson, the psychologist who coined the term behaviorism, stated:

> Give me the baby . . . I'll make it a thief, a gunman, or a dope friend. The possibilities of shaping it in any direction are almost endless. Even gross anatomical differences limit us far less than you may think. . . . Make him a deaf mute and I will build you a Helen Keller. Men are built, not born (Watson, 1927, p. 233).

Thus, the radical environmental view of language acquisition takes the position that language is entirely a learned activity. The sheer variety of human languages is often cited as evidence for the behaviorist theory.

According to behaviorists, if language is innate, how does one explain the variety of different languages around the world? After all, a toddler in Norway learns to speak Norwegian, while a toddler in Saudi Arabia learns to speak Arabic. These two toddlers learn completely different languages. A behaviorist would argue that if language was an inborn trait, then languages should show a much greater similarity.

An analogy could be made concerning the types of food that the child eats: A Norwegian child learns to eat Norwegian food, while an Arabic child eats Arabic food. There is no inborn preference for different cuisine anymore than there is for language. We basically eat what we are taught to eat, just as we speak what we are taught to speak.

Behavioral views of language acquisition stress the role of reinforcement and imitation in language learning. Children learn a language because their parents and caretakers positively reinforce them for learning it. The excitement and social reinforcement that parents demonstrate when a baby makes its first approximately meaningful sound are obviously reinforcers for that behavior.

How is language acquired in this model?

Therefore, in the viewpoint taken by Skinner (1957), the meaningful sound made by the child is an operant response, which is then reinforced by the parents. This meaningful sound is repeated by the child and is subsequently reinforced by the parents. Parents tend to ignore sounds by the baby that do not approximate sounds in their native language. Thus, those sounds are less likely to be used by the child in the future. In this sense parents shape the sounds made by the infant. They reward the sounds that approximate their native language.

Children also learn a language because adults in their environment constantly use it and the child imitates their speech sounds just as they imitate their social behavior. Thus, a child is more likely to produce a speech sound that he constantly hears in his environment than one he has not regularly heard.

In summary, the behavioral theory of language development emphasizes the role of traditional behavioral principles in language acquisition. Skinner (1957) stated that positive reinforcement of speech sounds can completely explain the acquisition of language in infancy.

Psycholinguistic Theory of Language Acquisition. The psycholinguistic theory of language acquisition was largely developed by linguist Noam Chomsky (Chomsky, 1957; 1975). This theory is sometimes referred to as a nativist perspective. Chomsky published an important critique of Skinner's viewpoint on language in 1959 (Chomsky, 1959). This critique helped establish psycholinguistic theory in the psychology field. Chomsky's work and the subsequent work by Eric Lenneberg (Lenneberg, 1967) emphasized the neural and biological basis for language acquisition.

The central tenet of the psycholinguistic theory is the concept of the language acquisition device (Chomsky, 1959). The language acquisition device (LAD) is an innate "prewired" structure in the temporal lobes of the neocortex. It is prewired in the same sense as the neocortical centers that control voluntary muscle movements. The voluntary motor centers in the central nervous system are located in virtually the same site in any person. They appear to be part of a genetic program for neural structures. In adults, brain damage to the site that controls the voluntary muscles will result in temporary or permanent loss of voluntary muscle movements (Teuber, 1975).

In Chomsky's view, the language acquisition device in the central nervous system appears to follow a similar genetic program. As with the motor centers, the language centers in the central nervous system are located in a particular site that basically is the same for each individual. As noted by Chomsky (1980) in his discussion of why he believed chimpanzees would not learn human language: "One thing is missing: that little part of the left hemisphere that is responsible for the specific structures of human language" (p. 181).

Chomsky does not exactly specify the nature of the language acquisition device. The question arises as to the degree of innate language ability in the child. Are there specific concepts that are genetically programmed? Are there structural aspects of language that are genetically programmed?

Chomsky speculates that the innate aspects of the LAD must include some of the basic underlying rules of language. In effect, the rules that are used to put words together into meaningful sentences or phrases. The term usually applied to these structural rules of language is syntax. Chomsky states that certain types of syntactical aspects are universal and apparently innate.

Thus, part of the innate aspect of the LAD is in the organizational and structural method of putting together a meaningful phrase or sentence. All human languages have a sentence structure that includes a noun and a verb. All languages have a method for negating a proposition and for distinguishing between different moments in time, such as past, present, and future. Thus, at least part of syntax is innate in Chomsky's model.

Two other terms of importance to Chomsky's model are deep structure and surface structure. Deep structure is the actual meaning or intention of a communication. Surface structure is the sound produced during the communication. In a common-sense way, surface structure is what we say, and deep structure is what we mean to say.

Clearly, the surface structure of a communication can produce one or more deep structure meanings. For instance, there is the sentence: "Nobody hurts like Barry Manilow." We could interpret this sentence to mean that no one feels pain like Barry Manilow. On the other hand, we could interpret the sentence to mean that no can cause pain like Barry Manilow. The speech sounds or written symbols in the sentence are the surface structure. The meaning derived from the sentence is the deep structure. The division of communications into a surface structure and a deep structure also is considered to be an innate aspect of the language acquisition device.

Chomsky points out that language acquisition develops at about the same time and in the same sequence in children, regardless of culture or country. The universality of the timing and sequence in language development is often cited as evidence for some type of innate program for language.

Interactionist Theory of Language Acquisition. As previously indicated, the interactionist perspective on language focuses on a balance between environmental and innate aspects of language acquisition. The interactionist model was developed by a number of researchers in the 1970s to explain some of the research anomalies found with both the behaviorist and psycholinguist theories.

How would gender or ethnic differences in language ability be explained by Chomsky?

Although the interactionist model is distinct from the two previous theories, the interactionist viewpoint is currently split between two camps: the cognitive interactionists and the social interactionists (Lombardo, 1990; Owens, 1988). To some degree the differences between the cognitive and social interactionists reflect the earlier divisions between the behaviorists and the psycholinguists. The cognitive interactionists are more supportive of the innate aspects of language, while the social interactionists are more supportive of the environmental contributions.

One of the differences between the interactionist perspective and the psycholinguistic perspective is best illustrated by the role of semantics versus syntactics in language acquisition. Chomsky's view is that syntax (the way that words are put together to form sentences) is partly innate and drives other aspects of language such as semantics (the meaning or definition of an individual word).

A series of studies published in the 1970s (Bloom, 1970; Brown, 1973; and Slobin, 1970) indicated that in the course of language development, semantics developed before syntax and that semantics developed from experience. In effect, the first words that a child appropriately uses stem from experience. These words precede other linguistic structures. These findings began what has been termed the "Semantic Revolution" in the study of language. These findings also created the basis for the interactionist model.

Which model of language acquisition do you support?

What Are the Major Points Concerning the Individual's Language Development in Childhood?

The acquisition of language ability in early childhood is a remarkable feature of human development. Children will appropriately use their first word at eleven to twelve months after birth. By twenty-four months, the average child will have a vocabulary of 270 words. By thirty-six months, the typical child will have a repertoire of 1,000 words (Lenneberg, 1967). As a parent once said to this writer, "By their first birthday, you can hardly wait for them to talk. By their third birthday, you can hardly wait for them to shut up."

There is a discernible sequence to language development. As previously discussed, children throughout the world learn their first language at about the same time and in the same order.

Prior to these first stages of language development, the newborn uses an important communication system: crying behavior.

What Role Is Ascribed to Crying Behavior?

The first communication system used by a human infant is crying behavior. Crying is viewed by some as a reflex activity that evolved as a signaling system for the infant to indicate distress (Bowlby, 1969).

Wolff (1969) differentiated between four separate types of crying behavior: (1) the basic or hunger cry; (2) the anger cry; (3) the pain cry; and (4) the attention cry. Wolff found that both the pitch and intensity of the cries were relatively

Crying is the first communication system used by infants. Crying decreases as language is acquired.

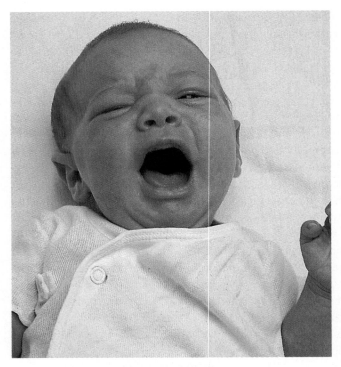

easy to distinguish. Parents of infants were able to make distinctions between the different types and to react accordingly. (Practice did enhance such ability.)

Bell and Ainsworth (1972) studied methods of soothing the crying behavior of an infant. The most successful method of soothing was picking up and holding the infant to the adult's shoulder. Feeding the infant was the second most effective method of soothing. Offering toys or pacifiers, vocalizations by care givers, and tactile and rhythmic stimulation were other methods of effectively soothing an infant.

Crying behavior remains as a signaling system for distress and emotional trauma throughout the life cycle. The development of language does not stem directly from crying behavior (Lenneberg, 1967). However, with the childhood onset of prelanguage and spoken language behaviors, the incidence of crying behavior decreases.

What is the relationship between crying and language?

What Is the Sequence for Language Development?

Figure 3.2 presents the overall sequence for language development.

Cooing Behavior. The first category of prelanguage behavior is termed cooing behavior (Lenneberg, 1967). Cooing behavior has been described as "squealing, gurgling sounds, usually called cooing, which is vowel-like in character and pitch modulated; sustains cooing for 15–20 seconds" (Lenneberg, 1967, p. 128). Examples of cooing behavior are the sounds "ooooooh" or "aaaaaaah." Lenneberg indicated that cooing may begin between six and eight weeks after birth. It becomes quite noticeable by ten to twelve weeks after birth.

Babbling Behavior. The second category in prelanguage development is called babbling behavior. Babbling behavior consists of a wide variety of vowel and consonant sounds, expressed either separately or together. An example of a babbling sound is "pakapakapaka" (Lenneberg, 1967, p. 139). Babbling sounds begin at three months after birth and are fully evident by six months after birth. Babbling behavior continues well past the child's first birthday, even when the child has started talking.

As previously indicated, the fixed sequence for language development would appear to indicate a partial contribution from an innate genetic program. This type of genetic sequence can readily be found with motor development. The parallel development of motor ability with language ability has been noted by Lenneberg (1967).

Figure 3.3 shows the relationship between motor development and language development.

Although the possibility of some innate contribution seems evident, it also is clear that children need the interaction with other people to successfully complete the stages of language development.

First Words. The type of first words spoken by children seems to have a degree of uniformity. Nelson (1973) found that 65 percent of first words were nouns referring to persons, animals, or objects in the child's immediate environment. These nouns included such words as milk, mama, dada, doggie, and ball. Action verbs, the next largest category, accounted for 14 percent of first words. The action verbs included such words as give, go, and bye-bye. Certain modifiers, such as dirty, mine, and nice, accounted for another 8 percent of first words.

First words typically occur between eleven and twelve months after birth with the normal range extending from eight to eighteen months. First words are often used to designate not only the object or person but other related objects or people. For instance, dada may be initially applied by the child as a label for any adult male, whether it is the biological father, an uncle, or a postman.

This aspect of language demonstrates the phenomena of overextension. Overextension involves using a word or grammatical rule to cover a broader category than is acceptable by adult usage.

FIGURE 3.2
Language Development

Behavior	Age Onset
Cooing	2 months
Babbling	3 months
First words	12 months
Holophrastic speech	12 months
Telegraphic speech	18 months

Describe the types of first words that a child uses.

Age	Motor Development	Language Development
3 months	Supports head in prone position	Cooing and smiling behavior
6 months	Sits up without support	Babbling behavior replaces cooing
10 months	Pulls self to standing position with support	Imitation of sounds
12 months	First steps without support	First words
24 months	Can run; walk up and down stairs	Uses two-word phrases

(Lenneberg, 1967)

FIGURE 3.3
Motor Development and Language Development

Holophrastic Speech. The next development in language acquisition is termed the holophrastic stage. During this stage, the child will use one word to express an activity or concept. For instance, when the child says the word "milk," the child's intention would be to have a drink of milk. Holophrastic speech is quite common between twelve and twenty-four months.

Telegraphic Speech. From holophrastic speech the child moves to two-word utterances. These types of simple two-word expressions are termed telegraphic speech. For example, the expressions "Go store" and "Want cookie" are types of telegraphic speech. As with a telegram, telegraphic speech leaves out modifiers and prepositions. The greatest frequency of telegraphic speech is during the period between one and a half and two and a half years of age.

After the development of telegraphic speech, the expansion of the child's vocabulary occurs at a rapid rate. Estimates of the speaking vocabulary of a child at age six range from eight thousand to fourteen thousand words (Carey, 1977). As pointed out by de Villiers and de Villiers (1978), the rate of vocabulary acquisition for a child from her first birthday to her sixth birthday is about five to eight new words per day. By adulthood the vocabulary repertoire includes approximately thirty thousand words (Berk, 1989).

What Are the Different Aspects of Metalinguistic Awareness?

During the period between ages five and eight, the child will begin to develop the capacity for what is termed metalinguistic awareness. Metalinguistic awareness is the ability to reflect about the nature of language; about the rules underlying sentence construction; and about correct word usage. The process of acquiring metalinguistic awareness occurs on several separate levels, such as syntactical awareness, semantic awareness, and contextual awareness. By age eleven, most children are able to demonstrate an ability for metalinguistic awareness.

Language skills are crucial to academic and vocational success. Parental interaction and reinforcement are critical to the development of language.

Clearly, there is a relationship between cognitive development and metalinguistic development. Just as mathematical ability is related to the development of concrete and formal operational thinking, metalinguistic awareness appears related to appropriate cognitive developments.

There is a continuing debate over the relationship between metalinguistic awareness and literacy. As with many of the debates in this area, the question is a chicken-and-egg question. Which comes first—metalinguistic awareness or the ability to read and write? Is the ability to read and write dependent on the emergence of metalinguistic awareness? Can metalinguistic awareness be accelerated by reading and writing exercises?

This type of issue is at the crux of early childhood enrichment programs that purport to teach children to read at age three or even earlier. Can the ability to read be taught before the child reaches a certain level of development? Can the ability to read be taught prior to awareness of the rule systems for reading?

Piaget (1952) believed that language development must wait on appropriate cognitive development. For instance, children who appear to read at age three are just demonstrating rote memorization of the material. There is no real transference of what they read to other similar reading material.

The research appears to support Piaget in this respect. Attempts at teaching the Piagetian concept of conservation through language training were unsuccessful (Peisack, 1973; Holland & Palermo, 1975). In these studies, children were provided with definitions of conservation through language instruction.

Can metalinguistic awareness be acquired through just instruction?

WHOLE LANGUAGE LEARNING

One of the recent trends in education is the movement toward integrating various parts of the curriculum and the classroom into a unified whole. This trend has resulted in a number of different modifications in some schools. Among these modifications are: whole class instruction, which is the attempt at ending grouping in the classroom; and full inclusion, which is the attempt to fully place all special education students in regular classrooms.

Another such area is whole language instruction, which is the attempt to integrate reading, writing, speaking, listening, and spelling into one single instructional method. Whole language instruction has a number of other important points.

Whole language instruction focuses on integrating the language arts curriculum and on teaching the class as a group.

1. The focus is on everyday life issues and their use as language arts material. For instance, the teacher might have as a theme for the week the following issue: Logging versus the spotted owl in Oregon. This issue would then be integrated into the student's reading, in class discussions, in student presentations, and in writing and spelling activities.

2. A second focus is on the meaningful aspects of the language activity first, with analysis of constituent parts coming later. Thus, the concentration is on extracting meaning first from the language material, with other analysis such as phonetic aspects later. In our example of the spotted owl and logging, the teacher might bring in magazine and newspaper articles. The class would read them together and examine them for their underlying meaning. For instance, the teacher might frame the following questions for discussion: What does this mean to the families of people who are in the logging business? What does this mean to future generations who will never see a spotted owl? What impact does logging have on the local tourist and outfitting industries?

3. A third focus is on solving problems. Students are asked to come up with a variety of possible solutions. They would work in a variety of settings to do this. They might work in small groups, pairings, or alone. After this work, though, everyone would meet as a whole class to share their solutions.

In summary, this type of method attempts to take one everyday issue and apply it across an integrated language arts curriculum. If effectively applied, children should be able to read about the focus issue, write about it, spell new words learned from the issue, and speak about it. If taught correctly, there is no reason that certain aspects such as spelling should suffer in whole language instruction.

Even with the correct definitions, the children were unable to correctly apply the concept of conservation to the experimental situations.

Although the debate on early childhood enrichment programs continues, the dominant view today is similar to that of Piaget. This viewpoint is that there is an absolute upper limit as to how much one can accelerate cognitive development. Attempts to accelerate beyond that upper limit may result in severe frustration and withdrawal by the child.

Language Development: Adolescence and Adulthood

Although much of language development research focuses on the school-age child, it has become increasingly clear that important developments occur well beyond childhood. Since language ability is so crucial to educational and professional success, it is important to understand some of these later developments.

Describe the major changes in language during this time.

Linguists and psychologists measure changes in language ability during these periods in a number of ways. Included among these ways are: the use of abstract, figural, or metaphorical language; the complexity of syntax and the use of conjunctives. In addition to these methods, it should be noted that increases in both vocabulary ability and appropriate syntax may occur throughout the adult years.

The use of abstract, figural, or metaphorical language appears to be associated with cognitive developments that occur during adolescence. These cognitive changes produce the ability to understand analogies and abstract principles. The ability to understand abstractions appears to produce a reorganization in how we define words in general. School-age children define words in terms of concrete aspects or activities. Adults define words in terms of abstract categories or abstract descriptions.

The ability to understand and explain proverbs, idioms, and metaphors increases during the adolescent years. This ability only reaches its full potential during the adult years (Rowe, 1992). Again, the key developments appear to be cognitive first, then linguistic.

Syntax developments during adolescence involve increases in the complexity of syntactical use but also in sentence and clause length. Syntax complexity includes the use of more complex sentence structures, especially the use of subordinate clauses. The appropriate use of a variety of verb tenses, particularly the passive voice, also tends to be a late linguistic development.

The use of conjunctives is another area that continues to develop during adolescence. Conjunctives join sentences or clauses together. Conjunctives include words such as "because," "therefore," and "although." The appropriate use of the more abstract conjunctives, particularly in writing, is a comparatively late development (Rowe, 1992).

What Are Some Factors Involved in the Acquisition of a Second Language?

One of the more intriguing aspects about language development is the ability to acquire a spoken second language in childhood. Lieberman (1984) reported the difficulty that adults have in acquiring a second language:

> We know that acquiring the sound pattern of a foreign language with native proficiency is essentially impossible for most adults. The syntax and semantic structure of a foreign language usually can be acquired by adults, given sufficient study and motivation. However, it is almost impossible to attain the phonetic proficiency of any normal child. There appears to be a critical period, a time after which we cannot master the sound pattern of a foreign language (p. 194).

It does appear that there is a critical period for learning to speak a foreign language that parallels the critical period for native language acquisition. This

Why do you think a
second language is more
easily acquired during
childhood?

critical period is between infancy and puberty. It is one of the few cognitive abilities that can be acquired with greater facility in childhood than in adolescence or adulthood.

A critical period for a spoken second language has major implications for providing second language instruction. It is obvious from the research that a second language should be taught during elementary school. In fact, to effectively speak a second language, training should begin as early as possible. By waiting until high school or college for second language instruction, we are limiting the ability to speak a second language.

One of the major research questions about teaching a second language after childhood is in regard to the acquisition/learning dichotomy (Krashen, 1981). This is perhaps better known as the language immersion question.

Krashen (1981) takes the position that full second language acquisition is only accomplished in the following manner: a naturalistic setting where the focus is on communication; where learning occurs with a low level of anxiety; and where learning is spontaneous and automatic. Usually, this is best accomplished in an immersion setting—living and learning a second language in a country that uses the language as its native tongue.

Obviously, such a view of language learning is not very satisfactory for foreign language classroom instructors. The question arises as to effective methods in teaching second languages. Some researchers present evidence indicating that effective second language learning for adults may occur in the classroom setting (Bialystok & Frohlich, 1977). There appear to be a number of classroom methods that may appropriately substitute for immersion procedures for acquiring a second language. Lombardo (1990) presents a thorough review of these methods. (see Applications from the Text 3.4)

What Are Some of the Important Gender Differences in Language Ability?

Gender differences in language ability have been frequently debated. For the school-age child and adolescent, the National Assessment of Educational Progress (NAEP) scores may provide some of the best overall information in this area. Mullis, Owens, and Phillips (1990) reported that across all age groups since 1970, females consistently outscored males on the reading and writing parts of the NAEP.

List some reasons why
gender differences in
language narrow during
adolescence.

However, these gender differences have been narrowing—a finding supported by other research. Gender differences in language ability also appear greatest at younger ages. These may be due to child-rearing patterns: Mothers apparently talk more to girls than to boys. It does appear that females have an early advantage in both the fluency and frequency of their vocabulary skills.

During the adolescent years, standardized test scores indicate fewer and fewer gender differences. In fact, on college aptitude tests, males outscore females on the verbal sections.

Speech and conversational patterns differ as well (Owens, 1988). Males are more likely to interrupt other speakers. Expletives are much more likely to be used by male speakers. Females are more likely to use "polite language." Females

What are some of the more effective classroom methods for learning a second language in adolescence or adulthood? (Adapted from Lombardo, 1990).

1. The number one method is to expose the students to language aspects that are used for normal purposes; language that has meaning for them.
2. Another method is to use speech practices that facilitate understanding. These include higher than normal voice pitch; greater than normal variations in intonation; louder than normal volume; frequent pauses between words or phrases; and frequent repetitions of key words and phrases.
3. A third method is greater individualization of instruction through a combination of small-group and paired-partner instruction. This method can potentially increase the amount of talking time per student, which appears to be critical in second language acquisition. However, the role of the teacher has to be structured appropriately to provide effective small-group learning.
4. The teacher's role in small-group language learning needs to ensure the following: that students take turns talking on a consistent basis; that students develop an effective two-way communication exchange of listening and speaking; that the content and form of the utterances are appropriate; that the teacher interacts with each group on an equal basis; and that questions and feedback occur within each group in a way that facilitates a communication exchange.

are more likely to take turns in conversations. Topics for conversation also are different: males choose nonpersonal topics, such as sports or politics, while females choose interpersonal topics.

What Are Some Ethnic and Regional Differences in Dialects in the United States?

Owens (1988) reviewed some of the regional and ethnic dialects in the United States. Owens made the point that Standard English or Standard American English is an idealized version that rarely occurs in ordinary conversational use. Owens claimed that Standard English primarily is used in textbooks and in network news broadcasts. Americans use a number of different dialects in their daily lives.

Owens also made the point that there are at least ten regional and two major ethnic dialects in the United States. Although these primarily are due to ethnic or regional variations, the use of these dialects also is influenced by socioeconomic and educational factors.

The two major ethnic dialects are Black English and Hispanic English. Both of these dialects are languages in their own right and are not deviant or substandard forms of English. (This also is true of the regional dialects.)

In his discussion of dialects, Nist (1966) prepared a map to illustrate the regional variations in the United States. This map (see figure 3.4) indicates the ten major regional dialects in the United States. As Nist states, the greatest variation in dialects is in the Northeast. Variations generally decrease as one moves west.

FIGURE 3.4
Major American English Speech Varieties

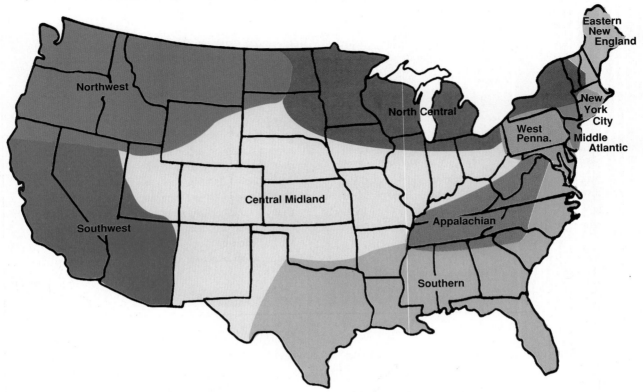

Source: Adapted from J. Nist, A Structural History of English, p. 371. Copyright © 1966 by St. Martin's Press, Inc. Reprinted by permission.

SUMMARY

This chapter reviews the various theories and research areas that are concerned with cognition and language. The focus of this chapter is on the relationship of cognition and language in terms of development and learning.

The major points about cognition are that cognitive development follows an invariant timetable that in all likelihood is not subject to acceleration by instruction and that instruction needs to address the developmentally appropriate level of each individual student.

According to Vygotsky, thought and language have different roots in childhood. By adulthood, the two separate processes have largely become united. This allows the unique human feature of creating abstract concepts.

Three theories of language acquisition were presented: the behavioral theory, the psycholinguistic theory, and the interactionist theory. The research on these theories of language acquisition would appear to indicate more support for the interactionist model. This type of model claims that language acquisition is partly dependent on innate factors and partly dependent on social interaction.

Individual language development follows a certain fixed sequence. This sequence appears to be universal across human cultures. This sequence also seems to parallel milestones in motor development, which may indicate some type of genetic program.

There does seem to be a critical period for second language acquisition that occurs in the period between infancy and puberty. Therefore, the education field may need to initiate second language training at a much earlier age. Immersion programs may be the most important types of language instruction. Programs that approximate immersion training also may work.

■ ■ ■

EPILOGUE

A Teacher Adapts Using Piaget and Vygotsky Models

In reviewing this chapter, what types of recommendations would you now make for the teacher in the case study at the beginning?

The issues raised in the case study are addressed by some of the following sections in this chapter:

1. Piaget's theory of cognitive development;
2. The Constructivist model;
3. Vygotsky's model of concept development;
4. The Applications from the Text 3.4 on whole language learning.

Piaget indicates that a child's level of cognitive development determines what she is capable of learning. For instance, many children in second grade may be incapable of understanding certain math operations because they have not yet grasped the concept of conservation.

Thus, a developmentally appropriate curriculum means that the teacher should tailor instruction to the individual level of each student. Piaget's model indicates that children at the same age level may be at different cognitive levels. Therefore, some changes in how the school determines who belongs in each grade may be necessary. An ungraded system or a system in which different age groups are combined into the same classroom may be necessary to implement a combination of developmentally appropriate curriculum and whole language instruction.

Some other questions about implementing a combination of developmentally appropriate curriculum and whole language instruction are:

1. What are some ways to determine the developmental level of the individual child?
2. Is whole language instruction more appropriate at earlier developmental levels or at later developmental levels?
3. Besides basing the classroom groups on developmental levels, are there any other ways that the individualized instruction needed for a developmentally appropriate curriculum can be made compatible with the whole class instruction so frequently used in whole language learning?
4. What might a Constructivist state about the use of a whole language learning model?
5. Using the Vygotskian model detail the relationship between cognitive development and whole language instruction.

CHAPTER REVIEW

1. What are the key developments in each of Piaget's four stages of cognitive development?
2. What are some of the distinctions between Piaget's model, the Constructivist model, and Vygotsky's model?
3. List and describe the criticisms of Piaget's model, the Constructivist model, and Vygotsky's model.
4. How does Vygotsky describe the relationship between thought and language?
5. How is the relationship between thought and language influenced by development?
6. Is language a unique ability of Homo sapiens?
7. What is the relationship between motor development and language development?
8. What is the relationship between metalinguistic awareness and cognitive development?
9. Is there a critical age period for language development?
10. Is language acquisition an innate ability, a learned ability, or a combination of the two?
11. What is the best age to learn a second language?
12. How many dialects are indicated in the United States?

REFERENCES

American Psychiatric Association. (1987). *Diagnostic and statistical manual of mental disorders–III–R*. Washington, DC: American Psychiatric Association.

Bell, S. M., & Ainsworth, M.D.S. (1972). Infant crying and maternal responsiveness. *Child Development, 43*, 1171–1190.

Berk, L. E. (1989). *Child Development*. Boston: Allyn and Bacon.

Bialystok, E., & Frohlich, M. (1977). Aspects of second language learning in classroom setting. *Working Papers on Bilingualism, 13*, 2–26.

Black, A. & Ammon, P. (1992). A developmental-constructivist approach to teacher education. *Journal of Teacher Education, 43 (5)*, 323–335.

Bloom, L. (1970). *Language Development: Form and function in emerging grammars*. Cambridge, MA: MIT Press.

Bowlby, J. (1969). *Attachment and loss: Vol. 1. Attachment*. New York: Basic Books.

Brown, R. (1973). *A first language: The early stages*. Cambridge, MA: Harvard University Press.

Carey, S. (1977). The child as a word learner. In M. Halle, J. Bresnan, & G. A. Miller (Eds.), *Linguistic theory and psychological reality*. Cambridge, MA: MIT Press.

Chomsky, N. (1957). *Syntactic structures*. Hague: Mouton.

Chomsky, N. (1959). Review of verbal behavior by B.F. Skinner. *Language, 35*, 26–38.

Chomsky, N. (1975). *Reflections on language*. New York: Pantheon.

Chomsky, N. (1980). Initial states and steady states. In M. Piattelli-Palmarinia (Ed.), *Language and learning: The debate between Jean Piaget and Noam Chomsky*. Cambridge, MA: Harvard University Press.

Crain, W. (1992). *Theories of development: Concepts and applications.* Englewood Cliffs, NJ: Prentice Hall.

de Villiers, J. G., & de Villiers, P. G. (1978). *Language acquisition.* Cambridge, MA: Harvard University Press.

Flavell, J. H., Miller, P. A., & Miller, S. A. (1993) *Cognitive development* (3rd ed.). Englewood Cliffs, NJ: Prentice Hall.

Fosnot, C. T. (1989). *Enquiring teachers, enquiring learners: A Constructivist approach for teaching.* New York: Teachers College Press.

Holland, V. M., & Palermo, D. S. (1975). On learning "less": Language and cognitive development. *Child Development, 46,* 437–443.

Kamii, C. (1985). *Young children reinvent arithmetic: Implications of Piaget's theory.* New York: Teachers College Press.

Krashen, S. (1981). *Second language acquisition and second language learning.* Oxford: Pergamon Press.

Lenneberg, E. (1967). *Biological foundations of language.* New York: John Wiley and Sons.

Lieberman, P. (1984). *The biology and evolution of language.* Cambridge, MA: Harvard University Press.

Lombardo, L. (1990). *Some implications of research in second language acquisition for foreign language teaching.* Paper presented at the World Congress of Applied Linguistics, April 1990. (ERIC Document Reproduction Service No. ED 330 213)

Mosenthal, J. H. & Ball, D. L. (1992). Constructing new forms of teaching: Subject matter knowledge in inservice teacher education. *Journal of Teacher Education, 43* (5), 347–356.

Mullis, I., Owens, E., & Phillips, G. (1990). *Accelerating academic achievement: A summary of findings from 20 years of the NAEP.* Washington, DC: U.S. Department of Education.

Nelson, K. (1973). Structure and strategy in learning to talk. *Monographs of the Society for Research in Child Development, 38* (1–2, Serial No. 149).

Nist, J. (1966). *A Structural History of English.* New York St. Martin's Press, Inc.

O'Loughlin, M. (1992). Engaging teachers in emancipatory knowledge construction. *Journal of Teacher Education, 43* (5), 336–346.

Owens, R. E. (1988). *Language development: An introduction.* (2nd ed.). Columbus, OH: Merrill Publishing Company.

Peisack, E. (1973). Relationship between knowledge and use of a dimensional language and achievement of conservation. *Developmental Psychology, 9,* 189–199.

Piaget, J. (1952). *The origins of intelligence in children.* New York: International Universities Press.

Rowe, V. (1992). *Language development in adolescence and beyond.* (ERIC Document Reproduction Service No. ED 341 055)

Skinner, B. F. (1957). *Verbal behavior.* New York: Appelton-Century-Crofts.

Slobin, D. I. (1970). Universals in grammatical development in children. In G. B. Flores d'Arcais & W. J. M. Levelt (Eds.), *Advances in Psycholinguistics* (pp. 237–280). New York: American Elsevier.

Teuber, H. L. (1975). Recovery of function after brain injury in man. In *Outcome of severe damage to the nervous system.* Ciba Foundation Symposium 34. Amsterdam: Elsevier-North Holland Publishing Company.

Vygotsky, L. S. (1962). *Thought and language.* Cambridge, MA: MIT Press.

Watson, J. B. (1927). The behaviorist looks at instincts. *Harper's Magazine,* no. 155, 233.

Wolff, P. H. (1969). The natural history of crying and other vocalizations in early infancy. In B.M. Foss (ed.), *Determinants of infant behavior.* New York: John Wiley and Sons.

Managing the Classroom

■ ■ ■

CHAPTER 4

Classroom Management

Theory and Practice

■ ■ ■

Chapter Outline

DEVELOPING A CLASSROOM MANAGEMENT STYLE

Lynne is a ten year old in the fourth grade. She has been disruptive in her classroom and is constantly leaving her seat. She never completes any of her school assignments.

Lynne's IQ test scores are in the high average range. She is a good reader and has the ability to do all fourth-grade assignments. Lynn has a brother who is three years older. Her parents are in their thirties and manage their own business. Upper middle class would describe the socioeconomic level of Lynne's family. Lynne relates fairly well with her peers. Her closest friend is a classmate named Sandra. Lynne frequently tells lies to other children even though they tell her they do not like it when she tells lies. She brings money and jewelry to school to share with Sandra. Her parents report that she is a behavior problem at home and acts like a spoiled child who always demands her own way. As Lynne's teacher, what strategies would you develop to help Lynne modify her behavior in class and help her achieve her potential as a student?

INTRODUCTION

One of the most important concepts to learn in the field of education is that of classroom management (CRM). The best of teachers can become ineffective if the learning environment of the students is inconsistent, unexpected, and without regulation. Therefore, it is vital for teachers to learn effective methods for developing classroom discipline policies, rules, plans for solving problems between students, educators, and the community, and ideas for enhancing the learning experience.

This chapter will discuss the theory behind many classroom management approaches and how teachers can begin to put theory into practice in the classroom. Of the three most common styles of classroom management, this chapter will focus on the student-centered and teacher-centered approaches. The eclectic style, although mentioned, will be further discussed in chapter 5.

KEY CONCEPTS

- Nondirective approaches to classroom management are based on the idea that heredity is the critical factor in development.
- Directive approaches to classroom management are based on the concept that environment is the key factor in development.
- Eclectic CRM models are based on the idea that development results from an interaction between heredity and environment.

- Learning styles of the students and the teaching style of the teacher greatly affect which management approaches will work best in the classroom.
- Discipline should be tailored to student needs for producing desired outcomes and not be merely a punitive system.

■ ■ ■

CLASSROOM MANAGEMENT STYLES

There are three philosophical bases from which teachers can develop a classroom management style: nondirective, directive, and eclectic. Each style is based on a psychological concept about the nature of people.

Nondirective (Student-Centered)

The first approach, nondirective or student-centered, is based on the idea that nature is the most critical factor in human development. Derived from the old nature-nurture debates of development, the nature argument states that people have within them a certain amount of potential to grow and develop. That is, people develop from an inner unfolding of potential. The teacher's task using this approach is to manage the classroom in light of what the students are able to do given their stage of development.

In relation to learning, the nondirective method has a student-centered focus. Students are given considerable freedom to make choices in what and how they want to learn, as well as choices in establishing class rules and consequences for breaking those rules. Students also help develop individualized learning and instruction. The assumption is made that students' curriculum must begin from where they are in their learning. For example, page forty-four in the textbook may not mark the spot where each student is ready to begin. Some may need to be on page twenty-two, some on page eighty-four, and others in the library or out in the community doing projects and research.

Teacher communication, when using this approach, is also student-centered. Teachers typically interact with their students through the use of active listening when a student brings a problem to them. When the teachers have a problem with a student, they communicate through assertive "I" messages. A high priority is placed on creating a climate in which students will be able to resolve their own conflicts. Student-centered teachers prefer that students work out their own conflicts and are more likely to use accommodation and avoidance policies as their principal conflict-management styles. However, if the students are not able to find their own solutions to conflicts, student-centered teachers will often use collaboration methods to resolve problems.

In summary, nondirective or student-centered teachers try to create a classroom environment that will best encourage the development of each student's inner potential. As Rogers (1969; 1983) points out, the key to creating a good classroom climate is to provide students with the freedom to learn while also building trust. The classroom should promote relationships of mutual caring and respect between teachers and students. Teacher involvement should be

Do you think that children in the primary grades are developmentally ready for a non-directive style of management?

focused on the unobservable parts of the students' personalities such as feelings, thoughts, motivations, and needs. The student-centered approach is based on the belief that students have a natural desire to learn. Thus, nondirective teachers lean toward a laissez-faire leadership style and support the students' freedom of choice whenever possible.

Directive (Teacher-Centered)

The second approach to classroom management is derived from the nurture side of the nature-nurture debate. In this approach, human development depends entirely on the quality and diversity of the environment. According to Skinner (1971), environment, not free choice, is what determines behavior. Teachers, operating under the nurture viewpoint, adopt a directive or teacher-centered approach to classroom management. The teacher directs the classroom through a behavior-analysis procedure designed to analyze the causes and effects of student behavior. After analyzing student behavior, the teacher implements an intervention plan designed to make on-task and socially accepted behaviors more attractive to the students. Interventions are directed toward the observable part of students' personalities—their behaviors. Teachers keep records of undesired behaviors to monitor the frequency of a behavior prior to, during, and after an intervention procedure.

When using the directive or teacher-centered approach to counseling a student, teachers focus more on what the student is doing rather than on why the student is doing it. By keeping students focused on what they do, teachers require students to take responsibility for their own behavior. Letting students

Nondirective classroom management is student centered. This model of management encourages student independence and inner development.

focus on why they behave in certain ways allows them to place responsibility or blame for their behavior on someone or something else. Directive teachers typically favor a competitive style of conflict resolution. They implement structured classroom management plans through behavior analysis and environmental planning. The teacher-centered approach to classroom management employs more of an autocratic leadership style with the teacher maintaining most of the decision-making power.

Eclectic (Combination)

Proponents of the eclectic classroom management style, the third broad philosophy of classroom management, believe that students and teachers benefit most from a combination of the elements contained in both the hereditary and environmental perspectives. The eclectic teacher relies on interventions from a variety of approaches to tailor interventions to the needs of the students rather than vice versa. In some cases, students will be able to assume more responsibility for their behaviors than in other cases. When nondirective approaches don't work, directive approaches will provide the structure students need to solve their learning and behavior problems. The eclectic teacher, having a wider range of alternatives available, is typically skilled in five basic approaches to conflict resolution and should know when to use each one. The five approaches are collaboration, compromise, competition, accommodation, and avoidance. The more democratic styles of leadership are generally employed as first-line measures in conflict resolution. The backup conflict-management style is typically focused on compromise solutions if a win-win, collaborative solution cannot be achieved.

Teachers successfully employing the eclectic style need to be well informed about the methodologies in both the student-centered and teacher-centered methods. In addition, they need to know how to use both methods in combination. Eclectic teachers are often criticized for knowing a little information about a lot of methods but not knowing enough about any one method to be successful classroom managers. Having sufficient information about a variety of methods enables teachers to be successful in whatever method they choose. Some have personalities and leadership styles that fit the student-centered model, others prefer the teacher-centered method, and still others will prefer to use parts of both styles. Opportunities to practice a variety of methods help in deciding what is best individually.

Do you think that there are gender differences in management styles? Are male teachers more inclined to one management style and female teachers to another? Are male students more responsive to one style of management and female students to another style?

What Is your Classroom Management Style Preference?

As discussed earlier, the three classroom management categories are not mutually exclusive. The styles often overlap because they have the common goal of providing students with the best learning environment possible. It is the ratio of student-teacher control that distinguishes the three styles. Completing a classroom management style inventory, such as the one in Application 4.1, can help prospective teachers make an assessment of which style best fits their personality.

CLASSROOM MANAGEMENT STYLE SURVEY

Instructions

Every school and every classroom situation is characterized by the style used to handle interpersonal concerns. As a teacher in a school, the manner in which you handle the various interpersonal relationships associated with your career will determine your success, as well as contribute to the success of your school. The quality of your relationships with your students can ultimately be determined by your understanding of these relationships and the knowledge of the consequences of the interventions you use with them.

The Classroom Management Style Survey is designed to assess the understanding and behavior of teachers and their classroom management style. There are no "right" or "wrong" answers. The best answer is the one that comes closest to representing your practices when you are teaching.

For each of the following 16 classroom situations or CRM philosophies, you are requested to indicate which of three, alternative interventions would be most characteristic of the way you would think and behave as a teacher. Try to answer as you think you do or would behave, not as you think you should. Some alternatives may be equally characteristic of you or equally uncharacteristic. Choose the alternative that is most relatively more characteristic of you. For each situation, you will have seven points to distribute in any way you choose among the three, alternative interventions.

Be sure the numbers you assign to (a), (b), and (c) under each situation sum to equal "7." Relate each situation in the survey to your own experience or to how you imagine you will act in the future. There is no time limit, so take whatever time you need to make true and accurate responses. Attempts to give "correct" or "ideal" responses will distort the meaning of your answers and make the survey results valueless.

To be successful, teachers must have healthy working relationships with their students. Below are a few situations and philosophical beliefs that can directly affect the type of relationships teachers will have with their students and indirectly affect the type of relationships teachers will have with their colleagues, administrators, and parents of their students. What do you believe, and how would you handle these encounters with your students?

■ ■ ■ ■ CLASSROOM MANAGEMENT STYLE QUESTIONNAIRE

1. I believe that:
___ a. students are free to make choices.
___ b. students' choices are conditioned by the environment.
___ c. students' choices are determined through interaction between their heredity and environment.

2. I believe that:
___ a. students are basically rational and have the power to reason and think; however, their decisions are not as yet fully mature, rational, and morally correct.
___ b. students should be given the opportunity to develop their decision-making skills by making choices within the scope of their school and home rules.
___ c. students should be given more freedom to make decisions because they have the emotional stability and decision-making ability to do it well.

3. I believe that:
___ a. students are basically self-centered and cannot be trusted to do the right thing.
___ b. students by nature are neither good nor bad; they do, however, have the potential to do both good and bad things.
___ c. Students are basically good and can be generally trusted to do the right thing. Hence, they should be given the benefit of the doubt until they prove themselves unworthy.

4. Regarding the classroom setting:
___ a. seating policies should be negotiated during classroom meetings.

___ b. classrooms should have open seating and students should be allowed to sit wherever they want.

___ c. students should have assigned seats in order to ensure better classroom management.

5. Regarding evaluation of students' learning:

___ a. all students should be evaluated in the same way on the same tests.

___ b. evaluation should be individualized to meet the needs of each student.

___ c. it is possible to ensure that competency standards are met without penalizing those students who need and desire individualized learning plans.

6. When a responsible student who has never missed a deadline for completing homework fails to do so, you should:

___ a. treat the student just as you would any student who turns in a late assignment. For example, each day late results in the loss of one letter grade.

___ b. make a new contract with the student for turning in the assignment.

___ c. assume that the student has a good excuse, say nothing, and wait for the assignment to be done.

7. Regarding student choices:

___ a. students should be given the freedom and responsibility to make some choices and decisions.

___ b. while the influence of the school may have a large impact on student choices, we need to realize the significant impact that other environmental influences have on student choices.

___ c. students are free to make choices in spite of environmental influences.

8. In violation of a school rule, Steve brings a small computer game to class. The game was broken when Bill borrowed it and dropped it on the floor. You, as a teacher, would:

___ a. act as a mediator should a conflict arise.

___ b. reprimand Steve for breaking the rule and Bill

for becoming irresponsible in taking care of another's property.

___ c. let the students work out the problem, it's none of your business.

9. Regarding your classroom management plan, you believe that spontaneous expressions of creativity and personal thoughts:

___ a. should be both nurtured and encouraged.

___ b. are OK as long as they do not interfere with your students' right to learn and your right to teach.

___ c. usually prevent the teacher from teaching and students from learning and should be restrained.

10. When classroom noise levels exceed the teacher's tolerance level during an activity period, the teacher should:

___ a. insist that the students follow the classroom rule about noise during the activity period.

___ b. ignore the noise until it bothers a student or students taking part in the activity.

___ c. deliver an "I" message. "I'm having a hard time trying to work with this excessive noise, and I want to work out a plan to make the activity period pleasant for all of us."

11. Your students complain that one of the classroom rules is unfair and want you to remove it. What would you do if you liked the rule and wanted to keep it? You would:

___ a. retain your veto power and exercise it if needed.

___ b. let the students decide on what would be a better rule.

___ c. negotiate a new rule that all would agree would be fair to everybody.

12. Regarding discipline, good educators:

___ a. maintain good discipline by creating a relationship of trust and unconditional positive regard with their students.

___ b. enforce school rules by taking firm but fair disciplinary action when rules are broken.

continued

___ c. meet with the student one-on-one and discuss alternative consequences when a school rule is broken.

13. While leading a group activity, you notice that one of your students is not participating. You should:

___ a. let the student exercise her right to pass or not participate in the activity.

___ b. encourage the student to participate by explaining the purpose and value of the activity.

___ c. ask the student why she is not participating and work out a plan that meets the student's needs.

14. Regarding the establishment of classroom rules during the first week of school, you would:

___ a. hold a classroom meeting for the purpose of establishing rules in a cooperative manner.

___ b. present a list of five or six rules and the consequences when the rules are broken.

___ c. let the students interact in an unstructured manner until they see a need for some structure and rules.

15. When a student interferes with my right to teach by bothering his neighbor, I would:

___ a. ignore the student and continue my teaching.

___ b. isolate the student from the other students by asking him to do his work in seat two (in the back of the room) or in the quiet corner (study carrel).

___ c. the student to comment on the lesson topic and arrange to meet with him later to discuss the interruption.

16. The best way to resolve conflict over an issue is to:

___ a. compete against others for your point of view when you are convinced beyond a doubt that you are right and they are wrong.

___ b. avoid conflict when possible and let it resolve itself.

___ c. collaborate with others in an attempt to find win-win solutions that will help everybody meet their needs.

Classroom Management Style Questionnaire Scoring Key

Scoring Instructions; For each of the 16 items, record the point totals given to each response you made indicating how you think and behave as a teacher. Add the total number of points for each category. Scores could range from 0 to 112 on any *one* of the three classroom management styles: nondirective, directive, and eclectic.

Item #	Nondirective (Student-Centered)	Directive (Teacher-Centered)	Eclectic (Combination)
1	a ___	b ___	c ___
2	c ___	a ___	b ___
3	c ___	a ___	b ___
4	b ___	c ___	a ___
5	b ___	a ___	c ___
6	c ___	a ___	b ___
7	c ___	b ___	a ___
8	c ___	b ___	a ___
9	a ___	c ___	b ___
10	b ___	a ___	c ___
11	b ___	a ___	c ___
12	a ___	b ___	c ___
13	a ___	b ___	c ___
14	c ___	b ___	a ___
15	a ___	b ___	c ___
16	b ___	a ___	c ___
Totals	___	___	___

Interpretation

A score of 40 or above on the student-centered scale indicates that you use this style most of the time; a score of 20 or below on this scale indicates that you might want to consider when you could use this style more often. The mean score for the student-centered scale is 30 with a standard deviation of 10.1

A score of 42 or above on the teacher-centered scale indicates that you use this style most of the time; a score of 18 or below on this scale indicates that you might want to consider when you could use this style more often. The mean score for the teacher-centered scale is 30 with a standard deviation of 11.7.

A score of 65 or above on the combination scale indicates that you use this style most of the time; a score of 41 or below on this scale would indicate that you might want to consider when you could use this style more often. The mean score for the combination scale is 53 with a standard deviation of 12.5. The scale with the most points above the mean is a close estimate of your preferred style. While most teachers have a primary CRM style and a secondary style, many teachers find they use all three CRM styles equally.

A teacher's CRM behavior can be described along two dimensions: (a) student-centered, the extent to which the teacher empowers students by giving them control over their learning, and (b) teacher-centered, the extent to which the teacher maintains control of the classroom learning activities. A combination of the two approaches results in an eclectic style that represents an attempt to integrate the student- and teacher-centered approaches. All three styles are useful in some situations. The effectiveness of any classroom management style depends upon the unique requirements of your classroom and the skill with which you use the intervention methods.

Classroom Management Models

Each of the three styles of classroom management is characterized by two prominent classroom management models as shown in figure 4.1. The directive or teacher-centered CRM style uses either behavior modification based on Skinner's (1968; 1971) operant conditioning methods or the assertive discipline model developed by Canter (1976; 1981). The nondirective or student-centered CRM style is best facilitated by the person-centered model developed by Rogers (1983) and by Gordon's (1974) adaptation of Rogers's work into the teacher effectiveness training model. Finally, the eclectic or combination CRM style uses Glasser's (1969; 1990) reality-based method and the individual psychology method of Dreikurs (1968) and Dreikurs, Grunwald, and Pepper (1982). The teacher-centered and student-centered approaches are discussed in chapter four. The eclectic approaches will be discussed in chapter five.

Teacher-Centered CRM Methods

How are behavioral methods used in classroom management?

Behavior modification methods are based on the idea that students behave in ways that they perceive as meeting their needs. Therefore, behavior change will not occur unless a behavior is perceived either as not meeting a need or as being punishing. A brief review of Maslow's (1970) hierarchy of human needs can be helpful to teachers in understanding the reasons students do what they do to meet their needs.

Self-fulfillment or self-actualization needs occupy the highest rung in Maslow's hierarchy. These needs receive most attention after the needs in the preceding levels have been met. At this level, students are trying to make their best selves even better. They work to develop new skills, interests, and talents.

Self-esteem needs refer to the need to feel worthwhile and important. These needs may be met through successful achievement of any task students perceive as being significant. Such tasks include, among other things, success in aca-

FIGURE 4.1
Classroom Management
Systems

Directive (Teacher-Centered)	Nondirective (Student-Centered)	Eclectic (Combination)
Behavior Modification	Person-Centered Teaching	Reality-Based Teaching
Assertive Discipline	Teacher Effectiveness Training	Individual Psychology

Dealing with student misbehavior is one of the most difficult tasks of being a teacher.

demic work, sports, music, part-time jobs, and social events. When students do not find success through socially acceptable avenues, they may seek to build their self-esteem through less desirable activities.

Social needs refer to the need to feel connected to a group such as family and peer groups. They also refer to the need to give and receive affection. Much behavior is directed toward developing and maintaining fulfillment of social and self-esteem needs.

Security needs refer to the need to feel safe and the need for adequate shelter or housing. Students who fear for their safety from abuse of any type will find most of their time and energy directed toward protecting themselves or being consumed in worrying about what to do. Family financial problems that actually threaten the family residence also can consume vast amounts of the students' time and attention that could be directed toward meeting higher level needs.

Physiological needs refer to the need for oxygen (clean air), clean water, food, and sleep. As in the case with security needs, any threat to fulfillment of physiological needs detracts from the time and energy given to meeting the higher-level needs. For example, it is difficult to teach hungry children to read.

In summary, people behave in ways that make sense to them. They also behave in ways that maintain or enhance their self-image, whether their self-image is positive or negative. Students repeat behaviors that they believe are helpful in meeting their needs. They will tend to discard behaviors that do not help them meet their needs.

An understanding of human needs is helpful to determining why students do what they do and is also useful in helping to modify their behaviors. A behavior analysis is a procedure for putting their knowledge of human needs into practice.

Apply Maslow's hierarchy to individuals you know. Do you know anyone who operates at the self-fulfilled level? Are most people fixated at the social and self-esteem levels?

How Do You Conduct a Behavior Analysis?

The process of conducting a behavior analysis of a student or of an entire classroom of students involves careful study of three things: (a) antecedent conditions, (b) the behavior itself, and (c) consequences following the behavior. Antecedent conditions refer to the setting and time in which a behavior occurs, as well as other conditions that might stimulate student behaviors. For example, a class may become disruptive at 11:00 each morning following a long period of time doing math problems and thirty minutes before the students go to lunch. The antecedent conditions in this scenario are fatigue, hunger, and restlessness caused by the time of day and the task just completed.

Studying a behavior involves describing an exact account of what the students have done and how often they have done it. For example, the students may interrupt the teacher without permission an average of one time every three minutes.

Consequences refer to everything that happens to the students following their behavior, either good or bad. If the "bad" consequences of a certain behavior exceed the "good" consequences, the students will discard that behavior for something that has more favorable consequences.

To change student behavior, teachers have to change the antecedents, the consequences, or both. Changing the setting (an antecedent condition) serves as a good way to prevent undesired behaviors. For example, a teacher may give students a short stretch break following a lengthy period of working on math. The break serves to relieve the tension that causes the disruptive behavior.

Behavior analysis can be used to determine the causes of and solutions to performance problems. For example, John has not been turning in his math assignments, even after promising his teacher that he would do better. Taking the following four steps could help him both identify and solve the problem.

Step One: It is important to determine what type of problem John is having. Is it a problem of working with people or is it a problem of performing a task? In other words, is someone preventing John from getting his work done or does he fail to perform the task? Perhaps in John's case, he does not have a problem working with others. His problem is failing to complete his work.

Step Two: It is then important to determine why John is failing to complete his task. Is it a problem of being unable to do the work or a problem of being unwilling to do the work? In other words, could John do the work if his life depended on it?

If it is a case of lacking ability, is it because of (a) the lack of knowledge about what, when, or how the task is to be done or (b) an obstacle in the environment (e.g., John cannot see the chalkboard from the back of the room)? If the answer is (a), the teacher could respond by providing training or tutoring for John's lack of knowledge. If the problem is (b), the teacher can remove the obstacle by moving John's seat closer to the chalkboard.

If the problem is that John is unwilling to do the work, is it because of (c) a lack of knowledge about why the task needs to be done or (d) simple refusal? If the problem is (c), the teacher can provide John with information or feedback on why the task is important and why it needs to be done. If John is aware of the importance of completing the task and still refuses to do the work (d), the teacher should change the balance of positive and negative consequences.

Step Three: If the teacher needs to change the balance of positive and negative consequences, he will have to discover what is going on in John's situation that reinforces the undesired behavior and punishes the desired behavior. The

Complete a behavior analysis of one of your own problems. For instance, analyze why you always procrastinate about writing your term papers.

REWARD INTERVIEW QUESTIONS

1. What are your five favorite things to do?
2. What are five things you would like to buy with your allowance?
3. What activities do you like to do with your friends?
4. What are your favorite television shows?
5. What things do you like to do with your family?
6. What things do you enjoy doing with your mother?
7. What things do you enjoy doing with your father?
8. What classroom activities do you enjoy?
9. Would you like to earn a bigger allowance? If so, how?
10. What are your favorite games?
11. Who are the people you like to talk with, play with, or visit?
12. What things do you like to collect?
13. What are your favorite foods and drinks?
14. What are your favorite school activities?
15. What do you like to read?
16. What are your favorite video games?
17. Where would you like to travel?
18. What are your favorite sports?
19. What are your favorite hobbies?
20. What pets would you like to have?

first step in changing the behavior is to reduce or remove those things that either reinforce the current behavior and/or punish the desired behavior. Perhaps John is reinforced by his peer group for refusing to do his work or perhaps John finds that homework takes up too much of his play or television time.

Step Four: The final step is to find ways to reward or reinforce the desired behavior. For example, conducting a reward survey with John, such as the one in application 4.2, will determine what types of reinforcers he would like to earn by completing his homework. The teacher has three options, other than punishment, to encourage John to complete his work: (1) decreasing the reinforcement John receives from the undesired behavior, (2) removing the punishment received from doing the desired behavior, and (3) reinforcing the desired behavior. Punishing the undesired behavior can cause the side effect of disturbing the teacher-student relationship. One method available to teachers, if punishment is necessary, is the use of logical consequences (discussed in the next chapter). Logical consequences do have a punishing effect on undesired behavior with a minimum of damage to the teacher-student relationship.

How Do Reward Surveys Work?

Reward surveys can be helpful first steps to teachers when trying to change the balance of positive and negative consequences to modify student behavior. If any behavior, grade contract, or contingency plan is to be effective in changing a student's behavior, the teacher must know what the student finds rewarding—what will stimulate her to accomplish the behavior and academic goals established in

Directions: The items in this questionnaire refer to things or activities that you may like or that may be of interest to you. Beside each item, place a check in one of the three columns to show how much you like it—very much, somewhat, or not at all.

	Not at all	Somewhat	Very much
1. Foods			
a. ice cream	—	—	—
b. candy	—	—	—
c. fruit	—	—	—
d. peanuts	—	—	—
e. cookies	—	—	—
f. gum	—	—	—
g. popcorn	—	—	—
h. marshmallows	—	—	—
i. chips	—	—	—
j. pretzels	—	—	—
k. other (——)	—	—	—
2. Beverages			
a. water	—	—	—
b. milk	—	—	—
c. soft drinks	—	—	—
d. other (——)	—	—	—
3. Dancing	—	—	—
4. Playing a musical instrument	—	—	—
(List your favorite instrument _____)			
5. Listening to music			
a. classical	—	—	—
b. country	—	—	—
c. rock	—	—	—
d. folk	—	—	—
e. heavy metal	—	—	—
f. alternative	—	—	—

g. jazz	—	—	—
h. rap	—	—	—
i. other (___)	—	—	—
6. Reading (Media)			
a. comic books	—	—	—
b. magazines	—	—	—
c. newspapers	—	—	—
d. books	—	—	—
Reading (Topics)			
e. famous people	—	—	—
f. travel	—	—	—
g. humor	—	—	—
h. science	—	—	—
i. adventure	—	—	—
j. sports	—	—	—
k. romance	—	—	—
l. classics	—	—	—
m. poetry	—	—	—
7. School			
a. Language Arts	—	—	—
b. Math	—	—	—
c. Science	—	—	—
d. Lunch	—	—	—
e. Music	—	—	—
f. Art	—	—	—
g. Gym	—	—	—
h. Recess	—	—	—
i. Social Studies	—	—	—
j. Foreign Language	—	—	—
k. Other (___)	—	—	—
8. Talking			
a. with a friend	—	—	—
b. with mother	—	—	—
c. with father	—	—	—
d. with brother	—	—	—

the contract. The purpose of administering a reward survey is to find what things are appealing to the student. When teachers know what their students like, they can give those things to the students when they behave appropriately. The rewards provide students with an incentive to repeat the behavior in the future. Teachers hope that, eventually, appropriate behaviors will become reinforcing in themselves. Teachers can then gradually eliminate extrinsic rewards in favor of the intrinsic rewards of doing helpful and appropriate behaviors. Students who improve their performance will often find that their parents or guardians are more likely to help them get what they want.

Reward surveys may be done with interviews or printed survey forms such as the ones in Applications from the Text 4.2 and 4.3. Some teachers may prefer to

e. with sister	___	___	___
f. with adults	___	___	___
g. with a teacher	___	___	___
h. with a counselor	___	___	___

9. Animals
   a. dogs ___ ___ ___
   b. cats ___ ___ ___
   c. horses ___ ___ ___
   d. birds ___ ___ ___
   e. fish ___ ___ ___
   f. turtles ___ ___ ___
   g. other (___) ___ ___ ___

10. Games
    a. chess ___ ___ ___
    b. checkers ___ ___ ___
    c. cards ___ ___ ___
    d. Trivial Pursuit ___ ___ ___
    e. video games ___ ___ ___
    f. backgammon ___ ___ ___
    g. board games ___ ___ ___
    h. other (___) ___ ___ ___

11. Play
    a. clay/pottery ___ ___ ___
    b. painting ___ ___ ___
    c. drawing ___ ___ ___
    d. coloring ___ ___ ___
    e. dolls, puppets ___ ___ ___
    f. cars ___ ___ ___
    g. Legos ___ ___ ___
    h. other (___) ___ ___ ___

12. Objects you like to own
    a. pencils/pens/ etc. ___ ___ ___
    b. paper ___ ___ ___
    c. stickers ___ ___ ___
    d. coloring books ___ ___ ___

e. videotapes ___ ___ ___
f. flowers ___ ___ ___
g. sports cards ___ ___ ___
h. books ___ ___ ___
i. other (___) ___ ___ ___

13. TV/Programs ___ ___ ___
    (List your three favorite programs:)

14. Going to movies ___ ___ ___
15. Hiking ___ ___ ___
16. Camping ___ ___ ___
17. Peace and quiet ___ ___ ___
18. Being praised ___ ___ ___
19. Helping in the classroom ___ ___ ___
20. Using the computer ___ ___ ___
21. Shopping for:
    a. clothes ___ ___ ___
    b. toys ___ ___ ___
    c. food ___ ___ ___
    d. sports equipment ___ ___ ___
    e. music tapes/cds ___ ___ ___
    f. electronics ___ ___ ___
    g. other (___) ___ ___ ___
22. Games or sports
    a. football ___ ___ ___
    b. baseball ___ ___ ___
    c. basketball ___ ___ ___
    d. golf ___ ___ ___
    e. swimming ___ ___ ___
    f. volleyball ___ ___ ___
    g. running ___ ___ ___
    h. soccer ___ ___ ___
    i. tennis ___ ___ ___
    j. other (___) ___ ___ ___

use a reward survey checklist, rather than an open-ended questionnaire. In either case, teachers need to give assistance to students who do not read well enough to complete the form independently. Be sure that students understand all the items and questions on the form and make sure that the check marks are made in the appropriate columns.

How Are Contingency Contracts Designed?

Once teachers identify the activities that students find reinforcing, they can write and negotiate contracts with students that outline ways they can earn these rewards. For example, a student who has difficulty in completing daily assign-

APPLICATIONS FROM THE TEXT 4.4

CONTINGENCY CONTRACT

Classroom Behavior	Points*
1. Walking into classroom on time without running	1
2. Checking out personal assignment folder	1
3. Asking the teacher or aide for daily assignment	1
4. Responding to the teacher or aide with completed assignment	1
5. Checking and correcting completed work (no points are earned for incorrect work)	1
6. Working without disturbing others	1
7. Achieving at least 80 percent accuracy on each work sheet on the first attempt	1
8. Returning personal assignment folder to the file	1
9. Leaving the room quietly without running	1

*100 points equals 30 minutes free time

ments could earn one hour per day of free time outside of school hours with friends each time he completes daily assignments. A perfect completion rate for one week could earn a bonus of three hours that could be accumulated until the student has enough hours for an overnight visit or a weekend trip with a friend's family.

A more formal contract can be written for an entire class in which students can earn points for doing on-task and socially appropriate classroom behaviors. Points can be exchanged for free time that can be used for a variety of fun activities that do not prevent the other students from learning. For example, students can listen to music with earphones, read about their favorite subjects, or play quiet games. A typical contingency contract for a classroom developed by Thompson, Prater, and Poppen (1974) is presented in Applications from the Text 4.4.

Contracts work best when the students are able to choose their own free-time activities, as long as they do not bother students who are working. For example, if a rule is broken under the contract in Applications from the Text 4.4, the remaining free time is forfeited. The teacher may even add that a student must earn two hundred points for the next thirty minutes of free time. The teacher

How do you feel about whole class contingency contracts? Are they fair? Can one bad apple spoil the contract?

also could subtract points from a student's total each time the student disrupts either teaching or learning. Teachers should chart each student's point total for the day and inform students of their daily and running point totals. Points can be accumulated to earn up to one week off from class. Students are motivated by receiving daily feedback on their performance and by observing their classmates enjoying free time.

How Is the Assertive Discipline Method Used in Classroom Management?

The assertive discipline approach developed by Canter (1976; 1981) is another method to help teachers establish a structured discipline approach when faced with certain classroom situations. As with the behavioral methods described earlier, the assertive discipline model is focused on changing student behavior by altering the balance of negative and positive consequences to promote appropriate classroom behavior. Although the term assertive discipline tends to connote behavior control through punishment, Canter (1989) points out that many applications of assertive discipline do include rewards for on-task and socially appropriate behavior. Canter prefers that teachers put most of their emphasis on noticing students in good behavior. The best way to begin an assertive discipline plan is to send a letter to each student's parents or guardians on the first day of school. The letter should begin with a short statement of the teacher's philosophy about discipline, expectations of students, classroom rules, consequences for breaking classroom rules, and rewards for appropriate behavior. The letter can take the form of a proclamation or nonnegotiable contract if the teacher prefers. Parents are asked to read the contract letter and to sign and return the bottom portion indicating that they have read and understand the discipline plan for their child's classroom. A sample letter for a third-grade classroom is presented in Applications from the Text 4.5 and a sample letter for a high school classroom is presented in Applications from the Text 4.6

As a teacher, what would you do if a parent failed to sign the contract? What if the parents simply do not respond to anything that you send home to them? What would you do?

Evertson and Harris (1992), in a review of the research literature on classroom management, found considerable support for approaches such as assertive discipline, which communicate clearly the classroom rules and which are implemented at the beginning of the school year. Both strategies are focused on problem prevention.

The assertive discipline plan has helped many teachers, nevertheless, it has been received with mixed emotions from other teachers and some parents. Some teachers are opposed to writing the names of misbehaving students on the board. Although writing names on the board facilitates record keeping and allows the teacher to continue teaching, it could be humiliating to students. Canter (1989) proposes that teachers use a clipboard or roll book for check marks and give the students a short, verbal warning or notification of a penalty.

Many parents say that assertive discipline is what their children need because the children have not been taught discipline. Other parents find the letter to be a negative way to start off the year because of the heavy emphasis on controlling student behavior. As is true with all CRM models, complete success cannot be

ASSERTIVE DISCIPLINE PLAN
FOR A THIRD-GRADE CLASSROOM

Dear _____,

In order to guarantee your child, and all the students in my classroom, the excellent learning climate they deserve, I am utilizing the following discipline plan starting today.

My Philosophy:

I believe all my students have the ability to behave appropriately in my classroom. I will tolerate no student stopping me from teaching and/or any student from learning.

My Class Rules:

1. Talk and move so quietly I cannot hear you.
2. Follow directions.
3. Finish all work on time.
4. Never interrupt reading group.
5. Keep hands, feet, and objects to self.
6. Always have necessary supplies (paper, two pencils, eraser, books, etc.).

If a student chooses to break a rule:

1. Name on board (A warning).
2. Check by name—ten minutes off recess.
3. Two checks by name—in isolation for all recess.
4. Three checks by name—isolation for recess, plus thirty minutes isolation in classroom.
5. All of the above, plus call parents.
6. Severe disruption: all of the above plus thirty minutes isolation in a fifth grade classroom..

Students who behave will earn:

1. Verbal praise.
2. Free-time activities.
3. Superstar awards.
4. Other varied, teacher-designated activities.

I will rely on your help and cooperation.

Thank you,

Please sign the tear-off sheet and return to me tomorrow.

I read and understood the discipline plan for your classroom.

_____   _____

Student's Signature   Parent(s)/Guardian(s) Signature(s) guaranteed. In fact, the proper use of any one model depends in large part on the creative ability of teachers in adapting the approach to fit the unique qualities of their classroom, school, and community.

Teachers who find teacher-centered methods too controlling may want to consider some of the student-centered approaches discussed in the next section. However, many teachers find that their degree of student-centered or teacher-centered practice depends on the developmental levels of their students or the students' readiness to accept responsibility for their learning.

Student-Centered CRM Methods (Nondirective)

How are the student-centered models developed by Carl Rogers and Thomas Gordon used in classroom management?

Carl Rogers (1969; 1983), regarded by many as the founder of the person-centered movement in psychology and education, believes that people are basically good. His positive view of people includes the idea that people have the capacity and right to self-direction (self-actualization) and, when given the opportunity, will make wise judgments and decisions about what they need to learn and how to learn it. He also believes that people have the ability to learn how to make constructive use of responsibility when given the opportunity to exercise self-directed learning. Rogers's philosophy includes the belief that people have the capacity to handle their own feelings, thoughts, and behaviors as they go about the process of making productive changes in their lives. Rogers's respect for the worth and dignity of all people allows him to view individuals as doing the best they are capable of doing at the moment.

Translating Rogers's positive view of people into an educational program requires that learning environments be characterized by a climate in which the teacher acts as a facilitator and initiator. Rogers believes that such a climate helps students to feel respected, provides students with opportunities to make responsible choices, and helps students feel excited about learning. According to his theory, students will move toward the goal of becoming effective, concerned citizens who are well informed, competent, and confident in possessing the knowledge and skills required to face the future. In other words, from Rogers's perspective, the best-managed classrooms will be those with the least amount of traditional management by the teachers. His ideal classroom is most simply described as being student-centered rather than teacher-centered. It is a classroom where students are empowered by being given both choices and the freedom to make decisions and solve problems. To make the student-centered approach work, teachers have to be able to do several things:

1. Create a climate of trust in the classroom that encourages and nourishes curiosity and the natural desire to learn. Such trust begins with the teacher's belief that students are fundamentally trustworthy or have the potential to be so.
2. Provide participatory decision making in regard to learning activities. Such decision making should be based on reaching group consensus through collaboration and compromise rather than through voting.

Do you agree with Rogers's view of people? Is he overly optimistic?

ASSERTIVE DISCIPLINE PLAN FOR
A HIGH SCHOOL CLASSROOM

Dear _____,

I believe that the best learning takes place in an atmosphere of mutual trust and respect.

I expect my students to:

1. be good listeners—sit quietly, take notes when appropriate, raise their hand and wait to be called on if they have questions or comments about the subject being discussed.
2. be eager participants in small- and large-group discussions.
3. come to class on time (be in their assigned seat when the second bell rings) with their textbook, paper, pen/pencil, and completed assignment(s).
4. keep all their graded assignments in a three-ring notebook and keep their assignment sheet up-to-date.
5. keep the classroom clean (use the trash can), neat (do not deface or move any furniture, fixtures, or materials), and orderly (push their chair under their desk before leaving the classroom).

Failure to fulfill these expectations will result in the following:

1. First offense—name on board, warning.
2. Second offense—name on board and one check, one detention served the following Thursday from 3:30 P.M. to 4:15 P.M.
3. Third offense—name on the board and two checks, two detentions served the following Wednesday and Thursday from 3:30 P.M. to 4:15 P.M.

==> Failure to serve detention(s) or a fourth offense will result in the student's referral to the Assistant Principal.
==> Exceptions to serving detention other than Wednesday or Thursday after school will be considered only after you have contacted me.

As your teenager's teacher, you may expect me to:

1. be a good listener who is sensitive to individual needs and the needs of the class as a whole. Extra-help sessions are provided each Thursday after school (see me in advance).
2. come to class prepared to offer a variety of learning experiences.
3. maintain an orderly classroom conducive to learning.
4. reward my students for work well done with an appropriate grade and provide opportunities for your child to work on independent projects related to our class.
5. provide opportunities for my students to earn appropriate free-time activities and other rewards.

Please sign the tear-off sheet and return to me tomorrow. Thank you.

I hereby agree to work with you to uphold the STUDENT-TEACHER CONTRACT so that we may have an excellent learning experience this year.

Teacher _____ Date _____

Student _____ Date _____

Parent/Guardian _____ Date _____

3. Provide ways to help their students value themselves and to build their self-esteem and confidence. This process begins when teachers show that they value their students and care for them in a nonpossessive way.

4. Develop a sense of empathic understanding of their students. Basically, teachers need to be able to understand their students' reactions, thoughts, and feelings from the inside. Teachers need to maintain a sensitive awareness to the way students react to learning. Teachers then need to be able to communicate this understanding to students. Students appreciate being understood rather than evaluated and judged.

5. Maintain a transparent realness with their students. In other words, teachers need to show their feelings and thoughts. Playing phony roles with students destroys trust. When teachers are open with students, students tend to be open in return.

What Are Some Specific Ways to Put Student-Centered CRM into Practice?

Because the best climate for learning is one that fosters good interpersonal relationships in the classroom, student-centered CRM strategies generally favor cooperative learning over competitive learning activities. Teachers emphasize collaborative or win-win methods to resolve conflict, as well as individualized instruction and independent learning activities. The teacher and students feel free to voice complaints through group meetings that both set and challenge classroom rules and policies when problems arise. Teachers spend most of their time as learning facilitators and consultants rather than as lecturers and test administrators. Good student-centered teachers are able to maintain a healthy balance between "tell me," "show me," and "let me do it" learning activities. Teachers also should be counted upon to be good and trusted empathic listeners when their students need help with problems. An examination of the ways the above ideas can be put into practice follows.

What Are Some Cooperative Learning Activities?

Cooperative learning activities allow students to teach each other. One method often used is to set up learning dyads that afford teaching opportunities. Teachers can create dyads by ranking their classes according to students' achievement and pairing students by ability level. For example, in a class of twenty-four, the teacher would pair student No. 1 with student No. 13, student No. 2 with student No. 14 and on up until No. 12 is paired with student No. 24. Students should not know the rationale for the pairs, and the dyads can be modified from time to time. This method of pairing students creates a balanced achievement gap that is wide enough to allow one student to teach another, yet not so wide as to cause frustration and discouragement on the part of either student.

Cooperative learning teams offer another avenue for peer teaching and tutoring. Using this method, a class of twenty-four students would be divided into teams of four. Each team would have a high-achieving student, two students in

As a student do you like cooperative learning activities? Do you often find that someone does most or all of the work in cooperative learning teams?

the middle range, and one from the lower range. The higher-achieving students can function as teaching assistants if given some training in modeling student-centered, facilitative teaching styles. The teams can select team names to give added unity. As students complete assignments, they win points for their team. The first completion earns ten points; the second, twenty; the third, thirty; and the fourth, forty. Thus, a team may earn a total of one hundred points for each assignment. Students must do more than turn in a copied form of someone else's work. They must pass a skill test (oral or written) over the assigned lesson to earn the points. Groups earning all one hundred points can earn free time or other low-cost rewards such as popcorn.

Are group grades fair to all children? Will students be graded down because of a low-ability student in their group?

Competition among groups can be a fun experience if the students are protected from the possible shame or embarrassment of holding a team back. One way to prevent embarrassment is to use a handicapping system similar to those used in golf matches. That way some lower-ability students would earn more points for mastering a task than other students.

There are several benefits to using such cooperative learning activities. Peer teaching enhances learning for both the tutor and the learner. Group interaction keeps each student involved in the learning process. Teachers also can provide more individualized instruction as they move from group to group as facilitators and consultants. Finally, students are given the opportunity to develop responsibility through the choices and commitments made in helping themselves and their group to meet their achievement goals. Most important of all, the group cooperation with competition model encourages relationship building.

What Are Ways to Provide Individualized Learning Experiences for Your Students?

Teachers can develop individualized learning by asking students to submit learning proposals that, after negotiation, become learning contracts. Negotiation and renegotiation are characteristic elements of the student-centered class-

Cooperative learning activities can encourage individual responsibility and interpersonal relationships.

I, _____ , wish to contract for the grade of _____ . If I do not complete the requirements for the grade I have chosen, I will accept the grade for which I have qualified or a grade of incomplete. I understand that I have the option to renegotiate this contract any time prior to the end of the grading period. I understand that I can participate in my final evaluation by arranging a conference with my instructor. I will complete the following outline before the contract is signed.

Individualized Contract Terms

1. Learning objectives
2. Method for meeting objectives
3. Sequence and time schedule of procedures
4. Evaluation of attainment of objectives
5. Nature of final report or product

Date _____   Subject Area _____

Renegotiation Date _____   Student _____

Teacher _____

room. Rather than failing students, teachers allow second chances and the assignment of "I" grades or "incompletes" until a task is completed. Two examples of independent learning contracts that are derived from student proposals are shown in Applications from the Text 4.7 and 4.8. These contracts are for students who are capable of doing science fair type projects.

Independent learning contracts for younger students can be simplified and drawn up for shorter periods of time. In summary, the value of independent learning lies in the contribution it makes toward teaching our students how to learn.

How Does Democracy in the Classroom Work?

The student-centered approach to classroom discipline is characterized by a heavy emphasis given to student choices and student government. Teachers use group meetings to make and evaluate classroom rules and to resolve conflicts either between the teacher and students or between groups of students. Successful student-centered teachers give considerable attention to teaching students how to negotiate collaborative conflict solutions. Win-win solutions generally offer new positions or alternatives that make it possible for all those involved to get what they want. Such solutions are often difficult to find and generally require considerable time and effort.

Students learn how team building works by reaching decisions through group consensus rather than by voting. When a group votes on a decision, members who lose often become less than enthusiastic about supporting the majority deci-

Independent study can be done in lieu of any class requirement, such as a term paper, assigned project, or examination. The scope and depth of the study depend upon the requirement it is replacing. The process of proposing independent study can be accomplished by completing the following outline.

1. What do you want to learn?
2. How are you going to do it?
3. How do you plan to evaluate it?
4. How do you plan to report it?
5. What class requirement does your study replace?

Subject area _____

Student _____

Date _____

I certify that my proposed study will be a new learning experience for me.

_____

Student's signature

Approved by:

_____

Teacher's signature

_____

Date:

sion. It is better to take time to reach a consensus decision by finding resolutions that give everybody a piece of the pie. Additionally, learning team-building skills will help students eventually enter a world of work that is embracing team management systems.

How Do Student-Centered Teachers Handle Discipline Problems?

Thomas Gordon (1974), a former student of Carl Rogers, has translated the Rogerian theory and practice into classroom applications. Many of Gordon's classroom applications evolved into his teacher effectiveness training method, which will be discussed in this section.

When classroom problems arise, Gordon encourages teachers to ask themselves one important question: "Who owns this problem?" The problem can be owned by the teacher (who is the only one that is upset about it), by a student (who is the only one upset), or by the entire classroom including the teacher. Gordon's theory encourages the owner to confront the source of the problem in an assertive manner as opposed to an aggressive or passive manner. The owner of the problem also is encouraged to use "I" language as opposed to "you" language, which casts blame on another. For example, a teacher might say to a student, "Bill, I feel angry when I see you talking to Frank when I'm trying to explain how to do a math problem. I would like to work out a plan with you so this won't happen anymore." In using "I" messages, teachers cover three topics: the problem, how they feel about the problem, and what they would like to have happen.

After a problem is addressed, the teacher and student should develop a workable plan for resolution, as well as a backup plan in case the first plan does not work. Plan one might be moving Bill's seat during math and the backup plan might be time out of the classroom. Another example of a good "I" message conversation can be in the form of a dialogue:

> TEACHER: "Bill, I've got a problem, and I would like to have you help me with it. Do you know what it might be?"
>
> BILL: "Yeah, I talk too much during math."
>
> TEACHER: "That's it! Will you be willing to work out a plan with me to help me with my problem?"
>
> *or*
>
> BILL: "No, I have no idea what it could be."
>
> TEACHER: "That's what I thought, too. If you had known how difficult your talking makes my teaching, I think you would have stopped it. Let's see if we can agree on a way to solve my problem."

Delivering an appropriate "I" message is the key to making an effective complaint. Gordon believes that complaints need to be made whenever someone infringes upon someone's rights or treats someone unfairly. Colleagues and students who are allowed to take advantage of a teacher will soon lose respect for that person. To maintain the trust required for effective nondirective strategies, it is important to retain teacher respect. Therefore, someone wins every time a justifiable complaint is made. If the complaint helps negotiate a better working relationship with students, colleagues, or administrators, the person is a double winner. Making effective complaints is an art. To do it well, it is best to follow a

What should a teacher do when a student refuses to talk about the problem?

"Who owns this problem?" The identification of responsibility for owning the problem is a major step in resolving the problem.

GUIDELINES FOR MAKING A COMPLAINT

Preparing the complaint

1. Ask what is the worst possible thing that could happen if the complaint is made. Developing the courage to complain may be the hardest thing to do because people often exaggerate about what will happen if a complaint is stated. Unfortunately, worse things will sometimes happen if a complaint is not expressed.
2. Complain only to the person who is infringing on your rights.
3. Write out the complaint and rehearse how to state it. Role playing with a third party also may help.
4. Make the complaint as soon as possible, but wait until your bad feelings are under control. It is difficult to negotiate agreements when tempers are hot.

Making the complaint:

1. Use an "I" statement such as: "I feel disappointed that you did not come to the tutorial session I scheduled for you, and I would like to work out some way to prevent this from happening again."
2. Refrain from asking people "why" they infringed on your rights. You simply want them to stop the infringement. If you ask "why" and they tell you or rationalize their behavior, the session may be over.
3. Avoid comparisons with others. Do not say, "I wish you were as good a student as your sister was." Such remarks will make the other person defensive.
4. Give people the opportunity to correct their behavior before continuing with the complaint. For example, "Were you aware there was a line and it ends back there?"
5. Make one complaint at a time. Avoid saying, "and furthermore. . . ."
6. Avoid sarcasm because it may detract from your statement and damage the relationship with the other person.

Following your complaint

1. Thank the other person for listening, for his time, and for anything he has agreed to do to remedy the situation.
2. Be willing to listen to a complaint the other person may have.
3. Offer to help the other person resolve the conflict.
4. Schedule a meeting at a later date if a follow-up meeting is needed.

set of guidelines, as shown in Applications from the Text 4.9, for preparing the complaint, making the complaint, and following up the complaint.

If the students or student owns the problem, the teacher should respond with an empathic "you" message (as opposed to a blaming "you" message). This process also is known as active listening because the teacher takes an active role in responding to what the student has said. For example, a student may come to the teacher with a problem saying, "Ms. James, I broke up with my boyfriend two days ago and all I seem to get done is a lot of crying. I can't even get started on my assignments." The teacher should reply, "Sandy, it sounds like this breakup has you feeling really depressed and upset and you are worried about how you are going to be able to pull yourself together and get your work done."

The empathic "you" message covers three important topics: the problem, feelings about the problem, and what Sandy would like to have happen. By responding with this kind of a message, the teacher leaves the door open for the student to talk about the problem in depth and to eventually move toward taking a first step to solve it. This Rogerian approach to counseling places a heavy emphasis on active listening and on summarizing the content of the problem, the feelings generated by the problem, and the expectations of what the student would like to have happen. Feelings are emphasized because they are the best indicators regarding what is best. The Rogerian approach emphasizes feelings because they identify what is right and wrong to a person. By having students frequently summarize the content, feelings, and expectations of a problem, they will take on the role of teaching the listener about the problem. In teaching, the students learn more about their problems and what they need to do to solve them. Teacher summaries act as oral quizzes to see if the teacher is learning what the student is trying to teach. Remember, one pillar supporting the student-centered philosophy is the goal to teach students how to become inner-directed and independent.

Student-centered teachers avoid trying to make decisions for their students and do not offer advice. Giving information can be helpful, but giving advice makes students feel like the teacher is telling them what decisions are best for them. Teachers should, however, take every step possible to prevent students from being injured, injuring themselves, or injuring others. In summary, when counseling students using the person-centered approach, teachers refrain from giving advice, asking questions, and offering interpretations. Teachers focus, instead, on active listening by making summarizing statements about a problem, the student's feelings about the problem, and the expectations of what the student would like to have happen.

Carkhuff (1973; 1981) developed a system that can help teachers rate the level of empathy they express when responding to students who come to them with problems. He classifies responses as belonging to one of five possible levels: levels one and two are harmful, level three marks a break-even point, and levels four and five are helpful. An example of each level is shown in Applications from the Text 4.10 in response to a student named Sam.

The level-I response indicates that the teacher is really not attending to Sam and his problem. The teacher misses both the problem and the feelings associated with the problem. Furthermore, the teacher discounts both Sam's problem and his feelings, making them seem unfounded and of little consequence. The level-II response, although an attending response, is still harmful because it offers advice or solutions before giving Sam the opportunity to tell the complete story and to suggest his own ideas for solving the problem.

The level-III response can sometimes be better than a break-even response because it can reflect the accurate empathy the teacher has for the student. Two topics need to be included in the Level III response: a summary of what the problem is and how Sam feels about it. This response fails, however, to address how Sam wants to solve the problem.

Level-IV responses go beyond accurate empathy by personalizing the situation for the student. With this kind of response, the teacher demonstrates to the student an understanding of the problem, how Sam feels about it, and what Sam would like to do. It reflects Sam's desire to change things.

Level-V is rated by Carkhuff (1973) as being most helpful because it helps the student initiate a plan for solving the problem.

The active-listening method, as explained earlier, is helpful because it allows people to identify where they are in their lives in regard to where they would like

Are feelings overrated in Rogers's model? Can teachers become too involved in responding to only feelings?

APPLICATIONS FROM THE TEXT 4.10

Sam:
"George is always trying to pick a fight with me, and I don't know how to make him stop."

Level-I response:
Teacher:
"Don't worry about it, I knew a kid like George once, and he never amounted to anything."

Level-II response:
Teacher:
"Maybe you should carry a ball bat around with you."

Level-III response:
Teacher:
"You're feeling annoyed and angry with George because he always tries to start trouble with you."

Level-IV response:
Teacher:
"You're feeling annoyed and angry with George because he always tries to start trouble with you and you'd like to know how you can make him stop this behavior."

Level-V response:
Teacher:
"Sam, just to make sure I understand the situation completely, let me try to put it together one more time. George's picking a fight annoys you to the point of getting serious about finding a good way to stop it. If you are ready, we could begin by looking at what you have already tried to do to solve the problem."

to be. Once a discrepancy (if any) is discovered, people can make better decisions about what they need to do to fill any gaps between where they are and where they want to be.

SUMMARY

Teacher-centered models of classroom management are characterized by the increased control the teacher retains in planning and implementing the classroom rules, consequences, and interventions. Behavior methods and assertive discipline are two teacher-centered CRM models that have research and popular support among those teachers who prefer an active role in directing their students' behavior. However, most teachers realize that student participation in developing classroom rules builds a better foundation for teacher-student cooperation. "Our" rules are easier to follow than "my" rules. Behavioral and assertive-discipline methods offer the most organized and systematic approach to classroom management. On the other hand, student-centered approaches are preferred by teachers who are comfortable in releasing some of their control over their students and classroom. Person-centered education and teacher-effectiveness training provide two models for operating a student-centered classroom. A high premium is placed on self-directed learning and cooperative-learning activities in student-centered classrooms.

■ ■ ■ ■

BEHAVIORAL CONTRACTS AS POSITIVE REINFORCEMENTS

EPILOGUE

As Lynne's teacher, you developed a behavioral contract designed to increase her desired behavior while decreasing her undesired behaviors in the classroom. First, you listed Lynne's problem behaviors and consequences. Second, desired behaviors were listed with rewards. Positive reinforcement included praise and points earned for "fun-time" activities. Positive reinforcers were withdrawn by loss of points when undesired behaviors occurred. Points could be earned by such on-task behaviors as bringing appropriate materials to class, completing assignments, working at her desk, and doing extra assignments. Points earned could be exchanged for such "fun-time" activities as working on the computer, playing various board and card games, and watching videotapes. Then you worked with Lynne in selecting the activities she likes to

do best. The goal for behavior contracts is to reinforce desired behaviors so that doing desired behaviors becomes reinforcing in itself. For example, as work performance and behavior improve, grades improve, parents and teachers will be happier, and the student's life also should be happier as the adults in her life become more accommodating and a lot less punitive.

After reviewing the behavior analysis method in the chapter, how might the plan be altered? What would you do if the behavioral plan designed by you and Lynne did not work? How could the assertive discipline plan have been used? Perhaps you favor a student-centered classroom management approach. How would a student-centered teacher handle Lynne's problem situation?

CHAPTER REVIEW

1. Compare and contrast the underlying assumptions of nondirective, directive, and eclectic models of classroom management.
2. Which of these management models appears to most facilitate student involvement in managing the classroom?
3. Which of these management models might be most appropriate in addressing student diversity needs?
4. Are some models more developmentally appropriate for some age groups than other models?
5. In completing a behavior analysis of students, what three aspects of behavior should the teacher examine?
6. To which model is behavior analysis most closely linked?
7. List some of the characteristics of the assertive discipline model of classroom management.
8. What management model is most closely linked to the assertive discipline model of classroom management?
9. To what degree does the assertive discipline model of management purport to assert teacher control over students?

10. What classroom model is most closely associated with cooperative learning? (What aspects of this model appear to facilitate cooperative rather than competitive classroom environments?)

11. How do we make an effective complaint? List the steps and procedures for making an effective complaint.

REFERENCES

Canter, L. (1976). *Teacher effectiveness training*. New York: Peter H. Wyden.

Canter, L. (1981). *Assertive discipline follow-up guidebook*. Santa Monica, CA: Lee Canter & Associates.

Canter, L. (1989). Assertive discipline—More than names on the board and marbles in a jar. *Phi Delta Kappan, 71* (1), 57–61.

Carkhuff, R. (1973, March). *Human achievement, educational achievement, career achievement: Essential ingredients of elementary school guidance*. Paper presented at the Second Annual National Elementary School Guidance Conference, Louisville, KY.

Carkhuff, R. (1981, April). *Creating and researching community based helping programs*. Paper presented at the American Personnel and Guidance Association Convention, Saint Louis, MO.

Dreikurs, R. (1968). *Psychology in the classroom* (2nd ed.). New York: Harper & Row.

Dreikurs, R., Grunwald, B., & Pepper, F. (1982). *Maintaining sanity in the classroom*. New York: Harper & Row.

Evertson, M., & Harris, A. (1992). What we know about managing classrooms. *Educational Leadership, 49* (7) 74–78.

Glasser, W. (1969). *Schools without failure*. New York: Harper and Row.

Glasser, W. (1990). *The quality school: Managing students without coercion*. New York: Harper and Row.

Gordon, T. (1974). *Teacher effectiveness training*. New York: Peter H. Wyden.

Maslow, A. (1970). *Motivation & personality* (2nd ed.). New York: Harper & Row.

Rogers, C. (1969). *Freedom to learn*. Columbus, OH: Charles E. Merrill.

Rogers, C. (1983). *Freedom to learn for the 80's*. Columbus, OH: Merrill.

Skinner, B. (1968). *The technology of teaching*. Englewood Cliffs, NJ: Prentice-Hall.

Skinner, B. (1971). *Beyond freedom and dignity*. New York: Knopf.

Thompson, C., Prater, A., & Poppen, W. (1974). One more time: How do you motivate students? *Elementary School Guidance & Counseling, 9*, 30–34.

CHAPTER 5

CLASSROOM MANAGEMENT
Eclectic Models

■ ■ ■

Chapter Outline

IDENTIFYING SOME SOURCES OF BEHAVIORAL PROBLEMS

Kevin Butterfield is a 16-year-old student in an eleventh-grade English class at Oakmont High School. Recently the teacher caught him cheating on his semester examination.

According to school records, Kevin is a high achiever with a 3.85 grade point average. Kevin's recent performance in the class, however, has been down. The test he cheated on could have brought his low grades up had he done well on it. School policy requires that zero grades be awarded when students are caught cheating, and, as a result, Kevin's academic standing is worse than ever. Kevin is the older of two boys who live with their mother, an office manager for a department store. Other teachers have indicated that Kevin's mother expects him to make straight A grades. According to teacher reports, Kevin is well liked by his peers; however, he has not developed any close friendships. The teacher has noticed recently that he has become quite attached to a tenth-grade female student. As Kevin's teacher, what strategies would you develop to help Kevin with the problems he has, as indicated by his cheating?

INTRODUCTION
What Is Classroom Management?

Classroom management is anything teachers do to establish and maintain a healthy and productive learning environment in the classroom. Well-managed classrooms protect both the teacher's right to teach and the students' right to learn. In a more formal sense, classroom management programs are structured around the teacher having an organized plan to handle situations when students infringe on these two basic rights. Well-managed classrooms are places where students want to be and where they believe that something important is happening. Students will behave well in such classrooms so as not to miss out on the opportunities they offer.

Classroom management also may be defined as anything teachers do to increase the quality and quantity of students' learning. This chapter will be directed toward helping teachers learn to make classrooms useful places where students want to be.

KEY CONCEPTS

■ Goals of misbehavior are based on faulty logic.

■ Corrective interventions for misbehavior are determined by the goal the student is trying to achieve.

■ Natural and logical consequences are related to a student's irresponsible behavior.

- Reality-based classroom management provides a counseling method for teaching problem solving.
- Classroom meetings offer an exciting way to stimulate learning and thinking while reducing classroom management problems.

EFFECTIVE CLASSROOM MANAGEMENT

Maintaining good classroom discipline is often equated with effective classroom management. Today's society is highly concerned about good discipline as stories appear in the news daily about violence and weapons in schools. In many areas, teacher safety has become the number one priority of the school. Schools with appropriate discipline do exist, however, and such schools often have some good discipline and classroom management practices in common. Many of these common practices involve measures that prevent disruptive student behavior from occurring, rather than simply addressing it once it has happened (Wayson, DeVoss, Kaeser, Lasley, & Pinnell 1982, the U.S. Department of Education, 1986). Professionals identify several commonalties shared by schools with good discipline.

Discipline Is Considered a Basic Skill. Discipline is perhaps the most important basic skill for students to learn. Without self-discipline, learning other basic skills is difficult. If a student has not learned good discipline elsewhere, the teacher will often have to teach discipline as part of the regular curriculum. Much of the material in this chapter will address this subject of teaching discipline.

Teachers make Classrooms Inviting and Exciting. Classrooms are places where students want to be and where they believe important learning is taking place. In general, teachers make this happen by doing two things: (a) persuading the students that the teacher genuinely cares about their well-being and (b) persuading students that they can be successful in the classroom.

> Reflect on how you might feel if you were a teacher in a school with metal detectors and security guards. How would this situation impact the climate in your classroom?

The teacher sets the tone and atmosphere for the classroom. For the most part students give back to us what we give to them.

Fuhr (1993) reminded teachers that they should always pose this question to themselves, "Would I like to be a student in my class?" Follow this question by reflecting on the traits of your favorite teacher (discussed in chapter one). Fuhr maintained that most classroom problems can be prevented if teachers behaved as their favorite teachers behaved. That is, if they were enthusiastic, knowledgeable, and caring.

Tierno (1991) is in agreement with Fuhr. He views teachers as role models for appropriate classroom behavior and for handling interpersonal relationships. He believes students will learn how to respect each other if the teachers model respect for their students.

Students Are Treated with Respect. When students are treated with respect, they, in turn, are more respectful of others. There is a direct correlation between poor discipline methods and the incidence of school vandalism and violence toward teachers. If teachers respect students, they will find less threat to themselves.

Teachers Empower Students. Teachers are able to win their students' cooperation by empowering their students. Students feel empowered when teachers let them have a say in the structure of classroom learning by giving them choices in both how the classroom will operate and how they will master the material for their grade level. Teachers who attempt to run their classrooms by overpowering their students often succeed only in maintaining yearlong, energy-draining power struggles.

Teachers Know How to Manage and Structure Classroom Rules. The number of classroom rules should be limited to five or six. (Remembering a list of ten rules is difficult for most people, even one as well known as the Ten Commandments.) There should be no mystery rules or rules that students do not know. The list of rules should be clearly written and posted in a place with high visibility in the classroom. There should be no unknown consequences for not following the rules. Students should understand what will happen when a rule is broken before they break it. Furthermore, consequences for breaking a rule should be logically related to the nature of the misbehavior. For example, if a window is broken, the student should have to pay for having it fixed either by paying for it directly or by working off the debt doing extra work around the school or classroom.

The students also should have a voice in establishing the rules and consequences. If they feel they are part of rule-making decisions, students are more willing to abide by the rules. The best way to achieve the ownership and cooperation needed regarding rules and consequences is to conduct classroom meetings where the teacher and the students work toward reaching consensus on the rules and consequences.

Finally, all rules should be given a trial period to see how well they work. For example, the rules and consequences could be reviewed in a classroom meeting after twenty school days. The class should consider several things in reviewing

Write what you would consider to be the three most important rules for your own classroom. List a logical consequence for not following each rule.

rules: (a) Does the rule work? (b) Is the rule needed? (c) Does the rule help learning in a positive way? (d) Are students following the rule? (e) Does the rule apply to adults as well as to the students? and (f) Are the rules and consequences fair to everybody? A teacher should retain veto power in the event that the group process does not work as well as desired. As students move toward developing more responsibility for conducting classroom business, veto power will become necessary.

Teachers Notice Good Behavior. Teachers realize that sometimes the best discipline can be accomplished by noticing students' good behavior. Teachers with good classroom management skills have a process for rewarding individual and group behavior with things and activities that do not cost much money.

Many teachers use jars that they fill with marbles as students complete tasks to help their classes move toward group goals. In one school the principal begins popping corn about 10:00 each morning. As the smell of popcorn wafts its way around the building, students begin working harder to fill the glass marble jar by noon, since classes with full marble jars receive coupons for free popcorn. Marbles are added to the jar at the discretion of the teacher who has the freedom to reward classroom discussion, written work, and other productive student behaviors.

Another way to reward students for good behavior is to send happygrams to students and/or their parents. Happygrams are short notes designed like telegrams in which the teacher describes the good work or other positive behaviors of the student. Happygrams also can be used by teachers as thank-you notes for various helpful student behaviors.

Still another way to catch students in good behavior is to call their parents and tell them how well their child is doing. One high school teacher makes two short calls each day to different parents. In the calls, he spends about three to four minutes describing the accomplishments of the student. The teacher reports that these positive telephone calls have done more for his classroom discipline than anything else he has tried.

Good Teaching Results in Good Discipline. Many educators believe that good classroom discipline is a by-product of good teaching. That is, if the teacher is able to teach the subject matter in a way that has relevance and purpose for students, students will be more interested in learning than in disrupting the classroom. Packer (1992) describes such a class where the students were learning chemistry by doing research on the type of lawn chemicals used by the school system. The class project was to find the most effective, economical, and environmentally safe grass fertilizer for use on the grounds of 104 schools. In addition to learning the chemistry involved in using various fertilizers, the students learned many skills required for successful careers, including how to (a) develop budgets and schedules (allocating resources), (b) work with teams of classmates, experts, and grounds keepers (interpersonal skills), (c) conduct research and organize and evaluate data (information processing skills), and (d) evaluate alternative solutions to problems (application of technology).

What type of rules would you develop for different age levels? Is there such a thing as a "developmentally appropriate classroom management system"?

Will all discipline
practices work with all
students? Can you
individualize discipline
practices? What
problems might occur in
tailoring discipline
policies to individual
students?

In summary, the good discipline practices mentioned here contribute in a positive way to student learning and academic achievement. Careful attention to the establishment, communication, and enforcement of fair and consistent rules and consequences should make the teacher's work easier to do. In general, the conclusions reported by Wayson et al. (1982) and the U.S. Department of Education report (1986) are that schools with good discipline have the following things in common:

1. closer than average ties to home and community;
2. causes, rather than symptoms, of discipline problems are treated by making the curriculum relevant to the students and to success in the outside world;
3. high expectations for student success;
4. frequent encouragement and reinforcement for each student's achievement;
5. a strong principal who works cooperatively with a dedicated and energetic staff in making policy decisions.

Eclectic CRM Methods

Several models of classroom management employ a combination of both directive and nondirective methods derived from several theories and approaches. The Adlerian model popularized by Rudolph Dreikurs (1968) and Dreikurs, Grunwald, and Pepper (1982) and the reality-based model of William Glasser (1969; 1990) are two of the most popular eclectic models.

Adlerian/Individual Psychology Model
How Can the Adlerian or Individual Psychology Model Help Teachers Manage their Classrooms?

Perhaps the single, best contribution Dreikurs and the Adlerians have made to teachers is a system for understanding student misbehavior. This system includes an analysis of the goal the student is trying to achieve, as well as a set of recommendations on what to do about the problem. Proponents of Adlerian psychology believe that all people strive to find a place in every social situation. This desire to belong begins with finding a place in the family, then progresses in preschool play groups, and classroom groups to finally seeking a place in the work world. If frustrated in their efforts to find a place or desired status, people may resort to various forms of misbehavior to fulfill their unmet needs. Children generally employ one or more of four primary types of misbehaviors that will help them achieve attention, power, revenge, and/or withdrawal. The Adlerians provide a surefire method for detecting which goals a child is trying to achieve. Teachers simply have to consult their own inner feelings when students misbehave to determine the cause. *Attention-getting* behaviors make the teacher feel *annoyed* with the student. *Power struggles* cause feelings of *anger* and being *threatened*. *Revenge-seeking* behavior causes a deeply felt *hurt*. Students withdrawing through *displays of inadequacy* make the teacher feel despair and *discouragement* about trying to help the student in question. Two students exhibiting the same misbehavior (e.g., coming for help in retying shoelaces for the fourth time) can generate two different feelings. For one child, the behavior can be attention getting and the teacher feels annoyed, while for the second child, the behavior is a display of inadequacy causing the teacher to feel like giving up on the student.

The four goals of misbehavior progress in order from the least damaging goal (attention) to the most serious and difficult goal to remediate (withdrawal). Examples of the goals and how to treat them are shown in figure 5.1.

Withdrawal through displays of inadequacy is the most difficult behavior to remediate. In working hard to convince others that they are truly inadequate, goal-four students begin to believe in their lack of ability.

How Do You Use the Four Goals of Misbehavior in Counseling Students?

The Adlerian counseling method focuses on helping students understand the goals they are trying to achieve with their misbehavior. The teacher and student discuss the student's behavior in the nonpunitive, friendly atmosphere of a private conference. It is important that the conference not be held when either one or both parties are disturbed or angry. In the conference, the teacher asks the student a series of "could it be" questions that serve as hypotheses to examine the student's behavior. For example, the teacher might treat attention-getting by saying, "Henry, could it be that you want me to pay more attention to you and the only way you know how to get my attention is to ask me questions you already know how to answer?" Henry might shake his head no and say no; however, he might crack a sheepish smile or blush indicating through a recognition reflex that the teacher has understood his motive. The teacher could continue by saying, "We may need to find a way where I can give more attention, recognition, and reinforcement for the good work you can do." Henry might reply, "Well, I never seem to get complimented in front of the class as much as some students do." Or, Henry might say, "I'm not trying to be the teacher's pet or anything. I'd just like to get to do some of the things you let other students do." From this beginning dialogue, the teacher and student can develop a plan to both correct the behavior and meet the student's needs. The agreement should include what consequences will occur if the misbehavior reappears.

Questions for the other three goals can proceed in the same manner:

a. "Could it be that you want to be your own boss and the only way you know how to do this is to refuse to do everything I ask you to do?"
b. "Could it be that I have hurt your feelings or someone else has hurt you and the only way you know how to handle your hurt is to hurt back?"
c. "Could it be that you want me to stop asking you to do so much homework, so you are trying to prove you cannot do it by turning in failing work?"

Manly (1986) developed a checklist of questions for the goals of misbehavior to help teachers discover what the student is trying to achieve. An example of Manly's chart appears in Applications from the Text 5.1.

Which of the four types of misbehavior do you think is most common in the classroom?

Think back about an incident (your own or that of someone else) of classroom misbehavior during school. Do the four goals of misbehavior apply to this incident?

FIGURE 5.1 The Four Goals of Misbehavior

Goal Number One—Attention

1. Child's Faulty Logic:
   "Life is not good when I'm not the center of attention. I belong only when I'm being noticed or being served."
2. Teacher's Feelings:
   Annoyance
3. Corrective Procedures:
   Ignore the misbehavior
   Use nonpunitive isolation to isolate the student in an attractive, time-out room conducive to working.
   Catch the student doing good behavior.
   Avoid helping the student too much.
   Give attention for positive behavior when the student is not making a bid for it.
   Let the student know it is OK to have tantrums as long as they are done privately and out of hearing.
   Resist the temptation to lecture or nag the student.

Goal Number Two—Power

1. Child's Faulty Logic:
   "Life is not good when I don't get my own way. I belong only when I do get my own way or when I am the boss or when I prove nobody can boss me."
2. Teacher's Feelings:
   Angry, Threatened, Provoked
3. Corrective Procedures:
   Take your sail out of the child's wind. Remember that it takes two to fight and one to stop the fight. In other words, refuse to engage in the conflict and also refuse to give in.
   Empower your students whenever possible by giving them choices and decision-making powers that you can live with in your particular classroom situation.

Goal Number Three—Revenge

1. Child's Faulty Logic:
   "Life is good when I am able to handle my hurt feelings by hurting others. I belong when I am able to avenge all the hurt I feel. I cannot be loved."
2. Teacher's Feelings:
   Deeply hurt
3. Corrective Procedures:
   Resist the urge to retaliate by punishing the child.
   Work on building a trust relationship while trying to teach the child that she is lovable and loved.
   Find the child a friend or buddy to help the process along. Perhaps another adult can be helpful if your relationship with the child is not good.

Goal Number Four—Withdrawal

1. Child's Faulty Logic:
   "Life is good when I'm able to convince others not to expect anything from me. I belong when I am able to get adults off my back by doing a poor job on anything they ask me to do. In reality I am not very capable. In fact, I am helpless."
2. Teacher's Feelings:
   Discouraged, Despair, Hopelessness, The urge to give up
3. Corrective Procedures:
   Resist the urge to give up on the child. You may want to suspend all grading and negative evaluations of the child's work until there is some improvement. Instead, write thank-you notes on the work that is completed.
   Use large doses of encouragement as you work to help your student experience some daily success in your classroom.
   Help your student to get started on assignments he is able to handle.
   Direct your focus to your student's positive attributes rather than to any negative traits.

PURPOSE OF YOUR MISBEHAVIOR

When you get into trouble for what you do, is it because you . . .
- —— want people to notice you?
- —— want people to do more for you?
- —— want to be special?
- —— want some attention?
- —— want to be boss?
- —— want to be in charge?
- —— want people to do what you want?
- —— want people to stop telling you what to do?
- —— want power?

- —— want to get even?
- —— feel like you have been treated unfairly?
- —— want people to see what it is like to hurt?
- —— want people to know you do not like what they do?
- —— want people to feel sorry for what they have done?
- —— want to be left alone because you cannot do it?
- —— want to be left alone because you might fail?
- —— want people to stop asking you to do things?
- —— want people to stop expecting too much from you?
- —— want people to feel sorry for you?

How Many Goals of Misbehavior Do Adolescents Have?

As mentioned earlier, children's goals of misbehavior generally are confined to the four goals of attention, power, revenge, and withdrawal. Adolescents, while also having these four goals, unfortunately develop other goals of misbehavior for each irrational thought they entertain about themselves or their behavior. For example, the irrational idea, "I must be perfect" could lead a student to engage in several types of perfectionist behavior that make life miserable for the student. Most irrational goal messages produce failure because the goals they set are unattainable. Therefore, when counseling adolescent students, it is important to help them examine the faulty logic behind their behavior as well as the goal of the misbehavior. According to Albert Ellis (1989), changing the word "must" to "it would be nice if" seems to help adolescents put irrational messages in better perspective. For example, *"It would be nice if* I were perfect, but since I'm human and humans make mistakes, it is OK to make mistakes, and I'm OK when I do."

What Are the Advantages of Using Natural and Logical Consequences Rather than Punishment to Treat Misbehavior in Your Classroom?

Teachers following the Adlerian method favor the use of natural and logical consequences over reward and punishment to direct student behavior. Consequences allow children to experience the actual good and bad results of their behavior. *Natural consequences* of irresponsible behavior are those unfavorable outcomes that occur naturally without any prearranged plan administered by others. For instance, if a ball glove is left outside and ruined by the rain, a natural consequence of the glove being ruined is experienced. Likewise, if a passenger fails to arrive at the airport on time, she will miss the flight.

Finding out the goals of misbehavior is an important aspect of counseling adolescent students.

Were you ever paddled in school or at home? What effect did it have on your misbehavior?

Logical consequences, established through classroom rules, are fair, direct, consistent, and logical results of a student's behavior. If Carolyn interferes with someone's right to learn, she will be asked to move to a place where her behavior will not cause a problem. If Mark breaks a window at school, he will be asked to fix it himself, pay to have it fixed, or work off his debt by doing some other type of work for the school. *Punishment* is defined by the Adlerians as being any illogical consequence for irresponsible behavior. For example, if David cannot come up with an acceptable excuse for his absence from school, he is punished with a three-day suspension. The punishment has no direct relation to the crime. In-school suspension programs in which students are allowed to complete their work in isolation are more logical than out-of-school suspensions with zero grades (an illogical punishment).

Corporal punishment works in the same way—it does not address the problem. Some students may even prefer corporal punishment because it may be easier to take three swats than to make restitution for a mistake. This form of punishment teaches students that it is OK for people with power to hit those with less power.

Corporal punishment continues to be an ineffective way to manage discipline problems in schools. In schools where it is still used, paddlings tend to increase rather than decrease during the school year with the same students getting most of the paddlings. Perhaps the most compelling reason why paddling should not be considered a logical consequence for disruptive behavior is that public floggings at the whipping post are no longer accepted forms of behavior control in our society.

In summary, by using natural and logical consequences in their classroom management (CRM) plan, teachers (a) help establish good relationships with their students, (b) teach students to accept the responsibility for the outcomes of their own behavior, and (c) expose students to the reality of the social order.

WILLIAM GLASSER'S REALITY-BASED MODEL

William Glasser's (1965; 1969; 1990) ideas on classroom management are based on his twelve years as the head psychiatrist at the Ventura School for Girls. The institution is operated by the state of California for the treatment of seriously delinquent adolescent girls. During his tenure at Ventura, Glasser was instrumental in reversing the school's 80 percent to 90 percent relapse rate. He believes that the success was achieved because he and the staff were able to replace the students' failure identity with a success identity. Building on Freud's idea that mental health is a function of the quality of a person's love life and work life, Glasser began to create success identities for the students. He started by encouraging the faculty to focus on two important human needs that students at Ventura were not getting met: the need to feel loved by a caring person and the need to feel a sense of achievement. Teachers were asked to direct their efforts toward filling both student needs. Those who found the young women difficult to like were asked to transfer to a new job. The focus of each classroom session was to help each student experience some success every day.

Glasser's "schools without failure" concept was born at the Ventura School if for no other reason than because of the impossibility of flunking out of a reform school. As mentioned earlier, Glasser's method worked. Consistent with Rogers's emphasis on creating the proper classroom climate, Glasser believes that efforts should be directed toward making the classroom a place where students want to be because they would miss something important and valuable if they do not come to class. Glasser also endorses the use of cooperative learning groups as discussed in the student-centered CRM model in chapter 4 (Glasser, 1986). Glasser (1990) emphasizes that teachers need to function as lead managers (rather than boss managers) who motivate by empowering students with the responsibility for learning. He believes that two- to five-member learning teams are powerful learning motivators because the teams help meet the students' needs for belonging, power, friendship, and achievement.

Do you agree with the focus of Glasser's program?

How Does the Reality-based CRM Approach Work?

Glasser has developed an eight-step program for putting reality therapy into practice.

Step One: The first step concerns the most important aspect of teaching—building a good relationship with students. Teachers need to develop positive student relationships that are honest, open, warm, and helpful. Teachers should build a classroom climate that fosters encouragement, support, and reinforcement among the students. No time should be spent on ridicule and sarcasm unless these topics have become a problem and need discussion.

Step Two: The second step begins the problem-solving process inherent in Glasser's method. When a student has a problem, whether academic or personal, the teacher should listen carefully to help both of them clarify and understand the problem. Once the problem is identified, the focus shifts to an examination of what alternatives the student has already used to try to solve the problem.

Step Three: In the third step, students are requested to or given the invitation to examine how helpful or harmful each alternative has been, Perhaps step three is the key to the change and problem-solving process. People do not generally change their behaviors or look for new problem-solving approaches until they are thoroughly disgusted with the approach they are currently using. In this step students are taught how to make value judgments about their decisions and behavior.

Step Four: If nothing useful turns up in step three, the student is encouraged to brainstorm a new list of alternative problem-solving behaviors. The teacher's task is to avoid advice and suggestions as much as possible so that students learn how to think for themselves. Students have more commitment to follow through on a plan that they design.

Step Five: The task in step five is to make a commitment to use one of the alternatives developed in step four to solve the problem. Handshakes and two signed copies of an agreement or contract can help students keep their commitments.

Step Six: A follow-up meeting should be held to find out how well the student or students carry out the plan. A student might say, "Well, I did commit to turn in one homework paper a day, and I was not able to do it" and begin to list all the reasons why. Teachers following the reality-based model are not interested in having their students dwell on rationalizing "whys" when students behave irresponsibly. At this point, the teacher will cut the "whys" off and suggest that a new contract be written or a new, more feasible plan developed. Teachers do not need to accept excuses if a student does not meet a commitment. Excuses are designed to avoid punishment. When students learn they will not be punished for not meeting a commitment, there will be no need for excuses.

Step Seven: Teachers should not interfere with the natural and logical consequences resulting from a student's irresponsible behavior. Such consequences may be receiving lower grades for not completing homework.

Step Eight: The final step is designed to prevent teachers from becoming discouraged when they are not as successful as they would like to be with a student. Glasser (1969) recommends that teachers stick with problem students three or four more times than students expect and that teachers continue to build the relationship begun in step one.

How Do You Confront Misbehaving Students with the Reality-based Method?

Glasser (1965) suggests that teachers use the same reality-therapy method counselors use when students misbehave. The reality-therapy method, like any counseling approach, is used when tempers have cooled. Before tempers have cooled, the teacher could say, "Robby, I need to have you stop what you are doing. I'll need to talk with you about this later." When later comes, the process follows these basic questions.

a. What are you doing? or
   What did you do in our class this morning?

Glasser's approach is to force students to take responsibility for their behavior. By avoiding the use of punishment, do you think that students will become more responsible?

b. What good did your behavior do?
   How was your behavior helpful:
       to you?
       to me?
       to our class?
c. If what you did was not all that helpful, what could you do that would be helpful?
d. Which one of *your* suggestions do you want to try?
e. When can we get together to check up on how your plan is working?
f. Shake hands on the commitment or use a written contract signed by teacher and student.
g. Recycle the process if the first plan does not work.

How Are Glasser's Reality-based Methods Applied to the Total Classroom Group?

Perhaps the most useful reality-based method for teachers to use with their class group is the classroom meeting. Glasser (1969) developed three types of classroom meetings: educational-diagnostic, social-problem solving, and open-ended.

Educational-diagnostic classroom meetings. These are designed to assess the breadth and depth of knowledge students have of a topic before beginning a new unit of study on the topic. The educational-diagnostic meeting also can be used to find out how much students have learned at the conclusion of the unit.

Classroom meetings are an important aspect of Glasser's Reality-based model of classroom management.

Paper-and-pencil tests can be used to test the students' recall of content; however, the classroom-meeting format tests their understanding and application of the content. Participation in classroom meetings is not graded and the students are not permitted to ridicule any ideas. The students need to feel free to express their thoughts without fear of grades and "put downs." The meetings work best when the teacher withholds negative value judgments while collecting diagnostic data about how much the students know. An educational-diagnostic meeting could start with questions like these:

> "What is the Constitution?"
> "Does it exist?"
> "How do you know that?"
> "Do constitutional rights pertain to you and me?"
> "What are some of those rights?"
> "What if you do something on your own property that is against the law?"

Open questions stimulate more discussion than closed questions that require one-word answers. Some teachers use educational-diagnostic meetings to get student feedback on what they like and dislike about how the class is being run. A teacher may want to ask the class, "What would you do if you were the teacher?"

Social–problem-solving classroom meetings. These are designed to help the classroom group solve any problems concerning the class as a group or any individual or individuals in the class. Problems may include such things as homework, teacher/student relationships, friends, drug use, vandalism, fighting, school and classroom rules and policies, and health issues. Once again the teacher should attempt to help students make value judgments about their own behavior regarding how their behaviors are helpful, not helpful, or even harmful to themselves and others. Once the problem topic has been established, the discussion moves toward solving the problem by using the sequence of the reality-therapy questions mentioned previously. Classroom meetings work best if everyone is seated in the front row or in a circle, the only requirement being that each student can see everyone else's face without having to lean forward or backward. The circle arrangement allows the teacher to have eye contact with each student during the times when the class needs to be together. This arrangement is desirable most of the time because improved eye contact is an automatic way to improve classroom discipline as well as group discussion. The circle arrangement, however, may not be helpful in classes that already have too much interaction.

Open-ended classroom meetings. These should be used most often because they offer the students the opportunity of bringing up and discussing thought-provoking questions related to their lives. The most attractive thing about the open meeting is that it is one of the few school times that students are not directed to find the "right" answers. The emphasis is on speculation and creativity. Teachers and students can bring their favorite "what if" questions to the meeting. For example:

a. "What if we were all born the same color?"
b. "What if all but the highest mountains were covered with water?"
c. "What if we won a lot of money and did not have to work or go to school?"
d. What would happen if people everywhere refused to fight in the next war?"
e. What would you do if you had one pill that would allow you to live two hundred years?"

Classroom meetings are most effective when they are an integral part of the regular school program. They are great examples of one way the schools-without-failure concept can be implemented in the classroom. In classroom meetings, students have the opportunity to explore questions that are not answered in textbooks. For example, the dictionary will contain a good definition of pollution; however, it will not tell students ways to fight pollution in their own area. Answers to world peace, human relations, hunger, homelessness, unemployment, health issues, shortages of natural resources, economic problems, environmental problems, and various moral dilemmas are generally not found in a textbook. Practice in using the problem-solving skills necessary to solve such complex problems can occur in classroom meetings. These meetings work best when the guidelines in Applications from the Text 5.2 are followed.

Are there age limits with these types of classroom meetings? Do you think that any one type of classroom meeting might be more appropriate for primary grade students?

RESEARCH SUPPORT FOR THE THREE STYLES OF CLASSROOM MANAGEMENT METHODS
Student-centered CRM

Radd (1987) developed a process to integrate self-concept development into life-skills education, a theme consistent with the application of student-centered methods to the classroom. Radd's process includes several classroom activities that are focused on building self-concept. The students are taught how to apply their learning to living more effective lives. Omizo and Omizo (1988) found activities similar to Radd's to be successful in working with learning-disabled students. Williams and Lair (1991) presented a rationale for using Rogers's conditions (genuineness, unconditional acceptance and caring, and deep, emphatic understanding) to help build self-acceptance in disabled students. Similar support was found in a study by Bayer (1986) who found person-centered methods to be effective in increasing the self-concept of seventh graders.

Herman (1990) and Aspy (1988) have made significant contributions in detailing successful applications of person-centered theory to the classroom. Aspy and Roebuck (1975) summarized seventeen years of research conducted by the National Consortium for Humanizing Education in forty-two states and seven foreign countries. They found that students learn more and behave better when they receive high levels of *understanding, caring,* and *genuineness* than when they are given low levels of the same. In other words, it does pay to treat students well. Wiggins's (1982) research supports the findings of Aspy and Roebuck. He found person-centered counseling to be effective in helping second-grade students improve their behavior. The students counseled by higher-functioning counselors on the Carkhuff scales made the greater gains; however, gains were

APPLICATIONS FROM THE TEXT 5.2

GUIDELINES FOR LEADING CLASSROOM MEETINGS

a. Identify the topic clearly:
   "The question for today is _____." or "Can someone restate what we will discuss today?" or "Today we can discuss _____ or _____. Which will it be?"

b. Ask for definitions:
   "What do you mean by _____?" or What is _____?"

c. Ask for specifics:
   "What else do you need to know about _____?" or "Tell me more about _____."

d. Ask for personal examples:
   "Do you know anyone who uses _____?" or "Do you ever use _____?" or "How does _____ relate to your life?"

e. Ask for agreements and disagreements:
   "Who agrees with you?" or "Who disagrees with you? Why?"

f. Challenge the group:
   "How can you find out more about that?" or "Would you like to learn more about that topic or idea? What?"

g. Present hypothetical situations involving the topic:
   "What would happen if we did not have _____?"

h. Withhold personal judgment of right and wrong about students' answers and opinions. Instead, use your Socratic line of questions to help them arrive at their own value judgments of their thinking and behavior.

i. Ask no embarrassing questions or questions that you would not be willing to answer yourself. Each student, as well as the teacher, has the right to pass on any question asked.

j. The right to state an opinion is to be respected even when one does not agree with it. Remember that answers to questions calling for personal opinions are always right for the student expressing the opinion. It is important that students feel good about valuing something that the majority does not value.

k. Employ the reality-therapy problem-solving model to help your class group solve a particular problem.

l. Using the classroom meeting circle, in which the students have easy eye contact with each other, enables the teacher to facilitate group discussions by encouraging members to talk with each other rather than through the teacher. Only one person at a time is allowed to speak.

also recorded for the students counseled by lower-functioning counselors. Rogers (1967) was successful in applying his principles in an educational institution that was seeking ways to bring about positive and productive change. One result was an increase in student-centered teaching. Robinson and Hyman (1984) found that twenty to thirty hours of human-relations training for teachers was the most effective program for producing positive changes in teacher attitudes and corresponding changes in improved classroom learning climates.

Some possible discussion questions in a lesson plan for conducting a problem-solving meeting on classroom rules follow.

Identify the Topic:

The question for our first classroom meeting is, "What rules do we need to have in our classroom this year?"

Ask for Definitions:

What do we mean when we talk about classroom rules?

Personalize the Discussion and Ask for Specifics:

What classroom rules have you had in other classes?

What rules do you have at home?

Can you think of other places in which you have or had to observe rules?

Ask for Value Judgments and Agreements/Disagreements:

Why do we have rules?

Why are some good rules? Why?

What are some bad rules? Why?

What rules would you like to have for our class?

Do you know someone who would agree with you about the rules that you like for our class? Who?

Do you know someone who would probably disagree with you about the rules you like? Why?

How many of us should agree on a rule before we make it a classroom rule?

Challenge the Group:

What rules would you be willing to follow in our class?

What should we do if our rules are broken?

What should we do if someone makes it hard for you to learn or hard for me to teach?

In what specific ways do some students bother others in the classroom?

What should we do when this happens?

Would two people volunteer to list our rules and consequences for breaking our rules on the bulletin board?

Teacher-centered CRM

Blechman, Kotanchik, and Taylor (1981) found that school-based contingency contracts written by families are helpful in inspiring inconsistent students to become more consistent in classroom performance. In addition to building better academic achievement, the home/school collaboration increases students' self-confidence.

Harrop and McCann (1984) found that shaping (reinforcing successive approximations of the desired behavior) improved the performance of third-year

In-class isolation or time-out are possible consequences of classroom misbehavior.

If you were a teacher, would student-centered CRM or teacher-centered CRM better complement your own personality? Would a combination of approaches suit you better?

students in creative writing. The dependent variables included influence, elaboration, and flexibility.

Chirico (1985) found that behavior management programs in three schools were successful in reducing problem behavior. The student of the week award was a key reinforcer in the program. Darveaux (1984) found similar success with a good-behavior game and a two-team competition/cooperation game.

Little and Kelley (1989), Abramowitz and O'Leary (1990), and Stratton (1989) all studied the effectiveness of various types of punishment and response cost in reducing off-task and socially inappropriate behavior in children. The following interventions all proved to be effective: removal of reinforcers, immediate rather than delayed reprimands, and time-out.

Genshaft (1982), Christie, Hiss, and Lozanoff (1984), Silverman and Kearney (1990), and Kahn (1989) have all found success with various self-management and behavior-skills training programs in reducing undesired student behaviors. Specific successes were recorded for anxiety reductions, increased attentiveness, on-task behavior, and school phobia.

Canter (1989) summarized a number of studies that have supported the use of assertive discipline in California, Oregon, Ohio, and Arizona schools. Hill (1990), however, presents the argument against assertive discipline, referring to it as dehumanizing, humiliating, and dangerous. It is important to remember that any CRM approach could be misused to the point of being dehumanizing and dangerous.

Eclectic CRM

Bundy and Poppen (1986), in a review of the research on the consultation role of school counselors, found that in eight successful studies on consultation with parents, four counselors used Adlerian psychology (eclectic), one used a multi-modal approach (eclectic), and three used parent effectiveness training (student-centered). Gamble and Watkins (1983), in a case study approach, were successful in combining Adlerian psychology and reality therapy in helping a twelve-year-old boy with several school and relationship problems. Pepper and Roberson (1983) combined interventions from Adlerian psychology and behavioral psychology in designing successful programs for eight males (ages twelve to fourteen) in special education classes.

Barkley, Wilborn, and Towers (1984), in an attempt to develop the Adlerian concept of social interest in teenage students, were successful in training the students to become helpers and listeners to people from a wide population range. The students also increased their scores on a social-interest index given at the beginning, middle, and end of the study.

Mattice (1976) found that children were able to understand the concepts related to the four goals of misbehavior when examining the goals of their own behavior. Nystul (1986) recommends that educators look beyond the goals of children's misbehavior to the special reasons for misbehavior. He points out that the most basic psychological need is for positive relationships with significant others. He also states that students have four life choices: to be a "good somebody," a "good nobody," a "bad somebody," or to have severe mental health problems.

Porter and Hoedt (1985), in a study of fourth- and fifth-grade students from inner-city schools, found focusing on the four goals of misbehavior to be more helpful than asking students *why* they misbehaved. Similarly, Glasser (1965) has always rejected the use of "why" questions when working with a person who behaves irresponsibly.

Pety, Kelly, and Kafafy (1984), in an attempt to discover students' preferences for praise (reinforcement) or encouragement, found that students in grades four through eight preferred praise; however, as the students matured they began to prefer encouragement to a greater degree. Males had a stronger preference for praise than did females. Rathvon (1990) found that encouragement decreased off-task behavior in all five first-grade children but failed to increase academic performance in six out of ten measures used.

In addition to the books written by Glasser that have already been mentioned and quoted, considerable research and writing has been done to support the use of reality-based methods in classroom management. The ten-step lesson plan mentioned earlier has been heavily researched over the years. The following researchers have reported success with their own versions of the ten-step method: Gang (1976), Thompson and Cates (1976), Fuller and Fuller (1982),

Each method of classroom management appears to have some research support. Can you discern any pattern to the research? Would you conclude that the research is mixed or somewhat supportive of one CRM over another?

Reflect on your own responses to different forms of social/verbal reinforcement. Would you agree that there are developmental differences in the use of social/verbal forms of reinforcement?

Lack of discipline can be as serious a handicap as failure to master any of the basic skill subjects. In fact, failure to learn discipline often prevents successful learning of any subject. If a student has not learned discipline at home, the teacher may need to give the student remedial instruction in this important basic skill. To that end, a ten-step plan for teaching discipline to students is presented in this application. The plan includes many of the interventions discussed in this chapter. In fact, it provides a chapter summary organized into a hierarchy ranging from the softer, beginning interventions to the harder and more severe interventions used for repeat offenders. The ten-step plan may be modified to fit the individuality of students and their situations. The plan is frequently used as an individual educational plan (IEP) for students who need special instruction in discipline. The ten steps have been grouped into three phases: *relationship, counseling,* and *time-out.*

Relationship Phase

The purpose of the relationship phase is to build a better working relationship with your student.

Step 1. Ineffective interventions
a. List what you have already tried with the student that has not worked.
b. Make a personal commitment to stop doing those things that do not work. Just stopping the ineffective interventions often causes an improvement in the student's behavior.

Step 2. Change of pace
a. List some change-of-pace interventions designed to disrupt your student's expectations.
b. Do the unexpected. For example, catch the student in good behavior no matter how brief it might be.
c. Ask yourself what your student expects you to do and do not do it.
d. Act shocked and surprised when the student does the same old misbehavior.
e. Try the paradoxical strategy of asking the student to do the thing you would like him to stop.

Step 3. Better day tomorrow
a. List the things you could do to help your student have a better day tomorrow.
b. Give your student three, twenty-second periods of your undivided, positive attention.
c. Ask your student to run an errand for you.
d. Give your student choices in how assignments can be done.
e. Let your student do a favorite classroom job.
f. Ask your student's opinion about something of interest.

Counseling Phase

The purpose of the counseling phase is to work out better plans for helping students meet their needs.

Step 4. One-line counseling approaches
a. Ask the student to stop the undesirable behavior. Use nonpunitive, nonverbal communication as much as possible in getting the student to stop.

Engelhardt (1983), Chance (1985), Johnson (1985), Dempster and Raff (1989), Hart-Hester, Heuchert, and Whittier (1989), and Heuchert (1989).

Classroom meetings and cooperative learning groups also have received some attention in the literature. Omizo and Cubberly (1983) found classroom meetings helpful in working with learning-disabled students. MacDonald (1989) describes how she teaches Glasser's control theory in classrooms for grades one, two, and three. Sullo (1990) developed a plan for using reality therapy and control theory in cooperative learning groups. Similar work with reality therapy has been done in the college setting. Fried (1990) designed a plan for teaching college students

b. Try the "Could it be?" questions (see page 141).

c. Reinforce only cooperative efforts by the student.

Step 5. Reality therapy and rules
a. What did you do?
b. What is our rule?
c. What were you supposed to do?
d. What will you do?

Step 6. Standard Reality therapy (see page ___)
a. What are you doing?
b. How does this help you?
c. What could you do that would help you?
d. What will you do?
e. Have the student dictate or write and sign a contract.
f. Hold a follow-up meeting and write a new contract if needed.

Isolation Phase

The purpose of the time-out or isolation phase is to teach students that their behaviors will likely keep them isolated most of their lives. If not isolated in some institution, they will find themselves isolated from family, friends, and jobs.

Step 7. Time-out or isolation in the classroom
a. Move the student's seat
b. Quiet corner
c. Study carrel
d. Private work area

Step 8. Isolation outside the classroom
a. Time-out room
b. Isolation in a classroom two years above or below the student's age.
c. In-school suspension with organized study periods.

Step 9. Isolation from school
a. Systematic exclusion—the student remains at school each day up to the time she breaks a rule on the plan or contract (IEP). The student returns the next day and begins the day with a clean slate.

Step 10. Field trip to juvenile court
a. Attends a court hearing.
b. Has an interview with the judge.
c. Attends school classes in the facility.
d. Has interviews with teachers, counselors, other court officials, and inmates.

The purpose of the field trip is to increase the student's awareness of the logical consequences existing outside the school and home settings should his irresponsible behavior continue. Failure to help students with the ten-step plan could mean that they should be referred to a community agency better equipped to help find them appropriate ways to meet their needs.

This ten-step plan is simply an example. Teachers can follow this model or develop a plan of their own to best fit their style of classroom management. Remember that an intervention plan needs to include the types of intervention to be used and the order in which they will be applied.

the concepts of reality and self-control in decision making and problem solving. Lincoln (1993) described an approach similar to reality therapy which is designed to help students develop self-discipline. She is an advocate of student input through classroom meetings and has described six steps for helping students solve a problem. Her steps parallel those used in reality therapy.

The APA Task Force on Psychology in Education (1992) supports many of the classroom management plans presented in chapters 4 and 5. The task force recommends several things: (a) cross-age and peer tutoring; (b) presentation of learning materials at different developmental levels for same-age students;

(c) creating supportive learning environments that promote security and a sense of belonging; (d) establishing teacher-student relationships based on understanding and mutual respect that reduce stress and insecurity; (e) conducting group activities that foster cooperative learning; (f) using student-centered projects that provide for student choice and responsibility; and (g) create learning activities that accommodate a variety of learning styles and social interactions such as working alone, competing with others, cooperating with others, and competing with other groups as a member of a team.

In summary, there is strong body of research supporting the practice of the various classroom management plans and interventions presented in chapters 4 and 5. The purpose of chapters 4 and 5 is to provide a wide variety of classroom management plans to allow teachers to select those interventions that fit their personal style of teaching as well as the special management requirements posed by individual students, classrooms, and schools.

SUMMARY

Adlerian and reality-based models of classroom discipline lend themselves to an eclectic or integrative model of classroom management. Each approach incorporates a number of methods and interventions drawn from a variety of other approaches. The Adlerian approach is characterized by an emphasis on the goals of misbehavior and interventions based on logical and natural consequences.

Punishment with illogical interventions is rejected in both Adlerian and reality-based methods. Reality-based methods are directed toward helping students face and evaluate their current behaviors. Unhelpful behaviors are discarded in favor of useful behaviors that can help students meet their needs in responsible ways.

CHAPTER REVIEW

1. What are some management practices associated with schools that have good student discipline?
2. According to Adlerian psychology, what are the four major goals of misbehavior?
3. What types of corrective procedures can be instituted to help children work through each of the four types of misbehaviors?
4. How is corporal punishment viewed as a classroom procedure?
5. What kind of lessons does the use of corporal punishment teach to students?
6. According to Glasser, what type of questions should be asked of a student after misbehavior has occurred?
7. What are the major research findings that support using student-centered classroom management procedures?
8. What are the major research findings that support using teacher-centered classroom management procedures?
9. What are the major research findings that support using eclectic classroom management procedures?

USING A REALITY-BASED APPROACH IN THE CLASSROOM

EPILOGUE

As Kevin's teacher, you might choose to use reality therapy as a way of handling individual behavior problems in class. The teacher wishes to help Kevin evaluate his behavior as to how it is helping him get what he wants. The teacher also wants to help Kevin develop a plan for doing better work without cheating. The plan for helping Kevin will follow seven steps: (a) Maintain a positive relationship with Kevin; (b) Identify what the problem is and what has been done to solve the problem; (c) Evaluate how the behavior is helpful or unhelpful to Kevin; (d) Develop a list of alternative plans for helping Kevin meet his needs; (e) Formulate a plan; (f) Help Kevin commit to a plan he can complete; and (g) Schedule a follow-up interview. For example:

Teacher: I guess you know why I wanted to talk with you today.

Kevin: I guess it's about the cheating.

Teacher: Yes, I was wondering how cheating on the test was supposed to help you.

Kevin: Well, I guess it really hurt more than it helped. I was trying to bring up the low grades I have been making this grading period. My mom expects me to do well and this puts a lot of pressure on me.

Teacher: Maybe it would help to explore what you are doing that has caused your grades to go down.

Kevin: I'm not spending much time on my school work since I started going with Gwyn. We spend a lot of time together and talk a lot on the phone when we are not together.

Teacher: It sounds like your relationship with Gwyn is very important to you, and you find all of your time going to her.

Kevin: Yeah, that's it. That's what I'm doing.

Teacher: I wonder if we can find a way where you can maintain your relationship with Gwyn and still keep up with your studies.

Kevin: Well, I guess I could budget my time better.

Teacher: How could you do it in a way that would work for you and Gwyn?

Kevin: Well, I'm sure she will understand that I need to get myself out of this hole I'm in.

Teacher: That sounds good. What might be some other things you could try?

Kevin: Well, maybe we could spend some time studying together rather than just talking.

Teacher: How can you get these ideas into a workable plan?

Kevin: What do you mean?

Teacher: I mean that a specific plan usually works better than a general plan to study more.

Kevin: OK. How about I finish all the work I can at school and finish the rest before I see Gwyn? If that doesn't work out, I'll do the rest of my work when I study with her.

Teacher: All right. Let's talk again on Tuesday to see how well your plan is working.

During your follow-up conference on Tuesday, you learn that Kevin did not keep any of his commitments. What is your next step, since the reality-based approach had not worked with Kevin? What should be the logical consequence for cheating on a test? How would this logical consequence differ from punishment?

REFERENCES

Abramowitz, A., & O'Leary, S. (1990). Effectiveness of delayed punishment in classroom setting. *Behavior Therapy, 21,* 231–239.

American Psychological Association. (1992). *Learner-centered psychological principles: Guidelines for school redesign and reform (Draft #3).* Washington, DC: American Psychological Association.

Aspy, D. (1988). Carl Rogers's contributions to education. *Person-Centered Review, 3,* 10–18.

Aspy, D., & Roebuck, F. (1975). Client centered therapy in the educational process. Invited paper for the Proceedings of the European Conference on Client Centered Therapy. Wurtzburg, Germany: University of Wurtzburg Press.

Barkley, H., Wilborn, B., & Towers, M. (1984). Social interest in a peer training program. *Individual Psychology: The Journal of Adlerian Theory, Research, and Practice, 40,* 295–299.

Bayer, D. (1986). The effects of two methods of affective education on self-concept in seventh-grade students. *The School Counselor, 34,* 123–134.

Blechman, E., Kotanchik, N., & Taylor, C. (1981). Families and schools together: Early behavioral intervention with high risk children. *Behavior Therapy, 12,* 308–319.

Bundy, M., & Poppen, W. (1986). School counselors' effectiveness as consultants: A research review. *Elementary School Guidance and Counseling, 20,* 215–222.

Canter, L. (1989). Assertive discipline—More than names on the board and marbles in a jar. *Phi Delta Kappan, 71* (1), 57–61.

Chance, E. (1985). *An overview of major discipline programs in public schools since 1960.* Unpublished doctoral dissertation, University of Oklahoma, Norman, OK.

Chirico, J. (1985). Three guidance programs in Providence, Rhode Island. *The School Counselor, 32,* 388–391.

Christie, D., Hiss, M., & Lozanoff, B. (1984). Modification of inattentive classroom behavior: Hyperactive children's use of self-recording with teacher guidance. *Behavior Modification, 8,* 391–406.

Darveaux, D. (1984). The good behavior game plus merit: Controlling disruptive behavior and improving student motivation. *School Psychology Review, 14,* 84–93.

Dempster, M., & Raff, D. (1989). Managing students in primary schools: A successful Australian experience. *Journal of Reality Therapy, 8*(1), 13–17.

Dreikurs, R. (1968). *Psychology in the classroom* (2nd ed.). New York: Harper & Row.

Dreikurs, R., Grunwald, B., & Pepper, F. (1982). *Maintaining sanity in the classroom.* New York: Harper & Row.

Ellis, A. (1989). Using rational emotive therapy (RET) as crisis intervention: A single interview with a suicidal client. *Individual Psychology: Journal of Adlerian Theory, Research, and Practice, 45,* 75–81.

Engelhardt, L. (1983, April). *School discipline programs that work.* Paper presented at the National School Boards Association Convention, San Francisco.

Fried, J. (1990). Reality and self-control: Applying reality therapy to student personnel work in higher education. *Journal of Reality Therapy, 9*(2), 60–64.

Fuhr, D. (1993) Effective classroom discipline: Advice for educators. *NASSP Bulletin, 76* (549), 82–86.

Fuller, G., & Fuller, D. (1982). Reality therapy: Helping LD children make better choices. *Academic Therapy, 17,* 269–277.

Gamble, C., & Watkins, C., Jr. (1983). Combining the child discipline approaches of Alfred Adler and William Glasser: A case study. *Individual Psychology: The Journal of Adlerian Theory, Research, and Practice, 39,* 156–164.

Gang, M. (1976). Enhancing student-teacher relationships. *Elementary School Guidance and Counseling, 11,* 131–134.

Genshaft, J. (1982). The use of cognitive behavior therapy for reducing math anxiety. *School Psychology Review, 11,* 32–34.

Glasser, W. (1965). *Reality therapy.* New York: Harper & Row.

Glasser, W. (1969). *Schools without failure.* New York: Harper & Row.

Glasser, W. (1986). *Control theory in the classroom.* New York: Harper & Row.

Glasser, W. (1990). *The quality school: Managing students without coercion.* New York: Harper & Row.

Harrop, A., & McCann, C. (1984). Modifying creative writing in the classroom. *British Journal of Educational Psychology, 54,* 62–72.

Hart-Hester, S., Heuchert, C., & Whittier, K. (1989). The effects of teaching reality therapy techniques to elementary students to help change behaviors. *Journal of Reality Therapy, 8*(2), 13–18.

158

Herman, W. (1990). Helping students explore the motives, medium, and message of Carl R. Rogers. *Person-Centered Review, 5,* 30–38.

Heuchert, C. (1989). Enhancing self-directed behavior in the classroom. *Academic Therapy, 24,* 295–303.

Hill, D. (1990). Order in the classroom. *Teacher Magazine, 7*(1), 70–73, 75–77.

Johnson, E. (1985). Reality therapy in the elementary/junior high school. *Journal of Reality Therapy, 5*(1), 16–18.

Kahn, W. (1989). Teaching self-management to children. *Elementary School Guidance and Counseling, 24,* 37–46.

Lincoln, W. (1993). Helping students develop self-discipline. *Learning 93, 22* (3), 38–41.

Little, L., & Kelley, M. (1989). The efficacy of response cost procedures for reducing children's noncompliance to parental instructions. *Behavior Therapy, 20,* 525–534.

Manly, L. (1986). Goals of misbehavior inventory. *Elementary School Guidance and Counseling, 21,* 160–161.

Mattice, E. (1976). *Dreikurs' goals of misbehavior theory: Child and teacher generation of a neo-Adlerian construct.* Unpublished doctoral dissertation, University of Tennessee, Knoxville, TN.

MacDonald, A. (1989). Me and my shadow: Teaching "control theory" in elementary school. *Journal of Reality Therapy, 8,*(2), 30–32.

Nystul, M. S. (1986). The hidden reason behind children's misbehavior. *Elementary School Guidance and Counseling, 20,* 188–193.

Omizo, M., & Cubberly, W. (1983). The effects of reality therapy classroom meetings on self-concept and locus of control among learning disabled children. *The Exceptional Child, 30,* 201–209.

Omizo, M., & Omizo, S. (1988). Group counseling's effect on self-concept and social behavior among children with learning disabilities. *Journal of Humanistic Education and Development, 26,* 109–117.

Packer, A. (1992). Taking action on the SCANS report. *Educational Leadership, 49*(6), 27–31.

Pepper, F., & Roberson, M. (1983). The integration of Adlerian behavioral approaches in the classroom management of emotionally handicapped children. *Individual Psychology: The Journal of Adlerian Theory, Research, and Practice, 39,* 165–172.

Pety, J., Kelly, F., & Kafafy, A. (1984). The praise-encouragement preference scale for children. *Individual Psychology: The Journal of Adlerian Theory, Research, and Practice, 40,* 92–101.

Porter, B., & Hoedt, K. (1985). Differential effects of an Adlerian counseling approach with pre-adolescent children. *Individual Psychology: The Journal of Adlerian Theory, Research and Practice, 41,* 372–385.

Radd, T. (1987). *The Grow with Guidance system section: Classroom behavior management.* Canton, OH: Grow with Guidance.

Rathvon, N. (1990). The effects of encouragement on off-task behavior and academic productivity. *Elementary School Guidance and Counseling, 24,* 189–199.

Robinson, A., & Hyman, I. (1984, April). *A meta-analysis of human relations teacher training programs.* Paper presented at the Annual Convention of the National Association of School Psychologists, Philadelphia. (ERIC Document Reproduction Service No. ED 253 521)

Rogers, C. (1967). A plan for self-directed change in an educational system. *Educational Leadership, 24,* 717–731.

Silverman, W., & Kearney, C. (1990). A preliminary analysis of a functional model of assessment and treatment for school refusal behavior. *Behavior Modification, 14,* 340–363.

Stratton, C. (1989). Systematic comparison of consumer satisfaction of three cost-effective parent training programs for conduct problem children. *Behavior Therapy, 20,* 103–115.

Sullo, R. (1990). Introducing control theory and reality therapy principles in cooperative learning groups. *Journal of Reality Therapy, 9*(2), 67–70.

Thompson, C., & Cates, J. (1976). Teaching discipline to students in an individual teaching-counseling approach. *Focus on Guidance, 9,* 1–12.

Tierno, M. (1991). Responding to the socially motivated behaviors of early adolescents: Recommendations for classroom management. *Adolescence, 26* (103), 569–577.

U.S. Department of Education. (1986). What works: Research about teaching and learning. Washington, DC.

Wayson, W., DeVoss, G., Kaeser, S., Lasley, T., & Pinnell, G. (1982). *Handbook for developing schools with good discipline.* Bloomington, IN: Phi Delta Kappa.

Wiggins, J. (1982). Improving student behaviors with Carkhuff-model counseling. *The School Counselor, 30,* 57–60.

Williams, W., & Lair, G. (1991). Using a person-centered approach with children who have a disability. *Elementary School Guidance and Counseling, 25,* 194–203.

CHAPTER 6

MOTIVATION

Chapter Outline

HOW TO IMPROVE MOTIVATION

Two educational psychologists were asked by the principal of a high school if they would meet with the school faculty during an in-service meeting to deal with the topic of "motivation." The day began with the faculty listening to a group of high school students who were participating in a discussion of the topic, "What if you were asked by the board of education to try to improve the level of motivation of the students here at our school?" During the thirty-minute discussion, the students were asked if they knew students who were really motivated and what they would do to get more students to become motivated to do better work in school subjects.

The discussion followed the format of an "open meeting," a concept developed by William Glasser (1969) as part of the Schools without Failure Model. The actual "lesson plan" used for the meeting, composed of provoking questions, is presented below. Prospective teachers can find the structure of such a lesson plan helpful in leading their own discussions with groups of students.

What these students discussed during the open meeting were questions that have continually plagued parents, administrators, and teachers. No doubt every teacher has developed ideas about how students can be motivated. We suspect that most teachers base their ideas about motivation upon what motivates them. In effect, the teachers take motivational approaches that work for them and try to apply them to their students.

LESSON PLAN FOR AN OPEN MEETING ON MOTIVATION

William Glasser (1969)

Questions for Presenting the Topic

Imagine that you are a member of a student board charged with the task of increasing the motivation of the students at your school. What would you do? How would you feel?

Questions to Clarify Definitions about Terms and Specifics about the Topic

What is meant by motivation? What is meant by increase? What is the present level of motivation?

Questions to Promote Personal Judgment

Is it a good thing to be motivated? Why? What is the difference between those students who are motivated and those who seem unmotivated?

Questions to Identify Agreements and Disagreements

Do you know anyone who agrees with you about motivation? Disagrees with you? What do you think most people think about how to motivate students?

Questions to Personalize the Discussion

Have you known students who were really motivated? If so, what were these students motivated to do? Do you know students who are really motivated to excel in school-work? What seems to motivate them?

Questions to Challenge the Group to Continue Thinking About the Topic

Are you motivated for schooling? How much? What would have to happen to increase your motivation? Do many students drop out or say they want to drop out? Do you think that it would be a bad idea or a good idea for the school board to ask the opinion of students about motivation?

INTRODUCTION

Although some psychologists have questioned whether the study of motivation should be a concern of psychology, educational psychologists have shown a renewed interest in why some students are "motivated" to learn educational subjects while others are not. Motivation is a topic that has seen its popularity "wax and wane," according to Ball (1984). By studying research published in the *Journal of Educational Psychology*, Ball concluded that the topic of motivation has been more popular every other decade since 1919. He thus contends that the study of motivation will become a consistent topic in research literature during the 1990s and into the twenty-first century.

Some of the questions raised by educational psychologists are: Can teachers benefit by studying the numerous approaches to motivation? If so, what do they need to know? One place to begin is to attempt to define a motive. A motive is a thought that leads to action; it is an inner drive or an incentive.

Psychologists study people's behaviors, emotions, thoughts, and motives. Behaviors are the easiest to study because behavior can be observed. Usually two people making an observation of a student on a playground or in a classroom can come to agreement about what behavior they are seeing. Emotions, thoughts, and motives are more difficult to study because they cannot be directly observed.

Most of us assume that students think about things. We also assume that some thoughts cause students to act, while others are merely dispelled or suppressed. A thought that leads to action is called a motive. A motive is said to affect a person's desire to begin or continue a behavior.

KEY CONCEPTS

- Motivation is a complex topic vital to teachers in understanding how to evoke learning.
- Students are motivated by needs that may vary according to priority.
- Motivation is most often hierarchical, progressing from one form to another or back.
- Student desires and motivations change with aging.
- Behavior is not always a result of motivation.

WHAT ARE THE TRADITIONAL VIEWS OF MOTIVATION?

To what extent are motives solely based on biological drives?

Traditionally, motivation has been viewed as an instinct, drive, need, or state of arousal (Ames & Ames, 1984). The study of instincts has been, historically, one of the first explanations for why people act in certain ways. Instinctive behavior patterns have been both demonstrated and documented by biologists in the study of animals, such as Lorenz and Leyhausen's study on the imprinting of ducklings (Lorenz, 1973). The application of instinct theory to explain how humans become motivated to achieve and learn, however, has remained largely unfulfilled. Because of the complex nature of human development, current psychologists believe that instinct theory has little value in explaining human behavior. With scientific advancement, geneticists may become able to determine a link between instinctive behavior and critical periods for learning and motivation. For now, it is best to assume that instinct theory has little relevance to education.

One theory that explains human motivation is based on the premise that needs are the motivating element of human behavior. The most well-known need theory was proposed by Abraham H. Maslow (1970), a prominent humanistic psychologist. Maslow's theory (as discussed in chapter 4) assumes that human beings have a hierarchy of basic needs. Progression from level to level in the hierarchy depends on the satisfaction of the need at each level. This idea has some practical applications to nearly every learning situation.

Examples of applying Maslow's hierarchy of human needs to education are readily available. For instance, basic needs like food and water must be met for any successful learning to occur. School breakfast and lunch programs, funded through Federal and state agencies, are attempts at satisfying physiological needs so that learning may occur. Teachers are also involved in providing for the safety of children. For instance, in nearly all states teachers are required by law to report any incident of child abuse. A sense of belonging is also provided by the school system through such extracurricular activities as school clubs, athletic programs, or fine arts programs.

Maslow also noted two other needs that schools need to more fully address. One was a set of cognitive needs or the need to know and understand. Maslow included under this set the desire to explore, to acquire further knowledge, and to satisfy more than a mild curiosity. Esthetics is another set of needs that did not fit neatly into the school's structure. Someone pursuing esthetics has an active craving for beauty, an abhorrence of ugliness, and seeks order, symmetry, and completion.

> Describe some other areas that the educational system currently attempts to satisfy needs listed by Maslow.

■ ■ ■

WHAT ARE THE CURRENT THEORIES OF MOTIVATION?
Cognitive View of Motivation

Kagan and Lang (1978) point out that one of many factors which distinguish human beings from animals is the ability to generate a cognitive representation of a future event. These ideas, or cognitive representations about what a person wants to experience, are what they define as motives. More specifically, a motive is a state of mind "created by the tension between the unsatisfactory reality of the present and the presumably more satisfying state later" (p. 246). Motives are more than mere ideas. A motive is a visual image that can be compared with a current state of events. For example, a student notices that a recent assignment is not finished. The graphic representation of placing the completed assignment on the teacher's desk is a motive or anticipated state. The motive may prompt the student to act if the student can see how to achieve this state. The student may be unsure about having the ability to complete the task but does know what to do to accomplish the desired state and knows the consequences associated with the completion of the task. What this scenario has described is the cognitive view of motivation. The cognitive view is currently the most popular among educational psychologists because it is seen as offering the most promise for increasing student motivation in school settings.

Do Motives Lead to Action? Educators know that strong motives do not always lead to action. Sometimes students do not have the competence to do what they want to do. They don't act because they expect to fail despite the effort they exert. How a motive results in behavior is a very complex process. A student may have many motives that coexist at one time. Which motive will activate a student's behavior? Most theorists agree with Maslow and say that these motives exist in some sort of hierarchy. The most potent motive would activate the behavior. Students may exhibit the same behavior in the same situation for different motives. For example, on Monday a student may work hard to get a high grade because he wants to please the teacher. On another day the student may work to get a good grade because he wants the social status that comes with getting high marks.

Students develop the ability to inhibit the expression of behavior associated with a motive. As children become older, it is harder to determine their motives because they become more inhibited by anxiety. Fear of failure may keep a ten-year-old child from trying out for a sports team even though she wants very badly to be a "star." A seven-year-old child may be willing to risk trying to make the team because he has not previously experienced the feelings of failure on the athletic field.

Are There Basic Motives? Another dilemma to plague psychologists over the years has been the listing and categorizing of motives. Adlerian psychologists have hypothesized four basic goals or motives for appropriate behavior and misbehavior that apply to children age ten and under (Dreikurs, Grunwald, & Pepper, 1982). Contemporary Adlerians note that adolescents develop additional basic goals of misbehavior. For instance, Kagan and Lang (1978, pp. 266–304) contend that children and adolescents have six major motives that operate in schools: (1) desire for teacher and peer approval, (2) desire to be like the teacher, (3) desire for mastery, (4) desire to resolve uncertainty, (5) desire for control, power, and status, and (6) desire to vent hostility. A brief description of each follows:

1. *The desire for teacher and peer approval.* A dominant motive for children is to have the approval of parents, teachers, and other significant adults. Those students who have clear parent approval have a lower need for teacher approval than those students who are a little uncertain of their value. Children, who are certain they are not valued, will not seek the teacher's approval because they think they will be unable to satisfy the teacher.
2. *The desire to be similar to the teacher.* Children often identify with a significant adult and try to imitate that person's behaviors. The attempt to model

As children mature, are they more likely to develop motives that lead to actions?

Which of the six major motives listed by Kagan and Lang do you think is usually the most important motive? Rank order the motives in order of importance.

is stronger if the child sees the adult as being like the child in some way and as being happy with her life.

3. *The desire for mastery.* Mastery is the desire to increase one's knowledge, skill, or talent. Mastery or achievement is a student's attempt to match his behavior to a standard he has set. White (1959) suggested that children strive to become competent; specifically, they have an "autonomous capacity to be interested in the environment" (p. 13). The idea of an internalized view of one's own competence has remained one of the important parts of the current view of motivation.

4. *The desire to resolve uncertainty.* Children become uncertain about whether adults like them, whether peers will reject them socially, or whether they can gain the friendship of their peers. Children also are curious about new and different events that happen in their lives.

5. *The desire for control, power, and status.* Young children seek to control their parents, often struggling for power in an attempt to show that they can get others to do their bidding rather than give in to the wishes of adults. The desire for control, power, and status is especially important during adolescence. Peer relationships, particularly, play a vital role in status development.

Johnson (1980) has listed a number of contributions that peers make to the cognitive and social development of children and adolescents. First, peers are of primary importance in socialization because interactions with peers are more frequent, intense, and varied than interactions with teachers and other adults in the school. Attitudes, values, and information about sex are critical areas in which peers "teach" each other how to think and

The desire for mastery includes an interest in understanding one's environment.

behave. This considerable influence of peers is maintained even through the college years.

Peers serve as role models and sources of reinforcement, thereby teaching social behaviors and attitudes that are essential for maintaining interdependent, cooperative relationships. There is evidence that the behavior of someone who is dominant and well liked in a peer group leads to other students modeling the dominant person's behavior (Parke, 1985). Poor peer adjustment is a good predictor of emotional difficulty in adult life (Cowen, Pederson, Babijian, Izzo, & Trost, 1973).

Peers have considerable influence on students' achievement motivations and educational aspirations. Actual achievement is more affected by fellow students than by other factors in the school (Damico, 1975). The peer group influence can be desirable or undesirable; however, some studies imply that when students who have poor study habits are associated with peers in moderate size groups, achievement increases (Stallings & Kashowitz, 1974).

6. *The desire to gratify hostility.* Hostility and revenge are strong motives that, according to theorists, become priorities whenever other motives are not gratified. Students often attempt to satisfy this motive by overt and aggressive acts of rebellion. Other actions may be less obvious, such as the desire to punish parents by failing to achieve in school.

Hostility is a negative emotion and usually has a negative impact on the teaching-learning act, except when a student demonstrates ability to show that a teacher is wrong ("I'll show Mrs. Jones, who I think hates me, that I'm OK. I'll ace her test just to show her she is wrong about me.") Negative motivations are seldom used for positive purposes; therefore, most educators have tried to get rid of them in classroom situations.

Are peer contributions basically positive or negative? What about children who are home-schooled? Are they missing essential peer contributions to their socialization?

The array of motives that each student may possess during childhood and adolescence has an impact on the teaching-learning process. These motives affect the student's behavior and adherence to the rules of the school. This chapter will address these motives and suggest ways for teachers to motivate students by appealing to each of the six major motives presented by Kagan and Lang.

Negative Motivation

Ames and Ames (1991) are among those who have considered what conditions promote negative student motivation and consequently have determined ways to eliminate those conditions in the classroom. Negative motivation is defined as the student having the mental image that the assigned task cannot be finished. In effect, the student has no strategy or intent for getting from the beginning to the end of the task. More specifically, students (a) do not persist on the task, (b) engage in tasks that distract others, and (c) are off-task in their thinking.

"What do students think about?" and "What type of thinking evokes negative motivation?" are questions Ames and Ames (1991) ask. They answer the questions as follows.

Thoughts about self-worth. Beliefs or perceptions about self-worth relate to the value a student puts on her attributes and qualities. The thought pattern that leads to failure is to avoid "trying hard." Students want to succeed without showing effort. When students do not succeed without trying, they begin procrastinating, giving up, and engaging in other off-task behaviors. The ideal self-worth belief that leads to continued positive motivation is that "I can succeed without apparent effort." Some students will do extensive homework and "goof off" during school hours in an attempt to look so smart that they hardly need to study.

Covington (1984) is credited with being an advocate of the self-worth motive. He makes a distinction between private and public images and suggests that students attempt to develop these images as internally consistent with each other and as accepted by others. "Doing nothing" might be a motivated behavior if it is intended to keep one from failing. Covington and Omelich (1979) demonstrate through their research how excuses help students maintain higher self-perceptions under conditions of failure. They believe that students are faced with the "double-edged sword" of either using no effort, which can produce failure, or of exerting high effort, which indicates low ability if one fails. Students find that excuses work as a shield against those two outcomes. Teachers make allowances for students with good explanations of failure and students maintain their own self-images if they come up with good excuses.

Thoughts about ability. Self-concept of ability is a narrower component of belief about self-worth. Students identify with their own abilities in each of the academic areas such as writing, reading, and mathematics. The thought pattern of "I do not have ability in mathematics" results in negative motivation.

Goals. A student will persist in a task if he sees it as related to a goal. The student thinks, "Will completing this task help me get what I want?" Educational psychologists have identified two major, but unequal, types of goals. A mastery goal, the desire to learn for the sake of mastery, generally is more related to pos-

Some research indicates that there are gender differences in feelings of self-worth. Do you agree? If so, why might there be such gender differences?

Do you believe that there is such a thing as learning for learning's sake? Or do people always learn because it will get them something that they want?

itive motivation than is an ego or performance goal. Ego or performance goals reflect the urge to do better at a task than others. Current research shows that performance goals tend to be more anxiety producing because of the competitive nature of the goals (for example, the desire to make a high or the highest grade). Nicholls (1989) says that it is important to emphasize the goal of personal accomplishment over the goal of winning. He argues that it is hard to locate an academic psychologist who will encourage the increased use of interpersonal competition as a motivator. Nicholls concludes that the best that can be said for the competitive orientation is that it is better than no orientation at all.

Student self-efficacy. Self-efficacy, as measured by researchers, is the estimate a student makes about her ability to accomplish a special task (e.g., solve a mathematics problem). Students think to themselves, "Will I be good at doing this task?" Students who have a high sense of self-efficacy know what they know. These beliefs are often referred to as the "how-to" beliefs, knowing that one knows how to do something. Schunk (1989) points out that there is considerable evidence that these personal expectations influence achievement behaviors.

Beliefs about the use of learning strategies. Learning strategies is another name for study skills. The strategies include, among others, the ability to plan, set goals, reread material, and relate new information to previous knowledge. Ames and Archer (1988) have identified two critical factors that students think about when deciding to use or not use learning strategies. One factor is knowing how to use the strategy and the other is putting forth the effort required to do the strategy. The self-talk that students use in this situation is, "Do I have a method for doing this task?"

Attribution about success and failure. Students also think about why they do or don't accomplish what they attempt. Weiner (1984) suggests that there are four reasons students use to explain their successes and failures. The basic causes are ability, effort, task difficulty, and luck. What students think about that causes their failure can evoke negative motivation.

In Figure 6.1 are examples of the six types of negative thoughts identified by Ames and Ames. The first five thoughts are related to students' *expectations* for success and number six concerns *attributions* about why a student succeeded or failed.

Attribution Theory

Bernard Weiner (1984) has developed a theory about a student's attempt to know why an event occurred, particularly in relation to the student's achievement. Causal attributions (ideas about why a student succeeds or fails) are produced when there has been either an unexpected outcome or an aversive outcome. Students generate a variety of explanations for these unexpected outcomes. Some of the ways students explain their success or failure are that it has been caused by (a) high or low ability or aptitude, (b) good or poor effort, (c) task ease or difficulty, (d) good or bad luck, (e) effective or ineffective strategies, (f) help or lack of help from other persons, or (g) other factors. Researchers tend to focus on the four most prominent of these—ability, task difficulty, effort, and luck—as the major categories of causes of success or failure in achievement set-

FIGURE 6.1
Six Negative Thoughts
Ames and Ames (1991)

> 1. "I cannot succeed without letting others know that I had to make an extreme or apparent effort."
> 2. "I do not have ability in this subject."
> 3. "Completing this task will not help me get anything that I want."
> 4. "I will not be good at solving this problem."
> 5. "I do not have a method for doing this task."
> 6. "Why did I succeed or fail?"
>   a. "was it because I was lucky or unlucky?"
>   b. "was it because the task was easy or hard?"
>   c. "was it because I do or do not have ability?"
>   d. "was it because I did not or didn't make an effort?"

tings. Attempts have been made to classify the major causes according to three dimensions: stability, locus of control, and whether the factors are controllable or uncontrollable. More recently, Weiner has suggested other dimensions, such as intentionality. The bulk of most studies, however, have focused on the initial three causal dimensions.

Students do not try to explain why all outcomes were obtained; however, when confronted with the bad news of failure, or the good news of an unexpected success, students will seek an answer to why they failed or succeeded. The student, according to Weiner's (1984) attribution theory, will base the cause on either internal or external factors. The internal factors are ability (i.e., level of aptitude or skill) or effort (i.e., degree of work or self-discipline). In effect, the student sees success or failure as related to ability, to effort, or to both. The student who is externally oriented will attribute performance outcomes to luck or task difficulty.

The internal versus external dimensions appear to be related to how students feel about their performance. A success attributed to internal factors usually leads to pride and satisfaction. Failure, though, would evoke feelings of shame, incompetence, or guilt. Guilt would occur if the attribution was lack of effort.

The stability factors are said to determine the student's expectations about future performance. In other words, students will expect to succeed if they believe that high ability (a stable factor) instead of luck (an unstable factor) affected the success. Students who are confident in their ability to succeed will persist even at the first sign of difficulty. Furthermore, if students do attribute failure to a stable factor, such as low ability, they will have lower future expectations than if they had attributed the failure to bad luck.

One point about the controllability dimension is important to note. If a student considers success to be related to controllable factors, he will assume responsibility for the success and therefore experience pride and satisfaction. If, on the other hand, success is thought to have been brought about by an uncontrollable factor, the student will feel gratitude toward that factor. If failure is viewed by the student as caused by some uncontrollable factor, the student may feel anger or self-pity.

Weiner presents two scenarios that reflect his current thinking about attribution theory and clearly show the importance of the theory for the classroom setting.

Do you attribute your successes to your own ability? Do you attribute your failures to your parents, bad luck, or other external factors?

Scenario 1: A student tried hard but failed at a relatively easy task. This student has a history of failure, while all the other students were able to do well at this activity. On the basis of the specific past history and social norm data, as well as causal rules specifying that only little ability is needed for success at a relatively easy task if the person has tried, the inference made by the student is that she is "dumb." Low ability is a stable cause, producing low expectancy of future success. In addition, it generates feelings of humiliation and a lack of confidence. The teacher also notes the student's past history, the effort expended, and the performance of others and concludes that this student is incompetent. This elicits pity and unsolicited help. These communications to the student serve as additional low-ability cues. The low expectancy of future success, accompanied by feelings of humiliation and expressions of pity and help, contributes to lack of persistence in the face of future failure and performance decrements at achievement-related tasks.

Scenario 2: A student did not study for a relatively difficult test and failed. This student has a history of success, and few of the other students did well on this test. On the basis of this information and use of causal rules, the inference is made by the student that he did not put forth sufficient effort. Lack of effort is an unstable cause, leading the student to anticipate the possibility of doing better on the next test. The lack of effort will produce guilt if the test is of some importance. The teacher also notes the student's past history and the performance of others and concludes that the student was "wasting time." This elicits anger and perhaps withdrawal. The communications to the student serve as added low-effort cues. The maintenance of a high expectancy of success in the face of failure, accompanied by feelings of guilt and expressions of anger from the teacher, contributes to increased intensity of performance (given the anticipation of the next exam) and produces increments in achievement-related behaviors.

What are the desirable attributions to promote among students? Forsterling (1985, p. 501) summarizes the concept as presented in figure 6.2 modified from his review of attribution research.

How students look at the causes of their performance outcomes can affect future achievement. Furthermore, studies show that patterns develop for students who are success motivated and those who are failure motivated. Heckhausen (1987), who categorized students as success-motivated and failure-motivated, notes that when the outcome is success, success-motivated students attribute their success primarily to internal factors (high ability). When failure-motivated students experience success, they will tend to note external factors, such as good luck and low-task difficulty. Whenever failure is experienced, stability as a factor seems to be important. As might be expected, success-motivated students attribute failure to lack of effort. Failure-motivated students see the failure as caused by their own lack of ability or to great task difficulty. The facts support a bleak outlook, at least for the failure-motivated student. Whenever she does succeed, it is explained as good luck or an easy task. A failure outcome produces discouragement because the cause is seen as the student's own lack of ability, which is viewed as a stable factor.

It is possible to do something to influence the attributions that students make for their successes and failures. Forsterling (1985) has reviewed fifteen attribu-

Do you think that there are any socioeconomic or ethnic differences in the likelihood of being a failure-motivated student?

FIGURE 6.2
Desirable and Undesirable
Attributions
Forsterling (1985)

	Success	Failure
Desirable	When students succeed, it should be attributed to high ability, which results in high esteem, motivating achievement.	When students fail, it should be attributed to lack of effort, which results in optimism and leads to persistence.
Undesirable	When students succeed, it should not be attributed to luck, which results in indifference and low motivation.	When students fail, it should not be attributed to lack of ability, which results in depression and further low achievement.

tional training studies and concludes that programs generally produced both cognitive and behavioral changes. Usually, those in the training increased their attributions for failure to lack of effort (the desired direction) and improved in both performance and persistence. Many other programs for use in changing student attributions have been reviewed by Wittrock (1986). His conclusions agree with Forsterling that the training programs are effective.

DeCharms (1984) reports on one ten-week training unit designed to emphasize four major concepts: (a) the self-concept, (b) achievement motivation, (c) realistic goal setting, and (d) the origin-pawn concept. The last goal was important in that students and teachers were taught to see themselves as "origins" (people who can take responsibility and control outcome) as opposed to "pawns" (people who cannot take responsibility and whose outcome is controlled by others). The trained students were compared with a control group who did not receive any training. Results significantly favored the trained group on composite scores of the Iowa Test of Basic Skills. The trained students also had fewer absences and less tardiness. DeCharms has conducted other studies to train teachers to see themselves as origins instead of pawns. The most important thing a teacher can do to maximize motivation in educational settings, according to deCharms, is to believe that all students can be origins.

McCombs (1984) also has demonstrated the effectiveness of a motivational skills training program that includes attributional retraining. The training program was evaluated as effective in producing increased learning and in reducing absenteeism. Green-Emrich and Altmaier (1991) used a structured group counseling approach to retrain people to learn more desirable attributions. Teachers, who would like to be sure that they are encouraging the student to attribute failure to effort, should communicate to the student that he may be able to do the assigned tasks if he puts forth effort.

Reflect on one of your own successes in school and one of your own failures. List the attributions that you made concerning each one. How do they relate to what you have just read?

Expectations about success or failure can dramatically affect student performance.

Do you think that there is any relationship between age and the amount of learned helplessness? Do younger children or do adolescents demonstrate more learned helplessness?

Learned Helplessness. One area that has been studied recently that relates to achievement motivation and the motive to avoid failure is learned helplessness. The original theory of "learned helplessness" has been reformulated. Originally, Seligman (Peterson & Seligman, 1987) proposed that uncontrollable negative events in someone's life would lead to deficits in learning and motivation. This idea has been changed to the view that an individual's causal attributions about these events influence the impact of the events. Learned helplessness may be an outcome that can lead to low motivation and a negative emotional state (such as depression) but is dependent upon individual differences in attributional causes of the events.

How does this concept relate to teaching and learning in the classroom setting? Dweck (1986) reports that learned helplessness is related to the student developing an internal and stable explanation for failure. Therefore, both successes and failures that students view as noncontingent and uncontrollable promote the feelings of helplessness. In effect, students learn from their experiences in the classroom that they will continually fail.

Achievement Motivation

McClelland (1965), who used projective tests to study motivation, determined that people expressed four major motives: the need for affiliation, the need for approval, the need for power, and the most important one for educators, the need for achievement. Since the original research in 1953, several studies have investigated the characteristics of people with a high need for achievement. These studies have resulted in practical materials that teachers and counselors can use in school settings to help students make better plans for their own achievement.

Achievement motivation is defined by McClelland, Atkinson, Clark, and Lowell (1953) in terms of standards of excellence and competition. Those people who have a high need for achievement set high goals for themselves and try to obtain a chosen level of excellence. McClelland viewed parenting, especially the stress the mother placed on independence and self-reliance at an early age, as influencing the development of a high need to achieve. Atkinson (1957) made a contribution to the work on achievement motivation by distinguishing the need for achievement from the need to avoid failure. While some students put forth effort because they desire to succeed, others will exert themselves to avoid failure. Atkinson believed that both needs exist in all people but at different levels. Coexisting within each person is an interest in success and an anxiety about failure.

If the motive to succeed is stronger than the motive to avoid failure, the person will set goals of moderate difficulty. However, when people follow a motive to avoid failure, they have the tendency to pick either very easy or very difficult objectives. The rationale for the behavior of those who want to avoid failure is that they will be off the hook either way. The easy task is a sure thing, and if they fail at the more difficult task, they can explain it away because the task was too hard to accomplish (Atkinson, 1964).

Teaching strategies should be varied for students who appear to have a high achievement need. Students with a high need for achievement can benefit from setting their own learning goals, at least some of the time, and being asked to demonstrate works of high quality. Conversely, students with a motive to avoid failure can benefit from sequentially paced learning exercises and considerable reinforcement for goal attainment. Another strategy to help students become better at developing their need to achieve is by using training in the methods and characteristics of effective achievers. Johnson and McClelland (1984) have written materials to help students "learn to achieve," such as the curriculum in figure 6.3.

Six Steps to Achievement

1. Study self.
2. Get goal ideas.
3. Select a goal.
4. Plan.
5. Strive.
6. Evaluate.

Four Characteristics of a Goal

1. The goal is your choice.
2. The goal involves medium risk.
3. The goal is specific enough to be measured.
4. The goal has a time limit.

Eleven Characteristics of Achievers

1. Achievers are self-reliant.
2. Achievers feel responsible for their own actions.
3. Achievers set high but not impossible goals for themselves.
4. Achievers think about success and failure.
5. Achievers plan carefully and intelligently to meet their goals.
6. Achievers take obstacles into account.
7. Achievers know how to find and use help to reach their goal.
8. Achievers check their progress as they work toward their goal.
9. Achievers don't waste time and they use skills efficiently.
10. Achievers enjoy achieving their goal.
11. Achievers want to do a better and better job.

FIGURE 6.3
Learning to Achieve
Johnson and McClelland (1984)

Applications from the Text 6.1

Introduction

Chris once heard a veteran colleague say, "I'm not interested in impossible cases anymore. I'll teach the kids who want to learn." The strategy had an allure. "But," Chris told herself, "some kids don't know they want to learn until you put it in their heads that they do." Again she heard, "I'll teach the ones who want to learn." She turned those words over in her mind and realized that her own son might not get taught if his teachers followed that strategy. Yet, still, the thought was alluring. You can't fail with the impossible cases if you don't try to teach them.

Chris Zajac in *Among Schoolchildren* (Kidder, 1989) states what many teachers undoubtedly have thought a number of times: "I'd be a great teacher if I had students in my classes who wanted to learn or were really motivated." A good way to get an argument going in a teacher's lounge is to make the comment that a student or a class is ". . . just not motivated." Without fail some other teacher in the room will make the comment, "Oh, they are motivated, but not to do school work. I saw one of your students at the mall last night and he was working hard selling candy bars for the band field trip. He told me he had been the top salesperson for the last two years and he wants to make it three years in a row." The argument has moved from whether students are motivated to what motivates them to take action. Wlodkowski (1986) states that one of the myths about motivation is the idea that students are unmotivated. Students have the energy and the volition—the motivation—to do many things, but not necessarily the assignments given in the classroom. For example, the farm boys in the Midwest complain long and hard about the work they have to do in the fields, but as soon as the chores are done and they get cleaned up, they are ready to play ball, go swimming, or dance until nearly dawn.

Practical Applications

What can be done by a teacher to attempt to "motivate" students to achieve in the classroom? It is helpful to think in terms of four categories of motivation, each one of which can be influenced in some way by the teacher to provide positive motivation and eliminate conditions that can stifle motivation. The four categories are adult-figure motivation, peer motivation, intrinsic/internal motivation, and reward/external motivation. Each category states basic assumptions drawn from the chapter research and provides practical suggestions for promoting positive motivation in school and classroom settings.

Adult-Figure Motivation (Teacher-Student Relationships)

Teachers, by making changes in how they function, can affect the thought patterns and actions of students in their classes. It is important for teachers to understand the interaction between the assumptions, concepts, and actions listed in the following table.

For instance, the first assumption derived from the research is: *students imitate satisfied and enthusiastic adults.* To fully conceptualize this assumption, a general principle or concept is developed: *students learn from role models.* The action teachers should then take is: *have a plan to enjoy the day.*

More specifically, students want to imitate teachers who seem to enjoy themselves and who seem satisfied with their career. Research shows that students are influenced by adults whom they like, admire, and respect. Teachers, at least those who are trying to energize high-risk students in the classroom, should experiment with various methods to establish a good relationship with students. Researchers say that the best way to establish a good relationship with students is for teachers to take good care of themselves and their jobs; thus, providing a good role model. One idea to help teachers be sure that they are enthusiastic and appear satisfied with their teaching is for teachers to include in the daily lesson plan an activity that they really enjoy.

A good example of this method is an elementary school at which faculty members practice letting their students "catch" them reading. The idea behind the plan is that it is important for the teachers to carry with them one of the current books they are reading and to read it in an obvious way. Faculty members want the students to see the teachers enjoying reading. This simple plan guarantees that the students would see teachers being satisfied and enthusiastic for at least part of the day.

The second assumption derived from the research is: *students want to be similar to adults,* especially those whom they see as like themselves. The general concept that is developed: *students emulate adults whom they see as similar to themselves.* The plan of action for teachers is: *to share ideas about themselves.* At one

inner-city middle school, teachers were asked to bring some of their students to a consultation meeting with an educational psychologist. In a discussion with the students, who all lived near the school, the students mentioned that they didn't know much about their teachers. Most of the teachers lived in the suburbs and drove to the inner city to work. The students wanted to know if their teachers had children and, if so, how many. They also wanted to know how old the teachers' children were and how they treated their children. The important concept gleaned from the discussion was that the teachers were sharing very little information about themselves with their students. Consequently, it was hard for the students to see any similarity between themselves and their teachers. It is no wonder that few of the students were motivated to be like their teachers. The teachers were not letting the students discover who the teachers were as people, what interests they had, or what ideas they

continued

Adult-Figure Motivation

Assumption	Concept	Action
Students imitate satisfied and enthusiastic adults	Students learn from role models	Teachers should have a plan to enjoy the day
Students want to be similar to adults, especially those whom they see as like themselves	Students emulate adults they see as similar to themselves	Teachers should share ideas about themselves
Students want adult approval	Students want unconditional positive regard from respected adults	Teachers should interview students and use other adults in classrooms

thought were important about life. Prospective teachers should note that sharing is not telling students how the teacher thinks they should live their lives but rather teachers expressing honest opinions about what they believe and what they do with their lives.

As indicated in the table, the third assumption derived from the research is: *students want adult approval.* The concept developed is: *students want unconditional positive regard from respected adults.* In effect, students want to be accepted, at least partially, without having to demonstrate a specific skill, learning outcome, or behavior. A plan of action for astute teachers, especially elementary school teachers, is to try and show this type of acceptance by doing an individual interview with each student very early in the school year or doing something unusual to let each student know they care about the student. Teachers who send postcards to students' homes a day or two before the new school year are likely to have students anticipating coming to school.

Another idea for showing teacher approval that would work at the secondary school level is for the teacher to use some type of inventory or interview with each student to find out about each of the students.

Peer Motivation
(Student-Student Relationship)

As in the previous section, teachers need to be aware of the interaction between assumptions, concepts, and actions in dealing with peer motivation. For instance, one assumption derived from the research is: *students want peer approval.* A general concept for this aspect is: *students want to belong to a peer group.* A plan for action is: *teachers should use sociometrics to show peer involvement.*

As indicated in Chapter 2, sociometrics is a measurement technique used to determine peer friendships and groupings. By using a sociometric technique, the teacher can determine which students may need help in their peer relationships. The teacher can check to see which students may feel left out of peer groups. Peer tutoring may be used with those students who do not seem to "fit in" with any established groups in the classroom.

Peer Motivation

Assumption	Concept	Action
Students want peer approval	Students want to belong to a peer group	Teachers should use sociometrics to show peer involvement
Students want to cooperate with each other	Students have a social need for positive peer interaction	Teachers should use cooperative group methods and group work

A second assumption is: *students want to cooperate with each other.* The concept derived from this assumption is: *students have a social need for positive peer interaction.* An action for this aspect is: *Teachers should use cooperative group methods and group work.*

Cooperative methods have become popular in many schools, and a variety of methods are available for teachers to use in the classroom. Using groups of four (putting students in teams) is a method that has been used in a number of class situations as a means to accomplish some of the management and organizational tasks in the classroom.

Intrinsic/Internal Motivation

There are two assumptions/concepts/actions in the area of intrinsic or internal motivation. The first assumption is: *students want to be seen as important and want power and status.* The general concept derived from this assumption is: *students want to be involved in decisions about what and how they learn.* A plan of action for this area is: *teachers should give choices and accept suggestions.*

In addressing this first assumption, teachers should be aware that students in a "participatory environment" for two or more years tend to have more positive reactions to school life. Students want a piece of the action in making decisions. They want to take part in the educational process. For example, an elementary teacher reported to the authors on the success of a cooperative school project. The fifth grade students helped the second grade students make "arts and crafts" for Christmas and Hanukkah. The teacher said: "The project was a success because the classes were doing what they had planned to do, not something that teachers thought up for them to make together."

The second assumption is: *students want to master skills.* The concept that follows is: *students can be internally motivated by learning relevant skills.* The action for this area is: *teachers should use techniques that apply content to real life situations.*

In this second area the important tasks are to determine what students need to master and what is relevant in their lives. As indicated in chapter 5, Glasser (1969)

continued

Intrinsic Motivation

Assumption	Concept	Action
Students want to be seen as important and want power and status	Students want to be involved in decisions about what and how they learn	Teachers should give choices and accept suggestions
Students want to master skills	Students can be internally motivated by learning relevant skills	Teachers should use techniques that apply content to real life situations

promoted the idea of classroom meetings to discuss items of interest. The educational diagnostic meeting can be used to determine what is relevant and important for students. It can also be used to apply information to real life situations. Simulations of real life situations are another technique that can be used to make learning relevant. Advance organizers and framers can also make learning more relevant for students.

Extrinsic/External Reinforcement

The assumption derived from the research is: *students will respond for a desired reinforcer*. The concept is: *if you reinforce a response, you increase the likelihood of that response*. The action is: *teachers should use a variety of reinforcers*.

In regard to this area, it is important to remember a number of points. First of all, reinforcers are not all things to all people. Some individuals prefer free time in the library, while others prefer free time in the gym. To the extent possible, teachers should try to implement reinforcement practices that meet the desired reinforcers of individual students. Secondly, constant reinforcement does not work as well as varied reinforcement.

Finally, there are two types of social reinforcement or praise: task relevant and non-task relevant. Task relevant social reinforcement is given for appropriate classroom behavior. Non-task praise can be used as a motivator of students. Praising students for achievements outside the classroom, such as their performance in the school band, can serve as a motivator.

Another example of non-task social reinforcement is to use forms of moderate distraction. For example, a bus driver in Anderson, Indiana, uses the idea of dressing up like Elvis Presley two days each week. The driver then plays tapes of Elvis' music during the bus ride to school. Few discipline problems are ever noted on the bus. Schools can do similar things by having "dress up" days. For example, once a month a special time period or style can be the theme for the "dress up" day. These special days tend to distract students from seeking other forms of attention.

Extrinsic Motivation

Assumption	Concept	Action
Students will respond for a desired reinforcer	If you reinforce a response, you increase the likelihood of that response	Teachers should use a variety of reinforcers

Intrinsic Motivation

Csikszentmihalyi and Nakamura (1989) note that prior to the 1950s, the study of motivation had nearly disappeared. The "optimal arousal hypothesis" developed then was a concept supporting the prevailing view that behavior depends on genetic programming or stimulus-response learning. Shortly after that hypothesis was introduced, thinking about motivation was split into two categories, extrinsic motivation and intrinsic motivation. Extrinsic motivation was the label given for the idea that behavior is a product of psychological drives and external stimuli. Intrinsic motivation was related to those behaviors chosen as a goal by the organism. Intrinsic motivation supports the idea that people can respond to curiosity and can determine some of their behaviors despite instinctive and behavioral learning.

Csikszentmihalyi and Nakamura (1989) used an Experience Sampling Method to determine what students were doing and their mood and state of consciousness at random times, eight times a day for a week. The method, combined with interviewing, allowed the researchers to gather extensive information about what thoughts motivated student behavior. The researchers determined the amount of "flow" experience exhibited by teenagers in Italy and the United States. Flow experience is what people feel when they actively enjoy what they are doing. The experience of "flow" is its own reward. People would not choose to do any other activity at that time. They are completely involved in what they are doing and their concentration is intense. Time passes quickly and there is no concern about failing or succeeding. The flow experience is rare. Fewer than 10 percent report it to happen daily. The theory of flow experience suggests that both the challenge and the skill of a task must be high to evoke flow. Students in Italy experience

List the activities that you engage in that produce a "flow" experience. Are there any educational methods that can create the "flow" experience for students?

Certain activities, called flow experiences, provide their own reward.

flow more often than a comparable sample in the United States. Talented, higher-achieving students report "flow" more often than equally talented but lower-achieving students.

■ ■ ■

RELATIONSHIP OF DEVELOPMENT AND MOTIVATION

Recently, a fourth-grade teacher expressed her distress to an educational psychologist about being transferred to teach the fifth grade. "The fifth-graders won't like to do many of the things that I do in my room that fourth-grade students love. The fifth-graders might think that giving tokens is kids stuff." Although little data exist to support such a clear distinction between what motivates children in one grade level versus those in the next grade, there is evidence that motivation is significantly affected by maturation. Children's ideas about a number of variables associated with motivation change as they become older and as they progress through school.

Stipek (1984) contends that educators have neglected the study of developmental changes in achievement motivation. Ball (1984) tells the story about how first-graders are quick to try to please the teacher who says, "I like children who sit up straight." On the other hand, few, if any, sixth-graders would change their posture in response to this statement. Rather, they would smile and assume that the teacher had some kind of quirk about how students should sit. Current investigations in this area provide limited comparisons of children at different age levels. One accepted conclusion is that for younger children, about age five, higher effort is seen to equal higher ability. By the time the child is age twelve, higher effort can imply lower ability. As children become older, ability comes to mean being able to do better than others and gradually becomes seen as capacity.

Stipek (1984) summarizes some ideas about achievement motivation by noting that children increasingly come to value academic achievement as they become older. Simultaneously the children's expectations for success decline, as do their perceptions of their own competence. Attitudes toward school become more negative and intrinsic motivation decreases. (See figure 6.4.)

Several factors contribute to the changes depicted in figure 6.4. Classroom environment has a profound effect. As students get older, the classroom becomes more formal and structured. For example, whole-class instruction increases and use of letter grades increases. Both changes in the school environment and the modifications in how students process feedback on their performance may contribute to the changes noted in Stipek's chart.

Nicholls (1989) has distinguished three levels of differentiation of ability and difficulty (egocentric, performance, and normative) and four levels of differentiation of ability and effort (overlap, cause and effect, partial differentiation, and capacity). These ideas are important because they have implications about when and how to use attribution and motivation training.

Distinctions are made about how children see difficulty and ability, luck and skill, and effort and ability. Difficulty and ability before age seven are egocentric (tasks are judged in terms of how each child thinks she will do). Between the

Do you agree with Stipek's contention that children increasingly value academic achievement as they grow older?

FIGURE 6.4

Achievement-Related Cognitions	With Age
Expectation for future success	declines
(correlation of expectation and past performance)	increases
Evaluation of competence	declines
(correlation of self-evaluation and performance indicators)	increases
Casual attributions for performance:	
importance of effort	decreases
importance of ability	increases

Figure modified from Stipek (1984; p. 167)

ages of seven and eleven, tasks are judged based on the performance of others. In effect, the child is becoming more objective in judgment even though no distinction is made about whether failure is caused by low ability or high difficulty. After age eleven, most children are on a par with adults and have adopted the normative view of ability and difficulty in which the two terms are completely differentiated.

Developmental stages of thinking about effort and ability have been noted by Nicholls. The first stage, which occurs before age seven, has the child seeing overlap in effort and ability. Students who do better are seen as working harder even if they don't. Those students who try harder are seen, at times, as smarter even if they get low scores. At the second stage, a cause and effect relationship is noted as students about age seven believe that effort is the cause of outcome. In the next stage, somewhat before age eleven, ability and effort are partially differentiated. In the final stage, ability is seen as capacity and the effect of effort is limited by capacity.

Nicholls also reports several levels of differentiation between luck and skill. At the first stage, effort is expected to affect outcome on both luck and skill tasks. About age seven, skill tasks are seen as more affected by effort, but students do not have a clear reason as to why. At the next level, students hold on to the belief, primarily through a matter of faith, that outcomes can be influenced on luck tasks. At age eleven and older, luck and skill are clearly differentiated and effort is believed to have no impact on the outcome of tasks that involve luck.

Some research indicates that, during middle school, children separate into two academic tracks: the achievers and the drop-outs. Thus, children who eventually drop-out in high school begin to give up in middle school. How does this research fit in with Nicholls' work?

What Are the Major Issues in the Study of Motivation?

The major issues in motivation parallel the debate that has gone on in education for decades, whether quality education represents "development from within" versus "formation from without." The formation from without view has been advocated by Skinner (1983), who argues that the main reason education has failed to meet the needs of our society is because educators have not been allowed to use behavioral psychology. Skinner claims that there is enough known about human behavior to solve the problems in education if teachers would use behavioral science. More recently, William Glasser (1984) takes

One of the major questions about motivation is in regard to the use of reinforcement by the teacher.

The Skinner/Glasser debate over motivation impacts on a variety of educational decisions. Whose side of the debate do you support?

exception with Skinner's view, by saying that educators who fail to educate students do so because there is too much reliance on behavioral methods and not enough on a more complete view of motivation. Control theory, the method developed by Glasser, emphasizes the idea that everything people think, do, and feel is generated by what happens inside of them. Nothing people do is caused by what happens outside of themselves.

"I'm not saying that what happens outside of us means nothing, far from it. What happens outside of us has a lot to do with what we choose to do, but the outside event does not cause our behavior. What we get, and all we ever get, from the outside is information; how we choose to act on this information is up to us" (Glasser, 1990, p. 41). The belief that teachers can do something to students to get them to learn is inferior to trying to motivate students by doing things for them. Schoolteachers need a plan for the long-term motivation of students. Behavioral (stimulus-response) theory may work, but only for a short time and only if the reinforcements are potent. The bottom line for Glasser is that there is no teacher who can teach a student who does not want to learn.

Chapter 8 presents the primary aspects of the behavioral view of learning. Evidence shows that an "engineered" learning environment with appropriate and adequate rewards is especially effective in special education settings and with younger students in elementary school classrooms. "Token economies" have been shown to help teachers and students obtain specified behavioral outcomes (Allyon & Azrin, 1968). Even the critics of extrinsic methods have granted that when rewards are used under appropriate conditions, they promote learning and enhance motivation (Bates, 1979). The defense of the behavioral approaches has been that when they have failed, they have not been properly implemented. Either reinforcers have been given inappropriately or rewards are either too simple or too difficult to obtain.

It is possible to observe imperfections in any school setting. A student reported to one educational psychologist how frustrating it was to do homework for three days in a row and have the teacher not notice it. On the fourth day the student neglected to do the work and was reprimanded for not having it. Slavin (1991) makes the point that extrinsic rewards are a part of life. ". . . just about every school in the world uses grades, praise, recognition, and other rewards to maintain student motivation" (p. 91). It is important for teachers to be consistent with extrinsic rewards, however, if they are to be effective.

There are many arguments, also, that question reliance on behavioral learning methods. Lepper and Hodell (1989) have identified two main functions of rewards in the teaching-learning situation that have negative effects. The first is the instrumental function, which is the idea that the rewards help the students see clearly how the "game is played" in the classroom. The student has tangible evidence about the bonuses or bribes used by the teacher. If the student assumes that the game will continue to be played in that way, the student knows what consequences to expect for his behavior. The rewards become an indication to the student of success. Of course, the unanswered question is whether those rewards serve to enhance or lower the student's view of his own competence. Research has shown that under certain conditions, obtaining rewards leads to lower student self-esteem.

The second negative function of rewards is said to be one of social control. The argument is that students will do what is wanted because they want the offered reward. Evidence indicates that this is not always so. For example, students who had a high initial interest in an activity and pursued it without reward may lower that interest if teachers or other adults start providing a reward for it (Deci & Ryan, 1985).

A natural extension of the argument over intrinsic or extrinsic rewards is to argue about the use of competition versus cooperation in educational settings. A newspaper columnist (Raspberry, 1991) berated one school in Indiana for attempting to deemphasize competition. The columnist was not opposed to the use of cooperation but was distressed because the principal was using it in extracurricular activities rather than in academic activities. Like the columnist, many educational psychologists believe that academics ought to be less competitive. Kohn (1991) has gone so far as to contend that the use of extrinsic rewards with cooperative learning activities may in the long run destroy an effective educational method. Slavin (1991) disagrees with him and reports that nearly all of the studies about cooperative learning support the idea that it works because of the use of group rewards.

Teachers need to be aware that a variety of motivational techniques should be used. Individual and group variations should determine the practice of competitive, cooperative, extrinsic, or intrinsic motivational methods. Teachers should not exclusively use one technique, but allow student needs and circumstances to determine which is the appropriate method.

Do you believe that conspicuous reinforcement techniques simply serve to produce reinforcement dependency in students? What are the alternatives to positive reinforcement?

What other problems might occur with group reinforcement procedures?

DEVISE AND FOLLOW A PLAN

In reviewing this chapter, what suggestions would you have for the high school principal in the case study who wanted to increase the level of motivation among the students who attended his school?

The issues presented in the case study are addressed throughout the chapter but especially in the following sections:

1. *Traditional views of motivation (need theory).* In terms of school policies, to what extent can the high school administration and faculty provide an environment that allows students to fulfill some of their basic needs?

    Is it possible for the school curriculum to help students meet both deficit and growth needs?

    Can students be motivated to fulfill growth needs even if they have major deficit needs?

2. *Current views of motivation.* What steps can be taken to provide learning experiences that are responsive to student desires to resolve uncertainty and develop mastery of knowledge, skills, or talents?

    What can teachers do on a day-to-day basis to decrease the prevalence of negative thoughts students have about their abilities and performance in school?

    How can administrators and teachers promote desirable attributions among students? How can they decrease undesirable attributions?

    Should the curriculum teach students the steps to achievement and the characteristics of achievers?

    Do students, teachers, and administrators have ideas about how the amount of "flow experience" can be increased in the daily lives of students?

The material in this chapter, especially the "Applications from the Text" section, contains a number of ideas about methods and procedures that can contribute to providing a more motivating school and classroom climate. What is needed, too, is for the school administrators and teachers to develop a plan that uses some of the ideas to enhance motivation among the students. The plan should include at least some of the ideas expressed by the students in a meeting similar to the one described in the case study. Students are more likely to respond positively if they see that teachers and administrators are willing to incorporate some of the thoughts students have about their own needs, motives, and goals. The plan does not need to be complicated to have an impact. The major difficulty in increasing motivation in the high school in the case study will not be devising a plan but rather in following the plan. Consistent adherence to the plan is a must!

SUMMARY

The study of human motivation has progressed in a number of new directions in recent years. For instance, one view about human motivation that has changed is the idea that motives are solely based on biological drives. Most psychologists now believe that motives are based on a complex interaction of cognitive, emotional, and behavioral components.

Another new aspect of contemporary motivation research is that people are able to cognitively represent a motive and a plan for action. Thus, humans are not tied to just drives and instincts. People can be motivated by inner needs, such as self-fulfillment.

Student motivation in the classroom is seen as affected by a variety of factors. These factors include: their need for approval by the teacher and by their peers; their need to master educational skills; and their need to feel that they are empowered in the educational process.

Attribution theory also indicates that students have different ways in which they attribute success or failure in the classroom. Attributions are based on such things as locus of control, task difficulty, and ability. Achievement motivation research indicates that teachers should be aware of differing needs for achievement. Teachers should tailor teaching strategies based on whether students are motivated out of a need to achieve or a need to avoid failure.

CHAPTER REVIEW

1. Why study motivation?
2. What are the basic motives?
3. What are the traditional views of motivation?
4. What are the current models of motivation?
5. How can teachers modify the teacher-student relationship to promote motivation?
6. How can teachers use student-student relationships to enhance motivation?
7. How can teachers use internal motivation methods?
8. How can teachers use external motivation methods?

REFERENCES

Allyon, T., & Azrin, N. (1968). *The token economy: A motivational system for therapy and rehabilitation.* New York: Appleton-Century-Crofts.

Ames, C., & Archer, J. (1988). Achievement goals in the classroom: Student learning strategies and achievement motivation. *Journal of Educational Psychology, 18,* 409–414.

Ames, C., & Ames, R. (1984). Introduction. In C. Ames & R. Ames (Eds.), *Research on motivation in education: Student motivation* (Vol. 1, p.1–11). Orlando, FL: Academic Press.

Ames, R., & Ames, C. (1991). *Motivation and effective teaching.* In L. Idol & B. F. Jones (Eds.), *Educational values and cognitive instruction: Implications for reform* (pp. 247–269). Hillsdale, NJ: Lawrence Erlbaum Associates.

Atkinson, J. (1957). Motivational determinants of risk-taking behavior. *Psychological Review, 64,* 359–372.

Atkinson, J. (1964). *An introduction to motivation.* Princeton, NJ: Van Nostrand.

Ball, S. (1984). Student motivation: Some reflections and projections. In C. Ames & R. Ames (Eds.), *Research on motivation in education: Student motivation* (Vol. 1, pp. 313–326). Orlando, FL: Academic Press.

Bates, J. (1979). Extrinsic reward and intrinsic motivation: A review with implications for the classroom. *Review of Educational Research, 19,* 557–576.

Covington, M. (1984). The motive for self-worth. In C. Ames & R. Ames (Eds.), *Research on motivation in education: Student motivation* (Vol. 1, pp. 78–108). Orlando, FL: Academic Press.

Covington, M., & Omelich, C. (1979). Effort: The double-edged sword in school achievement. *Journal of Educational Psychology, 71,* 688–700.

Cowen, E., Pederson, A., Babijian, H., Izzo, L., & Trost, M. (1973). Long-term follow-up of early detected vulnerable children. *Journal of Consulting and Clinical Psychology, 23,* 112–119.

Csikszentmihalyi, M., & Nakamura, J. (1989). The dynamics of intrinsic motivation. A study of adolescents. In C. Ames & R. Ames (Eds.), *Research on motivation in education: Goals and cognition* (Vol. 3, pp. 45–71). San Diego: Academic Press.

deCharms, R. (1984). Motivation enhancement in educational settings. In C. Ames & R. Ames (Eds.), *Research on motivation in education: Student motivation* (Vol. 1, pp. 275–308). Orlando, FL: Academic Press.

Damico, S. (1975). The effects of clique membership upon academic achievement. *Adolescence, 6,* 281–294..

Deci, E., & Ryan, R. (1985). *Intrinsic motivation and self-determination in human behavior.* New York: Plenum.

Dreikurs, R., Grunwald, B., & Pepper, F. (1982). *Maintaining sanity in the classroom: Classroom management techniques* (2nd ed.). New York: Harper and Row.

Dweck, C. (1986). Motivational processes affecting learning. *American Psychologist, 41,* 1040–1048.

Forsterling, F. (1985). Attributional retraining: A review. *Psychological Bulletin, 98*(3), 495–512.

Glasser, W. (1990). *The quality school: Managing students without coercion.* New York: Harper and Row.

Glasser, W. (1984). *Control theory: A new explanation of how we control our lives.* New York: Harper and Row.

Glasser, W. (1969). *Schools without failure.* New York: Harper and Row.

Green-Emrich, A., & Altmaier, E. (1991). *Attribution retraining as a structured group counseling intervention,* 69(4), 351–355.

Gronlund, N. (1959). *Sociometry in the classroom.* New York: Harper and Brothers.

Heckhausen, H. (1987). Causal attribution patterns for achievement outcomes: Individual differences, possible types and their origins. In F. Weinert & R. Kluwe (Eds.), *Metacognition, motivation, and understanding* (pp. 143–184). Hillsdale, NJ: Lawrence Erlbaum Associates.

Johnson, D. (1980). Group process: Influences of student-student interaction on school outcome. In J. McMillian (Ed.), *The social psychology of school learning* (pp. 123–168). New York: Academic Press.

Johnson, E., & McClelland, D. (1984). *Learning to achieve.* Glenview, IL: Scott, Foresman.

Kagan, J., & Lang, C. (1978). *Psychology and education: An introduction.* New York: Harcourt, Brace, & Jovanovich.

Kidder, T. (1989). *Among schoolchildren.* Boston: Houghton Mifflin.

Kohn, A. (1991, February). Group grade grubbing versus cooperative learning. *Educational Leadership,* 83–87.

Lepper, M., & Hodell, M. (1989). Intrinsic motivation in the classroom. In C. Ames & R. Ames (Eds.), *Research on motivation in education: Goals and cognition* (Vol. 3, pp. 73–105). San Diego: Academic Press.

Lorenz, K., & Leyhausen, P. (1973). *Motivation of human and animal behavior: An ethological review.* New York: Van Nostrand Reinhold. Pleasant Hills, PA: *The Worldwide Student & Teacher Network.*

McClelland, D. (1965). Toward a theory of motive acquisition. *American Psychologist, 20,* 321–333.

McClelland, D., Atkinson, J., Clark, R., & Lowell, E. (1953). *The achievement motive.* New York: Appleton-Century-Crofts.

McCombs, B. (1984). Processes and skills underlying continuing motivation to learn: Toward a definition of motivational skills training interventions. *Educational Psychologist, 19,* 199–218.

Maslow, A. (1970). *Motivation and personality* (2nd ed.). New York: Harper and Row.

Nicholls, J. (1989). *The competitive ethos and democratic education.* Cambridge, MA: Harvard University Press.

Parke, B. (1985). A field adaptation of the SYMLOG adjective rating form suitable for populations including children. *International Journal of Small Group Research, 1,* 89–95.

Peterson, C., & Seligman, M. (1987). Helplessness and attributional style in depression. In F. Weinert & R. Kluwe (Eds.), *Metacognition, motivation, and understanding* (pp. 185–215). Hillsdale, NJ: Lawrence Erlbaum Associates.

Raspberry, W. (1991, December 20). The plainfield paradigm: Competition less right in the classroom than gym. *The Knoxville News-Sentinel,* p. A16.

Schunk, D. (1989). Self-efficacy and cognitive skill learning. In C. Ames & R. Ames (Eds.), *Research on motivation in education: Goals and Cognition* (Vol. 3, pp. 13–41). San Diego: Academic Press.

Skinner, B. (1983). Origins of a behaviorist. *Psychology Today, 17*(9), 22–33.

Slavin, R. (1991, February). Group rewards make group work. *Educational Leadership,* 89–91.

Stallings, J., & Kashowitz, D. (1974). *Follow-through classroom observation evaluation.* Menlo Park, CA: Stanford Research Institute.

Stipek, D. (1984). The development of achievement motivation. In C. Ames & R. Ames (Eds.), *Research on motivation in education: Student motivation* (Vol. 1, pp. 145–170). Orlando, FL: Academic Press.

Weiner, B. (1984). Principles for a theory of student motivation and their application within an attributional framework. In C. Ames & R. Ames (Eds.), *Research on motivation in education: Student motivation* (Vol. 1, pp. 15–36). Orlando, FL: Academic Press.

White, R.W. (1959). Motivation reconsidered: The concept of competence. *Psychological Review, 66,* 297–333.

Wittrock, M. (1986). Students' thought process. In M. Wittrock (Ed.), *Handbook of research on teaching* (3rd ed.). New York: Macmillan.

Wlodkowski, R. (1986). *Motivation and teaching: A practical guide.* Washington, DC: National Education Association.

CHAPTER 7

Individual Differences
Cultural Diversity and Gender Issues

■ ■ ■

Chapter Outline

SHOULD EDUCATION AND TRAINING FOR DIVERSITY BE REQUIRED?

SHOULD EDUCATION AND TRAINING FOR DIVERSITY BE REQUIRED?

You teach American History and Western Civilization courses at a large, suburban high school in a major metropolitan area in the Northeast. You are just beginning your third year of teaching history at the school. The school system is facing increasing pressure from a number of community groups to better address diversity issues. In particular, the problems cited by these groups are curriculum changes, the special needs of minority students in the schools, and the recruitment of more women and minorities into administrative positions in the school system.

The school superintendent creates a School/Community Task Force to address these issues. You are one of the faculty members appointed to the task force.

In the school district the number of female teachers is greater than that of men. However, there are very few minority faculty members. There also are virtually no minority or female administrators.

Recently, a number of racially charged fights have occurred among students at the high school. The school system administration is accused of being insensitive to diversity needs by some local groups.

At the first meeting of the School/Community Task Force the local community groups present a number of demands of the superintendent. Included in these demands are that the school district:

1. require a Diversity Issues course for all students at the high school, require teachers at the middle school and high school levels to address diversity issues in each course, and have a curriculum oversight committee that will examine syllabi and course content for sensitivity to diversity issues;
2. have a priority recruitment program for minority teachers so that within five years the number of minority faculty members will equal the percentage of minority students in the district;
3. hire either female or minority administrators for the next three vacant administrative posts in the school district;
4. require diversity issues sensitivity training through workshops and continuing education programs for all faculty members and all administrators in the district;
5. initiate a speech and conduct a code at the middle school and high school levels that prohibits any speech or conduct that demeans or discriminates against minorities or women;
6. require changes in the history curriculum at the high school to deemphasize Eurocentric courses and refocus on non-Western cultures and history.

As a history teacher and a member of the task force, what position will you take concerning the questions of minority hiring practices, speech codes, and curriculum modifications?

INTRODUCTION

The purpose of this chapter is to examine diversity issues and gender differences. In particular, this chapter focuses on the impact of cultural, ethnic, and gender issues on the individual. This section reviews individual differences based on culture, ethnicity, and gender. This chapter presents the public debate concerning diversity and multiculturalism. Related aspects, such as bilingualism and school alienation, are also presented. Individual differences in learning styles and classroom behavior that are attributed to ethnicity or gender are also examined.

KEY CONCEPTS

- Historical background for cross-cultural issues in educational psychology.
- Major points of debate concerning diversity and multicultural issues.
- Relationship between school alienation and the issues of cultural diversity in education.
- Differences in learning styles among various ethnic groups.
- Problems with today's textbooks in public schools in terms of diversity issues.
- Relationship between gender, intelligence, and overall academic ability as described in this section.
- Relationship between gender and classroom academic performance.
- Relationship between gender and classroom behavior.

DIVERSITY AND MULTICULTURALISM

According to John Dewey, an educational philosopher, one goal of teaching is to make the familiar strange and the strange familiar. In other words, a good teacher is able to take a familiar piece of knowledge and provide a novel perspective to it. A good teacher also is able to take an unknown, difficult subject and make it clear and understandable to students. One of the best places to see this principle at work is in the area of cultural studies.

In examining other cultures, students discover that each culture has its own worldview and perspective of human life. If the study of other cultures is approached with an open mind, students can learn to view the world from these various perspectives. Thus, the new, unknown culture will become understandable and the native or known culture will become novel when examined through the new outlook.

This type of comparative, multicultural education provides teachers with the opportunity to make the familiar strange and the strange familiar. These cross-cultural comparisons are an essential part of many academic disciplines.

For example, one controversy influenced by cultural issues concerns the debate on human intelligence. Researchers Sir Cyril Burt and Arthur Jensen

What is the purpose for studying cultures?

strongly supported the genetic basis of intelligence. Burt and Jensen's arguments state that IQ differences between ethnic groups are due to genetic factors. Other psychologists, however, cite strong evidence that cultural and socioeconomic factors are the major determinants of IQ scores.

Cultural differences also influence learning in the area of language development by affecting how students conceptualize certain ideas. In the same manner, sex-role development appears to be basically influenced by culture rather than genetics.

The effects of cultural differences such as these have been debated in psychology and educational psychology for some time. It is important to understand the role of cultural differences in teaching and learning. In some respects, the recent debate over multicultural education appears to be a continuation of previous controversies that have occurred in psychology and other social science disciplines.

What Are the Key Aspects in the Debate over Diversity and Multicultural Education?

What type of cultural tradition should be taught in public schools?

Writers frame the debate over multicultural education in different ways. One writer, Diane Ravitch (1990), states that the controversy over multiculturalism is a debate between a particularist vision of culture and a pluralist vision of culture.

Ravitch indicates that a particularist view of culture emphasizes the special history, literature, and artistic efforts of particular ethnic groups. The particularist view emphasizes specific ethnic studies for minority groups that are often developed to raise self-esteem among those particular groups. The particularist viewpoint also was developed to protect or preserve certain cultural or subcultural identities. In this sense, it is akin to a protectionist trade policy in which certain economic assets of a country are protected by social and political policy.

The pluralist position, according to Ravitch, is the view of culture as a melting pot. Different ethnic groups are studied to examine their overall contribution to the common culture of a country. This viewpoint assumes that there is a common or dominant cultural tradition in a country that is subscribed to by a significant majority of its people. To some, this position has been characterized as a form of cultural imperialism because it seems to advance only one dominant cultural tradition.

How Is Diversity Associated With School Alienation?

Proponents of multicultural education state that a diversity of cultural viewpoints should be taught in schools. They believe that the lack of appropriate multicultural perspectives and role models causes ethnic minority groups to be alienated from schools. This alienation, in turn, may increase school dropout rates, racial tensions, and possibly criminal activity. Educators who agree with this position believe that a multicultural curriculum and multicultural textbooks will reduce problems causing school alienation.

Sleeter and Grant (1991) assert that textbooks also can cause alienation. Their research shows that textbooks in grades one through eight are still dominated by whites in terms of story lines and accomplishments, show women and nonwhite ethnic groups in a more limited range of social and job roles than white males, and contain little information about race relations or other issues that concern minority ethnic groups.

Nieto (1992) expands on the school-alienation argument, stating that if minority students choose to identify with their own culture or background, they feel alienated not only from school but from mainstream U.S. society. If these students identify with mainstream society, they often feel like traitors to their family and community. Nieto continues with this theme, contending that:

> there is an inherent and natural tension between Americanization, with its commonly accepted meaning of assimilation, and keeping one's culture and language. As we approach the beginning of the twenty-first century, however, the question shifts a bit. No longer a choice of whether one should assimilate or not, the question now becomes, how far can society, and the institutions of society such as schools, be pushed to accommodate the changing definition of America? (1992, pp. 271–272).

Opponents of the multiculturalist viewpoint state that multicultural education results in an incorrect focus for a state-run public school system. In multicultural education, the focus is too often on self-esteem and cultural pride rather than on basic skills and knowledge. Those who subscribe to this viewpoint claim that there has been a serious overall decline in basic knowledge and literacy in the United States. The correction of this decline must be the paramount issue of education (Hirsch, 1988).

Is the melting pot concept outdated in the United States?

Can textbook reform reduce school alienation?

What should be the
focus of a state run,
public school system?

Opponents of multicultural education state that a purely multicultural focus results in a lowering of academic standards and a dilution of the curriculum. The question often asked by opponents of multicultural education is: "How can we teach a multicultural curriculum when our students are currently unable to handle a monocultural curriculum?"

Other questions raised by the opponents of multicultural education include the question of "Balkanizing" the curriculum (Will, 1992). This means that if each ethnic group is allowed to teach its own version of cultural education, then American society may end up reinforcing the existing divisions in its society.

The debate over multicultural education raises questions that do not lead to easy answers. Clearly, a person's culture and language profoundly influence behavior and even cognitive processes. As Ravitch states, the problems raised by the debate over multicultural education reflect a fundamental question in American education: Should the United States develop an educational system that represents a common, integrated cultural tradition or should it represent an amalgamation of many diffuse, separate cultural traditions?

How Do Learning Styles Tie in to Multicultural Education?

Some supporters of multicultural education cite a number of research studies that indicate learning style differences between white students and ethnic minority children. These supporters believe that learning styles should be tailored to meet the needs of minority children to help those students achieve their maximum levels of learning.

Vasquez (1990) reviewed a series of studies on learning styles among Hispanic, African American, and Native American students. In this review, Vasquez maintains that some learning style differences do occur when different ethnic groups are compared. One example Vasquez cites indicates that Hispanic children achieved better in cooperative rather than competitive learning environments. Vasquez stipulates that the extended-family environment of Hispanic children is most likely the reason for their preference of cooperative learning. The culture typical to most Hispanic students places a high value on the extended and immediate family with a primary sense of loyalty toward their own extended family. According to Vasquez, this produces a sense of cooperation rather than competition toward same-age peers. Often, Hispanic students will refuse to participate in competitive activities, even if those activities involve areas in which the students excel.

Vasquez recommends that instead of openly reinforcing Hispanic students for classroom achievement, teachers should have a system in which students' families are informed of their academic achievement. Vasquez also recommends that teachers use more cooperative learning activities with Hispanic students.

In his review of research on African American children, Vasquez suggests that African Americans are more person-centered than white children. According to Shade (1982), the cognitive style and interests of African American children are more interpersonal than the object-centered approaches that characterized the responses of the white child. As noted by Vasquez (1990, p. 300):

Are there real
differences in learning
styles among ethnic
groups?

Some researchers believe that school alienation can cause a number of social problems. For instance, individuals may dropout from school and seek membership in gangs.

This distinction between Black and white children takes on considerable importance when we become aware of the requirement in typical classrooms to focus on objects (mathematics, natural phenomena, letters of the alphabet, rules, etc.), not people, for extended periods of time in order to learn well.

In regard to Native American children, Vasquez's review suggests that Native Americans are more field dependent than field independent in their learning styles. Field independent means that individuals are able to learn better without contextual cues. Vasquez characterized it as a learning style that is analytical and that develops first from details and then puts together the whole picture. Field dependent means a learning style that is holistically oriented. This is a style that sees the big picture first and then focuses on the details. Students who learn in this manner appear to focus more on the context of a figure or an object (its environment) and less on the prominent aspects of the figure or object itself. This tendency for Native American children to be more field dependent or context bound in how they perceive and process information indicates to some extent the degree to which some white students were more familiar with objects and abstracting information than were some minority students.

In a related study, Sanders and Wiseman (1990) compared teacher behaviors and their effects on four categories of ethnicity: Caucasian, Asian American, Hispanic, and African American. The primary variable Sanders and Wiseman studied was the effect that teacher-immediacy behaviors have on various types of student learning. Teacher-immediacy behaviors are those behaviors that show that the teacher wants positive communication and interaction. They include eye contact, smiling, physical proximity, encouraging students to talk or ask questions, and praising student's work.

How should teachers handle learning style differences in teaching different ethnic groups?

APPLICATIONS FROM THE TEXT 7.1

The following applications are observations and comments from current educators concerning the area of individual differences. The first application details one perspective on teaching to the needs of minority students. As you read this application, consider this essential question: Can certain academic areas, such as art or music, serve as a bridge between different ethnic and cultural groups?

LINDA W. ANDERSON
Art Educator

In teaching minority students, I have often found them to be more perfectionistic and self-critical than mainstream students. Such an attitude may surprise some people. My findings could be due to the fact that I teach art, rather than English or math.

I believe many African American students do feel alienated from the public school system. It causes them to disconnect from academics. Yet many African American students, once given reinforcement in my art classes, are more productive and interested in their work than mainstream students.

I have had a number of other minorities, but once activated, African American students do about the best. I have to work through a sort of self-critical phase with them and get them to believe in what they are doing, to trust themselves and their skills. If they get through this part, they are about the best that I have. When they discover that art is a form of personal self-expression, it is much more meaningful for them, and they seem to be delighted with artwork. Their level of enthusiasm is much greater than other students.

In my art classes I also allow a higher noise level. This loud talking can be mistaken as a behavior problem, but if dealt with properly, it can be seen as just noise, not a behavior problem at all. In art class I give them the freedom to talk as long as they continue their work, an allowance very much different from what is experienced in most middle school and high school classes.

I think that there is also a lot more give-and-take in my classes between student and teacher. There is a high degree of interaction between student and teacher in developing the skill of drawing, leading to a more informal teacher-student relationship. The informal setting allows minority students to interact in a way that is different from the traditional forms of student-teacher interaction.

Again, I think that the flexibility I have in my art classes does reduce the disaffection from school that I see in some minority students. It allows these students to interact in ways that they are more used to in their own lives.

The following application details one person's life experience as a member of an ethnic minority. It also provides a unique view on ethnic and cultural diversity issues.

DR. TERRY L. SMITH
Director of Special Education Services for the Regional Education Services Agency, II

Family Background

My mother, she was under five feet tall, coal-black hair, and her maiden name was Yuki Miyahara. My maternal grandfather came over to this country to work for several years before he sent for his wife. It was not unusual for Japanese men to leave their families and come here, to find the land of milk and honey, and then send for their wives.

My mother was born in Seattle, Washington—an American citizen of Japanese descent. When World War II started and she was just a young girl, my mother's family was given two weeks' notice that they had to sell everything and move. They were then sent to a series of internment camps where all they could take was what they could carry. (They tried to store some of their goods, but everything was gone when they returned.)

The internment camps were pretty bad, especially in the beginning. They were first put in horse stables

Dr. Terry L. Smith working at the Regional Education Services Agency.

and had to sleep on straw. They were always under armed guard and the camps were surrounded by barbed wire fences. The men and women were separated. Later, they spent most of the war at a camp in Idaho. There, my mother lived in one large barracks with a number of other families.

My maternal grandfather was a respected man, a leader in the Japanese community, both before and after the war. My mother, however, was a risk taker. She was the first Japanese descendant in Seattle to marry what they called a Hakujin, a white person.

My father was from West Virginia. He had just been assigned to Seattle when he met my mother. Before his Washington assignment, he had been stationed with MacArthur in the military occupation of Japan. He had gone into the military at the age of fourteen and had just celebrated his sixteenth birth-

day in Tokyo. He was reassigned stateside to Seattle. That's how a native West Virginian met and married the daughter of a Japanese couple.

My parents were both just teenagers when they married that year and both spoke fluent English and Japanese. My father's spoken Japanese was actually better than my mother's. Not everyone, however, was pleased with the marriage.

Soon thereafter, my mother left on a bus with my father to live in West Virginia and did not return to Seattle for thirteen years. In the 1950 census, she was the only person of Japanese descent listed in the whole state of West Virginia.

Childhood Years

A short time after their arrival in West Virginia, I was born, their first child. In my early years of growing up in West Virginia, I really was not aware of my minority status. My mom and dad never said anything about it. We had certain Japanese traditions, particularly about the food we ate, but I never really thought anything about it.

In middle and late elementary school, however, the other kids made me aware of my ethnicity. I remember many times at that age period being called "Jap" or "Chink." Older middle- and upper-class kids generally were the ones who did it. They chased me home from school, started fights with me, threw things at me, and called my mother various names.

At the time I didn't really understand why they were so cruel. I'd just think that they were pickin' on me. As I got older, about junior high age, I began to realize the main reasons for it. In late elementary school and early junior high school, the fighting and abuse were the worst. I got in fights almost every day and was attacked by both individuals and gangs.

In late junior high school, however, I blossomed. I grew to the extra large size that I am today. I also earned belts in the martial arts in high school where I became the state judo heavyweight junior champion. I got a reputation, and people left me alone in high school. *continued*

I even started dating in high school, going to parties, and going to dances. It was the first time since early elementary school that I was accepted.

I think what happened in childhood motivated me to strive to be the best that I could. It made me compete with myself. It's probably why I pursued a doctorate. People always seemed to be whispering that I was different, that I was not good enough, or that I was not smart enough. It became an issue for me to prove myself and to prove them wrong.

Ethnic and Multicultural Issues

I certainly had a taste of what it is like to grow up as a discriminated minority. I think that it was bigotry as much as racism. I really had no community like African Americans have. Therefore, I'm not sure that what I experienced was the same as the institutional racism seen by that community. The African American people faced a form of community or group racism. My situation did not carry quite the same type of legacy of historical antagonism.

What I faced was more a form of personal bigotry. No one in West Virginia had ever dealt on a personal level with someone of my ethnic background. The problems were compounded by attitudes derived from World War II. The parents of many of the kids who attacked me probably had lost family in the war and blamed all Japanese people for it. I grew up in a time when the Japanese were looked down upon and were openly derided. I was guilty by association.

In terms of other minorities in my school, there were virtually none. The schools in West Virginia were segregated until the late 1960s, so there were no African Americans. There was an Italian boy in my elementary school who spoke little English. The other kids called him a Hunnkee. (This is a coal miner's slang term for the Hungarians who were employed in the West Virginia mines in the 1920s and 1930s.)

My teachers in elementary school saw me as a novelty. I don't ever recall them mistreating me. They just saw me as the little kid with shiny dark hair, almond eyes, who looked different, and was cute.

In terms of what I think about multiculturalism and diversity, I have a couple of ideas. I think that everyone should be treated with respect as individuals. Treat people on a one-to-one basis with consideration and respect, regardless of their background. This practice is the key to resolving ethnic alienation. If we all did this, the discrimination issue gradually could be settled.

I think people should be proud of their culture and their heritage. Everyone should be. I know that I am proud of both my parents' backgrounds.

I also think teachers should foster an appreciation of all ethnic groups. If teachers see that a child has an interest in a particular group, they should foster that interest in the form of book reports, research, and show-and-tell opportunities. This ethnic encouragement should be at the individual level.

I have a problem with requiring all students to take a particular ethnic-studies curriculum in public schools. To say that you have to study this group or that group is going to leave out a lot of other groups. By accenting national or ethnic groups, are you not putting a priority on ethnicity? Are we all going to end up being Irish Americans, Chinese Americans, or Mexican Americans? In effect, we will no longer be just Americans. We will be something else first.

I don't buy that sort of thing. You have to be an American first and part of an ethnic group second. There are certain things like democracy, free speech, and individualism that are a part of this country's heritage, part of all Americans. I also feel the same about a national language. I'm all in favor of learning other languages. As many as possible. But we do have a national language and that is English. It seems to me that any other system will create hundreds of separate ethnic groups that will be like special interest groups or social classes. A house divided that way cannot stand.

One of the major research questions about learning and cultural diversity is the degree to which ethnic differences influence learning styles.

Sanders and Wiseman's study shows that positive teacher-immediacy behaviors enhance student outcomes in all ethnic groups. Although the results indicate more similarities in student responses than differences, the researchers did discover some important ethnic differences. Using personal examples is particularly important to Hispanic and African American students. In contrast, using students' names and making appropriate gestures are more important for Caucasian and Asian American students. Asian American students also prefer teachers who ask for student viewpoints on class material. African American students prefer teachers who use humor and who maintain relaxed body positions.

Opponents of multicultural education criticize these ideas and studies on a number of grounds. One major point of contention is that the overall differences between ethnic groups are sometimes fewer than the overall differences within each ethnic group. For instance, the overall variations between African Americans as a group are sometimes as great or greater than the overall differences between African American and Hispanic students.

In tandem with this contention is the viewpoint that by reinforcing ethnic differences in learning styles, educators may simply end up stereotyping different ethnic groups. In effect, Hispanic students may be stereotyped as not wanting leadership roles in extracurricular activities or not wanting solo performances in musical productions. If reinforced, stereotypes such as these may produce negative educational expectations about minority student performance and could end up producing more harm than good.

What Are the Important Instructional Aspects of Multicultural Education?

To some degree the instructional aspects of multicultural education hinge on which side of the debate a teacher favors and to what extent she supports those beliefs. Among some of the issues currently being considered in multicultural education are curriculum policies, textbook policies, bilingual education, and hiring practices.

Both sides of the multicultural debate condemn present curriculum and textbook policies. As indicated in the previous section, proponents of multicultural education condemn textbooks and curriculum for being white-male oriented or for stereotyping minority groups. Opponents of multicultural education condemn textbooks and curriculum for being "watered-down" in academic content so as to avoid the appearance of bias.

What is the role of bilingual education in the public schools?

Perhaps the most explosive multicultural issue is the question of bilingual education. When a majority of students in a district are not native English speakers, a plethora of problems arises. To what extent should students, who speak other than Standard English, be required to use Standard English in public schools? Should equal weight be given to Spanish as well as English in school districts where Hispanics are a majority? Should school districts require all teachers to be bilingual when Hispanics are a majority of the district? Should state legislatures mandate that schools require an English-only policy?

Such questions are being debated by state legislatures and local school boards. A number of states have already passed English-first or English-only requirements that have been severely criticized by multicultural advocates. One advocate states:

> By representing the class and ethnic-group interests of traditionally disempowered groups, bilingual education has been characterized by great controversy and debate. The issue is not whether or not it works but the real possibility that it might. Bilingual education is a political issue because both its proponents and opponents have long recognized its potential for empowering these traditionally powerless groups (Nieto, 1992, p. 160).

The issue of bilingual education cuts to the heart of the debate concerning the degree of cultural differences that should be accepted as part of a public education system. Questions arise over the extent of accommodations that should be made in state-run schools for languages other than Standard English and whether or not bilingualism should be a goal that is promoted by the state.

What Is Diversity Training in Education?

An issue closely related to the instructional aspects of multicultural education is the question of whether or not to require diversity training in education programs. Public school systems and colleges across the United States are using various methods to promote sensitivity to diversity issues in the classroom. These attempts at diversity education range from specific Ethnic Studies and Women Studies courses to Sensitivity Training Workshops on Diversity Issues and even requiring a Diversity Issues component in all courses.

Perhaps the most publicized diversity program is the "Rainbow Curriculum" instituted by Chancellor Joseph Fernandez, formerly the chief executive officer of the New York City public schools. The "Rainbow Curriculum" was an attempt by the nation's largest public school system to address the diversity needs of cultural, racial, and ethnic minorities.

Among the most controversial aspects of the new curriculum was the attempts to address the diversity needs of the gay community. Included among the optional texts in the curriculum was "Daddy's New Roommate," a book concerning a boy's experience with understanding about his father's new gay roommate. The book was designed for children in elementary school. The curriculum also included a teacher's guide on how to teach Columbus' voyage to the New World from a multicultural perspective.

The "Rainbow Curriculum" produced an apparent political backlash in New York City. A number of the curriculum offerings were dropped, including "Daddy's New Roommate."

Deutsch (1993) interviewed experts in top university business schools and in major companies about the issue of diversity training and education programs. Deutsch cites several opinions as shown in figure 7.1.

In a July 5, 1993, cover story, the *New Republic* magazine criticized the diversity training industry for charging millions of dollars for programs that sometimes failed to solve the problems that they purported to address.

Murray (1993) reviewed the diversity training program at Lucky Stores, a California-based chain of grocery stores, and relates the following story.

> To what extent should diversity training be mandated in public education?

"Stereotyping happens at an unconscious level and can only be overcome through experience."
James I. Cash, chairman of the Harvard Business School's M.B.A. program

"There is a body of knowledge out there, and yes, it can be taught."
Thomas P. Gerrity, dean of the Wharton School at the University of Pennsylvania

"The biggest barrier to managing diversity has not been racism or sexism or any ism, but simply poor management."
R. Roosevelt Thomas, Jr., president of the American Institute for Managing Diversity

"I am cynical about the extent to which navel gazing and deep thought can produce real change. I've seen more mutual respect and stereotype shattering and advances in this subject by people working together than by any other means."
B. Joseph White, dean of the University of Michigan School of Business Administration

"Since so many M.B.A. graduates go directly into management positions, business schools that do not provide training in managing diversity are doing a disservice to their students and to the companies that hire them."
Beatrice J. Vidal, manager of Corporate Work-Force Diversity, Xerox Corporation

FIGURE 7.1
Opinions on
Diversity Training

(Deutsch 1993, 22–24)

Lucky Stores wanted to find out why more women and minority group members were not being promoted. So the company held a workshop to increase sensitivity among its store managers. As part of an exercise common in such sessions, the supervisors were asked to mention stereotypes they'd heard about women and minority group members. 'Women cry more,' one said. 'Women don't have as much drive to get ahead,' volunteered another manager, 'Black females are aggressive,' said a third. 'The work force would not perform for a black female manager,' added a colleague. The idea was to expose potential prejudice and to deal with it. But to management's horror, notes from this session later turned up as evidence in a sex discrimination lawsuit (Murray, 1993, p. 5).

Murray also points out that the employees at Lucky Stores were able to use the notes from the session as evidence of employer bias. The stereotypes voiced by the managers were accepted as evidence in court and were cited by the court as indicating management bias.

Despite problems in this area, many school systems and colleges are moving ahead with some type of diversity issues curriculum reform. As one professor pointed out in Murray's article, most diversity programs are better than none at all.

What Are Some Other Diversity Issues?

Other controversial multicultural education issues include job quotas, hiring policies, and college admissions requirements. Debates arise over whether or not ethnic minorities should be given special consideration in hiring policies if there is a large ratio of minority students in a school district or if ethnic minorities should be hired when more educated or more experienced White teachers are available. Colleges are faced with decisions about admitting certain quotas of minority students and providing special scholarship funding for minority students.

As with other questions relating to the issues of diversity and multicultural education, these situations have become both political and economic questions. Although these questions are often answered by political expediency or political correctness, it is important for educators to realize that the essential question must be: "What is in the long-term, best interests of all the children?"

Several questions are related to this essential question. To what extent are we preparing children to be successful in a highly competitive twenty-first century global economy? Are children better served by multilingual and ethnic studies in our schools? Are children better served by teaching Standard English and a core curriculum based on traditional studies? Is there some way to synthesize the different perspectives about multicultural education?

In addressing the long-term, best interests of all children, it is important to remember three specific educational goals: (1) transmission of a knowledge base; (2) critical, rational, logical reasoning about our world; and (3) tolerance for different viewpoints, ideas, and cultures.

The first goal reflects the basic reason for an institutionalized educational system. From its roots in Classical Greece twenty-five hundred years ago, formal education in Western culture was developed as a time-saver. Someone who has already learned something can save someone else time by teaching him what she

What lessons can be learned from the "Rainbow Curriculum" and the Lucky Stores training program?

What type of hiring policies will best support diversity issues?

has learned. In effect, it is quicker to be taught than to have to learn all on one's own. (Having to learn everything on one's own is like reinventing the wheel.) Thus, at its best, formal education is economical: in terms of both time saved and monetary costs.

The second goal reflects a fundamental belief in the value of critical intellectual inquiry to make decisions based on deductive and inductive reasoning. Objective decision making, based on rational reasoning, is a fundamental aspect of our academic tradition.

The third goal reflects a belief that tolerance for diversity is a necessary prerequisite for any intellectual or educational activity. Preconceived beliefs and cultural ethnocentrism can blind anyone as to what is actually occurring in an educational or research situation. It is important to emphasize that teachers should not prejudge without sufficient data and that they should not allow their expectations to predetermine how they treat students. The type of intellectual tolerance that is developed when educators engage in research is equally important in teaching students.

The second and third goals are vitally important because teachers should do more than just disseminate knowledge. In addition to the transmission of the knowledge base in a discipline, teachers also provide intellectual models for their students. The abilities and attitudes displayed by teachers, particularly regarding the nature of ideas, are critical to the educational process. Most teachers do not realize that they can be the most effective models available for critical reasoning and tolerance, regardless of their own viewpoint or culture.

The essential nature of the debate over multicultural education, however, reflects a conflict between these three basic goals. It is essentially a conflict between the intellectual tradition of Western culture and a tolerance for or a sensitivity to those perspectives that do not share this tradition. Finding a balance between these two perspectives is the key to developing educational programs that will be in the best, long-term interests of all students. Multiculturalism does not necessarily need to involve a lowering of academic standards or a dilution of the curriculum. In the same manner, high academic standards do not require a singular ethnic focus, nor does it need to involve social or school alienation. Educators must be willing to find what will provide the best chance for their students' social and economic success in the twenty-first century.

What are the essential problems in the debate over multicultural education?

■ ■ ■

GENDER ISSUES

There are a number of questions about gender differences often cited in educational research literature. The major questions in this area are: Are there any innate gender differences in intelligence test scores or on subtest measures of intelligence? Can any gender differences in overall academic performance be found? Are there any gender differences in classroom achievement within specific academic subjects? Are there any gender differences in classroom behavior? Can any gender differences in classroom academic performance or classroom behavior be attributed to innate differences?

Are There Gender Differences in Intelligence?

The issue of overall gender differences in performance on intelligence tests is no longer an important consideration to most researchers. It is now generally assumed that the total or full-scale IQ scores are not different for males and females. There is, however, considerable debate about the differences between the scores of males and females on certain subtests.

In regard to both intelligence test scores and general academic ability, there has been the perception that females have better verbal ability, while males have better visual-spatial ability (Maccoby & Jacklin, 1974). Thus, females tend to do better on vocabulary, spelling, and reading tasks. Males tend to do better on map reading, puzzles, and other types of spatial-relation tasks. Another suggested difference is that males have an advantage in mathematical performance, particularly those areas related to spatial ability such as geometry.

The reasons for these gender differences can be explained by either hereditary or environmental causes. On the hereditary side, some research has indicated specific neurological or genetic differences to account for the verbal-visual discrepancies between females and males (Waber, 1976; Parsons, 1982).

Heredity may not be a complete explanation, however. Although these differences were consistently found in the literature in the 1960s and 1970s, recent research indicates that these gender differences have narrowed considerably (Feingold, 1988; Hyde & Linn, 1988).

If such gender differences are narrowing, the conclusion would be that these differences were due to environmental causes (social and cultural effects) rather than any innate neurophysiological differences between the sexes. For instance,

What are some recent changes in gender differences on test scores?

There appear to be few, if any, innate gender differences in intellectual ability.

the belief that there are inborn gender differences in math ability has been large-ly disqualified by research showing that males are much more likely to take col-lege prep math classes in their high school years. When these differences in aca-demic preparation are factored into the research studies, gender differences in math performance appear to be virtually nonexistent.

Therefore, caution should be used in interpreting gender differences on indi-vidual subtests of intelligence or concerning general academic ability. Research is clear that there is considerable overlap between the sexes on many of the ver-bal and visual tests that outwardly appear to be due to gender differences.

How Does Gender Cause Classroom Differences?

Another category of possible gender differences is in classroom performance. Girls generally perform better in a classroom environment, particularly on mea-sures of academic performance developed or scored by classroom teachers (Serbin, Zelkowitz, Doyle, Gold, & Wheaton, 1990). Boys, however, generally perform better on college aptitude tests. Thus, girls perform better on classroom evaluation procedures, while boys generally perform better on standardized col-lege aptitude tests. Girls also are cited as having fewer classroom behavioral problems than boys. Such findings may point to a relationship between class-room academic performance and classroom misbehavior.

Research has led some educators to claim that traditional public schools are not a place where boys feel comfortable (Sexton, 1965). This claim has led some researchers to develop a number of different hypotheses to explain why there is such a gender difference in classroom behavior.

How do the genders score on actual classroom measures?

How Does Sex-Role Development Affect Classroom Behavior?

The work of Chodorow (1974) and Gilligan (1982) on sex-role development provides one explanation for some of the sex differences in school adjustment. Both Chodorow and Gilligan state that appropriate male sex-role development is predicated on the condition that male children establish autonomy from their mothers. In effect, males must establish a separateness from their mothers for normal sex-role development. They must separate themselves from the gender identity and gender role of the mother. Gilligan states:

> For boys and men, separation and individuation are critically tied to gender identity, since separation from the mother is essential for the development of masculinity (1982, p. 8).

This need for boys to establish autonomy from female figures may be trans-ferred to female teachers in early elementary school. The end result is that males often identify school as a feminine activity and feel they must disassociate them-selves from it. This disassociation, in turn, causes a greater proportion of dis-ruptive behaviors from males in the classroom. This explanation may be one rea-son for the gender differences in classroom grades and in problem behaviors.

How do we explain the greater proportion of classroom misbehavior in males?

How Does Gender Create Activity Level Differences?

Another possible contributing factor to classroom performance is that boys appear to have much higher physical activity levels, aggression levels, and classroom misbehavior levels than do girls. For instance, males are more likely to engage in strenuous play activities, to be physically aggressive, and to act out in class. As previously noted, this may produce a cumulative, interactive effect between classroom performance and classroom misbehavior.

At the elementary level, there may be a mismatch between the classroom environment and the classroom behavior of males. This mismatch produces more disruptive behavior, which has a negative effect on their academic performance. Negative academic performance causes boys to act out more in the classroom. This cycle subsequently snowballs through the public school years. In the end, it may be a factor causing the higher dropout rate among males in high school.

How Is Teacher Responsiveness Affected by Gender?

Does gender affect teacher behaviors?

Another noted gender difference concerns teacher responsiveness. Teachers appear to be more likely to respond to questions from males and to provide feedback to males. Research shows this trait to be consistent from elementary school through college (Sadker, Sadker, & Klein, 1991). When this finding is compared with the previous information concerning females' superior classroom performance, there is an obvious paradox. On the one hand, females have superior classroom performance. On the other hand, males receive more attention from teachers.

One explanation for this paradox is that there may be some type of subtle, social reinforcement that rewards female passivity in the classroom. In some way or another, females seem to take a more acquiescent role. When males and females work together, females may defer to males in classroom interactions.

It also could be that teachers overcompensate for the classroom academic and behavioral performance of males and undercompensate for the performance of females. Perhaps because boys have a greater likelihood of negative classroom behaviors, teachers are much more likely to respond to males when they do act appropriately.

Is there again some sort of cumulative interactive effect operating in the classroom? Males have such a history of greater behavioral problems that when they behave appropriately, teachers may go overboard in responding to them. Females are expected to behave appropriately, so teachers simply pass over them. This type of "mind-set" of expectations also may figure prominently in how teachers treat academic as well as behavioral aspects of the classroom environment.

What Self-Esteem Differences Are There between Genders?

Recent research on self-esteem and self-concept appears to indicate that self-esteem in both genders declines during the early high school years. The reasons for this decline, however, are unclear and under much debate. Some professionals

Boys are more likely than girls to act out and to be physically aggressive in school.

say that the decline may be due to maturational changes because of the onset of puberty or to the increased social pressures of being an adolescent in today's world.

A recent report by the Wellesley College Center for Research on Women states that the self-esteem decline is considerably more obvious in adolescent females than in males. The report claims similar findings to the Sadker et al. studies. The Wellesley study states that females are less likely to be acknowledged or responded to by teachers than are their male peers, which appears to be linked to the drop in self-esteem. This study also states that there is a link between the enjoyment of math and science and self-esteem. Those students, regardless of gender, who like math and science score higher on self-esteem ratings. One example of the relation between gender and self-esteem is shown in figure 7.2.

Is there a link between academic performance and self-esteem?

How Does Gender Affect Variability in Academic Performance?

One issue related to gender differences concerns the recent findings of greater male variability in academic achievement. Research provides some indications that males are more variable in their academic performance (Feingold, 1992). The greater variability among males may provide clues as to the nature of gender differences.

Some research shows that males are more likely to separate into two different educational tracks in school. One track of students will continue to develop in academic achievement and in academic self-concept. The second track of students will gradually decrease both in academic performance and in academic self-concept from approximately fifth grade to high school where many of them tune out or drop out.

This discovery about male educational patterns may explain why males drop out at higher rates than females and why males score better on college aptitude

FIGURE 7.2
The Wiz

The sound comes from the back of the throat, a tiny noise that is doomed to failure even as it begins. "Wait," Elizabeth Mann is trying to say, attempting to slip into a discussion that is swirling around her. It is a loud discussion with overlapping voices, but Elizabeth is a close listener, and she has heard something that needs correcting or at least elaboration. She also is a patient listener who doesn't blurt out her thoughts but waits for an opening to fit into.

The setting for this is Montgomery Blair High School in Silver Spring, Maryland. It is third period, Quantum Physics, the most difficult class in the school's math, science and computer magnet program. Seven of the country's brightest high school seniors sit around a table, working their way through a book on Einstein's general theory of relativity. There is Steve Chien, Blair High's valedictorian. There is Josh Weitz, the salutatorian. There is an intense looking boy named Sudheer Shukla, and another boy named Danilo Almeida, and another named Jeff Tseng, and another named Jeff Wang, and lastly there is Elizabeth. The girl.

As soon as the bell rings, the discussion is off and running, and very quickly as is usually the case, it is dominated by Steve, who sits to Elizabeth's right, and Josh, who sits to her left. Steve talks. Josh interrupts. Steve mumbles. Josh interrupts that . . .

And through it all, Elizabeth sits, listening. She tries to say, "Wait," and falls silent.

By David Finkel (1993)

What is an explanation for gender differences on college aptitude measures?

tests. The males who take college aptitude tests are the "survivors"—the ones who stayed in school. The males who did poorly in school have already dropped out or have forgone taking college aptitude tests.

As with cultural differences, gender differences present a series of difficult educational and political problems. Many of the same questions that occur with multicultural issues are also found with gender differences. In particular, controversies about textbook stereotyping, curriculum decisions, and hiring policies also are found in this area. These controversies may have profound consequences for women in the areas of self-esteem and career tracking.

For the most part, psychologists no longer claim any major, innate gender differences in academic ability. The present viewpoint on academic gender differences it that differences are relatively minor and generally are caused by socialization. These differences appear to have narrowed considerably in the past two decades, presumably because of the Women's Movement. It is important, however, for educators to be sensitive to the differences and needs of both males and females as individual students.

SUMMARY

Ethnic diversity and gender differences are two crucial areas of debate in American education. Many supporters of cultural diversity argue that school alienation is caused by a public school system that is disconnected from the cultural background of many minority students. By reforming textbooks and school curriculum, it is believed that school alienation and its negative effects, such as school drop-out, can be lessened.

Ethnic differences in learning styles also are thought to be a neglected area of multicultural education. Learning styles, academic performance, and classroom behavior differences that are attributable to ethnicity or gender appear to be addressed infrequently by teachers.

In terms of gender effects, males seem to be more likely to be responded to by teachers. However, females have better overall grades in public schools. Other research indicates that gender-difference measurements on college aptitude tests seem to be narrowing.

EPILOGUE

THE RESULTS OF DIVERSITY TRAINING

In reviewing this chapter, what types of recommendations would you now make for the teacher in the case study at the beginning of the chapter?

The issues raised in the case study are addressed by some of the following sections in the chapter:

Diversity and School Alienation—To what extent can curriculum reform decrease school alienation among minority ethnic groups? Will the hiring of more minority teachers also decrease school alienation?

Many writers who favor multicultural education believe an appropriate curriculum reform will bring about less school alienation in minority groups. It also seems that hiring minority teachers would provide more appropriate role models for minority children. With both curriculum reform and minority hiring the schools are providing more appropriate sources with whom minority children may identify.

In terms of curriculum reform, should we have a general curriculum with outside assignments made for minority children to focus on their own cultural heritage? Perhaps teachers should be directed to teach cultural differences or comparative cultures. If they are directed to teach such issues, then it would guarantee coverage of certain cultural heritages.

Diversity Training in Education—Will mandated diversity training sessions increase sensitivity to diversity issues or will such training exacerbate existing differences? Will speech and conduct codes decrease problems or will such codes prove impossible to enforce?

We generally assume that education can produce cognitive changes that can lead to subsequent emotional and behavior change. We want to change people's attitudes and behaviors about ethnicity and gender. If training in diversity issues cannot produce positive changes, then what will produce these changes?

Finally, the most important question again may be: Are these proposed changes in the best interests for the maximum number of children?

CHAPTER REVIEW

1. What are the major points of difference between the comments made by Nieto and Hirsch in this chapter?
2. Describe the relationship between school alienation and the cultural values of American education.
3. Describe the differences in learning styles among the various ethnic groups as indicated by Vasquez.
4. What are some of the problems with today's textbooks, as indicated by both proponents and opponents of multiculturalism?
5. Describe the relationship between gender and specific academic abilities.
6. Describe the relationship between gender and classroom behavior.

REFERENCES

Chodorow, N. (1974). Family structure and feminine personality. In M. Z. Rosaldo and L. Lamphere (Eds.), *Woman, Culture and Society*. Stanford: Stanford University Press.

Deutsch, C. H. (1993, April 4). Diversity bedevils M.B.A. programs. *New York Times*, sec. 4A, pp. 22–24.

Feingold, A. (1988). Cognitive gender differences are disappearing. *American Psychologist, 43*(2), 95–103.

Feingold, A. (1992). Sex differences in variability in intellectual abilities: A new look at an old controversy. *Review of Educational Research, 62*(1), 61–84.

Finkel, D. (1993, June 13). The Wiz: genius and gender. *The Washington Post Magazine*. pp. 8–13; 22–27.

Gilligan, C. (1982). *In a different voice*. Cambridge, MA: Harvard University Press.

Hirsch, E. D. (1988). *Cultural literacy*. New York: Vintage Books.

Hyde J. S., & Linn, M. C. (1988). Gender differences in verbal ability: A meta-analysis. *Psychological Bulletin, 104*, 53–69.

Maccoby, E. E. & Jacklin, C. N. (1974). *The psychology of sex differences*. Stanford: Stanford University Press.

Murray, K. (1993). The unfortunate side effects of diversity training. *New York Times*, 1993, August 1 sec. F, p. 5.

Nieto, S. (1992). *Affirming diversity*. New York: Longman.

Parsons, J. E. (1982). Biology, experience, and sex-dimorphic behaviors. In W. R. Grove and G. R. Carpenter (Eds.), *The fundamental connection between nature and nurture*, (pp. 137–170). Lexington, MA: Lexington Books.

Ravitch, D. (1990, October 24). Point of view. *The Chronicle of Higher Education*, A42.

Sadker, M., Sadker, D., & Klein, S. (1991). The issue of gender in elementary and secondary education. *Review of Research in Education, 17*, 269–334.

Sanders, J. A. & Wiseman, R. L. (1990). The effects of verbal and nonverbal teacher immediacy on perceived cognitive, affective, and behavioral learning in the multicultural classroom. *Communication Education, 39*, 341–353.

Serbin, L. A., Zelkowitz, P., Doyle, A. Gold, D., & Wheaton, B. (1990). The socialization of sex-differentiated skills and academic performance: A mediational model. *Sex Roles, 23*, 613–627.

Sexton, P. O. (1965). Schools are emasculating our boys. *Saturday Review, 48,* 57.

Shade, B. J. (1982). Afro-American cognitive style: A variable in school success? *Review of Educational Research, 52,* 219–244.

Sleeter, C. E., & Grant, C. A. (1991). Race, class, gender and disability in current textbooks. In Michael Apple and Linda Christian-Smith (Eds.) *The Politics of the Textbook.* New York: Routledge and Chapman Hall.

Vasquez, J. A. (1990). Teaching to the distinctive traits of minority students. *The Clearing House, 63*(7), 299–304.

Waber, D. P. (1976). Sex differences in cognition: a function of maturation rate? *Science, 192,* 572–574.

Will, G. F. (1992, December 29). Clinton's promise of quotas returns to bedevil him. *Washington Post,* 7A.

SECTION III

THE BASIS FOR LEARNING

CHAPTER 8

BEHAVIORAL APPROACHES TO LEARNING

■ ■ ■

Chapter Outline

CASE STUDY

ACCOMMODATING DIFFERENT LEARNING STYLES

It was time for the high school Social Studies class to continue its discussion on a psychology unit about operant conditioning and differences between positive reinforcement, negative reinforcement, punishment, and extinction. The teacher, Ms. Brooks, continued her lecture about how each of the four terms refers to consequences that can occur after a person or organism does certain behaviors. She explained that two of these consequences tend to make the behavior occur again while the other two tend to decrease that behavior. Within three minutes, several students raised their hands. "Could you explain these terms in a differ-

ent way?" they asked. Ms. Brooks suddenly realized that she was not reaching her "right-brain" thinkers who need graphic and tangible examples to create the mind pictures they need to assimilate new learning. They are the deductive learners who reason and think by moving from an understanding of the whole concept to an understanding of its parts or from the total picture to the elements of the picture. In other words, they do better on jigsaw puzzles when they can view the complete picture of the puzzle before starting.

What should Ms. Brooks do?

INTRODUCTION

In chapter 8, readers are asked to identify and analyze their own preferred learning style. Next, the reader is challenged with the question of how learning recall can be increased and what teachers can do to help their students recall more information. The full range of learning definitions is presented with a discussion of why teachers should study learning. The various behavioral approaches to learning are considered in the light of how they contribute to the understanding of how people learn. In fact, the reader would do well to evaluate each behavioral theory according to its potential usefulness to teachers.

KEY CONCEPTS

- People have preferred styles of learning that require teachers to accommodate their teaching methods to the different learning style preferences of their students.
- Quality and quantity of learning varies in direct proportion to the student's level of involvement in the learning.
- Learning refers to any relative permanent change in behavior or potential performance due to experience.
- Teachers are developing increased interest in how their students are learning because teacher performance ratings and merit salary increases may be based on how much their students learn.

- Classical conditioning offers teachers an avenue for making their classrooms and subject matter more attractive to their students.
- Operant conditioning offers teachers a method for changing their focus from punishing inappropriate and off-task behavior to reinforcing appropriate and on-task behavior.

■ ■ ■

HOW DO PEOPLE LEARN?

People learn best when they are able to personalize their learning. This chapter on learning theories will begin by asking you to develop your own theory about how you prefer to learn. To help you in your search, consider identifying your favorite and most efficient ways of learning about new subjects and skills. In fact, you will be diagnosing your own personal learning style (Applications from the Text 8.1). Many educators believe that people learn best when they maximize the use of all of their senses: hearing, seeing, touching, tasting, and smelling. Some of you will find that you are active learners who learn best when you can

APPLICATIONS FROM THE TEXT 8.1

Suppose you have just received a "state-of-the-art," new personal computer and that you had your choice of ways to learn about it. Rank order the following learning alternatives by giving your first choice a rank of one down to your last choice, which would receive a rank of fifteen.

I would like to learn about my new computer by:

___ a. Reading a book.
___ b. Viewing a videotape.
___ c. Listening to an audiotape about it when jogging, driving a car, or just relaxing.
___ d. Attending a lecture about it.
___ e. Obtaining an annotated reading list of books and articles about it that are in the local library.
___ f. Reading an owners manual containing detailed pictures and diagrams of how to use it.
___ g. Viewing a live demonstration.
___ h. Participating in the live demonstration.
___ i. Participating in a group discussion with people who know how to use it.
___ j. Working one-on-one with a consultant.
___ k. Attending a series of ten classes.
___ l. Working in a group of four people with a consultant.
___ m. Teaching what you have learned to another person.
___ n. Working in a competitive setting with prizes for achievement.
___ o. Working in a cooperative learning group.

After ranking the fifteen ways to learn about your new computer, study your top five selections to see if you can recognize a pattern regarding your individual learning style. You may prefer to rely on auditory, visual, tactile, or kinesthetic modalities. Or, you may find that you like a combination of all four modalities in which you involve ears, eyes, hands, and participatory activities in your learning.

see and touch the item you are studying. Others of you will find that you like an interactive learning situation in which you work cooperatively with others in reaching your goals. Many people prefer a one-on-one teaching-learning situation in which the learning is personalized for the individual. You may also find that you work best under the excitement or pressure of competition. Competitive learning can occur between individuals as well as between cooperative groups. Finally, we need to recognize that many people are independent learners who prefer to work alone and who are quite adept at digging out the information for themselves from books and manuals. So, learning styles may vary on the continuums of active-passive learning and interactive-independent learning.

From your diagnosis of your own personal learning style, write a short note to your professor describing how your class can be structured to accommodate your personal learning style. In other words, how much of the class would you prefer to be "tell me," "show me," and/or "let me do it?" How much of the class would you prefer to be passive learning: lecture, tapes, demonstration, and reading? How much of the class would you prefer to be active learning: participation, teaching others, practicum, internship, and laboratory?

As teachers you will want to conduct a similar diagnosis with all your students so that your teaching style will complement their various learning styles. In general, most of your students will prefer active learning methods over the traditional passive approaches of lectures and reading.

More formal ways to assess learning styles are available in learning style inventories such as the inventory developed by Dunn, Dunn, and Price (1989). These authors attempt to identify learning styles through a series of questions addressing the learner's environmental, emotional, sociological, and psychological preferences for optimal learning conditions.

Do you learn best from lecture, demonstration, or hands-on experience? Rank them one, two, and three according to your preference.

Students have a variety of learning styles. Individualizing instruction means finding the right style for the right student.

Learning is enhanced by using a variety of the senses to understand an object or experience.

Environmental factors would include the learner's preferences for *sound, light, temperature, and design. Sound* preferences could range from absolute quiet to preferences for background music. Some learners are able to block out noise when they study. The ability to block out surrounding distractions is often referred to as being field independent. Other learners have difficulty studying without some background noise. *Light* preferences may range from low to high, direct to indirect, and indoor to outdoor. Likewise, *temperature* preferences would fall into a high to low range. *Design* preferences range from formal to informal seating in a classroom and from comfortable to less comfortable in the home or library. For example, some learners prefer to study on the floor or in a comfortable chair while others require a desk and chair.

Emotional factors include *motivation, persistence, responsibility,* and the need for *structure. Motivational* preferences range from intrinsic (intangible) to extrinsic (tangible) rewards and from self-motivation to motivation from others. *Persistence* refers to the degree of commitment the learner will give to completing assignments. Commitment levels range from preferences for long- or short-term assignments to preference for structured or unstructured assignments. *Responsibility* refers to the learner's ability to follow through on various assignments without relying on continuous direction and reinforcement from others to do so. The need for *structure* varies from the highly unstructured, often creative learners who want to design their own learning plan to those very structured learners who want others to tell or show them exactly what needs to be done.

APPLICATIONS FROM THE TEXT 8.2

LEARNING STYLE PREFERENCES

Environmental

Place a check on the line nearest your preferences

Quiet	___	___	___	___	___	___	___	Background noise or music
Direct, bright light	___	___	___	___	___	___	___	Dim, indirect light
Warmer temperatures	___	___	___	___	___	___	___	Cooler temperatures
Formal seating	___	___	___	___	___	___	___	Informal seating

Emotional

Motivation: ___ self ___ parent(s) ___ teacher(s) ___ peers ___ others (list)_____

Persistence: High	___	___	___	___	___	___	Low
Responsibility: High	___	___	___	___	___	___	Low
Need for structure: High	___	___	___	___	___	___	Low

Sociological

Prefer to work with: ___ self(alone) ___ peers ___ team ___ teacher(s)

___ parent(s) ___ pairs ___ others (list)_____

Physical

Perceptual: ___ visual ___ tactile ___ auditory ___ kinesthetic

Intake

Nutritional intake: High	___	___	___	___	___	___	Low
Time of day: Morning	___	___	___	___	___	___	Night
Mobility: High	___	___	___	___	___	___	Low

Do you work and learn best alone or in small groups? Why?

Once again, as was true with many other categories, we will find preferences in the higher, medium, and lower range for the need for structure. Accommodating such wide preferences ranges in one classroom or even in one school is the challenge toward which this text is directed.

Sociological factors include the degree to which the learner prefers to work alone or with others in small or large groups. Some students prefer to work in teams while others prefer to work in pairs. Some students prefer working with peers while others prefer working with adults. Finally, there will be some learners who like a varied approach that provides a balance between several combinations of working alone and working with others.

Physical factors include perceptual preferences, nutritional intake, time of day, and mobility. *Perceptual* refers to the different learning modalities: visual, auditory, tactile, and kinesthetic. Does the learner learn best by telling, showing, hands-on experience or by some combination of all three? *Nutritional intake* refers to whether or not the learner learns best when eating or drinking nutritional foods when studying. *Time of day* relates to the most productive study time for the learner be it morning, noon, or night. Finally, the mobility factor is considered. Some learners work best by sitting in one place, while others have to move around and change positions.

Having reviewed the factors on the *Learning Style Inventory* (Dunn, Dunn, & Price, 1989), you may want to rate yourself on a checklist containing each factor (see Applications from the Text 8.2).

As teachers, we can assist our students by providing a variety of learning environments that can accommodate their varied learning style preferences. We also can help students by providing mediational steps to help them move from structured learning and outer direction to higher levels of self-motivation, direction, and responsibility for their own learning.

Learning is enhanced when teachers involve as many of the learner's sensory modalities as possible. A healthy teaching balance between telling, showing, and participation should provide optimal learning (see Applications from the Text 8.3).

Barkman (1991), quoting the Secony-Vacuum Oil Company studies, pointed out that we remember 10 percent of what we read, 20 percent of what we hear, 30 percent of what we see, 50 percent of what we see and hear, 70 percent of what we say as we talk, and 90 percent of what we say as we do it. Gagné and Rohwer (1985) found that learners have preferences for pictorial over verbal, concrete over abstract, and grammatical structure over nonstructured presentation. Barkman (1991) further noted that a blend of telling and showing is superior to either telling or showing for enhancing a learner's ability to recall what has been learned.

In addition to the recall advantages of combining telling and showing, it has been found that active learning is superior to passive learning in strengthening recall of learned material. Mackenzie and White (1982) found that generative, active learning in which students were participants in the learning produced better recall of learned material than did passive learning in which the students were merely recipients. The generative, active learning group retained 90 percent of what they had learned as compared with 58 percent for a passive learning group and 51 percent for a control group.

The American Psychological Association (1992) Task Force on Education made several recommendations regarding effective instruction. It views effective instruction as actively involving students in their own learning with opportunities

> Is your learning affected by the time of day? If so, what are your best hours for studying?

Methods of Instruction	Recall after 3 Hours	Recall after 3 Days
Telling when used alone	70%	10%
Showing when used alone	72%	20%
Blend of Telling and Showing	85%	65%

FIGURE 8.1

Concept Trees (grades 5–12)

Student knowledge and comprehension are facilitated through using concept trees. These graphic illustrations reveal the connection between subject ideas and encourage motivation because of the student's feeling of acquired success. This visual communication method can demonstrate the sequential and logical order of events and is particularly useful for developing the visual style of student learning. The needs of the aural style learners can be met through the teacher's explanation and class discussion, while the kinesthetic learner can be served by drawing the concept tree from personal notes (Hirumi & Bowers, 1991).

The concept tree diagram (see figure) can be used for depicting the mathematical combinations in the following problem example. Suppose solid blue and gold paper, bows, and tags have been purchased. How many different combinations can be created without repeating any previous selection (McGehe, 1991)?

Concept Tree Diagram

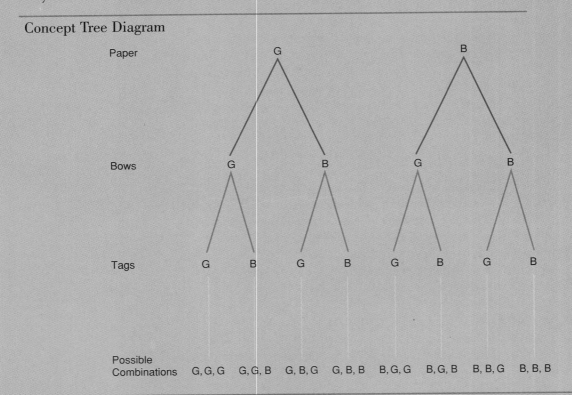

Vivian Haun, a student in Educational and Counseling Psychology at the University of Tennessee, wrote the applications for this chapter.

Two-on-Two Word Competition (grades 1–12)

This technique can be adapted to any grade level and can involve peer tutoring. A new word is presented daily to the class. The presentation should be a visual demonstration using role playing, photographs, or drawings. The definition is obtained individually from dictionaries and recorded on 3" × 5" note cards. The cards are kept by the students and used for individual practice. Vocabulary partners also can work together. If a competitive spirit is desired, have a word competition with other competing partners scheduled at predesignated times (weekly, biweekly, or monthly). By maintaining balance in ability levels, everyone of each set of partners will get to be winners at some time (Berentsen, 1991).

for interaction with teachers and peers (see Applications from the Text 8.4). Auditory, visual, and kinesthetic methods of presenting information were supported. The task force also recommended that opportunities should be created for acquiring and practicing a variety of learning strategies involving problem solving, debates, and group discussions.

In summary, the amount of learning students retain varies in direct proportion to their level of involvement in the learning. Dale (1969) presented a cone of experience model that can serve as an illustration of the points we are trying to make regarding sensory input and learning (see Figure 8.2).

> What is your best learning situation on Dale's experiential learning cone? Why?

HOW IS LEARNING DEFINED?

Learning generally is defined as a relatively permanent change in behavior or potential performance due to experience. Changes resulting from drugs, maturation, and illness are *not* classified as learning. Learning includes:

> Write a correct definition of learning in your own words. This should help you understand the topic.

a. good and bad habits;
b. observable behavior, skills, and knowledge, as well as the unobservable attitudes, thoughts, and feelings;
c. both conscious and unconscious behaviors;
d. values and opinions.

Why should learning be studied? First, as mentioned on a previous page, it is helpful to understand how both teachers and students learn. Teachers should be able to assess the preferred learning styles of their students and then adapt their instruction to fit students' learning styles. Second, teachers need to know the best conditions or classroom environments for enhancing the learning process. Third, teachers need to be as efficient as possible in teaching a variety of skills and information. With teacher advancement and merit pay beginning to be based on student achievement, teachers may begin to pay more attention to the

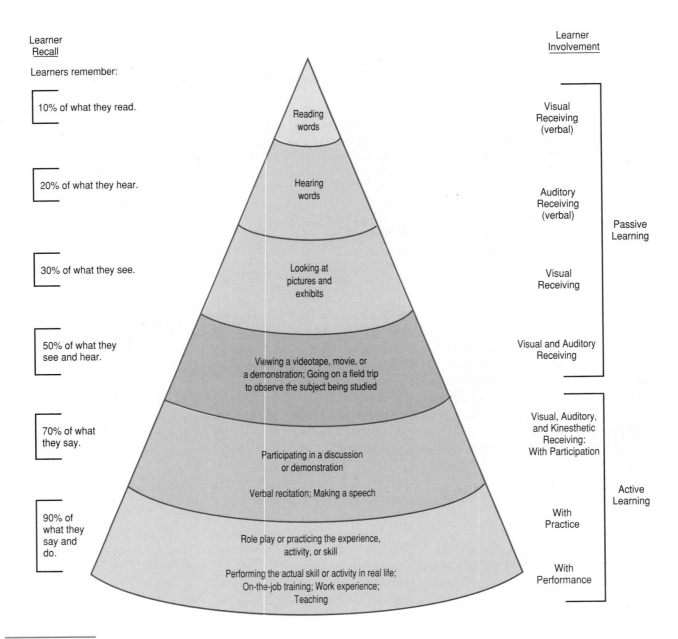

Learner Recall

Learners remember:

10% of what they read.

20% of what they hear.

30% of what they see.

50% of what they see and hear.

70% of what they say.

90% of what they say and do.

Reading words

Hearing words

Looking at pictures and exhibits

Viewing a videotape, movie, or a demonstration; Going on a field trip to observe the subject being studied

Participating in a discussion or demonstration

Verbal recitation; Making a speech

Role play or practicing the experience, activity, or skill

Performing the actual skill or activity in real life; On-the-job training; Work experience; Teaching

Learner Involvement

Visual Receiving (verbal)

Auditory Receiving (verbal)

Visual Receiving

Visual and Auditory Receiving

Passive Learning

Visual, Auditory, and Kinesthetic Receiving: With Participation

With Practice

With Performance

Active Learning

FIGURE 8.2
Experiential Learning Cone

question of how students learn. Learning is a continuous process that goes on all day long, often in an unorganized and uncontrolled manner. Learning about learning should help teachers find ways to organize and direct learning into productive channels without stifling creativity.

The question of how people learn divides learning theorists into one of three major groups: behavioral (classical and operant conditioning), cognitive (insight, latent, and observational learning), and eclectic (combinations of behavioral and cognitive theories). Contributions from theorists in each group will be examined in the light of what they have to contribute to effective teaching.

Behavioral theorists, also referred to as connectionist theorists because they hold that all learning is the result of connections between stimuli and responses, are divided into two subgroups: classical conditioning theorists and operant conditioning theorists. Classical conditioning proponents include Ivan Pavlov, John B. Watson, and Edwin Guthrie. Operant conditioning proponents include Edward Thorndike and B. F. Skinner.

Ivan Pavlov

Ivan Pavlov's (1849–1936) contribution to education and learning theory came as a by-product from his research on the function of various digestive fluids. While attempting to collect saliva from dogs for his research, he noted that the dogs salivated when they were fed and when they heard any noise, such as the click of opening the gate to the dog pen, that preceded their feeding. His observation led to further experiments with his classical or respondent conditioning model and to more efficient methods for collecting saliva for his research. Classical or respondent conditioning may be defined as a form of learning that occurs when a neutral stimulus (the conditioned stimulus) elicits a response after multiple pairings with another stimulus (the unconditioned stimulus). In other words, classical conditioning occurs when two stimuli are presented together and the response originally elicited by one of them, the unconditioned stimulus, comes to be elicited by the other stimulus, the conditioned stimulus (see Figure 8.3).

FIGURE 8.3
Classical or Respondent
Conditioning

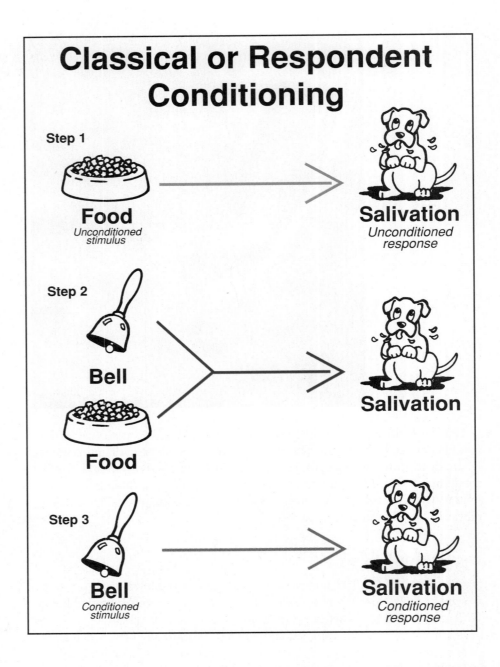

Classical or Respondent Conditioning

Step 1

Food
Unconditioned stimulus

Salivation
Unconditioned response

Step 2

Bell

Food

Salivation

Step 3

Bell
Conditioned stimulus

Salivation
Conditioned response

Write a correct definition of classical or respondent conditioning in your own words and write one example of it.

In other words, classical conditioning is based on stimulus-response learning that results from the stimulus substitution that occurs when two stimuli are paired together (contiguity). The stimulus-response bond is strengthened by the presence of the unconditioned stimulus, which was food in Pavlov's experiment.

The process can be demonstrated in a common student activity by having an experimenter blow gently through a straw into a willing participant's eye, causing the eye to blink. One second before each puff of air, a loud noise is made such as blowing a whistle or ringing a bell. After twenty to thirty pairings of the unconditioned stimulus (puff of air) with the conditioned stimulus (whistle), the conditioned stimulus should be able to produce the conditioned response of the eye blink without the puff of air. Several repetitions of the conditioned stimulus (whistle) alone without the unconditioned stimulus (air) should extinguish the eye blink (the conditioned response). A lapse in time often results in the spontaneous recovery of the conditioned response.

Pavlov used his classical conditioning methods to teach dogs how to discriminate between circles and squares in locating meat behind the "correct" door. However, he discovered that the dogs became neurotic when they were unable to discriminate between circles and ellipses as the diagrams became more alike. He found that the dogs developed one of two types of personalities: the excitatory personality and the inhibitory personality. When frustrated by the difficult discrimination decisions, the excitatory dogs seemed to follow the philosophy of when in doubt do something or do anything. The inhibitory dogs, on the other hand, seemed to believe that when in doubt it is better to do nothing. Pavlov believed that humans acted in similar ways when confronted with difficult and conflicting decisions.

Pavlov's work has many applications for teachers. Making classrooms nice places to be has the effect of making learning fun and pleasant. Unattractive and cold school environments reinforce school phobia and fears and anxiety about certain school subjects. Pairing fun activities and games with learning mathematics can turn a potentially painful class into one the students look forward to having (see Applications from the Text 8.5). Presenting difficult subject matter

Can you think of at least three ways to make one of your teaching lessons effective, pleasant, and even fun?

APPLICATIONS FROM THE TEXT 8.5

Lucky 7 Game (grades 1–6)

Fast, accurate recall of the place value system is fundamental for good estimating skills. (United States Department of Education 1986). A method for acquiring this adeptness is to play the Lucky 7 Game (Cox, 1990). Draw one large, blocked 7 on 40 different, small index cards. Within this open-blocked number 7, print one set of multiple digit numerals using one "7" somewhere within each number. For example, two and three digit numbers (57, 79, 713) may be used for beginning learners. For more advanced learning, larger numerals (471,950) and decimal digits (258.057) may be written on each card. The place value of the 7 digit is to be written on the back of each card. An option would be to have the cards laminated for future use. To play Lucky 7, the cards are shuffled and stacked face up in front of the two or three players. The first player takes as many cards as is rolled on the die—1, 2, 3, 4, or 5. A turn is lost if a 6 is rolled. The player must accurately read the numeral and give the place value of the 7 on each card as received. The card is kept when correct and is returned to the bottom of the center stack when incorrectly identified. When the stack is gone, the game is over; the player with the most cards is the lucky winner. An advantage of this game is its adaptability. Other subjects can be used: grammar, literature, social studies, art, and music. Students can contribute questions and answers to be written on the cards. They also can "practice" (study) during their own free time. The advantages of cooperative learning can be introduced by having two individual players teamed together (as in the card game of bridge) to play team against team.

My Pal (grades K–3)

A teaching aid for beginning readers kindergarten through third grade is "My Pal." Have the students choose one of their own stuffed toys or dolls as a reading partner. First, the student brings the toy to school and introduces it to the class. Then, the child and pal take a book home and read it together, preferably with a parent. Teacher's discretion will determine whether the book needs to have been read earlier for practice by the student.

After what is to be a pleasurable reading experience, the student rewrites the story in a notebook. Any reactions to the experience also can be recorded. The notebook is returned the next day after the parent signs it, the student signs it, and the pal signs it (with the student's assistance). At the end of the year, each student has a journal of the year's readings and fond memories. Parents of younger children can write the child's dictated stories in the journal.

The teacher needs to be prepared for students who do not have any stuffed toys available. To prevent any embarrassment, take the initiative and collect some "pals" from personal friends or other teachers. Stuffed but friendly toys can be purchased inexpensively (as little as a quarter) at thrift stores or garage sales and machine washed (gentle cycle and air dried) at home. Circumspective inquiries regarding availability of toys can be made ahead of time. This behavioral approach relies on the positive association with "the pal" to be transferred to the activity of reading (Crosson, 1991).

in small steps ensuring success experiences for all your students is another helpful application of classical conditioning methods. Bad habits can be eliminated by the adversive conditioning method of pairing a painful rubber band snap on the wrist with the habit itself or with the thought of doing that habit. For example, a student could snap the rubber band on her wrist each time she had the urge to daydream. Basically, teachers use Pavlov's method each time they pair pleasant and reinforcing things with their learning activities (see Applications from the Text 8.6). Teachers get themselves in difficulty when they do the opposite by assigning extra schoolwork and detention to punish their students. School and studying then become regarded as a punishment rather than as a privilege.

John B. Watson

John B. Watson (1878–1958), known as the father of American behaviorism, introduced behaviorism and Pavlov's classical conditioning model to the American public in the academic period of his life 1903–1920. Watson believed that observable behavior was the most important thing for psychologists to study. Watson considered finding answers to the questions of what an individual is doing and how behavior can be changed to be the goals of psychology.

Watson is, perhaps, most remembered for conditioning eleven-month-old Albert B. to fear white, furry objects and animals. When a white rat was presented to him, Albert showed only curiosity. However, when Albert reached for the rat, a steel bar located out of Albert's sight was struck by a hammer. Albert reacted to the noise with a startled response and hid his face in the mattress. A second trial produced the same response but seemed to disturb Albert more than the first trial. One week later, five more trials pairing the loud noise (unconditioned stimulus) with the white rat (conditioned stimulus) produced the fear response (conditioned response) when white, furry objects or animals were presented to Albert.

Watson, working with Mary Cover Jones, later demonstrated that children's fears could be removed with the same classical conditioning methods. Such applications of the model included emotional flooding, counterconditioning, and systematic desensitization. Emotional flooding includes frequent presentation of the feared object in "safe" situations (see Applications from the Text 8.7). Counterconditioning refers to pairing a strong, reinforcing stimulus (favorite food treat) with the feared object (see Applications from the Text 8.8). Desensitization is a process that allows presentation of the feared object in a series of steps that gradually increases the intensity of the exposure to the stimulus.

Watson's focus on the importance of the learning environment led him to believe that, given the proper conditioning, he could shape people into whatever he wanted them to be regardless of their innate abilities and talents.

Watson did believe that people are born with the basic emotions fear, rage, and love. Fear was produced by loud noises and loss of support. Rage was produced by restraint of movement; love, by affectionate touching. Stimuli paired

Do you believe that John Watson's methods can be used to shape people into whatever we want them to be regardless of their innate abilities and talents? Why or why not?

Teachers who pair enjoyable and reinforcing events with learning activities are using a form of classical conditioning.

APPLICATIONS FROM THE TEXT 8.7

Journal Writing (grades 1–12)

Much anxiety can be experienced by ESL (English as a second language) students. Journal writing can help ESL students express themselves. This activity also can promote writing and reading skills in some learning-disabled students as well. The basis of the technique is founded on a nonthreatening interchange. Model correct punctuation, grammar usage, and spelling by rephrasing, correcting, or rewriting words in the journal. Prompt attention to feedback is important in journal writing. Confidence and self-esteem can be nurtured into intrinsic motivation through positive reinforcement of what students write (Gaustad & Messenheimer-Young, 1991).

Foreign Folktales (grades K–12)

Ask foreign students to share folktales with the class in their native languages. Focus on the student's fluency and theatrical flair. Have the class guess the subject of the story. Afterward, the student can retell the same story in English. Sharing books in the student's native language also will assist in the acceptance process (Harbaugh, 1990).

Practicing speaking and listening skills provides a strong basis for improving reading proficiency. This is particularly critical for ESL students and for those who live with families primarily speaking another native language (United States Department of Education, 1986).

These previous activities accomplish two ends. They allow the foreign students to feel more comfortable and be a part of the classroom experience and give the other students more contact with the foreign culture and language. Thus, the cultural diversities and commonalties can be acknowledged, appreciated, and integrated with the American culture.

with any of the above stimuli could evoke the same three basic emotions. Hence, the white rat paired with the loud noise evoked fear in Albert.

Watson viewed learning as a trial-and-error process that continued until the error responses dropped out. In solving a problem, the response that changes the stimulation gains in frequency and recency of use until it becomes a habitual response when the stimulus (problem situation) is presented. In addition to the applications to teaching that were listed under Pavlov's model, we could add the importance of enhancing learning by using a problem-solving approach to teaching. The method would allow learning through using the scientific method to systemize the trial-and-error learning postulated by Watson. Teachers also may want to provide opportunities for students to benefit from the use of Watson's frequency-recency principles. In other words, teachers should want their students to experience frequent and recent success in applying the following scientific method to problem solving:

a. Defining the problem;
b. Hypothesizing possible solutions to the problem;
c. Controlled trials of viable solutions;
d. Collection and accurate analysis of data;
e. Formulation of conclusions and problem solution.

Watson's formal academic career ended when he was forced to resign his professorship because of a scandal involving his affair with a graduate student and subsequent divorce from his wife. Landing on his feet, he became an extremely successful advertising executive as he applied his work on the basic fear, rage, and love reactions to selling products and services. Baby powder became associated with mother's love. Rage was used to help sell commuter train services as people were shown being trapped in traffic jams. Fear was used to sell safe toilet tissue (Malone, 1990).

Do you believe that a system of motivating student learning could be based on fear, rage, and love? If so how? If not, why?

Edwin R. Guthrie

Edwin R. Guthrie (1886–1959), favoring objective psychology, supported Watson's behaviorism and Pavlov's conditioned reflex. He rested his theoretical concepts about learning on the concept of contiguity. Contiguity refers to events that occur closely together in time and space. In other words, an association or connection will be formed between a stimulus (S) and response (R) when they occur at approximately the same time. It is not necessary for the stimulus to cause the response, but both are present when learning occurs. However, Guthrie believed that the same stimulus will be accompanied by the same response each time it recurs. The stimulus is a cue for the response that is made. For example, people may feel like eating something each time they step into a kitchen.

Guthrie stressed the importance of physical activity and movement as behavior to be studied. He believed that a stimulus or combination of stimuli that has

APPLICATIONS FROM THE TEXT 8.8

Pizza Fractions (grades 4–6)

This idea increases the learning "appetite" for fractions. Four different-colored circles and an individual-size pizza box are needed for each student or small group. Elicit pizza box donations from students and friends. Each student should receive the four "pizza" circles: one whole, and the others cut in halves, in thirds, and in fourths.

To make the instructions and demonstrations a little simpler to follow, have each differently divided circle represented by a single color for all students: red for the half-cut, green for the third-cut, and yellow for the fourth-cut pizzas. The single whole pizza can be colorfully garnished by each student according to individual preferences. Finally, the students can maneuver the other colors to identify, apply, analyze, and cognitively organize the proportional properties of fractions. Additional fractions (sixths, eighths, ninths, etc.) can be explained and shown by using the same four proportioned circles. This fun, hands-on teaching technique allows the students to progress from the basic to the higher-order thinking skills (Heese, 1990). Additional motivation can be created by using real pizzas. All the students can be rewarded by eating the fractions of their choices.

accompanied a movement will, on its recurrence, tend to be followed by that movement. In short, if you do something in a given situation, the next time you are in that situation, you will tend to repeat it whether right or wrong.

Application of Guthrie's principle could help you improve your next test performance. Try studying for your next exam in the same seat in the room where you will be taking the exam. You can increase the stimulus cues by chewing the same strongly flavored gum during the test that you chewed while you studied. Grape-flavored gum is a favorite among those who have used the technique to help their recall of subject matter. Of course Guthrie's principle probably works best when you are actually taking a practice test while you are studying in your classroom seat. As was mentioned in chapter 1, you can construct your practice test questions from textbook chapter headings and lecture subheadings. Providing you recite the correct answers to good questions, the stimulus conditions should help you to recall more of what you learned when you are taking the actual test.

Guthrie believed that the presence of an unconditioned stimulus was not necessary for learning to occur as long as the conditioned stimulus and response occurred together (e.g., the conditioned stimulus of chewing grape-flavored gum and the response of remembering the answer to a test question). Guthrie did not agree with Watson about learning being increased by the frequency of response or by practice. He believed you either had a stimulus-response connection or you did not. Only one trial was needed to form the connection. Practice or response frequency does not strengthen the S–R connection except as it affects recency of response. This is not to say that practice is not helpful in increasing skill performance. Practice or frequency of response does help the coordination of the many S–R bonds required to accomplish such skills as playing a piano, hitting baseballs, and riding bikes. Many of the S–R bonds represent mediational learning steps that bridge the gaps between failure and successful performance. For example, the new bike rider learns that balance can be maintained by turning the front wheel in the direction the bike is leaning or falling.

Guthrie did not hold with traditional uses of reward and punishment. He believed behavior is not based on reward but on whether it changes the problem situation so that it becomes the last behavior tried. Such behaviors could include:

a. problem-solving behaviors;
b. task-oriented (helpful) behaviors;
c. defense-oriented behaviors (escape responses, denial, and other unhelpful behaviors).

Guthrie believed that reward and punishment are best defined by what they make the person or subject do. Rewards cause subjects to stop what they are doing and effectively change the situation. For example, the completion of a project or task would effectively bring about changes in behavior and the situational context. Punishment leads to strong, new behaviors in the old situation (Malone, 1990). Guthrie considered rewards effective when they changed a situation without disengaging the subject's last response from the stimulus cues of that situation.

What do you think of Guthrie's method for improving your test performance? Would you be willing to give it a try?

Guthrie's most interesting and best applications of his theory of learning can be found in his methods for breaking habits. His methods all involve identifying the stimulus or stimuli that evoke the undesirable response and then finding a way to make the desirable response occur in the presence of that stimulus or those stimuli. Three methods will be discussed: threshold, fatigue, and incompatible stimuli.

The *threshold* method involves presenting the stimulus weakly at first and gradually increasing it in small steps. To "break" a horse from bucking when saddled with a rider, you would want to begin by getting the horse used to walking around with a saddle blanket. The blanket would be followed by a blanket and saddle. When the horse was comfortable with the saddle, a rider would be tried. Confronting the horse with all these things at once would evoke a bucking response. The same threshold method could be used to teach any difficult subject, particularly one that frightens students (see Applications from the Text 8.9).

The *fatigue* method involves repeating undesired behavior over and over again until you wear it out. You may want to try it the next time you develop a blinking tic in your eye during a high-stress period. Simply blinking your lid one hundred times in rapid succession is generally enough to wear out the response.

One frequently quoted application of the fatigue method involved a young girl who was overly fascinated with lighting matches. She was given the option of lighting all the matches she wanted to light until she tired of the activity. Her final response, pushing the match box away and not lighting the match, became her lasting response. The girl was cured of her match-lighting habit. We might add that the method seems to work even better when the habit behavior is made an assigned task. For example, the girl could have been assigned the task of lighting all the matches in a large box one at a time. As noted in the chapters on classroom management, a teacher could assign the task of staring to a student who bothered others by staring at them during class.

Results from the fatigue method for breaking habits reject the law of frequency in favor of the law of recency. After several repetitions (frequency) of the

Would you like to rid yourself of an undesirable habit or change some unhelpful behavior? If so, which one of Guthrie's three methods might you choose and why?

behavior, the most recent or last response in the situation was stopping the behavior. Continuous smoking for thirteen hours has proved to be a successful method for some people who wanted to quit smoking. In addition to the fatigue factor, nausea adds to the urge to throw the remaining cigarettes away (the most recent response).

The method of *incompatible stimuli* involves pairing stimuli for undesired behavior (response) with new stimuli that can produce a desired response. For example, a student who suffers from text anxiety can be trained through systematic desensitization to learn to replace anxiety with relaxation. Wolpe's (1969; 1958) desensitization methods involved breaking the test anxiety experience down into a hierarchy of twelve to fifteen steps or mental images culminating in the actual testing experience. People are taught relaxation techniques to practice while they visualize each step in the hierarchy until relaxation is achieved with each image. For example, the first step in using the hierarchy may be practicing relaxation while visualizing the experience of reading the class syllabus and noting that a test is scheduled in three weeks. The pairing of relaxation and visualization of each step in the test anxiety hierarchy continues until the test is taken.

Another educational application of the incompatible stimuli method could be helpful to you when you are trying to study in a noisy dormitory. Put down the textbook and begin reading a book or article you find entertaining. If the book is sufficiently entertaining, you will soon be reading without the distraction of the noise. After a short period, switch back to the textbook. The noise becomes detached from the listening response and attached to the reading response. Help for rejected lovers can be found in the same method. Each time the rejected lover has lonely or grieving thoughts about the former partner, a good sniff from a mason jar containing rotten eggs will produce nausea rather than grief pains. Soon thereafter, just the thought of the former lover will induce nausea and the nausea will soon become the stimulus for forgetting or not grieving over lost love. The freedom from grieving will give the rejected lover the time and energy to develop new and better relationships.

Edward L. Thorndike

Prior to Edward L. Thorndike's work, the study of psychology was limited to the introspective study of internal mental events or the analysis of conscious experience. In other words, it was thought that human behavior was caused by mental processes such as ideas, thoughts, hopes, dreams, feelings, and expectations.

Thorndike (1874–1949) preferred to study behavior directly. Behavior, viewed by Thorndike, was something that could be observed and quantified. In fact, Thorndike believed that even the above mental events could be studied as a part of what we do. He believed that learning did not result from thinking about a problem. Rather, he viewed learning as a product of the associations or connections that developed between stimuli and response. He worked hard to establish psychology as a science by publishing more than 450 books, articles, and monographs in a career spanning 51 years including his retirement.

Thorndike's research with cats in a puzzle box was his most well-known work. The cats were required to find the mechanism, such as a loop of string,

According to Thorndike's Law of Effect, reinforcing a student's response will increase the strength and likelihood of that student responding in the same way again.

that would open the box and allow them to escape and receive a food reward. Thorndike noted that the cats used a trial-and-error (selecting and connecting) approach to learning, and, although they decreased the time it took for them to escape, they never did seem to obtain insight into how the escape problem could be solved. He therefore concluded that learning resulted from connections (associations) that develop between stimuli and responses rather than resulting from thinking about a problem and developing problem-solving conclusions leading to insight and concept formation. Hence, Thorndike labeled his learning theory connectionism. Eventually the connections between stimulus and response became known as S–R bonds.

Thorndike's work with the cats led to the development of his most well-known law of learning, the law of effect. The law of effect stated that when a response made in the presence of a stimulus is followed by a satisfying event, the connection or bond between that stimulus and response is strengthened (see Applications from the Text 8.10). The same connection would be weakened if it led to an annoying event. He later modified the latter half of the law to read that punishment or an annoying event serves to increase the variability of responding, thereby increasing the likelihood that a person or cat would select a response that led to a satisfying or rewarding state of affairs. Thorndike concluded that punishment merely directed the response to a satisfying event. Punishment did not, however, contribute to the unlearning of the punished responses. In other words, punishment may serve only to encourage our students to be more clever about

What would Thorndike tell teachers about the effectiveness of punishment? Why would you agree or disagree with Thorndike?

Game Show (grades 6–12)

A fun and simple teaching technique incorporates TV quiz games as an incentive for learning social studies and current events. Be sure that each student has at least one source of written news: newspapers and/or magazines. Write on the chalkboard the clue words to particular news stories. Examples of current stories may include rain forests, the environment, ozone, recycling, and nature. Attention to these clues are important as their stories are to be the major focus of the week's quiz game. Some students will choose to draw additional information from television's nightly news. On the "game" day, become an amusing "game show host" and read a "round" of four questions aloud concerning a specific topic to the small groups/teams (four to six students). Allow time for the team to talk quietly among themselves and to write the answers on a piece of paper. Sufficient, yet brief, discussion time permits all team members an opportunity for information input. The answers are handed to the "game show host," and each correct topic is worth ten points. Opportunity is given to discuss any surrounding stories concerning the subjects. Suggested time is approximately five to six rounds in thirty to thirty-five minutes. Following each round, a bonus question involving a general unassigned topic is auctioned to all teams. Each team quietly discusses and writes down its bid; no bid can exceed total points previously awarded the team. The team with the highest bid receives the bonus question and gives an oral answer after team discussion. The game fosters student interaction, cooperative learning, enhanced listening skills, and increased attention to news. The clue words provide cues for the students to be attentive. The bonus points reinforce attention to unmentioned subjects. A wide variety of subject/topic areas can be addressed during the same week and any implicit relationships among them noted accordingly. This behavioral teaching method provides a thorough approach to expanding news information, as well as an effective strategy for incorporating other historical aspects of social studies (Smith, 1980).

hiding their misbehavior. Thorndike was highly critical of the heavy use of punishment in families, schools, and churches. In addition to being an ineffective discipline technique, punishment generally is accompanied by the unwanted side effect of building anger and destroying the relationship between the person doing the punishment and the person receiving it.

Thorndike developed two other major laws of learning: the law of readiness and the law of exercise. The law of readiness refers to preparation for action. The law of readiness also refers to a conduction unit of neurons and synapses ready to conduct and to do so is satisfying to the learner. Learning depends on the readiness of the learner to learn. The law of readiness also is concerned with the conditions that affect what the learner may consider as a satisfier or an annoyer or what is reinforcing or punishing at a particular time. For example, it would be easier to train a hungry dog with food as a reinforcer than it would be to train a dog that has just been fed.

Generalizing to the classroom, an evaluation of the content and method used to teach that content in the light of the readiness of our students to learn it is needed. Is teaching leading to satisfying or annoying conditions for our students? In too many classes, the only satisfying condition is the end of the class

How can you increase your students' readiness to learn?

hour. In fact, avoidance and escape behaviors often bring more satisfaction than any other class-related behaviors. In summary, learning is facilitated when the student is able, willing, and eager to engage in a learning activity. In fact, students in the above state of readiness would find it most annoying to be deprived of the opportunity to learn (see Applications from the Text 8.11).

The law of exercise or repetition draws on practice for strengthening S–R connections. In other words, the more a stimulus-induced response is repeated, the longer it will be retained. Thorndike believed that frequency of response had a significant positive influence on learning and that S–R bonds were dissipated by disuse. Many have experienced the "lose it if you do not use it" phenomenon in past academic endeavors, particularly regarding foreign language learning. Thorndike, himself, was not able to validate the law of exercise in his own research; however, work by Heff (1961) and Estes (1969) did support the law of exercise.

APPLICATIONS FROM THE TEXT 8.11

Study Buddies (grades 3–12)

A technique to increase learning time both at home and in the classroom is with the use of peer tutoring and a chalkboard. Allow small groups of appointed "homework buddies" or "board buddies" to use the chalkboard during any free or assigned time to practice, share, and check their assigned homework problems. If the available board can be away from the front of the class or out of the class's direct vision, the students may be more relaxed and willing to practice. The board buddies can talk quietly among themselves at the board concerning concepts and methods. This not only increases active learning time but allows small-group questions and answers in addition to positive reinforcement from the other buddies (Hallinan & Williams, 1990). Board buddies also could be expanded to computer buddies with two or more keyboards wired to a common monitor. In fact, computer buddies also could be played on any computer network.

Question Cards (grades K–12)

Technical theory can be both difficult and boring whether the subject is science, math, grammar/punctuation, or vocational-technical training. To make it more fun, the teacher can give the students a handout with a sizable number of questions, perhaps as many as one hundred. The students have two weeks to learn the answer to each question. After two weeks, divide the class into two teams. A randomly chosen question from the original list is presented to one student volunteer from the first team. The correct answer given within five seconds is worth five points. After an individual incorrectly answers (or runs out of time), his team gets a chance to answer for three points. If that team is incorrect within the additional five seconds, the opposing team gets a chance for the correct answer and three points. This challenging, fun game reinforces the desire to learn important technical concepts and terms that could otherwise be boring material (Martin, 1988). Different lists can be saved throughout the school term and used for review for the BIG game (final exam preparation). As an extra bonus, the winning team or those teams who have achieved above a predetermined score may be exempted from an exam.

Thorndike's five principles or subsidiary laws of learning include the principles of multiple response, set, selective response, response by analogy, and associative shifting. These five principles serve to support and explain Thorndike's three main laws just described.

Principle of Multiple Response. The principle of multiple response states that when a particular response fails to produce satisfaction, a new response is initiated. When one attempts to learn a new skill, the person does the best possible with the repertoire of behaviors and skills brought to the situation. Basically a person tries, as Piaget (1930) noted, to assimilate the new learning into the present system of functioning. Failing to master the new learning by assimilation, a person will accommodate to the new learning situation or problem by mastering new skills and concepts that become part of our functioning system (schema).

Principle of Set. The principle of set refers to disposition, attitude, experience, expectations, and needs of the learner regarding readiness to learn. In fact, the principle of set is another way of defining the law of readiness as it pertains to the necessity of drive or motivation for learning to occur. As mentioned when discussing the law of readiness, many factors affect whether or not the learner will be successful in learning what is being taught (see Applications from the Text 8.12). Again, the goal of educators is to create the conditions that will make students enthusiastic and invested in what is being taught. The task is to relate teaching to what is important or motivating to students. Once again, teachers need to consider the level of skill, knowledge, and experience students bring to their classes.

When you lose something are you more likely to rely on trial and error or systematic problem-solving? Why?

Principle of Selective Response. The principle of selective response refers to the stimulus discrimination that occurs as one progresses in learning. That is, as learning takes place, one begins to respond selectively to some factors of the situation while ignoring others. Whether ineffective behaviors are eliminated by trial and error or by scientific problem solving, those responses that have been rewarded in the past will be repeated. Once again, the assimilation/accommodation principle is at work. Educators should recognize that students are helped most when they are taught efficient methods of eliminating unproductive problem-solving behaviors. The game of twenty questions can be used to teach students how to ask good questions. For example, students have twenty yes or no questions to ask to solve a problem or guess what is in the mystery box. In addition to guessing the mystery box contents, students could ask twenty yes- or no-type questions for guessing a number. The group or individual needing the fewest questions wins. Competition between student teams makes the twenty-questions contest a fun and exciting way to teach students how to apply the selective response principle.

Principle of Response by Analogy. The principle of response by analogy refers to transfer of learning from one situation to another. The learner is likely to be successful in transferring learning if there are elements common to both learning situations. This is another application of Piaget's assimilation principle. People do tend to react to new situations in much the same way they did in past similar situations. Perhaps this principle is most central to educators because instruction is based on the idea of transferring knowledge from the course to useful activities beyond the course. The transfer principle makes an excellent case for "hands-on" learning, on-the-job training, practicums, internship experiences, and applied learning in general.

Associative Shifting Principle. The associative shifting principle states that responses learned for one stimulus may be learned for a new stimulus. The best example is the Pavlovian classical conditioning model of converting the neutral stimulus of a bell to a conditioned stimulus producing the conditioned response (salivation by the dogs) to the bell. Educators would do well to pair their instruction with attractive (satisfying) unconditional stimuli. Classrooms need to be attractive and fun places to be (see Applications from the Text 8.13). Teachers also need to be warm, friendly, and reinforcing. Pairing these good stimulus qualities with mathematics, reading, and composition should help generate the performance responses sought from students (see Applications from the Text 8.14).

In summary, Thorndike's laws and subsidiary laws were somewhat mechanical with no provision for cognitive operations such as thought or insight. He did introduce the concepts of reinforcement and, to some extent, the role of punishment in learning. He eventually concluded that punishment did not directly weaken S–R connections. Rather, he believed that punishment served to direct behavior to more satisfying S–R connections. Thorndike's laws do provide an explanation of how S–R bonds are stamped-in, strengthened, weakened, and stamped-out.

For example, the teacher asks the class, "What is the square root of 144?" A student raises her hand and answers, "12." The teacher says, "excellent." The S–R connection that the square root of 144 equals 12 is stamped in and strengthened.

Rewarding Learning Time (grades K–5)

The amount of time the student is actively engaged in learning correlates positively with the achievement level (United States Department of Education, 1986). To make the best use of the student's learning time, props can be used as an enticement for strengthening math skills. The teacher can make one-dimensional, construction-paper facsimiles of pencils and big erasers. Math problems can be written on the pencils with the answers on the underside of the erasers. The matching color and decoration of pencils and erasers can denote the corresponding level or type of math problem (yellow pencil and eraser for simple addition, yellow pencil and eraser with blue stars for column addition, green for fractions, red for word problems). A cardboard container, decorated as a pencil sharpener, can be used to hold both pencils and erasers. In their spare time, the students can go to the chalkboard with the pencils and erasers to work, master, and check the problems. These colorful teaching aids can be used as rewards upon completion of assigned desk work (Hancock, 1991).

Stimulus: The teacher asks the class, "What is the square root of 144?"
Response: The student answers, "12."
Consequence: Reinforcement and approval from the teacher (satisfaction).
S–R Connection: The square root of 144 equals 12.

Thorndike's contribution to stimulus-response or connectionist learning theory laid the groundwork for the related work done by Clark Hull and Neal Miller.

Hull's deductive behaviorism or reinforcement theory was focused on what occurs between the stimulus and the response. Hence, for Hull, the S–R model became an S–O–R model with "O" representing the organism. He viewed learning as occurring through the biological adaptation of the organism to its environment in ways that promoted survival (drive reduction). Drive reduction was viewed as a state of need existing within the organism such as the need for food or water. The organism, when confronted by any shortage or pain (drive or stimulus), goes into action. Actions or behaviors (response) that reduce the shortage or relieve the pain are reinforced. Hull explained differences in response among organisms as being caused by several intervening variables within the organism such as habit strength, deprivation level (drive), incentive, fatigue (reactive inhibition), and rest (conditioned inhibition).

Miller believed that learning could be broken down into four elements: *drive, cue, response,* and *reward. Drive* was defined as an aroused state of the organism (stimulus). *Cue* was defined as the stimuli that direct the organism toward a specific response. *Response* referred to the behavior that reduced the drive. *Reward* was the actual drive reduction. Using Miller's theory, Thorndike's puzzle-box escape problem would be explained as follows:

Drive—the level of the cat's hunger or its annoyance about being confined,
Cue—the loop of string,
Response–the cat pulled the loop of string,
Reward—escape and food.

Using Miller's theory, how would you teach one of your classes?

Grammar Usage (grades K–12)

Correcting oral grammar intensifies negative perspectives regarding foreign language learning for the traditional student. The same can be said for those learning English as a second language (ESL) and for learning-disabled students. Focusing on the actual communication through behavioral modeling is best for reinforcing positive learning attitudes. By rephrasing the student's statement or idea correctly, the attention is on the process and not the mistake (Gaustad & Messenheimer-Young, 1991).

Students are given a grammatical rule with its examples. After a few correct prototypes, give an example of the exceptions. The students will use the rule incorrectly, of course, with the "exception" example. The teacher acknowledges the class's error and gives immediate feedback with the corrected answer and reason for it. A higher retention rate of the exceptions to the rules is learned when this prompted trial-and-error correction method is used.

Applying Miller's drive reduction theory to your next snack, you would have the following sequence:

Drive—You feel hungry,
Cue—Refrigerator,
Response—Fix and eat a sandwich,
Reward—Hunger is gone, and you feel good.

In bonding terms, the above sequence or chain of events could be represented as Drive—Cue—Response—Reward.

Let us apply Miller's theory to teaching mathematics. How could the drive or need for our students to learn math be developed? It could be taught before lunch with popcorn as a reward for successful work. Ways could be found to challenge students by teaching math with games or with computers (Hammer, 1986; 1987). Class could be made fun and people will work when the reward is fun. Cooperative learning teams could be formed to use the rewards of working together as a team in competition with another team. Teacher verbal approval of work well done is rewarding as is the intrinsic reward of mastering a difficult subject. Teachers have the responsibility to provide the mediating learning steps (cues and responses) that take students step-by-step from where they are in their learning to where they need and want (if the job has been done) to be.

As was true with Hull, drive reduction in Miller's system became the basic operation in learning and motivation as it reinforced the response that came before it. The heavy emphasis on reward separates Thorndike, Hull, and Miller from Pavlov, Watson, and Guthrie.

Burrhus F. Skinner

Burrhus F. Skinner is perhaps the most famous name associated with behaviorism or connectionist theories of learning. Lattal (1992), writing on the career of

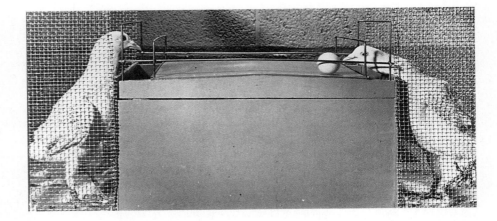

Skinner demonstrated the effectiveness of behaviorism in a variety of ways. In 1950, he trained two pigeons to play soccer through the use of operant conditioning.

Write, in your own words, a correct definition of operant conditioning. Include one classroom example of operant or instrumental conditioning.

B. F. Skinner, pointed out that his death in 1990 ended six decades of prominence in psychology. His first paper was published in 1930 and his last in 1990. In fact, he worked on his final paper the evening before his death. According to Cook (1991), in 1989 the citation of Skinner's name in psychological literature exceeded that of Sigmund Freud's. Contrary to popular belief, Skinner (1904–1990) was not a stimulus-response theorist in the same sense as were Watson, Guthrie, Thorndike, and Hull. Rather, Skinner was more of a response-stimulus theorist who believed that our random behavior continued or discontinued depending on the consequences following the behavior. In effect, he viewed the behavior-reinforcement process as a circular process in which the reinforcing stimulus acted as a stimulus for repeating the behavior that elicited the positive consequence.

Skinner was influenced by Thorndike's writings and his work on the law of effect. Skinner's (1938) principle of reinforcement was a modification of the law of effect. He believed that if the occurrence of an operant is followed by the presentation of a reinforcing stimulus, the strength [of the operant] is increased.

Skinner defined operant behavior as that behavior that is instrumental in achieving a desired goal. In fact, operant behavior also is known as instrumental behavior. Operant behavior refers to how people change or operate upon their environment to meet their needs.

Operant conditioning is a learning process that is based on the consequences of behavior. Rewarded behaviors are likely to be repeated while punished behaviors are not. Skinner was not as preoccupied as were Thorndike and Hull about why a particular reinforcer was reinforcing. He was content with identifying effective reinforcers and those operants that they influenced because that was all he needed to predict and control behavior. Thus, he was able to ignore the concepts of readiness and intervening variables. Skinner believed that Pavlov's work on respondent conditioning was adequate for explaining reflex behaviors that are automatically elicited by certain stimuli such as an eye blink following a loud noise or a puff of air.

Skinner was more interested in studying operant behavior, which he believed to be the basis for learning more complex behaviors such as playing the piano. He defined behavior as an observable, measurable action produced by the organism. Learning was defined as occurring when a new behavior was produced or an existing behavior was modified.

Skinner's primary contribution to psychology and education may be the organization of behavior theory into a workable technology available for use by teachers, parents, psychologists, counselors, school administrators, and business executives.

Skinner's technology is centered in the operant conditioning method (also known as instrumental conditioning). Basically, the method is directed toward increasing or decreasing the frequency of certain existing behaviors. It also is used to teach or condition new behaviors and to unlearn old behaviors. Basically the method works by applying one of four possible consequences following the occurrence of a specific behavior. Two of the consequences are designed to initiate or to increase the frequency of behavior: positive reinforcement and negative reinforcement. Just remember that the term reinforcement always refers to building up or strengthening a behavior. Positive reinforcement refers to the presentation of a positive or rewarding consequence following a desired behavior. For example, students could be granted free time for accumulating points for academic achievement and on-task behaviors. Negative reinforcement refers to the removal of a negative or punishing consequence following a desired behavior. For example, if your students do well on their class project, they could be excused from taking the final examination (a definite negative consequence).

The other two consequences are designed to extinguish or decrease the frequency of a behavior. Punishment refers to the presentation of something negative or the removal of something positive following an undesired behavior. For example, students could be required to repair damage they did to their school building or they could lose free-time points. Extinction refers to the withholding of a reinforcing consequence following an undesired behavior. For example, when one of your students is seeking attention through disruptive behavior, attention can be withheld by ignoring the student or by removing the student's audience by isolating the student in a time-out room until the student is finished doing the disruptive behavior.

Skinner preferred to focus his attention on reinforcing appropriate behavior rather than punishing inappropriate behavior. He believed that punishment served to bring about short-term suppression of the misbehavior but did little to extinguish it on a permanent basis. Skinner also was concerned about the undesirable side effects of punishment, which include deteriorating relationships, revenge, anger, aggressiveness, anxiety, and fear.

Skinner's behavioral technology included the use of unconditioned and conditioned reinforcers. *Unconditioned reinforcers* or *primary reinforcers* have inherent value. Examples of unconditioned reinforcers are food and water. *Conditioned reinforcers* or *secondary reinforcers,* such as points, money, tokens, and grades, acquire their reinforcing value through their association with primary reinforcers. For example, one hundred points earns thirty minutes of free time.

Schedule of Reinforcement. Two schedules of reinforcement are used in reinforcing the acquisition and establishment of a new behavior: continuous and intermittent schedules. Continuous reinforcement, the reinforcement of each

What types of reinforcers would you use in your classroom? Primary, secondary, both, or none? Why or why not?

successful response, is best when the new behavior is first being learned. However, once the new behavior is established, continuous reinforcement actually has the effect of extinguishing the behavior through satiation of the learner. Therefore, it is better to switch to one of four intermittent schedules: fixed interval, variable interval, fixed ratio, and variable ratio.

Fixed Interval Schedule. On fixed interval schedules, reinforcement is provided on the first response occurring after a fixed time has elapsed. The best example of a fixed interval schedule is the hourly wage paid on a weekly basis. Level of production on a fixed interval schedule is unrelated to reinforcement and, therefore, is likely to be lower. Production would tend to increase right before the next pay period and decrease after it. In experimental settings, laboratory animals on a fixed interval schedule could be reinforced every thirty seconds regardless of the number of correct responses they might make. Again, responses would tend to increase before the reinforcement period and decrease shortly thereafter. Teachers may have noted how study behavior increases before scheduled examinations and decreases after the examinations.

Variable Interval Schedule. Variable interval schedules provide for reinforcement on the first response occurring after some average period of time. One example of a variable interval schedule would be to give your students a series of unscheduled pop quizzes during the semester with different lengths of time between quizzes. The variable interval schedule quizzes have the effect of increasing study behavior but at the price of increasing your students' anxiety and decreasing your popularity as their teacher. In a laboratory setting, animals could be reinforced at different time intervals that would average thirty seconds over a daylong period. Once again, reinforcement would not depend on production; however, production would increase as more time elapses from the last reinforcement period. The U.S. mail, often delivered on a variable interval schedule, induces mailbox-checking behavior as the anticipated delivery time nears.

Which reinforcement schedules would work best in your classroom? What are the strengths and weaknesses for each schedule?

Fixed Ratio Schedule. Piece work in a business setting is a good example of fixed ratio reinforcement. The worker is paid for a certain number of products completed. Laboratory animals would be reinforced for every five, ten, or twenty responses made. Constant, high rates of performance are produced on fixed ratio schedule; however, quality controls may be needed to ensure that quality does not suffer as quantity increases.

Variable Ratio Schedule. Playing a slot machine would be a good example of variable ratio reinforcement. The player could be reinforced on a schedule varying from five to twenty-five handle pulls averaging ten pulls per reinforcement. As people with a gambling addition can attest, the variable ratio schedule of reinforcement is most resistant to extinction and produces the greatest responses frequency. The same finding holds true for animals reinforced on a variable ratio schedule.

Shaping is the principal technique developed by Skinner to demonstrate operant conditioning. Shaping is a process whereby the subject or participant is reinforced for successive appropriations until the target behavior is mastered. For example, in teaching a pigeon to peck a ball, the pigeon would be reinforced each time it moved near the ball until it touched the ball and then until it actually pecked the ball. When shaping is occurring, all the unwanted behaviors are extinguished because they receive no reinforcement. Eventually using shaping, Skinner was able to teach pigeons to engage in a spirited game of soccer where reinforcement (food) could only be earned by pecking the ball past the opponent.

Chaining is a concept used to explain how complex behavior such as piano playing is learned through operant conditioning. In chaining, stimuli function as both secondary reinforcers for the correct behavior and discriminative stimuli for the next behavior in the chain of responses leading to the primary reinforcer.

Summary

The chapter begins with a review of personal learning styles followed by a historical discussion of behavioral learning theory from Pavlov to Skinner. The teaching machine, pioneered by Sidney Pressey in the 1920s and developed into programmed instruction by Skinner (1987), reinforces students by giving them immediate feedback on their responses to questions. Computer-assisted instruction is today's version of the teaching machine. Skinner viewed the computer teaching machine as a way to provide each student with an individual tutor. Skinner's teaching machine provided a method for breaking major learning tasks down into a sequence of smaller steps. Learners are provided with information and direction as they are reinforced for correct responses and corrected for wrong answers. Computer-assisted instruction (CAI) is individualized and permits students to work at their own pace. Skinner (1968 and 1990) believed that students needed something more than being told or shown how to do something. He recommended that teachers arrange the contingencies of reinforcement to facilitate learning. Three variables are involved: (a) an occasion upon which the behavior occurs (antecedent conditions), (b) the behavior, and (c) the consequences. Teachers have the task of providing the best possible learning environments, observing the behaviors, and reinforcing the resulting appropriate behaviors.

Chapter Review

1. Identify your preferred and backup style of learning. Explain how you adapt to a style of teaching that does not accommodate your learning style preference.
2. What can you do to assure that your instructional methods will accommodate the different learning styles in your classroom? Be specific in the examples you present for each learning style.
3. Define learning in your words using examples to make your point.
4. If you could interview Pavlov, Watson, Guthrie, Thorndike, Miller, and Skinner, what would they give as their best advice to teachers on how to increase their students' learning? Rank orders the theorists according to the degree of help given to teachers. Be prepared to defend your ranking.

ACTIVE LEARNING TECHNIQUES SUCCEED

The disruption from the students asking questions in Ms. Brooks's Social Studies class did not seem to bother their teacher. Ms. Brooks said, "I forgot, again, and I have been doing too much talking and too little demonstration and practice. We'll switch to more active learning for you right-brain thinkers. Tell you what; suppose you wanted to help a person stop certain irritating behavior, how could you use operant conditioning to make it happen?" The students looked challenged and seemed to perk up as they involved themselves in the discussion. It was not long before the students came up with ways to apply each of the four operant conditioning methods; then the teacher let the students practice ways to conduct each of the four conditioning processes. For example, shaping through positive reinforcement and extinction was practiced by sending students out of the room (one at a time), naming a task for them to do such as writing on the board, bringing them back into the room, and teaching them the task through *positive reinforcement* and *extinction*. The students were applauded when they made a "good" move and ignored when they made a bad move or did nothing. *Punishment* was taught the same way by booing other students each time a wrong move was made as the students tried to discover the task. *Negative reinforcement* was taught by having the class members hiss when the student reentered the room and continue to hiss until the student made a right move. Hissing resumed the moment a wrong move was made and continued until the next right move. The class was fun and ended too soon for the students. Best of all, they learned how to define and use the four operant methods. The teacher accommodated the learning styles of those students who do not respond well to lecture classes without demonstration and practice.

Discuss some ways that you could use to involve your "right-brain" thinkers in the subject matter that you teach. Remember that learning and recall are directly related to the degree to which we use the student's visual, auditory, and kinesthetic senses in processing the information we are teaching. In other words, how can you use active learning in your classroom?

REFERENCES

American Psychological Association (1992). *Learner-centered psychological principles: Guidelines for school redesign and reform (Draft #3).* Washington, DC: American Psychological Association.

Barkman, D. (1991). *Training others.* Knoxville, TN: The Business Center.

Berensten, J. (1991). Word of the day. *Instructor 100*(9), 100.

Cook, D. (1991). B. F. Skinner: The man with pigeons and persistence. *Bostonia*, 56–58.

Cox, G. (1990). Game plans: lucky 7. *The Mailbox, 12*(3), 39.

Crosson, B. (1991). Overnight reading Buddy. *Instructor, 100*(5), 62–70.

Dale, E. (1969). *Audiovisual methods in teaching* (3rd ed.). New York: Holt, Rinehart, and Winston, Inc.

Dunn, R., Dunn, K., & Price, G. (1989). *Learning style inventory.* Lawrence, KS: Price Systems.

Estes, W. (1969). Reinforcement in human learning. In J. Tapp (Ed.), *Reinforcement and behavior.* New York: Academic Press.

Gagné, R. & Rohwer, W. (1985). Instructional psychology. In W. E. Jeffrey (Ed.), *Psychology of work behavior.* Chicago: Dorsey Press.

Gaustad, M. G., & Messenheimer-Young, T. (1991). Dialogue journals for students with learning disabilities. *Teaching Exceptional Children, 23*(3), 28–32.

Hallinan, M.T., & Williams, T.A. (1990). Students' characteristics and the peer-influence process. *Sociology of Education, 63*(2) 122–132.

Hammer, C. (1986). *Math shop.* New York: Scholastic, Inc.

Hammer, C. (1987). *Algebra shop.* New York: Scholastic, Inc.

Hancock, S. (1991). Teachers express: Sharpen your skills. *Instructor, 100,* (7), 106.

Harbaugh, M. (1990). Celebrating diversity. *Instructor, 100*(2), 45–48.

Heff, D. (1961). Distinctive features of learning in the higher animal. In J. F. Delafresnoye (Ed.), *Brain mechanisms and learning.* Oxford: Blackwell.

Heese, V. (1990–91). Let your fingers do the figuring: Incorporating math manipulatives in the classroom. *The Mailbox, 12*(6), 43.

Hirumi, A., & Bowers, D. (1991). Enhancing motivation and acquisition of coordinate concepts by using concept trees. *Journal of Education Research, 84*(5), 273–279.

Lattal, K. (1992). B.F. Skinner and psychology. *American Psychologist, 47*(11), 1269–1272.

Macintyre, P., & Gardner, R.C. (1991). Investigating language class anxiety using the focused essay technique. *The Modern Language Journal, 75*(3), 296–304.

Mackenzie, A. & White, R. (1982). Fieldwork in geography and long-term memory structure. *American Educational Research Journal, 19*(4), 623–632.

Malone, J. (1990). *Theories of learning: A historical approach.* Belmont, CA: Wadsworth Publishing Company.

Martin, R. (1988, August). Play the game: Make technical theory fun. *Vocational Education Journal, 63*(5), 39.

McGehe, C.A. (1991). Mathematics the write way. *Instructor, 100*(8), 36–38.

Piaget, J. (1930). *The child's conception of physical causality.* New York: Harcourt, Brace, Jovanovich.

Simpson, J. (1991). Students learn math skills by playing the stock market. *Curriculum Review, 31*(1), 20.

Skinner, B. (1938). *The behavior of organisms.* New York: Appleton-Century-Crofts.

Skinner, B. (1968). *The technology of teaching.* New York: Appleton-Century-Crofts.

Skinner, B. (1987). Programmed instruction revisited. *The Education Digest, 52,* 12–16.

Skinner, B. (1990). Can psychology be a science of mind? *American Psychologist, 45*(11), 1206–1210.

Smith, P.C. (1980). Electrifying current events. *Teacher, 98*(3), 74–80.

United States Department of Education. (1986). *What works: Research about teaching and learning.* Washington, DC: Office of Educational Research and Improvement.

Wolpe, J. (1958). *Psychotherapy by reciprocal inhibition.* Stanford, CA: Stanford University Press.

Wolpe, J. (1969). *The practice of behavior therapy.* New York: Pergamon Press.

CHAPTER 9

COGNITIVE APPROACHES TO LEARNING

■ ■ ■

Chapter Outline

UNCERTAIN ABOUT INNOVATIVE INSTRUCTIONAL PROGRAM

Margaret was beginning a new teaching job in a fifth-grade classroom in the West Creek District noted for its innovative instructional program. She had been informed that all teachers were expected to use cooperative learning in their curriculum. In researching the subject, Margaret found that teachers generally are reluctant to alter the traditional, control-oriented classroom environment. The majority of teachers preferred the authoritative, teacher-centered environment typified by lecture, reading, paper and pen, and quiet students. The comfort and safety of this conventional teaching style is preferred despite the overwhelming data indicating the strength of the more nontraditional, cooperative learning methods and peer tutoring techniques (Blanton, 1991). She read that the overall success of cooperative learning depends on two factors: (1) shared group goals and (2) individual accountability (Slavin, 1990). The enhancement of interpersonal skills, flexibility in thought, and increase in motivation are the desired outcomes of this mutual learning and sharing of information.

Margaret discovered that cooperative learning can be divided into three models: jigsaw, investigative, and cybernetic. The scenario for the jigsaw format, the first model, has the teacher presenting a subject to the class, which has been divided into small groups. The subject is then divided like a jigsaw puzzle among the individual group members for further exploration and problem solving as the group members work to fit the pieces of the puzzle or problem together. The second model, group investigation, has the total subject or "puzzle" given to each team to work or solve. Group members cooperate as they compete with other groups. Cybernetics, the third model, provides a problem-solving approach to cooperative learning. A direct or implied concept, subject, or problem is introduced in question form by the teacher.

INTRODUCTION

Chapter 9 begins with a discussion of how four different cognitive approaches to learning contribute to our understanding of how people learn. Contributions from Edward Tolman, Max Wertheimer, Jean Piaget, and Jerome Bruner are presented with the best ideas they have to offer teachers. Implicit in all learning theories is a concept of what motivates people to learn. As was true with their behavioral colleagues in chapter 8, the cognitive theorists also discuss the motivational factors in their systems of learning. The chapter concludes with a discussion of eclectic approaches to learning which integrate the best information from behavioral and cognitive theories into one approach to learning. Robert Gagné's eclectic theory of learning provides a useful summary of how parts of behavioral and cognitive learning theory can be combined in one comprehensive approach to understanding the learning process. He classified learning theories into a hierarchy of eight levels ranging from the lowest to the highest form of learning.

A crescendo effect can be gained by presenting escalating problems or questions (three to five) to each group to be encountered on a rotating basis. For example, the teacher would state the time allocated per question and give a one minute closure announcement for each time period. Each group may prefer to assign timekeeping responsibilities to a particular member (Guiton, 1991). Sample questions for an environment unit could include: "What do you or your friends recycle?" "What could be the personal advantages or problems of recycling?" "What would be the consequences of recycling on a global scale?" and "What can you do regarding this subject?" These different inquiries draw the students through a process of sharing experiences and information with others and expanding personal boundaries of thought.

Cooperative learning groups or teams should include students who do not normally work together. Teachers may enjoy a competitive element by instructing each student to place all subject-pertinent materials (handouts, study sheets, and homework) into an individual folder that is then placed into a team envelope. After sufficient time to organize materials, each student is given a teacher-prepared questionnaire. If done individually, collect all the team members' correct/incorrect numbers to compute the team score; if done as a team, simply obtain the numbers from the teams' questionnaires. The winning team is the one with highest ratio of correct to incorrect answers. Everyone can be a winner in this enjoyable activity (Roblee, 1991).

Vivian Haun, a doctoral student in Educational and Counseling Psychology at the University of Tennessee, wrote the material on cooperative learning in the case study and the classroom applications.

KEY CONCEPTS

- Discovery learning and problem-solving learning are most likely to lead to the development of cognitive maps that will help the learner in future problem solving.
- Creative solutions to problems usually come from a person's ability to view the problem in several different ways.
- Achievement of insight requires the learner to group the separate parts of a problem situation into a meaningful system (whole), which leads to the solution of the problem.
- Levels of readiness to learn, as well as levels of cognitive development, must be considered for each school subject taught. Developmental and readiness levels may differ across school subjects.
- Teaching methods should be balanced between telling, showing, and doing.

COGNITIVE APPROACHES TO LEARNING

Cognitive theorists include Max Wertheimer, Kurt Koffka, and Wolfgang Kohler, who developed and supported insight learning that became the hallmark of their Gestalt learning theory. Other cognitive theorists include Edward Tolman, who supported the concept of latent learning (learning that occurs without reinforcement), Jean Piaget, who identified and studied four stages of cognitive development, and Jerome Bruner, who is interested in how people organize, classify, and store information for future use.

Edward C. Tolman

Edward C. Tolman (1886–1959) referred to himself as a behaviorist; however, in addition to being influenced by Watson, he also was influenced by Gestalt learning theory. Tolman might even be classified as a cognitive theorist in the behavioral tradition. At least he did find some common ground between behaviorism and Gestalt psychology. As a behaviorist, Tolman opposed introspective psychology, which was directed toward the study of mental processes and subjective individual experience. On the other hand, Tolman did embrace the Gestalt view of molar behavior as being the important unit of study rather than the behaviorist emphasis on molecular behavior. In other words, he considered the behavioral act (molar behavior) to be the unit for psychological study rather than the individual behaviors (molecular behavior) contained within the act. Playing the piano is a molar behavior made up of several smaller or molecular behaviors.

Tolman was committed to the concept of purposive behavior. He believed that all behavior was goal directed, be it securing a reward or avoiding a punishment. He also believed that several things happened between the stimulus and the response to that stimulus. However, his definitions of these intervening variables were not as precise as Hull's. Tolman concluded from his many studies of rat learning that an organism learns about the environment rather than just reacting to it. He believed that organisms made use of tools, signs, and pathways to find the shortest route to their goal; Tolman concluded that their behavior was both purposive and cognitive. He found that rats that had learned to walk through a maze also could swim through it even though swimming required different muscle responses. In fact, learning even occurred when the rats were pulled through the maze in a basket with no responses being reinforced. He found that rats that earned no reward for the first days in a maze may have learned more about the maze than did the rats that were totally focused on the food in the goal box. He referred to this learning without reward as latent learning. Incidental or hidden learning that occurred unobserved also was classified by Tolman as being latent learning. All of the experiences mentioned above contributed to the forming of cognitive maps that, according to Tolman, serve to guide a person through the next problem-solving or decision-making situations.

Purposive behavior and cognition were central to Tolman's theory. He believed that behavior was purposive and was directed to the goal of securing something good or avoiding something bad. In contrast to the stimulus-response theories that hold that the learner is encouraged by stimuli, Tolman believed that

Can you think of a skill you learned which required you to learn how to do some smaller skills before mastering the larger skill?

the learner followed signs to a goal. In other words, the learner learned a behavior route (cognitive map) rather than movement patterns implied in S–R theory. Tolman defined two classes of signs or behavior supports the learner needs to reach or avoid a goal: discriminanda and manipulanda. Discriminanda are the characteristics and qualities of objects that enable the learner to make the sensory discriminations necessary to discover how to reach or avoid goal objects. These qualities include taste, odors, colors, and tones. Manipulanda are the characteristics of objects, such as a maze pathway, that can be used to reach or avoid the goal object. These qualities include length, width, solidity, fluidity, and weight. A third behavior support required for the successful learning environment was something Tolman referred to as means-end-relations or cognitive maps. If the learner is to achieve a purpose or goal, he will need to have the knowledge and skills necessary to compete the task. For example, the knowledge of direction and distance would be helpful in planning and completing a journey. Another example would be the cognitive map you have of your hometown that allows you to find alternative routes to your destination when a street is blocked.

Tolman (1932) wrote that behavior is a function of the situation and other antecedent causes (B = F [S, A]). He believed that several variables intervened between stimulus and response and referred to these variables as behavior determinants. In fact, he developed three classes of these intervening variables: *capacities, behavior adjustments,* and *immanent determinants.*

Capacities refer to the learner's talents, knowledge, skills, and aptitudes that are products of the learner's heredity and environment. *Behavior adjustments* refer to the problem-solving process the learner employs to find alternative solutions to problems. Strategies could run from trial and error to the scientific method (see Applications from the Text 9.1). In fact, the process would be sim-

> When you find yourself confronted by a new problem situation, do you try old problem-solving methods before experimenting with new ones or do you plunge right in with new problem-solving methods?

APPLICATIONS FROM THE TEXT 9.1

Simulated Shopping (grades 1–6)

Familiar, physical objects are effective as learning tools for elementary-level mathematics (United States Department of Education, 1986). Simulated shopping is a good technique for practicing money skills, addition, and subtraction. Have the students bring a variety of clean, empty, unbreakable grocery containers (such as plastic ketchup containers, Styrofoam egg cartons, empty soup/sauce envelope packets) to class. Place a purchase price on each item and stock it in an appointed shopping area. Play money should be located at the shopping area. First, have the students purchase one item daily using the play money. Subsequently, have the students make a shopping list of a few items to purchase. The bill should be added and correct change can be counted. Students can also bring their home grocery receipts to school for practicing addition and calculating taxes. (Dywan, 1991). The ability to estimate mathematical answers indicates an understanding of the problem. This leads the student either to reject unreasonable answers or to proceed further. The learned skill of estimating is both practical for everyday activities and beneficial for numerous areas of math and science (United States Department of Education). Grocery shopping receipts are a practical and plentiful resource to be used for rounding numbers and estimating totals.

Vivian Haun wrote the applications for this chapter.

ilar to Piaget's assimilation-accommodation model in which the learner attempts to assimilate the problem into the old cognitive map or schema (see Applications from the Text 9.2). When the problem cannot be solved in the old way, the learner has to accommodate or revise the old system to handle the new problem. Tolman believed learning occurred when previous learning was no longer appropriate or found lacking to solve a problem. *Immanent determinants* refer to purposes and cognitions, neither of which can be directly observed in the laboratory setting. Purpose can be compared with the drive a learner has to achieve or to avoid a goal object. There are two types of cognitions or cognitive maps: *means-end-readiness* and *sign-Gestalt-expectation*. Means-end-readiness is a belief that certain behaviors will lead to a desired goal or avoidance of an undesired situation. Sign-Gestalt-expectation refers to an expectation or a hypothesis that an object will be helpful in obtaining a desired outcome when the need arises. For example, you feel hungry and immediately recall where the nearest snack is located (drive reduction).

Tolman believed that all behavior is purposive or goal directed. Each action is undertaken as a means to achieve an end.

Guessing Games (grades K–4)

Early grade students can acquire the concept of number values and enjoy a guessing game at the same time. This involves their guessing how many items are in a clear plastic jar. The guesses can be recorded and any winner can receive a prize, for example, of free reading time. The jar's contents can be changed weekly using items of different shapes and sizes. Their guesses will be more accurate as the year progresses and as their concepts of number and volume develop. (Shires, 1991).

In summary, Tolman's theory makes a case for discovery learning and problem-solving teaching methods if students develop broad and comprehensive cognitive maps of their environment. Extrinsic reinforcement of learning may even cause our students to focus more on the reward than on the concepts that are being taught. Rewarding academic achievement with extrinsic rewards may even detract further from learning. Students may get the message that learning without pay is a bad deal and learning, by itself, is not rewarding. Tolman also makes a good case for considering students' readiness levels for learning new material (see Applications from the Text 9.3). In fact, he would seem to support an individualized approach to teaching that would include a thorough consideration of his long list of intervening variables that affect learning.

Gestalt Psychology: Wertheimer, Kohler, and Koffka

Gestalt psychology was founded in Germany in the years surrounding 1916 by Max Wertheimer (1880–1943). He enlisted the aid of Wolfgang Kohler (1887–1967) and Kurt Koffka (1886–1941), who acted as research subjects for his experiments on the perception of motion. The two subjects became his junior partners in developing Gestalt psychology. These three Gestalt psychologists opposed the introspectionists' attempts to analyze the mind of breaking it down into its basic elements, as well as the behaviorists' attempts to analyze behavior by studying its basic stimulus-response elements. They believed that experience cannot be broken down into ideas, affect, sensations, and behaviors that are connected by the laws of association. Instead, they believed that people organized their worlds into meaningful wholes (Gestalten). Reduction of those wholes or Gestalten into their basic parts would cause the loss of the experience of the object itself. In other words, the whole is greater than the sum of its parts. For example, the experience of listening to a total band or orchestra is lost if one isolates each player and listens only to that player's part. In fact, it is the interaction of all the parts that creates the total effect or experience. Just adding all the parts together will not give the total effect.

Gestalt is a common German noun that refers to a form, pattern, or configuration consisting of interdependent but separate parts (Malone, 1990; Hill,

Can you explain how a coach might use Gestalt learning theory to teach athletes to play more effectively as a team?

Book Baskets (grades K–7)

A big basket filled with engaging picture and word books can be an enticing stimulus to enjoy. Have the basket placed in a low traffic area where students can relax and read for leisure (Puetz, 1990).

Reading Dyads (grades 1–3)

Greater improvement is made when reading aloud relatively difficult books rather than silently reading easier books. Best results occur when two students have an individual copy of the same book. Each student takes a turn reading to the teacher as the other student simultaneously reads silently. When the reading becomes eloquent for both partners they choose a new book to begin (Eldredge, 1991).

Once Upon a Time Around the World (grades 3–12)

Multicultural experiences can be promoted through reading. Share ideas and concepts concerning folktales with the students. Have a class discussion after reading a popular folktale. Then discuss the purpose that folktales serve for the indigenous culture. Small groups can discuss reading from examples that include from India "How the Duck Got His Bill," and the African "Why the Sun and the Moon Live in the Sky." The librarian can assist in acquiring a list of available cultural folktales. The students can select and read their own choices. Finally, have the students create their own folktales and share in either a large or a small group (Reckord, 1988).

Do you think it is possible to learn how to focus and concentrate on one thing at a time while putting other distractions in the background? How would this ability to make the task at hand figural while relegating everything else in your perceptual field to ground make you a better student or athlete?

1985). The parts are integrated into the whole because of their proximity and function. As a whole the parts have order and meaning; each part points beyond itself and implies the larger whole (Koffka, 1935). In other words, an example of a Gestalt could be a jigsaw puzzle in which each part derives its meaning from its contribution to the order and meaning represented in the completed puzzle.

Wertheimer's work on visual perception showed that when a stationary object was presented at different positions successively during brief intervals of time (e.g., motion picture film), the object appeared to move. Obviously the apparent movement could not be explained by just one part of the progression. The individual components or summation of these components were meaningless without seeing the totality of all components together.

The Gestalt is the totality of what Wertheimer (1924) referred to as the total structure. According to his perceptual theory, perceptions included an integration of thoughts, feelings, emotions, attitudes, and sensations. Perceptions consist of the figure, or point of interest, and the ground, or context, in which the figure occurs. For example, in a photograph or painting of a landscape, a tree could be the figure with the rest of the picture serving as background or ground. However, should we focus on those parts of the painting other than the tree, those parts would become the figure. The behavioral environment, which comprises everything in our conscious awareness, is differentiated into figure and ground. Gestalt learning theorists would argue that we must understand the whole before we can find meaning in the parts. For example, in studying geography, the Gestalt point of view would be to start with the solar system and work back through the planet earth to individual countries, states, and counties.

Wertheimer (1945; 1959) emphasized the importance of centering and recentering on the significant parts of a problem situation. The *centering* process is a type of reorganization or reorientation that allows one to view a problem in a different light or from a different perspective. Creative solutions to problems usually come from a person's ability to view the problem several different ways or at least in uncommon ways.

Centering is what people perceive. The meaning they derive from a perception depends on the significance of the figure and their frame of reference. Wertheimer (1959) wrote that centering is the way one views the meaning and role of the parts in regard to the center or core of the situation. Objectivity in centering may be clouded by emotions and egocentric thinking. Consequently, people must change or recenter their frame of reference until they become sufficiently objective to solve the problem. Reframing and recentering are part of the learning process. In fact, Wertheimer described productive thinking as a process of successive restructuring of a problem. The structural features of the problem create stresses and tensions within the learner. The stresses and tensions hold the learner to successive problem restructurings until the solution emerges. Through thoughtful reflection, the learner can combine what she already knows with what she is learning from the present situation (assimilation and accommodation) to reach a new understanding (equilibrium).

The process of reframing changes the figure as the ground is changed. It allows one to see new solutions and alternatives that were not previously seen. The behavior of changing one's perspective produces learning through insight. Gestalt learning theorists view learning as a thinking process that involves interactions within the learner that lead to a search for a solution. They believe that people do not use simple trial-and-error problem-solving approaches. Rather, they use a repertoire of past learning and a hypothesis-testing approach that allow them to restructure and change their problem-solving methods in a systematic way (see Applications from the Text 9.4). They also believe that learning is much more than a conditioned habit. Wertheimer (1959) believed that learning involved a perception of the situation as a whole as well as a perception of those parts that provide pathways to the goal. The transition from unknowing to mastery defines insight.

Wertheimer also coined the principle of Pragnanz, which asserts that the organization of the field tends to be as simple and clear as the given conditions allow. In other words, the Pragnanz principle is the tendency to form the good Gestalt or a clear, perceptual understanding of the whole situation and its parts (see Applications from the Text 9.5). There are wholes that behave in ways that are independent from the behavior of their individual elements; however, the behavior of these elements in combination are determined by the nature of the whole. For example, in water, H_2O, you have the two separate elements of hydrogen and oxygen, which have their own individual properties. When these two elements

Can you think of a time when you stepped back and took a different view of a problem and suddenly found a way to solve it?

Volleyball vs. Ping-Pong Ball (grades 5–8)

Scientific explanations may dispute what the students consider to be naturally correct. Observing a volleyball fall at the same speed as a Ping-Pong ball can disprove the wrongly held assumption that the heavier weight and the larger size will cause the volleyball to fall faster. Despite both the teacher's explanation and the textbook, the student may not completely release the false assumption and comprehend the theory until it is observed in a hands-on demonstration (United States Department of Education, 1986). Many students need the opportunities to investigate and witness scientific experiments. Direct observation can alter the most rigid misconceptions. For best results, students should be given the opportunity to predict the experimental results. As in the earlier mathematics example, tally the students' predicted results regarding the first ball to hit the ground: volleyball or Ping-Pong ball. After the tally has been noted and the experiment's results have been observed, the teacher can reveal why the students' first prediction was erroneous. Participation and observation of scientific methods can assist students in detecting facts from fallacies. Both cognitive comprehension and analysis can be strengthened through the experiment's application. (United States Department of Education.)

are combined in the right proportions and under the right conditions they form the compound of water, which also has its own individual properties.

A good Gestalt has such properties as regularity, stability, and simplicity. Gestalt theorists believe that learners act as intelligently as they can under the circumstances that confront them in order to achieve insightful solutions to problems. Kohler (1925) attempted to prove the concept of insight learning in his study with a caged chimpanzee who was given two sticks that could be fitted together and the task of reaching a banana that was out of reach of either stick. After the chimp made several unsuccessful attempts to reach the banana with each stick, he paused, joined the two sticks together, and retrieved the banana. Kohler argued that the chimp had suddenly developed insight into the problem (often referred to as an "aha" experience). Such insight is thought to be the result of internal cognitive restructuring (reorganization) of the perceptual field (environment) that helps the learner solve a problem or achieve a goal. Once again, notice the similarity to Piaget's concept of accommodation of the learner's cognitive structure to handle new material and experiences. Behavioral learning theorists believe that such insightful problem-solving examples are the result of prior conditioning. For example, how do we know that Kohler's chimp did not learn how to join sticks to reach bananas in the jungle prior to his capture? Recently crows were observed dropping walnuts in the street for cars to run over and crush, thereby making the nuts available for their food. Is this insight or the result of conditioning?

The achievement of insight requires the learner to group the separate parts of a problem situation into a meaningful system (whole), which leads to the solution of the problem (see Applications from the Text 9.6). For example, the learner is able to define the problem, visualize the goal, and think of a means to reach the goal. Bringing these three aspects of the problem together to solve the problem closes the Gestalt and provides the learner with the intrinsic reward of the self-satisfaction that results from solving the problem and reducing the tension that accompanies any "unfinished or incomplete" Gestalt.

Koffka (1935) pointed out that some laws of perception proposed by Wertheimer also could be used as a locus of learning because the laws explain how the learner integrates the separate parts of a problem situation into a workable solution (Gestalt). For example, the law of closure acts as a reinforcer when the learner solves the problem. The law of closure states that incomplete objects tend to be completed by the learner. Incomplete circles are viewed as complete circles as the learner fills in the incomplete part of the circle. The same completion would be done for a square or rectangle missing parts of two sides. The law of proximity relates to how the learner organizes units or parts into meaningful groupings. For example, a straight line of dots becomes a line, while the same line of dots spaced differently can become groups of two, three, four, or more.

Wertheimer believed that teachers could help students with insight learning by teaching their students how to view the problem as a whole and work from the whole to the parts of the whole. He recommended that we teach our students to use "A solutions" rather than "B solutions." A "B solution" to a problem is a memorized rule such as finding the area of a rectangle by multiplying the base times the height. "A solutions," on the other hand, teach the principles of calculating area in a way that will allow your students to generalize their learning to finding the area of figures other than rectangles. An example of this would be teaching understanding of what constitutes a square foot so that students transfer the ability to calculate area of rectangles to other geometrical figures such as parallelograms, triangles, and trapezoids.

APPLICATIONS FROM THE TEXT 9.5

The Homemade Ice Cream Principle (grades 4–6)

Science and math can be linked in a demonstration requiring a thermometer, ice cubes, salt, and a cup of water. It is advisable to have a timekeeper to announce every fifteen-second interval point. Students are to record temperature degrees at each of the intervals. First, announce the temperature of a cup of water; keep the thermometer in the cup. The temperature is announced and recorded simultaneously as one ice cube is dropped into the cup of water and stirred at each fifteen-second interval. When thirty-two degrees Fahrenheit is obtained, add salt to the same thirty-two degree water and continue adding salt at fifteen-second intervals. Individual students can later graph the results of each interval. The outcome will reveal salt's decreasing temperature effect on the freezing point of water. The experiment becomes more meaningful if ice cream is made as part of the experiment (Sherman, 1989).

Wertheimer (1959) wrote that two teaching approaches inhibited understanding. The first emphasized the importance of logic and rules that must be followed to reach a conclusion in both deductive and inductive logic. He believed that such an approach inhibited problem solving because it did not allow for emotions, attitudes, perceptions, and intellect to reach an understanding of the problem. Logical steps should be omitted in favor of rearranging the problem components until a solution is reached. The second method emphasized the doctrine of association, which fractured connections through drill, memorization, and reinforcement. Wertheimer believed both approaches ignored the important characteristics of thought processes.

He contended that if learners continually implement productive thinking techniques, solutions to problems become obvious. Wertheimer (1959) presented the following example. How would you compute the sum of $1 + 2 + 3 + 4 + 5 + 6 + 7 + 8 + 9 + 10$? Most students might want to mechanically add the numbers. However, the learner with a productive thinking attitude or learning set might notice that from the two ends of the series going toward the middle, the terms increase and decrease at the same rate. Since $1 + 10 = 11$, $2 + 9 = 11$, $3 + 8 = 11$, and on down the series, the learner notes that there are five pairs of eleven and, therefore, $5 \times 11 = 55$. In this example, a regrouping or reframing has taken place that allowed a new organization to emerge.

Luchins (1942), in a series of problems involving measuring quantities of water in hypothetical water jugs, found that students persisted in using "B solutions" even when the problem was changed and no longer fit the formula they had memorized. A sample of problems included:

If you had three jugs (A, B, and C) that held 21, 127, and 3 units respectively, how could you measure out 100 units?

The formula was B–A–2C for all the problems. However, problems such as the next one, not fitting the old formula, were missed by those students who were relying on "B solutions."

Do you find yourself relying on "B solutions" to solve math and science problems? Do you think "A solutions" might work better during final exams and other times when you have forgotten memorized rules?

APPLICATIONS FROM THE TEXT 9.6

Capillary Action (grades 8–12)

Capillary action can be easily demonstrated by sharply cutting a celery stalk's bottom portion. Place overnight in a glass jar with approximately five centimeters of dark red (red food coloring) water. (If you feel lucky, you may let the students do this; otherwise, it may be safer for you to handle the food coloring.) Let the students hypothesize what they think will happen. The next day the students will see that the red coloring has risen upward through the fine lines to the stalk's top and leaves instead of outward. The explanation of the liquid sticking to the celery's tubes illustrates capillary action. Allow the students to make other associations such as water and a tree and its leaves. Student participation, anticipation, and observation reinforce learning and the higher-order thinking skills (O'Connor, 1990).

If you had three jugs (A, B, and C) that held 23, 55, and 3 units respectively, how could you measure out 20 units?

B–A–4C

Even though Luchin's work was done over fifty years ago, many teachers continue to teach "B solution" for solving problems that emphasize drill and rote memorization of ready-made answers and formulas for ready-made problems that require none of the productive thinking outlined in Gestalt learning theory.

Jean Piaget[1]

As indicated in chapter 3, Jean Piaget provided a theory devoted to the description of cognitive development. Piaget also provided the groundwork for a cognitive model of learning. The framework for his approach to learning and instruction is provided in this section. Piaget (1896–1980) described himself as a genetic epistemologist indicating his interest in growth and his concern with the understanding of knowledge. His research was conducted by using a system of observation, description, and analysis of behavior. From these studies he proposed a theory about the nature and level of conceptual development in children (Piaget, 1952, 1960, 1967, 1969; Piaget & Inhelder, 1969; and Inhelder & Piaget, 1958, 1964). An excellent and more complete explanation of Piaget's thoughts can be found in Wadsworth (1989), Furth (1970), Crain (1992), and Flavell (1963), from which much of the following has been drawn.

Generally, his conclusions were that children are not merely uninformed adults. Rather children have distinctly different ways of viewing the world than

1. Donna A. Henderson Ph.D. wrote the material on Jean Piaget. Henderson is a professor in the Department of Human Development and Learning at East Tennessee State University in Johnson City, Tennessee.

adults do. For Piaget, intelligence is the process of actively constructing an understanding of reality. Interactions with the world are the foundation of that understanding. The basic assumptions of this theory of development are as follows:

1. When they are born, children have some primitive strategies for interacting with the world. These primitive ways of interacting are the starting point in developing thinking.

2. As the child encounters new experiences, changes in these beginning strategies are gradually produced. These changes are the result of assimilation and accommodation. An active interaction with the environment is essential in the developing processes.

3. During childhood and even adolescence, the child constructs a series of theories, or ways of thinking, which are based on the level of understanding that has been achieved so far. According to Piaget, children have consistent ways of changing the abstractions and complexity of thought. Evidence of this consistency, he says, is that all children seem to go through a series of discoveries about the world, make similar mistakes, and arrive at the same solutions. Piaget's theory of cognitive development is founded on the sequence of changes. His theory is an explanation of stages in which children pass through one period before moving to another.

4. Learning skills, maturation, and social interaction are important parts of the developmental process, but the essential ingredient is the child's construction of reality. This construction involves the child actively exploring and experimenting with the environment.

With these basic assumptions as a background, the specifics of the theory can now be considered. To understand Piaget, one must recognize that to him cognitive intelligence includes function, content, and structure. Function refers to the processes of mental activity that continue throughout the developmental process. These functions are cognitive processes that are innate, universal, and independent of age. They will be defined. Content refers to what children know. This knowledge or content varies between ages and between people. Content, therefore, is a part of intelligence that is person specific. Structure consists of the mental categories and strategies that are constructed (schema or schemata). Changes in the structure are what Piaget calls development. The sequence of these structural changes are the developmental stages.

Piaget began his professional studies as a biologist and was influenced by his early work in this field. He originally studied mollusks and was impressed by the interaction of the organism with the environment. Believing that living organisms constantly adapt to their environment, he proposed the principles of adaptation and organization to cognitive development. He theorized that adaptation involved the changes that happen within an individual as a result of interacting with the environment. These are changes in thinking or behaving that allow the person to function more effectively in a situation. Two processes basic to adaptation include assimilation and accommodation. Piaget also theorized that two other important functions occur in the thinking process.

These functions are organization and equilibrium. The following will include further descriptions of these four functions and the processes involved. Before these processes are discussed, Piaget's term schema needs to be explained.

The next time you have the opportunity to play with a toddler in the sensorimotor stage you may want to see if they look for the ball after you place a cup over it. If so, the youngster is beginning to develop an awareness of object permanence.

Through the process of exploring and experimenting with the world, infants begin to understand the objects and people that make up their world. At first children have a few simple action patterns used for this interaction, such as grabbing, sucking, or throwing. Piaget called these action patterns schemes. As they grow older, children's schemes for understanding the world become more complicated and less overt. The child can carry out the scheme mentally. These mental categories and strategies are schemata (the plural of schema). Schema is a sequence of acts that will lead to the solution of a problem. Different kinds of schema emerge during development, but some kind is always present in cognitive functioning. Schemata, therefore, are the substructures that are the foundation of specific types of functioning, which may now be investigated.

The function of adaptation involves the processes of assimilation and accommodation. Assimilation involves a person integrating new matter into an existing mental structure (schema). The object or person or experience is noticed and included into earlier experiences or categories. An example that is often used to illustrate this concept is a child who sees a horse for the first time. The child may call the horse a dog because, for the child, the horse has the characteristics of a dog—an animal with four legs. The horse was assimilated, taken into, the dog

Can you see how developing schemata might be compared to a mental file where old files are continually modified, discarded, or expanded as we encounter new situations?

According to Piaget, children go through a series of discoveries about their world. Each new discovery changes how they think and view their would.

Have you ever been frustrated in trying to convince a six-year-old that the rules of a favorite game needed changing?

schema the child previously had established. Thus that schema becomes larger to incorporate this new material. Assimilation is the process of applying existing ways of thinking to new circumstances.

Sometimes assimilation is not possible. For some reason the new material may not fit into any existing schema. In that case the child can either create a new schema or modify one that already exists. The child who had seen the horse would have to accommodate the four-legged animal schema if someone was riding the horse. For that child, no other experience with four-legged animals included a rider. The child could then either change the schema about animals or develop a new schema. Accommodation is the modification of an existing way of thinking to meet new demands. These two processes, assimilation and accommodation, are the mechanics of the function of adaptation.

Another function is organization, which for Piaget is the natural tendency to build theories and to organize those ideas into some kind of mental system. This process includes the notion of building from a simple process such as seeing or naming into a higher order of mental functioning such as looking at a ball, saying "Ball," and grabbing it.

The final function to be considered is equilibrium, the tendency to maintain a state of balance. As noted previously, children begin life with a few simple schemes. The child is always striving for a mental structure that includes all experiences, all the assimilations and accommodations from the past. When this is possible, a child is in a state of cognitive equilibrium or balance. When the thought strategies fail, the child experiences disequilibrium and is off balance. The resulting feeling of discomfort remains until a more advanced approach for accommodating new information is acquired. This process of struggling to resolve discrepancies between what one understands currently and a disruption in this ordinary way of thinking leads to advances in cognitive organization. This self-regulating process is concerned with ensuring that the developing child is interacting efficiently with the environment, balancing between equilibrium and disequilibrium. The process is called equilibration and is important in motivating learning according to Piaget.

In summary, adaptation, organization and equilibration are the processes involved in learning new skills or concepts. In Piaget's viewpoint, children should be allowed, as much as possible, to generate their own levels of adaptation or organization. These levels of adaptation or organization reflect the child's developmental level. In effect, Piaget initiated and supported "developmentally appropriate practices" in schools. Instruction should guide but not direct students. To a certain extent, Piaget's model harkens back to Rousseau's idea of the "natural child" approach to instruction.

Jerome S. Bruner

Jerome Bruner (1915–) led the movement away from behavioral learning theory in the 1950s and 1960s that helped begin a new interest in cognitive learning theory. Many learning theorists were objecting to the restrictive prescriptions of behavioral theory. As was discussed in the Gestalt learning theory section, it was obvious to many that much more was involved in learning than a chain of

Applications from the Text 9.7

Role Playing (grades K–12)

Role playing can be a fun, imaginative, and informative technique to help students understand different perspectives concerning controversial issues. Select different people within small groups to play specific roles assigned to them for research. The basic information may be covered in class, but informal research pertaining to their designated roles can be directed by the students. An example would be the subject of recycling. Some possible roles and issues could be a young mother with small children (paper diapers), an active ecologist (recycle every possible thing), a young working couple (no time to recycle anything), a student (recycles newspapers), a semiambulatory eighty-year-old person (cannot maneuver objects well), a politician (patronizes people), two different economists (opposing views concerning costs), and a teenager (foil & Styrofoam packaged fast food and soft drinks), and a homeowner (lives near dump site). The students can get personal insight by interviewing different people within the community. Some students may need additional help to appreciate the various positions. The role playing will be expressive of different perspectives, thus allowing the student to see different sides and problems of the same issue. Role playing helps students work through egocentrism and is also beneficial for the different learning styles used by the students (Geddis, 1991).

stimulus-response events. Bruner attempted to convince others that the conscious processes in learning could be studied experimentally (Bruner, Goodnow, & Austin, 1956).

Bruner (1983), as a cognitive psychologist, focused on learning as a thinking process. He developed a threefold learning theory emphasizing the rational, structural, and intuitional parts of the learning process.

The rational part regards the mind as a method applied to solving problems or achieving tasks. For example, rather than thinking about science, you think science. Science is more than just a collection of facts about the environment; it is the method you use to get the facts. Once again, using the scientific method for problem solving would be an example of using the mind as a method.

Bruner (1973) borrowed from Piaget in defining the structural dimension of his theory. The structural dimension refers to how the learner organizes, classifies, and stores information for future use. In other words, the process is similar to developing your own concept filing system. For example, certain animals are filed under the bird category or schema (Piaget's term), while others are filed in a four-legged-animal category or schema labeled dogs. Models and categories of experiences are constructed for two reasons: (a) to represent what we encounter and (b) to use the data from what we encounter to move beyond those experiences to new problem-solving situations.

Perhaps Bruner's largest contribution to education originates from the structural dimension in his reaffirmation that there are ways to frame ideas to fit the level of development each child has reached. Hence, we have Bruner's (1977) famous quotation that any subject can be taught to any child at any stage of

"Money to Burn" (grades 7–12)

The use of chemical experiments not only depicts chemical processes and reinforces concepts but also reduces fear and focuses attention upon the immediate learning task. A quick, inexpensive, and relevant demonstration regarding the heat of vaporization is the "Money to Burn" experiment. Soak a dollar bill in a mixture of two parts rubbing alcohol with one part water. Take the dollar bill out and light it. The alcohol will burn but the dollar bill will not. This attention-grabbing "magic trick" coupled with an explanation becomes a visual depiction of a scientific concept. Other equally fast and fun experiments are given in an article titled "Dynamic Demos" (Sae, 1991).

Natural cause and effect is more easily understood when demonstrated through experiments (United States Department of Education, 1986).

Do you think it is possible to teach any subject providing it is structured to meet the learner's level of cognitive development?

development if it is presented to the child in the proper way. Proper way refers to teaching the subject in an interesting and meaningful way at the appropriate level of difficulty (see Applications from the Text 9.8). The teacher also would consider mediational learning where critical "halfsteps" help the learner to bridge the distance between difficult steps in each learning task.

Intuition, Bruner's third area of emphasis in the learning process, refers to the generativeness of knowledge. He believed that knowledge was something more than a storehouse of information. He saw learning as being an extension of this stored knowledge that would enable the learner to move beyond what is already known. Bruner viewed intuition as an invitation to further exploration, hypothesis-testing, examination, and creativity (see Applications from the Text 9.9).

Bruner (1966) wrote that humans use three systems of representation of ways of knowing or learning about something: *enactive, ikonic, and symbolic.* These modes represent knowledge that can be used to master a problem and organize experiences for future use.

Comparing Bruner with Piaget, the enactive mode is similar to how sensori-motor stage learning operates. The ikonic corespondents to Piaget's preoperational or preconcrete thinking stage and the symbolic to the concrete and formal stages.

The *enactive* stage of representation involves gaining knowledge through motor actions and responses. Actions stimulated by an object serve to define them. For example, an object will be defined by how it registers with the basic sensory impressions from touching, smelling, hearing, seeing, and tasting. The classification ability of children in the enactive stage is limited by their narrow frame of reference and lack of autonomy.

The *ikonic* stage is focused on the use of mental images or pictures to represent the world. We use images as models to remember how to perform certain tasks. For example, an image of a city street map can help people arrive at their destination.

Newspaper Reporters (grades 5–12)

Reporting creative news as a junior journalist using news style can improve writing skills. Have the students bring magazine pictures from home. Give each student one picture and instructions to formulate a story to go with it. The creative news story should answer the questions: Who? What? When? Where? and Why? (Dunagan, 1991).

A similar idea includes using daily newspapers to heighten awareness of figurative language. Give each small group of students a daily newspaper. After finding and listing the attention-grabbing headlines, the groups exchange the lists and proceed writing the stories to go with the headlines (Reisman, 1991). Another idea is to have the different groups write stories using the "same" headlines. This will show diversity of interpretation and creativity.

Symbolic representation involves changing ikonic images into language to make logical decisions. Language provides one with the ability to consider propositions rather than objects. Language also helps classify objects and concepts in hierarchies and to consider wider ranges and combinations of alternative problem solutions.

All three stages can be illustrated in learning a new dance step. Through the repeated act of dancing, a habitual pattern is developed. This pattern enables the person to do the steps without thinking about them. If the dance follows a pattern like a waltz or a slide dance does, a person can picture the image of making a box or a plus sign. These visual images show how the dance should be done. Putting the dance steps into symbolic language allows one to tell self and others how to do various dances.

Bruner makes an excellent case for balancing teaching between showing, telling, and doing. Bruner (1966) stated that symbolic systems must have categoriality, hierarchy, prediction, causation, and modification. The same could be said for Piaget's schemata systems in which things with common properties are categorized in hierarchies. The animal kingdom is one such example. If children are not taught how to represent experiences symbolically, they will have to rely on the enactive and ikonic systems of representation. All three systems are needed to enhance the growth of invariance that is the recognition of the continuity in things transformed in shape, size, location, and appearance. Piaget defined this concept as conservation.

Also like Piaget, Bruner was interested in blocks to logical thought. Bruner (1973) wrote about transcending momentariness where a five-year-old child was not able to realize that he was contradicting himself when he said a beaker of water was both fuller and emptier than a smaller beaker containing the same volume of water. Development of new representational models will allow the child to experience a wider range of connection.

> Did you use the ikonic stage of Bruner's theory the last time you learned a new dance?

What Motivates People to Learn?

Bruner proposed four motives for intrinsic learning. Can you list at least one personal learning experience from each of the four types?

Bruner (1966) wrote that the single most characteristic thing about human beings is that they learn. Learning is so deeply ingrained in people that it is involuntary. He favors intrinsic motivation because he believes that intrinsic motives for learning are built into all children. He believes that external reinforcement might get a certain behavior performed, but the only sustaining motivation to learn has to come from within. These motives for learning are as follows: (a) curiosity, (b) the drive to achieve competence, (c) aspiration to emulate a model, and (d) a deep sense of commitment to the web of social reciprocity.

Curiosity ensues when a person sees something that is unclear, uncertain, or unfinished. The curiosity nature fits well with Gestalt learning theory, which states that curiosity maintains interest until one finishes the unfinished, unclear, or uncertain object or thing. In other words, the success and self-satisfaction of finishing, clearing up, or making the uncertain certain are sufficiently rewarding so that extrinsic reward is not needed. Successful teachers teach by using curiosity to keep their students interested in what is coming next. A good way to end class is to leave some unfinished discussion for the next class.

Bruner believes that effective teaching involves a balance among doing, showing and telling. Effective learning involves a balance among the physical, the visual and the symbolic aspects.

Globe Trotters (grades 5–12)

An imaginary trip (adapted from Novelli, 1990) can advance planning and decision-making skills as well as increase knowledge and an appreciation for ethnic diversity. Allow each student to choose a specific travel destination from a teacher-prepared list of cities or countries. Mode of transportation and mileage can be determined by using a map and or globe. Students then research the chosen destinations.

A handout can be provided to the students as a guide for assigned topics of interest—for example, history, population and geographic size, weather and geological conditions, language and cultural aspects, and means of monetary exchange. Oral presentations can be completed with visuals and cultural-specific music to allow all the students to become familiar with the locations. Each student can then pack a suitcase with symbolic articles indigenous of the country. These representations can be any available sources: photographs, magazine pictures, travel guides, drawings, stuffed animals, toys, or clothing.

The research for the imaginary trip is an opportunity to gather information and familiarity with the destination. Creativity is sparked by choosing items to represent the country. The handout, used as a learning guide, can assist the student with acquiring a greater confidence for public speaking. The imaginary trip is a good technique to allow minorities or "English as a second language" (ESL) students to share their culture.

Another method to enhance minority/ESL participation is to dedicate a bulletin board to a specific ethnic group every few weeks. Have designated students research famous people and relevant facts pertaining to the particular ethnicity/culture. The students' ages will be a contributing factor regarding the bulletin board responsibility. The students' expertise also promotes public speaking skills and self confidence (Nicholas, 1988).

The drive to achieve competence also is a powerful source of intrinsic motivation. Anyone who has had the opportunity to observe toddler-age children has witnessed the drive to achieve competence. From the time they are able to reach for things, children constantly explore everything they can to find better ways to meet their needs and to adapt to their environment (see Applications from the Text 9.10). They take great pride in mastering the various developmental tasks they face in each stage of development. This drive to achieve competence continues through the life span and is verified by the large number of older adults taking chances and taking on new challenges. Teachers need to capitalize on this drive to achieve mastery by building skill attainment into classes. The Scouts have always benefited from the drive to achieve competence by designing a series of skill attainments into their educational programs. By offering merit badges for each skill attained, Scouts add extrinsic reinforcement to the stronger intrinsic reward of mastering the skill. Maybe each class taught should be built around a series of merit-badge skills. Report cards would reflect how many badges have been passed, and the course would be completed when all badges had been passed. Passing a badge test would qualify the student to become a peer tutor to those still working on that skill. The APA Task Force on Psychology in Education (1992) recommended that instructional practices be focused on individual mastery rather than competitive performance goals.

The aspiration to emulate a model, the third source of intrinsic motivation in Bruner's theory, stems from the belief that people have an internal desire to please the people in their reference group and to model the behavior of those they respect and admire to get their approval. The work of Maslow, Bandura, and Adler is supportive of this motive. People do have a need to belong to a group and to receive recognition for their productive efforts. Behavior is also affected by those models who one finds attractive, a fact which has not been lost in the advertising business. Successful teachers have always been able to "win over" their students by first winning the cooperation of those students who serve as models for the older students. These "models" can become your best peer tutors for those students needing extra help. Teachers themselves, often become successful models for their students. Most people can name several teachers who have had a positive effect on their own learning and development.

The final intrinsic motive for learning in Bruner's system is a *deep sense of commitment to the web of social reciprocity,* a concept similar to the Adlerian focus on social interest. Social reciprocity refers to the deep human need to help others and to work together to make the world a better place to live. Most subject areas have direct relevance to the human condition. Bruner would advocate the practice of making applications of subject matter to the improvement of the world. The "world" focus could start in the family and the neighborhood and move outward. In doing so teachers would be able to harness this natural drive for social reciprocity.

In summary, Bruner has little regard for rote learning and extrinsic reinforcement in any learning environment. His four sources of intrinsic reinforcement provide an automatic reward each time one engages in the learning process. In other words, learning is its own reward. Bruner does favor teaching basic skills as steps to learning the application of higher-level skills (see Applications from the Text 9.11). In agreement with John Dewey, Bruner believes in experiential learning and learning by doing. He recommends augmenting the students' own experiences with experiences in the school curriculum; both are important to learning. Instruction should be specific, relevant to the learner, and taught in the correct sequence. He believes that teachers severely limit learning by failing to go beyond the "what" questions and the recitation of facts. "Why" and "how" questions must be raised and answered. For example, the sky is blue, but why is it blue? Bruner (1973) supported a balanced education that enables the learner to proceed intuitively when necessary and to analyze when appropriate. Ideas emerge from intuition and then need to be analyzed. The earlier this skill is taught to children, the easier it will be for them to understand abstract ideas as they begin to develop formal thinking skills prior to adolescence.

■ ■ ■

ECLECTIC APPROACHES TO LEARNING

Eclectic theorists, employing the best parts of behavioral and cognitive theories, include Albert Bandura and Robert Gagné. Bandura focused on observational learning and Gagné on the sequencing of learning based on an eight-stage hierarchy of learning.

At this point, after having reviewed behavioral and cognitive theories of learn-ing, you may wonder why more effort has not been directed toward combining the best of both approaches into an eclectic theory of learning. Behaviorists make a strong argument for limiting the study of learning to observable behavior that can be counted and analyzed for its meaning. Observable behavior is easy to val-idate and changes are recognizable. Self-report data, such as are collected in phe-nomenological studies, may not be trusted as data based on overt responses. People do not always practice what they preach. For example, a dated definition of a conservative is a liberal who has just been mugged (likewise a liberal could be defined as a conservative who has just had his civil rights violated). In other words, a person's values may not always stand up against the rigorous test of putting the values into practice during crisis periods. If you speak like a liberal but behave like a conservative, behavioral psychologists will record you as a con-servative. Phenomenological psychologists, via the interview, may record you as a liberal if the interviewer fails to capture what the person has experienced in acting on her beliefs.

On the other hand, learning is more involved than stimulus-response associ-ations. Learning how to learn, developing insight, being creative, drawing con-clusions about new relationships, problem solving, and doing research seem to find a better fit with the viewpoints expressed by cognitive theorists. In an effort to combine the best of both approaches to learning, Robert Gagné developed a hierarchy of eight types of learning.

Robert Gagné

Robert Gagné's (1916–) eclectic theory of learning (1977) was an attempt to clas-sify learning theories into a hierarchy of eight levels ranging from the lowest to highest form of learning. With the exception of the first level, each level of learn-ing was presented as a prerequisite for the level that followed it in the hierarchy. In other words, each lower-level skill is needed to move to the next higher-level skill. For example, the ability to discriminate is necessary for classification; con-

Whom do you think
would be most unhappy
with Gagné's theory,
Skinner or Bruner? Why?

cept formation and combination are necessary for rule learning; and rule learning is necessary for problem solving. A description of each of the eight types of learning will begin with signal learning, the lowest level in Gagné's hierarchy.

Level of Learning	Description
Signal Learning	Pavlov's classical conditioning model for the acquisition of involuntary behavior; for example, salivation or eye blink. The learner responds to a signal.
Stimulus-Response Learning	Skinner's operant conditioning model in which the learner forms S–R bonds from trial-and-error learning; for example, the baby's crying brings relief.
Chaining	Sets of S–R learnings are connected in sequence to allow the performance of more complex behaviors—for example, playing the piano. Each response acts as a stimulus to the next response in the chain.
Verbal Association	Forming S–R connections between words and objects. Naming objects is an early form of verbal association. S–R connections also can be made between word pairs.
Learning Discrimination	The learner is able to distinguish between objects or concepts that are similar; for example, all four-legged animals with wet noses are not dogs. This level is required for learning to distinguish letters in the alphabet from one another.
Concept Learning	The classification of objects, concepts, and other stimuli based on their common characteristics; for example, color, number, size, shape, and position.
Rule Learning	A rule is a chain consisting of two or more concepts; for example, water freezes if the temperature is zero degrees centigrade; and there are ten centimeters in one decimeter and one hundred centimeters in one meter.
Problem Solving	The learner uses rules to meet a goal or solve a problem; in so doing, the learner continues to develop the capacity for learning and the strategies to do so. The significant aspect of problem solving is the use of the discovery method to find solutions to new problem situations. For example, "How can we pay off the national debt?"

Gagné (1977) was interested in the varieties of learning outcomes that might result from the eight prototypes listed above. He identified five categories of learning outcomes: verbal information, intellectual skills, cognitive strategies, attitudes, and motor skills. *Verbal information* refers to what the learner knows. It is the ability to recite what has been learned. *Intellectual skills* refer to what the learner can do. Contrasting verbal and intellectual skills, verbal skills would allow a person to state a theory and intellectual skills would provide the ability to put the theory into practice (see Applications from the Text 9.12). Problem solving is an intellectual skill (see Applications from the Text 9.13).

Cognitive strategies, a form of intellectual skill, describe how a person learns. They refer to methods a person uses to manage the process of attending, perceiving and encoding, remembering, and thinking. Cognitive strategies also are referred to as executive control processes that enable the learner to know when and how to employ verbal and intellectual skills (see Applications from the Text 9.14).

Attitudes refer to the expectancies control process that represents the specific motivation of the learner to choose and reach a goal of learning. Attitudes are internal beliefs that affect a person's actions toward people, places, events, and things (see Applications from the Text 9.15).

Motor skills refer to those skills people use when driving a car or playing the piano. Motor learning can be broken down into three phases: (a) cognitive—where the skill is learned; (b) association—where the parts of the skill begin to come together; and (c) autonomous—where the skill can be done like a habit without too much thought.

Gagné (1974) dissected the act of learning into an eight-step process often referred to as his eight phases of an act of learning. Listed in order the steps are (a) motivation, (b) apprehending, (c) acquisition, (d) retention, (e) recall,

APPLICATIONS FROM THE TEXT 9.12

Calendars (grades K–4)

Using familiar manipulatives in class assists not only in the acquisition of knowledge and in understanding future mathematical concepts (United States Department of Education, 1986). Since the beginning of time, one such manipulative has been the calendar. This technique can be used to teach many concepts: the concepts of yesterday, today, and tomorrow, days of the week, counting by tens, addition, months of the year, weather, and birthdays.

Word Problems (grades K–12)

Mathematics can be more easily understood by having the students develop their own word problems. The following examples tap several levels of cognitive development: write a story about fourteen children; write an addition problem that has an answer of eighty-six; while a story involving the addition, subtraction, and multiplication of fractions; write a story involving geometry and a soccer play (McGehe, 1991).

The Price Is Right or Wrong (grades 5–12)

Real-life interests can be used to learn the concept of interest rates. First, students can choose any item to purchase on loan. Next, have them determine the total amounts of money owed using different interest rates for the loans. Give different rates of interest for comparison; quarterly and monthly conversion rates can be identified, as well as compound interest rates. Through knowledge acquisition and multiple comparisons, the students gain skills in distinguishing and evaluating different purchasing opportunities (Cook, 1990).

Consider a subject topic you would like to teach to the students of your choice. List one thing you could do to assist your students through each one of Gagné's eight learning process steps.

(f) generalization, (g) performance, and (h) feedback. Gagné's eclecticism is reflected in the phases that are influenced by both external events and internal processes.

Motivation Phase. Gagné seems to support intrinsic motivation over extrinsic rewards. He would advise teachers to capitalize on the human tendency to be curious about how the environment works and how to master it. Discovery learning used to solve real problems should go far to capture students' interest. Such problems need to be relevant to the students' world and often the teacher's role requires making the subject relevant. Clearly stated outcome or performance objectives help build intrinsic motivation. For example, following successful completion of the unit of study, the student will be able to write a poem, to dismantle and rebuild a car engine, or to organize and begin a small business. Teachers need to be expert sales representatives on the topic of why their subject matter is important and useful.

We are in favor of using extrinsic rewards in addition to the intrinsic rewards. For example, teachers could promise to teach their students how to legally become millionaires. The money topic always makes for a lively class session. Topics range from saving two thousand dollars a year in a tax-sheltered annuity to writing and earning royalties on books and computer software. In summary, the purpose of the motivation phase is to build positive outcome expectancies in your students.

Apprehending Phase. Capturing and maintaining students' attention during the apprehending phase is important. Novel and active approaches to learning generally help. Humor also helps. As mentioned in the classroom management chapters, many successful teachers put all their students in the front row (one large circle) as a way of holding their attention through better eye contact. Thorough explanation of the skill being taught, complete with samples, examples, and demonstration, helps students to attend selectively to the correct stimuli the teacher wishes to present (see Applications from the Text 9.16).

Word Web (grades K–12)

It is helpful to know what information students bring into a new subject area. A "word web" can furnish this data and also contribute insight into the students' feelings and thoughts concerning the new material. This cognitive teaching technique is a visual representation of thought organization.

Write the principal word (such as decimals) in the middle of the chalkboard. Ask the students to reply with any reactions, feelings, or facts about the principal word. Sort their responses into categories that are unknown to the students. When the students have exhausted all their thoughts, they can then identify the individual categories (see figure). The word web is beneficial to both the teacher and students. As mentioned earlier, the teacher gains valuable information from the students. The students benefit by sharing their knowledge, learning from others, and realizing that others may share the same thoughts and feelings. Visualizing problem solving and decision making are additional benefits of the "web." Write the question that is to be examined on the chalkboard. First, determine the goal to be accomplished or the problem to solve. Categorize the possible methods for achieving the goal or resolving the problem, and then list the advantages and disadvantages of each, as well as the anticipated outcome of each method. The visual illustration enables students to observe the critical thinking and problem-solving process (McGehe, 1991).

A Word Web Is a Thought Organization Strategy

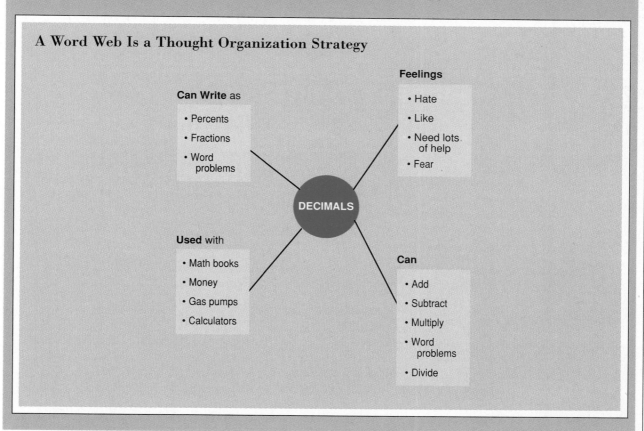

277

Living Maps (grades 4–8)

Geography, politics, and economics can be taught by the living map activity. A world map needs to be drawn (chalked) on a large flat surface (playground or gymnasium floor). Divide and position the students proportionately to the populations of the major world powers (North America, Japan, Europe, etc.).

Distribute items to the students that are symbolic of the particular area's economic statistics—for example, used small batteries for energy supplies, individual cereal boxes for food supplies. As the teacher, you can decide how specific the representative types of energy and food can be. The geography books generally indicate the major gross national product divisions. Disproportions of resources and populations will become visually apparent. The students can then negotiate for things needed by their particular country. This life-size visual and interactive activity helps the students to understand the importance of economics and politics from the world's perspective (Lambert, 1990).

Mother Goose Revisited (grades K–3)

A fun activity for any age group is to have the students rewrite a popular, familiar story/fable from a different perspective; for example, the Giant's view of that pesky little Jack in "Jack and the Beanstalk." Younger students can draw and tell their own picture stories.

Cartoon Graffiti (grades 1–12)

Give the students newspaper cartoons with the captions cut out. Individual humor and creativity blend together for a more personal approach as students write their own cartoon captions.

Short Story Lottery (grades 3–12)

Have each student write two familiar subjects/nouns, each on a separate piece of paper and deposit them in a box. Action verbs are written and placed in a separate box. After all pieces have been shuffled in the boxes, each student draws two papers from the noun box and one from the verb box. Ask the students to write a short story concerning their two subject nouns and one verb. The students will be entertained and surprised at their creativity (Faggella, 1990).

Gagné's hierarchy of learning indicates that problem solving ability is the highest level of learning.

Acquisition Phase. The important event in this third phase is to code the material or subject matter in a form that can be stored in the short- or long-term memory. Having students put the subject matter into their own words helps the process. Others find it helpful to use mnemonic devices such as visual imagery, rhyming, and using words for phrases. Further information on memory is presented in chapter 10.

Retention Phase. After the learning has been coded, it is moved from the short- to long-term memory for storage. Information entering the short-term memory is limited to a storage capacity of five to nine items and a life span of twenty to thirty seconds. Frequent rehearsal and practice of the material helps to maintain it in the short-term memory as well as helping to encode it in the long-term memory. When perceptual learning moves from the short- to long-term memory, it is transformed into conceptual learning. New learning may interfere with old learning. For example, new telephone numbers tend to squeeze out memory of the old numbers.

Recall Phase. Retrieval is the function of the recall phase and, as such, is the source of verification of learning. Learning strategies as well as general information may be retrieved to solve old and new problems. Skilled learners use their recall strategies to make their long-term learnings available for use in the accessible short-term memory. Two things can happen when learning is returned to the short-term memory: (a) it can combine with new information and be returned to the long-term memory or (b) it can activate the response generator that organizes it for performance functions.

Generalization Phase. Generalization refers to the transfer of learning for applications to new situations. Discovery learning, in which students are exposed to problems without ready-made solutions, is the best way to teach the transfer of learning. The process can be achieved by asking students for alternative solutions to the problems posed in class. Finding new uses for old products is another way of developing transfer of learning. For example, which of the following would most likely be helpful in sewing cloth: (a) comb, (b) mirror, (c) apple, or (d) fish?

Performance Phase. Perhaps the best test of our learning lies in its direct application because it is both observable and measurable. As such, one can verify how successful the instruction has been. Gagné (1974) defined learning as occurring when a stimulus situation causes learners to perform differently than they did before being introduced to the learning situation. For Gagné, learning is a change in performance. Good teachers provide a variety of ways through which performance can be verified.

Feedback Phase. The eighth and final phase of the learning process is the feedback learners receive on their performance. Some feedback is obvious to the learner performing a certain skill such as playing a piece of music, working a math problem, or repairing a machine. Success helps fix the learning in our long-term memory. Teachers can provide positive reinforcement for honest improvement (shaping) and corrective feedback when students need more work on how to perform a skill. Motivation is built by promising reinforcement and delivering on the promise during the performance phase. Encouragement, which does not depend on performance, can be offered to help students who became blocked on any one of the eight phases of learning.

Bloom's Taxonomy. Bloom, Englehart, Furst, Hill, and Krathwohl (1956) developed a model of educational objectives that is similar to the eight levels of learning and the eight phases of the learning act proposed by Gagné. Bloom et al.'s model, incorporating information similar to both of Gagné's models, helps teachers to present information to their students in ways that will reach beyond their memory level of recall. In short, Bloom et al. believed that information can be learned and stored on six levels: knowledge, comprehension, application, analysis, synthesis, and evaluation.

Knowledge Level. Information learned at the knowledge level is similar to the short-term memory in Gagné's system. Unfortunately, the information learned (memorized) at the knowledge level only is often quickly forgotten after the test

Weather Watchers (grades 2–12)

Use the Weather Channel as a colorful visual aid when teaching weather. Watching the spectacular footage and listening to the meteorologist can reinforce the daily lessons. Videotape a few different weather graphs/reports prior to beginning the topic so that the students will not remember seeing them on television. When the subject has been covered in class, let the students view the videotape without the sound. Afterwards, the students can present their own interpretations and compare with the replayed videotaped meteorologist's report. This fun and challenging activity can be used by individuals; small groups can be used for consultation (Mernit, 1991).

if not before. Typical level-one memory-level information includes things such as definitions, mathematical formulas, historical dates, biological classification systems, and memorized quotations, poetry, and recitations. A level-one question would ask the learner to quote the textbook definitions of reinforcement and punishment.

Comprehension Level. Information learned at this level will be retained longer because definitions are translated into the learner's own words and the learner will be able to compare the new concept with its opposite concept. For example, the learner will be able to compare the differences between reinforcement and punishment and to give examples of each.

Application Level. Moving up the levels of learning, one finds that each level depends on the mastery of each of the levels preceding it. Information learned at the application level can be translated to performing a task or skill. The learner can put theory into practice at the application level (see Applications from the Text 9.17). For example, the learner would be able to design and implement a classroom management plan based on the principles of reinforcement rather than punishment.

Analysis Level. Analysis-level learning requires the learner to be able to debate the pro-and-con issues surrounding the subject matter and to draw conclusions based on these pro-and-con arguments. For example, the learner could debate the issues surrounding the use of corporal punishment as the issues related to behavior modification programs in schools.

Synthesis Level. The hallmark of synthesis-level learning is creativity. The learner at this fifth level knows enough about the topic to create original material about it. Examples include things such as writing a poem, essay, or short

Do you find the six-step levels of learning developed by Bloom et al. to be more useful than Gagné's eight-step process? Why or why not?

story, composing music, or inventing a new procedure or machine. In keeping with the reinforcement example, the development of a new and creative classroom management plan would qualify as level-five or synthesis-level learning.

Evaluation Phase. In the sixth and highest level of learning, the learner is required to establish the criteria required for evaluating a program or concept and then examining that program or concept against those criteria (see Applications from the Text 9.18). For example, the learner, required to evaluate a particular presidential administration, would begin by establishing the criteria of what makes an effective administration. Such criteria would set standards for foreign and domestic policy, the economy, education, health, defense, employment, and the budget against which the particular administration would be evaluated. Once again, in staying with the reinforcement example, one could design an evaluation-level question for researching the effectiveness of behavioral management systems.

Gagné, basing his own information-processing model on the information-processing work of Atkinson and Shiffrin (1971) and Shiffrin and Atkinson (1969) wrote:

> The processes that one must conceive in order to explain the phenomena of learning are those that make certain kinds of transformations of "inputs" to "outputs" in a fashion somewhat analogous to the working of a computer. . . . The various forms of transformation are called learning processes. It is these processes, their characteristics, and their manner of functioning, which constitute the essence of modern learning theory (Gagné, 1975, 15).

Gagné's model describes the flow of information. Stimulation from the environment is picked up by receptors and is transmitted by neural connecters to the sensory register. The new information in the sensory register remains as long as

Enhanced Learning Techniques (grades 5–12)

Crib notes provide another effective learning technique. Simply apply the SQ3R format (as identified in chapter 1) with note cards. The question is written on one side with the answer written on the back side of the card. The student analyzes, synthesizes, and evaluates information from the textbook and class notes required for developing the note cards. Similarities and contrasting points between or among items are sometimes easier for the student to discern because of the attention necessary for crib note formulation. The textbook's page number or the class note's date is written in the corner of the cards for further referencing. Strengthening organizational skills and increasing attention to details are additional benefits of this learning procedure (Whitworth, 1991).

the learner attends to it. The act of attending moves the information into the short-term memory where further attending to it by the learner will encode it as input into the long-term memory (see Applications from the Text 9.19). Perceptual information in the short-term memory becomes conceptual information in the long-term memory. Successful retrieval of information from the long-term memory is necessary for the verification of learning. The retrieval process begins with an environmental or internal cue that starts the search process. Once located, the information is returned to the short-term memory where it is accessible to the learner for combination with new information or for activating the response generator that allows the learner to perform certain skills by activating the effectors. Performance verifies that learning has occurred. The last event in the information-processing model is the feedback, which confirms to the learner that the information has been learned. Generally, the learner will be able to judge the success of the learning process. For example, the learner will be able to observe the success of his efforts to repair a television set. The feedback fixes the learning in the long-term memory in a way that makes it available to the learner.

Two processes individualize learning for each learner: executive control and expectancies. Executive control processes refer to the choices the learner makes regarding what information in the sensory register to save and discard. It also determines how information is processed, stored, retrieved, and utilized. Expectancies refer to the degree of motivation the learner has to reach a particular learning goal. As such, expectancies will influence the entire information-processing system beginning with what information is attended to and ending with how the information is used. Gagné believes that the information-processing model under the influences of executive control process and expectancies has the effect of making people truly intelligent beings who can learn how to learn (see figure 9.1).

> What is the best method you have found for moving information from your short-term to long-term memory?

FIGURE 9.1
Gagné's Information
Processing Model

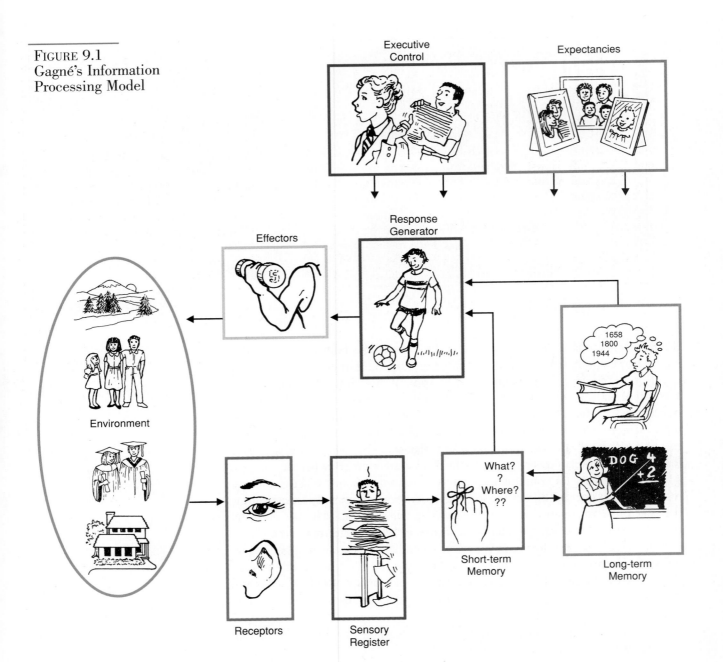

Executive Control

Expectancies

Effectors

Response Generator

Environment

1658 1800 1944

Receptors

Sensory Register

What? ? Where? ??

Short-term Memory

Long-term Memory

DOG 4 +2

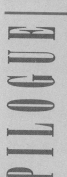

EPILOGUE

COOPERATIVE LEARNING—EXCITING NEW CHALLENGE FOR TEACHERS AND STUDENTS

Margaret felt encouraged after her research on cooperative learning. She began immediately to think of ways to select her teams in a way to keep them balanced academically and ways to provide rewards for each team completing its assigned tasks. What advice and support could you give to Margaret and other teachers who are insecure about relinquishing some of their classroom control and moving toward some cooperative learning activities?

Cooperative learning activities afford students the opportunity to teach subjects to their peers. We know that teaching a subject develops higher-level learning within the "teacher." How would you use cooperative learning in your classroom? Do you think it is possible to use cooperative learning and competition at the same time? If so, how would you do this in your classroom?

SUMMARY

Cognitive approaches to learning regard learning as something much more than observable behaviors that can be quantified. Definitions of learning are extended to include insight learning, latent learning, and information processing. A strong case is made for discovery learning and problem-solving teaching methods. Students are encouraged to become productive thinkers who are able to reorganize data and facts into workable units for solving problems. In other words, students are taught to solve problems without relying on ready-made formulas. In conclusion, learning theorists have understood learning as a stimulus response connection, as a Gestalt experience, and as an integration of these two. Gagné's eclectic model incorporates ideas from each and can serve as a summary of learning theories.

CHAPTER REVIEW

1. Discuss the three, principal ways cognitive approaches to learning differ from behavioral approaches.
2. Consider the subject matter you teach and describe how you could use cognitive methods to teach it. Be specific in your examples.
3. If you could interview Tolman, Wertheimer, Piaget, and Bruner, what would each recommend for improving your teaching? Rank the theorists according to their helpfulness and be prepared to defend your ranking.
4. From the cognitive viewpoint, what motivates people to learn and how is this different from the behavioral view?

5. How could a person train her executive control (in the Gagné model) to become a more efficient learner? As a teacher, how could you help your students train their executive control?

REFERENCES

American Psychological Association. (1992). *Learner-centered principles: Guidelines for school redesign and reform (Draft #3).* Washington, DC: American Psychological Association.

Atkinson, R., & Shiffrin, R. (1971). The control of short-term memory. *Scientific American, 225*(13), 82–90.

Blanton, M. (1991). Teaching reading in the math classroom. *Clearing House, 64*(3), 162–164.

Bloom, B., Englehart, M., Furst, E., Hill, W., & Krathwohl, O. (1956). *Taxonomy of educational objectives: The classification of educational goals, Handbook 1: The cognitive domain.* New York: Longman.

Bruner, J. (1966). *Toward a theory of instruction.* New York: W.W. Norton.

Bruner, J. (1973). *The relevance of education.* New York: W.W. Norton.

Bruner, J. (1977). *The process of education.* Cambridge, MA: Harvard University Press.

Bruner, J. (1983). *In search of mind: Essays in autobiography.* New York: Harper & Row.

Bruner, J., Goodnow, J., & Austin, G. (1956). *A study of thinking.* New York: John Wiley & Sons.

Cook, D. (1990). Envisioning change in the practice of mathematics teaching. *School Science and Mathematics, 90*(16), 510–515.

Crain, W. (1992). *Theories of development: Concepts and applications.* Old Tappen, NJ: Prentice Hall.

Dunagan, L. (1991). Highlight it. *Teaching Pre K-8, 20*(3), 92.

Dywan, J. (1991–92). Shopping for groceries. *The Mailbox, 13,*(6), 45.

Eldredge, J. (1991). Increasing the performance of poor readers in the third grade with a group-assisted strategy. *Journal of Educational Research, 84,*(2), 69–77.

Faggella, K. (1990). Brain busters. *Instructor, 100*(2), 104.

Flavell, J. H. (1963). The developmental psychology of Jean Piaget. New York: Van Nostrand.

Furth, H. (1970). *Piaget for teachers.* Englewood Cliffs, NJ: Prentice Hall.

Gagné, R. (1974). *Essentials of learning for instruction.* Hinsdale, IL: Dryden Press.

Gagné, R. (1975). *Essentials of learning for instruction* (rev. ed.) Hinsdale, IL: Dryden Press.

Gagné, R. (1977). *Conditions of learning* (3rd ed.).

Geddis, A. N. (1991). Improving the quality of science classroom discourses on controversial issues. *Science Education, 75*(2), 169.

Guiton, E. (1991). Cooperative learning and elementary social studies. *Social Education, 55*(5), 313.

Hill, W. (1985). *Learning: A survey of psychological interpretations.* New York: Harper & Row.

Inhelder, B., & Piaget, J. (1958). *The growth of logical thinking from childhood to adolescence.* (A. Parsons & S. Pilgram, Trans.). New York: Basic Books.

Inhelder, B., & Piaget, J. (1964). *The early growth of logic in the child.* London: Routledge and Kegan Paul.

Koffka, K. (1935). *Principles of Gestalt psychology*. New York: Harcourt, Brace, and Company.

Kohler, W. (1925). *The mentality of apes* (E. Wister, Trans.). New York: Harcourt, Brace, & World.

Lambert, C. (1990). Bucky Fuller's big game goes on. *Tennessee Teacher, 58*(1), 16–18.

Luchins, A. (1942). *Mechanization in problem-solving: The effect of Einstellung.* Psychological Monographs, *54* (Whole No. 248).

Malone, J. (1990). *Theories of learning: A historical approach.* Belmont, CA: Wadsworth Publishing Company.

McGehe, C. A. (1991). Mathematics the write way. *Instructor, 100*(8), 36–38.

Mernit, S. (1991). Get with the program: Teach with TV. *Instructor, 100*(8), 42–44.

Nicholas, A. (1988). Hidden minorities. *Instructor, 98*(2), 8.

Novelli, J. (1990). Great starts. *Instructor, 100*(2), 62–122.

O'Connor, B. (1990). Understanding, appreciating, conserving. . .our world's forests. *The Mailbox, 12*(4), 26.

Piaget, J. (1952). *The origins of intelligence in children.* New York: International Universities Press.

Piaget, J. (1960). *The child's conception of the world.* London: Routledge.

Piaget, J. (1967). *Six psychological studies.* New York: Vintage Press.

Piaget, J. (1969), *The mechanisms of perceptions.* New York: Basic Books.

Piaget, J., & Inhelder, B. (1969). *The psychology of the child.* (H. Weaver, Trans.). New York; Basic Books.

Puetz, S. (1990). Reading incentives. *Learning, 19,*(4), 123.

Reckford, N. (1988, October). Focus on reading: Pourquoi stories. *Instructor, 98*(3), 13.

Reisman, R. (1991). Headline hunt. *Learning, 19*(5), 34.

Roblee, K. M. (1991). Cooperative chemistry. *The Science Teacher, 58*(1), 20–23.

Sae, A. (1991). Dynamic demos. *The Science Teacher, 58*(7), 23–25.

Sherman, L. G. (1989). Making the math/science connection. *Instructor, 98*(7), 44–48.

Shiffrin, R., & Atkinson, R. (1969). Storage and retrieval process in long-term memory. *Psychological Review, 76*(2), 179–93.

Shires, J. (1991). Guessing jar. *Learning, 19*(7), 14.

Slavin, R. E. (1990). Research on cooperative learning: Concensus and controversy. *Educational Leadership, 47*(4), 52–54.

Socha, S. (1991). Questions with multiple answers. *Mathematics Teacher, 84*(8), 638–840.

Tolman, E. (1932). *Purposive behavior in animals and men.* New York: Appleton-Century-Crofts.

United States Department of Education. (1986). *What works: Research about teaching and learning.* Washington, DC: Office of Educational Research and Improvement.

Wadsworth, B. J. (1989). *Piaget's theory of cognitive and affective development* (4th ed.). New York: Longman.

Waldron, S.L. (1990). All hands-on lab! *The Science Teacher, 57*(4), 35–37.

Wertheimer, M. (1924). Gestalt theory, In W. D. Willis (ed.), *A source book of Gestalt psychology* (pp. 1–11). New York: Harcourt, Brace, and Company (1938).

Wertheimer, M. (1945) *Productive thinking.* New York: Harper Row.

Wertheimer, M. (1959). *Productive thinking: Enlarged edition.* (Michael Wertheimer, Ed.). New York: Harper Row.

Whitworth, R. (1991). Using crib notes as a learning device. *Clearing House, 64*(1), 25–27.

Memory

FORGETTING CAN LEAD TO FRUSTRATION

Charles, a ten-year-old fourth-grade student in Mrs. Wheeler's class, seemed to be unable to remember to do his assignments, locate his writing materials, or possess any idea of how to study for tests. Mrs. Wheeler had just finished a parent conference with Charles' mother in which both of them agreed to attempt to help Charles do better at these tasks.

Charles' grades are below average, although his attendance has been very good. His academic achievement test scores are declining gradually each year. Scores during the early years were near the fiftieth percentile when compared with his grade-level classmates. The most recent scores are between the thirty-fifth and fortieth percentile. Charles is poor in spelling and has his greatest success in mathematics. Charles is an only child from an intact family. His father operates a small business. His mother, who does not work outside the home, does some volunteer work. Charles has a winning personality and a pleasing disposition. He is liked by his classmates but is not one of the more popular students in his classes. He does become frustrated at times about his schoolwork not being completed or having to miss certain school events because he has forgotten to bring either his permission slip for the event or the money required to attend.

INTRODUCTION

Teachers know that one of their most important functions as educators is to help students learn to remember significant information that is presented in the classroom. Equally important is instructing students in ways to get organized to study, in habits to plan to study, and in strategies to use in effective studying. The ideas, concepts, and applications contained in this chapter will give teachers a basis for learning to accomplish these difficult educational objectives.

Included among the ideas and concepts in this chapter are a number of different models of memory. These models can be divided into two types, based on how they examine memory.

One type of model examines what we remember: in effect, the different ways of representing and storing information. This type of model investigates different mental abilities, such as verbal, visual or abstract abilities, and the way they are stored as memory systems.

The second type of model investigates how we remember. This type of model examines memory as a process. This model includes the ways in which stimuli register on the sensory systems, are processed through different stages of the memory system, and then stored as a long-term memory.

Both types of models are critical to understanding the theories, the research, and the applications of memory to the educational process.

- The relationship of memory systems to sensory systems.
- Tulving's concepts of procedural memory system, semantic memory system, and episodic memory system.
- The relationship among the procedural, semantic, and episodic systems.
- The different aspects of the multistore model of information processing.
- The relationship of attention to learning and memory.
- The effects of levels of processing information on memory.
- The interrelationship between learner and task in Jenkins' model of memory.
- The effectiveness of metamemory strategies on memory performance.

WHAT IS MEMORY?

Webster defines memory as "the power or process of reproducing what has been learned and retained. . . ." It is the mental (cognitive) activity of recalling to present awareness a past experience. As evident in these definitions, memory is a concept closely related to learning and cognition. Understanding memory involves studying how knowledge is acquired, modified, manipulated, used, stored, and processed (Neisser, 1967).

Definitions of memory have been dominated by two distinct views:

1. Memory is in one way or another a neurophysiological reproduction of the original experience;
2. Memory is a mental reconstruction of the original experience.

The first definition of memory assumes that remembering involves a specific neurophysiological activation of a memory trace that is stored in a distinct site in the brain. The second definition of memory assumes that memory is a generalized mental ability distributed throughout substantial areas of the brain. In the second definition of memory, there is little or no relationship between a specific memory and a specific neurophysiological site.

WHAT DO WE REMEMBER?

Before reading any further, please take a moment and pinch yourself. For at least a few seconds, you can remember where you pinched yourself and how it felt. This, and other sensations, are a type of memory. Memory can involve any or all of the five basic senses: sight, sound, smell, touch, taste. The more senses involved and the more vivid the sensory experience, the more likely it will be remembered.

In addition to the sensory memory systems, there appear to be a number of other memory systems. There is a separate memory system for language. There is a separate memory system devoted to music. There is a memory system for mathematics. There is a motoric/physical memory system. There also appears to

Reflect on your own memory ability. Which of the following memory systems produces the most vivid memories: seeing, hearing, smelling, tasting, or touching?

Memory appears to be enhanced by vivid sensory experiences that utilize a number of senses.

How far back in your own life history can you remember? Can you remember back as far as age four or five? Can you remember your first-grade teacher? Anecdotal accounts indicate that most of us can recall episodic memories from ages four or five.

be a personal history memory system: in effect, a memory system exclusively devoted to remembering one's own personal life.

One of the most widely used categorizations of memory systems was developed by Tulving (1985). Tulving (1985) has identified research support for three possible types of memory systems: procedural, semantic, and episodic.

Tulving (1985) indicates that the procedural memory system enables people to make stimulus-response connections. Procedural memory encodes behavioral responses to the physical world. Semantic memory enables people to make the additional step of internally representing aspects of the world that are not physically present. The semantic system includes those cognitive activities that allow sign and symbol formation—usually but not exclusively words. Episodic memory allows individuals to personally place themselves in space and time. For instance, this system enables people to mentally place themselves in their own personal world at a given point in time. (I will meet you next Saturday. I visited New York in 1969.) The episodic memory system also includes relational understanding: the ability to understand the relationships between events, objects, or people.

Although each system has its own specific attributes, there is a hierarchical aspect to the three memory systems. Tulving (1985) states that the procedural memory system is the most basic system. The semantic system must use the procedural system to function. The episodic system depends on both the procedural and semantic system to function as a system. Thus, the episodic system involves the most complex types of cognitive functions.

A number of research questions have been raised about the basic unit of memory (called a memory trace or an engram) in these different memory systems. It seems clear that each of the systems listed by Tulving may have its own separate, basic unit of memory. With procedural memories, the basic unit appears to be a behavioral response or a response associated with a specific stimulus. With the semantic system, it appears to be a word, concept, or number.

Within the episodic system, the basic memory unit appears to be what is termed as a proposition (Martindale, 1981). Propositions are abstract cognitive units that code an event in terms of its meaning. The difference between a semantic unit and a proposition can be illustrated in the following manner: The words "George Washington" are a semantic unit. However, the words "George Washington became the first president of the United States" is a proposition.

A number of research questions have been raised about how a basic unit of memory like a proposition is stored and recalled. It is apparent from the research that a variety of factors are involved in memory performance. For example, reinforcement, repetition/rehearsal, novelty, attention, meaningfulness, organization(chunking), and depth of processing have all been listed as factors.

Besides these separate systems, there also appear to be different levels of processing and encoding memories. For instance, there does seem to be a time lag involved from when a stimulus registers on a sensory organ and when the memory is permanently stored in a specific memory system. Thus, each memory that is transferred to some type of permanent storage system is processed at a variety of levels.

Memory research and memory models involve a variety of approaches. It may be useful to keep in mind the distinction between different types of memory systems and different models of processing of memories. The next section examines the different models of how we process memories.

■ ■ ■

How Do We Remember?

There are several models that attempt to explain how the memory process works. Though models provide a way to describe the memory process, recent neurological research has made strides in actually mapping the brain and the specialized functions of its various regions (Van Essen, 1985). Perhaps in the future we will know exactly how the brain functions in remembering information, displacing the current metaphorical models described here. Until that happens, however, educators and psychologists must use these models in developing practical applications.

The models described in the next section examine memory processing from the perspective of the following models: an information processing viewpoint, a depth of processing viewpoint, and an integrated learner/task viewpoint.

The Multistore Model of Information Processing

Atkinson and Shiffrin (1968) developed the multistore model, or information processing model, drawing on the pioneering work of William James (1890) and the twentieth-century field of computer science. This model is illustrated in figure 10.1 and described in the following sections.

FIGURE 10.1
A Multistore Model of
Memory Structures and
Processes
*Modified from Schneider and
Pressley (1989)*

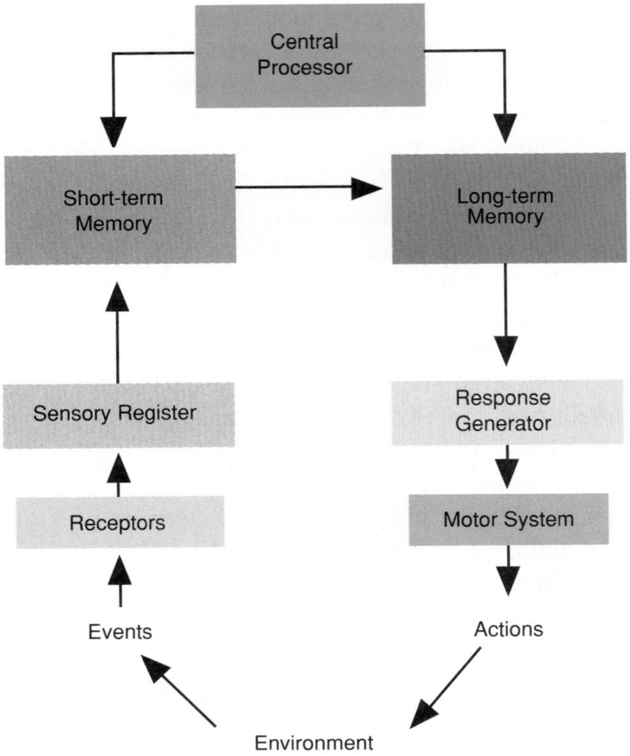

Step One: Environmental Stimuli. The act of remembering begins when you interact with your environment. The quality of your environment influences what you remember. Environments can be impoverished, providing inadequate stimulation, or they can be overstimulating and distracting. Either extreme can disrupt the memory process.

Step Two: Receptors. The receptors receive stimuli from the environment. If a stimulus is not in your environment, then obviously you cannot process and remember it. If a stimulus is received at below the threshold for a sensory receptor, it will not activate the receptor. If the receptors are not fully developed or are impaired, your ability to learn and recall will be affected. Thus, the nature of the environmental stimuli and the adequacy of the receptors are fundamental to appropriate learning.

In applying this information, teachers need to remember that classroom lectures must have appropriate volume and pitch. (Not only must there be a certain decibel level to grab students' attention, but variations in the volume and pitch will help to maintain attention.) Teachers also need to ensure that all students can hear and see in their classroom. Student problems with learning are sometimes due to poor vision or hearing.

Step Three: Attention. To learn or remember something, we must first attend to it. As you sit reading this paragraph, there are many stimuli impinging on your senses from your surrounding environment. From this end, as I write this paragraph, I can selectively attend to various stimuli in my environment. For exam-

Intense stimuli such as a loud noise can cause a reflexive startle response. Is there a relationship between the intensity of a stimulus and the likelihood of the stimulus being recalled?

ple, I can attend to the feel of the pen in my hand, the sight of the blue ink on the white paper, the smell of lunch cooking in the kitchen, the sensation of my stomach growling in anticipation, the sound of my child ripping pages out of a catalog, or I can block out all of this and attend only to the information I want to convey to you regarding selective attention. The point is, to remember, one must first attend, and we are constantly exercising selective attention as stimuli bombard our senses. The Selective Attention Theory (Reynolds & Shirey, 1988) supposedly works like this:

1. Learner processes information and grades it according to importance.
2. Extra attention is paid to important elements.
3. Elements judged more important, and therefore attended to, are more likely to be remembered.

Although there is general agreement that there is much more data in our environment than we can attend to, there is debate about whether we can pay attention to more than one stimulus at a time. Broadbent (1958) found that we filter out one stimulus to attend to another. More recent research has demonstrated, however, that many of us can attend to more than one stimulus at a time, depending on the distinctiveness of the stimulus and the amount of effort required to attend to it (Kahneman, 1973). For example, most people react to hearing their name called even though attending to another conversation or task.

Barkley (1988) contends that attention is a multidimensional construct involving several components. Figure 10.2 lists these components and briefly describes each one. Each of these components appears to be at least moderately correlated.

Step Four: The Sensory Registers. The receptors receive the information selected from the environment and send it to the sensory store in the sensory register. Klatzky (1980) assumes that there is one "register" or "store" for each sense so that audio stimuli are stored in the audio register, etc. Each stimulus is stored intact and unchanged but only for a very brief time unless further processed into short- or long-term memory stores. Auditory stimuli seem to remain the longest in the sensory register—up to four seconds. Visual stimuli, on the other hand, remain for only one second (Darwin, Turvey, & Crowder, 1972).

Describe what you attended to the last time you drove a car. Did you attend to multiple stimuli? Did you listen to music, talk to a passenger, stop at a red light, avoid other cars?

Components of Attention	Description
Alertness	Degree of general sensitivity to the environment
Selectivity	Ability to focus on stimuli that are essential to the task and ignore other elements
Distractibility	Response to irrelevant aspect of a task
Impulsivity	Rapid and inaccurate responding
Sustained attention	Duration of response to a task; vigilance
Span of attention	The number of stimuli attended to simultaneously

FIGURE 10.2
Components of Attention

Teachers who vary the pitch, tone and volume of their presentations can help to maintain student attention.

Models of forgetting state that interference from competing stimuli may cause memory loss. List some personal situations where interference might have caused problems in memorizing for a test.

Information in the sensory register follows a process somewhat like "Ping-Pong balls in a box." If the box is full, a new ball can be placed in the box only by pushing out another ball. Or, using a different analogy, once a computer disk is full, the only way more information can be stored is by erasing something on the disk to "make room." Likewise, when the sensory register is full, new stimuli replace old stimuli—another way to say we "forget."

Attention to information is essential if it is to be stored in a sensory register; however, pattern recognition also is required if the information is to be further processed by the system. Pattern recognition functions to convert the raw information into a form that the system can use. Before moving on to short- or long-term memory stores, information in the sensory register must be matched with information in long-term memory. This information or patterns in long-term memory are often called memory codes or codes of information.

According to Klatzky (1980), pattern recognition happens in three steps.

1. The pattern is analyzed.
2. The information is compared with existing information stored in long-term memory.
3. A decision is made to either "toss out" the information or further process it into the system.

The complexity of pattern recognition is belied by the relatively simple steps listed here. For example, to recognize and store this visual pattern, we must be able to match it with other patterns in the same category such as A, **A, a,** and α. In conclusion, once the complex process of pattern recognition is complete, information is ready to be stored in short-term or long-term memory.

Step Five: Short-term Memory (STM). Although the information processing model refers to STM as a "store," much more goes on than merely the holding of data. In fact, the concept of STM as a "container" gradually is being replaced by the concept of STM as a very active mechanism that performs a variety of functions (Dempster, 1985).

STM is the processing center between the sensory register and long-term memory. This processing center interacts with information in both the sensory registers and the long-term store. As the name implies, the STM holds recognized patterns of multisensory input for a short duration, estimated to be somewhere between five and twenty seconds (Peterson & Peterson, 1959). Unlike stimuli in the sensory registers, information stored in short-term memory is not identical to what was perceived. The raw material has now been coded, transformed, and modified in some way. This transformation makes storage and retrieval easier.

Traditionally, psychologists and educators have assumed that, unless information in STM is rehearsed and transferred to long-term memory, it is forgotten or displaced by new information. Most research supports the idea that the capacity of short-term memory is limited. Miller's (1956) classic study demonstrated that people have difficulty remembering more than nine items or concepts at a time. Furthermore, it seems that seven is the magic number, plus or minus two.

The research indicates that short-term memory capacity is limited. How many chunks or bits of information can you remember in your short-term memory?

Pattern recognition involves a complex sequence of analysis, comparison, and identification of the pattern with similar patterns that were previously encountered.

That is, most people can comfortably remember between five and nine pieces of information at one time. To illustrate the seven plus or minus two phenomenon, consider the conclusion drawn by a minister friend of one of the authors. This minister is convinced that this phenomenon is what keeps him in business, so to speak. He jokingly says that if Moses had brought down five, seven, or nine commandments from Mount Sinai, folks would have no problem remembering all of them. As it is, however, no one seems capable of remembering all ten. Therefore, for this minister, business is booming!

On the other hand, Chase and Ericsson (1981) have demonstrated that with practice, memory capacity can be increased to as many as eighty items or chunks of information. Some methods for increasing the capacity of short-term memory and some ideas for using short-term memory more effectively are presented in the Applications from the Text with this chapter.

Step Six: Long-term Memory (LTM). Long-term memory contains information that has been transformed and processed by STM and then stored for future use. The process of moving information from STM to LTM is called encoding.

One of the major research questions in this area is in regard to the process that makes long-term memory possible. The debate centers on what, if any, neurophysiological changes occur during the process of encoding a memory. One point about the encoding process seems apparent from the research: there does appear to be a fixed time period in which the encoding of a memory occurs. This time period for encoding begins at the moment the stimulus impacts on the sensory organ. The time period lasts anywhere up to sixty minutes after the original encounter with the stimulus.

Severe disruptions in the process of encoding can cause the loss of a memory. For instance, brain trauma or severe electric shock can disrupt the encoding process. Certain types of amnesia may be caused by this disruption in the encoding process.

Central Processor (Executive Control). Processing and depth of processing for memories are assumed to have a decision-making aspect to them. What happens when a stimulus is registered and transferred to the short-term memory system for further processing is assumed to be under a person's control. The person controls the process by deciding what information to keep, where to place it, what to retrieve, and how to use it. Information in long-term memory usually is assumed to be organized in some fashion and interconnected in some manner. There is a central processing function that associates the pieces of information with one another. Some argue that information is arranged in a hierarchy (Collins & Quillian, 1969). A more contemporary idea is that there is a network arrangement with information being connected through a variety of associations (Anderson, 1985).

As indicated in the preceding sections, memory is a complicated process. There clearly are multiple levels of storage and multiple systems of memory. Although such models still only approximate the relationship between the brain and cognition, they clearly have aided researchers in identifying some aspects of the memory process. One area of research on remembering that stems directly from the previous section is the levels of processing model.

Do you believe that long-term memory capacity is unlimited? Do you believe that some long-term memories are discarded as new memories are stored?

List some factors that appear to be used in deciding to process or not to process a memory.

The Levels of Processing Model

Craik and Lockhart (1972) developed the levels of processing, or depth of processing, model of memory. The basic assumption of the levels of processing model is that a stimulus from the environment enters the system and produces a perception or memory trace that may be processed at various levels on a continuum from shallow to deep. Transient traces result when only physical or sensory features of a stimulus are processed. Deeper levels of processing, on the other hand, result when the memory trace is moved into semantic and episodic forms. The assumption is that the deeper the level of processing, the deeper the memory trace. Likewise, the deeper the memory trace, the easier the recall.

Perhaps an illustration of the levels of processing model will help you to process this concept at a deeper level. The word "snow" for example, can be processed at many levels. I can process the word literally as a group of four letters or markings on a page. This would represent a very transient or shallow level of processing, and one that is most likely to result in forgetting.

Also I could process the word "snow" at a deeper level by sounding out the word and experiencing it acoustically. At a still deeper level, I could attach meaning to the sight and sound of the word by learning that snow is a type of precipitation—but different from rain, hail, or sleet. This level of processing is still not as deep as the level involved when my environment provides me with an actual, firsthand experience with snow. When I have tested it, romped in it, and crunched it under my feet and in my hands, the memory trace is more likely to become permanent. Eskimos, whose environment necessitates remembering snow at deep levels (excuse the pun), can distinguish between various types of snow (i.e., heavy snow, wet snow). This is a depth of processing that the typical Floridian will never achieve, simply because the environment in Florida does not provide "in-depth" experiencing!

Consider an analogy. A memory trace begins as a perception that may be fleeting and transient, like a feathery line drawn in the wet sand. If processed at a deeper level, the faint line may become a small furrow. At the deepest level, and most permanent, the memory trace may have become a trench, clearly defined, strong, and indelible.

One example of the depth of processing model is that an object, such as an airplane, can be processed on a number of different levels. For instance, an airplane can be processed at the purely physical level—what Tulving (1985) termed the procedural level. This might be simply the physical response made to the sight and sound of the plane. Identifying sight and sound made by the plane with the word "airplane" would place it at the semantic level of processing. Making the statement that "the airplane is a Boeing 747 and my wife is on board" would be an episodic memory.

It appears that increasing the depth of processing is associated in some way with increasing memory performance. However, other factors also appear to be important. For instance, certain other strategies and characteristics of the learner appear to affect memory performance. One example of another strategy is elaboration. Elaboration involves transforming information into the learner's

Do you think that creating a word or concept about an experience aids in memory performance? Are we more likely to process those experiences on which we can "hang a conceptual peg?"

own words or concepts. Such a transformation and assimilation increases memory performance. The type of learning task also appears to affect memory performance. The next section presents a model of memory that examines both the characteristics of the learner and the characteristics of the task.

The Learner and the Task

Another view of memory was proposed by Jenkins (1979). This viewpoint examines the interaction of the characteristics of the learner and the nature of the task. One advantage of this view is that it encompasses both the learner and the task. Both factors interact to increase or decrease memory performance.

Part I. The Learner. Characteristic: The individual characteristics of the learner affect her ability to encode, store, and retrieve information. Unlike other factors, these individual characteristics may fluctuate from day to day. Is the learner fatigued, distressed, or disadvantaged in some way? Additionally, level of maturation and development will play a critical and continuing role in memory processing. Motivation is still another dimension of the individual learner. Boyd (1988) points out that educational and school psychologists primarily concentrate on assessing these individual characteristics of learners.

It has been demonstrated that if learners have a need to remember certain material, the level of recall is enhanced. For example, Istomina (1975) has shown that young children recall more information if they understand the purpose for remembering it. Specifically, when children were presented a five-word grocery list during a play activity involving shopping, they recalled twice as many words from the list as when they were taught simply as a memory exercise.

Part II. Task. Nature/Characteristics of the Stimulus Materials: According to Jenkins, the characteristics of the material to be remembered affect the memory process. Salient characteristics of the materials include the physical structure, the sensory modality, the sequence of presentation, and the level of conceptual difficulty. Perlmutter and Meyers (1979), for example, demonstrated that changing the structure of material without changing the type of material can influence a learner's success on a memory task. Manning (1991) has demonstrated that changing the structure of material by using color dots to highlight important points to remember can improve retention and recall. Presenting material in a variety of sensory modalities and a variety of levels of processing enhances the memory process. Finally, making sure that the material is appropriate for the learner also will facilitate memory.

In conclusion, the nature of the learning materials varies considerably from school to school. While some students have access to multimedia learning centers, others must share a single textbook (Kozol, 1991). The fact remains that the characteristics of the task have significant impact on memory.

Did you ever know a student who could look at a text one time and remember everything that was written? Do you think that there is an inborn ability for memory?

In addition to the characteristics of the task, do you think that there is an order effect involved in the sequence of materials presented in a task? Do you find that you can more easily recall the first and last parts of a task?

How Is Memory Measured?

The ability of a student to remember material usually is either a recognition task or a recall task (Kagan, 1971). On a recognition task or test, the student must sort out the correct answer or item from similar but incorrect material. For example, students may be given an opportunity to listen to a list of words read to them and then asked to identify those words that were included in the list. In other cases, students may be shown a series of pictures and then asked to note whether a particular picture was included among those shown.

A recall test would present information to the student and ask for a report of some or all the information given. Some recall tests are called "free recall" because the student is given no clues about the possible answer and must search his memory for the necessary information. For example, a student may be asked to remember how to spell the word "continuum" or complete a mathematics problem $12 \times 4 = ?$.

Boyd (1988) reviewed methods for the clinical assessment of memory and has noted that tasks for assessing memory can be any of those presented in figure 10.3.

The stimulus for the test can be verbal, visual, or auditory and the response can be verbal, visual, or motor. Memory tests occur daily for all of us. Could you find your keys this morning? Did you remember to send your mother a birthday card? Did you remember to bring your pencil to class for the test? Did you remember the test? Teachers use memory tests as one of the major ways to report learning and most frequently these are tests that are made up of questions that

Long-term memory recall of general information,
Long-term memory of numerical reasoning,
Replication of a sequence of beads placed on a string,
Repetition of sentences,
Sequential pointing to an object previously displayed,
Short-term memory span for digits,
Short-term memory span for a tapping sequence,
Short-term memory for pictures,
Short-term memory for objects
Short-term memory for faces,
Short-term memory for sequential hand movements,
Short-term story recall,
Recall locations of picture arrangement,
Perform orally directed series of actions,
Draw geometric form(s) from memory,
Recall sequence of letters,
Reproduce visual-spatial configurations,
Draw shapes and location of blocks from memory,
Timed exposure (ten seconds) to shapes with immediate recall reproduction,
Timed exposure (ten seconds) to shapes with recall after a delay (fifteen seconds).

FIGURE 10.3
Tasks Assessed by Tests of Memory

Adapted from Boyd (1988)

require either recall or recognition. School psychologists, the frontline workers who measure a learner's ability to remember, use a variety of test batteries that contain items like those listed here.

■ ■ ■

USING MEMORY PROFICIENTLY: THE ROLE OF METAMEMORY

It is one thing to measure memory, it is another thing to help a student use her memory proficiently. Ultimately, however, the purpose of understanding the memory process is to accomplish this goal. Thinking about memory and how to best use it is called metamemory. Flavell (1971) coined this term, which refers to a person's potential for verbalizing knowledge about memory storage and retrieval.

Metamemory involves devising strategies for using memory processes. The techniques and applications discussed in the next section are examples of using metamemory to enhance learning in the classroom.

Metamemory: Practical Applications in the Classroom

What characteristics does a good memory strategist possess? In a nutshell, good strategists "try smart" rather than "try hard." That is, they are reflective without focusing on negative self-doubts concerning memorization. They know that "trying hard" to memorize is not enough. In fact, anxiety works against effective memorizing efforts. Good strategists know that their memory competence gradually will increase as they continue to discover, use, and refine more effective strategies (Dweck, 1987).

What kind of strategies are effective? Good memorizers use external and internal strategies for remembering things. External strategies include making "to do" lists or placing an object in a certain place so it won't be forgotten on the way to school the next morning. An example of an internal strategy, on the other hand, would be mentally rehearsing information.

Good strategists learn which strategy to use in which situation. There are three ways to learn memory strategies:

1. Trial and error or self-discovery;
2. Formal instruction in strategy use by teachers and role models;
3. Emulating teachers, parents, or other good models who demonstrate effective strategies.

One step in training good memory strategists would be to replicate the following experiment to assess what strategies students use on a day-to-day basis. The same process can be used to assess instruction and to practice with strategies for remembering. Kreutzer, Leonard, and Flavell (1975) did an interview study of children's memory that showed, that by the time they reached grade five, children knew many of the principles of remembering taught in study skills and psychology classes! The students demonstrated "metamemory" (i.e., they

Anecdotal accounts of graduate students indicate that one memory strategy used in studying for a test is to know what not to study. How do you determine what is important and what is not important when you study?

Strategy	Number
Write it down (assignment book or calendar)	19
Write it on my hand; tie string on finger	7
Have someone remind me	7
Place note on dresser, etc.	5
Repeat it over and over	5
Put it in an obvious place (school bag)	5
Total	48

FIGURE 10.4
What Fifth-grade Students
Do to Remember a Task

thought about what strategies they used to remember things). For example, the students said they would place an object they wanted to remember to bring with them to school the next day in a place where it would be obvious. Students also said that they would use written reminders, tie strings on their fingers, or ask another person to remind them to help them remember. Internal methods, such as deliberately thinking about it the night before, also were mentioned. One of the authors replicated this study and obtained similar results. Twenty-four fifth-graders were asked to list all the things they do to remember to do something tomorrow. Forty-eight responses were gathered. The results are presented in figure 10.4.

Students also were asked a question related to using short-term memory. Imagine that your parent dropped you off at school and asked you to give your teacher a message as soon as you got to school. "What would you do to try to remember?" Fifteen said that they would ask their parent to write a note. (Not a strategy that shows a good deal of confidence in one's memory.) Fourteen said that they would repeat it over and over until they saw their teacher. Other responses were "cross my fingers" (one answer) and "write it on my hand" (one answer). Replicating the study would be only a beginning in developing good strategy users in the classroom. A next step would be to look at the memory process as described in the earlier part of this chapter and identify strategies to use at the various stages of the multistore model and the depth of processing model. Figure 10.5 outlines some ideas that might be appropriate at the various stages of the process of remembering.

Describe a memory strategy that might be used for the example on this page.

Attention. What can be done at the preattention or attention stage? Obviously the first step in the memory process is to get the attention of the student and to have him focus on the task at hand. Gordon (1974) notes that most teachers know how to enrich the learning surroundings. In *Teacher Effectiveness Training,* he lists thirteen ideas for increasing students' attention by adding attractive features to the classroom. Included in the list are items such as a creative-writing center, an art center, a listening station, bright-colored displays, and a puppet stage.

List some other classroom features that might enhance attention.

FIGURE 10.5
Practical Applications at
the Various Stages of
Remembering

Memory Process	Application
Attention	Modify the environment (enrich or impoverish)
Sensory Registers	Cue for attention
	Multisensory presentations for perception
Short-term Memory	Rehearsal chunking
Encoding	Elaboration;
	Organizational and other mnemonic techniques
Long-term Memory	Avoiding interference
Retrieval	Cueing to aid search

Modified from Gagné and Driscoll (1988)

A current list would include a computer center complete with interactive video programs and access to data bases. Many students benefit by the teacher enriching the classroom climate. Their curiosity is aroused and their motivation to respond to stimuli is increased. Not all students excel in an enhanced environment; rather, some with attention deficit disorder (ADD) or attention deficit hyperactivity disorder (ADHD) are distracted by too much stimulation. Gordon makes this point and has urged that teachers look at how to impoverish the classroom setting, at least for certain students. Teachers have for years used study carrels, room dividers, special arrangements of furniture, and removal of distracting objects to help those students who are easily distracted or drawn "off-task."

The parallel between engaging students in the remembering process and handling discipline problems in the classroom is noted. Gordon's suggestions are intended to improve "discipline" in the class but sound very similar to Jones' (1987) plan for good instruction. The first phase of a structured lesson should begin with "raising the level of concern," which is the pivotal part of the lesson plan. A necessary skill in teaching is the ability to engage students when the teacher wants attention. Writing for a different audience, Frank (1986) says it best: "What allures, entices, tempts, tantalizes, fascinates, captivates, enchants, attracts, bewitches, catches, hypnotizes, makes you remember, and gets you to buy a product, stay tuned to a show, or keep reading? A hook" (p. 40). Frank describes numerous hooks, such as visual hooks, humor as a hook, and a single sentence, question, or slogan as a hook. Sounding a lot like Dr. Seuss, Frank suggests that people keep a "hook book," which is a notebook of ideas to be used to set the stage for a lesson.

Problems in dealing with students with attention deficit disorder (ADD) differ only in degree from those of any other learner. The problem remains: How to get and maintain the attention of the student? Attention to what is important is a critical component of effective study skills.

Some research indicates that we have about a twenty-minute attention span for classroom lectures. Describe some techniques for maintaining attention after the first twenty minutes.

What happens to bring about learning and recall of information? Grossman (1990) has listed ideas that can be used to help gain the attention of impulsive and distractible students. One, require students to leave pencils and material on the desk until the teacher is ready for them to begin work. Two, have the students keep their desks free of any materials not needed for the assigned task. Three, keep all items that might be distracting in a separate area of the classroom. Four, use unmarked plain paper to cover finished work on the page so that the student can focus only on the current problem or question.

Cueing is one way to promote attention to important elements and to improve concentration. Manning (1991) describes three methods of cueing: cue cards, cue audiotapes, and cue colors. Cue cards can be pictures or written reminders. For example, a secondary school history class may be cued by an overhead transparency that illustrates that underlined material in a reading assignment is important! Cues also can be used in other forms. Students will benefit from making their own cue cards and posters. Cards should be taped in an obvious place: on the desk or inside a notebook cover. Elementary school students like to write cues on paper bracelets and wear them during the school day. As previously noted, many students do not hesitate to write cue notes on their arm or hand!

Cueing can be done by using an audiotape with a bell or tone repeated at various times during a study period. Manning (1991) notes that the procedure

Can teachers go too far in cueing students about what information to attend and to study? Will students still learn how to filter out extraneous information?

According to Gordon (1974), adding classroom features such as learning centers or special displays can aid children in attending to the information. By aiding attention the memory of the information may be increased.

works best if the students are trained to monitor their behavior by responding to a check sheet that records whether they are concentrating or not. Color dots or stop-and-go signs can be used to call attention to important features of a lesson or important rules to remember. Learning is more efficient if the learner attends to the right information. Most students benefit from the ideas listed here as a means to help them perceive the items to be learned and to filter out the many other stimuli available to their senses. Older students gradually will learn to be more selective by becoming able to sort out key words and maintain ideas from the other material presented. Teachers cannot wait for selective perceptions to develop naturally. One important component of teaching is training the student to discriminate. Many students may attend but still be unable to comprehend what is deemed to be important to learn.

Sensory Registers. In applying metamory techniques, the idea of sensory modality is important. Many students who find it difficult to understand math when it is presented in a verbal mode find it easy when exposed to manipulatives. The manipulatives allow them to use additional senses to understand the concepts. One of the authors' daughters came home from school humming a tune about the states in the United States. Obviously, her teacher had used a memory aid to help the fourth-grade students commit to memory the names of the fifty United States. The teacher was using the idea that imposing a rhythm to the presentation helped student recall. Support for this tactic comes from a study by Bower and Springston (1970). Specifically, research subjects had better recall for TVFBIJFKYMCA when the reader of the list paused in a pattern of TV. . .FBI. . .JFK . . .YMCA rather than TVF. . .BIJ. . .FKY. . .MCA.

Short-term Memory. A variety of procedures have been listed in this chapter that can help increase memory performance. Included among these procedures are reinforcement, repetition/rehearsal, novelty, attention, meaningfulness, organization (chunking), elaboration, and depth of processing. Teachers can use some of these procedures to help students increase the efficiency of their short-term memory system.

A key process is the combining of pieces of information, or chunking. Students find it easier to remember a string of nine digits if the numbers are grouped in sets of three. For example, 615–693–547 is easier to remember than 615693547. Phone numbers are presented in chunks to aid memory. The capacity of short-term memory has been demonstrated to be limited. As noted earlier in this chapter, the number seems to be seven plus or minus two (Miller, 1956).

The idea of chunking is useful because more information can be stored in short-term memory. Imagine you have twenty items to wrap in packages. If you can wrap some of the items into packages of three or four items, you can decrease your work load and spend less time wrapping packages. Similarly, if you can only take seven packages with you on a airplane trip but wanted to take twenty items, you would wrap them into no more than seven packages. Can a teacher give students help in remembering by training them about grouping

Describe some of your own personal methods for chunking. Are these methods listed in this chapter?

APPLICATIONS FROM THE TEXT 10.1

Do you remember that the time span for short-term memory was described previously in this chapter as brief? One way of compensating for this time limitation is rehearsal. Teachers can help students to remember by teaching them rehearsal techniques. One of the authors' sons, a thirteen-year-old, suffers from a common ailment of adolescence. He has trouble remembering what he has been told to do while on his way to doing the task. This is especially true if he is given two tasks to remember. Often he will do one task and forget the other. Rehearsal, the idea of saying the two tasks over and over, will improve recall in these situations.

Ellis and Lenz (1987) describe using rehearsal in the classroom by having students recite silently or orally specific information to be learned. For example, to remember the parts of the circulatory system, the student would list all of them and recite the list a number of times. A more engaging approach would be to have the student or a teacher copy the terms on three-inch by five-inch cards and say each term a number of times while writing it. If the teacher or an adult is writing the card, the student can be asked to say the letters and then trace them with a finger after the card has been completed. Ellis and Lenz (1987) have developed a CAN DO strategy for helping students, especially learning disabled, to cue themselves to use verbal rehearsal. Students are taught the acronym, "can do" and trained to follow specific steps. The steps are: C—create a list of words to be learned, A—ask yourself if the list is complete, N—note the main ideas and details using a tree diagram, D—describe each component and how it relates to the others, and O—overlearn the main ideas and supporting terms. The strategy is a nontransformational strategy because it does not embellish, exaggerate, or transform the material to be learned.

---

items? Perhaps, but with limitations. The prediction that instructing students in chunking would help them be able to remember as well as those who intuitively chunk information has not been supported (Lyon, 1977). The key is how you as a teacher present information. Presenting the information in clusters can aid student recall.

The teacher also needs to remember that there is a relationship between prior knowledge and the student's ability to chunk the information. Chi (1978) found that children who knew a lot about the game of chess were better able to chunk information than adults who were less knowledgeable about chess.

Encoding. The use of aids for short-term memory can help to make the day less complicated (i.e., fewer phone numbers are forgotten, more tasks are completed). However, the teacher is looking for a more long-term payoff. What can be done to help students commit important information to long-term memory? How can students be assisted in encoding information into the long-term memory file? The student using the good strategies will learn how to use elaboration as a means to get information into the long-term files. Schneider and Pressley

With what type of knowledge is rehearsal necessary? Is rehearsal necessary in learning basic skills, particularly with arithmetic and reading skills?

Do you agree that if elaboration is an effective strategy, then teachers should encourage more note taking and less teacher-made handouts? Do you think teachers are too likely to "spoon-feed" information?

(1989) list ideas about elaboration skills that may be useful when planning instruction and when presenting information to children at different age levels. Their list is modified and presented here. The general conclusions are that older children are more likely than younger children to do the following:

1. Use elaboration strategies even if they are not instructed to do so. It also is interesting that elaboration is used infrequently by the adult population as noted by Pressley, Levin, and Ghatala (1984). Although many adults have learned the memory strategy by their own self-discovery or via instruction, there is still plenty of need for instruction about elaboration techniques.

2. Carry out elaboration strategies that cannot be used by younger children. An example of a study comparing older and younger children contrasted second-grade and sixth-grade students. The students were asked to use a keyword elaboration strategy. Younger children need pictures to help in generating elaborative images, while sixth-grade students could do so without pictorial support (Pressley & Levin, 1978). The point is that much more precise elaboration is necessary if the strategy will work for younger students. Also, the best strategy is for the learner to respond to "Why?" about the item to be learned. Bransford et al. (1982) found that, when students developed their own elaboration by making it more precise, learning improved. For example, if students turned the statement, "The hungry man got out of the car" into a more precise elaboration like, "The hungry man got out of the car to go into the restaurant," recall increased. When students generated their own response to a "Why?" question, it promoted their learning.

3. Retrieve and use elaborative mediators that they have created. Even if young children do use elaborative mediators they have constructed while learning material, they are less likely to use the mediator at test time (Pressley & Levin, 1980).

4. Transfer elaborative strategies. The most important study in this area compares transfer of the strategy with other curriculum areas for ten- to sixteen-year-olds and sixteen- to nineteen-year-olds (Pressley & Dennis-Rounds, 1980). There was little or no transfer for the ten-to-sixteen-year-olds and significant transfer for the older group. One conclusion would be that use of elaborative strategies needs to be applied in all subject areas rather than taught as a general study strategy, especially to younger students.

5. Coordinate elaborative strategies with the knowledge base. Studies show that younger children benefit from having associated pairs presented to them that can be easily elaborated. For example, needle-balloon (the needle popping the balloon) rather than an unrelated pair (lamp-key). A study by Pressley and Levin (1977) showed that instruction in elaboration helped the younger students, who possessed less prior knowledge, more than older students, who because of their prior knowledge, seemed to form elaborations almost immediately and automatically.

6. Use metamemory about elaboration strategies. Older children have more insight into their own memory performance. Appell, Cooper, McCarrel, Sims-Knight, Yussen, and Flavell (1972) looked at this issue by showing four-, seven-, and eleven-year-old children two sets of pictures. The

instructions for one set was to look at the pictures and try to remember them. The instructions for the other set was that looking at the pictures would help performance on a later task. The idea was to see whether the children behaved any differently when they were expecting a recall test. As might be expected, the eleven-year-olds used more rehearsal and their performance on the recall test was significantly better. Kreutzer, Leonard, and Flavell (1975), using an interview to gather data from children, found that there was a clear developmental increase in understanding, indicating that verbal elaboration facilitates learning.

There are a number of other elaboration strategies that teachers can use to help students commit facts and concepts to long-term memory. Most people faced with a learning task will try to change the material in some way so that it will be more memorable. Prytulak's (1971) study showed that people will try to make words or phrases out of nonsense syllables as a way to remember the syllables. This example illustrates a transformational elaboration. To transform is to change the content in some way other than what would be naturally or meaningfully associated with the content. Nontransformational elaborations (discussed previously) are not additive, but transformational elaborations are because they embellish what is to be learned in some manner. For example, elaboration to learn paired associates (noun-paired learning) would be to join the items together into a common phrase or an image. Imagery mnemonics has been shown to greatly assist in the learning of paired associates. A verbal elaboration could be the learning of cat-apple. A verbal elaboration might be "The cat rolled the apple on the ground." An imaginal elaboration would be to think of your childhood pet cat playing with the kind of apple you remember eating as a child (Schneider & Pressley, 1989).

Research on long-term memory storage indicates that we retain an abstract or outline of conceptual material. In effect, the salient aspects of the concept are retained while the "fluff" is forgotten. Is it possible to develop a memory strategy based on this idea?

The keyword method has been frequently used in teaching children a second language.

The keyword method was brought to prominence by Atkinson in 1975 when he applied the learning method to assist in learning a foreign language. The first step in the method is to find a concrete English word (the keyword) that sounds like a salient part of a foreign word you want to know. Next, using ideas from imagery, you form a visual image of the two words interacting in some manner. An example is the Spanish word "carta," which means letter and sounds like the English word cart (the keyword). An image or picture of a stamped, addressed letter loaded into a shopping cart would assist the student in remembering the meaning of the word "carta."

Atkinson and Raugh (1975) used the keyword approach to successfully teach elementary Russian words to beginning language students. Students who used the keyword method recalled 72 percent of a list of 120 words as compared with a recall of 42 percent for students who used traditional methods. Numerous studies have replicated these results with adults and children. Furthermore, the method has been extended and used in other content areas such as social studies. Shriberg, Levin, and McCormick (1982) taught about famous people via the keyword method. The approach incorporated a prose method rather than a paired associate approach. Students were shown a picture illustrating the keyword (in this case "raccoon," which sounded like the name of the person to be remembered: "McCune"). The students also were asked to remember McCune for her major accomplishment of teaching her cat to count. The students in the experimental groups had significantly improved performance over a control group that used more traditional methods. In an interesting later study, Levin, Shriberg, and Berry (1983) demonstrated the importance of including a keyword in an illustration. Student recall of the attributes of a hypothetical town "Fostoria" (the keyword was frost) was significantly greater than a similar organized picture without the people dressed warmly because of the frost.

Organizational and Other Mnemonic Methods

Memory aids or mnemonics can be useful to hold items in storage until needed. One of the authors often uses the rhyme, "Thirty days has September, April, June, and November. All the rest have thirty-one, except February, which has twenty-eight or twenty-nine" to remember the days in the months. According to Bower and Bolton (1969), the meter and rhyme force recall because there are few if any other pieces of information that would fit the particular pattern. The teacher we mentioned before who taught a jingle was using a single-use, chain-type mnemonic (Bellezza, 1981). Many of us have used a rhyme to remember important information. We also use acronyms (first letter technique) such as, ROY G. BIV to recall the colors in the color spectrum. One of our sons uses I'M NO WIMP to be able to list the states around the Great Lakes (Indiana, Michigan, New York, Ohio, Wisconsin, Illinois, Minnesota and Pennsylvania). One of our daughters has used an acrostic (first letter of each word in a sentence) "My Very Evil Mother Just Served Us Nine Pizzas" to remember the planets in their respective order: Mercury, Venus, Earth, Mars, Jupiter, Saturn, Uranus, Neptune, and Pluto. You might want to study a dictionary of mnemonics to identify others (Dictionary of Mnemonics, 1972).

What other academic areas might effectively use a keyword method?

Mnemonic aids can take many different forms. The key aspect of a mnemonic is to pair something that is easily remembered with whatever it is you are trying to learn. Perhaps the oldest such technique is the method of loci. This method dates to Roman times (Yates, 1966). As an example, you might visualize one of your favorite rooms. Imagine some of the obvious objects in the room. You might imagine six objects. One might be your dresser, a second could be your desk, a third might be your compact disc player, etc. You always use the same series of objects. In effect, you have establish an external framework of locations (loci) on which to place what items you want to remember. Try it the next time you are trying to remember a number of items from the store. Modern psychologists have developed a contemporary version of the loci method called the pegword approach. The pegword method uses visual imagery and organizes information by placing or hanging the items on "pegs." The method is similar to the loci methods. The learner must first learn a list to serve as the "pegs." Many experts suggest a poem that is easy to remember. Minninger (1984) suggests ten always available memory pegs on your body.

1. The top of your head. Use an image of the object you want to remember perching on your head. (Make it funny to make it easier to remember.)
2. Your forehead. Pretend that it is a flashing billboard advertising the second item you want to recall.
3. Your nose. It's a vending machine spurting out the third thing you want to remember.
4. Your mouth. It's a garage for parking the fourth item.
5. Your throat. An object that is hard to swallow is placed here.
6. Your chest. This object is stored in your lungs.
7. Your belly button. This object is glued there.
8. Your hips. This object is attached to your belt and hangs on your hips.
9. Your knees. You are kneeling on the ninth object.
10. Your feet. You stand on the tenth object. How does it feel standing on the object?

The story method also can be used to help students memorize. Here the student uses each successive word on a list in a story that he makes up. Students seldom confuse the important words with the words they added to the story and recalling the story prompts the students to remember the significant items. Because each story is different, the new stories rarely interfere with remembering previous stories and vital information they contain.

Retrieval

There is considerable overlap between the concepts of encoding and retrieval. Murdock (1974) defined retrieval as the utilization of stored information. Obviously, effective encoding should result in better retrieval of information from long-term memory. The setting and environment seem to have some influence on this ability. For example, scuba divers are able to remember words learned underwater better than words they practiced and rehearsed on shore (Godden & Baddeley, 1975). Secondly, even aromas in the environment are proving to be a factor. Schab (1991) had students list antonyms for adjectives. Those who did

Research indicates that items learned in one environment are more likely to be recalled in a similar environment. What impact might such an effect have on studying and test taking?

Do interference effects operate in an elementary school classroom? Does material learned in the afternoon interfere with the recall of material learned in the morning?

this task while smelling the aroma of chocolate had better performance than students in a control (no chocolate aroma) situation.

More practical methods have been presented by Ormrod (1990), who described cues as important aids to the retrieval process. Multiple-choice questions generally require less familiarity with the material to be learned because an identity cue is provided in the answer. Associate cues also improve retrieval. For instance, if I asked you to remember a list of twenty-five animals and gave you only a short time to study them, you would probably be unable to recall some animals from the list. If I prompted you or gave you associate cues (farm animals, house pets, and zoo animals), you would no doubt be able to come up with at least another name or two.

Many colleges have a policy that no undergraduate student must take more than two final examinations on the same day. The rationale for this is the phenomenon of interference. If you were given twenty words to try to remember and then given another similar list, you would find that learning the second list interfered with your ability to recall the words from the first list. Therefore, the teacher in the classroom should not teach two similar concepts closely in time. Furthermore, teachers can reduce interference if they use different methods to teach similar content. A study by Andre (1973) showed that varying organization and presentation decreased student confusion. In one case, the teacher also aided organization by using different-colored paper.

Metamemory Strategies

As previously noted, metamemory is the term used to refer to how students can have more complete control over the process of committing information to memory. Manning (1991) is among those who have developed plans for helping students use metamemory in the classroom on a day-to-day basis. She credits a student teacher with developing a set of steps for learning spelling words. It is presented in Applications from the Text 10.3 as an example of cognitive self-instruction. Other models have been developed for other content areas.

Schneider and Pressley (1989) provide an excellent summary of things for teachers to consider about trying to develop good strategy usage among their students. Their points are modified somewhat and listed here:

1. There are many strategies to learn and they should become a part of the school curriculum.
2. Teachers do not think in information-processing terms. Education programs should consider teaching an entire course of strategies to use in schools.
3. It takes effort for use of strategies to occur. Direct instruction, modeling, and practice are required before students will use good strategies.
4. More evaluation work is being done and needs to be made available to teachers.
5. There are numerous individual differences in students. No one strategy will work for all students. It is important to be familiar with a wide variety of strategies and be prepared to implement them to meet varying student needs. For example, some special education students may need more extensive modeling and rehearsal. With persistence and help, any student can benefit from learning good memory strategies.

SUMMARY

Memory theory and research has still not fully solved the relationship between mind, memory, and brain. A number of different models of memory exist. However, no one single model appears to fully explain the relationship of memory to neurophysiological functioning.

It is clear that multiple memory systems exist. The number of systems appears to be linked to the various sensory systems. For instance, it is clear that there are memory systems for vision, for hearing, and for other sensory systems. However, it also appears that there are other memory systems distinct from the sensory systems. For instance, there is research support for a memory system of one's personal life history.

Even though multiple memory systems exist, there is research evidence to support some type of central processor or centralized control. This evidence means that there is some type of decision making or volition involved in processing memories. The decisions that are made about the type of processing and the depth of processing appear to play a role in effective memory strategies.

Information processing models of memory offer some direction to how memories are processed and stored. There does seem to be research support that information is processed from a sensory register, through a short-term memory system, and maintained in a long-term memory system.

Metamemory strategies offer some hope in aiding the memory process. A number of different memory strategies are presented. Teachers should be aware of such techniques and make them available to students. Such techniques can effectively enhance student learning.

SMART METHODS OF ORGANIZING, PLANNING, AND STUDYING

In reviewing this chapter, what recommendations would you have for Mrs. Wheeler, Charles, or Charles' mother in the case study at the beginning of the chapter?

The problem described in the case study can be addressed by some of the following applications presented in this chapter, such as having students use both external and internal strategies. In the case study, the teacher and Charles's mother used external strategies to promote better organization and study habits for Charles.

Mrs. Wheeler enlisted the help of the mother to have Charles practice two things at home each evening. One plan was to have him report to his mother each day after school what assignments he had for the next day and what homework he had to do that evening. A second idea was for Charles to get his "stuff" together for school before he went to bed at night rather than to wait to do it in the morning before school. At school the plan was for Charles to carry a three-inch by five-inch card in his pocket and to write on one side his assignments for each of his subjects each day. On the other side of the card, he was to note anything he had to bring to school the next day or anything he had to plan to do in the future, such as a project for class that might be due in two weeks.

Mrs. Wheeler decided to try using cueing methods with Charles in the classroom. The plan would be to have a cue card taped to Charles' desk with a set of instructions for him to follow each time before he started to do assigned work. For example, the card could list the following questions: Do I have pencil, paper, and other materials needed to do this assignment? Do I understand the assignment? How will I know when I am finished with this assignment?

The purpose of the strategies to be used by both Mrs. Wheeler and Charles's mother was to teach Charles a set of habits to help him get organized about his schoolwork. After he develops these habits, other methods might need to be used to help him improve other short-term and long-term memory practices.

After these methods have successfully improved his achievement, other internal methods can be used. Charles could be taught to use a method that changes the way he thinks about his school assignments. The CAN DO strategy described in the chapter is one example of an internal method that when used properly helps to develop new patterns of how students think about their studies and how they go about learning the information assigned to them. Instruction in remembering methods can be specific to the various stages of the multistore model. For example, enrichment of the environment can be used to improve the likelihood of students "paying attention." Elaboration and other mnemonic techniques can be used to aid encoding, which is the commitment of information to a long-term memory.

Mrs. Wheeler has many options available to her to use with Charles to help increase his effectiveness as a student. Teachers are required to do more than know the subject they teach. Imparting study skills is an important component of providing for the complete needs of the students in the classroom. Mrs. Wheeler might want to replicate the study described in this chapter where students were asked what they did to remember to do things. Conducting the study with the students also is a form of instruction or review of what students know about good organizational practices. The teacher also might check to see if she is demonstrating good planning methods for her class. Furthermore, is she describing what she is doing and why she is doing it to the class? If she is, she is serving as a good model of someone who is trying smart methods of organizing, planning, and studying.

CHAPTER REVIEW

1. How might sensory memory be effectively engaged in the learning process in the classroom?
2. Can you think of examples from the classroom that illustrate each of Tulving's categories?
3. What might a teacher do to provide a more stimulating learning environment for the classroom? What might be done to keep the environment from being too stimulating for students? List some answers to these questions and compare your ideas with those listed in the Applications from this chapter.
4. How can learning be enhanced by making use of the concept of selective attention in the classroom?
5. Since attention is the starting place for learning and memory, what are some ways that teachers can enhance the attention of students in the classroom?

REFERENCES

Anderson, J. (1985). *Cognitive psychology and its implications.* New York: Freeman.

Andre, T. (1973). Retroactive inhibition of prose and change in physical or organizational context. *Psychological Reports, 32,* 781–782.

Appell, L., Cooper, R., McCarrel, N., Sims-Knight, J., Yussen, S., & Flavell, J. (1972). The development of the distinction between perceiving and memorizing, *Child Development, 43,* 1365–1381.

Atkinson, J., & Shiffrin, R. (1968). Human memory: A proposed system and its control processes. In K. Spence & J. Spence (Eds.), *The psychology and learning of motivation: Advances in research and theory* (Vol. 2). New York: Academic Press.

Atkinson, R. C., & Raugh, M. R. (1975). An application of the mnemonic keyword technique to the acquisition of a Russian vocabulary. *Journal of Experimental Psychology: Human Learning and Memory, 1,* 126–133.

Barkley, R. (1988). Attention. In M. Tramontana & S. Hooper (Eds.), *Assessment issues in child neuropsychology* (pp. 145–176). New York: Plenum.

Bellezza, F. (1981). Mnemonic devices: Classification, characteristics, and criteria. *Review of Educational Research, 51,* 247–275.

Bower, G., & Bolton, L. (1969). Why are rhymes easy to learn? *Journal of Experimental Psychology, 82,* 453–461.

Bower, G., & Springston, F. (1970). Pauses as recording points in letter series. *Journal of Experimental Psychology, 101,* 360–366.

Boyd, T. (1988). Clinical assessment of memory in children: A developmental framework for practice. In M. Tramontana & S. Hooper (Eds.), *Assessment issues in child neuropsychology* (pp. 177–204). New York: Plenum.

Bransford, J., Stein, B., Vye, N., Franks, J., Auble, P., Mezyniski, K., & Perfetto, G. (1982). Differences in approaches to learning: An overview. *Journal of Experimental Psychology; General, 111,* 390–398.

Broadbent, D. (1958). *Perception and communication.* London: Pergamon.

Chase, W., & Ericsson, K. (1981). Skilled memory. In J. Anderson (Ed.), *Cognitive skills and their acquisition.* Hillsdale, NJ: Erlbaum.

Chi, C. (1978). Knowledge structures and memory development. In R. Siegler (Ed.), *Children's thinking: What develops?* (pp. 73–96). Hillsdale, NJ: Erlbaum.

Collins, A., & Quillian, M. (1969). Retrieval time from semantic memory. *Journal of Verbal Learning and Verbal Behavior, 8,* 240–247.

Craik, F., & Lockhart, R. (1972). Levels of processing: A framework for memory research. *Journal of Verbal Learning and Verbal Behavior, 11,* 671–684.

Darwin, C., Turvey, M., & Crowder, R. (1972). An auditory analogue of the Sperling partial report procedure: Evidence for brief auditory storage. *Cognitive Psychology, 3,* 255–267.

Dempster, R. (1985). Short-term memory development in childhood and adolescence. In C. Brainerd & M. Pressley (Eds.), *Basic processes in memory development: Progress in cognitive development research* (pp. 209–248). New York: Springer-Verlag.

Dictionary of Mnemonics. (1972). London: Eyre Methuen.

Dweck, C. (1987). *Children's theories of intelligence: Implications for motivation and learning.* Paper presented at the annual meeting of the American Educational Research Association, Washington, DC.

Ellis, E., & Lenz, B. (1987). A component analysis of effective learning strategies for LD students. *Learning Disabilities Focus, 2,* 94–107.

Flavell, J. H. (1971). First discussant's comments: What is memory development the development of? *Human Development, 14,* 272–278.

Frank, M. (1986). *How to get your point across in 30 seconds or less.* New York: Simon and Schuster.

Gagné, R., & Driscoll, M. (1988). *Essentials of learning for instruction.* Englewood Cliffs, NJ: Prentice Hall.

Godden, D., & Baddeley, A. (1975). Context-dependent memory in two natural environments: On land and underwater. *British Journal of Psychology, 66,* 325–332.

Gordon, T. (1974). *T.E.T: Teacher effectiveness training.* New York: David McKay.

Grossman, H. (1990). *Trouble-free teaching: Solutions to behavior problems in the classroom.* Mountain View, CA: Mayfield.

Istomina, Z. (1975). The development of voluntary memory in preschool-age children. *Soviet Psychology, 13,* 5–64.

James, W. (1890). *The principles of psychology.* New York: Henry Holt.

Jenkins, J. (1979). Four points to remember: A tetrahedral model of memory experiments. In L. S. Cermak & F. Craik (Eds.), *Levels of processing in human memory* (pp. 429–446). Hillsdale, NJ: Erlbaum.

Jones, F. H. (1987). *Positive classroom instruction.* New York: McGraw-Hill.

Kagan, J. (1971). *Understanding children: Behavior, motives, and thought.* New York: Harcourt Brace Jovanovich, Inc.

Kahneman, D. (1973). *Attention and effort.* Englewood Cliffs, NJ: Prentice Hall.

Klatzky, R. (1980). *Human memory; Structures and processes.* San Francisco: Freeman.

Kozol, J. (1991). *Savage inequities.* New York: Crown.

Kreutzer, M., Leonard, C., & Flavell, J. (1975). An interview study of children's knowledge about memory. *Monographs of the Society for Research in Child Development, 40*(1, Serial No. 159).

Levin, J., Shriberg, L., & Berry, J. (1983). A concrete strategy for remembering abstract prose. *American Educational Research Journal, 20,* 277–290.

Lyon, D. (1977). Individual differences in immediate serial recall: A matter of mnemonics? *Cognitive Psychology, 9,* 403–411.

Manning, B. (1991). *Cognitive self-instruction for classroom processes.* Albany, NY: State University of New York Press.

Martindale, C. (1981). *Cognition and consciousness.* Homewood, IL: Dorsey Press.

Miller, G. (1956). The magical number seven, plus or minus two: Some limits on our capacity for processing information. *Psychological Review, 63,* 81–97.

Minninger, J. (1984). *Total recall: How to boost your memory power.* Emmaus, PA: Rodale Press.

Murdock, B. (1974). *Human memory: Theory and data.* New York: Wiley.

Neisser, U. (1967). *Cognitive psychology.* New York: Appeleton-Century-Crofts.

Ormrod, J. (1990). *Human learning: Theories, principles, and educational applications.* Columbus, OH: Merrill.

Perlmutter, M., & Meyers, N. (1979). Development of recall in 2- to 4-year-old children. *Developmental Psychology, 15,* 73–83.

Peterson, L., & Peterson, M. (1959). Short-term retention of individual verbal items. *Journal of Experimental Psychology, 58,* 193–198.

Pressley, M., & Dennis-Rounds, J. (1980). Transfer of a mnemonic keyword strategy at two age levels. *Journal of Educational Psychology, 72,* 575–582.

Pressley, M., & Levin, J. (1977). Task parameters affecting the efficacy of a visual imagery learning strategy in younger and older children. *Journal of Experimental Child Psychology, 24,* 53–59.

Pressley, M., & Levin, J. (1978). Developmental constraints associated with children's use of the keyword method for foreign language vocabulary learning. *Journal of Experimental Child Psychology, 26,* 53–59.

Pressley, M., & Levin, J. (1980). The development of mental imagery retrieval. *Child Development, 51,* 558–560.

Pressley, M., Levin, J. R., & Ghatala, E. S. (1984). Memory strategy monitoring in adults and children. *Journal of Verbal Learning and Verbal Behavior, 23,* 270–288.

Prytulak, L. (1971). Natural language mediation. *Cognitive Psychology, 2,* 1–56.

Reynolds, R., & Shirey, L. (1988). The role of attention in studying and learning. In C. Weinstein, E. Goetz, & P. Alexander (Eds.), *Learning and study strategies: Issues in assessment, instruction, and evaluation* (pp. 77–100). San Diego, CA: Academic Press.

Schab, F. (1991). Odors and remembrance of things past. *Journal of Experimental Psychology: Learning, Memory and Cognition, 17,* 648–655.

Schneider, W., & Pressley, M. (1989). *Memory development between 2 and 20.* New York: Springer-Verlag.

Shriberg, L., Levin, J., & McCormick, C. (1982). Learning about "famous" people via the keyword method. *Journal of Educational Psychology, 74,* 238–247.

Tulving, E. (1985). How many memory systems are there? *American Psychologist, 40,* 385–398.

Van Essen, D. (1985). Functional organization of primate visual cortex. In A. Peters & E. Jones (Eds.), *The cerebral cortex* (Vol. 3). New York: Plenum.

Yates, F. (1966). *The art of memory.* London: Routledge and Kegan Paul.

SECTION IV

Evaluation, Assessment, and Special Education

■ ■ ■

CHAPTER 11

STANDARDIZED TESTING

■ ■ ■

Chapter Outline

THE TRACKING CONTROVERSY

You are in your second year of teaching a fourth-grade class in a medium-sized city in central Ohio. Your school system has decided to review a new policy that will completely "detrack," or end tracking, within the school system. You have been assigned to a planning committee that will make recommendations about this proposed policy. The planning committee is composed of various community, school, and parent groups.

The old policy on tracking included the assignment of students to within-class groups in elementary schools. For instance, in your fourth-grade class you had within-class groupings for reading and math. Achievement tests and grades were used to place students to within-classroom groupings in your school.

At the high school level, students were assigned to either a college preparatory or a vocational track. There also was a special magnet school for gifted students. Assignment to these tracks or magnet programs was based on achievement test scores, grades, and in the case of the gifted program, intelligence test scores.

The new detracking policy would end all of the following: any within-classroom groupings, any within-school tracks, and any magnet school programs. At the elementary school level, teachers would be required to institute whole-class learning in all subject areas. Cooperative learning programs would be instituted at the elementary school level. Cooperative learning teams would assign high-ability students with low-ability students. Student grades would be based on the cooperative learning teams' overall performance. The same grades would be given to all students on each team.

Many members of the minority ethnic communities in the school district strongly support the detracking policy. Some minority-group members on the planning committee state that the old policy of testing and tracking smacked of racism. They believe that standardized tests are biased against minorities. They say that using the test scores for placement in groups or tracks resulted in a disproportionate number of minorities in the lower groups in elementary school and in the vocational track in high school.

Parents of students in the gifted programs and in the college-preparatory programs are opposed to the detracking. Parents of these students on the planning committee state that their children will lose out because teachers will have to teach to the average in their classrooms. These parents say that their child will become bored and lose interest in school because teachers will "teach down" to accommodate other students in the class. Parents of students in the preparatory track point out that a detracking policy will make high school students less competitive in applying for the more selective colleges.

What position would you take on detracking on the planning committee to review the policy? How would such a change in policy affect your own teaching and curriculum decisions?

INTRODUCTION

The purpose of this chapter is to examine intelligence, aptitude, and achievement tests; to explore the issues relating to standardized testing; and to discuss contemporary problems regarding standardized testing. Some of the problems include discussions of test bias, test administration, the decline in college aptitude scores, and the integrity of standardized achievement tests.

KEY CONCEPTS

- History of standardized testing.
- Contemporary models of intelligence.
- Differences and similarities among intelligence, aptitude, and achievement tests.
- Effects of socioeconomic factors on test performance.
- Administration of survey achievement tests.
- Role of diagnostic achievement tests.
- Interpretation of standardized test scores.
- Contemporary issues in standardized testing.

STANDARDIZED TESTS

What Is Standardized Testing?

Standardized tests were developed in the early part of the twentieth century. The term standardized test means that all students answer the same questions, take the test under similar conditions, and are scored the same way. All student scores are compared with a uniform reference group.

What Are the Types of Tests Available?

The three types of standardized tests that are most commonly used in public schools are intelligence tests, academic aptitude tests, and achievement tests. Intelligence tests attempt to measure the overall aspects of mental ability. Academic aptitude tests attempt to measure the aptitude or potential for learning in an educational setting. Achievement tests attempt to measure present knowledge levels in specific academic areas.

There are several interrelationships among standardized intelligence, aptitude, and achievement tests. Students' scores on any one of these tests have a relationship with how they score on the other two tests. For instance, a student who scores above average on any one of these tests tends to score above average on the other two tests. A student who scores below average on one test tends to score below average on the other tests. Another aspect of these tests is that they tend to consistently and positively relate to actual classroom performance on teacher-made tests.

Reflect on your own experiences with standardized tests? Did your test scores predict your classroom grades?

INTELLIGENCE TESTS

Historical Background of Standardized Testing

The history of standardized testing begins in 1904 with the French psychologist, Alfred Binet. Among his many accomplishments, Binet is credited with creating the first modern test of intelligence. It is from Binet's test that nearly all subsequent IQ tests were derived. In fact, much of the standardized testing field owes its original impetus to Binet's work.

To understand the impact of Binet, one must realize how intelligence and mental retardation were determined prior to Binet's test. In most cases a medical doctor would look for certain "degenerative physical signs," particularly small skulls or specific facial features that were considered "evolutionary throwbacks" (Gould, 1981). The doctor also would sometimes attempt to assess language ability by simply conversing with the patient. Thus, a child with certain particular facial features, who was shy and spoke very little in front of the doctor, could have been a prime candidate for the diagnosis of retardation.

In 1904, Binet received an appointment to a special commission mandated to develop a program to diagnose and place children of subnormal intelligence in special schools. Binet then began the task of devising a measurement instrument that would distinguish between normal children and retarded children. Thus, in addition to developing the first IQ test, Binet completely changed the method of diagnosing retardation.

In essence, the task of Binet and the special commission set a pattern both for special education and for measuring intelligence. One of the eventual roles of contemporary special education was defined by this commission: to provide an alternative educational program so that the mentally retarded might be able to attain some type of skill or vocation. Another aspect of contemporary special education programs also was established by Binet: to develop an appropriate diagnostic evaluation for determining who should receive special education.

What Is Binet's Model of Intelligence?

Binet had to start from scratch in developing this new field of study. He began by forming a definition of what is intelligence. According to Binet, intelligence is the "ability to judge well, to comprehend well, to reason well, these are the essential activities of intelligence. A person may be a moron or an imbecile if he is lacking in judgment; but with good judgment he can never be either" (Binet & Simon, 1973, p. 43). As a reflection of this concept, Binet's model and the Binet test are heavily oriented toward verbal reasoning skills, comprehension, and judgment.

Binet also believed in a general or unified view of intelligence, meaning that a single core factor exists that can be given the label of general intelligence. Included in this assumption is the viewpoint that, for the most part, intellectual abilities are interrelated. For example, a person who is highly intelligent in an ability such as verbal reasoning should be highly intelligent in other areas.

Do you believe that Binet's approach to diagnosing retardation is an improvement over the previous approach? Are using intelligence tests better than a physical exam?

How do you feel about Binet's definition of intelligence? What one intellectual skill do you believe is most important?

In devising his test, Binet had to use a trial-and-error method. Binet would ask different questions to a particular age group. If 50 percent of an age group could successfully answer a question, then a norm for that age was established for that question. With enough questions across enough age groups, the basis for his test began to take shape. Presented in figure 11.1 are examples of the types of questions used in Binet's test.

Binet's test was designed as an individual measure of intelligence. This designation means that the test is given by one psychologist to one student at a time. Binet never developed a group form of his test—where an examiner administers a test to more than one person at a time. In Binet's original version, testing stopped when the subject missed three questions in a row. The point on the scale where the last correct answer occurred became the child's mental age. At that point, Binet compared the child's mental age with his chronological age. If the child's mental age was significantly lower than the chronological age, he received special education.

What Is the Intelligence Quotient?

After Binet's death, Stern revised the Binet scoring system and developed the first version of the intelligence quotient (IQ score). Stern's system, called the ratio method for scoring the intelligence quotient, uses the following formula:

$$IQ = \frac{\text{Mental Age}}{\text{Chronological age}} \times 100$$

Do you think that intelligence can be summarized into one single score?

FIGURE 11.1

Sample Questions from Binet's Test

Age 3:
1. Point to your nose, then your eyes, and now your mouth.
2. Repeat these two numbers: 7, 2.
3. What is your last name?
4. Repeat this sentence: I want to play at school.

Age 6:
5. Fill in the blank in the sentence: Summer is hot; winter is ___.
6. Tell me what this word means: What is an orange?
7. What is the difference between a bird and a dog?

Age 12:
8. Tell me what this word means: What is a brunette?
9. Repeat these numbers in reverse order: 9, 4, 12, 3, 7.

Using this formula, a child whose mental age is six and whose chronological age is five would have an intelligence quotient of 120.

$$IQ = \frac{6}{5} \times 100 = 120$$

A child whose mental age is nine and whose chronological age is ten would have an IQ equal to 90.

$$IQ = \frac{9}{10} \times 100 = 90$$

Stern's intelligence quotient quickly became identified with Binet's test, though Binet had apparently opposed using one single number to represent a person's intelligence (Gould, 1981). Binet also issued a cautionary note to regular classroom teachers about misusing his test to place students in special education:

> They seem to reason in the following way: "Here is an excellent opportunity for getting rid of all the children who trouble us," and without the true critical spirit, they designate all who are unruly, or disinterested in school (Binet & Simon, 1973, p. 169).

How Did Lewis Terman Create the Stanford-Binet Intelligence Scale?

List the advantages and disadvantages of taking an individually-administered IQ test as compared to a group-administered IQ test.

In 1916, a group of American psychologists translated Binet's test into English. Included among this group were Lewis Terman, Henry Goddard, and Arthur Otis. While revising the Binet test for individual use, they also developed a group form of the test. The revised/translated individual form was called the Stanford-Binet Intelligence Scale. The group form of the test became known as the Army Alpha test and later the Otis Tests of Mental Ability.

What is Terman's Model of Intelligence?

Terman's model of intelligence includes the belief that intelligence is almost completely determined by genetics. Terman, Goddard, and their co-workers also accepted Binet's assumption that intelligence is a general unified factor. Furthermore, this group's theoretical view states that Binet's test appropriately measures the underlying nature of intelligence.

This belief, that the IQ test measures the innate nature of intelligence, can be best understood by relating it to an analogy with the vision test given by an optometrist. When an optometrist measures a person's vision and determines that she has 20/30 vision, it is accepted as a measure of the inherent physical properties of the person's vision. To the group associated with Terman and Goddard, the IQ score is interpreted the same way: as a measure of the inherent physical properties of intelligence.

Unfortunately, the assumptions of these early testers led to some of the worst abuses made in the standardized testing field. The worst single abuse probably was in racial and ethnic discrimination.

Is There Racial and Ethnic Discrimination in Intelligence Testing?

From the earliest use of the American group version of the intelligence test, differences were noted between African Americans and whites. On the Army Alpha tests during World War I, the average scores of African Americans were fifteen points below the average scores of whites (Yerkes, 1921). However, African Americans from certain northern states had a higher average score than whites from certain southern states. In fact, the testing program found that the recruits, regardless of race, had an average mental age of thirteen (Yerkes, 1921).

Another IQ study was completed at Ellis Island, the central receiving center for European immigrants entering the United States. In this study of adult immigrants, Goddard (1917) claimed that 83 percent of Jewish immigrants, 80 percent of Hungarians, 79 percent of Italians, and 87 percent of Russians were feebleminded. Feebleminded adults had a mental age of less than twelve. As noted by

Describe some other world events where similar attitudes about ethnic differences have played a major role.

Many American psychologists during the early twentieth century believed that intelligence was almost completely due to heredity. In effect, like physical attributes, intellect was determined almost solely by genetics.

Goddard, Nordic immigrants from northwestern Europe had decidedly higher IQs than did immigrants from southern and eastern Europe.

Although most psychologists now believe such differences are due to socio-economic and educational factors, Terman and Goddard assumed these differences were due to heredity. Such views reinforced existing beliefs in the early twentieth century about racial differences in the United States. One result of this view was that intelligence test scores were sometimes used to support racist policies in American education and society.

Who Developed Early Standardized Testing?

Terman and Otis were responsible for much of the initial work in the testing field in the United States. Besides developing the Stanford-Binet Intelligence Scale, Terman and his associates also contributed to the development of some of the first comprehensive tests of achievement and of aptitude (Cunningham, 1986). These tests were known as the Stanford Achievement Test and the Scholastic Aptitude Test. Thus, many of the standardized tests used today were based on earlier tests developed by Terman and his associates.

What Are some Contemporary Models of Intelligence?

Do you believe intelligence is composed of one factor or many factors?

While some psychologists still hold to the view of the general or unified theory of intelligence, many others subscribe to various models that view intelligence as a number of disparate and even unrelated factors. Psychologists, who subscribe to this latter viewpoint, believe that intelligence has many different components.

Because of the different and unrelated factors in a multi-factor model of mental abilities, appropriate intelligence testing would have to be composed of multiple factors or even multiple tests.

Among the multiple factor models of intelligence, the theories of intelligence developed by Cattell (1971), Gardner (1983), and Sternberg (1988) are presented.

Raymond Cattell. Cattell (1971) proposed that intelligence is composed of two basic factors: fluid intelligence and crystallized intelligence.

Fluid intelligence is largely the genetic aspects of intelligence, though it can be affected by disease or malnutrition. For the most part fluid intelligence is the ability of the central nervous system to process and recall information in a given time span. This type of intellectual ability is not based on accumulated information or educational training.

The types of items on intelligence tests that relate to the fluid factor are usually timed tests of visual-spatial performance. For instance, test items that require arranging different geometric figures in a correctly prescribed pattern are an example of fluid intelligence. These types of items are relatively unaffected by cultural or educational background.

Crystallized intelligence is the aspect of intellectual ability that is largely due to our education and experience. It is the part of intelligence that is culturally valued and culturally biased. To some degree crystallized intelligence is based on the cultural norms of what is appropriate reasoning, judgment, and knowledge at a given age. The crystallized factor is related to test items that measure reasoning, vocabulary, and general information. For instance, correctly defining a given word is a type of item that measures crystallized intelligence.

When different age groups are compared across the human life span, distinct differences can be found between fluid and crystallized intelligence. After young adulthood fluid intelligence decreases at a fairly stable rate. Crystallized intelligence does not decrease in this fashion and may even show slight gains during the middle adult years.

Howard Gardner. Gardner (1983) based his view of intelligence on research completed in the areas of memory and neurophysiology. Gardner's theory of intelligence states that there are seven distinct learning and memory systems in the human brain. The seven intelligence systems are: linguistic, musical, logical-mathematical, spatial, bodily-kinesthetic, interpersonal, and intrapersonal. Each of these separate systems forms its own distinctive type of intelligence. Thus, damage to one system does not necessarily mean a corresponding loss in the other systems.

The linguistic system provides the ability to comprehend both expressive and receptive language. It includes the skills of vocabulary ability and verbal reasoning and the potential for both spoken and written language. In the past, tests of intelligence have largely been oriented toward the linguistic system—even to the exclusion of the other systems.

The musical system is the ability to effectively produce music. The musical system generally is lateralized in the right cerebral hemisphere, while language usually is lateralized in the left hemisphere.

Which one of Cattell's factors would be more influenced by ethnic or gender differences?

According to Gardner musical ability is one of the seven separate forms of intelligence.

Which one of Gardner's factors is most likely to be addressed by public education? In other words, is educational instruction oriented toward a specific intelligence?

The logical-mathematical system initially develops as the ability to apply a numerical series when grouping or classifying objects. From this ability stems the capacity to manipulate the quantity of a series of objects in an exact and accurate manner. It also involves the ability to understand the relationship between one object and a second object and to derive causal rules about objects and events. Thus, the logical-mathematical system is more than just simple arithmetic. It is the development of the logic system that underlies the mathematical and scientific basis of Western culture.

Spatial ability includes the capacity to correctly perceive and recognize the different aspects of the visual world. It also includes the ability to recreate the visual world in the mind's eye and to transform those perceptions.

Bodily-kinesthetic ability is the capacity to coordinate and initiate the various neural and muscular movements involved in motor behavior. These movements range from the completely voluntary acts of motor control to highly automatic habitual activities. Some of the different activities included in bodily-kinesthetic ability are dance, athletic ability, acting, and miming.

There are two types of personal intelligences in Gardner's model. These are interpersonal and intrapersonal. Both forms are reflections of the highly social nature of Homo sapiens. They also reflect the way that symbol systems, such as language, have affected human behavior.

Interpersonal intelligence involves the ability to deal effectively with the behavior, feelings, and motivations of other people.

Intrapersonal intelligence involves the ability to deal effectively with one's own internal feelings and motivations. There is an obvious overlap to these two types of ability.

The central key to both types of personal intelligence appears to be a highly developed sense of self. Both personal intelligences are reflections of the sense of self-concept and self-awareness that each person develops. As noted by Gardner, interpersonal intelligence is the ability to acquire and process information about the external social world. Intrapersonal intelligence is the ability to acquire and process information about one's internal world.

Gardner's model of intelligence raises some serious concerns for the testing field. For example, not even the most comprehensive of intelligence tests adequately measures the variety of abilities listed in Gardner's model. If Gardner's model generally is valid, then a test or tests of mental ability may need to be devised to cover this broad range of intelligences.

Gardner's model also presents some real problems for gifted programs in public schools. Most gifted programs base at least part of their determination of giftedness on an IQ test score. Again, if Gardner's model is valid, the present basis for selection and placement of children in gifted programs must be questioned. Obviously, a more comprehensive definition and placement procedure would be necessary for gifted programs.

If placement decisions for gifted education were based on Gardner's model, list some criteria for each of the different intelligences.

Robert Sternberg. Sternberg (1988) also has developed a multiple-factor model of intelligence. Sternberg claims that human intellect is composed of three basic manifestations. He uses the term the triarchic mind to refer to his model.

Sternberg's three manifestations are: the relationship of intelligence to the internal world of the individual; the relationship of intelligence to the experience of the individual; and the relationship of intelligence to the external world of the individual.

The relationship of intelligence to the internal world refers to the kinds of processes that result in intelligent thinking. Sternberg devotes most of his analysis of human intelligence to this manifestation. For this part of intelligence, Sternberg lists three processing components: (1) metacomponents, "which are used to plan, monitor, and evaluate your problem solving" (1988, p. 78); (2) performance components, which Sternberg most closely identifies with the actual process of inductive reasoning. Performance components are used to understand relationships, to classify objects, and to complete a series; and (3) knowledge-acquisition components, which are used to learn new information. According to Sternberg, all three of the processing components must work together for intelligent thinking to be possible.

All three of the components are used to deal with the second and third manifestations of intelligence. For example, the processing components are used to deal with the two key areas in the relationship of intelligence to the experience of the individual: coping with novelty and automatizing complex cognitive and behavioral activities.

With the third manifestation, the relationship of intelligence to the external world of the individual, the processing components are again used to relate to the everyday world. Sternberg lists three key functions where the processing components are applied to the everyday world: "adaptation to existing environments, selection of new environments, and shaping of existing environments into new environments" (1988, p. 65).

Sternberg's complex model of intelligence takes a somewhat different approach from previous models. Sternberg tends to focus on more than just the factors that compose intelligence; he attempts to relate information processing to its interaction with the external world. This model may offer more practical applications than some models of intelligence.

Which of the three contemporary models of intelligence seems most valid? In terms of their validity, rate the three models on: comprehensiveness, educational applicability, and research support.

What Are the Most Frequently Used Contemporary Individual Intelligence Tests?

While there are a number of mental ability tests used in public schools, the two most frequently used contemporary individual intelligence test batteries are the Stanford-Binet Intelligence Scale (1986) and the Wechsler Intelligence Scale for Children–III (1992). Different school psychologists may use either of these tests.

How Is the Stanford-Binet Intelligence Scale (Fourth Edition) Organized?

The Stanford-Binet Intelligence Scale (1986) has undergone a number of transformations from the original English-language version developed by Terman (1916). The latest revision of the Stanford-Binet (1986) is the fourth edition.

For this category of tests do you agree that mental abilities or cognitive abilities are more appropriate terms to use than intelligence?

This edition attempts to address some of the criticisms that have been leveled at the Stanford-Binet test and intelligence tests in general.

In responding to these criticisms, the Stanford-Binet Intelligence Scale (1986) generally has avoided using the term intelligence quotient or IQ score. The IQ score has been replaced with the standard age score (SAS). This change in terminology came after the term IQ score was removed from a number of the standardized group intelligence tests. The group tests are now termed mental abilities or cognitive abilities tests. Now, the only major individual intelligence test to consistently use the term IQ score is the Wechsler Battery.

The editors of the Stanford-Binet also have responded to critics by expanding the areas of material covered by the test. The Stanford-Binet had long been criticized as too heavily weighted toward vocabulary and reasoning skills. The new version attempts to correct for such biases by increasing the variety of subtests included in the battery. There are now fifteen subtests in the latest Stanford-Binet scale, which are grouped into four ability scales.

The Verbal Reasoning ability scale contains four subtests. These tests are designed to measure the ability to define words; to comprehend the use of items, objects, or events; to determine what is missing in a picture; and to identify differences and similarities in a series of words.

The Abstract/Visual Reasoning ability scale contains four subtests. These tests attempt to measure the ability to compete different visual patterns. The subject is asked to use blocks to complete a pattern or design; to copy figures; to complete a matrix; and to identify what a folded paper object would resemble once it is unfolded.

The Quantitative Reasoning ability scale is composed of three subtests. These tests involve pictorial and verbal arithmetic problems; different types of numerical series with the last two digits in the series absent; and equations that the subject must unscramble and solve.

The Short Term Memory scales contain four subtests. These tests involve repeating word for word a sentence that is read aloud; a visual presentation of a stack of beads that must be correctly repeated in a certain sequence; repeating and reversing a series of digits; and a series of pictures of various objects that must be correctly recalled in the order in which they were presented.

How Is the Wechsler Test Battery Structured?

The Wechsler Battery of Intelligence tests is divided into three separate versions. The Wechsler Preschool Primary Scale of Intelligence-Revised (WPPSI–R) (1989) is for ages three to seven. The Wechsler Intelligence Scale for Children–III (WISC–III) (1992) is for ages seven to sixteen. The Wechsler Adult Intelligence Scale–Revised (WAIS–R) (1981) is for ages sixteen years and older. The WISC–III test is the one most commonly used in public schools. With a few exceptions, the WPPSI–R and WAIS–R follow the same general format.

The WISC–III is divided into two basic sections: verbal and performance. The verbal section examines reasoning and vocabulary skills. The performance section examines visual-spatial skills. The combined score from these two sections yields a full-scale IQ score. Thus, the examiner can obtain three IQ scores from this test.

The verbal section contains six subtests: the Information test, which involves general knowledge questions about the culture and the environment; the Similarities test, in which the subject is asked to compare two items and determine the ways in which the items are similar; the Arithmetic test, which involves presenting the subject with verbal arithmetic problems in sentence form; the Vocabulary test, in which the subject is asked to define specific words; the Comprehension test, in which the subject is asked what would be appropriate in a given situation (for example, why is it wrong to set off a fire alarm when there is no fire?); and the Digit Span test, in which the subject is asked to repeat a series of digits and if completed correctly is then asked to repeat another series of digits.

The performance section of the WISC–III contains the following subtests: the Picture Completion test, in which the subject is shown a series of pictures each of which has a part missing that the subject is asked to identify; the Picture Arrangement test, in which the subject is presented with a series of pictures in a mixed-up order that the subject must then arrange in a logical format that tells a coherent story; the Block Design test, in which the subject is presented with a cube with red and white designs (somewhat like a Rubik's cube) that the subject is asked to change into a number of different designs that are displayed on cards; the Object Assembly test, which is like a child's puzzle where pieces are provided that the subject must place together in the correct manner; the Coding test, in which the subject is provided with a series of nonverbal symbols that the subject must copy correctly in a space below the symbol; and the Mazes test (a supplementary test that is not generally used in the standard WISC–III test), which involves the subject correctly tracing a path through a series of mazes.

> Does the WISC-III or the Stanford-Binet appear to be a more appropriate test? Should either test be used as part of a test battery to determine special education placement?

APTITUDE TESTS

What Is the Purpose of Aptitude Tests?

Academic aptitude tests attempt to assess a student's potential for school performance. By this definition, academic aptitude tests are quite similar to intelligence tests. Some writers, in fact, include intelligence tests under the heading of aptitude tests (Hopkins, Stanley, & Hopkins, 1990). There is a considerable difference, however, between the use of academic aptitude tests and intelligence tests. Intelligence tests are often used as part of the psychoeducational evaluation to refer students for special education. Aptitude tests are not used for this purpose. The assumption is that intelligence tests measure a greater sample of intellectual abilities than do aptitude tests. Some intelligence tests also have subtest norms that aid in the diagnosis of students with special education needs. Therefore, intelligence tests are assumed to provide the most accurate measure of general mental ability in students, while aptitude tests measure potential school performance.

> Should admission to a selective college program be based partly on college aptitude tests like the ACT or SAT? List some other types of criteria that selective admissions programs could use to determine their admissions criteria.

What Types of Academic Aptitude Tests Are Available?

There are three major aptitude tests that are most commonly used today: the Differential Aptitude Test (DAT); the American College Test (ACT); and the Scholastic Aptitude Test (SAT).

How Is the Differential Aptitude Test (DAT) Used?

The DAT is designed for junior and senior high school students. It is used primarily as a counseling and placement tool to provide students with information about what courses or academic tracks to take in high school. The DAT also can be used as a vocational guidance inventory.

The DAT provides eight separate subtest scores for various academic and vocational aptitudes: verbal reasoning, numerical ability, abstract reasoning, clerical speed and accuracy, mechanical reasoning, spelling, space relations, and language usage. Usually, these skills are treated as independent abilities. Thus, students who score high on one subtest will not necessarily score high on other subtests. Each separate subtest is assumed to predict certain academic and/or vocational abilities. In their review of the DAT, Hopkins, Stanley, and Hopkins (1990) state:

> The basic rationale underlying these tests is that various academic and occupational pursuits require different patterns of aptitude and, hence, a decision in which a profile of aptitudes is available should be more appropriate than a decision based on a single omnibus score (p. 371).

The DAT is a widely used instrument in public schools. Engen, Lamb, and Prediger (1982) reported that 34 percent of secondary schools use the DAT in assessing and counseling students. In a practical sense the DAT is used to counsel students who are unsure of what their next step should be in an educational or training program. The DAT can give students an idea of their vocational strengths and weaknesses and is often used along with vocational interest tests like the Strong-Campbell Vocational Interest Inventory. Vocational interest inventories measure the similarities of a student's personality and career interests with a norm group of people who are currently working in specific jobs.

It does appear that adolescents engage in a certain amount of unrealistic fantasizing about their occupational future (Ginzberg, 1972). One major developmental hurdle in adolescence is to come to grips with some type of career preparation (Levinson, 1978; Super & Hall, 1978). Used together, the DAT and a vocational interest inventory can provide the student with a type of reality check. These tests can give an indication of how vocational aptitudes and interests might crystallize around a particular vocation. They also may give the student some direction for the next step to take in preparing for a career.

What Is the American College Test (ACT)?

The ACT, first used in 1959, is designed as an aptitude test to predict college success. A number of colleges base part of their admission requirements on ACT scores. The ACT contains four subtests and a composite score. The four subtests

When did you decide that you wanted to major in education? Describe the factors that led up to this decision.

are: English Usage, Social Studies Reading, Natural Science Reading, and Mathematics Usage.

In 1991 the ACT was administered to nearly 800,000 high school students (Wilson, 1991). The average composite score for that group was 20.6 with a standard deviation for the test being approximately 5.

Officials administering the ACT program note that students who took at least 4 years of English, 3 years of math, 3 years of social studies, and 3 years of natural sciences in high school had an average composite score of 22.1, almost 2 points higher than the average (Wilson, 1991). This finding would seem to indicate that scores on the ACT test can be affected by academic preparation, especially with math scores.

Some professionals claim that the ACT is more directly related to high school performance than its competitor, the Scholastic Aptitude Test. It appears that both tests, however, are about equally effective in predicting college grades.

How Is the Scholastic Aptitude Test (SAT) Used?

The SAT, developed in 1926, is the oldest and most frequently used academic aptitude test. It generally is given to high school seniors as part of admission requirements for entrance to college. Slightly more than one million students took the test in 1991 (Dodge, 1991).

The SAT consists of two separate subtests, Verbal and Mathematical, which are then combined to give a composite score. The Verbal component is largely based on reading comprehension. The Mathematical component consists of basic mathematics with some elementary algebra and geometry. The average SAT scores in 1991 were Verbal—422, Mathematical—474 (Dodge, 1991). The standard deviation for each subtest is approximately 100 with a total of 800 points possible for each subtest.

At the present time, the SAT is considered the assessment method closest to a national test of educational ability. Because of this fact, SAT scores at the national level are closely scrutinized each year, producing a number of major controversies. Chief among these controversies are SAT test bias and the decline of SAT scores since 1963.

Is There Test Bias in the SAT?

As with intelligence tests, a number of claims have been made that the SAT is biased against minority groups. The claims have centered on possible vocabulary and cultural biases in the test questions. For example, Dodge (1991) reported that in 1991 the SAT average scores were as follows: Verbal—351, Mathematical—385 for African Americans; Verbal—441, Mathematical—489 for whites.

Such score differences appear to indicate a test bias. However, defenders of the test point out that an actual bias because of vocabulary differences is difficult to claim. The average difference between African Americans and whites on the Verbal part is 90 points. On the Mathematical part, the difference is 104. A vocabulary bias or a cultural bias in the Mathematical section is difficult to claim, since it deals with basic mathematical skills. Math skills would appear to be relatively independent or cultural bias. If there is a vocabulary or cultural bias, the differences should be greater on the Verbal section.

On the other hand, many researchers agree that the SAT scores reflect an overall socioeconomic bias in this country. As indicated previously, many minority groups make up a larger portion of the lower socioeconomic ranges. Since socioeconomic status is a key variable in predicting academic success, it is inevitably reflected in academic aptitude test scores. In this sense the SAT is a reflection of an economic and social bias in the United States.

It would appear that minority group members, as well as whites who are from lower socioeconomic groups, often do not receive the educational opportunities needed to ensure equal education. This exclusion produces lower scores on standardized tests and raises questions about how to ensure equal educational opportunity at the college level for groups that have been previously denied such opportunities.

Should tests like the SAT simply not be used for such groups? Should quotas for these groups be available? Should special scoring procedures be instituted to ensure proportionate selection of disadvantaged groups? Clearly, these are controversial political and educational policy issues that are far from being settled.

Do Preparatory Programs Help Students on These Tests?

A number of companies claim that they can produce a significant increase in students' scores with a preparatory class for the SAT or ACT. Messick (1982) presents evidence that coaching and preparatory programs are able to substantially improve SAT scores.

On the other hand, in his review of the effects of coaching on the SAT, Cunningham (1986) states that short-term courses only result in modest improvements in SAT scores. Cunningham does acknowledge, however, that intensive training may produce greater increases in scores. Cunningham also points out that the scores on the math section are more likely to be improved than are vocabulary scores. This finding appears to be consistent with other research.

Many intensive preparatory courses take fifteen to twenty hours to complete and cost hundreds of dollars. If such courses do significantly improve outcomes, then the courses may be reinforcing the socioeconomic bias already inherent in American education, since students of lower socioeconomic levels would not be able to afford the courses.

What Has Caused the Decline In SAT Scores?

Many articles have been written concerning the decline in average SAT scores since 1963. The average SAT scores in 1963 were Verbal—478, Mathematical—502 (Wirtz, 1977). In 1981, the average SAT scores were Verbal—424, Mathematical—466 (Cunningham, 1986). The average SAT scores in 1991 were Verbal—422, Mathematical—474 (Dodge, 1991), with Verbal continuing to decline and Mathematical rising slightly. The overall decline from 1963 to 1991 is 9.1 percent. Although this decline appeared to be halted in the mid-1980s, the 1991 score for the Verbal section was the lowest ever recorded in the history of the SAT.

Many explanations have been presented to account for the decline in SAT scores. In the late 1960s and early 1970s, there was a massive increase in the college student population. With a broader pool of students, it is logical that scores declined. Yet this reasoning can hardly explain the declines in test scores that have occurred since that period. Although some researchers have questioned the SAT itself, it appears that any effect the test had on scores has been eliminated (Cunningham, 1986) in light of the fact that the ACT, the other major aptitude test, has shown a similar decline.

Social causes for the decline also have been cited. Among these are the increases in teenage pregnancies and single-parent families, and the growing number of working two-parent families. Other explanations include the increases in television viewing and the corresponding decreases in reading.

Although these explanations may have contributed to the decline, the fact of the matter is that the average college freshman today has considerably less academic aptitude than the average freshman of the preceding generation. Although other explanations have contributed, the root of the problem is a failure in our educational and socialization systems. On the part of teachers, it appears to be a failure to maintain academic standards and a willingness to cave in to grade inflation syndrome. On the part of parents, it seems to be a failure to expect and motivate their children to achieve in school. There is plenty of blame to go around for the decline. It is important to remember that nearly every educator and parent shares some responsibility for the "dumbing down of America."

Do you believe that there is a relationship between the decline in SAT scores and the economic decline in the United States?

■ ■ ■

STANDARDIZED ACHIEVEMENT TESTS
What Is the Purpose of Achievement Tests?

The purpose of achievement tests is to measure specific knowledge that is acquired through classroom learning. These kinds of tests are geared toward specific areas of instruction. For example, a reading achievement test measures a student's present reading ability. Thus, standardized achievement tests are more directly geared toward actual classroom experiences than are intelligence or aptitude tests.

What Is the Educational Context for These Tests?

Standardized achievement tests have become the dominant form of standardized test in American public school systems. Because of the controversies involving group intelligence tests, most school systems have now opted for group achievement tests. The result is a massive and sometimes questionable industry revolving around these tests.

The extensive use of standardized achievement tests by different school districts and different states has led to various national movements for achievement test reforms. Since 1969, the National Assessment of Educational Progress has measured a relatively small sample of schoolchildren on a uniform national achievement test to try to monitor achievement levels and promote reform. One proposal made by the reform movements is to establish a single, national standardized achievement test that all children will take in specified grades.

What Are the Uses of Standardized Achievement Tests?

The uses of standardized achievement tests include two main areas: overall grade-level testing and individualized testing.

The first area, overall grade-level testing of students in group situations, involves testing all students in a particular grade in a school district to determine how those students compare with local, state, or national standards. Decisions about curriculum changes and funding formulas are made based on the test scores. In some school districts, merit pay for teachers is based on how their students score on these achievement tests.

The second area, individualized testing, involves testing a student to determine whether he has a learning difficulty or is in need of special education placement. This use of achievement testing often centers on a discrepancy between the potential ability of the student as measured by an IQ test and actual performance as measured by an achievement test. For example, if a child scores above average on an IQ test but significantly below average on a reading achievement test, it could be a sign of a severe reading disability such as dyslexia. (More information on using testing as a diagnostic procedure is provided in chapter 13.)

List the positive and negative attributes of having a national test. Do you believe it would be helpful or harmful to the educational process?

How would you feel about having merit pay decisions be determined by your students' achievement test scores?

What Types of Achievement Tests Are Available?

There are two major types of achievement tests: (1) survey achievement tests, which are used for measuring the overall academic ability of large groups of students; and (2) diagnostic achievement tests, which are used to determine specific learning problems. Survey tests are used to determine grade-level norms, school-level norms, and school-district norms. Diagnostic tests, on the other hand, are used to help determine placement in special education. Diagnostic tests usually focus on one specific academic area, such as reading, while survey tests cover all areas of classroom learning.

What Survey Achievement Tests Are Available?

There are a number of survey achievement test batteries available for public school use. This aspect of the testing business has been increasingly dominated by major publishing houses or their subsidiaries.

Thorndike, Cunningham, Thorndike, and Hagen (1991) list six major survey achievement batteries: the California Achievement Test, the Comprehensive Test of Basic Skills, the Iowa Tests of Basic Skills, the Metropolitan Achievement Tests, the Science Research Associates Achievement Series, and the Stanford Achievement Test. Cannell (1988) provides a list of the states that use each test, as shown in figure 11.2.

In terms of the quality of these tests, Thorndike et al. state:

> These tests are similar in terms of the time and effort that has gone into their development, and their overall quality is high. They cover the same range of students and have similar content areas. The test development and norming procedures are generally exemplary (p. 336).

The major types of survey achievement tests listed by Thorndike et al. have very similar test quality. Therefore, making a clear distinction between the tests is difficult. In deciding which survey achievement test battery to use, the best

Iowa Test of Basic Skills: Arizona, Colorado, Georgia, Idaho, Iowa, North Dakota
Stanford Achievement Test: Alabama, Hawaii, Mississippi, Nevada, South Dakota, Tennessee.
Comprehensive Test of Basic Skills: Delaware, Kentucky, New Mexico, South Carolina, Utah, West Virginia, Wisconsin.
California Achievement Test: Maryland, New Hampshire, North Carolina.
Metropolitan Achievement Tests: Arkansas, Oklahoma, Washington.
Science Research Associates: North Dakota, Virginia.
Locally Developed Tests: California, Maine, Oregon, Pennsylvania, Rhode Island, Texas.
Test Chosen by School Districts: Alaska, Connecticut, Florida, Illinois, Indiana, Kansas, Louisiana, Massachusetts, Michigan, Minnesota, Missouri, Montana, New Jersey, New York, Ohio, Vermont, Wyoming.

Cannell (1988)

FIGURE 11.2
Achievement Tests
Used by State

advice is to choose the test that has been most recently revised. There is some indication that the more recently revised tests have more accurate norms and also may include the latest advances in test development and item construction.

What Is the Content of Survey Achievement Tests?

The content of survey achievement tests is geared toward specific goals and objectives that the test authors believe are appropriate to certain age or grade levels. Although there are some minor variations among tests, all of the survey achievement batteries listed earlier attempt to cover a broad range of academic knowledge that would be expected of most students. The areas that are measured involve reading comprehension, vocabulary, spelling, mathematical computation, and mathematical concepts. Some of the upper-level forms, developed for high school students, also cover the science and social science areas. For example, on the High School/College Form of the Stanford Achievement Test (Stanford Test of Academic Skills, Basic Battery Booklet, 1981), the following subtests are presented: Reading Vocabulary, Reading Comprehension, Mathematics, Spelling, and English. An example of the type of content available in achievement tests is in figure 11.3.

As can be seen in these questions, the type of item used is multiple choice. This item format tends to be used in nearly all standardized achievement tests.

Scores on standardized tests indicate that 25 to 30 percent of entering college students are academically deficient in at least one academic areas. Many colleges provide developmental classes for these students. Should such students be admitted to college?

FIGURE 11.3

Example Achievement Test Questions

A blacksmith is someone who:

a. makes horseshoes
b. fixes pipes
c. builds houses
d. chops wood

33 is 50% of:

a. 16.7
b. 60
c. 66
d. 96
e. None of the above

Which volume of the encyclopedia should be examined for Kit Carson?

a. Volume C
b. Volume F
c. Volume K
d. Volume S

Gronlund (1985) makes the following points concerning multiple choice items:

> The multiple choice item is one of the most widely applicable test items for measuring achievement. It can effectively measure various types of knowledge and complex learning outcomes. The wide applicability of the multiple choice item, plus its advantages, makes it easier to construct high quality test items in this form than in any of the other forms (pp. 177–178).

Thus, the survey achievement test batteries are oriented toward multiple choice items that measure basic skills in specific academic areas. While this type of test item is widely used, it also has been criticized for a number of reasons. Multiple choice items are particularly criticized for being unable to measure problem-solving ability. They also have been criticized for not being able to measure critical thinking. Nor does a multiple choice test measure how well a student can develop and express an idea. Multiple choice tests appear to best measure specific knowledge levels but not the application of that knowledge to new situations.

How Are Survey Achievement Tests Administered?

Survey achievement test batteries present a series of academic subtests that must be completed in a particular time frame. For example, a reading subtest may have a thirty-minute time limit, while a math subtest may have a forty-minute time limit. The tests usually are administered in group situations, such as in a classroom or lecture hall. The test administration must be monitored by appropriate school personnel to ensure the integrity of the test and to maintain the time limits and protocols for the tests.

Recently, there has been a great deal of concern that the integrity of achievement tests may have been compromised. Several problems are created if the tests are not properly administered. One major problem is that the test norms become invalid if the integrity of the test is compromised. If the norms are invalid, comparisons between schools or school systems become invalid.

In responding to these problems, the American Psychological Association, in conjunction with the American Educational Research Association and the National Council on Measurements in Education, has developed a series of standards for test administration, scoring, interpretation, and evaluation (American Psychological Association, 1974; 1985).

The APA guidelines have strict instructions for those who administer the tests: (1) the test administrator is responsible for strictly following the procedures given in the test manual; (2) the test administrator is responsible for eliminating the possibility of cheating by using special seating arrangements, proctors, or identification methods for the examinees; (3) the test administrator also is responsible for ensuring the security and integrity of the tests by keeping them in a locked storage area.

In addition to the test, standardized test scores and results from teacher-made tests must be kept confidential. The Family Educational Rights and Privacy Act of 1974 (also known as the Buckley Amendment) is a federal law designed to protect the confidentiality of academic records. Teachers cannot release any test

Are you personally aware of test situations where the integrity of the test has been compromised? What should be the consequence for not following appropriate testing procedures?

Applications from the Text 11.1

One of the best ways prospective teachers can learn to use standardized testing and understand the importance of such testing is to accept mentoring from more experienced teachers. Several seasoned veterans have shared their opinions and tips about understanding testing, preparing students, and getting full use of the benefits of standardized testing in this application section.

Linda Parker
Third-grade Teacher

I use a testing and instructional program called Scoring High to prepare students for the Comprehensive Test of Basic Skills (CTBS). I use it so children can test in a format like the CTBS. I also use this program as a review. I check the results of the CTBS to see if modifications are needed for students who are having trouble. But I do not use them to put them into levels. I teach whole-class instruction; I do not track. I think that these types of tests are only one indicator. Some children cannot test well but do well otherwise. I think tracking and labeling can have a real negative impact if you are placed in a low group.

Nancy Thompson
Third-grade Teacher

I do not do any special preparation for the Comprehensive Test of Basic Skills. Unless everyone does it, it would be unfair.

Nancy Goheen
First-grade Teacher

As a school, we do a test item analysis of our standardized achievement scores. Our whole faculty senate looks at strengths and weaknesses. We go to work on the weaknesses.

Rebecca Queen
Second-grade Teacher

I use standardized achievement scores only when another indicator, such as classroom performance, observations, verbal or nonverbal ability, would indicate a need to use them. Very high or very low achievers would be checked. I think my own classroom measures are more helpful. The standardized tests take up too much time. I would rather use the time for classroom instruction.

Sheila Leach
Sixth-grade Teacher

On some of these tests I think that students are tested on materials that have never been covered in class. Keep in mind that learning outcomes vary from school system to school system, from county to county, and from state to state, etc. It is unfair to assume that a standardized test or a national exam can take all this into account.

Mary Russell
First-grade Teacher

We use these types of tests to chart student progress and the weaknesses of each child. We pass the information along to the next teacher to see what skills are weak. That way she will know what needs to be worked on. It cuts wasted time for the next teacher.

score or grade to any person without the permission of the parents of children in their classroom. They cannot display such scores or grades in any way that can identify who made a particular score.

Another area of concern in test administration is in teachers attempting to teach the test. It is not ethical for teachers to examine the content of standardized tests to determine what is to be taught in their classrooms. Teachers should not use standardized test items on their own exams or tutor students on the specific subject matter of an expected exam based on their knowledge of the exam from the previous year. If a teacher does any of these things, the integrity of the exam is compromised and it ceases to be a valid instrument to measure all students.

A final area of concern in test administration is in providing special testing conditions for those with handicaps. Those students with handicapping conditions do have the right to special testing conditions. This provision includes not only those with physically handicapping conditions, such as the visually impaired, but also those with diagnosed learning disabilities.

■ ■ ■

DIAGNOSTIC ACHIEVEMENT TESTS
What Are Diagnostic Achievement Tests?

Diagnostic achievement tests generally are used as screening tests to pinpoint specific academic weaknesses or to diagnose learning disabilities. For this reason, they usually are given in an individualized situation. Most diagnostic achievement tests are either reading tests, writing tests, or mathematics tests. As reported by Salvia and Ysseldyke (1988), reading difficulties are the single most frequent reason for referring a student for any type of psychoeducational assessment.

If you have a disabling condition, including a learning disability, a certain amount of extra time on standardized tests may be provided. How do you feel about such a policy?

What Types of Diagnostic Tests Are Available?

There are many different types of diagnostic achievement tests. Included among the more common ones are: the Woodcock-Johnson Psycho-Educational Battery–Revised, the Woodcock Reading Mastery Tests–Revised, the Key Math–Revised Inventory, the Peabody Individual Achievement Test–Revised, the Test of Reading Comprehension, and the Gates-McKillop Reading Diagnostic Tests.

In their discussion of diagnostic achievement tests, Mehrens and Lehmann (1991) make the conclusion that two newly developed diagnostic batteries, the Stanford Diagnostic Reading and Mathematics Tests and the Metropolitan Diagnostic Reading, Mathematics, and Language Tests, appear to provide the best format for diagnostic testing. These two batteries appear to meet the same quality standards that are found in the survey achievement batteries. Mehrens and Lehmann also make the point that "there is a paucity of valid diagnostic tests" (p. 354).

What Is the Content of Diagnostic Achievement Tests?

The content of diagnostic achievement tests tends to be much more specific than the content of survey achievement tests. For example, certain reading diagnostic tests cover such skills as visual and auditory discrimination, phonetic analysis, reading comprehension, vocabulary, word-attack skills, and reading rates. Math diagnostic tests cover such areas as time measurement, word problems, fractions, numeration, numerical reasoning, and geometry, as well as the traditional areas of addition, subtraction, multiplication, and division.

How Are Diagnostic Achievement Tests Administered?

There is considerable controversy in the educational and psychological communities about who is qualified to administer and interpret tests that lead to a psychoeducational diagnosis. Survey achievement tests are available for teachers to administer and interpret. Individual intelligence tests, such as the Wechsler Battery, are available only to qualified school psychologists. Diagnostic achievement tests fall somewhere in between.

Are classroom teachers qualified to administer and interpret diagnostic achievement tests? McLoughlin and Lewis (1990) address the problem in their discussion of the Key Math–R, a diagnostic achievement test for mathematics. They state: "No special training is required to administer the Key Math–R. . . . Test interpretation, however, is best accomplished by professionals with training in psychometrics and experience in teaching mathematics" (p. 342).

Thus, McLoughlin and Lewis claim that classroom teachers are quite capable of administering such tests. Their background and training for appropriate interpretation, however, may be lacking. Many classroom teachers do not have the basic training in testing and measurement necessary to appropriately interpret certain tests.

On the other hand, present practices in public schools often require teachers to administer and interpret a series of screening tests, which may include a diag-

Should classroom teachers be able to interpret these types of tests? Would you support additional educational training for teachers in tests and measurements?

nostic achievement test. These screening tests are completed prior to a referral for a complete psychoeducational evaluation. (The psychoeducational evaluation is administered by a school psychologist prior to special education placement.) Such practices force the classroom teacher to play an important role in administering and interpreting tests. These tests often become a factor in determining special education placements.

Any decision to place a child in special education, however, must be based on the federal guidelines developed as part of the Federal Public Law 94–142. Although the controversy over who should give what tests will continue, the federal guidelines are quite specific about the decision-making process.

■ ■ ■

STATISTICAL MEASURES IN TESTING

A number of statistical techniques were created in conjunction with the standardized testing movement. Many of these techniques are crucial for understanding the results of standardized tests. For teachers, it is essential that they are able to understand and interpret the test scores of their students in order to explain these results to both students and parents.

Besides interpreting the tests, teachers also have to make many educational decisions based on students' test scores. Included among them are decisions about whether or not a child needs special education and what types of individualized educational programs are needed for students.

This section will explain the test score information using several statistics terms: mean, median, mode, range, percentile rank, standard deviation, and stanine scores. Besides these statistical elements, there are several other concepts that teachers need to understand for scoring, administering, and interpreting tests: these are raw scores, standard scores, age-equivalent scores, grade-equivalent scores, basals, ceilings, and test reliability and validity.

What Are Measures of Central Tendency?

Measures of central tendency provide a description of the middle or central points of a particular distribution. The three basic measures of central tendency are the mean, the median, and the mode.

Among the various measures of central tendency, the best known and most commonly used measure is the mean, or arithmetic average. To refresh your memory for computing the mean, the formula is the sum of the scores in the distribution divided by the number of scores in the distribution.

The median is the middle most case in a distribution. In effect, the median is the number that splits the distribution into two equal halves. The median will always split the cases into two equal parts. When the distribution contains an odd number of cases, the median will be the middle value in the distribution. When the distribution has an even number of scores, the median is found by averaging the two middle scores. The median is the middle-most case in a distribution with no regard to the values of the cases. For example, in the distribution 190, 100, 75, 50, 45, the median is 75.

Students often dislike reading and studying statistics. Yet as teachers, you will have to interpret these statistical measures to parents and students. Imagine a meeting with parents where you discuss each of the scores in this section.

The mode is the most frequently occurring number in a distribution. For example, in the distribution 120, 100, 100, 85, 72, 40, the mode is 100 because it occurs the most often. There can be more than one mode in the distribution. When there are two modes, the distribution is termed bimodal. When all the numbers occur with the same frequency, the distribution is called unimodal.

Because of the way standardized tests are constructed, the mean, median, and mode on such tests will nearly always have the same value. The mean, median, and mode on both the Stanford-Binet and the WISC–III is 100. A number of other standardized tests, such as the Wide Range Achievement Test–Revised, also have 100 as their mean, median, and mode.

What Are Measures of Variability?

Measures of variability are used to reflect the degree of dispersion or variation in a distribution. Like measures of central tendency, they provide a method for summarizing one part of a distribution of scores into a single number.

There are three commonly used measures of variability in the educational field: range, standard deviation, and stanine scores. The range is simply the highest number in the distribution minus the lowest number.

Standard deviation represents a standard method of determining how scores deviate from the mean. The standard deviation also has an important relationship in describing the normal curve. The formula for deriving a standard deviation involves the four steps shown in figure 11.4.

Your class this year has a greater range of test scores than last year's class. What does this mean to you as a teacher?

FIGURE 11.4

1. Subtract the mean from each raw score. The remainder will be the difference score; X (the number) − M (the mean) = d (the difference).

$$
\begin{array}{ccc}
X & M & d \\
18 - 14 & = & 4 \\
16 - 14 & = & 2 \\
14 - 14 & = & 0 \\
12 - 14 & = & -2 \\
10 - 14 & = & -4 \\
\end{array}
$$

2. Square each difference score and sum the squares.

$$
\begin{array}{l}
4^2 = 16 \\
2^2 = 4 \\
0^2 = 0 \\
-2^2 = 4 \\
-4^2 = 16 \\
\end{array}
$$

$$16 + 4 + 0 + 4 + 16 = 40$$

3. Divide the sum of the squares by the number of scores. $40 \div 5 = 8$
4. Take the square root of this dividend. $8 = 2.828$

The final answer of 2.828 is the square root of the average of the squared deviations from the mean. In effect, 8 is the average of the d^2 column and 2.828 is the square root of the average of the d^2 column. In conceptualizing standard deviation, it should be viewed as a method of obtaining a single value that is representative of how scores deviate from the mean.

FIGURE 11.5

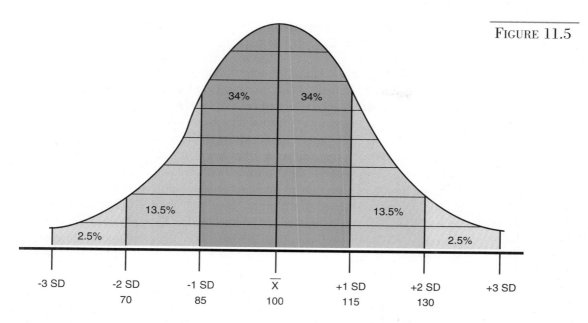

-3 SD	-2 SD	-1 SD	X̄	+1 SD	+2 SD	+3 SD
	70	85	100	115	130	

As indicated in the figure, the standard deviation represents a standard method for determining how scores deviate from the mean. This relationship of standard deviation is represented by the normal curve, which has considerable use in educational practices. Figure 11.5 shows the relationship between the normal curve and standard deviation.

In this normal curve, the percentage of scores between the mean and one standard deviation above the mean is approximately 34 percent. The percentage of scores between one standard deviation above the mean and two standard deviations above the mean is approximately 13.5 percent. The percentages in the graph will always remain constant as long as the distribution is normal, and the percentages will always be symmetrical as long as the distribution forms a normal curve.

In counting the percentage of scores between one end of the distribution and the mean, the result is 2.5 percent + 13.5 percent + 34 percent = 50 percent. In effect, 50 percent of the scores are below the mean and 50 percent of the scores fall above the mean. The percentage of scores falling between the end of the distribution and two standard deviations from the mean is approximately 2.5 percent.

Along with the mean, the standard deviation is reported in manuals for standardized tests. For the WISC–III, the overall mean is 100 with a standard deviation of 15. This information provides a gauge for determining if a sample of students taking the test is like the population for whom the test was normed. If the sample is normally distributed, then approximately 34 percent of the subjects should fall between the mean and one standard deviation below the mean. Thus, 34 percent of the sample should fall between 85 (–1 SD) and 100. Most of the sample (68 percent) should fall between 85 and 115.

The Stanford-Binet Intelligence Scale has a mean of 100 and a standard deviation of 16. The same distribution of scores occurs with this test. Therefore, 34 percent of the sample should fall between 84 (–1 SD) and 100. Thus, a score of 68 on the Stanford-Binet is the same as a score of 70 on the WISC–III.

How Is Standard Deviation Associated With Special Education?

Standard deviations are critical in understanding test scores. Many state laws for determining who receives special education are based solely on standard deviation scores. Generally, IQ scores that are two standard deviations below the mean or lower are a diagnostic sign of mental retardation. On the Wechsler test, it would be an IQ score of 70 or lower. As shown by the normal curve table, the percentage of the population that will score 70 or less is approximately 2.5 percent.

Basing the determination for receiving special education on standard deviation scores from IQ tests has been criticized. What do you see as some problems with this particular practice?

In many school systems, the determination for gifted children also is based on standard deviation scores on an intelligence test. Many school systems state that a child will be considered in the gifted category if she scores two standard deviations or above on an individual test of intelligence. On the WISC–III, this score would be 130 or above. Only about 2.5 percent of the population will score 130 or better.

In determining if a child has a learning disability, a frequently used diagnostic sign is a one standard deviation or greater difference between the Verbal and Performance parts of the WISC–III. For example, if a child's Verbal score is 84 and his Performance score is 101, it could be indicative of a language-related learning disability such as dyslexia.

Stanine scores are another measure of variability based on the normal curve. Stanines are a scoring system with a mean of 5 and a standard deviation of 2. On the WISC–III, an IQ score of 115 would produce a stanine score of 7. Stanines have limited use and generally can be used only with scores that fall within 2 SDs from the mean. On the WISC–III, an IQ score of 100 would result in a stanine score of 5.

While not generally included as a measure of variability, percentile ranks are a frequently reported measure of student ability. They do provide a measure of how a student scores in relationship to other students. The percentile rank is a point in a distribution of scores, indicating the percentage of people who scored below that point. For instance, scoring at the 50th percentile rank means the student scored above 50 percent of the people taking the test. A student who scored at the 10th percentile rank would have scored above 10 percent of the people taking the test.

What Are the Scoring Procedures for Standardized Tests?

Raw scores are the actual responses of the subject to the test items—the number of items on a given scale or subscale for which the student obtained a correct response. For example, on the WISC–III, the raw score on the Vocabulary subtest is the number of words the subject correctly defined multiplied by two. (The WISC–III gives two points for each correct definition of the stimulus word.)

Standard scores are raw scores that are transformed to some type of common scale, standard scale, or normal curve distribution. For example, on the WISC–III, a raw score of 50 on the Vocabulary test means that the subject correctly answered 25 of the items on that subtest. This raw score of 50 is then transformed to a standard score of 10 based on a statistical procedure.

The deviation IQ score developed by Wechsler is a standard score system with a mean of 100 and a standard deviation of 15. This type of score system, commonly called the Deviation Score System, has become a popular standard system for a number of standardized tests. This system allows accurate comparisons between the scores from different types of tests.

For example, on the Wide Range Achievement Test–Revised (WRAT–R), a commonly used measure of student achievement, the mean is 100 and the standard deviation is 15. If a student scores 130 on the reading section of the WRAT–R, a teacher can predict that the students' equivalent score on the verbal section of the Wechsler IQ test also will be 130. Standard score systems provide the basis to compare different test scores to determine whether they are equivalent from test to test.

Age-equivalent scores are scores normed for a given age group. For example, if a student correctly answers an appropriate number of items designed for the average five-year-old, the student will receive an age-equivalent score of five years old.

Grade-equivalent scores are scores normed for a given grade level. For example, if a student answers an appropriate number of items for the average third-grader, the student receives a third-grade equivalent score.

Basals are the baseline level or initial testing level of the child. It is any point on a test where the subject successfully passes enough items to establish a reasonable starting point for the test administration. For example, a basal may be the most advanced point on the test where the child obtained five correct responses in a row.

Ceilings are the upper limit of the test administration. The ceiling is the point where the subject obtained the last correct response before missing the designated number of items that ended the testing on that particular scale.

What Is Test Reliability and Validity?

To judge the quality of a standardized test, there are two basic methods used: reliability and validity. Reliability measures the consistency of the test. One form of reliability is called test-retest reliability. When the same subjects take the same test and then retake the test, do they score approximately the same? If they do, the test scores are consistent. Therefore, the test is judged to have appropriate reliability.

Validity is used to determine whether or not the test measures what it claims to measure. One form of validity is called criterion-related validity. In this case a test is given to a group of subjects and then compared with their scores on some external criterion, generally considered to be related to what the test should measure. With IQ tests, validity is often measured by giving the IQ test to subjects and then comparing it with their grade point average. If the subjects' IQ scores are closely related to their grade point average levels, then the test is considered valid.

The statistical technique used to measure reliability and validity is correlation. Correlations are calculated and placed on a measurement scale that ranges from −1.00 to +1.00. Correlations measure the degree of relationship or association between two factors, variables, or tests.

Which measure of test quality do you think is more important: reliability or validity?

In determining reliability and validity, the important aspect of correlation is to determine how close to + 1.00 the correlation will come. The closer to +1.00, the more reliable or valid a test is considered to be.

■ ■ ■

INTERPRETATION OF STANDARDIZED TEST SCORES

As indicated by the material in this chapter, standardized testing is a complicated, controversial subject. It can be a virtual mine field for teachers if they are not familiar with the problems that can arise. Research studies have shown that a number of factors have a relationship with intelligence, aptitude, and achievement test scores. One of the best single predictors of these test scores is the socioeconomic status of the individual who takes the test. For children, socioeconomic status is generally indicated by their parents' socioeconomic status. Thus, the trend is that the higher the socioeconomic status, the higher the test scores (Ornstein & Levine, 1985). This same pattern is duplicated in the relationship between socioeconomic status and general school performance (Coleman et al., 1966).

The reasons for the strong relationship between socioeconomic status and test scores have been debated since World War I. In general, the contemporary view is that a higher level of socioeconomic status provides better nutrition, health care, motivation, and environmental stimulation. These four factors seem to be the main reason for the trend toward higher test scores as one moves up the socioeconomic ladder (Cronbach, 1970).

Extreme caution, however, should be used in basing any educational decisions for individual children on just the relationship between socioeconomic level and test scores. There is a wide variation in intellectual and academic ability both within and between socioeconomic groups. Any educational decision by the classroom teacher should be based on the individual performance of the child and not on her background.

Individual intelligence test scores may be presented with both an overall score and subtest scores. Interpretation of these scores generally requires a trained psychologist. For the most part, these scores are interpreted in terms of their relationship to special education criteria. Aptitude test scores are provided with overall scores, subtest scores, and general percentile ranks.

Usually, achievement test scores are presented as percentiles and standard scores. Sometimes, grade-equivalent scores and age-equivalent scores also are provided, despite being sharply criticized in recent years (Sax, 1989).

As indicated, percentiles are a measurement unit that serves as a marker for a given percentage of scores. A percentile rank of 70 means that a student outscored 70 percent of the other students taking the test. Percentile ranks are easily understood by most students and parents. This type of score procedure also allows quick comparisons of individual test scores with other scores in the class as well as with state and national norms.

Figure 11.6 shows a student profile from the Iowa Tests of Basic Skills, Form 07, Level 12 (University of Iowa, 1983). The student's name is Barbara. She is 11 years old and attends 6th grade.

The relationship between socioeconomic level and academic achievement often is a vicious cycle, with the gap between the haves and have-nots growing rather than receding. What can teachers do to decrease the problems that occur because of this relationship?

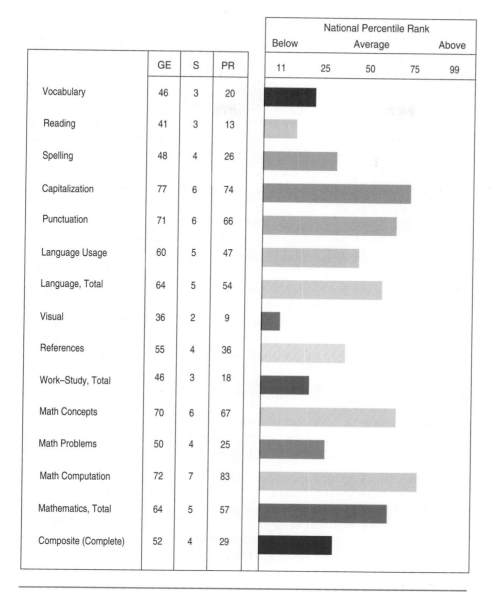

	GE	S	PR	National Percentile Rank				
				Below		Average		Above
				11	25	50	75	99
Vocabulary	46	3	20					
Reading	41	3	13					
Spelling	48	4	26					
Capitalization	77	6	74					
Punctuation	71	6	66					
Language Usage	60	5	47					
Language, Total	64	5	54					
Visual	36	2	9					
References	55	4	36					
Work–Study, Total	46	3	18					
Math Concepts	70	6	67					
Math Problems	50	4	25					
Math Computation	72	7	83					
Mathematics, Total	64	5	57					
Composite (Complete)	52	4	29					

FIGURE 11.6

University of Iowa (1983). Iowa Tests of Basic Skills. Chicago: The Riverside Publishing Company.

Beginning with the Vocabulary subtest, each subtest in the Figure is provided with three scores: GE—grade equivalent score; S—stanine score; and PR—percentile rank. A chart is provided to further indicate Barbara's percentile rank.

In interpreting these scores, the test authors first recommend that the Composite score be examined. On Barbara's profile her Composite GE score is 52. This means that her overall achievement level for the entire test is at a grade equivalent level of 5th grade, second month. For Barbara, this means that her overall performance is approximately one year behind what the average performance level is for a sixth grader. Her stanine score of 4 indicates that she is approximately one half of a standard deviation below the mean.

The most important score for teachers to interpret is the percentile rank. (As indicated in the previous discussion of scoring systems, grade equivalent scores have been criticized. Stanine scores tend to be limited because of the small range of values.) Barbara scored at a percentile rank of 29 on her Composite score. This means that she scored better than 29 percent of all sixth graders nationally. However, 71 percent of all sixth graders scored as well or better than Barbara.

It is also important to emphasize that Barbara is doing quite well in some areas. Her math computation skills and her understanding of math concepts place her well above average in these areas. For instance, her math computation skills are at the 83rd percentile.

Among the most troublesome of the subtest scores are Barbara's scores in Vocabulary, Reading, and Visual. All three of these scores have percentile rankings of 20 or less. Vocabulary and Reading scores tend to strongly predict classroom grades. Taken in combination with the Visual scores, these three scores may be indicative of some type of learning difficulty, learning disability, or vision problem. It may be necessary to have an eye exam, classroom observation, or diagnostic testing completed on Barbara to ascertain if she has a problem.

In summary, Barbara has an extremely wide variation in her subtest scores. Such a variation may indicate some type of problem.

Are There Any Gender Differences in Test Scores?

What can teachers do to change these types of gender differences in test scores?

Gender differences on achievement tests also are similar to what one sees on aptitude and intelligence tests. Sax (1989) discussed sex differences in his review of the Iowa Tests of Basic Skills:

> The average female outperforms the average male on vocabulary, reading, language, work-study skills, and mathematics; the boys, in contrast, show higher scores in the use of maps, graphs, and in mathematics only for those students who are in the upper 10 percent of the achievement distribution. The average and below-average male obtains lower scores than females on virtually every subtest of the ITBS. On tests having science or social studies subtests, however, the tendency is for the boys to do somewhat better than the girls (p. 453).

How Do Age Differences Affect Test Scores?

Age differences play a prominent role in standardized test scores. At the primary grade levels, age becomes a prominent predictor of scores on standardized mental ability tests. For example, a six-year-old child born in February may have a significant developmental advantage over a six-year-old child born in December of the same year. This seemingly slight age difference can have a profound impact on test scores.

Some aspects of the relationship between age and intelligence were previously indicated in the earlier discussion of Raymond Cattell's model of intelligence. As indicated in that section, intellectual abilities that deal with processing information in a given time span appear to decline during the middle and later adult years. Such abilities include reading speed and the ability to quickly recall mem-

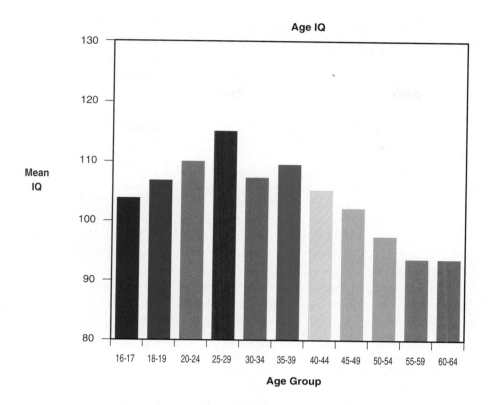

Age IQ

FIGURE 11.7
Age IQ

orized information. On the other hand, some abilities apparently do not show such a decline. For instance, comprehension does not necessarily decline during the middle adult years. Understanding the relationships between events and the ability to apply knowledge to practical situations also do not decline during the middle adult years.

Figure 11.7 summarizes another view of age and intelligence from Wechsler's original work on intelligence testing (Wechsler, 1958). This graph represents how different age groups performed on similar test items. This type of design is referred to as cross-sectional research.

As can be seen in the figure, intellectual performance increases rapidly throughout adolescence. Intelligence peaks in early adulthood in the mid-to-late twenties. After that point, intellectual performance shows a decline on Wechsler's test. When different age groups are compared across the life span, the young adult group shows the best performance levels.

Other research, however, has indicated considerable variation in how intelligence changes over the life span. When the same group of subjects is tracked across the life span (termed longitudinal studies), the results are different from the cross-sectional studies. The decline in intelligence test scores is generally less in the longitudinal studies than in the cross-sectional studies (Anastasi, 1988).

Despite this conflict in the research between cross-sectional and longitudinal studies, most IQ tests now use different test norms and scoring procedures for different age groups. For instance, on the Wechsler test, the subject is only compared with the standardization sample for the year in which he is born. Thus, a five-year-old child would only be compared against other five-year-old children.

Do you agree with the findings that intellectual ability may decrease after the mid to late twenties? Do you think that occupational ability decreases in a similar manner?

The interpretation of standardized tests by teachers must be qualified by both the socioeconomic level of the student and her age. Gender differences appear on certain specific verbal and visual tests, though such differences generally are of small magnitude. It generally is believed that ethnic differences are due to socioeconomic factors.

How Should Teachers Conduct Conferences about Test Scores?

One of the roles that teaches play is to interpret test scores to students and parents in a conference. A few simple guidelines apply. Conferences about test scores, as well as about grades, must be completed in private. There are both legal and ethical reasons for private conferences. The Buckley Amendment protects the confidentiality of academic records. Ethically, it creates serious classroom problems if testing records become commonly known. Students will make unfavorable comparisons with their classmates, which may engender a great deal of unnecessary and unwanted competition in the classroom.

Another aspect of these conferences is to view test scores in a formative rather than summative manner. Test scores generally should be viewed as a way of making improvements. Among the goals of the conference should be a plan or contract with the student for necessary improvements. A teacher should ask several questions: Where do we go from here? How do you want to change or improve? What is our specific plan for improvement?

Conferences also should help teachers and students examine discrepancies between different subtests of the achievement test or discrepancies between classroom performance and achievement test performance. Such discrepancies may indicate a lack of motivation or may indicate some type of specific learning problem. In either case, these types of discrepancies need to be explored until a satisfactory explanation can be found.

One of the most difficult aspects of teaching is conducting parent conferences when a student is having difficulty. How might a teacher best handle explaining the scores in Figure 11.6 to the student's parents?

Conferences with parents about test scores or grades should be conducted in private. The release of academic information about tests or grades must follow guidelines established by the Buckley Amendment.

CONTEMPORARY ISSUES ABOUT SURVEY ACHIEVEMENT TESTS

What Causes High-Stakes Testing and Cheating?

Popham (1987) coined the term high-stakes testing to refer to school districts where major educational decisions are based on achievement test scores. Such decisions include school funding allocations, placement decisions, in tracks or groups, merit pay for teachers, and evaluations of teachers and principals. Popham believed that standardized tests can serve as "instructional magnets." Such "magnets" focus and improve instruction by concentrating it on specific outcomes.

Other researchers disagree with this view, stating that high-stakes testing may improve test scores without a commensurate gain in learning (Cannell, 1988; Shepard, 1990; Shepard & Dougherty, 1991). Part of the reason for such a discrepancy between test performance and learning is the extensive time spent in preparation for taking the tests.

Various types of achievement test preparation programs were studied by Smith (1991). These different preparation programs included no specific preparation; test-taking skills; exhortations by the faculty; teaching content known to be covered by the test; teaching to the test; stress inoculation; practicing parallel tests items; and cheating.

In their survey of high-stakes testing, Shepard and Dougherty (1991) found that 6 percent of teachers believed that changing incorrect answers to correct ones on answer documents occurred in their school. The study reported that 8 percent of teachers indicated that students who might have trouble on the test were encouraged to be absent in their school. Additional findings indicated that 23 percent of teachers believed that hints to correct answers were given and that 18 percent believed that questions were rephrased to help students in their school.

As indicated in the previous section, these types of teacher behaviors are considered unethical by the major professional educational and psychological associations. Such practices compromise the integrity of the tests and call into question the entire educational process. The problem created by these practices is now referred to as the Lake Wobegone Effect.

> What type of ethical considerations or consequences should govern teachers' behavior in this area? Should teachers be terminated, placed on probation, or reprimanded when they are involved in "High Stakes Cheating?"

What Is the Lake Wobegone Effect?

Cannell (1988) published a survey of state scores on standardized achievement tests. On these standardized tests, all fifty states were above average at the elementary school level. Obviously, it is impossible for all fifty states to be above average. These types of results raise additional questions about the administration and scoring of the tests themselves.

Cannell's finding was named the Lake Wobegone Effect (Thorndike et al., 1991). This name is taken from Garrison Keillor's radio show, "A Prairie Home Companion." Lake Wobegone is a place "where all the women are strong, all the men are good looking, and all the children are above average."

Cannell's report was an embarrassment to a number of professions and organizations. Cannell was a pediatrician in West Virginia who had no background in psychometrics. He discovered the testing problem by accident, through reading reports on local and state school test results in West Virginia. Clearly, the people who research, design, and evaluate standardized tests should have been the first to discover the problem.

For instance, federal and state officials who monitor the administration of these tests should have noted the problem before 1988. Some states, that traditionally have had poor funding for schools, high numbers of high school dropouts, and high levels of adult illiteracy, had above average achievement test scores (Cannell, 1988). It is extraordinary that the education officials in these states did not discover that the scores were inflated or invalid.

Others who should have noted the problem are the test publishers themselves. It is difficult to impossible to believe that these publishers had no idea of the Lake Wobegone Effect. After all, they publish the scores and norms for the tests.

In their review of the Lake Wobegone Effect, Thorndike et al. (1991) indicated some of the responses of the test publishers to this problem. One statement made by publishers was that the norms for the tests were dated. In effect, the achievement levels of the students had increased from the time that the original norms for the tests were developed. Some publishers stated that the test norms were not changed for as long as seven to eight years. Thus, though the norms were at one time accurate, they had simply been outdated by increases in student achievement levels.

As pointed out by Thorndike et al., this explanation does not seem very convincing. Scores on the SAT and ACT have been declining for a generation. Students could hardly have been dramatically increasing on one set of tests and dramatically decreasing on the other set of tests.

Three other explanations are given by school officials and test publishers. First, teachers become more familiar with the test each year. They now teach material directly from the text. This type of explanation is clearly related to the above point about the increases in achievement test scores. As previously noted, this type of teaching compromises the integrity of the test. The result is to artificially inflate the students' scores.

If this explanation is true, then the tests need to be changed each year by the test publishers. Both the SAT and the ACT change their tests each year. Other than the cost, there is no good reason for the publishers of the six major achievement tests not to revise their tests each year.

Second, local school officials sometimes exclude special education students, remedial students, and vocational track students from the testing programs. Thus, they cause a change in the population of students who take the tests. This change artificially inflates the test scores of local school districts.

If this answer is true, local school officials need to change how they administer the test program. All students should be tested in a school district. If that is not being completed, then the school system needs to note what population is being tested and what population is not being tested. If school systems are being compared, then there must be equivalency in the populations being tested.

Third, the publishers of the tests offer special norms for schools and school districts with large numbers of minority and low-income students. These norms provide special weighted scores, a type of handicapping of scores, based on the

Do you think that part of the reason for the Lake Wobegone Effect may be the behavior of teachers and administrators, who have compromised the integrity of the standardized tests?

number of low-income or minority children in the district. Such special norms inflate the overall scores on the tests.

This explanation would almost appear to involve a type of collusion between the test publishers and the local school officials. School officials want their school system to be presented in the best light. Test publishers want the school system to keep buying their tests. If this explanation is true, then the test publishers should be required to publish the results with the special weighting procedure and without the special weighting procedure. This would provide an index of just how much of an effect the social and economic biases produce in the test scores.

The Lake Wobegone Effect may have further eroded the public's confidence in the testing process and in the credibility of public schools. Given that the public's confidence in the educational system was already low, this problem could hardly have come at a worse time.

What Are some Cross-Cultural Comparisons?

A number of studies have compared American schoolchildren with students from other countries on standardized tests (Comber & Keeves, 1973; Lynn, 1982; Stevenson et al., 1985). Many of these studies have found that American schoolchildren score well below comparable samples of children from other countries on math or science achievement tests (Lapointe, Mead & Phillips, 1989; National Research Council, 1989; Schaub & Baker, 1991).

For example, Schaub and Baker (1991) found that children in Japanese middle schools averaged 20 percentage points higher on a math achievement test than did their American age-equivalent counterparts. As the authors noted, this finding is quite consistent with other research findings in math and in science.

Schaub and Baker's research also explored the instructional predictors of these differences. They found that Japanese teachers spend significantly more time in instructional preparation and in teaching the whole class. American teachers spend significantly more time in having students work alone, work in groups, and take tests. These researchers found that American teachers spend significantly more time in keeping order in their classrooms. American students also had much more variation in achievement levels at the beginning of the school year.

One recent comparative study of American schoolchildren with other countries did provide some good news for U.S. public schools. The International Association for the Evaluation of Educational Achievement (1992) conducted a thirty-two nation study of reading achievement. At age nine, the sample of American schoolchildren was second highest. At age fourteen, the American sample was fifth highest. Although there were some methodological problems with the study (Rothmann, 1992), the findings do provide some encouragement for reading teachers in the United States.

What Are the Related Professional Tests?

Minimum competency tests and professional skills tests are different names for tests that are closely related to survey achievement tests. In general, the major

Many states have now gone to a practice of developing their own test because of the problems associated with the major standardized tests. What problems may occur with this practice of each state having its own test?

Some research findings indicate that American children in the elementary school years do comparatively better on cross-cultural tests than their older American counterparts. What factors might cause such a difference?

Should minimum competency tests be required of all graduating high school students? What should the policy be toward special education students?

differences between these categories are the uses of the tests, their scoring procedures, and the age levels at which they are given.

Minimum competency tests are standardized tests that assess certain basic skills. They are used to determine whether a certain criterion or competency level has been reached by the student. For instance, a number of states have mandated minimum competency tests for students receiving a high school diploma. Thus, a student would have to take the necessary course work in high school and in his senior year to pass the competency test to receive the diploma.

Minimum competency tests have been justified because they provide a method of ensuring accountability in the schools. The public can be shown that a certain number of students have reached a certain level of skill performance on a standardized test. However, these tests have been criticized because they prevent a disproportionate number of minority children, children from lower socioeconomic levels, and special education children from attaining a high school diploma.

Professional skills tests are used in a similar manner to minimum competency tests. A number of states have required that students majoring in teacher education and in certain other areas take a professional skills test to certify that they have a given level of competency. In the teacher education area, preprofessional skills tests examine such aspects as reading, writing, and mathematical performance. Like minimum competency tests, preprofessional skills tests are used to determine whether the student has met a certain performance level. If they do not meet this level, they cannot become a teacher.

SUMMARY

In this chapter, the use of intelligence tests, academic aptitude tests, and standardized achievement tests is reviewed. Intelligence tests attempt to measure overall mental abilities. Aptitude tests attempt to measure the potential for academic performance. Achievement tests attempt to measure present knowledge levels in specific academic areas.

The three major academic aptitude tests that are administered to public school students are: the Differential Aptitude Test, the American College Test, and the Scholastic Aptitude Test. There have been a number of questions raised concerning SAT test bias. There also has been an ongoing debate concerning the decline in SAT scores that has occurred since 1963.

There are two basic types of standardized achievement tests that frequently are used in public schools. The two types are survey achievement test batteries and diagnostic achievement tests. Survey achievement batteries are used as group achievement tests. Diagnostic achievement tests are used to determine individual learning problems and psychoeducational evaluations.

Many questions have been raised about the present uses of standardized tests in public education. In particular, the use of standardized tests to make major educational decisions has produced considerable criticism. One aspect of the problem was termed the Lake Wobegone Effect.

How to Best Instruct the Maximum Number of Children

In reviewing this chapter what types of recommendations would you now make for the teacher in the case study at the beginning?

The issues raised in the case study are addressed by some of the following sections in the chapter:

1. Test bias in standardized tests—Are the tests biased against minorities or are the tests "the messenger" indicating a general socioeconomic bias in the society? Standardized tests appear to be more affected by the students' socioeconomic background than by ethnic background. Minority ethnic members apparently have lower test scores and disproportionate numbers in lower academic tracks because of adverse socioeconomic factors rather than because of test bias.

2. Should test scores be used to make placement decisions? Is there a rational relationship between the standardized tests and the decisions made about students in placing them in tracks or groupings? Are the tests valid enough to be used to place students in a vocational track or a low reading group? Test scores are used in a variety of ways to place students. They are used to place students at the college level and they are used to place students in special education. Numerous studies have indicated that such tests have a strong and significant relationship with classroom grades assigned by teachers. Research indicates the tests are valid and can reliably be used to make academic decisions. Thus, the debate about tracking is an instructional issue; not a testing issue. The debate should be framed in the following terms: What is the best way to instruct the maximum number of children?

In reflecting on the new policy on detracking are there any other possibilities? Is there any middle ground between the positions on tracking and testing? Is detracking more feasible at the elementary level than at the secondary level? What will detracking do to teachers? Will teachers' jobs become more difficult, since they will be teaching students who have a wider range of academic ability?

Chapter Review

1. Describe the differences and similarities among intelligence tests, aptitude tests, and achievement tests.
2. Describe the different points of views with regard to test bias on the SAT.
3. What factors have been cited in the decline of SAT scores?
4. What are the differences between a survey achievement test and a diagnostic achievement test?
5. Describe what is meant by high-stakes testing.
6. What are the different types of preparation methods that teachers employ in preparing for high-stakes testing?
7. Describe the Lake Wobegone Effect and the problems associated with this controversy.

REFERENCES

American Psychological Association (1974). *Standards for educational and psychological tests.* Washington, DC: American Psychological Association.

American Psychological Association (1985). *Standards for educational and psychological tests.* Washington, DC: American Psychological Association.

Anastasi, A. (1988). *Psychological testing* (6th ed.). New York: MacMillan.

Binet, A., & Simon, T. (1973). *The development of intelligence in children.* Reprint of the 1916 edition by Classics in Psychology. (Elizabeth S. Kite, Trans.). New York: Arno Press.

Cannell, J. J. (1988). Nationally normed elementary achievement testing in America's public schools: How all 50 states are above the national average. *Educational Measurement: Issues and Practice, 7*(2), 5–9.

Cattell, R. B. (1971) *Abilities: their structure, growth and action.* Boston: Houghton Mifflin Company.

Coleman, J. S., Campbell, J., Wood, A. M., Weinfel, F. D., & York, R. L. (1966). *Equality of educational opportunity,.* Washington, DC: U.S. Department of Health, Education and Welfare.

Comber, L. C., & Keeves, J. (1973). *Science achievement in nineteen countries.* New York: Wiley.

Cronbach, L. (1970). *Essentials of psychological testing.* New York: Harper & Row.

Cunningham, G. K. (1986). *Educational and psychological measurement.* New York: MacMillan.

Dodge, S. (1991). Average score on the SAT verbal falls to all-time low. *The Chronicle of Higher Education, 38,* 2, 45.

Engen, H. B., Lamb, R. A., & Prediger, D. J. (1982). Are secondary schools still using standardized tests? *The Personnel and Guidance Journal, 60,* 287–190.

Gardner, H. (1983). *Frames of mind: theory of multiple intelligences.* New York: Basic Books, Inc.

Ginzberg, E. (1972). Toward a theory of occupational choice: A restatement. *Vocational Guidance Quarterly, 20,* 169–176.

Goddard, H. H. (1917). Mental tests and the immigrant. *Journal of Delinquency, 2,* 243–277.

Gould, S. J. (1981). *The measurement of man.* New York: W. W. Norton and Company.

Gronlund, N. E. (1985). *Measurement and evaluation in teaching* (5th ed.). New York: MacMillan.

Hopkins, K. D., Stanley, J. C., & Hopkins, B. R. (1990). *Educational and psychological measurement and evaluation* (7th ed.). Englewood Cliffs, NJ: Prentice Hall.

International Association for the Evaluation of Educational Achievement (1992). *How in the world do students read?* Hamburg, Germany: International Coordinating Center, University of Hamburg.

Lapointe, A., Mead, N., & Phillips, G. (1989). *A world of differences: An international assessment of mathematics and science* (Report No. 19-CAEP 01). Princeton, NJ: Educational Testing Service.

Levinson, D. J. (1978). *The seasons of a man's life.* New York: Knopf.

Lynn, R. (1982). IQ in Japan and the United States shows a growing disparity. *Nature, 297,* 222–223.

McLoughlin, J. A., & Lewis, R. B. (1990). *Assessing special students.* Columbus, Ohio: Merrill.

Mehrens, W. A., & Lehmann, I. J. (1991). *Measurement and evaluation in education and psychology* (4th ed.). Fort Worth, Texas: Holt, Rinehart and Winston, Inc.

Messick, S. (1982). Issues of effectiveness and equity in the coaching controversy: Implications for educational and testing practice. *Educational Psychologist, 17,* 67–91.

National Research Council (1989). *Everybody counts: A report to the nation on the future of mathematical education.* Washington, DC: National Academy.

Ornstein, A. C., & Levine, D. U. (1985). *An Introduction to the Foundations of Education* (3rd edition). Boston: Houghton Mifflin.

Popham, W. J. (1987). The merits of measurement-driven instruction. *Phi Delta Kappan, 68,* 679–682.

Rothmann, R. (1992). U.S. ranks high in international study of reading. *Education Week, 12,* 4, 1.

Salvia, J., & Ysseldyke, J. E. (1988). *Assessment in special and remedial education* (4th ed.). Boston: Houghton Mifflin.

Sax, G. (1989). *Principles of educational and psychological measurement and evaluation* (3rd ed.). Belmont, CA: Wadsworth Publishing Company.

Schaub, M., & Baker, D. P. (1991). Solving the math problem: Exploring mathematics achievement in Japanese and American middle grades. *American Journal of Education, 99*(4), 623–642.

Shephard, L. A. (1990). Inflated test score gains: Is the problem old norms or teaching the test? *Educational Measurement: Issues and Practice, 9,* 15–22.

Shephard, L. A ., & Dougherty, K. C. (1991). *Effects of high-stakes testing on instruction.* Paper presented at the annual meeting of the American Educational Research Association, Chicago.

Smith, M. L. (1991). Meanings of test preparation. *American Educational Research Journal, 28*(3), 521–542.

Stanford-Binet Intelligence Scale. (1986). 4th edition. Chicago: Riverside Publishing Co.

Stanford Test of Academic Skills, Basic Battery Booklet. (1981). San Antonio, Texas: The Psychological Corporation.

Sternberg, R. J. (1988). *The triarchic mind.* New York: Viking.

Stevenson, H. J., Stigler, S., Lee, G., Lucker, S., Kitamura, S., & Hsu, C. (1985). Cognitive performance and academic achievement of Japanese, Chinese and American children. *Child Development, 56,* 718–734.

Super, D. E., & Hall, D. T. (1978). Career development: Exploration and planning. *Annual Review of Psychology, 20,* 333–372.

Terman, L. M. (1916). *The measurement of intelligence.* Boston: Houghton Mifflin.

Thorndike, R. M., Cunningham, G. K., Thorndike, R. L., & Hagen, E. P. (1991). *Measurement and evaluation in psychology and education.* New York: MacMillan.

Weschler, D. (1958). *The measurement and appraisal of adult intelligence* (4th ed.). Baltimore: Wilkins and Wilkins.

Weschler, D. (1981). *Manual for Weschler Adult Intelligence Scale–Revised.* New York: The Psychological Corporation.

Weschler, D. (1992). *Manual for the Weschler Intelligence Scale for Children–III.* New York: The Psychological Corporation.

Weschler, D. (1989). *Manual for the Weschler Preschool Primary Scale of Intelligence–Revised.* New York: The Psychological Corporation.

Wilson, R. (1991). Average score on ACT held steady. *The Chronicle of Higher Education, 38,* 2, 42.

Wirtz, W. (1977). *On further examination: Report of the advisory panel on the Scholastic Aptitude Test score decline.* Princeton, NJ: College Entrance Exam Board Publication.

Yerkes, R. M. (1921). Psychological examining in the United States Army. *Memoirs of the National Academy of Sciences,* (Vol. 15, pp. 1–890).

CHAPTER 12 ::

EFFECTIVE CLASSROOM EVALUATION

■ ■ ■

Chapter Outline

SPECIAL TREATMENT FOR ATHLETES

It is your first year as a teacher in a large, suburban high school. You teach English Literature and Composition classes. You have a wide cross-section of students in all your classes, including five starting members of the varsity football team.

The head football coach stops by at the end of the second week of the fall semester. He emphasizes how important it is "for his boys to pass." The coach asks to see your syllabus. Looking at the syllabus, he shakes his head and says that your attendance policy will not work. His boys have to miss more than your policy will allow. The coach then provides a list of all the "excused class absences" that they will miss for games.

The coach also explains the tutoring program for his players, which is funded by wealthy athletic boosters. The Coach leaves, saying, "You let me know what our boys need to do to pass. We'll tutor them just the way you like."

The Coach checks with you at least once a month on his boys' progress in the class. However, after midterm exams, three of the players are failing. The Coach calls and complains that you are not helping his boys make up the lost class time. He implies that you are discriminating against football players.

On the next out-of-class writing assignment all three of the failing football players' term papers appear to have been written by someone else. Although it is in their handwriting, the sentence structure and syntax are not at all like previous papers. In fact, the papers are all of A-level quality. Previously, their best grade was a D.

The next day the coach calls you. He asks if you would like to be paid at a very substantial rate to tutor "his boys" after school. He claims that he has talked to the principal who is in favor of the idea. Two parents of the football players call you and ask you to tutor their sons. The parents ask if there is anything else the students can do to make up for their failing grades. They specifically request make-up work to compensate for the bad grades.

What should you do about the grades, the term papers, the make-up work, and the tutorials?

INTRODUCTION

The purpose of this chapter is to provide the beginning teacher with a basic understanding of teacher-constructed evaluation techniques. This chapter takes the point of view that classroom evaluation and instruction are two sides of the same coin. Thus, classroom evaluations must be tailored to suit particular types of instructional methods.

Among the major areas reviewed in this chapter are: (1) an examination of the rationale for teacher-made tests; (2) a discussion of the different categories of classroom evaluations, such as formative and summative evaluations; (3) the different types of test items and how they relate to various cognitive skills; (4) the role of grading with evaluation; (5) the relationship of evaluation to diversity issues; and (6) the various methods used to decrease academic dishonesty.

EVALUATION DECISIONS

What Is the Rationale for Teacher-Constructed Evaluations?

To appropriately evaluate students, it is necessary for teachers to develop a variety of their own evaluation techniques. For the most part, evaluation instruments constructed by the classroom teacher best address the particular needs of each instructional module.

Although many standardized achievement tests are available, these are too general to use as the basis for student grades. Certain programmed instructional packages for reading and arithmetic offer test items. However, these tend to be limited in scope. They measure only those areas that are specific to the part of the programmed instruction for which the student is studying. Thus, teachers must develop their own evaluation methods just as they must develop their own instructional methods.

Devising appropriate tests, term paper requirements, and homework assignments are among the more burdensome tasks of being a teacher. Assigning grades and dealing with students' reactions to grades can be even more onerous. Evaluation, classroom management, and parent-teacher interaction are among the most difficult areas for teachers.

Yet good instruction and good evaluation go hand in hand. If completed in an appropriate manner, evaluations can increase student motivation. On a practical level, most students appear to respond at a higher achievement level when they are effectively evaluated. Effective evaluations provide necessary feedback to students. Evaluations key students as to what the teacher believes to be important. Once the first evaluation is completed, students have a better idea of what the teacher wants them to learn.

List as many ways as you can think of for evaluating your students' learning.

Devising appropriate classroom tests are among one of the more difficult tasks for teachers.

Therefore, an evaluation serves as a guide to students and as a measure of performance. In this sense, effective evaluation techniques can enable students to perform at a higher level by guiding them to specific information. Effective evaluations provide reinforcement and they provide direction for additional work.

Another reason for effective classroom evaluation revolves around the issue of accountability. As mentioned in the chapter on standardized tests, this is of growing concern. School boards and state legislatures increasingly demand a certain level of educational accountability. Classroom evaluation measures and grades are a major area in which the question of accountability arises.

Part of the reason for the increasing pressure on public schools for accountability may be due to grade inflation. The general perception is that the educational system has become increasingly lax in its grading of students and in its quality control.

This perception appears justified by the research. For example, Hopkins, Stanley, and Hopkins (1990) reviewed the relationship between ACT composite test scores and high school grade point averages. They found that in the ten-year period from 1969 to 1979, ACT average scores declined from 20 to 18.5, while the average grade point average increased from 2.65 to 2.95. The decline in ACT scores matched a corresponding decline in SAT scores. Classroom grades increased while standardized aptitude test scores declined. Thus, grades appear to have become increasingly inflated in the past two decades.

With effective classroom evaluations, teachers can combat some of the negative public perceptions brought about by grade inflation. By accurately verifying to the public a certain level of student performance, teachers can help change the image of a "lax, permissive educational system where everyone receives an A."

The more effective the evaluations in assessing student performance, the better the teachers' ability to verify student learning. This verification will enable teachers to make better overall judgments about student grades. This, in turn, may provide a way of ensuring to the public a more acceptable degree of accountability.

What Are the Distinctions between Evaluation, Testing, and Grading?

In defining evaluation, testing, and grading, there are some crucial distinctions to be made. Generally speaking, evaluation is the most comprehensive term in use (Gronlund & Linn, 1990). Evaluation is the process of quantitatively describing students, qualitatively describing students, and making judgments about student learning (Gronlund & Linn, 1990).

According to Gronlund and Linn, a test is a type of evaluation that is used to quantitatively describe a student. An observation is a type of evaluation used to qualitatively describe a student. Judgments about student learning are educational decisions about student progress—Mary needs some more work in learning fractions; John is making noticeable improvements in learning Euclidean geometry.

Grading is another term used in conjunction with the evaluation process. Grading is the measurement of student progress in a way that can be communicated to others. In this sense, grading is the aggregate or sum of the formal evaluations conducted in a classroom.

Assessment is sometimes used as a synonym for evaluation. However, assessment appears to be increasingly used as the specific term for the process of testing, diagnosing, and making decisions about individuals who have an exceptionality or a mental disorder (Tallent, 1992). Thus, in education, assessment tends to be used in special education testing, diagnosis, and placement decisions.

Which type of test or evaluation method do you prefer for evaluating what you have learned? Why?

How Do Instructional Decisions Determine Evaluation Decisions?

In considering this area, the first recommendation is to view evaluation and instruction as two sides of the same coin. They are intertwined to such a degree that evaluation should not be seen as a separate process from instruction. As classroom teachers develop their own instructional materials, they need to make decisions about evaluations and about how these evaluations relate back to the instruction.

In a practical sense, instruction is guided by instructional objectives. The instructional objectives are the goals, objectives, and learning outcomes for a grade or a course. Instructional objectives for a particular grade may be mandated by a state department of education, a local school board, or a curriculum committee at each school.

Instructional objectives may involve general or specific aspects of the curriculum. For instance, a general instructional objective for third grade would be for students to demonstrate appropriate levels of proficiency in their cursive writing performance. For fourth grade, a general instructional objective would be for students to demonstrate appropriate levels of proficiency in recalling and using multiplication tables. Instructional objectives can be detailed for the semester or term. They may specify daily or weekly objectives.

Appropriate instructional objectives for use in the day-to-day activities of a class should be defined in such a way that they can be effectively evaluated. The evaluation method should be constructed in such a way that it meets two goals: appropriate measurement of the instructional objectives and appropriate feedback to the students. In other words, an instructional objective should contain a well-defined learning outcome that can be evaluated. In this sense, instructional objectives should guide evaluation decisions just as they guide instructional methods.

In relating instructional objectives to evaluations and in preparing the evaluations, teachers face a number of questions. The questions that need to be answered are:

1. What is a working definition of a specific instructional objective?
2. What is the relationship between a particular instructional objective, a particular learning outcome, and a particular evaluation?
3. What type of evaluation procedure should be conducted?
4. Are objective items or essay items better suited for evaluating a particular instructional objective?
5. How will an evaluation method provide feedback to the students?
6. What weight or value does a particular evaluation have with respect to other evaluations in the course?
7. How will a particular evaluation be used to determine overall grades in the class?
8. Is the evaluation a fair and appropriate measure of the students?

The scout merit badge system has been effective for evaluating the attainment of various scouting competencies. Could such a system be adopted for your classroom? How? or Why not?

APPLICATIONS FROM THE TEXT 12.1

One instructional objective for fourth grade is to have the student learn five assigned spelling words in a given week. The learning outcome of this objective is to demonstrate mastery of the five new words by correctly recalling them. The evaluation method is to devise a test or a measure that will allow the student to demonstrate the correct recall of the five words.

Such a measure involves a multiple choice test with five items. On each item, the student is asked to identify the correct spelling of each word from among a list of alternatives.

Another example of an instructional objective is to demonstrate an understanding of the scientific method. The learning outcome is to demonstrate mastery of the scientific method by recalling the four steps in the scientific method and by providing examples of how the scientific method is applied in research. A test to measure the outcomes would involve the following: a series of multiple choice items, quizzing the students about each step; and two restricted-response essay questions requiring the student to detail two separate examples of how the scientific method would be applied to study two given phenomena.

As previously noted, stating instructional objectives in a manner that can be measured is one aspect of an effective evaluation. Thus, instructional objectives should include an outcome that can be measured. To be measured, the learning outcomes derived from the instructional objectives should be stated in concrete and tangible terms. Then an evaluation procedure is instituted that can appropriately measure the learning outcome.

CATEGORIZING AND COMPARING EVALUATIONS

What Are the Different Categories of Evaluations?

In a broad sense, evaluations can be categorized in a number of different ways. Two widely used methods of categorizing evaluation procedures are: (1) formative versus summative evaluation procedures; and (2) criterion-referenced versus norm-referenced evaluation procedures.

Formative versus Summative Evaluations

According to Popham (1990), "formative evaluation takes place when we assess the merits of an instructional program in order to ameliorate its deficits" (p. 387). In effect, formative evaluations are undertaken to improve instruction or to improve student performance. In contrast, summative evaluations are used to determine final outcomes. Generally speaking, formative evaluations are not used as part of an overall classroom grade. Summative evaluations are used as a part of the overall grade.

In conducting formative evaluations, Popham (1990) suggests that teachers complete the following: "Design tests that measure the key en-route (enabling) skills that learners must master on their way to acquisition of terminal skills" (p. 387).

Popham states that such tests should be designed based on the guidelines that follow:

Formative evaluations are used to improve either instruction or student performance.

As a student, would you prefer formative or summative evaluations? Why? Would you like to have both?

What does the learner need to be able to do in order to perform this skill? Having identified a precursive en-route skill, then focus on that en-route skill and once more ask, What does the learner have to be able to do in order to perform this en-route skill? Do this until a reasonable chain of en-route skills has been isolated (Popham, 1990, p. 387).

After the above sequence is determined, the teacher should construct items that measure each key en-route skill. (See Applications 12.3.)

In contrast, summative evaluations are completed at the end of an instructional module or program. They are used to determine whether the student passed the academic program. Usually, they summarize the students' overall achievement on a specific instructional segment. Summative evaluations can be used in a number of ways. They can be used to determine whether students should pass a course or whether students should receive a high school diploma. A final exam and a minimum competency test are examples of summative evaluations.

Criterion-Referenced versus Norm-Referenced Evaluations

One of the major questions about evaluation is in setting overall standards for tests and grades. Should teachers grade students on the basis of how they perform on some objective standard? Or should teachers grade students on the basis of how they compare with other students?

When students are graded on the basis of a specific performance standard, it is termed a criterion-referenced evaluation. For example, the teacher sets the performance criterion for a test at 80 correct responses out of 100 items. Regardless of how many students reach or surpass the criterion of 80 successful responses, all such students will have met the performance standard on that measure. Therefore, all the students who meet or surpass the standard will be considered to have completed the activity.

By contrast, norm-referenced evaluations are based on how well students do in regard to one another. Thus, students' scores are compared with other students' scores. The top scores receive the highest grades and the lowest scores receive the lowest grades. For instance, a student might have achieved a 90 percent correct response rate on an exam. However, many students had even higher scores. The student with a 90 percent achievement rate might have been given a B or even a C, since so many other students did better.

As a teacher, would you prefer norm-referenced or criterion-referenced evaluations of your students' work?

APPLICATIONS FROM THE TEXT 12.3

LINDA W. ANDERSON
Art Educator

One terminal skill in art for my students in middle school is to be able to demonstrate a mastery of simple portrait drawing.

In learning to draw a portrait, I begin by a motivational technique. I introduce the students to portrait drawing by showing a photograph of King Tut's funeral mask. We discuss its purpose and function in Egyptian culture.

We begin the actual drawing by learning to place features on a generic face. I draw on the board first and then have the students draw on their paper.

The first step or skill is to have students practice drawing an oval until they can demonstrate proficiency on this task. Then we work on the placement of the eyes in correct proportion to the rest of the oval or face. Eyes should be roughly halfway between the top and bottom of the oval. Each eye should be one fifth of the total width of the oval. We master this step in placing the eyes before moving to the next part.

The next step is placement of the nose. The tip of the nose should be drawn about halfway between the eyes and the chin. As with the eyes, the mastery of this step is to develop the proper placement.

The next step is to draw the mouth. We begin by drawing the line created by the lips touching. In effect, the midline of the mouth created when the upper and lower lips come together. Then we fill in the upper and lower lips. I make it a point to have the students observe the changes in this midline due to different expressions. We then work on mastering how the difficult expressions can be reflected in the midline of the mouth.

The next step is placement of the ears. The ears should be placed in the appropriate area on each side of the oval. The placement of the ears should be on a plane between the eyebrows and the tip of the nose.

At this point we go back to the eyes. We work on mastering the ability to draw eyelids, eyelashes, and expression in the eyes. We discuss how various expressions with the mouth are reflected with eye expressions.

The next step is to fill in the other parts. This includes eyebrows, hair, hairline, and facial hair.

The final step is the relationship of the head to the neck.

I evaluate this task on a credit/no credit basis. We continue redrawing until both the student and I are satisfied. The features must be well placed for the drawing to be given credit. Then we extend this by applying the same steps to a self-portrait by using a mirror and a ruler to actually measure their own features.

Do you think teachers should grade on a curve where you have the same number of "A's" as you do "F's" and the same number of "B's" as you do "D's" with the rest of the grades being "C's"?

Norm-referenced evaluations are often called grading on the curve. In effect, the assignment of grades is based on certain reference points on the normal curve. (However, in common classroom use, this term is frequently a misnomer. There should be the same number of F's as A's and the same number of D's as B's when you grade strictly on the curve. This is hardly what students want when they ask if test grades will be curved.)

Norm-referenced evaluations require some sort of transformation procedure to change the raw scores from the test to a grade. Teachers can use normal curve statistics to transform the scores. They can use some other type of scoring system to transform student scores.

Cureton (1971) reviewed the history of this procedure. He indicated that one of the most common forms of grading on the curve was to use 1.5 standard deviations above the average score as the cutoff for an A grade. If the grades were normally distributed, this would result in 7 percent of the class obtaining an A. The scores receiving an F would have scored 1.5 standard deviations below the mean or lower, which would encompass 7 percent of the scores. The scores for a B would be between .5 standard deviation above the mean to 1.5 standard deviations, which would encompass 24 percent of the scores. The opposite standard deviation cutoffs below the mean would receive a D. The scores for a C would be between .5 standard deviation above the mean to .5 standard deviation below the mean, which would encompass 38 percent of the scores.

Other points on the normal curve could be used to transform the scores. Again, in using norm-referenced evaluation procedures, the point is that students' scores are compared and then transformed to grades. This can be used to ensure a given number of A, B, C, and even D and F grades.

How Do the Different Evaluation Procedures Compare?

The same type of test item can be used for formative or summative procedures, as well as for criterion-referenced and norm-referenced procedures. Therefore, the purpose of the evaluation determines its categorization. The way the evaluation procedure is used in the grading system determines the way it is categorized.

In comparing evaluation procedures, there seem to be some important differences. Criterion-referenced methods may decrease unwanted competition among students. Formative evaluations may provide necessary feedback in a nonthreatening manner. Each of the different methods has positive and negative attributes. Different evaluation methods affect the tone and tenor of a classroom, as do different instructional methods.

If you went to a doctor for a physical examination and he gave you the following results: heart-B, lungs-C, blood pressure-C, cholesterol-A, and liver-D+, would you want to know more information or would the letter grade satisfy your information needs?

Because of their purpose, criterion-referenced evaluation procedures may be more appropriate to use in conjunction with formative evaluations (Gronlund & Linn, 1990). Norm-referenced methods may be more appropriate to use with summative evaluations (Gronlund & Linn, 1990).

The question of whether to use criterion-referenced or norm-referenced evaluations is debated by a number of people in the testing field. Norm-referenced evaluations tend to accentuate individual differences and to decrease cooperative

The problem with setting a certain criterion level often occurs with any new test. When the state of West Virginia decided to implement a minimum competency test as an entrance exam into teacher education programs, it had to develop a cutoff point or performance standard.

The test development question became: What is an acceptable performance criterion for college juniors on this type of standardized test? To answer this question, West Virginia decided to administer the new test on a trial basis to volunteer samples of undergraduate majors in teacher education and to currently practicing teachers.

Using these norm groups, the criterion level was then set at what approximately 60 percent of the norm group was able to pass. Thus, the state used a norm from volunteer sample groups to set a criterion for the test. This is not an uncommon practice in determining performance standards for minimum competency tests.

Classroom teachers may want to use a similar procedure in developing appropriate criterion levels. The performance level of previous classes should provide your best guide to setting a criterion for your evaluation procedures. You may want to discuss your criteria levels with more experienced teachers. Another possibility is to compare your classroom performance levels with grade-equivalent scores or other scores from standardized achievement tests.

learning and interaction among students. On the other hand, criterion-referenced procedures may result in artificially low or high cutoffs for the performance criteria. Unless carefully considered, criterion-referenced tests may result in grade inflation.

Hopkins, Stanley, and Hopkins (1990) note that most standardized tests are norm-referenced evaluations. They also present the argument that criterion-referenced procedures are most effective in measuring basic skills. However, they claim that it becomes increasingly difficult to use criterion-referenced tests with higher-level cognitive skills. In one way or another, a classroom norm must be established in such courses as Calculus, English literature, or Physics.

Therefore, teachers are often faced with a specific problem when they first develop criterion-referenced evaluation measures. Where does one set a criterion or cutoff for criterion-referenced tests? (See Applications 12.4.)

■ ■ ■

OBJECTIVE VERSUS ESSAY ITEMS
How Are Test Items Classified?

Gronlund and Linn (1990) divide classroom test items into two categories: "the objective item, which is highly structured and requires the pupils to supply a word or two or to select the correct answer from a number of alternatives, and the essay question, which permits the pupils to select, organize, and present the answer in essay form" (p. 121).

As a student, do you prefer short-answer and multiple choice tests over essay tests? Why or why not?

Gronlund and Linn state that the decision to use one or the other item should be based on the instructional objectives to be measured. Basic skills appear to be better measured by objective items, while more complex skills are better measured by essay items. They also state that, in general, essay questions should be used when measuring the ability to apply, organize, or integrate ideas into a common theme.

What Are the Positive and Negative Aspects of Essay Items?

Essay questions have certain positive benefits aside from the three aspects indicated by Gronlund and Linn. They may increase the student's writing skills by forcing the student to write in an organized and coherent manner. They also may increase higher-level cognitive skills by forcing the students to synthesize and defend their ideas.

However, as any college student knows, there is one major problem with essay questions. The grade assigned to an essay item is dependent on who is grading the essay. There is very little consistency from one person to another in determining essay grades. However, consistency of grading may be increased by restricting the types of responses available to the student in answering the essay question.

For instance, a restricted-response essay question would be:

In two paragraphs or less, compare and contrast intelligence tests and achievement tests by listing two similarities and two differences between intelligence tests and achievement tests.

An open-ended or extended-response essay question would be:

Describe intelligence and achievement tests and list as much basic information as possible about these two tests.

Even with restricted-response essays, it is clear that inconsistency in grading remains a problem for the essay test. It may be possible to specify the number of points in grading particular parts of the essay, such as the points for content, organization, application, and synthesis of ideas. Such specificity at the outset may decrease some of the problems associated with grading essay material.

As a teacher, do you prefer essay or short answer tests?

How Are Objective Items Constructed?

In choosing objective items, nearly all test authors agree that the multiple choice item is the most popular type of objective item (Gronlund & Linn, 1990; Popham, 1990). Gronlund and Linn (1990) state the multiple choice item is the best format for presenting objective items. The publishers of standardized tests generally agree that the multiple choice items offers greater consistency and flexibility than any other type of objective item.

The construction of quality multiple choice items involves a number of features. The two essential parts of the multiple choice question are the stem and the alternatives. The stem is the question or statement of the problem. The stem generally should be a positive question or statement, as opposed to a negative question. For instance, a positive statement is:

Which one of the following was a President of the United States?

A. Benjamin Franklin
B. Thomas Paine
C. Alexander Hamilton
D. Rutherford B. Hayes

A negative statement is:

Which one of the following was not a President of the United States?

A. James Madison
B. Benjamin Franklin
C. Grover Cleveland
D. James A. Garfield

The stem should be longer than any of the alternatives but as concise as possible. The stem should be meaningful by itself, containing as much of the content as possible. It should not be an incomplete or awkward question.

The alternatives should consist of the correct answer and three or four incorrect answers known as distractors. The goal of test construction is not to confuse students but to discriminate between those who have mastered the material and those who have not. The following points should be considered when constructing good multiple choice alternatives:

1. All the alternatives should be grammatically consistent with the stem. Grammatically inconsistent alternatives provide clues as to what the correct answer is.
2. Each of the alternatives should be plausible. However, someone who knows the material should be able to distinguish what the correct answer is.
3. If they do not know the correct answer or are unsure, there is a tendency for students, when guessing, to pick the first answer (item A on the multiple choice format) or to pick the longest answer. Thus, care should be taken in choosing A as the correct answer in constructing multiple choice questions or in choosing the longest answer as the correct answer.
4. Be careful of your own biases in constructing tests. There is a tendency to repeat the same correct answer on your own teacher constructed tests. In effect, there is a tendency to prefer either A, B, C, D, or E as the correct answer in designing one's own multiple choice tests. Students will quickly discover if you have a bias for picking one of the alternatives as the correct answer.
5. Avoid using "all of the above," "none of the above," or other combination answers as alternatives. As with negative stems, these only confuse students, and they reduce the consistency of scores on the test.
6. Increasing the number of items on a multiple choice test generally is beneficial. As long as the items meet these criteria, the more the merrier when it comes to the number of items on a multiple choice test.

> What mistakes do teachers make on multiple choice tests that "tip off" the correct answer?

■ ■ ■

EVALUATION ALTERNATIVES
What Are Some Alternatives to Traditional Evaluations?

A number of alternatives to the previously listed evaluation procedures have been proposed in recent years. This movement toward alternative forms of measurement has been called the "Authentic Assessment" or the "Authentic Testing" movement. Three of these alternative evaluation procedures are reviewed in this section: performance tests, portfolios, and exhibitions.

Performance Tests. Performance tests are similar to criterion-referenced measures. However, performance tests measure skills that require some sort of observable activity or ability. In his review of performance tests, Carey (1988) states: "They enable teachers to analyze students' performance and to comment on such aspects as timing, speed, precision, sequence, and appearance" (pp. 220–221).

How can objectivity in grading be maintained for alternative evaluations? Consider how you might do this for your class.

One example of a performance test is the driver's test required by each state for a driver's license. A typing test, required by many companies for hiring employees in a secretarial position, is another example.

Portfolios. Portfolios are an accumulated record of a student's performance in a particular academic discipline. In journalism, a portfolio is the repository for the articles that a student has written for the school newspaper or for journalism classes. The portfolio may contain material for just a semester or it may contain material needed to complete graduation requirements.

One example of an Exhibition is a recital that is performed for a music class.

Wiggins (1989) provides the following example of a portfolio:

> The requirements include a written autobiography, a reflection on work (including a resume), an essay on ethics, a written summary of coursework in science, an artistic product or a written report on art (including an essay on artistic standards used in judging artwork (p. 42).

Exhibitions. Exhibitions tend to be a more summative type of evaluation that indicates the mastery of a subject area (Wiggins, 1989). In one sense they are like a performance test but are used to determine whether the course of study is now completed. Some examples of exhibitions are the oral defense of a doctoral dissertation or the final recital performance at a music school.

How Do Alternative Forms of Evaluation Compare with Traditional Procedures?

In certain cases, alternative forms of evaluation may provide a better way of measuring performance abilities, higher-level cognitive skills, or creative abilities. However, it does appear that the degree of subjective judgment involved in grading some forms of alternative evaluations could cause similar problems to what is found in essay measures. It appears that alternative forms of evaluations may be more effective when using pass/fail grading policies.

As indicated in the preceding sections, there seems to be a relationship between the type of evaluation and the type of academic skill. Some writers have indicated that basic skills were more effectively measured by criterion-referenced techniques and objective items, such as multiple choice questions. There also may be a need to use formative evaluations more with basic skills learning.

Higher-level cognitive skills appear to be more appropriately measured with norm-referenced techniques, essay items, and with alternative evaluation measures, such as portfolios and exhibitions. There may be less of a need to complete formative evaluations when measuring higher-level cognitive skills.

■ ■ ■

EVALUATIONS AND GRADES
How Are Evaluations Used to Determine Classroom Grades?

The goal of each particular evaluation, its place in your grading policy, and its relationship to the curriculum are other areas for teachers to consider. Each evaluation should carry a particular weight or value in relationship to other evaluations in a given subject area. (In the elementary grades, formal evaluations also may affect the decision of whether to pass the student to the next grade level.)

Care must be taken in considering the relationship of each evaluation to the total grade. Each evaluation used to determine actual grades needs to have an explicit relationship both to the instructional methods and to the overall grading system in the classroom. The teacher needs to communicate the grading policies at the beginning of the grading period.

In fifth grade, each weekly spelling test accounts for 5 points or 5 percent of the total grade received for spelling on the 9-week report card. There are 9 such spelling tests that account for a total of 45 points or 45 percent of the total grade in spelling.

Spelling Grade

Weekly test:
5 points per test x 9 tests = 45 points
Midterm exam: 15 points
Final exam: 15 points
Writing assignment: 25 points
Total class points: 100 points

For the 9-week spelling grade, the following number of points is necessary to attain each grade:

Grade	Points
A	92–100
B	82–91
C	72–81
D	65–71
F	Below 65

In using point systems to determine student grades, should points be deducted for misbehaviors? Is it legal in your state to deduct grade points for misbehavior?

Students and parents have a right to know where each evaluation fits into the overall grading policy. By knowing exactly what is expected of them, students will be able to plan their own time better. It also sends a message to students and parents that the teacher wants to be fair and consistent to everyone in the class.

Frequent feedback about evaluations, completed in a nonthreatening manner, can help students correct their mistakes. Providing students an opportunity to privately discuss any questions about their grades can go a long way in avoiding disagreements and problems. Providing regular feedback to the parents also can prevent potential questions about why their child is having problems in school. It is imperative that parents be notified of problems as soon as possible. This can help reduce the knee-jerk reaction of many parents when informed their child is having academic difficulty.

In providing feedback, it is essential that it be done in ways that do not compromise the privacy rights of the student and the parents. As previously indicated, these rights are included in the Buckley Amendment, which protects the confidentiality of grades and test records of students. Grades should be discussed only with the student, her parents, and other school personnel who have direct instructional contact with the student.

What Are the Issues Associated with Grading Policies?

Grading practices are replete with the same problems as other areas of evaluation. No one likes to be graded, yet there appear to be few alternatives to the present system of letter grades. Although arguments can be made against testing and grading (most often by students), a number of reasons seem to preclude changes in the present system.

As previously indicated, the public's call for accountability in education is one major reason for the type of grading policies that are now in place. Parents, legislators, school boards, and employers want a concrete measure of student performance. The public's attitude is that there must be a certain knowledge base associated with a certain level of education. In essence, a given level of knowledge or competency should be associated with an eighth-grade education, a high school diploma, or a college degree.

Therefore, a passing grade for a given educational level should indicate a certain level of knowledge. The call for minimum competency testing of graduating high school seniors is just one example of the increasing demands by the public for educational accountability. Requiring beginning teachers to pass a professional skills test to be certified is another example.

A second reason for the present system of grading is communication. Each subsequent level of education requires some type of appropriately communicated standard from the previous level. Where does an individual student perform in relation to his same-age peers? Where does an individual student perform on some generally accepted criterion of achievement? A third-grade teacher needs that type of information from the student's second-grade teacher. A college admissions committee needs that information from high school teachers.

Beginning teachers also should be aware that assigning grades is almost as much a measure of the teacher as it is a measure of the student. Is the teacher able to judge student performance in a manner that is fair, appropriate, and without discriminatory intent? When grades have been challenged, these are among the considerations made by grade-appeal committees.

> Under what conditions is it permissible to discuss another student's grade with a student who claims that his grade should have been the same as her's?

How Can a Teacher Avoid Grade Challenges?

In general, the legal system in the United States has sided with teachers and schools in legal challenges to grades and related issues such as educational malpractice. Zirkel and Richardson (1988) state: "A long line of court decisions concur that academic evaluations of students are not amendable to the fact finding process of judicial and administrative decision making" (p. 46).

The burden of proving that a grade is incorrect is on the student. Potential problem areas for teachers involve two basic issues: (1) discriminatory intent on the part of the teacher and (2) the lack of a rational or appropriate relationship between the classroom instruction, the evaluation measures, and the academic decisions made with regard to the student.

If the teacher applies the same, uniform standards to all students in the instructional and grading process, then discriminatory intent would not be a viable argument. If there is a clear relationship between the evaluation and the instruction, it would be very difficult to prove a lack of an appropriate or rational relationship.

Terwilliger (1989) made a number of important comments about grading practices. Among them he included the following recommendations:

1. Data collected for purposes of judging student achievement should be expressed in quantitative form.

What do you think about
the practicality of a
"schools without failure"
policy? How could such
a policy work? Should
students be allowed to
retake tests until they
reach a passing grade?

2. Such data should be collected over time and should be formulated within an explicit set of guidelines available to each student.
3. Assignment of a failing grade should reflect a judgment that the student does not possess a minimum level of competency.
4. A minimum level of competency should be independent of other students' level of performance.
5. The minimum level of competency should represent the essential course objectives that all students must achieve to certify a minimum level of mastery of the course material.

Terwilliger presents the argument that failing a student in a course should be a decision based strictly on a pass/fail judgment. Evaluations used to measure the attainment of minimal competency also should be based on criterion-referenced measures. Terwilliger states that failure rates should be low and that failure should reflect serious deficiencies in achieving minimal competency.

What Effect Do Evaluations Have on Students?

One of the most frequently debated issues about evaluations is the question of whether they are really a positive motivational tool. There have been a number of studies measuring the effects of evaluations on student performance.

Williams and Ware (1976) found that students, who expected to be tested after viewing a videotaped instructional module, scored higher than a control group of students who did not expect to be tested immediately after viewing the videotape. Clark (1969) found that students performed at a higher level on research papers when they expected to be graded than did a control group of students who did not expect to receive a grade.

However, a review of the research by Holmes and Matthews (1984) found real problems with retaining or holding back students for a full academic year. They found that students who were retained demonstrated a lower academic, social, and behavioral performance level than comparable students who were promoted. It did not appear that retention increased later classroom performance. In fact, it may have further decreased student achievement.

Thus, the research appears to indicate that the expectation of being graded increases achievement. However, the ultimate negative grade, retention, does not appear to help students.

Some people believe that
a decision to retain a
student carries with it
the obligation to provide
a written plan describing
what will be done
differently for the
student than was done
during the preceding
year. What do you think?

What Is the Relationship between Classroom Evaluation Practices and Diversity Issues?

One of the most cited research findings is the impact of expectations on student achievement (Good, 1987). Essentially, teacher expectations of classroom performance can shape student achievement. For instance, if a student is expected to achieve at a high level, she tends to perform at a high level. Conversely, if the teacher expected few gains in achievement, the student again tended to perform as expected.

This point is particularly crucial when examining the effects of teacher expectations on evaluating women and minorities. A report by the American Association of University Women (AAUW, 1992) reviewed some of the problems with educational expectations.

With regard to teacher expectations, the AAUW's major finding was that females were still less likely to do well in the sciences. On virtually every index of science achievement or aspiration, females scored considerably lower than males. The AAUW report indicated that it was expectations for success in science that appeared to hinder females.

In the AAUW report, the above findings in science achievement were contrasted with the considerable gains by women in mathematics performance. Thus, the once-noted gender gap in math achievement is now almost nonexistent.

With the above exception in science, the AAUW report indicated that females do better than males on classroom grades. Thus, on virtually every measure of teacher-made evaluations, females outperform males. However, as mentioned in the previous chapter, males outscore females on college entrance exam tests.

One reason for this paradox appears to be that males of all categories drop out of high school at a higher rate than do females. This picture of dropout rates is somewhat complicated by ethnic variations. As indicated in the AAUW report, the gender gap in dropout rates is far more pronounced for African Americans than for other groups. On the other hand, the gender gap in dropout rates appeared to be less pronounced for Hispanics and Asian Americans than for other groups.

Among all ethnic groups, women appear to be more likely to aspire to a college education. The dropout rates for males and the college aspirations for females make for a decidedly different pool of individuals who take college entrance exams compared with those who are enrolled in high school. These two factors may explain the paradox of why women do better on classroom evaluations but men do better on college entrance exam scores.

Other factors in grading practices cited in the AAUW report (1992) are the interactive relationship between gender, socioeconomic status, (SES) and ethnicity. The AAUW report indicated that Asian American females had the highest overall level of classroom evaluation achievement.

Across all the different socioeconomic and ethnic categories, males were consistently more likely to be retained or failed in public school. Contrary to some popular stereotypes, there were no significant differences found among low SES African American, Hispanic, or white males in retention rates. However, low SES Native American males were retained at substantially higher rates than any other low SES group. Low SES Asian American males were retained at considerably lower rates than any other low SES male group.

Within the high SES groups, the AAUW report indicated that the gender gap in retention rates narrowed a great deal. In the high SES groups, the only major gender gap was among whites. High SES white males were twice as likely to be retained as their female counterparts.

As with other studies of academic achievement, the AAUW report showed the predominant effect of socioeconomic status on school achievement. This variable appeared to account for more differences than did gender or ethnicity. Although gender and ethnic differences still remain, educational and social programs that deal with the economic differences between income groups seem most warranted.

Do you agree with these findings about gender differences?

REDUCING TEST ANXIETY

A number of different programs have been developed to reduce test anxiety. Some of the methods used in these programs are readily available to teachers.

1. Legitimize anxiety—Tell students that it is OK to be anxious. Everyone has anxiety. It is only when we allow it to overwhelm us that we have a problem. Have students articulate and reflect on their own test anxiety.
2. Deal with expectations—Tell students exactly what is expected of them in class and on the test. Students with test anxiety allow their fear of the unknown aspects of the test to overwhelm their resources. By knowing exactly what is expected of them, you remove the fear of the unknown.
3. Relaxation training paired with imagery techniques—As with phobias, systematic desensitization techniques appear to have considerable success in reducing test anxiety. These techniques teach the student to relax while imagining the test situation. Pairing the relaxed state with the imagined test situation appears to be effective.

4. Rational cognitive scripts—Many test-anxious students develop irrational fears, beliefs, and attitudes about their own test performance. Have students articulate these irrational thoughts. Help students to replace them with positive scripts.
5. Time management—Many test-anxious students do not appropriately budget their study time. Develop student contracts about study time. Using buddy systems in which students study together also may help with time management.
6. Exam sessions—A number of techniques in administering the test may help test-anxious students. Extra time or untimed tests can help. Practice exams may desensitize students to test anxiety. Telling students to wait until they reach a relaxed state before they turn the exam over and begin the exam can help. Allowing test-anxious students to take an exam in a separate room from other students is another possible technique.

What Factors Are Associated with Test Anxiety?

What has worked well for you in combating test anxiety?

The AAUW report (1992) also indicated that women suffer more from test anxiety. Test anxiety ranges from the common queasy stomach feeling to an incapacitating phobia. Research and treatment programs examining test anxiety have increased in recent years.

The research indicates that, to some degree, people who have a high level of general anxiety tend to also have a high level of test anxiety. Thus, general anxiety and test anxiety are somewhat related. There are a number of other factors that also appear to be related to test anxiety. Included among these factors are negative attitudes and expectations about school; low self-esteem; negative expectations about the specific course or subject; and the type of test situation. The type of test situation that triggers test anxiety is a timed test.

What Factors Lead to Academic Dishonesty during Classroom Evaluations?

Recent media reports of academic dishonesty in high schools and colleges suggest that classroom cheating has reached massive proportions (Deutsch, 1988;

McLoughlin, 1987). The Carnegie Commission on Education (Singhal & Johnson, 1979) reported that 30 percent to 50 percent of college students admitted to cheating.

Evans and Craig (1990) stated that research findings indicate that the incidence of cheating among students from elementary grades to graduate school was 40 percent or more. They also stated that results of their own study on cheating in middle schools and high schools pointed to an increase in cheating with each successive grade level.

Students appear to cheat more in classes where they perceive the teacher to be incompetent or where the teacher does not take active steps to prevent cheating (Evans, Craig, & Mietzel, 1991). Evans, Craig, and Mietzel also indicated that students who have the following characteristics are more likely to cheat: low self-esteem, a defiance of authority, and an external locus of control. (External locus of control means that you believe that your behavior is largely controlled by external forces, such as parents, environment, luck or fate.)

Certain measures may curb cheating incidences. Among these measures are explicit definitions of academic dishonesty, written statements of policy provided to all students, and uniform enforcement of the negative consequences of cheating by all teachers in the school (Singhal & Johnson, 1979).

Certain evaluation procedures also appear to curb cheating incidences. Evans and Craig (1990) claim that cheating is decreased by avoiding evaluations "where grading is on a curve and where grades are based on just one or two exams or other products" (p. 50).

Other factors also may decrease cheating on exams. Included among these are appropriate test security, the use of in-class term paper assignments, the use of essay items, changing exam items each term, and administering multiple forms of the same exam. As with other aspects involved in the treatment of students,

Have you ever cheated on a test or an assignment? If so, how did you cheat? Is cheating ever justifiable?

Academic dishonesty is a growing problem in schools. There are a variety of methods that can curb this problem.

What should be the
logical and natural
consequences for
cheating?

consistency is of prime importance. Differential treatment of students in the evaluation process can only result in a loss of the teacher's personal credibility and integrity.

As with other aspects of effective evaluations, this area can help the teacher maintain the academic integrity of the classroom. Failure to prevent academic dishonesty will, in turn, contribute to the poor public perception of the present educational system.

What Are Some Ethical Issues Involved in Grading Practices?

A number of ethical issues have been raised in the area of classroom grading and evaluation. Many of the ethical issues focus on the questions of fairness, consistency, and a rational relationship between instruction and evaluation. As with the ethical problems in the standardized testing area, these issues affect the academic integrity of the educational process and the personal integrity of the teacher. Some additional ethical questions are:

1. Is it ethical to allow completion of out-of-class assignments or other make-up work to compensate for low test grades?
2. Can graded student work be displayed in any type of manner or form?
3. Should teachers be allowed to tutor their own students after school hours for financial gain?

In regard to the first issue, make-up work generally is not considered a good evaluation practice. In-class exams minimize cheating. Such exams should be utilized to the maximum extent possible. Out-of-class assignments are most susceptible to academic dishonesty. By accepting such make-up work, the teacher is allowing a less valid evaluation practice to take the place of a more valid evaluation practice.

In addition to the above, there is the ethical issue of fairness to all students. If a choice is made by the teacher to accept out-of-class work for poor test performance, the policy for this work has to be clearly stated and available to all students during the first week of each term. It would be unethical to allow some students to make-up tests or assignments without allowing all students the same opportunity.

Displaying graded student work is not a good evaluation practice. Not only may such displays engender unwanted competition and jealousy between students, it probably violates the Buckley Amendment. Student grades or any graded material cannot be displayed in a way that compromises the privacy rights of the students. Written permission from the parents of the students would be necessary to display any classwork that receives a grade.

Tutoring one's own students for financial gain also is not a good practice. Again, the fairness issue of a uniform instructional and evaluation policy toward all students is the major problem with private tutoring of one's own students. If teachers are paid money to tutor their own students, it becomes clear that those with the money will have an advantage. Those students without money will not have the same opportunity. Many schools have a policy that forbids teachers from tutoring their own students for financial gain. Some schools forbid teachers from tutoring any students who attend their school.

SUMMARY

Teacher-made evaluations should be determined by instructional objectives. These evaluations should directly relate to specific learning outcomes for the class. Teacher-made evaluations can be divided into a number of different categories, including formative versus summative evaluations and criterion-referenced versus norm-referenced evaluations. Each type of evaluation category has its positive and negative aspects.

Among objective test items, there appears to be general agreement that the multiple choice item is the most appropriate type. Essay items may be able to more effectively measure higher-order cognitive skills. However, the reliability of grading essay items remains a major problem.

Evaluations and how they relate to the total academic grade need to be carefully considered. Each separate evaluation needs to be given a numerical weight or score so that it can be related to other measures.

Any type of classroom evaluation technique must be applied fairly and consistently. There also should be a rational relationship between what is taught in the class and what is measured on the test.

Diversity issues are becoming an increasing concern in classroom evaluation procedures. Although gender and ethnic differences appear to be narrowing, there still appear to be areas of concern. Women still do not achieve as well as men in science disciplines. There remain complex socioeconomic, gender, and ethnic differences in the rate at which students dropout of and fail in school.

Academic dishonesty appears to be a major problem with evaluations in public schools. Cheating appears to increase with each grade level through the high school years. There also seem to be some methods of reducing the incidence of academic dishonesty.

CHAPTER REVIEW

1. Define the following terms: evaluation, testing, grading and assessment. What are the relationships between these terms?
2. Describe the relationship between instructional objectives, learning outcomes, and evaluation.
3. According to some researchers in the field, different evaluation techniques are more congruent with other evaluation techniques. Please list the ways that different evaluation techniques can be used in conjunction with one another. Included in this area are formative and summative evaluations, norm-referenced and criterion-referenced evaluations and objective and essay items.
4. What are the positive and negative aspects of objective test items?
5. What are the positive and negative aspects of essay items?
6. What are two rationales for the present grading practices in public schools?
7. What are two reasons given for the research finding that females do better on classroom evaluations but do worse on college aptitude tests?
8. What are four methods teachers can use to reduce test anxiety?
9. Describe three methods for reducing academic dishonesty during classroom evaluations.

INSTRUCTION AND EVALUATION SHOULD BE FAIR AND CONSISTENT

In reviewing this chapter, what types of recommendations would you now make for the teacher in the case study at the beginning?

The issues raised in the case study are addressed by some of the following sections in the chapter:

1. Discriminatory Practice and Ethical Issues—
   In terms of grading policies to what extent can a teacher provide students with extra out-of-class assignments to make up a failing grade?
   Is it a discriminatory practice to allow students to make up in out-of-class work what they have failed to do on an in-class exam?
   What if all the students in the class requested make-up work?
   Is paid tutoring by a teacher a legitimate and ethical activity?
   Can paid tutoring be construed as a type of discriminatory practice?
   What if all students requested paid tutoring services of the classroom teacher?

   As indicated in the section on ethical practices, the above questions involve a number of different issues. Yet these issues still come back to the basic principle of fairness. Students should be treated fairly and consistently. Instruction and evaluation practices cannot favor one student over another student. Tutoring a student for financial gain violates the fairness principle. It allows a student with money to receive more instruction than a student without money.

2. Academic Dishonesty—
   Should the teacher in the case study require the failing students to do in-class writing assignments to determine if they cheated on their term papers?
   If the teacher allows the failing athletes to make-up their work, will this problem continuously occur again?
   Will the Coach know that this is an 'easy teacher' and continue to expect favorable treatment for 'his boys?'

   As with the first section, this issue involves the principle of equal treatment for all students. A stated policy, that is not upheld for all students, sends a signal that the process is not fair and consistent. As the research on academic dishonesty indicates, uniform policies and consistency with regard to negative consequences are important measures that can curb cheating. By not being consistent, the academic integrity of the educational process and the personal integrity of the teacher may be damaged. In addition, if the teacher allows one group of students to get away with this type of activity, then the teacher can expect further attempts at such behavior.

   Reflecting on the material in this chapter, another possible suggestion for the beginning teacher in the chapter case study is to discuss school policies with some senior faculty members. After discussing policies with other teachers it might be useful to request a meeting with the Principal to determine exactly the Principal's position on academic and ethical policies related to the issues of grading, tutoring and make-up assignments.

REFERENCES

American Association of University Women (1992). *How schools shortchange girls.* Washington, DC: American Association of University Women Educational Foundation.

Carey, L. M. (1988). *Measuring and evaluating school learning:* Boston: Allyn and Bacon, Inc.

Clark, D. C. (1969). Competition for grades and graduate school performance. *Journal of Educational Research, 62,* 351–354.

Cureton, L. W. (1971). The history of grading practices. *NCME Measurement in Education, 2,* 1–8.

Deutsch, C. H. (1988). Cheating: Alive and flourishing. *New York Times Educational Supplement, 137,* April issue, 25–29.

Evans, E. D., & Craig, D. C. (1990). Teacher and student perceptions of academic cheating in middle and senior high schools. *Journal of Educational Research, 84,* 1, 44–52.

Evans, E. D., Craig, D. C., & Mietzel, G. (1991). *Adolescents' cognitions and attributions for academic cheating: A cross national study.* (ERIC Document Reproduction Service No. ED 335 612)

Good, T. L. (1987). Teacher expectations. In D. C. Berliner & B. V. Rosenshine (Eds.), *Talks to teachers* (pp. 157–200). New York: Random House.

Gronlund, N. E., & Linn, R. L. (1990), *Measurement and evaluation in education.* New York: MacMillan.

Holmes, C. T., & Matthews, K. M. (1984). The effects of nonpromotion on elementary and junior high school pupils: A meta-analysis. *Review of Educational Research, 54,* 225–236.

Hopkins, K. D., Stanley, J. C., & Hopkins, B. R. (1990). *Educational and psychological measurement and evaluation* (7th ed.). Englewood Cliffs, NJ: Prentice Hall.

McLoughlin, M. (1987, February 23). A nation of liars. *U.S. News and World Report,* 54–60.

Popham, W. J. (1990). *Modern educational measurement: a practitioner's perspective.* Englewood Cliffs, NJ: Prentice Hall.

Singhal, A. C., & Johnson, P. (1979). How to halt student dishonesty. *College Student Journal, 13,* 13–19.

Tallent, N. (1992). *The practice of psychological assessment.* Englewood Cliffs, NJ: Prentice Hall.

Terwilliger, J. S. (1989). Classroom standard setting and grading practices. *Educational Measurement: Issues and Practices, 8*(2), 15–19.

Wiggins, G. (1989). Teaching to the (authentic) test. *Educational Leadership, 46*(7), 41–47.

Williams, R. G., & Ware, J. E. (1976). Validity of student ratings of instruction under different incentive conditions. *Journal of Educational Psychology, 68,* 48–56.

Zirkel, P. A., & Richardson, S. N. (1988). *A digest of supreme court decisions affecting education.* Bloomington, IN: Phi Delta Kappa Foundation.

CHAPTER 13

CHILDREN AT RISK AND CHILDREN WITH DISABILITIES

■ ■ ■

Chapter Outline

IMPLEMENTING A FULL INCLUSION POLICY

You are a new second-grade teacher in a wealthy, suburban school district in the Northeast corridor. Your training has been exclusively in kindergarten through sixth-grade regular education. You have had one survey class in special education.

Your school district is noted for its innovative programs. There are a number of very active parents' groups. Among them is a local parents' advocacy group for children with disabilities.

Recently, this advocacy group announced its overwhelming support for full inclusion of all children with disabilities in regular education classrooms. This means that all special education children, regardless of their disability, will be placed in regular education settings such as your classroom. Such children with disabilities would include the blind, severely retarded, and those with physically challenged conditions.

Many of the teachers in your district have questioned their own ability to handle children with severe disabling conditions. Some principals have stated that their classrooms do not have the appropriate physical facilities to handle children with handicapping conditions. However, the local school board has agreed to implement this proposed policy.

What impact would this policy have on a new second-grade teacher? How would you feel about supervising a classroom of twenty-five children, which included some children with severe disabilities? What would you do about playground activities or physical education? What type of additional training or extra educational support would you need? How would this policy change your teaching methods?

INTRODUCTION

This chapter examines two key, related areas in American education: children at risk and children with disabilities. One purpose of this chapter is to provide the beginning teacher with a knowledge base about the different factors associated with causing children to be at risk in public schools. An examination of early childhood programs for at risk children also is provided.

A second purpose of this chapter is to provide the beginning teacher with a basic understanding of special education regulations and categories. These regulations are becoming increasingly important for all teachers because of the growing movement for inclusion of children with disabilities in regular education classrooms. A basic overview of the different types of children with disabilities also is provided.

■ Relationship between maternal drug/alcohol use and at risk conditions.
■ Effects of lead exposure on causing learning disabilities.
■ Effectiveness of early childhood programs on helping children at risk.
■ Categories of children with disabilities.
■ Laws and regulations governing special education.
■ Methods for working with children with learning disabilities.
■ Role of the inclusion movement in special education.
■ Gender and diversity issues involved in special education.

■ ■ ■

CHILDREN AT RISK
Who Are the Children At Risk for School Failure?

Children at risk for school failure include children who have certain predisposing factors that may cause them to be low educational achievers. Among the factors causing children to be "at risk" are prenatal problems, maternal drug/alcohol use during pregnancy, birthing problems, environmental toxins, infant diseases, or adverse socioeconomic conditions.

These problems can produce a variety of physical, developmental, or psychological disorders. This area has become of increasing concern to educators because of the number of babies born to women who used crack cocaine or alcohol during pregnancy or who were HIV positive with the AIDS virus.

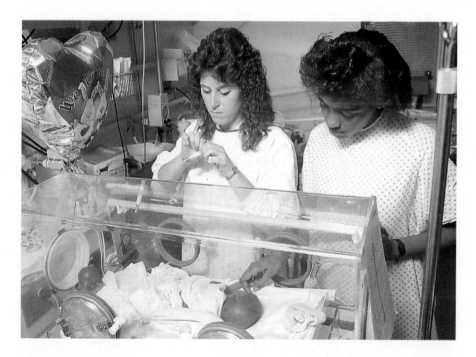

The number of at risk children born in recent years has increased significantly. This increase may pose special problems for our educational system.

Describe some social factors that you think might have contributed to the problem of children at risk.

Some of the numbers have become alarming. For instance, Stevens and Price (1992) reported the following data concerning at risk children: Each year, 350,000 newborns have been exposed prenatally to drugs, including alcohol; between 15,000 and 30,000 children are HIV positive; 3 million to 4 million children have been exposed to damaging levels of lead; and 37,000 children have significantly low birth weight.

The effects of these risk factors on mental and physical functioning are only now becoming fully documented. It is clear that the degree of problems produced by these conditions range from mild to severe effects. Thus, the mental abilities for at risk children range from normal intelligence to severe mental retardation (Stevens & Price, 1992). Their physical problems have a similar variability.

What Factors Are Associated with Fetal Alcohol Syndrome?

Researchers in this area claim that fetal alcohol syndrome (FAS) is the single leading cause of mental retardation in the world (Burgess & Streissguth, 1992). Fetal alcohol syndrome is caused by women who are heavy drinkers of alcohol during pregnancy. FAS is a medical diagnosis that is based on three distinct characteristics in the child (Burgess & Streissguth, 1992):

1. growth deficiency, such as low birth weight;
2. certain specific facial and physical abnormalities;
3. central nervous system dysfunctions.

Have attitudes changed about pregnant women drinking alcohol? Is it becoming more socially unacceptable to drink alcohol during pregnancy?

Burgess and Streissguth point out that a new term is being used in this area. This term is fetal alcohol effect (FAE). This syndrome also involves women who drink heavily during pregnancy. However, the physical effects of the drinking on the child are not nearly as pronounced as with FAS. For instance, the facial and physical abnormalities are much less present or even absent. However, the cognitive deficits are as severe in FAE as they are in FAS.

The question is always asked: How much alcohol is safe to drink when pregnant? Researchers indicate that no amount appears to be safe. Even as little as one or two drinks per day have been found to produce children "at risk" for learning disabilities (Streissguth, Barr, & Sampson, 1990).

In terms of distinctive behavioral effects, Burgess and Streissguth (1992) indicate some common characteristics of children with fetal alcohol syndrome and fetal alcohol effect. The major behavioral characteristics are high levels of activity, impulsivity, distractibility, and poor communication skills.

In terms of educational functioning, the average IQ scores for this population are between sixty-five and seventy (Burgess & Streissguth, 1992). The need for early diagnosis and intervention is stressed by researchers in this field. The most important areas of educational intervention are in teaching communication skills and in improving adaptive living skills.

What Problems Are Found in Children with Prenatal Exposure to Cocaine?

One group of much-publicized at risk students has been the so called crack babies. The controversy with this type of disorder stems from a series of sensationalized accounts of screaming, premature newborns hooked up to life-support machines. In his review of the research, Griffith (1992) sharply criticized these accounts of crack babies.

Griffith indicated a number of problems with these accounts of infants who were prenatally exposed to cocaine. Griffith listed three erroneous perceptions:

(1) that all cocaine-exposed children are severely affected;
(2) that little can be done for them;
(3) that all the medical, behavioral, and learning problems exhibited by these children are caused directly by their exposure to cocaine (1992, p. 30).

Griffith pointed out that there are a number of confounding variables in any of the studies completed on crack babies. Women who engaged in cocaine use during pregnancy generally did not receive prenatal education, medical care, or appropriate nutrition. The majority of these women were also multiple drug users (also referred to as polydrug users) and they continued to use multiple drugs after the birth of the children.

Griffith indicated that all these factors make it difficult for anyone to isolate the exact effect of prenatal exposure to cocaine. In addition to these confounding effects, Griffith stated that little long-term research has been completed on children who were prenatally exposed to cocaine.

Griffith (1992) reviewed an ongoing, unpublished study by the National Association for Perinatal Addiction Research and Education. This study was conducted on more than three hundred cocaine/polydrug-exposed children. At the time of his review, the children had been tracked through age three. On the Stanford-Binet Intelligence Scale, there were no overall differences between the drug-exposed children and a control group.

However, this study did find that approximately one-third of the drug-exposed children displayed problems in normal language development and in attention span. This subgroup displayed the types of impulsivity and distractibility that were characteristic of other categories of drug-exposed children.

It appears that children who are prenatally exposed to alcohol or other drugs may share a set of common behavioral effects. As Griffith pointed out, it is difficult to factor out the specific effects of alcohol or substance abuse from other prenatal problems. Generally speaking, women who were substance abusers during their pregnancies also demonstrated other problems that placed their children at risk.

What Problems Occur with Childhood Exposure to Lead?

The controversy concerning childhood exposure to lead has had a long and tortuous history. Research has linked childhood exposure to lead with neuro-

Do you believe that there have been actual increases in the number of at risk children? Or do you think that it has largely been the publicity surrounding "Crack Babies" that has drawn attention to the problem?

The state of Kentucky recently passed a law stating that women, who used illegal drugs during pregnancy, could be found guilty of child abuse. Is this law an appropriate method of dealing with the problem? Does this law discriminate against women?

The basic transmittal mechanism for lead is by young children ingesting paint as it deteriorates. Lead exposure is associated with learning disabilities.

behavioral problems since the 1890s (Needleman, 1992). However, a political combination of manufacturing industries and organized medicine prevented a ban on lead-based materials until recently in the United States (Needleman, 1992).

The basic transmittal mechanism of lead toxins is thought to be lead-based paints in homes. As paint deteriorates, it flakes or chips. Children who then touch the deteriorating paint may ingest lead particles through nail biting or thumb sucking. In addition, lead in gasoline, soil, or construction materials has contributed to the problem.

The Agency for Toxic Substances and Disease Registry estimated that 16 percent of all American children have blood lead levels in the neurotoxic range (Needleman, 1992).

The behavioral and cognitive factors that are most affected by lead exposure are in the areas of language functioning, distractibility, and attention span (Needleman, 1992). The association of lead exposure with both learning disabilities and attention deficit disorders now seems warranted. Lead exposure may be a leading cause of learning disabilities.

What Difficulties Develop in Children with HIV Infections?

With the AIDS epidemic, there are an increasing number of pediatric cases of human immunodeficiency virus (HIV) infections. Most of these cases are found where the AIDS epidemic has had its greatest impact: in the largest cities in the United States. However, children with HIV infections can be found throughout the country.

What can teachers and school systems do to help in reducing lead exposure problems? Are programs and workshops on awareness of the problem sufficient?

Although some of the stigma associated with AIDS may have lessened in the United States, a major difficulty children with HIV infections face in school is their treatment as social outcasts. All teachers should keep in mind that an HIV infection is a medical condition. Information about a child's condition is protected by the same legal and ethical codes that protect any other type of medical condition. Such information cannot be released by school personnel without parental consent.

As with adults who have HIV infections, children will not exhibit symptoms in the early stages of the disease. It is only when they begin to exhibit symptoms that special education programming becomes necessary (Seidel, 1992). It also appears that one difference between children with AIDS and adults with AIDS is in the progression of the disease. Seidel noted that developmental delays in reaching cognitive milestones are often the first symptomatic indication that a child has an HIV disorder.

Another apparent difference is that the course of the disease appears to affect the central nervous system more in children (Seidel, 1992). Thus, with children there will be a much greater progressive deterioration of central nervous system functioning than with adults. (For instance, adults with AIDS are much more likely to suffer from opportunistic infections in the respiratory system.)

The types of motor and cognitive impairments that occur in children with HIV infections appear to center on motor control difficulty, language loss, and decreased intellectual levels (Seidel, 1992). Children may attain certain developmental milestones, then regress and lose these milestones as the course of the disease continues.

Seidel (1992) also presented research evidence indicating that early compensatory education programs may delay the loss of cognitive and motor functioning. Although research in this area is only beginning, there may be some hope for delaying the motor and cognitive regression that occurs with this disease. However, at this time, the long-term prognosis for children with HIV infections is the same as that with adults.

Reflect on your own feelings about having a child who is HIV positive in your classroom. Describe how you would feel and handle such a situation.

What Are Other Causative Factors for At Risk Children?

A number of other factors may be associated with causing children to be at risk for school failure. Among these factors are premature births, low birth weight, and labor and delivery difficulties. In many cases these factors are related to the educational and socioeconomic status of the parents (Birsch & Gussow, 1970).

In fact, being from lower socioeconomic levels can be considered a factor in and of itself for being an at risk child. Parents from lower socioeconomic levels tend to participate less in prenatal education programs, have poorer nutrition, and have less adequate health care. These prenatal nutritional and health-care standards seem to be particularly associated with at risk problems.

Low socioeconomic status also seems to be associated with producing a subgroup of males who have low academic achievement, low academic aspirations, and low vocational aspirations (Mckee & Banks, 1994). In terms of its effect on

From your own personal experience, do you agree with the statements about low socioeconomic status sometimes producing a subgroup of apparently anti-social males?

academic and vocational aspirations, a low socioeconomic background appears to have a more pronounced, adverse impact on males (Mckee & Banks, 1994).

There are some indications that these males will become increasingly alienated from school during the latter part of their secondary education. It also appears that this group of adolescent males may provide the breeding ground for a host of social, educational, and vocational problems.

In adolescence and early adulthood, this subgroup appears to be more likely to drop out of school, or be unemployed or marginally employed, and to engage in criminal activity. Dealing effectively with this particular subgroup presents American education and society with one of its most difficult challenges.

What Effect Does Head Start Have on Helping Children At Risk?

Early childhood education programs appear to offer the best hope for effectively helping at risk children. Among the best known of these programs is Head Start, a federally funded compensatory program for low income preschool children that began in 1965.

Head Start was initiated by President Lyndon Johnson as a Great Society program. Head Start was designed as a comprehensive intervention program in the areas of education, health, parental involvement, and social services. It originally was created to provide services for three- and four-year-olds. As of 1991, Head Start had served twelve million children and their families.

Although appearing to be one of the singular success stories of the Great Society, Head Start has not been without its critics. Much of the criticism has centered on the question of short-term versus long-term gains resulting from participation in Head Start. The research has been both voluminous and contradictory.

How much can compensatory early childhood programs aid children? After the program ends, these children often return to the same environment. Therefore, are these programs helping children only while they are in the program?

The essential research questions are: (1) How do Head Start children compare on social and academic measures with children from similar socioeconomic backgrounds who do not receive Head Start? and (2) Do Head Start children show long-term gains over their socioeconomically matched non-Head Start comparison groups?

A number of research reviews in this area are available (McKey et al., 1985; Guralnick & Bennet, 1987). A careful review of this research indicates that most Head Start children do achieve some short-term academic gains over matched controls. However, in many instances these academic gains "fade out" by the end of the third grade. In effect, the early academic gains are not maintained after the primary grades.

However, other types of gains, particularly in the social sphere, seem to be maintained. One of the best-known examples of these gains was in the Perry Preschool Project (Schweinhart & Weikart, 1983). The Perry Preschool Project followed Head Start children and matched controls well into adolescence. Significant positive effects were found for Head Start participants over a control group in such areas as employment, arrest records, dropout rates, and years in special education (Schweinhart & Weikart, 1983).

Low socioeconomic status appears to cause many at risk conditions. These conditions may also produce a subgroup of alienated males who engage in a number of anti-social behaviors.

Because of the success of the Perry Preschool Project and other similar programs, there have been a number of experimental spin-off programs from Head Start. Many of these programs are specifically designed to compensate for the academic "fade-out" effect. Best known among the federal government programs in this area are Even Start and the Head Start Transition Project.

A new federal program called Early Start is now being developed for children under the age of three. This program is designed to specifically address some of the problems of very young at risk children.

One of the findings in this research is that social gains may be maintained, but not academic gains. List some factors that may produce these outcomes.

What Effect Do Other Programs for At Risk Children Have on the Participants?

A number of other highly intensive, experimental programs, formed by consortiums of public schools, early childhood agencies, and universities have consistently been able to demonstrate short-term positive outcomes with at risk preschool children. These programs maintained frequent, concentrated amounts of instructional time with a very favorable ratio of teachers to children. They also relied on a large cadre of educational specialists, social workers, and health providers.

1993 EARLY CHILDHOOD/HEAD START TRANSITION PROJECT

What's Out	*What's In*
Teaching children how to sit on the floor.	Allowing children to choose their own comfortable position.
Teaching listening skills.	Creating experiences for children that are worth listening to.
Teaching self-esteem.	Children acquiring confidence though competence.
Teaching how to share.	Providing enough materials and opportunities for children to negotiate.
Talking about history.	Talking about what happened on the bus that morning.
Following directions.	Figuring it out.
Getting into line.	Going where you need to go.
Workbooks.	Work time.
Staying inside the lines.	Stepping over the line.
Products on display.	Process is what counts.

Adapted from the June 1993 Head Start Transition Consortium Conference Manual.

A team of trained professionals may be able to successfully intervene with some at risk children. However, the time/cost factors involved are substantial. Some researchers believe that a better solution is to educate and support the parents of such children. Do you think parental training programs offer a better solution?

Breitmayer and Ramey (1986) studied the effects of one such early childhood program specifically designed to help at risk children. Their study determined at risk criteria based on factors such as family income, Apgar scores (Apgar scores are a measure of neonatal responsiveness and physical appearance that are determined immediately after birth), maternal IQ scores, and parental educational level. The researchers randomly assigned subjects either to a special compensatory program or to a control group immediately after birth.

Breitmayer and Ramey found that the children in the special compensatory education program performed significantly better on measures of cognitive ability when tested at fifty-four months after birth. An associated finding was that the early intervention program seemed to produce the most differences in those children who were most at risk. In effect, the program had the greatest positive increases in outcomes with those children who were considered to be in the highest risk categories.

In summary, being at risk for school failure should not be viewed as an "all-or-nothing" state. There is a wide variation in children who suffer from at risk conditions. There are a number of research studies indicating that early childhood education programs may help children with at risk conditions.

As with quality day care, early childhood education programs appear to be successful when two factors are present: a highly favorable student/teacher ratio and a very frequent amount of quality instructional time. When these conditions are met, such programs are successful. These same factors appear to be necessary for successful special education programs.

Head Start and other preschool programs appear to be most effective when there are frequent and intensive levels of instructional and professional support services.

CHILDREN WITH DISABILITIES AND SPECIAL EDUCATION
What Are the Defining Aspects of Special Education?

Special education involves the education of children with disabilities. As indicated in the previous section, such children have a variety of causes for their disabilities. Their skills and abilities also have a wide range of variation. In addition to the factors listed for the previous section, there are a number of other factors associated with these disabilities.

Special education involves providing a free and appropriate public education for every handicapped child between the ages of three and twenty-one, regardless of how serious the disability may be (Public Law 101–476, 1990). Public Law 101–476, now commonly called the Individuals with Disabilities Education Act (IDEA), is the culmination of fifteen years of federal legislation that began with Public Law 94–142, which was passed by Congress in 1975. This series of legislation established one of the most comprehensive special education programs in the world.

Along with racial integration, the integration of exceptional children into the public education system eventually may be viewed as one of the triumphs of twentieth century American education. It is difficult for many students who read these words to realize the advances made in the area of special education in this century.

Critics of special education programs claim that educating the typical special education child costs three to five times as much as the cost for regular education. Are the benefits worth the costs?

How Were Individuals with Disabilities Treated Prior to Public Law 94–142?

The following are some examples that will give you an idea of the treatment of exceptional students prior to this legislation.

Well into the early part of this century, the mentally retarded were frequently considered "evolutionary throwbacks" (Gould, 1981). In essence, they were stereotyped as degenerative or subhuman. Because of this stereotype, individuals who were retarded or severely emotionally disturbed were frequently institutionalized from childhood until their death.

This institutionalization policy, once called warehousing, provided basic maintenance care. However, there was little or no attempt at education, intervention, or training. Individuals, who were institutionalized under these conditions, were often involuntarily sterilized particularly from 1930 to 1960.

Moron, imbecile, and idiot were the standard clinical terms applied to the mentally retarded for a good part of the twentieth century. People with learning disabilities were given the labels brain injured or minimal brain dysfunction.

People with disabilities were, in some cases, subjected to unethical medical experiments. In one study conducted in Massachusetts from 1946 to 1956, 125 mentally retarded patients were fed a diet of radioactive iron and calcium (Wheeler, 1994). The purpose of the research was to determine the long-term effects of radiation. A similar study, using mentally retarded subjects, involved partial or full-body exposure to massive amounts of radiation. One purpose of this study was to measure the effects of high levels of radiation on the intellectual abilities of the retarded (Wheeler, 1994).

As late as 1970, the education of people with disabilities entailed a high degree of segregation from regular education. In many cases, even the highest functioning individuals with disabilities attended completely separate schools or segregated classes.

What Are the Different Categories of Children with Disabilities?

According to the Individuals with Disabilities Education Act (IDEA), the major categories for children with disabilities are listed in the table in figure 13.1.

The Individuals with Disabilities Education Act (Public Law 101–76), the amendment to PL 94–142, included two new categories: autism and traumatic brain injury to the categories of students that have the right to receive special education. Data for these categories were not available at the time of the above report. In addition to the above categories, a number of state school regulations mandate the right of gifted individuals to receive special education.

What Are the Various Special Education Regulations and Procedures?

As indicated earlier, policies for special education testing and referral are determined by federal and state laws. Because of the degree of litigation in this area, teachers need to be particularly aware of the different special education laws and regulations.

One aspect of any form of segregation is that it keeps us from being confronted with our biases. There is a sort of "out of sight, out of mind" syndrome that accompanies segregation. Is there a relationship with our openness about disabilities and our interest in including them in the educational mainstream?

Category	Percentage of Total Special Education Enrollment
1. mentally retarded	12.7
2. hearing impaired	1.4
3. speech impaired	22.7
4. visually impaired	0.5
5. emotionally disturbed	9.0
6. orthopedically impaired	1.1
7. other health impaired	1.3
8. deaf-blind	0.0
9. multiple disabilities	2.2
10. learning disabled	49.1

FIGURE 13.1
Categories of Children
with Disabilities

Adapted from the Fourteenth Annual Report to Congress on the Implementation of the Individuals with Disabilities Education Act (p. 6) by the U.S. Department of Education, 1992, Washington, D.C.: U.S. Department of Education.

The following requirements are prescribed by the Individuals with Disabilities Education Act (Public Law 101–476):

1. All handicapped children aged three through twenty-one have the right to free and appropriate public education.
2. All handicapped children have the right to the least restrictive environment. This means that handicapped children should be placed in as normal a setting as possible. They should be mainstreamed or placed in the regular classroom whenever possible.
3. Each handicapped child should have an individualized educational plan (IEP) written by a multidisciplinary team composed of the classroom teacher, the special education teacher, the school psychologist, and the child's parents.
4. All tests and assessments used to measure, diagnose, or place handicapped children must be free from racial or cultural bias. Testing should be completed in the child's native language. Assessment must not be biased because of a child's handicapping condition.
5. Handicapped children will be identified through a psychoeducational evaluation composed of a series of appropriate assessments.
6. The final decision for placement in a special education program will not be made until after a thorough evaluation. The decision for placement will be made by a multidisciplinary team composed of teachers, administrators, school psychologists, and the parents.

In a practical sense, special education referrals by classroom teachers follow a particular sequence. Initially, the regular classroom teacher in a primary grade has noticed that a child has a problem. The teacher will then observe, complete

Parents of children with severe disabilities have been successful in suing school systems to make the schools pay for special services. Sometimes, these services are outside the school district. Should school systems be required to pay for services that are not locally available?

What should be done if the parents refuse permission for special education placement? How would you discuss such a refusal with a parent?

Regular education teachers in primary grades are often the "front line" in the initial decisions for special education testing referrals. List some of the issues and problems a teacher might face in this situation.

informal assessments, and complete screening tests. After this point the teacher will contact the parents and discuss the situation. If the parents agree in writing, a referral for a full psychoeducational evaluation will be undertaken.

After the full evaluation by the school psychologist, the multidisciplinary team will meet and make a decision to place or not place the child in a special education program. Providing special education placements and bearing the costs of the placements are the responsibility of the local school system. It also should be noted that the parent's agreement with any special education placement decision is mandated.

How Are Special Education Diagnoses Determined?

Certain categories of children with disabilities tend to be diagnosed by specific personnel. Physicians generally diagnose those with physically challenged conditions. These may include the deaf, visually handicapped, orthopedically impaired, other health impaired, deaf-blind, multihandicapped, autistic, and traumatic brain injured. Speech pathologists and audiologists tend to diagnose the speech impaired or the hard of hearing.

Other disabilities tend to be diagnosed by psychologists after a referral from teachers or school personnel. These categories include the mentally retarded, the emotionally disturbed, and the learning disabled.

There are a variety of ways that the determination of gifted is made. Children in the gifted category are most often selected through standardized test scores or by teacher ratings.

In the previous chapters, there have been discussions of the diagnostic aspects of different standardized tests that measure intelligence and achievement. More detailed discussions of the characteristics associated with speech disorders, mental retardation, learning disabilities, attention deficit-hyperactivity disorder, behavior disorders/emotional disorders, and the gifted are presented in the following sections.

Speech Disorders

Speech disorders form one of the most common reasons for referral to special education. Speech disorders can be caused by factors ranging from detectable neurological/physical abnormalities to purely psychological/emotional problems.

The two major types of speech disorders that occur in school-age children are articulation disorders and stuttering. Articulation disorders are defined as a consistent failure to correctly express proper speech sounds or phonemes. Children may mispronounce the sounds, substitute other sounds, or omit the proper sounds altogether. Articulation disorders almost always involve consonant sounds, particularly *r, sh, th, f, l,* and *ch.* Articulation disorders are more common in males.

Stuttering is a marked impairment of speech fluency characterized by repetitions or perseverations of sounds. Stuttering is viewed as having a genetic basis (American Psychiatric Association, 1987). The likelihood of stuttering is increased by social conditions, especially where there is pressure to talk. Conversely, stuttering is decreased or even absent in singing, talking to pets, or talking to inanimate objects. The onset of stuttering is concurrent with the development of speech between ages two and seven.

With the initial onset of the stuttering, the child is often unaware of the problem behavior. However, as the awareness increases, the child will often demonstrate certain accompanying behaviors, such as eye blinks, tics, jerking of the head, or fist clenching. Stuttering is three times more common in males (American Psychiatric Association, 1987).

With either articulation or stuttering problems, early detection and referral for treatment can be critical. If treated at an early age, articulation problems can be completely eliminated. With stuttering, approximately 80 percent of stutterers will recover with proper treatment (American Psychiatric Association, 1987).

As with most disabilities, early intervention for speech disorders is critical for successful treatment. From your own experience, what other factors might play a role in successful intervention?

Mental Retardation

Mental retardation is defined by having significantly subaverage intellectual performance with accompanying difficulties in adaptive functioning in one's social environment. The onset must be prior to age eighteen.

Generally, IQ scores that are two standard deviations below the mean or lower are one diagnostic sign for mental retardation. In effect, IQ scores that are seventy or lower on the Wechsler Intelligence Scale for Children–III (WISC–III) signify mental retardation.

As indicated earlier, to be diagnosed as mentally retarded, the individual also must have a deficit in his level of adaptive functioning. Adaptive functioning is

Do you agree that adaptive level of functioning is just as important as intelligence test scores? If a person can adapt, is there any reason to give them a special education diagnosis?

Individuals with mental retardation have a wide range of intellectual, social, and vocational abilities.

the ability to complete the important tasks of daily living. This type of functioning means a significant deficit in performance on tests of adaptive functioning, on observational and behavioral measures, on teacher-made tests, or on standardized achievement tests.

For instance, one indication of problems in adaptive functioning are scores on a survey achievement test that are two standard deviations below the mean. Some regulations specify two grade levels below the norm as another diagnostic sign of mental retardation. The same degree of discrepancy between present age or grade level and the child's classroom performance also would be a possible sign for retardation.

What Are the Different Categories of Mental Retardation?

The American Association on Mental Deficiency (AAMD) has provided the most widely used classification system for the different categories of mental retardation (Grossman, 1983). Its subgroup classifications of the mentally retarded include four commonly accepted groupings based on WISC–III IQ scores:

Mild Retardation: 50–55 to 70 IQ
Moderate Retardation: 35–40 to 50–55 IQ
Severe Retardation: 20–25 to 35–40 IQ
Profound Retardation: Below 20–25 IQ

Another classification model used by some school systems is:

Educable mentally retarded: 55 to 70 IQ
Trainable mentally retarded: 40 to 54 IQ
Severe/profound mentally retarded: Below 40 IQ

The incidence of mental retardation in the general population appears to be between 1 percent and 3 percent, depending on the stringency of the various classification procedures (Haring, McCormick, & Haring, 1994). The majority of the mentally retarded are in the mildly retarded range. The gender ratio indicates that there are three males to every two females in the mentally retarded population (American Psychiatric Association, 1987).

What Are the Causes of Mental Retardation?

As indicated in the section on at risk children, there are a number of causes for mental retardation. Prenatal traumas, genetic disorders, chromosomal abnormalities, labor and delivery difficulties, and maternal substance use during pregnancy are among the causes of mental retardation.

The greater the degree of mental impairment, the more likely it is that there is a detectable physical or neurological cause for the mental retardation. For instance, McLaren and Bryson (1987) reported that in the mildly mentally retarded population, a detectable physical/neurological cause could not be found for 60 percent to 75 percent of the cases. However, when IQ scores were below 50, the results were reversed. Between 60 percent and 75 percent of this latter population did have a specific physical or neurological cause for their impairment.

Do gender differences in the incidence of retardation reflect innate genetic factors? Some researchers believe that males are more likely to be labeled as mentally retarded. List some factors that might support the genetic model for gender differences and list some factors that might support the labeling viewpoint.

Is it a surprise that the majority of the mildly retarded have no detectable cause for their retardation? As adults, many of these individuals will be able to keep jobs and contribute to society.

Down's Syndrome

The single most common congenital cause of mental retardation is Down's syndrome. Down's syndrome occurs in 1 out of every 660 live births (Berk, 1989). Down's syndrome is a chromosomal abnormality that produces an extra, or 47th, chromosome. The chromosomal abnormality occurs at the moment of conception.

The likelihood of having a child with Down's syndrome is most strongly related to maternal age. The likelihood of having a Down's syndrome child is 1 in 1,000 when the mother is 29 years of age (Shaffer, 1985). The likelihood of a Down's child is 1 in 65 when the mother is between 40 and 44 years of age (Shaffer, 1985). Research also has indicated that there is an increasing likelihood of having a Down's syndrome child with increasing paternal age (Hook, 1980).

The majority of Down's syndrome children have an average IQ of 50 or less (Berk, 1989). However, there is a wide range of variation in their scores. Some Down's syndrome children have IQ scores within normal ranges. Down's syndrome is more common in males. (See Applications 13.2.)

> What are the factors that might cause the likelihood of having a Down's syndrome child to increase with age?

■ ■ ■

LEARNING DISABILITIES
What Is a Current Definition of Learning Disabilities?

One of the most widely used definitions of learning disabilities was devised by the National Joint Committee on Learning Disabilities (1987):

> Learning disabilities is a generic term that refers to a heterogeneous group of disorders manifested by significant difficulties in the acquisition and use of listening, speaking, reading, writing, reasoning, or mathematical abilities. These disorders are intrinsic to the individual and presumed to be due to central nervous system dysfunction (p. 107).

Learning disabilities appear to affect between 5 percent and 10 percent of children in the primary grades (Lerner, 1989). It is the single most common type of exceptionality in public schools (Lerner, 1989).

There is considerable controversy about how to diagnose and treat learning disabilities. Part of the controversy centers on establishing an accurate and widely accepted standard for defining the various types of learning disabilities. Another related problem is the differing methods used for determining whether a child has a learning disability. Because of these two problems, there have been considerable differences among states and school systems in the frequency of children diagnosed with learning disabilities.

> The number of children diagnosed as learning disabled has increased dramatically in the last fifteen years. List some reasons why this increase occurred.

What Is the Basis for Using Discrepancy Scores to Diagnose Learning Disabilities?

In determining whether a child has a learning disability (LD), a generally used diagnostic sign is a significant discrepancy between aptitude and achievement. A significant discrepancy is a one standard deviation or greater difference between aptitude and achievement. (This is sometimes referred to as a discrepancy between ability and achievement.)

JEFF

Vince and Marilyn have three lovely children. There is David, a student at the University of Virginia, Jeff, 16, and Shannon, 10.

Although in many American households, it is the middle child who gets lost in the shuffle, in this household this is not true. Jeff, because of his personality and disposition, is a difficult guy to ignore. He also was born with Down's syndrome.

Some Down's children suffer from physical problems such as heart disorders, poor vision, or respiratory problems. Fortunately, Jeff has few such problems. However, he was born with a cleft palate and is unable to communicate verbally. He also suffers from frequent ear infections. Down's children have very small Eustachian tubes, making them prone to ear problems. Jeff also, like many children, has an allergy to corn products.

This is the second marriage for Marilyn. When her second husband, Vince, met Jeff, the youngster was about three years old. There was no question for him that Marilyn and her two sons were part of a package deal. It was a deal he was ready and willing to make. The couple have been together for eleven years. Daughter Shannon is the product of that union.

"I remember when I first met Jeff," Vince said. "He immediately impressed me with his need and ability to communicate even without words. At first glance, Jeff appears to live in his own little world. Yet nothing gets by him! He has the unique ability to sense when someone is feeling sad or down. He will always head straight for that person and try to comfort them by touching them or holding their hand. He communicates through touch and has a surprisingly wide range of facial expressions.

"He also has a weakness for pretty blondes, whether they're nurses, teachers, or just our friends."

According to Vince, his son also is a lover of good music. His tastes lean toward "oldies but goodies," ("Barbara Ann" by the Beach Boys is a favorite). He also likes the classical tapes Marilyn listens to around the house. Jeff often sits quietly, absorbing the strains of Bach, Mozart, or Beethoven. He also likes it when Shannon practices her piano lesson.

Marilyn is a woman who exudes both a keen intelligence and empathy. At the same time, she is quick to point out that parents of a special needs child must arm themselves for a struggle that never ends.

"When I first saw Jeff in the hospital, I knew at once that he was different," she said. "It was a shock, but I felt with the proper education I could cope."

The problem was, there were few resources available at that time. Marilyn was dismayed to discover that even the so-called professionals in her area actually knew very little about Down's syndrome.

"I had to educate myself," she said, "and I recommend that parents do the same. There are many more helpful books on the market today. There is a wealth of information we had no access to fifteen years ago."

Marilyn cautions, however, that parents should take care in what they read. Anything written before 1976 she considers the "Dark Ages."

Communication also is important, whether it is between spouses, parents, or caring professionals. "Other parents help a lot," Marilyn said, "and they are still the most knowledgeable group around. When looking for a professional, check out his attitude. Good attitude and a willingness to learn about your child can go a long way."

Marilyn said her mother, a former special education teacher, taught her a lot about patience. "I had to learn to take it one day at a time," she said, "and for me that was a hard lesson. But, it really does make a difference in how you handle things."

Vince added: "We try to avail ourselves of what's out there. It's also important to know your limitations, but not be limited to them. Parents can accomplish a lot, especially if they are able to keep their children at home."

"Sure you have to make adjustments. But we like having Jeff in our lives. We take him to Knoxville, Gatlinburg, wherever we go as a family. For now," Vince said, and Marilyn agreed, "we want to live life to the fullest and just enjoy him" (Adapted from Deskins, 1992).

Aptitude usually is measured by an intelligence test with achievement measured by an achievement test. An example would be a student who has an IQ score of 110 but a math achievement score on a diagnostic achievement test of 90. (This assumes that both tests are using the deviation standard score system, which has a mean of 100 and a standard deviation of 15.)

Another diagnostic sign is a significant discrepancy between the Verbal and Performance parts of the Wechsler Intelligence Scale for Children–III (WISC–III). (As previously noted, one standard deviation on the WISC–III is 15 points.) For instance, if the Verbal score was 84 and the Performance score was 101, this would be another diagnostic indicator of a language-related learning disability such as dyslexia.

Using the aptitude/achievement discrepancy score has been criticized by some researchers (Kamhi, 1992; Stanovich, 1991). The criticisms center on whether IQ scores offer an appropriate and independent measure. In effect, is an IQ test a measure that can be differentiated from achievement measures? Because of this criticism, some public school systems are currently examining other alternatives for assessing learning disabilities.

What Are the Causes of Learning Disabilities?

There is a great deal of debate over what causes learning disabilities. One important point must be stressed about the possible causes of learning disabilities: there is no one single cause. The etiology and progression of a learning disability are unique to each individual.

There is a growing body of research indicating that some LD children have a genetic cause for their learning disability (Defries & Decker, 1982). However, the exact nature of the genetic transmission is still undetermined. The percentage of LD children with a genetic cause also is undetermined. Some research points to a sex-linked trait (Vellutino, 1987). Estimates of the gender ratios for learning disabilities indicate that they are considerably more common in males. Different estimates of the male-to-female ratio for learning disabilities show that LD problems are anywhere from two to four times more common in males.

Yet, there also appear to be a number of environmental causes for learning disabilities. As noted in the children at risk section, there is a relationship between childhood exposure to lead and the development of some learning disabilities. Brain accidents and brain trauma during birth or early childhood also appear to have a relationship with the onset of some learning disabilities.

Some researchers in this area also cite as a cause for a learning disabilities diagnosis a syndrome called developmental delay learning disabilities (Coplin & Morgan, 1988). The concept of the developmental delay syndrome is somewhat akin to what is called a late bloomer. Some children, presumably because of a delay in central nervous system maturation, will demonstrate the type of academic problems associated with a learning disability.

This group of LD children will operate at delayed cognitive and academic performance levels. They will demonstrate the types of reading, writing, spelling, or arithmetic errors that would be expected of much younger children. With these children, the major problem is their delay in developing specific academic skills.

Because of the discrepancy between intelligence and specific academic achievement, some children with learning disabilities will also be gifted. What special procedures or programs would be needed for gifted, LD students?

A number of famous individuals were apparently learning disabled. Included among them were Nelson Rockefeller, Albert Einstein, and Winston Churchill. The latter two were noted "late bloomers." What can teachers do to help "late bloomers?"

However, they may be more likely to catch-up in academic skills or compensate for their disability than children in other LD subgroups.

What Is the Relationship between Neurological Problems, Degree of Impairment, and Successful Remediation?

Generally speaking, there appears to be a relationship between the frequency of detectable neurological problems and the pervasiveness of the learning disability. Thus, the more organic or "hard" neurological signs that an LD child has, the more pervasive will be her impairment. For example, those children with abnormal electroencephalograms (EEGs) or CAT scans may have a greater impairment.

Therefore, in addition to physical and psychological assessments, it is important to complete neurological assessments on children with possible LD indications.

Those with distinct neurological signs also may have greater difficulty in successful treatment and intervention. As with other types of exceptionalities, the more pervasive the impairment, the more difficult the treatment. However, successful remediation of learning disabilities of all types may be accomplished.

If diagnosed and treated at an early age, the likelihood for successful remediation from such a disability appears to be better than at later age periods. Thus, the likelihood for successful treatment appears to be dependent on both the initial severity of the problem and the age at which intervention is initiated. Even so, significant remediation has been found to occur as late as the college-age years (Guyer & Sabatino, 1989; Guyer, Banks, & Guyer, 1993).

Whatever the causes, learning disabilities are seen as a significant delay in the acquisition of a specific academic ability in children who are average or above average in intelligence. A learning disability diagnosis is given only when all other possible causes have been eliminated. For instance, physical, visual, or auditory impairments have been eliminated as possible causes for the learning disability by medical examinations. Mental retardation also must be eliminated as a possible cause, as well as emotional disturbance or cultural deprivation.

Language-Related Learning Disabilities

The most common type of learning disability is a language-related learning disability. This disability occurs when a student demonstrates average or better intelligence but exhibits a specific impairment in reading, spelling, or writing. This type of disorder is sometimes referred to as dyslexia. (In contrast, math disorders are termed dyscalculia.) Language-related learning disabilities are at least three times more common in males (Defries, 1989).

Some of the characteristics of language-related learning disabilities are indicated by how children process their reading or writing.

For example, a child with a language-related learning disability improperly rotates, inverts, or reverses letters or words when writing. Improper rotations involve writing a letter horizontally when it should be written vertically. For instance, a child writes a W for an E. Inverting a letter is done when a u is written for an n. Reversals are writing a b for a d or a p for a q.

Why do you think that age plays such an important role in successfully treating learning disabilities?

Among all the LD problems, reading problems cause the greatest academic difficulties for students. Why do you think that reading problems cause the most difficulties?

POSSIBLE SIGNS OF A LEARNING DISABILITY

In a practical sense, classroom teachers should note the following signs that may indicate a learning disability:

1. Difficulty in distinguishing left from right that is significantly delayed for the child's age/grade level.

    Examples: The child inconsistently shifts from right to left in the use of his hands or legs in classroom or physical activities. The child frequently is unable to follow directions in physical education activities that require her to use the left foot then the right foot or to use the right hand then the left hand.

2. Motor-coordination difficulties that are significantly delayed for the child's age level.

    Examples: The child has a frequent inability to successfully participate in physical education or activities such as dance. The child is unable to throw and catch a ball or to perform coordinated motor activities such as constructing crafts or models.

3. Language-processing difficulties in speech, reading, or writing that are significantly delayed for the child's age level.

    Example: When children first begin to read, they finger point to the words or they move their lips. They are unable to read silently as well. When a child consistently continues these three activities for a significant time after other children have stopped, this may be a sign of a reading disability.

4. Mathematical-processing difficulties that are significantly delayed for the child's age level.

    Examples: A child consistently is unable to grasp the concept of set or group. A child is pre-sented with a group of three apples, then asked to add a group of four oranges to the first group. The child must go back and count each item in each group rather than add the two groups together. A child has consistent difficulty in working through a series of mathematical steps in the appropriate sequence. However, he has no trouble with each individual step.

5. Visual/perceptual-processing difficulties that are significantly delayed for the child's age level.

    Examples: A child has trouble in constructing puzzles and block designs. A child has difficulty in tracing patterns or in recalling geometric designs and then tracing them correctly.

6. Attention-span and concentration difficulties that are significantly delayed for the child's age level.

    Examples: A child is easily and consistently distracted by extraneous stimuli. A child is unable to remain in one place long enough to finish a task.

None of the problems cited here should be taken as a sign in and of itself of a learning disability. The difficulties should only be used in conjunction with other problems and used with students who are consistently behind in a specific academic area. The key words are "consistently behind," since these difficulties also are stages that all children go through on the way to developing appropriate academic skills.

Extreme caution should be used in labeling a child with a learning disabilities designation. Only the school psychologist in consultation with the multidisciplinary team actually can make this determination.

What Are Some of the Educational Interventions Used for Children with Learning Disabilities?

Some of the widely used treatment programs include language based programs, such as DISTAR (Englemann & Osborn, 1976); data-based instruction (Blankenship & Lilly, 1981); and direct instruction (Rosenshine, 1978).

One of the more successful types of treatment for children with learning disabilities appears to be the Orton-Gillingham model (Guyer & Sabatino, 1989).

Orton-Gillingham is a multisensory phonetic approach for the remediation of language-related learning disabilities (Mercer & Mercer, 1987).

What are the factors in the multi-sensory approach that might be producing the successful remediation?

With this type of treatment, the child is taught to use as many sensory modalities as possible when reading or writing. For example, when reading, the student also is asked to trace the word, to speak the word out loud, and to try to picture in her mind what the word represents. There are exercises in which the individual sounds of the letters are made concrete by relating that sound to a particular object. For instance, the "ph" sound is mnemonically combined with phone and the "st" sound is combined with stick. Other aspects of this method include having the student make letter shapes by moving his arms and legs into the shape of the letters.

Attention Deficit Hyperactivity Disorder

Attention deficit hyperactivity disorder (ADHD) is characterized by developmentally inappropriate degrees of inattention, impulsiveness, and hyperactivity (American Psychiatric Association, 1987). There has been some question as to the classification of ADHD in the overall categories of special education: Is it a learning disability or is it a separate disorder?

Why would a stimulant drug like Ritalin help hyperactive children? Generally, it is thought that Ritalin works because it increases the attention span and concentration of ADHD children. By helping them focus on academic tasks, Ritalin makes ADHD children appear to be less distractible and less impulsive.

Part of the problem with independently categorizing attention deficit hyperactivity disorder is that between 15 percent and 20 percent of learning disabled students also have ADHD (Silver, 1990). Another problem is that children with ADHD also are frequently classified as having a behavior disorder.

Attention deficit hyperactivity disorder appears to be successfully treated by stimulant medications in approximately sixty percent to seventy-five percent of the cases (Lerner, 1989). Ritalin remains the drug of choice in treating ADHD. However, careful monitoring of these stimulant medications, particularly at the outset, is warranted. Adverse reactions to the medication can occur (Lerner, 1989).

Behavior Disorders/Emotional Disorders

Behavior disorders/emotional disorders include a range of responses that are characterized by their degree of departure from socially appropriate norms. These responses adversely affect the child's educational performance. They persist over a long period of time and they are exhibited to a marked degree (Haring, McCormick, & Haring, 1994). The prevalence of behavior/emotional disorders in children is listed at approximately 1 percent of the school-age population. However, this estimate does not count those children who may have a learning disability or attention deficit hyperactivity disorder with an accompanying behavior disorder.

To some extent, the younger a child is, the more a mental disorder is manifested in behavioral terms, such as withdrawal behaviors or acting-out behaviors. This is one reason for the semantic distinction between mental disorders in adults and behavior/emotional disorders in children. Other manifestations of a behavior/emotional disorder in children are:

1. a general, pervasive mood of unhappiness or depression;
2. an inability to build and maintain interpersonal relationships with peers or teachers;
3. overly aggressive behavior, including antisocial acts;
4. frequent displays of anxiety or inferiority.

These manifestations can be associated with disorders such as depression, antisocial activity, or eating disorders. As with mental disorders in adults, the etiology and treatment regimens for behavior/emotional disorders in children are varied. There is no general agreement in the psychological community on the causes for these disorders. There also is considerable debate on how to treat these problems. Yet, as with other disorders listed in this chapter, the earlier the intervention, the better the outcome.

■ ■ ■

GIFTED

In many school systems, the determination for gifted education also is based on standard deviation scores derived from IQ tests such as the WISC–III (Wechsler, 1992). For instance, some school systems state that a child will be considered gifted if she scores two standard deviations or better on an individual test of intelligence. On the WISC–III, this score would be 130 or above. The percentage of the population that would score 130 or better is approximately 2 percent to 3 percent. Other school systems may use a similar two-standard-deviation cutoff using survey achievement tests.

Some school systems base their determination of giftedness on teacher ratings. Teacher ratings can be based on the students' creative performances, exhibitions, or portfolios. This method of determining giftedness has the advantage of a broader interpretation of giftedness than simply using intelligence as the determination. Some school systems use a combination of these procedures.

One of the major questions about gifted programs is in regard to the best method to educate the gifted. The methods for educating the gifted fall into two broadly defined programs: enrichment and acceleration.

When gifted children are provided special instructional methods, special classes, or special magnet schools, the method is referred to as enrichment.

When gifted children are allowed or encouraged to skip grades in public schools, the method is called acceleration.

Gallagher and Gallagher (1994) provide an extensive review of both procedures. They conclude that both enrichment and acceleration methods can work. However, they do not necessarily work with all gifted children. The belief that acceleration is socially harmful does not appear to be borne out by the research. The belief that segregating gifted children by placing them in special magnet schools is socially harmful also does not appear to be supported by the research. Yet in both cases the social and psychological characteristics of the child should be the deciding factor—not the policy.

On the other hand, the use of special classes or special schools for the gifted has become a part of a prominent educational controversy. The use of segregated

Some researchers believe that most emotional disorders in children are related to problems directly caused by parental disorders. If emotional problems in the children are caused by the parents, what type of treatment should be used?

What is the best method for determining who is gifted? Who should we label as gifted? Should musically gifted children receive special education? What about artistically gifted children? What about mechanically gifted children?

classes and special magnet schools has become one of the controversial issues generated by both the Detracking Movement in regular education (detracking means to end all tracks or groups in public schools, including vocational or business tracks in high schools) and the Inclusion Movement in special education.

What Are the Goals of the Inclusion Movement?

Inclusion, full inclusion, least restrictive environment, and mainstreaming are all terms used to designate a policy goal that advocates the placement of children with disabilities in regular education classrooms.

The differences between these terms are the degree to which they support full placement. Least restrictive environment and mainstreaming are terms from Public Law 94–142. In both cases these two terms refer to placing children at the most appropriate level. However, both least restrictive environment and mainstreaming advocate the placement of children in regular education classrooms if appropriate.

The inclusion movement (also referred to as the regular education initiative) advocates the full merger of regular education and special education. Inclusion means a fundamental restructuring of education to provide appropriate education and services for the disabled in the regular classroom.

Thus, the orientation in inclusion means that placement in regular classrooms shall be the goal whenever possible. Inclusion indicates that the best place for all children with disabilities is in the regular classroom. The regular classroom and regular education should be restructured to meet the needs of children with disabilities.

Full inclusion is the most radical form of the inclusion movement. This form mandates the immediate change to complete inclusion of all children with disabilities, regardless of their disabling condition. This type of inclusion assumes that bringing about full inclusion will force school systems to make appropriate classroom changes.

Besides placing all children with disabilities in regular education, the types of changes proposed include:

1. Providing special education teachers for the regular classroom on the basis of being "collaborative, consulting teachers." This type of teacher would work with children with disabilities in the regular classroom on a regular basis. Thus, the consulting teacher would move from child to child and classroom to classroom as needed.
2. Designating cooperative learning as the basic form of instruction. This would include placing high- and low-ability students in cooperative groups. High-ability students would then tutor low-ability students. All members of the group would receive the same academic grade.
3. Providing intensive instruction in special education procedures to regular education teachers and aides.
4. Integrating team teaching for all classrooms and all teachers and providing both regular and collaborative consulting to further meet the needs of children.

Do you think that the Inclusion Movement is too idealistic? Is the Inclusion Movement in the best interests of all children?

5. Moving to a whole classroom instruction model and away from any homogeneous groupings.

What Are the Criticisms of the Inclusion Movement?

Shanker (1993) has sharply questioned the inclusion model. He states that there are a number of problems with this model: the time and expense involved in reeducating regular education teachers; the expense involved in providing collaborative consulting teachers; and whether this policy is best for all children in all classrooms.

Gallagher and Gallagher (1994) question whether this model will provide appropriate educational activities for gifted children. According to these writers, gifted children may not benefit from whole class instruction. They may be more academically successful with some type of homogeneous grouping.

The Council for Exceptional Children, one of the major associations in the special education field, also has raised questions about the inclusion movement. Its concerns are in the ability of regular education teachers to balance the needs of handicapped children with effective instruction for all children (Haring, McCormick, & Haring, 1994).

Despite all these questions, the inclusion movement appears to be gaining adherents in school systems across the country. A number of states are moving toward an inclusion model for combining regular education with special education.

> Are these criticisms of the Full Inclusion movement justified? If implemented, would Full Inclusion save money or will it cost more money?

What Are Some of the Gender and Diversity Issues Associated with Special Education?

A report by the American Association of University Women (AAUW, 1992) stated that the gender ratio in special education programs was greater than two males to every one female. In every single category of children with disabilities, there were more males than females. The report questioned whether this ratio was valid or whether males were identified at higher rates because of greater behavior problems.

The AAUW report indicated that gender differences were most pronounced in the area of behavior/emotional disorders. They were least pronounced in the area of the mildly mentally retarded (AAUW, 1992). There was some question as to whether males are diagnosed as learning disabled because of their LD problems or because teachers want them out of their classrooms.

Diversity issues also are noted as a problem in special education. The major difficulty has been the disproportionate numbers of minority children who are labeled as mildly mentally retarded. Although this problem apparently still persists, there has been some lessening of this frequency of labeling (Haring, McCormick, & Haring, 1994). Currently, these does not appear to be any major ethnic differences in such areas as learning disabilities or in the more severe forms of mental retardation.

> Is there some type of gender discrimination occurring in the special education field? Do regular education teachers want to get rid of male students because of their greater likelihood of behavior problems?

Summary

This chapter presents a review and an analysis of some of the issues involved in working with children at risk and children with disabilities. One major point emphasized in this chapter is the extraordinary variation in abilities that are found in children at risk and in children with disabilities. Parents and educators should also be aware of the ability for children in both groups to grow and develop their mental abilities.

This chapter provides a framework for examining the etiology and progression from being a child at risk to being a child with disabilities. The association between poor prenatal care and disabling conditions is now becoming fully recognized.

Other issues reviewed in this section include the effects of early childhood programs on children. It is noted that highly intensive programs with favorable teacher/student ratios seem to produce the most successful early childhood programs.

A presentation of the different categories of children with disabilities is included in this chapter. It is noted that learning disabilities are the single most common type of disability. The characteristics of the most common forms of each special education category are detailed. Methods for determining if a child has a disability are presented. Teachers are encouraged to be aware of these characteristics and methods, since they are the 'frontline' in the initial diagnosis of many children with disabilities.

The different types of programs for treating learning disabilities are reviewed. Among the intervention models for learning disabled children, one suggested program is the multi-sensory phonetic technique. This program has shown some promise in effectively remediating learning disabilities. A review of the Inclusion Movement is also presented. A number of questions are raised about the Inclusion Movement, particularly with regard to the time and expense of full inclusion.

Chapter Review

1. What prenatal factors appear to be most likely to cause children to be at risk?
2. What is the single leading cause of mental retardation?
3. What prenatal or early childhood factor seems associated with causing a learning disability?
4. What types of positive outcomes have been found with Head Start?
5. What is meant by the least restrictive environment?
6. How are IQ scores used to determine mental retardation, learning disabilities, and giftedness?
7. What are the commonly used categories for mental retardation?
8. What is the relationship between neurological signs and degree of impairment in the mentally retarded and in the learning disabled?

WHAT IS BEST FOR THE MAXIMUM NUMBER OF STUDENTS?

EPILOGUE

In reviewing this chapter, what types of recommendations would you now make for the teacher in the case study at the beginning?

The issues raised in the case study are addressed by some of the following sections in the chapter:

1. Early childhood educational programs— The research on these programs indicate that the amount of contact hours of instructional time (intensity of the program and student/teacher ratio) appears to be crucial in helping children at risk and apparently children with disabilities. Is there any reason to think that this would be different for a second-grade classroom? Will children with disabilities receive the same amount of contact in a regular classroom as they do in a special education classroom? Will provisions be made for extra help or will these children be dumped into regular classroom without any extra help?

2. Special education categories—Will some types of children with disabilities be more successful in a regular classroom than in a special education classroom? Will other types of children with disabilities suffer from being forced to attend regular education classrooms? What types of accommodations would have to be made in a second-grade regular education classroom for a child like Jeff, who has Down's syndrome? What policy would you have about group play activities during physical education? What impact will a full inclusion policy have on gifted children?

Again, the most important question to be asked is: Are the proposed changes in the best interests of the maximum number of children?

9. What is the most common form of learning disability?
10. What is the relationship between gender and the likelihood of having a disability?

REFERENCES

American Association of University Women. (1992). *How schools shortchange girls.* Washington, DC: American Association of University Women Educational Foundation.

American Psychiatric Association. (1987). *Diagnostic and statistical manual of mental disorders* (3rd ed. revised). Washington, DC: American Psychiatric Association.

Berk, L. E. (1989). Child development. Boston: Allyn and Bacon.

Birsch, H. G., & Gussow, J. D. (1970). *Disadvantaged children: Health, nutrition and school failure.* New York: Harcourt Brace.

Blankenship, C., & Lilly, M. S. (1981). *Mainstreaming students with learning and behavior problems: Techniques for the classroom teacher.* New York: Holt, Rinehart and Winston.

Breitmayer, B. J., & Ramey, C. T. (1986). Biological nonoptimality and quality of postnatal environment as codeterminants of intellectual development. *Child Development, 57,* 1151–1165.

Burgess, D. M., & Streissguth, A. P. (1992). Fetal alcohol syndrome and fetal alcohol effects: Principles for educators. *Phi Delta Kappan, 74*(1), 24–34.

Coplin, J. W., & Morgan, S. B., (1988). Learning disabilities: A multidimensional perspective. *Journal of Learning Disabilities, 21*(10), 614–621.

Defries, J. C., & Decker, S. (1982). Genetic aspects of reading disability: A family study. In R. N. Malatesha & P. G. Aaron (Eds.), *Reading disorders; Varieties and treatments* (pp. 255–279). New York: Academic Press.

Defries, J. C. (1989). Gender ratios in children with reading disability and their affected relatives: a commentary. *Journal of Learning Disabilities, 22,* 9, 544–545.

Deskins, C. H. (1992, March 8). One day at a time. *Bluefield Daily Telegraph,* p. 12.

Englemann, S., & Osborn, J. (1976). *DISTAR language: An instructional system.* Chicago: Science Research Associates.

Gallagher, J. J., & Gallagher, S. A. (1994). *Teaching the gifted child.* Boston: Allyn and Bacon.

Gould, S. J. (1981). *The mismeasure of man.* New York: W. W. Norton and Company.

Griffith, D. R. (1992). Prenatal exposure to cocaine and other drugs: Developmental and educational progress. *Phi Delta Kappan, 74*(1), 30–34.

Grossman, H. J. (1983). *Classification of mental retardation.* Washington, DC: American Association on Mental Deficiency.

Guralnick, M., & Bennet, C. (1987). *Effectiveness of early intervention.* New York: Academic Press.

Guyer, B. P., & Sabatino, D. (1989). The effectiveness of a multisensory alphabetic phonetic approach with college students who are learning disabled. *Journal of Learning Disabilities, 22*(7), 430–434.

Guyer, B. P., Banks, S. R., & Guyer, K. E. (1993). Spelling improvement for college students who are dyslexic. *Annals of Dyslexia,* V 43, 186–193.

Haring, N. G., McCormick, L., & Haring, T. G. (Eds.). (1994). *Exceptional children and youth* (6th ed.). New York: Merrill.

Hook, E. B. (1980). *Genetic counseling dilemmas: Down syndrome, paternal age, and recurrence risk after remarriage.* American Journal of Medical Genetics, 5, 145.

Kamhi, A. G. (1992). Response to historical perspective: A developmental language perspective. *Journal of Learning Disabilities, 25*(1), 48–52.

Lerner, J. (1989). *Learning disabilities: Theories, diagnoses, and teaching strategies* (5th ed.). Boston: Houghton Mifflin.

Mckee, J., & Banks, S. R. (1994, February 14). *Educating rural youth—what teacher education should know: A replication of the Maine study.* A presentation at the Association for Teacher Education, National Conference, Atlanta, GA.

McKey, R. H., Condelli, L., Granson, H., Barrett, B., McConsky, C., & Plantz, M. (1985). The impact of Head Start on children, families, and communities (Final report of the Head Start Evaluation, Synthesis, and Utilization Project). Washington, DC: CSR.

McLaren, J., & Bryson, S. E. (1987). Review of recent epidemiological studies of mental retardation: Prevalence, associated disorders, and etiology. *American Journal of Mental Retardation, 92,* 243–254.

Mercer, C., and Mercer, A. R. (1987). *Teaching students with learning problems* (3rd ed.). Columbus, OH: Merrill.

National Joint Committee on Learning Disabilities. (1987). Learning disabilities: Issues on definition. *Journal of Learning Disabilities, 10*(2), 107–108.

Needleman, H. L. (1992). Childhood exposure to lead: A common cause of school failure. *Phi Delta Kappan, 74*(1), 35–37.

Rosenshine, G. (1978). The third cycle of research on teacher effects. Content covered, academic engaged time, and quality of instruction. In *National Society for the Study of Education, 78th Yearbook* (pp. 272–290). Chicago: University of Chicago Press.

Schweinhart, L. J., & Weikart, D. P. (1983). The effects of the Perry Preschool Project on youths through age 15. In *As the Twig is Bent. . .Lasting effects of preschool programs*. Consortium for Longitudinal Studies (pp. 71–101). Hillsdale, NJ: Lawrence Erlbaum Associates.

Seidel, J. F. (1992). Children with HIV-related developmental difficulties. *Phi Delta Kappan, 74*(1), 38–40, 56.

Shaffer, D. R. (1985). *Developmental psychology: Theory, research, applications.* Monterey, CA: Brooks/Cole Publishing Company.

Shanker, A. (1993, September 19). A rush to inclusion. *New York Times,* E–9.

Silver, L. B. (1990). Attention deficit hyperactivity disorder: Is it a learning disability or a related disorder? *Journal of Learning Disabilities, 23,* 394–397.

Stanovich, K. (1991). Discrepancy definition of reading disability: Has intelligence led us astray? *Reading Research Quarterly, 26,* 7–30.

Stevens, L. J., & Price, M. (1992). Meeting the challenge of educating children at risk. *Phi Delta Kappan, 74*(1), 18–23.

Streissguth, A. P., Barr, H. M., & Sampson, P. D. (1990). Moderate prenatal alcohol exposure: Effects on child IQ and learning problems at age 7 1/2 years. *Alcoholism: Clinical and Experimental Research, 14,* 662–669.

Vellutino, F. R. (1987). Dyslexia. *Scientific American, 256*(3), 34–41.

Wechsler, D. (1992). *Manual for the Wechsler Intelligence Scale for Children–III* (3rd ed.). New York: The Psychological Corporation.

Wheeler, D. L. (1994, January 12). An ominous legacy of the atomic age. *The Chronicle of Higher Education, 40*(19), A7–A8.

GLOSSARY

Ability Grouping. An educational practice of placing students of similar ability levels together, either within groups in a classroom, also known as homogeneous grouping, or in separate classrooms, also known as tracking.

Accommodation. A Piagetan concept that means to change a cognitive structure or create a new one because of new information.

Accountability. In education, accountability is the practice of making administrators and teachers responsible for their students' achievement.

Achievement Motivation. The motivation to strive for success on a given task.

Achievement Tests. A type of standardized test that measures a student's present knowledge level in a given academic subject.

Adaptive Functioning. The present level of social, behavioral, and cognitive functioning that the individual demonstrates in a particular environment. Often used as one of two determinants for diagnosing mental retardation.

Advance Organizer. Presenting a well-known or generally understood concept to introduce and frame the subsequent instructional information.

Aptitude Tests. A type of standardized test that attempts to predict future academic performance.

Articulation Disorders. A speech disorder characterized by pronunciation difficulties, such as the distortion of a consonant sound.

Assertive Discipline. Developed by Canter, this is a teacher-directed classroom management model characterized by developing a rule-based management system in which everyone knows the rules and consequences.

Assimilation. A Piagetan term that refers to the integration of new information into an existing cognitive structure.

At risk. Children who are at risk for academic failure because of prenatal conditions, birthing problems, or low socioeconomic status.

Attention Deficit Hyperactive Disorder. A type of disorder in which the child demonstrates impulsivity, difficulty in concentration and attention, and behavioral overactivity.

Attributions. How students explain, rationalize, and justify their successes and failures.

Authentic Assessment. A type of evaluation method using measures that more closely approximate the actual abilities than do traditional evaluation measures. Performance tests, portfolios, and exhibitions are types of authentic assessments.

Basic Skills. What are considered to be the fundamental academic skills needed for higher-level learning. Often thought to be reading, writing, and arithmetic skills.

Behavioral Learning Theories. Explanations of learning that apply the principles of behaviorism. This model examines the associational links between stimuli or the relationship between a behavior and the reinforcement of that response.

Behaviorism. One of the major theoretical models of psychology and educational psychology. The term was coined by John Watson. This model focuses on behavior and in particular on the relationship between stimuli or the relationship between responses and their consequences.

Behavior Modification. A teacher-directed classroom management system based on applying the principles of behaviorism. This system focuses on the student's behavior and the consequences of that behavior.

Bilingualism. Individuals with two languages. Generally in reference to children who have a native language and are in the process of acquiring English.

Central Processor. The part of the memory system that involves the decision-making aspect of memory, such as whether to retain or not retain an experience.

Chaining. Linking together a series of reinforced responses so that they are seen as one behavioral sequence.

Chunking. A type of memory aid that involves grouping bits of information into larger chunks or units.

Classical Conditioning. Developed by Pavlov, this type of conditioning involves the association of a neutral stimulus with an unconditioned stimulus, such as food, so that the neutral stimulus will eventually elicit an unconditioned response such as salivation.

Classroom Management Models. The methods that teachers use to manage the classroom. They are divided into teacher-directed, student-directed, and eclectic management models.

Cognitive Development. Most closely identified with Piaget, this is the process of developing mental and cognitive skills from infancy through adulthood.

Cognitive Learning Theory. The application of cognitive psychology to learning. This approach focuses on how students acquire new cognitive structures and reorganize their existing cognitive structures.

Cognitive Psychology. One of the major models of psychology and educational psychology. This model focuses on the role of thinking processes in the mediation of behavior and emotions.

Computer-assisted Instruction. Using the computer as a teaching tool or instructional method.

Concrete Operational Thinking. The third stage in Piaget's model of cognitive development. The child is able to deal with concrete, logical thinking processes. During this stage, the child acquires conservation.

Conditioned Response. In classical conditioning, this is a response that has become associated with a previously neutral stimulus.

Conditioned Stimulus. A neutral stimulus that becomes associated with an unconditioned stimulus so that it elicits a physical response after conditioning.

Consequence. An event following a response that affects the likelihood of the response being repeated.

Conservation. Originated by Piaget, this is a cognitive structure that allows the child to understand the transformation of weight, shape, or quantity.

Constructivism. A model of cognition that examines the active construction, testing, and reconstruction of cognitive models of the student's world.

Contiguity. The association of two events because they occur together in space or time.

Contracting. A classroom management or instructional technique in which the student agrees in writing to complete certain behaviors or certain academic tasks.

Conventional Level of Moral Judgment. Developed by Kohlberg, this is the second level of moral judgment. This level involves viewing right and wrong as conformity to peer-group or societal rules.

Cooperative Learning. An instructional technique that involves students working in groups. Grades and rewards are based on group performance rather than on individual achievement.

Criterion-referenced Evaluations. An evaluation method in which each score is measured only against a previously determined performance standard.

Criterion-related Validity. A measure of test quality that examines whether the test measures what it purports to measure by correlating the test with an external criterion related to the test.

Crystallized Intelligence. Developed by Cattell, this type of intelligence is largely learned and most closely relates to vocabulary and general knowledge.

Detracking. The policy of removing all separate tracks or special programs within public schools. For instance, the removal of separate college preparatory or vocational tracks in high school.

Developmental Crises. Associated with Erikson, it refers to the major developmental hurdles that individuals have at various stages in the life cycle.

Developmentally Appropriate Curriculum/Educational Practices. Instructional methods and activities primarily designed to meet the appropriate developmental level of each student.

Deviation IQ. Developed by Wechsler, it is an IQ score based on comparing the individual's score with a norm group of people who are the same age.

Deviation Score System. A standard score system for standardized tests with a mean of one hundred and a standard deviation of fifteen.

Diagnostic Achievement Test. A standardized achievement test that usually focuses on a specific academic area such as reading. It usually is used to determine whether a student has a learning problem or a learning disability.

Differential Aptitude Test. A standardized aptitude test that attempts to predict vocational abilities.

Discovery Learning. An instructional method in which students are encouraged to discover solutions on their own.

Distractors. Alternatives to the correct answer on a multiple-choice test.

Down's Syndrome. The most frequent congenital cause for mental retardation. It is caused by the production of an extra (forty-seventh) chromosome at the moment of conception.

Egocentrism. A Piagetan term that refers to the assumption that others experience everything the same as you do. It is the critical developmental hurdle during the preoperational stage.

Elaboration. A method of increasing memory by rewriting or rewording new information so that it conforms to one's existing cognitive structures.

Enactive Mode. Developed by Bruner, it is the first mode of representing information in Bruner's model. It is characterized by understanding and representing information solely in terms of its physical aspects.

English as a Second Language (ESL). A type of language program designed to teach English to students for whom English is their second language.

Episodic Memory System. Developed by Tulving, this system allows the individual to remember a particular time and place. It is particularly used to remember the episodes in one's life.

Evaluation. The most comprehensive term used in making decisions about student performance and assigning grades.

Exceptional Students. Students with disabilities or problems that require special education services.

Executive Control. Similar to central processor, it is the part of the memory system involved in decision making, such as the organization of information in memory.

Exhibition. A type of authentic assessment that is often used as a final requirement in a course or educational program.

Extrinsic Motivation. A type of motivation caused by external reinforcement.

Field Dependence. Developed by Witkin, it is a cognitive style in which individuals see the total pattern or holistic structure before seeing separate aspects of the pattern.

Field Independence. Cognitive style in which separate parts of a pattern are perceived and analyzed.

Fixed-Interval Reinforcement Schedule. A schedule of reinforcement in which reinforcement is provided once the desired response has occurred during a fixed interval of time.

Fixed-Ratio Reinforcement Schedule. A schedule of reinforcement in which reinforcement is provided once the desired response has occurred a fixed number of times.

Flow Experience. Activities or experiences that are so positive that they provide their own reward.

Fluid Intelligence. Developed by Cattell, a type of intelligence that is largely genetic in its formation. Most closely related to the processing speed for dealing with new information.

Formal Operations. Developed by Piaget, it refers to cognitive structures that involve abstract thinking. It is the fourth stage in Piaget's model of cognitive development.

Formative Evaluation. A type of ungraded evaluation technique used to determine the student's abilities before instruction or to check on abilities during instruction.

Full Inclusion. The most radical form of placing special education students in the regular classroom. Full inclusion mandates the placement of all children with disabilities in the regular education classroom.

Gender Bias. An evaluation or instructional technique that is biased against one gender.

General Intelligence. A view of intelligence that believes there is a common or single general factor of mental ability.

Gestalt. A German word that literally translates as figure or pattern. Gestalt also is a theory of learning that emphasizes insight and holistic learning.

Giftedness. Often defined by extremely high scores on intelligence tests or other types of standardized tests of mental ability.

Grade-Equivalent Score. A scoring procedure based on norms for a given grade level, such as the grade-level achievement for third grade or fourth grade.

Grading on the Curve. A norm-referenced evaluation technique that compares students' achievement based on normal curve properties.

Heterogeneous Grouping. An educational practice of deliberately grouping students of separate ability together.

High-Stakes Testing. Developed by Popham, this type of testing uses standardized achievement test scores to make major educational decisions such as those involving funding or merit pay.

Holophrastic Language. A one-word utterance used by toddlers to designate an idea. For instance, "Milk" means "I want to drink some milk."

Iconic Representation. Developed by Bruner, it is the second mode of representing information in his model. In this mode, information is represented mentally in the form of images or pictures.

"I" Messages. Used as a method of making an effective complaint because of student misbehavior. It is an assertive statement that something is bothering you as the teacher.

Inclusion Movement. A trend or movement to place special education students in regular classrooms whenever appropriate.

Individual Differences. A method of examining differences with an emphasis at the individual level rather than at the group level.

Information Processing. A model of cognition and memory originally based on computer processing models.

Instructional Objectives. The objectives for teaching that include goals, instructional methods, learning outcomes, and evaluation techniques.

Intelligence Quotient (IQ). Originally developed as a scoring technique that compared mental and chronological ages. Now used primarily by the Wechsler Battery to indicate intelligence scores derived through the deviation score system.

Intrinsic Motivation. A type of motivation that is internal to the subject so that an action provides its own reward.

Keyword Method. A memory technique in which memorization of a new word is enhanced through association with a previously learned word or image.

Lake Wobegone Effect. The name given to a controversy caused by inflated standardized test scores, in which the test scores at the elementary school level in all fifty states were above average.

Law of Effect. Developed by Thorndike, this principle states that any response followed by a reinforcing stimulus will be more likely to be repeated.

Learned Helplessness. An internalized belief that no amount of effort will enable the student to achieve a positive outcome. This belief has developed because of a series of consistent failures that are believed to be beyond the student's control.

Learning. A relatively permanent change in behavior, thought, or feeling due to experience.

Learning Disability. A type of specific learning problem that is defined by a distinct discrepancy between overall intellectual potential and actual performance in a given academic area.

Learning Outcomes. Part of instructional objectives, this is a well-defined outcome of the instruction that can be readily evaluated.

Learning Styles. A preferred mode of learning and processing information. For instance, some students prefer learning through visual processing, while others prefer auditory processing.

Least Restrictive Environment. The placement of children with disabilities in as normal an educational environment as possible.

Levels of Processing. A model of information processing and memory that is based on the depth and breadth of associations that are made by the student to the material.

Locus of Control. The degree of control that people attribute to internal or external factors. For instance, the amount of responsibility attributed to success: is it attributed to internal factors, like ability, or external factors, like luck?

Long-term Memory. The last stage in the process of memory formation. This stage appears to involve a relatively permanent, long-term storage system for memories.

Mean. The arithmetic average in a distribution of scores.

Measure of Central Tendency. A type of measure that describes the middle or central aspects of a distribution. It includes the mean, median, and mode.

Median. The middle score in a distribution of scores.

Melting Pot. A view of culture based upon the assimilation of ethnic groups into the mainstream of society to the extent that ethnic differences largely disappear.

Mental Age. Used in intelligence testing, it is a score indicating the average ability level for a given age group.

Mental Retardation. A category of children with disabilities who have both significantly below-average intelligence and adaptive behavior. Mental retardation is manifested before age eighteen.

Metalinguistic Awareness. An understanding of language that allows the student to reflect on underlying rules such as grammar and syntax.

Metamemory. An understanding of memory that allows the student to reflect on and use memory strategies to enhance memory ability.

Method of Loci. A mnemonic technique that requires the student to visualize or mentally place information to be remembered in familiar locations, such as places around the student's home. In remembering the information, the student remembers the location, which then triggers the memory.

Minimum Competency Testing. A type of standardized achievement test that is used to determine whether students meet the minimum competencies needed for graduation or to be accepted into a program.

Mnemonics. Techniques that are used to aid in memory recall. For instance, the method of loci.

Mode. A measure of central tendency that indicates the most frequently occurring score in a distribution.

Moral Development. Most closely associated with Kohlberg, this involves the development of the judgment and reasoning processes involved in ethical decision making.

Motive. A thought or image that directs behavior.

Multicultural Education. An educational viewpoint that believes in the value of cultural diversity and teaches from the perspective of more than one culture.

Multiple Intelligences. The belief that there are many different intelligences, as opposed to a single general intelligence. Most closely associated with Gardner's theory of intelligence, which consists of seven separate abilities.

Nature-Nurture. A longstanding controversy in the social sciences over the contributions of heredity (nature) or environment (nurture) to such abilities as intelligence and personality.

Normal Curve/Distribution. A commonly occurring distribution in the natural world, in which scores assume a bell-shaped curve and are distributed in a standard pattern around the mean.

Norm Group. A sample group whose test scores provide a comparison standard for evaluating subsequent students' scores on the test.

Norm-referenced Evaluation. A type of evaluation technique in which individual students' scores are graded on the basis of how they compare with the performance of others.

Objective Test Items. Those types of test items for which there is one correct answer. Multiple choice, matching, and true-false questions are examples.

Object Permanence. Developed by Piaget, it is the cognitive realization that objects exist even though the child cannot sense them. It is the major developmental hurdle during the sensorimotor stage.

Operant Conditioning. Coined by Skinner, it is learning in which a response followed by a reinforcer is the basis for most, if not all, learning.

Overextension. Using a word or grammatical rule to cover a broader category than is acceptable by adult usage.

Percentile Rank. The percentage of scores that fall below a given point in a distribution.

Performance Test. A type of authentic assessment that attempts to develop a test situation that is similar to what the student would encounter outside the classroom.

Portfolio. A type of authentic assessment that involves a collection of the student's work in an area, such as newspaper articles for a journalism student.

Positive Reinforcement. Administering a reward that increases the likelihood of a response being repeated.

Postconventional Level of Moral Judgment. Developed by Kohlberg, it describes the highest level of moral development. At this level, the individual internalizes universal ethical principles that are consistently applied across situations.

Preconventional Level of Moral Judgment. Developed by Kohlberg, this level describes the first level of moral development. It is characterized by judgments made by external authority figures or by the direct consequences of the behavior.

Preoperational Stage. Developed by Piaget, this is the second stage of cognitive development. The major developmental hurdle is overcoming egocentrism.

Private Speech. According to Vygotsky, it is talking to oneself in childhood. This guides the child's thinking and action. This speech becomes internalized as silent inner speech and guides adult thinking processes.

Procedural Memory. Part of Tulving's model, it is the memory process for concrete, physical activities.

Programmed Instruction. A type of instructional method that presents the student with an organized series of informational frames, which allow for a student response, and then provides immediate feedback about the response.

Psychosocial Development. Coined by Erikson, it is the developmental sequence that describes the interactive unfolding relationship of individuals with their society.

Range. A measure of variation in a distribution. This indicates the difference between the highest and lowest score.

Reality-based Classroom Management. Developed by Glasser, this is an eclectic form of classroom management. It focuses on personal responsibility.

Reliability. A measure of standardized test quality. This indicates the accuracy or consistency of the test.

Response Cost. The removal or loss of reinforcers because of inappropriate behavior.

Second-Language Acquisition. The process of acquiring a second language.

Self-actualization. Coined by Maslow, it is the highest level of motivation in his hierarchy. It means to fulfill one's potential.

Self-concept. How we view ourselves. Usually due to how our parents or caregivers viewed us.

Self-efficacy. The student's belief about personal competence or success on an academic task.

Semantic Memory. Memory for defining the meaning of words.

Sensorimotor Stage. Coined by Piaget, it is the first stage in his model of cognitive development. The key development hurdle involves acquiring object permanence.

Sensory Register. The initial processing system in the formation of memories. This involves the sensory systems holding information in their receptors.

Shaping. Reinforcing successive approximations of the desired behavior in incremental steps.

Short-term Memory. The second step in the process of memory formation. This is an intermediate, or working, memory that retains a limited amount of information before a decision to retain or discard the information.

Social Learning Theory. Associated with Bandura, this theory focuses on imitation and observational learning.

Socioeconomic Status (SES). A combination of income, educational, and occupational status that appears to be a prime predictor of student achievement.

Standard Deviation. A measure of how scores deviate or vary from the mean. Associated with normal curve properties.

Standardized Tests. A type of test that is based on norms that are developed through sampling and research procedures so that the test can be administered and scored according to set procedures.

Stanines. A scoring procedure with a range of scores from one to nine. It has a mean of five and a standard deviation of two.

Stem. The question or statement aspect of multiple-choice test items.

Stimulus. An external event that produces a response.

Summative Evaluation. A type of evaluation that is used as an outcome measure to determine grades, achievement, and completion of a course or program.

Symbolic Stage. Coined by Bruner, the third mode of representation of information. It is characterized by the use of symbol systems such as language and mathematics.

Teacher Effectiveness Training. Developed by Gordon, this is a type of student-centered classroom management procedure. The focus is on "I messages" and "Who owns this problem?"

Telegraphic Speech. A level of speech development usually using two or three word utterances without pronouns, modifiers, or conjunctions. For instance, "Want drink" to indicate "I want to drink."

Test Bias. The extent to which a standardized test is found to be discriminatory against one ethnic or social group.

Tracking. Placing students into separate academic programs based on their abilities and aptitudes.

Unconditioned Response. Part of Pavlov's model of conditioning, this is a naturally occurring response such as salivation.

Validity. A measure of standardized test quality that indicates the degree to which a test measures what it claims to measure.

Variable-Interval Schedule of Reinforcement. Varying the administration of reinforcement based on a random amount of time. The subject must make a desired response in a given amount of time, but the amount of time varies randomly.

Variable-Ratio Schedule of Reinforcement. Varying the administration of reinforcement based on a random number of desired responses needed to receive a reinforcer.

Whole Class Instruction. A type of instructional technique that focuses on teaching the whole class together as opposed to dividing the class into groups.

Whole Language Instruction. An instructional method for language that emphasizes whole class instruction and integrates spelling and reading with other language arts skills into one unit.

Zone of Proximal Development. Developed by Vygotsky, this indicates the level of task difficulty in which a child will fail alone but will succeed with support.

International Association for the Evaluation of Educational Achievement, 357, 360
Istomia, Z., 300, 316
Izzo, L., 168, 188
Jacklin, C. N., 206, 212
Jackson, S. E., 21, 25
James, W., 6, 7, 8, 9, 25, 293, 316
Jenkins, J., 300, 306, 316
Jensen, A., 193, 194
Johnson, A., 47, 65
Johnson, C., 40, 66
Johnson, D., 49, 50, 66, 167, 188
Johnson, E., 154, 159, 175, 188
Johnson, M. L., 38, 39, 67
Johnson, P., 383, 387
Jones, F. H., 304, 316
Kaeser, S., 137, 140, 159
Kafafy, A., 153, 159
Kagan, J., 165, 166, 169, 188, 301, 316
Kahn, W., 152, 159
Kahneman, D., 295, 316
Kamhi, A. G., 407, 416
Kamii, C., 77, 99
Karniol, R., 58, 66
Kashowitz, D., 50, 67, 168
Kearney, C., 152, 159
Keeves, J., 357, 360
Kelley, M., 152, 159
Kelly, F., 153, 159
Kidder, T., 176, 189
Kitamura, S., 357, 361
Klatzky, R., 295, 296, 316
Klein, S., 208, 209, 212
Koffka, K., 254, 257, 258, 261, 287
Kohlberg, L., 45, 60, 61, 62, 66, 67
Kohler, W., 254, 257, 260, 287
Kohn, A., 185, 189
Kostelnik, M., 36, 59, 67
Kotanchik, N., 151, 158
Kozol, J., 300, 316
Krashen, S., 94, 99
Krathwohl, O., 8, 24, 280, 281, 286
Kreutzer, M., 302, 309, 316
Kulic, C., 34, 65
Kulic, J., 34, 65
Lair, G., 149, 159
Lamb, R. A., 334, 360
Lambert, C., 278, 287
Lampl, M., 38, 39, 67
Lang, C., 165, 166, 169, 188
LaPointe, A., 357, 360
Larson, R., 51, 65
Lasley, T., 137, 140, 159
Lattal, K., 243, 249

Lee, G., 357, 361
Lehmann, I. J., 344, 360
Lenneberg, E., 85, 87, 88, 89, 99
Lenz, B., 307, 316
Leonard, C., 302, 309, 316
Lepper, M., 185, 189
Lerner, J., 405, 410, 416
Levin, J., 308, 310, 316, 317
Levine, D. U., 350, 361
Levinson, D. J., 334, 360
Lewis, R. B., 344, 360
Leyhausen, P., 164, 189
Lieberman, P., 83, 93, 99
Lilly, M. S., 409, 415
Lincoln, W., 155, 159
Lindsey, S., 5
Linn, M. C., 206, 212
Linn, R. L., 367, 372, 373, 374, 387
Lipsitt, L. P., 31, 65
Little, L., 152, 159
Livson, N., 53, 67
Lockhart, R., 299, 316
Lombardo, L., 87, 94, 95, 99
Lorenz, K., 164, 189
Lowell, E., 174, 189
Lozanoff, B., 152, 158
Luchins, A., 262, 263, 287
Lucker, S., 357, 361
Lynn, R., 357, 360
Lyon, D., 307, 316
MacCoby, E. E., 206, 212
MacDonald, A., 154, 159
MacIntyre, P., 235, 249
MacKenzie, A., 223, 249
Magnusson, D., 52, 53, 67
Malina, R., 51, 52, 53, 67
Malone, J., 233, 234, 249, 257, 287
Manly, L., 141, 159
Manning, B., 300, 305, 312, 313, 316
Marcia, J. E., 57, 67
Martin, R., 239, 249
Martindale, C., 293, 316
Maslach, C., 21, 25
Maslow, A., 112, 123, 132, 165, 166, 189, 272
Matthews, K. M., 380, 387
Mattice, E., 153, 159
McCann, C., 151, 158
McCarrel, N., 308, 315
McClelland, D., 174, 175, 189
McColgan, E. B., 61, 66
McCombs, B.,173, 189
McConsky, C., 396, 416
McCormick, C., 310, 317

McCormick, L., 404, 410, 413
McGehe, C. A., 224, 249, 275, 277, 287
McKee, J., 395, 416
McKey, R. H., 396, 416
McLaren, J., 404, 416
McLoughlin, J. A., 344, 360
McLoughlin, M., 383, 387
Mead, N., 357
Mehrens, W. A., 344, 360
Mercer, A. R., 410, 416
Mercer, C., 410, 416
Mergendoller, J., 47, 67
Mernit, S., 281, 287
Messenheimer-Young, T., 232, 243, 249
Messick, S., 336, 361
Meyers, N., 300, 317
Mezyniski, K., 308, 315
Midgley, C., 38, 65
Mietzel, G., 383, 387
Miller, G., 297, 306, 317
Miller, N., 242, 243
Miller, P. A., 76, 77, 80, 99
Miller, S. A., 76, 77, 80, 99
Minninger, J., 311, 317
Mitman, A., 47, 67
Montessori, M., 77
Moore, W., 40, 66
Morgan, S. B., 407, 416
Mosenthal, J. H., 78, 79, 99
Mullis, I., 94, 99
Murdock, B., 311, 317
Murray, K., 203, 204, 212
Nakamura, J., 181, 188
National Board for Professional Teaching Standards, 16, 24
National Joint Committee on Learning Disabilities, 405, 417
National Research Council, 357, 361
Necco, E. G., 21, 25
Needleman, H. L., 394, 417
Neisser, U., 291, 317
Nelson, K., 89, 99
Newman, B., 57, 67
Newman, P., 57, 67
Nicholas, A., 271, 287
Nicholls, J., 170, 182, 183, 189
Nieto, S., 195, 202, 212
Nist, J., 95, 96, 99
Novelli, J., 271, 287
Nye, B., 11, 25
Nystul, M. S., 153, 159
O'Connor, B., 262, 287
O'Leary, S., 152, 158
O'Loughlin, M., 77, 99

Omelich, C., 169, 188
Omizo, M., 149, 154, 159
Omizo, S., 149, 159
Ormrod, J., 312, 317
Ornstein, A. C., 350, 361
Osborn, J., 409, 416
Otis, A., 326, 328
Owens, E., 94, 99
Owens, R. E., 87, 94, 95, 99
Packer, A., 139, 159
Paikoff, R., 51, 67
Palermo, D. S., 91, 99
Paolitto, D., 58, 60, 67
Parke, B., 50, 67, 168, 189
Parker, J., 50, 67
Parsons, J. E., 206, 212
Pavlov, I., 227, 228, 229, 230, 232, 243, 244, 274
Pederson, A., 168, 188
Peisack, E., 91, 99
Pepper, F., 112, 132, 140, 153, 158, 159, 166, 188
Perfetto, G., 308, 315
Perlmutter, M., 300, 317
Perry, J., 49, 67
Peskin, H., 53, 67
Peterson, A., 52, 65
Peterson, C., 174, 189
Peterson, L., 297, 317
Peterson, M., 297, 317
Pety, J., 153, 159
Phillips, G., 94, 99, 357
Piaget, J., 58, 60, 61, 62, 67, 70, 72, 73, 74, 75, 76, 77, 78, 79, 81, 82, 91, 92, 97, 99, 240, 241, 249, 252, 254, 256, 260, 263, 264, 265, 266, 267, 268, 269, 286, 287
Pinnell, G., 137, 140, 159
Pipp, S., 45, 66
Plantz, M., 396, 416
Popham, W. J., 355, 361, 369, 370, 374, 387
Poppen, W., 34, 36, 44, 59, 65, 67, 118, 132, 153, 158
Porter, B., 153, 159
Prater, A., 118, 132
Prediger, D. J., 334, 360
Pressey, S., 294, 307, 308, 309, 312, 317
Price, G., 220, 223, 249
Price, M., 392, 417
Prytulak, L., 309, 317
Puetz, S., 258, 287
Quillian, M., 298, 316
Radd, T., 149, 159
Raff, D., 154, 158

Ramey, C. T., 398, 416
Raspberry, W., 185, 189
Rathvon, N., 153, 159
Raugh, M. R., 310, 315
Ravitch, D., 194, 195, 196, 212
Reckford, N., 258, 287
Reed, R., 40, 66
Reese, H. W., 31, 65
Reimer, J., 58, 60, 67
Reisman, R., 269, 287
Reynolds, R., 295, 317
Richardson, S. N., 379, 387
Rickard, K., 50, 67
Roberson, M., 153, 159
Robinson, A., 150, 159
Robinson, F., 10, 25
Roblee, K. M., 253, 287
Roche, A., 40, 66
Rogers, C., 105, 107, 112, 118, 121, 126, 145, 149, 150, 159
Rohwer, W., 223, 249
Rosenshine, G., 409, 417
Rothmann, R., 357, 361
Rounds, T., 47, 67
Rowe, V., 93, 99
Ryan, R., 185, 188
Sabatino, D., 408, 409, 416
Sadker, D., 208, 209, 212
Sadker, M., 208, 209, 212
Sae, A., 268, 287
Salvia, J., 343, 361
Sampson, P. D., 392, 417
Sanders, J., 197, 201, 212
Sax, G., 350, 352, 361
Schab, F., 311, 317
Schaub, M., 357, 361
Schneider, W., 294, 307, 309, 312, 317
Schuler, R. S., 21, 25
Schunk, D., 170, 189
Schwab, R. L., 21, 25
Schweinhart, L. J., 396, 417
Scott, H., 4
Seidel, J. F., 395, 417
Seligman, M., 174, 189
Serbin, L. A., 207, 212
Sexton, P. O., 207, 213
Shade, B. J., 196, 213
Shaffer, D. R., 405, 417
Shanker, A., 20, 25, 413, 417
Shaw, M. E., 47, 65
Shepard, L. A., 355, 361
Sherman, L. G., 261, 287
Shiffrin, R., 282, 286, 287, 293, 315
Shires, J., 257, 287

Shirey, L., 295, 317
Shriberg, L, 310, 316, 317
Silver, L. B., 410, 417
Silverman, W., 152, 159
Simon, T., 324, 326, 360
Simpson, J., 241, 249
Sims-Knight, J., 308, 315
Singhal, A. C., 383, 387
Skinner, B., 6, 8, 9, 24, 84, 85, 99, 106, 112, 132, 183, 184, 189, 227, 243, 244, 245, 246, 247, 249, 274
Slavin, R., 185, 189
Slavin, R. E. 252, 287
Sleeter, C. E., 195, 213
Slobin, D. I., 87, 99
Smart, M. S., 62, 67
Smart, R. C., 62, 67
Smith, D., 44, 65
Smith M. L., 355, 361
Smith, P. C., 238, 249
Socha, S., 273, 287
Soderman, A., 36, 59, 67
Springston, F., 306, 315
Stallings, J., 50, 67, 168
Stanford Test of Academic Skills, Basic Battery Booklet, 340, 361
Stanford-Binet Intelligence Scale, 331, 332, 361
Stanley, J. C., 333, 334, 360, 366, 373, 387
Stanovich, K., 407, 417
Stattin, H., 52, 53, 67
Stein, B., 308, 315
Stein, L., 36, 59, 67
Sternberg, R. J., 328, 330, 331, 361
Stevens, L. J., 392, 417
Stevenson, H. J., 357, 361
Stigler, S., 357, 361
Stipek, D., 182, 183, 189
Stratton, C., 152, 159
Streissguth, A. P., 392, 416, 417
Sullo, R., 154, 159
Super, D. E., 334, 361
Tallent, N., 367, 387
Taylor, A., 36, 52, 65
Taylor C., 151, 158
Terman, L., 326, 327, 328, 331, 361
Terwilliger, J. S., 379, 380, 387
Teuber, H. L., 85, 89
Thompson, C., 118, 132, 153, 159
Thorndike, E., 6, 7, 9, 25, 227, 236, 237, 238, 239, 240, 241, 242, 243, 244
Thorndike, R. L., 339, 355, 356, 361
Thorndike, R. M., 339, 355, 356, 361
Tierno, M., 138, 159
Tikunoff, W., 47, 67

PHOTO CREDITS